SOVIET POLITICS:
CONTINUITY AND
CONTRADICTION

To Frank

SOVIET POLITICS
CONTINUITY
AND
CONTRADICTION

GORDON B. SMITH
University of South Carolina

St. Martin's Press   New York

First published in the United States of America in 1988

Printed in the U.S.A.

ISBN: 0-312-00795-7
ISBN: 0-312-74866-3 (pbk.)

21098
fedcba

cover design: Darby Downey
cover photo: "Moscow," Brian Brake/Rapho/Photo Researchers, Inc.
graphics: G&H Soho

Library of Congress Cataloging-in-Publication Data

Smith, Gordon B.
  Soviet Politics.

  Bibliography: p.
  Includes index.
  1. Soviet Union—Politics and government—20th
century. 2. Soviet Union—Social conditions—1917–
I. Title
JN6511.S56   1987   947.084   87-4610
ISBN 0-312-00795-7
ISBN 0-312-74866-3 (pbk.)

ACKNOWLEDGMENTS

Figure 1-1: David Hooson, *The Soviet Union: Peoples and Regions* (Belmont: California: Wadsworth Publishers, 1966), p. 43. **Figures 4-1 and 4-2:** Adapted from Ronald J. Hill and Peter Frank, *The Soviet Communist Party* (London: George Allen & Unwin, 1981), pp. 32 and 59. **Table 4-9:** Adapted from Jerry Hough and Merle Fainsod, *How the Soviet Union Is Governed* (Cambridge: Harvard University Press, 1979), pp. 412–417. **Figure 5-1:** Hélène Carrère D'Encausse, *Decline of an Empire* (New York: Newsweek Books), pp. 8–9. **Figure 6-1:** Thane Gustafson, *Reform in Soviet Politics* (Cambridge University Press, 1981), p. 72. **Pages 118–119:** Quotation by Theodore H. Friedgut in Everett Jacobs, ed., *Soviet Local Politics and Government* (London: George Allen & Unwin, 1983), pp. 159–160. Reprinted by permission. **Chapter 7** is revised, edited, and updated from Chapter 5 of *Public Policy and Administration in the Soviet Union,* edited by Gordon B. Smith. Copyright © 1980 American Society for Public Administration. Reprinted and revised by permission of Praeger Publishers. **Table 8-1:** Harriet Fast Scott and William F. Scott, *The Armed Forces of the USSR,* second revised edition (Boulder, CO: Westview Press), 1984, p. 143. **Figure 9-1:** David Lane, *Soviet Economy and Society* (New York: NYU Press, 1985), p. 10. **Table 9-3:** Adapted from A. Katsenelinboigen's table, "Coloured Markets in the Soviet Union," *Soviet Studies,* vol. 29, no. 1, 1977, p. 63.

Preface

Winston Churchill once remarked, "The Soviet Union is a riddle, wrapped in a mystery, inside an enigma." Soviet political behavior, whether it involves the selection of a new General Secretary of the CPSU, the direction of a centrally planned economy, or control over the press and artistic expression, is radically different than in most Western societies. Consequently, students are apt to conclude that the Soviet political system is unique. On the surface, the Soviet political system often appears to be monolithic, devoid of political conflict and the battle of self-interested groups, and free of regional and personal rivalries. In short, it is often difficult for students to see the *politics* in Soviet politics.

Soviet Politics: Continuity and Contradiction delves below the surface of political processes in the USSR to explore how political conflicts arise over a wide array of issues, how these conflicts are expressed, and how they are mediated, compromised, and resolved. Through case studies and drawing on my personal experiences in the USSR, I have attempted to go beyond the formal depiction of political institutions and their powers in order to illustrate how the political system works in practice. I hope that this approach will enable students to see behind the formal facade of the Soviet political system and appreciate it in a wider, comparative perspective.

The central themes of the book are continuity and contradiction. The USSR is an extraordinarily diverse and complex country. It is a society torn between the competing pressures for reform and resistance to change; between the centrifugal tendencies of nationalism and regionalism and the centripetal tendencies of centralization; between the competing ideals of a mass society and the reality of a class society; between the commitment to a centrally planned economy and the recognized need of an unofficial "second economy"; and between revolutionary rhetoric and bureaucratic reality. These contradictions shape political processes in the USSR in significant ways, and the manner in which the Soviet government attempts to ameliorate them has shown marked continuities through history.

The contradictions that pervade Soviet politics and society are reflected in my own ambivalence toward the USSR. Like many students of the Soviet Union, I have ambivalent attitudes about the country, its political system, and its people. To me, the Soviet Union is, and I suspect always will be, a collage of contrasting elements: the beauty of the Russian language and the depth of Russian literary and artistic expression contrasting with the stilted

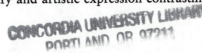
v

official rhetoric of the Soviet bureaucracy; the haunting strains of Russian folksongs; the interminable lines; the camaraderie of Russian friends sitting around a table, openly sharing their feelings; the constant need for caution and discretion in order to protect one's friends from the authorities; the commitment to social equality; and the fierce competition and jealousy over special perks and favors. Even after many visits, whenever I enter the Soviet Union, I do so with a mixture of excitement and apprehension.

Undoubtedly, my two-sided view of Soviet politics and society shades my analysis, but it also reflects real contradictions that exist in the USSR. I have endeavored to present here a balanced, comprehensive view of Soviet politics and society. The success or failure of that effort is for the readers to judge.

This book was written with the support of many individuals and institutions, and it is a pleasure to record my gratitude and indebtedness to them. I wish to thank the University of South Carolina, especially the Department of Government and International Studies, for supporting my work over the years. I am grateful to my colleagues for their encouragement, criticism, and friendship. A portion of the book was completed while I was in residence at the Slavic Research Center of Hokkaido University in Sapporo, Japan. I owe Professor Hiroshi Kimura and the entire faculty and staff of the center my profound thanks for providing a stimulating environment in which to work and to share ideas.

A number of individual scholars assisted me in the preparation of this book. Their comments and criticisms were invaluable and greatly appreciated. It goes without saying that they bear no responsibility for errors in the text. Specifically, I wish to acknowledge the assistance of Professors Barbara A. Chotiner, Tsyoshi Hasegawa, Jean-Claude Lanne, Ronald H. Linden, Donald C. Rawson, Daniel R. Sabia, Jr., Robert Sharlet, and John E. Turner.

Special thanks also go to a devoted friend who read this manuscript in every stage of its development.

I am indebted to two of my graduate assistants, Anita Floyd and William Clark, for assisting me throughout the process of completing this book. For her expert typing and efficient secretarial help, I wish to thank Lori Joye. I also thank Larry Swanson, Christine Pearson, and Patricia Mansfield at St. Martin's Press for their skillful assistance in bringing this project to fruition.

Finally, I would like to acknowledge the steadfast support and patience of my family.

GORDON B. SMITH

Contents

1

Russian Political Culture

Russia is a land of contradictions. It is a modern superpower, capable of challenging the military might of the United States. Yet, it is also a country in which citizens routinely stand in long lines to buy milk, meat, and potatoes, and where items such as fresh fruit, toilet paper, and typewriters are in chronic short supply. Soviet youth today wear Levis purchased on the black market and listen to the latest Western rock music, yet their attitudes and values are not Western. There is a mysticism, a fatalism, an attachment to the Russian soil that transcends simple patriotism. As one citizen remarked, "My parents and grandparents—like me—were born out of this black Russian soil. And when they died, they returned to the soil. This is my place, this is where I belong."[1]

Soviet society produces talented musicians and writers, distinguished scientists, and superb dancers. Yet, it also imprisons those who would push the boundaries of creative thought too far. Outwardly, the Soviet political system appears to be a grey bureaucratic monolith in which the Party has eliminated all controversy and conflict. But beneath the uniformity of Soviet politics and beneath the banners proclaiming the unity of the Party and the people, there are innumerable political conflicts that pit bureaucracies, regions, ethnic groups, and personalities against each other.

Russia is indeed a land of contradictions. It is best understood, not as a uniform mass, but as a patchwork quilt of geographic, ethnic, religious, economic, and political diversity. Our exploration of the Soviet Union and its political system begins with an examination of some of the contradictions that define and shape political attitudes and values in the USSR.

RICH LAND/POOR LAND

Although the Soviet Union is immense in size and rich in natural resources, it is inherently poor in sustaining existence. The USSR, which occupies roughly one-sixth of the earth's land surface, is by far the largest nation in the world; it is twice the size of the United States, larger than all of South America, and only slightly smaller than the entire continent of Africa. By sheer size and expanse, the Soviet Union is both a major European and Asian power. From its Pacific shores to the western frontier with Poland, the USSR stretches over 6800 miles, spanning eleven time zones. From the northernmost reaches above the Arctic Circle to the desert borders with Turkey, Iran, and Afghanistan, it covers more than 3500 miles. Yet, vast areas of the USSR are uninhabitable, and the bulk of the population resides in only a fraction of its territory.

The Soviet Union is so large that it is easy to lose sight of its immensity. For instance, the Caspian Sea is larger in area than the entire United Kingdom. Lake Baikal, which on the map of the USSR appears modest in comparison to the surrounding reaches of Siberia, contains one-fifth of the world's fresh water—more than all the water of the Great Lakes combined.

While the immensity of Russia has afforded it some degree of isolation throughout history, it has also raised problems. Transportation and communication, necessary ingredients to any modern state, were virtually nonexistent before the 1860s, when railway and telegraph communications were established in European Russia. Even today, there are obvious difficulties in coordination: at the same time that Muscovites are going to bed at night, the people in Vladivostok are having breakfast the next morning.

The Soviet Union has more than 26,000 miles of coastline—more than any nation in the world. Yet, most of its coasts are to the north, on the Barents, Kara, Laptev, East Siberian, and Chukchi Seas. Few ports are navigable during the long winters, when massive ice floes clog the Arctic Ocean. Ships leaving the warmwater ports of the Soviet Union in the Baltic Sea, Black Sea, and the Sea of Japan must pass through narrow straits to reach international waters. Over the years, much has been made of the quest for warmwater ports as a primary motivating force in Russian and Soviet territorial expansion in the Balkans and the Far East.

The northerly position of the Soviet Union on the Eurasian continent, compounded by the effect of the large continental landmass, results in a notoriously harsh climate. With no major bodies of water to moderate temperatures, the massive continental expanse allows rapid warming of the land in summer and cooling in winter. The northernmost 15 percent of the Soviet Union lies above the Arctic Circle and consists mostly of treeless tundra. The permafrost zone, in which the subsoil is permanently frozen, covers more than 40 percent of the country. In the tundra and permafrost regions, only moss and low shrubs will grow. At Verkhoiansk in northeastern Siberia, a world-record low temperature of −90° F was reported. During the winter, the sun does not shine, whereas in the summer, temperatures reach above 80° F and the sun never sets.

To the south of the tundra is a wide belt of taiga, or woodlands, extending across Russia's middle latitudes. The taiga accounts for more than one-third of all the forests in the world. In the European part of Russia, the forests have largely been cleared; this region provides the Soviet Union with much of its arable land, known as the "non–black-earth zone." In the taiga, winter turns to summer with such suddenness that spring is almost nonexistent. In April and early May, the rapidly melting snow floods the streams, the soil thaws, and "all Russia is an epic of mud."[2] (See Figure 1-1.)

Further south, stretching from Hungary to Mongolia, is the steppe, vast grasslands and semiarid plains that are suitable for grazing livestock. For centuries, the steppe was controlled by fierce, nomadic Mongol tribes who drove the pastoral Slavs into the forests to seek protection. The climate in the steppe is typical of continental regions; in the winter, temperatures

Figure 1-1. Regions of the Union of Soviet Socialist Republics

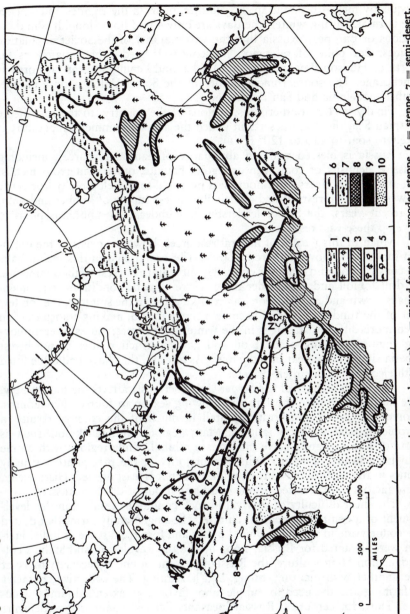

1 = tundra, 2 = tayga, 3 = mountain (vertical zoning), 4 = mixed forest, 5 = wooded steppe, 6 = steppe, 7 = semi-desert, 8 = Mediterranean, 9 = wet sub-tropical, 10 = desert

Source: David J. M. Hooson, *The Soviet Union* (London: University of London Press, 1966), p. 43.

frequently hit −40° F, and in the summer, highs in the eighties and nineties are normal. During winter, the days are only 4 to 5 hours long. It is in these regions of European Russia that the vast majority of the Soviet population resides. For point of reference, Moscow is located approximately as far north as Hudson Bay and Juneau, Alaska, and Leningrad is as far north as Anchorage. The southernmost border of the Soviet Union is on a parallel with Philadelphia and San Francisco.

Finally, in the southernmost regions of the country, to the east of the Caspian Sea, there are deserts in which the average summer temperature is likely to soar to 110 to 120° F.

Russia is blessed with an abundance of natural resources, including massive deposits of coal, iron ore, gold, bauxite, other nonferrous metals, oil, and gas. Its rivers offer boundless potential for developing hydroelectric power, and its forests afford a virtually endless supply of lumber and pulp. In recent years, the Soviet leadership has undertaken ambitious plans to develop these vast resources.

Much of this wealth of natural resources, however, exists in the northern tundra far above the Arctic Circle. The brutal cold in this region halts all construction and makes it extremely difficult to harvest timber, mine ore, or drill for oil and gas. Under these severe climatic conditions, equipment breaks down and rubber boots shatter like glass. In the summer, the top few feet of the tundra thaw and become a soggy marsh, making transportation even more difficult than it is in the winter. Sometimes, pieces of earthmoving equipment being used at oil and gas construction sites in northwest Siberia simply disappear into the mud. As a result, they have had to be fitted with ejector seats for their drivers.

The harsh climate of the Soviet Union seriously affects the food supply. The northerly climate shortens the growing season to four or five months. Moreover, limited and erratic rainfall in much of the country results in chronic agricultural crop failures. Many regions with black soil, such as parts of Kazakhstan, receive inadequate rainfall, while regions with ample rain have sandy or loamy soil. The majority of the precipitation usually comes in the second half of the summer when it is least needed. Historically, these factors have resulted in one bad harvest out of three in Russia.[3]

The sheer difficulty of survival in such conditions resulted in the development of a communal peasant culture. The single-family farms that dotted the countryside in the rural United States and fostered a sense of individualism were ill-suited for Russia. Long before the Revolution and Stalin's collectivization of agriculture, the Russian peasants found it necessary to assist one another with planting, tilling, and harvesting. The collective character of farming and the need for ample labor favored an extended family structure. Thus, for centuries, Russian peasants lived in communal settlements called the *dvorishche*. In some of the most northerly regions, Russian peasants conserved energy by living in communal housing rather than in the traditional cottage, or *izba*. Due to the short growing season, farm work was concentrated in a few months; cottage industries and alcohol consumed the long winters.

Finally, the harshness of the climate inevitably helped to shape the Russian mind-set. Russians often think of the world as cold and inhospitable. For centuries, Russian peasants had to cope with epidemics, toil, famine, and political and economic repression, but there were largely accepted as "God's will." This fatalism was compounded by the Russian Orthodox church, which taught that life is fraught with toil and trials and which made a virtue of asceticism and suffering.

DOGMATISM AND INTOLERANCE

The physical boundlessness of Russia initially found expression in a primitive natural paganism that later merged with Orthodoxy to mold Russian spiritual values. In pre-Christian Russian society, the illiterate peasants attributed supernatural powers to forces in their environment that they could not understand or control. For instance, the wolf, which preyed on the peasants and their flocks, became an object of worship. Fire also was ascribed a mystical power, being a necessity for life in the harsh winters, but also the cause of the destruction of whole villages and certain death.

With the conversion of Russia to Christianity, this paganism was not completely eradicated; rather, the primitive natural beliefs of the Russian people were absorbed into Orthodoxy. On the exterior of some of the oldest surviving Christian churches in the Soviet Union, one can still find pagan gargoyles and figures whose purpose was to keep away evil spirits. Remnants of these early beliefs can also be seen today in Russian *skazki,* or fairy tales, which depict Father Frost, fire, wolves, and other animals and natural forces.

The Christianization of Russia during the ninth and tenth centuries was a conscious decision by Grand Prince Vladimir of Kiev designed to modernize the country and forge stronger political ties with the Byzantine Empire centered in Constantinople. According to ancient chronicles, Vladimir was visited by religious delegations of various faiths: Roman Catholics from Germany, Khazars professing Judaism, Bulgar Moslems, and Orthodox Christians from Byzantium. Legend has it that Vladimir spurned Islam because it forbade alcohol; as the Prince noted, "Drink is the joy of the Russian."[4] Likewise, he decided against Judaism because he believed it was the faith of a defeated and homeless people. His choice of Eastern Orthodoxy for Russia determined the direction not only of the country's religious development, but also its political and cultural evolution. By choosing Orthodoxy, Vladimir opened Russia to influence from the highly developed Byzantine culture, and Kievan literature, art, architecture, law, and customs reflected this. The decision also meant that Russia would remain outside of the influence of the Roman Catholic church and thus contributed to the country's isolation from the rest of Europe and from such important intellectual movements as the scholastic tradition and the Renaissance.

The Eastern Orthodox church constructed an authoritarian hierarchy, which intertwined with and strengthened an equally authoritarian political structure. The values stressed by the Church were those of asceticism, self-denial, suffering, piety, and dogmatism. It was a religion that ensured the maintenance of power in the hands of a few and that discouraged the peasants from seeking power or change. The doctrines of the Church corresponded to the life experience of the Russian peasant. The Orthodox church taught that life is to be endured, not enjoyed. Not only were the peasants instructed to suffer the harshness of the climate and the authoritarian, often corrupt rule of the tsar and his provincial governors. They were also to learn piety from suffering; there was something noble about "bearing one's cross." As a result, in a few isolated Siberian villages, some sects took to the extreme of self-flagellation, extended fasts, isolation, and other acts of self-denial. Rather than focusing on this world, Russian Orthodoxy displayed a strong mystical and transcendental element that stressed the hereafter.

Orthodoxy helped to develop in the Russian peasant a mystical attachment to the soil, to Mother Russia. Some scholars believe that the origins of the word *Russia* (*Rus'*) are tied to those of *rodina* ("motherland").[5] It is significant that such concepts are usually of the feminine gender. The rich, black soil of Russia is likened to the womb, the source of all life. The Russian serfs of the seventeenth century through the first half of the nineteenth century were not only legally bound to the land, they were religiously and mystically attached to it. In small villages that could not afford to pay for a priest, peasants would go out into the fields and confess their sins not to the heavens, but to the soil, to Mother Russia.

Many of the attributes of Russian Orthodoxy spilled over into the social realm as well. When Russians adopted a belief system, they often did so dogmatically, totally and without reservation. This dogmatism, whether on religious issues or on political issues, has led to numerous apocalyptic events throughout Russian history.[6] For instance, in the seventeenth century, a schism occurred within the Russian Orthodox church over the introduction of certain liturgical reforms. A group that came to be called the Old Believers split from the Orthodox church because they opposed the triple "Hallelujah"—repeating the Hallelujah chant three times—and persisted in making the sign of the cross with two fingers, rather than three.

Russians, whether orthodox, heretics, or schismatics, have tended to be apocalyptic and nihilistic and to be willing, even anxious, to suffer for their beliefs. Belief systems are held and defended with equal fervor. Religious dogmatism has often translated itself into intolerance for those who stray from the true belief. Whether among the Old Believers in the seventeenth century, or the Russian revolutionaries, anarchists, and nihilists of the nineteenth century, or Marxist-Leninists of the twentieth century, dogmatism and intolerance have gone hand in hand. These qualities transcend religious issues and have permeated social and political values as well.

MESSIANIC STATE WITH AN INFERIORITY COMPLEX

Russian Orthodoxy also transcended the Russian Empire, upholding itself not only as the defender of the Slavic people (even those residing beyond the borders of the empire) but also as the defender of the true Christianity. After the fall of the Byzantine Empire, the Second Rome, the doctrine of the Third Rome emerged in the Muscovite state. In 1510, the monk Filofei wrote to Tsar Vasily III:

This examination copy of

Soviet Politics
CONTINUITY AND CONTRADICTION

is sent to you with the compliments of
your St. Martin's Press representative.

Your comments on our books help us estimate printing requirements, assist us in preparing revisions, and guide us in shaping future books to your needs. Will you please take a moment to fill out and return this postpaid card?

☐ you may quote me for advertising purposes

I ☐ will adopt ☐ have adopted ☐ am seriously considering it

Comments

Name_____ Department_____

School_____ Phone Number ( )_____

City_____ State_____ Zip_____

Course Title_____ Enrollment_____

Present Text_____

Do you plan to change texts this year? Yes ☐ No ☐ When is your decision due?_____

Is your text decision individual ☐ committee ☐ department ☐

If committee or department, please list others involved_____

BUSINESS REPLY MAIL

FIRST CLASS   PERMIT NO. 1147   NEW YORK, NY

POSTAGE WILL BE PAID BY

College Department
ST. MARTIN'S PRESS, INC.
175 FIFTH AVENUE
NEW YORK, N.Y. 10010

Of all kingdoms in the world, it is in thy royal domain that the holy Apostolic Church shines more brightly than the sun. And let thy Majesty take note, O religious and gracious Tsar, that all kingdoms of the Orthodox Christian Faith are merged into thy kingdom. Thou alone, in all that is under heaven, art a Christian Tsar. And take note, O religious and gracious Tsar, that all Christian kingdoms are merged into thine alone, that two Romes have fallen, but the third stands, and there will be no fourth. Thy Christian kingdom shall not fall to the lot of another.[7]

Thus, the Russian state was infused with a messianic zeal that justified territorial expansion. Nationalism and Orthodoxy were effectively merged into one powerful ethic.

The expansion of the Russian Empire continued from the sixteenth through the nineteenth century, beginning with the consolidation of the empire in the territories west of the Urals, including the Baltic, the Don region, and the North Caucasus, and then expanding into contiguous territories to the east and south. Territorial expansion in Russia was itself a contradictory process, vacillating between compulsion and voluntary assimilation. At times, the authorities dammed back the influx of new peoples into the empire; at other times, they pressed control over neighboring peoples by force.

The conquest of Siberia began in earnest in the late sixteenth century, and by the mid-eighteenth century, Russian outposts extended all the way to the Pacific. As a result of the Napoleonic Wars (1805–1814), the Caucasus was added to the empire. The consolidation of Russian influence in the Far East and Alaska was formalized from 1858 to 1860. In contrast, Russian occupation and control of Central Asia was a gradual and lengthy process spanning the period from 1868 through 1885.

The causes of Russian territorial expansion were many. First, the empire was surrounded by sparsely settled territories that invited incorporation. Second, lacking any natural borders, the empire tended to expand in search of security. Third, empires of the nineteenth century often measured their power and influence in terms of the extent of territory controlled and the size of their populations. Fourth, because much of the arable land in Russia was of poor quality and traditional farming techniques tended to deplete the soil quickly, the peasants were constantly seeking more fertile farming areas. Finally, because England, France, and other European powers could no longer expand their territories on the European continent without precipitating war, they turned toward the acquisition of extensive colonial holdings that would provide sources of raw materials for their industry and markets for their newly acquired industrial capability. The Russian Empire, anxious to compete and be recognized as a major European power, was afforded the opportunity to expand into contiguous territories that presented many of the same advantages of a colonial empire, but without some of the risks and costs.

Eventually, this rather constant territorial expansion brought the tsarist state into conflict with other empires: there were wars with the Napoleonic Empire in Europe, the Ottoman Empire in the South, the British Empire in the Crimea, the Japanese in the Far East and Manchuria (1904–1905), and the Austro-Hungarian and German empires in Eastern Europe (1914–

1917). These wars had important implications. They brought Russians into increased contact with Western nations and cultures. They also reinforced existing tendencies toward the centralization of power in order to mount an army and to support military ventures. In addition, they brought to the attention of the tsarist regime the necessity of promoting industrialization to free Russia from its dependence on imported steel and other products necessary for manufacturing military hardware.

The expansion of Russia, especially in Asia, the Caucasus, and the Baltic, inevitably introduced non-Slavic peoples into the empire. By the time of the Revolution, Russia was a multiethnic state consisting of peoples speaking more than 150 distinct dialects or languages. Religiously, they ranged from Catholics and Protestants in the western regions of the Ukraine, Belorussia, and the Baltic, to Orthodox believers in European Russia, to Shiite Moslems in Central Asia, Buddhists in the Far East, and Shamanists in isolated villages throughout eastern Siberia.

Non-Russian influences were also introduced during centuries of invasion and occupation by foreign powers. The list of invaders of Russia includes the Scythians, Mongols, Sarmatians, Goths, Huns, Avars, Khazars, Tatars, Swedes, Poles, Lithuanians, Turks, French, Japanese, and Germans. During the twentieth century alone, six major wars or foreign interventions have occurred on Russian soil. With no bodies of water or major mountain ranges to impede their assault, invaders have repeatedly occupied Russia and subjugated its people. The longest occupation came at the hands of the Mongol-Tatar invaders and lasted more than 250 years—from the thirteenth through the first half of the fifteenth century. The Mongol influence was such that Russian poet Alexander Pushkin wrote: "Scratch a Russian and he bleeds Mongol blood!" The repeated foreign incursions have ingrained a sense of vulnerability, and a feeling of being exposed into the Russian people.

EAST VERSUS WEST

Until the nineteenth century, Russia was largely isolated from the events and developments that influenced the course of Western Europe. As a result, Russia was shaped by profoundly different political, economic, religious, and cultural forces than those that molded Western Europe. In Russia, there was no Renaissance or Reformation. The separation of church and state, each with its own independent realm of authority, was totally foreign to Russian thinking. The Industrial Revolution came late to Russia; when industry developed, it was not due to the rise of a middle class of entrepreneurs but to state decree. Russia entered the twentieth century never having experienced elections nor legalized political parties and never having had a constitution to limit the powers of the tsar. In short, the idea of government as a social contract between the rulers and the ruled was foreign to Russian society. Civil liberties were unknown as legal or political concepts. Democracy was unheard of among the peasants and denounced by a nobility too frightened to conceive of sharing power with the common people. Thus, Russia entered the twentieth century as an authoritarian state with a largely backward, agrarian economy and a deeply divided social class system.

Russia was neither wholly Eastern nor Western, and the clash of Eastern and Western cultural traditions and values within the country has been the subject of repeated controversy. When the young Peter the Great assumed the throne in 1682, he immediately began a series of wrenching reforms designed to modernize and strengthen the Russian state. As a young man, Peter studied carpentry, shipbuilding, and navigation, because he recognized that Russia must have a modern navy to compete with its adversaries. From 1697 to 1698, he led a delegation of his advisers and craftsmen on an extensive tour of Europe to acquire Western technological "know-how."

Peter believed in enlightened despotism. He envisioned a modern Russian state, freed from the superstitions and corruption of the Church and the conservatism of the Muscovite establishment and all that it represented. He strove to raise the Russian people from their ignorance and backwardness, but in so doing, he was quite willing to resort to ruthless tactics. Peter promulgated a revolution from above. At great human expense, he built a new capital, St. Petersburg, which was intended to be Russia's "window on the West." He ordered all military officers to shave their beards "for the glory and comeliness of the State and the military profession," and levied a tax on those citizens who persisted in growing beards.[8] He established the Academy of Sciences and encouraged members of the nobility to study abroad.

Peter was especially severe in his policies toward the Russian Orthodox church, which he believed had retarded the development of the Russian state. Copying the relationship between church and state in Lutheran countries of northern Europe, he replaced the patriarch with the Holy Synod. When his policies encountered opposition, he dealt with his critics mercilessly; he imprisoned his wife and sister and executed his own son for opposing his reforms.

Much of Peter the Great's reign was occupied with the Great Northern War (1700–1721). In fact, only one year during his entire reign was without war. Many of his reforms were motivated by the desire to strengthen the State in order to enhance Russia's military capability. For example, Peter instituted general conscription and reorganized the army into more effective fighting units. He also helped to build the first Russian navy and aspired to turn Russia into a naval power that would rival the great navies of Britain, France, and Holland.

Peter reorganized the haphazard, unwieldy governmental bureaucracy into nine *collegia*, or ministries. In addition, he is credited with establishing the first treasury and universal system of coinage to replace the previous system of barter. This facilitated the collection of taxes to support his military campaigns. In short, Peter's reforms both strengthened the Russian state and forced Western enlightenment on a segment of the population. The changes, however, also served to widen the gulf between the peasants, who were largely unaffected by them, and the upper classes.

Another outcome of Peter's reforms was the gradual emergence in Russia of an intelligentsia—a class of well-educated persons, primarily from the nobility, who were profoundly influenced by Western ideas. The influx of Western culture, however, also generated a reactionary backlash among those who rejected these ideas and chose instead to preserve the uniqueness of Russian culture. By the nineteenth century, the conflict between the Western ideas introduced since the time of Peter and the indigenous Slavic mores became manifested in the Westernizer and Slavophile schools of philosophy. The Westernizers held that Russia must follow the Western model of development. On the other hand, the Slavophiles glorified the superior achievements and historical mission of Orthodoxy and of Russia. While the Westernizers promoted industrialization, secularization, and the rise of a middle class, the Slavophiles stressed the simple idealistic virtues of the Russian peasant (*muzhik*), the peasant commune (*mir*), Orthodoxy, and rural life.

The Westernizer-Slavophile debate continued throughout the nineteenth century, and analogies can be found even during the Soviet period. For instance, in the late 1960s, several members of the leadership lobbied for increased contact with the West as one method of easing tensions and alleviating the declining growth in the Soviet economy. However, many local party officials and propagandists were concerned that increased contacts would "infect" Soviet society with decadent Western values. In 1971, Leonid Brezhnev, who was initially skeptical of East-West dialogue and who favored increased integration with the Eastern bloc instead, was finally persuaded to announce at the Twenty-Fourth Party Congress his support for expanded trade, political, and cultural ties with the West. This episode is just one of many illustrating the historic Russian ambivalence toward the influx of Western ideas and Western culture.

FROM ANARCHY TO AUTOCRACY

Another dominant contradiction within Russian political culture is a tendency to seek anarchy and the absence of order and control on the one hand, and autocracy on the other. A noted authority on imperial Russian history observed, "The *muzhiki* (peasants) preferred absolutism to any other form of government except anarchy."[9] The immensity of the Russian landmass and the absence of boundaries is reflected in the preference for anarchy. While in the West geographic, social, and political boundaries were clearly established, in Russia organization, limits, and order did not come naturally. In a sense, the Russian political system fell victim to the size of the nation; it was incapable of establishing stability and order over such an extensive, diverse, and socially divided empire. V. O. Kliuchevsky, a distinguished Russian historian of the nineteenth century, remarked, "The state expands, the people grow sickly."[10]

Some Russian historians explain the despotic character of Russian government as necessary for creating order and setting limits for a country and a people for whom no limits existed. Traditionally, Russians have turned to the State to create order out of the chaos of their society. In doing so, they have often sacrificed their own interests to those of the State.

The concept of the State in Russia was originally derived from the role of the head of the extended family in the early peasant society. The father was sovereign of the household, an autocrat in the broadest sense of the word. He literally owned all the property of the clan as well as its members, who could be sold as one might sell a cow. He alone was responsible for punishing members of the family; whipping a son to death was not uncommon. In parts of Siberia, as late as the mid-nineteenth century, a father who murdered a family member was liable only to a penance issued by the Church.

Until the middle of the seventeenth century, Russians had no concept of the State as Westerners know it. The State, insofar as they thought of it at all, meant the sovereign (*gosudar'*)—that is, the tsar—his private staff, and his family. Like the father of an extended family, the prince or tsar emerged as the sole proprietor in public right of all the subjects and all the territory in his principality.

It was under Peter the Great that there first emerged a notion of the State as a power distinct from and superior to the tsar. Yet, the idea that legal norms were binding on the sovereign and could restrict his powers gained only shallow acceptance and was overshadowed by the traditional stress on the patrimonial state. Thus, the concept of the State in Russian political culture is synonymous with a fusion of power and proprietorship, with unchallenged authority. There were no recognized formal limits on the tsar's political authority and no rule of law, and individual liberties existed only insomuch as they were granted by the tsar.

The preeminent role of the State was officially recognized by Tsar Nicholas I (1825–1855) and promulgated into the doctrine referred to as "official nationality." Formally proclaimed in 1833 by Count Serge Uvarov, the tsar's Minister of Education, the degree contained three principles: Orthodoxy, autocracy, and nationality. *Orthodoxy* referred to the official church and its role as the ultimate source of ethics and ideals that gave meaning to human life and society. *Autocracy* meant the affirmation of the absolute power of the sovereign, which was considered the indispensable foundation of the Russian state. *Nationality* (*narodnost'*) referred to Russian nationality, which was preeminent over all other Slavic and non-Slavic groups within the rapidly expanding empire.

The Russian Orthodox church was fragmented, decentralized, and made subservient to the State's messianic interests and goals. It was unable to challenge the power or authority of the State and stood by silently while an Ivan the Terrible or a Stalin slaughtered thousands. Ultimately, the inability or unwillingness of the Church to speak out on issues of social and political injustice created a spiritual vacuum that was filled with secular ideologies.

THE RULERS AND THE RULED

In Western societies, the notion is that ultimate political power and authority derives from the people and that the State exists as the manifested will of the governed. In the Soviet Union, as in prerevolutionary Russia, the State and political power, while considered necessary elements of Russian life, were seen to derive from forces external to the people themselves. Political decisionmakers were so far removed from the average Russian peasant that policies and laws appeared to come "from above," "from outside." This we-they schism characterizing the Russian view of the State is symbolized by the tale of the earliest Russian ruler, Rurik (862 A.D.). According to the *Primary Chronicle,* a series of annals recorded by monks during the Kievan era, the Russians—a pastoral people residing in the region of Novgorod—were suffering from a lack of order and state discipline, so they sought leadership from abroad:

> The [Russians] set out to govern themselves. There was no law among them, but tribe rose against tribe. Discord thus ensued among them, and they began to war one against another. They said to themselves, "Let us seek a prince who may rule over us, and judge us according to the law." They accordingly went overseas to the Varangian Rus' (Scandinavia): these particular Varangians were known as Rus', just as some are called Swedes, and other Normans, Angles, and Goths, for they were thus named. The Chuds, the Slavs, and the Kirvichians then said to the people of Rus', "Our whole land is great and rich, but there is no order in it. Come to rule and reign over us." They thus selected three brothers, with their kinfolk, who took with them all the Rus', and migrated. The oldest, Rurik, located himself in Novgorod; the second, Sineus, in Beloozero; and the third, Truvor, in Izborsk. On account of these Varangians, the district of Novgorod became known as Russian (Rus') land. The present inhabitants of Novgorod are descended from the Varangian race, but aforetime they were Slavs. After two years, Sineus and his brother Truvor died, and Rurik assumed the sole authority.[11]

Thus, the Slavs, recognizing their own lack of ability to govern themselves, had to send out for government.

Serfdom developed in Russia, as in the feudal West, with peasants entering contractual arrangements with lords. During the latter sixteenth and early seventeenth centuries, serfdom spread as the tsar granted lands to his gentry class as a reward for loyal service. Serfdom in Russia appeared simultaneously with the emergence of a centralized monarchy, not with feudal dispersal of power, as in western Europe. As the tsar consolidated more political authority in Moscow, his power grew to award new lands to his supporters; thus, serfdom spread. There also was a growing economic dependence of the peasant on the landlord and active Muscovite government support of the gentry class. Initially, the peasants were bound to the land and became the property of the gentry when the lands they worked were granted by the tsar. Most peasants considered serfdom as an injustice, but they attributed the blame primarily to the local nobility, rather than to the tsar himself. An old Russian expression captures the flavor: "God is high in heaven and the tsar is far away." The peasants saw the tsar as endowed by God, as a benevolent father-figure and shepherd of his flock. On the other hand, they often saw the tsar's local governors and nobility as greedy and corrupt. It is said that the Russian peasant came into contact with the government through two officials—the tax collector, who took away as much as 60 percent of the peasant's harvest, and the conscription officer, who drafted young men to fight in wars. Nevertheless, the notion developed that this good and merciful tsar cared about his flock and would right these injustices if only he were aware of them. But like God, who is high in heaven, the tsar was far away.

The peasants, having a legal, economic, and spiritual attachment to the Russian soil, found it wrong that nobles should possess vast tracts of land.

The soil was God's, and all who toiled and labored on it might enjoy its use. Concepts of private property in early Russian law did not extend to the land; rather, most of the peasants' land was held in a primitive agrarian communal institution, the *mir*. (The word *mir* means both "peace" and "world," which conveys a great deal about how the Russian peasant viewed the peasant commune. It represented a harmonious and peaceful world, and the borders of the commune were almost literally the borders of the peasant's world.)

After the Emancipation in 1861, much like after the Emancipation Proclamation two years later in the United States, the serfs did not gain the financial means to exist as free persons. Many continued in a quasi-serf status, dependent upon local landlords who had fewer obligations to their tenant farmers than they had toward their serfs prior to the Emancipation. Other peasants migrated to the cities in search of employment in the newly emerging industries. Thus, they contributed to the rise of a working class, most importantly a class of uprooted and disaffected people who tended to gravitate to the cities, where they lived in makeshift hovels. Once these people were isolated from the supportive social structures of Russian village life, their individual woes became the widespread and sometimes violent political demands of an incipient working class.

At the time of the Revolution in 1917, the nobility constituted less than 5 percent of the total population. For the last 100 years of the tsarist regime, many nobles traveled frequently to European capitals to acquire Western fashions and education. French, German, Italian, and English tutors, architects, chefs, and artisans were imported by the gentry and nobility to raise the level of Russian culture. Some of the gentry and nobility even intermarried with other European aristocracies. Western culture affected only those at the top of Russian society, however, and served to further alienate them from the masses of the population.[12] Unlike the nobility in England that opposed the monarchy and succeeded in limiting the power of the throne, the Russian aristocracy had no rights independent of those granted by the tsar. Consequently, it became an arm of the tsarist autocracy, which also inhibited social and political change in Russia.

In contrast to the nobility, the Russian peasants, who constituted more than 80 percent of the population in 1900, were largely illiterate, conservative, superstitious, and above all devoutly religious. They looked with suspicion upon the Western ways adopted by the nobility. They were ruled by a relatively small class of people, some of whom were not Orthodox and a few of whom spoke only French and German. As the rift between the Russian peasants and the nobility widened, the tsarist regime responded with coercion and repression in a futile attempt to replace its eroding credibility and popular support with political control. It was this cycle of repression and revolution that culminated in the Bolshevik seizure of power in 1917.

Notes

1. From a conversation with the author in Leningrad, November 1975.
2. Cited in G. Melvyn Howe, *The Soviet Union: A Geographical Survey* (Plymouth, Devonshire, England: Macdonald & Evans, 1983), 33.

3. Quoted by Richard Pipes in *Russia under the Old Regime* (London: Weidenfeld and Nicolson, 1974), 5.

4. Quoted in Nicolas Berdyaev, *The Origin of Russian Communism* (London: Geoffrey Bles, 1937), 10.

5. The origin of the word *Rus'* is much debated. For the peasant attachment to the soil, see Georgi P. Fedotov, *The Russian Religious Mind* (Cambridge: Harvard University Press, 1966).

6. This theory was first developed by Nicolas Berdyaev in *The Origin of Russian Communism*.

7. From the *Primary Chronicle*, available in English in Serge A. Zenkovsky, ed., *Medieval Russia's Epics, Chronicles, and Tales* (New York: E. P. Dutton, 1963).

8. B. H. Sumner, *Peter the Great and the Emergence of Russia* (New York: Collier, 1962).

9. Pipes, *Russia under the Old Regime*, 250.

10. V. O. Kliuchevsky, *A Course of Russian History*, translated into English by C. J. Hogarth (London: J. M. Dent, 1911).

11. From the *Primary Chronicle*, in Zenkovsky, *Medieval Russia's Epics, Chronicles, and Tales*, 50.

12. Wladimir Weidle, *Russia: Absent and Present* (New York: Vintage, 1961).

Selected Bibliography

Benet, Sula, ed. and trans. *The Village of Viriatino*. Garden City, New York: Doubleday, 1970.

Berdyaev, Nicolas. *The Origin of Russian Communism*. London: Geoffrey Bles, 1937.

Clarkson, Jesse D. *A History of Russia*. 2d ed. New York: Random House, 1969.

Custine, Marquis De. *Journey for Our Time: The Russian Journals of the Marquis De Custine*. Translated and edited by Phyllis Penn Kohler. Chicago: Henry Regnery Company, 1951.

Fedotov, Georgi P. *The Russian Religious Mind*. Cambridge: Harvard University Press, 1966.

Harcave, Sidney. *Russia: A History*. Chicago: Lippincott, 1953.

Hingley, Ronald. *The Tsars, 1533–1917*. New York: Macmillan, 1968.

Howe, G. Melvyn. *The Soviet Union: A Geographical Survey*. 2d ed. Plymouth, Devonshire, England: Macdonald & Evans, 1983.

Mellor, Roy E. H. *The Soviet Union and Its Geographical Problems*. London: Macmillan Press, 1982.

Pipes, Richard. *Russia under the Old Regime*. London: Weidenfeld and Nicolson, 1974.

Pokrovsky, M. N. *History of Russia*. New York: Russell & Russell, 1966.

Riasanovsky, Nicholas V. *A History of Russia*. 2d ed. New York: Oxford University Press, 1969.

Schapiro, Leonard. *The Origin of Communist Autocracy*. Cambridge, Mass.: Harvard University Press, 1955.

Sumner, B. H. *Peter the Great and the Emergence of Russia*. New York: Collier, 1962.

Vernadsky, George. *A History of Russia*. 6th ed. New Haven: Yale University Press, 1969.

Zenkovsky, Serge A., ed. *Medieval Russia's Epics, Chronicles, and Tales*. New York: E. P. Dutton, 1963.

2

Russia's Revolutionary Heritage

In Russia, there is a legacy of repression and revolution. Throughout the nineteenth and into the twentieth century, an increasingly anachronistic regime, immobilized by fear and inertia, confronted rapidly changing social forces. Those who criticized the regime or spoke out for reforms were imprisoned or exiled. A self-perpetuating cycle developed: calls for reform resulted in police harassment, which further radicalized the dissidents and hardened their demands. With every repetition of the cycle, the political demands grew more strident, the protests more violent, and the responses of the authorities more repressive and brutal.

THE FIRST RUMBLINGS OF DISSENT

Opposition to the tsarist regime began with the rise of the intelligentsia in the early eighteenth century. As the intelligentsia—the educated and enlightened class—emerged as a social force, its members began to call for change. Their modest petitions brought them sacrifice, suffering, and imprisonment. One of the first critics of the regime was Alexander Radishchev. A member of the gentry and a government official, Radishchev was educated at the University of Leipzig, where he acquired a thorough knowledge of eighteenth-century European thought; he was especially influenced by the works of Rousseau. Radishchev returned to Russia, and in 1790, he wrote his famous book *Journey from Petersburg to Moscow*. In the book, written in the form of a travelogue, Radishchev described the lives of the Russian serfs he had seen during his journey: the auction of members of a peasant family to different buyers; serfs working their fields on Sunday, the only day they could work their own land; arranged marriages; and the poverty of peasant existence. The book shattered the facade of the "progressive and enlightened" character of the reign of Catherine the Great (1762–1796). Frightened by the events of the French Revolution and fearing similar occurrences in Russia, Catherine condemned Radishchev to death. The sentence was later commuted to banishment to Siberia. Such was the reward for criticizing the injustices of Russian society or advocating even modest political and social reforms.

Change was bound to come to Russia, however. During the reign of Alexander I (1801–1825), Russia experienced a cultural renaissance that resulted in, among other things, the golden age of Russian poetry. Freemasonry gained a wide following and was responsible for spreading education, thus opening Russian society to new ideas and social movements. The Napoleonic Wars brought Russia into direct contact with the West and Western ideas. Alexander himself was a man of enlightenment. On a visit to England, he met with Robert Owen, the English utopian socialist, and worshiped with Quakers. Alexander relaxed restrictions on travel abroad and on the entry of foreigners into Russia. He granted an amnesty to many political prisoners incarcerated during Catherine's reign. Torture and forced confessions were abolished, and censorship was eased. An 1801 law provided for the voluntary emancipation of serfs by their masters.

Although the first half of Alexander's reign was enlightened and progressive, it was followed by a period of reaction during which Alexander grew impatient and increasingly intolerant of his critics. The change in his policies can be attributed to several factors. The Napoleonic Wars and subsequent alliances with foreign powers preoccupied the Tsar for much of this period (1805–1812), distracting him from internal matters. From 1807 to 1812, the Tsar's chief assistant and adviser was Michael Speransky, who had risen not from the gentry, but from the poor village clergy. In 1809, Speransky proposed that the Tsar enact a constitution, recognize civil rights, and observe strict norms of legality, including the election of judges. Although these reforms were not acted upon, they indicate the liberal influence Speransky exerted on the Tsar. Speransky was removed from his influential role in 1812 and replaced with the reactionary General Alexis Arakcheev. Arakcheev's most notable innovation was the establishment of "military settlements." Villages were declared to be military property, and the peasants were forced to farm under military order. The coerciveness of the "military settlements" is illustrated by Arakcheev's regulations ordering married women to bear a child every year.

Another factor in the hardening of policies during the second half of Alexander's reign was the rise of a political and religious backlash to the Enlightenment ideas that had gradually filtered into Russia over the previous decades. Prince Alexander Golitsyn, president of the Bible Society in Russia, became Alexander's Minister of Education and imposed his extremist ideas on the universities. Golitsyn believed that all knowledge was contained in the Bible and that all other sources of learning were suspect. The faculties of the universities were purged, libraries were ransacked, and students were encouraged to report on one another.

THE FIRST RUSSIAN REVOLUTION

The reactionary turn of Alexander's reign gave impetus to the first revolutionary movement in Russian history, the Decembrist uprising of 1825. The Decembrists, a group of army officers from aristocratic families, well-educated and influenced by the ideas of the Enlightenment and the French Revolution, called for the establishment of a constitutional regime in

Russia and the abolition of serfdom. On December 26, 1825, using the death of Tsar Alexander as an opportunity to take power, regiments in St. Petersburg mutinied and marched to Senate Square, where they confronted troops loyal to the government. Artillery was brought in, and after several volleys, sixty to seventy of the Decembrists were dead and the others were arrested.[1] Nicholas I, who succeeded his brother, condemned several of the leaders to death and exiled more than three hundred to Siberia.

The reign of Nicholas (1825–1855) represented another downward turn in the cycle of reform and reaction that characterized Russia in the nineteenth century. Nicholas had been brought up during the Napoleonic Wars and the last years of Alexander's rule. He possessed a love and admiration for military life and engineering. As Tsar, he displayed cunning, decisiveness, and an iron will. The Decembrist uprising merely reconfirmed his determination to preserve autocracy and eliminate any vestiges of dissent.

During the time of Nicholas I, the Russian intelligentsia was crushed between a reactionary autocratic monarchy on one side and an unenlightened mass of peasantry on the other. It was perhaps inevitable that the attempts of Catherine, Alexander I, and Nicholas I to suppress even moderate proposals for reform would engender more radical demands in the future.

In the 1840s, the ideas of the utopian socialists Claude-Henri Saint-Simon, Charles Fourier, Pierre-Joseph Proudhon, Georg Hegel, and Friedrich Schelling were especially influential among the intelligentsia of Moscow and St. Petersburg. Utopian socialism helped to promote the Western philosophies espoused by Peter Chaadaev, among others. In 1836, Chaadaev, an influential member of Moscow society, published a letter in an intellectual journal denouncing Russia for being neither Eastern nor Western. He accused Russia of lacking the dynamic social principles of Catholicism that were the foundation of Western culture. Chaadaev was declared a madman and imprisoned in an insane asylum. After his release, he partially recanted in his *Apology of a Madman*. Nevertheless, Chaadaev raised the question that troubled many of the intelligentsia: Did Russia's destiny lie with the West or with the East? Clearly, he and others favored the adoption of Western values.

Of the many salon groups formed during the mid-nineteenth century, one of the most famous was the Petrashevsky circle. Heavily influenced by ideas of utopian socialism, these intellectuals, many of whom were of aristocratic origin, met regularly to discuss the ideas and philosophies that were abounding in Europe. Far removed from the diversity and pluralism of intellectual discourse that prevailed in Western Europe, however, the Russian intelligentsia tended to take the tentative ideas of Western thinkers and promote them as absolutist strains of doctrine. Fyodor Dostoyevsky, a prominent member of the Petrashevsky group, depicted the salon society and its rather naive calls for social reform in *The Possessed*. Although the Petrashevsky group merely discussed ideas and did not undertake actions to subvert the regime, Nicholas I ordered his secret police to round up and arrest its members. Dostoyevsky was condemned to death and received a reprieve only at the last minute, when he was standing before the firing squad. Twenty-one of his associates from the Petrashevsky group were not so fortunate. Dostoyevsky's near death represented a turning point in his life. He renounced his earlier liberal views, and his subsequent books reflect more conservative sentiments.

Most of the intelligentsia were members of the gentry. Well-schooled and knowledgeable about European affairs and philosophies, many were troubled by a nagging sense of guilt over owning serfs and enjoying special privileges. Their idealization of the simple, illiterate, God-fearing, Russian peasant—the *muzhik*—was an admiration from afar (often from the salons of Paris, London, and Vienna). Their humanitarian concern was for an abstract class of the downtrodden, not for the individual peasants with whom they had contact. In a sense, they were parlor liberals; they seldom attempted to translate their ideas into political action. Above all, they were painfully aware of the gulf separating them from the Russian masses whom they proposed to liberate "for their own best interest."

Alexander Herzen, who had witnessed the revolutions in Western Europe and had been disillusioned by their outcomes, was the first to advocate a uniquely Russian form of socialism. Herzen began an underground newspaper, *The Bell*, which voiced his socialist ideals; he was consequently harassed repeatedly by the Tsar's secret police. Nevertheless, each month, the latest issue of *The Bell* made its way to Nicholas's desk, a source of endless annoyance to the Tsar. Despite repeated investigation and interrogations, the newly created political police (the Third Section) were never able to ascertain who was responsible for smuggling the newspaper into the Tsar's chambers.

According to Herzen, Russia possessed the latent power to transform society, to fashion a new and more just social order. That power lay with the *muzhik*. Reacting to the dislocations of Western capitalism and the traumas of the Industrial Revolution, Herzen and the other *narodnik* socialists charted a special course for Russia.* They advocated a form of agrarian or populist socialism. *Narodnik* socialism believed, above all, in the character of the Russian people to redeem the society and, secondly, in the principle of communal socialist organization. *Narodnik* socialism repudiated Western philosophies and experience, but without accepting the Slavophile attachment to autocracy and Orthodoxy. Instead, *narodnik* socialism hailed the peasant commune—the *mir*—as a progressive socialist institution that would allow Russia to advance to socialism more quickly than the capitalist West. Herzen and the other *narodniki* also noted that the concept of private property was alien to the Russian people. In this sense, *narodnik* socialism was the intellectual antecedent of Marxist communism; unlike Marxism, however, it viewed the development of industry as an evil because it destroyed peasant life.[2]

ALEXANDER II'S REFORMS

In the mid-nineteenth century, Russia was alive with new ideas and social movements. Under the relatively enlightened and progressive rule of Alexander II (1855–1881), society was opened to change. Alexander con-

Narodnik is derived from *narod,* meaning "people."

cluded the manifesto announcing the end of the Crimean War with a promise of reform. Inexorable pressures—both economic and moral—were building for the abolition of serfdom. As agriculture grew more competitive, many landlords could no longer afford to care for their serfs. In addition, serfdom began to engender political unrest. While the Pugachev peasant rebellion of 1773 to 1775 is the most famous, peasant insurrections occurred more frequently and became more violent in the second half of the nineteenth century. Official records of the tsarist government report more than five hundred peasant uprisings in the nineteenth century prior to the emancipation of the serfs in 1861.[3] Furthermore, the intelligentsia of all philosophical orientations opposed the institution of serfdom as morally wrong. Ivan Turgenev, for example, indirectly condemned serfdom in his work *A Sportsman's Sketches,* which contained realistic descriptions of the plight of the serfs. Publications of the book led to Turgenev's forced exile on his estate in 1852.

Emancipation eventually came on March 3, 1861. At the time, approximately 20 million peasants owned 115 million dessiatins; only 30,000 of the gentry class owned more than 95 million dessiatins.[4] Except in the Ukraine, land was sold not to individual peasants, but to the peasant commune, which divided the land among its members and was responsible for taxes and the provision of recruits for the army. Because few peasants could afford to buy land from the gentry, the government acquired the land for them and was reimbursed through heavy redemption payments, which rapidly created a class of impoverished peasants. Thus, for many serfs, the so-called emancipation altered only slightly their everyday existence.

The emancipation was not the only reform undertaken by Alexander II. He also created district and city *zemstva,* or assemblies, which granted limited self-rule to the local units of government and representation for the peasants. The *zemstvo* system provided free health care and education and unintentionally fostered increased support for socialist policies among the peasant class.

Alexander II introduced a widespread reform of the judicial system in 1864. Under the new provisions, the judiciary became an independent branch of government. Trials had to be conducted in public. Judicial procedure was streamlined and codified, and the courts were reorganized into a single, unified system under the Senate. Other reforms of the 1860s included the creation of the State Bank, establishment of a single state treasury, publication of the state budget, liberalized rules in education, and relaxed censorship.

FROM THE SALON TO THE STREET

The reforms instituted by Alexander II invited increasingly strident political demands and sharpened the reactionary policies of the conservative aristocracy rather than placating those calling for change. Unrest swept the universities. At St. Petersburg University, students occupied the administrative offices and closed the university with strikes. Male students grew their hair long, while female students cut their hair short and wore rose-tinted glasses. Students boasted of breaking social norms and experimented with new institutions, such as coed communes. The parallels between the student radicalism in Russia in the 1860s and in the United States in the 1960s are striking.

A decisive change in Alexander II's policies came in 1866, in reaction to a deranged student's attempt to assassinate the Tsar. Count Dmitrii Tolstoy was named Minister of Education and ordered to reinstill discipline and control over the universities. Press censorship was stiffened, and political cases were exempted from regular judicial procedures.

The intelligentsia of Russia during the 1860s and 1870s was experiencing a generation gap. The "fathers" of the 1840s generation were isolated and bewildered by the "sons" of the 1860s and 1870s.[5] Whereas the older generation emphasized humanistic, metaphysical, and aesthetic approaches to Russia's salvation, the younger generation, led by radicals such as Nicholas Chernyshevsky, Mikhail Bakunin, Dmitri Pisarev, Sergei Nechaev, and Felix Dzerzhinsky, supported nihilism, anarchy, and violent revolution.

The rebels of the 1860s were political activists who took their philosophies to the streets. Earlier generations of Russian intellectuals had been social philosophers who criticized the regime on philosophical grounds while enjoying brandy and cigars in the salons; their defiance extended only to publishing their ideas in underground newspapers and pamphlets. In contrast, the younger generation advocated a more violent and direct course of action.

Many of the younger generation advocated nihilism as the spiritual liberation of the individual, a necessary first step toward political liberation. Nihilism (from the Latin *nihil,* or "nothing") was the negation of all value and order. A characteristically Russian phenomenon, nihilism sought absolute liberation for the individual in a quasi-religious, apocalyptic fashion. The nihilists wanted to break every established social norm and convention, to destroy all traditional institutions that they claimed enslaved humanity. True liberation could come, they maintained, only by the total destruction of the old regime. Nihilists demanded liberation from all concepts (soul, God, art, standards) as well as institutions (law, the state, marriage, family). For instance, they argued that marriage, by its very nature, enslaved women; the full emancipation of women would come only with the total destruction of the institution of marriage.

Nihilism embodied a strong religious element, a sense of seeking purification and spiritual rejuvenation through the total rejection and negation of conventional society and values. The ideas of nihilism were especially popular among seminarians and the children of priests, who were alienated by the intellectual corruption and decadence of the Russian Orthodox church. Chernyshevsky's utopian novel, *What Is to Be Done?,* is a virtual textbook of nihilism. The hero, Rakhmetov, sleeps on a bed of nails as a trial of will and self-sacrifice, while the heroine, Vera Pavlova, dreams of utopian cooperative workshops and free love. Karl Marx reportedly learned Russian just so that he could read Chernyshevsky's book.

While the nihilists rejected the decadence and moral decay of Russian society and sought the liberation of the individual, the *narodniki* of the 1860s, strongly influenced by Bakunin and Herzen, offered a program of political action aimed at the eventual overthrow of the tsarist regime. Bakunin and Herzen translated their earlier populist and agrarian socialism into a movement that came to be called "To the People"; it eventually evolved into the Socialist Revolutionary party. Responding to Herzen's admonition to "go to the people," more than twenty-five hundred students and intellectuals went into the countryside, some to teach and provide health care, others to radicalize the peasants. Much like the handful of American student activists of the 1960s and early 1970s who determined that they must radicalize the "hard hats" and "rednecks" in order to successfully challenge the Establishment, these Russian radicals were received in the villages with suspicion and sometimes violence. Bakunin had predicted that, if properly inspired, the peasants would rise spontaneously in revolt, but the populist campaign failed. The Tsar's secret police made mass arrests, and more than two hundred members of the movement were tried and exiled in 1877.

The failure of the peasants to rebel spontaneously prompted some of the radicals to reexamine the course of revolution in Russia. They concluded that an effective organization was needed to mobilize the populace for revolution. In 1876, Peter Tkachev published a tract, *Revolution and the State,* in which he argued that the seizure of power must precede the transformation of society. The revolution would not come about as the result of an uprising of the masses, but as a coup engineered by a small, conspiratorial group acting on behalf of the masses. Peter Lavrov and Sergei Nechaev felt that the masses would play a supporting role in the revolution, but that they must be led by a tightly organized band of professional revolutionaries. In *Catechism of a Revolutionary,* Nechaev advocated a revolutionary party organization consisting of highly centralized cells designed to force the masses to revolt. Lavrov predicted that, after a successful revolution, a transitional period of dictatorship would ensue, during which the illiterate, conservative, and deeply religious Russian peasant would be transformed through propaganda and education. The ideas of Lavrov and Nechaev were later adopted and perfected by Lenin and the Bolsheviks.

Others used the failure of the "To the People" experiment to rationalize still more coercive measures. Felix Dzerzhinsky, a dedicated revolutionary who would later become the first chief of the Cheka, Lenin's secret police, advocated creating suffering among the peasants to stimulate them to rise in revolution. Dzerzhinsky and his followers engaged in activities intentionally designed to inflict hardship on the peasants, such as setting fire to their fields to induce starvation in the countryside.

Many of the instances of violence in the early 1870s were spontaneous countermeasures against increasingly brutal tactics of the police. By the late 1870s, however, a well-organized conspiratorial anarchist society, the People's Will, had emerged. Members of the People's Will hoped that a few well-chosen terrorist acts would seriously disrupt the excessively centralized tsarist regime and inspire the peasants to rebellion. The People's Will called for Alexander II's death and made numerous bold attempts on his life. In one incident, the Tsar's dining room in the Winter Palace was totally destroyed by explosives, but the Tsar escaped unharmed. In 1878, Vera Zasulich shot and wounded the military governor of St. Petersburg, who had ordered the flogging of a political prisoner.

Alexander II, besieged by the activities of the anarchists and receiving little sympathy from the public, decided that a more moderate policy might lead to a rapprochement. He appointed Count Mikhail Loris-Melikov Minister of the Interior, instructing him to develop a plan to counteract the terrorism. Melikov's proposals called for sweeping reforms to broaden public participation in policy-making. Alexander approved the proposals and was to have signed them into law on the afternoon of March 1, 1881, but he was assassinated on his way to a ceremonial review of the troops that morning. The People's Will had carefully plotted the murder, placing members along all of the routes from the Winter Palace to the parade ground. Each terrorist carried a recently invented device—a nitroglycerin bomb. The two anarchists who lobbed their bombs at Alexander's carriage died instantly. The Tsar's legs were blown off by the force of the explosion; he died in the arms of his son and heir, Alexander III, who swore to avenge his father's death by initiating a reign of terror against the anarchists.

FROM REFORM TO REACTION

Alexander III, a dedicated reactionary, was determined to suppress revolution and maintain autocracy at all cost. He instituted counterreforms giving the authorities sweeping powers to deal with the press and political critics of the regime. Summary search, arrest, imprisonment, exile, and secret trials by courts-martial became common. A new university statute of 1884 outlawed student unions and placed the universities under the strict supervision of the Ministry of Education. Alexander II's liberal advisers and ministers resigned in protest and were replaced by well-known conservatives and reactionaries, such as Constantine Pobedonostsev and Dmitrii Tolstoy. Pobedonostsev, tutor to Alexander III and his successor, Nicholas II, feared Westernization, urbanization, and industrialization because they threatened to bring change. In fact, he once expressed the desire "to keep people from inventing things."[6]

In order to strengthen its hold on the increasingly restive peasants, the regime established the office of *zemskii nachal'nik* (land captain), whose responsibilities included exercising direct control over the peasants throughout the empire. The land captains, who were appointed by the minister of the interior, had the power to approve or disapprove peasants elected to local offices, to override the decisions of the communes, and to fine, arrest, and imprison peasants.

The reactionary character of Alexander III's regime manifested itself in the treatment of non-Orthodox denominations. Roman Catholics and Lutherans, who comprised a majority in some of the western regions, were discriminated against, and campaigns to convert Moslems and Buddhists in Central Asia and the Far East were organized. But the most coercive tactics were reserved for the Old Believers, Baptists, and Jews. The Jewish Pale, the area of western Russia in which all Jews had to live, was reduced in size, forcing many families to relocate. Jews were prohibited from farming, thus forcing them into the trades and professions. In 1887, the government imposed quotas on Jewish enrollment in institutions of higher learning, further restricting their ability to enter various professions. Throughout the late 1800s and early 1900s, violent popular outbreaks against the Jews swept Russia, resulting in the destruction of Jewish property and the deaths of many Jews. These pogroms occurred with the silent consent, if not the active encouragement, of the government. Pobedonostsev, the Tsar's most trusted adviser, once remarked that "the Jewish problem" in Russia would be solved by the conversion to Orthodoxy of a third of the Jews, emigration of another third, and the deaths of the remaining third.[7]

The counterreforms of Alexander III did not come without opposition, however. Despite the stepped-up measures of the secret police, remnants of the People's Will continued their underground activities. In 1887, a group that included Alexander Ulianov, Lenin's older brother, was arrested and executed for plotting to assassinate the Tsar.

The execution of his brother had a deep, lasting effect on the seventeen-year-old Lenin. Born Vladimir Ilich Ulianov in a small Siberian town in 1870, Lenin was the son of a provincial school inspector.[8] Radicalized by the death of his brother, he began to read the works of the German socialist Karl Marx. After finishing law school at St. Petersburg University, he devoted his time to revolutionary activity. In 1895, he was arrested and exiled to Siberia. In exile, he wrote his first major work, *The Development of Capitalism in Russia,* an attack on the populist ideas of the Socialist Revolutionaries. Lenin held no great admiration for the Russian peasants; his socialism was a product of the rapid industrialization that was transforming Russia into a more modern, capitalist state.

The reigns of the last two Romanov tsars, Alexander III and Nicholas II, were marked by reaction, repression, and a pathological fear of change. Support for the regimes lay almost exclusively with the gentry, whose political and economic power was waning. The provincial governors who controlled the countryside on the Tsar's behalf were a backward group who sought to preserve their own interests. They were the subject of derision in the satirical writing of noted nineteenth-century Russian authors, including Mikhail Saltykov-Shchedrin and Nikolai Gogol. Saltykov-Shchedrin had himself been deputy governor of Tver and the Riazan provinces under Alexander II. In *Provincial Sketches,* he portrayed one provincial governor as having a soup bowl in place of a head. Inevitably, the governor stumbled in a rutted street, shattered his "head," and was thereafter condemned to go through life headless—with no perceptible impairment of his mental faculties. Another of Saltykov-Shchedrin's fictional provincial governors, widely hailed as a progressive and forward-thinking man, was found dead one morning, devoured by his own fleas.

Graft and corruption were rampant among the provincial bureaucrats. Saltykov-Shchedrin wrote that it was more prudent to invest in bribes than in bank deposits, because bribes spared one harassment by the authorities, which could be even more costly.[9] Nikolai Gogol's story "The Nose" is a caricature of a provincial bureaucrat so concerned with advancing his own career and elevating his rank that he was transformed into nothing but an uplifted nose.

In 1894, Alexander III died unexpectedly at the relatively young age of forty-nine, leaving his twenty-six-year-old son, Nicholas II, ill-prepared to assume power. Unlike his father, Nicholas lacked the drive, authority, and determination to tackle difficult problems. He proved to be narrow-minded, weak, and most important, unusually dependent upon the advice of his ministers and aides. Toward the end of Nicholas's reign (1894–1917), the power behind the throne was his wife, the German-born tsarina Alexandra.

The one area of intelligent and farsighted policy under Nicholas II was in the Ministry of Finance, headed by Count Sergei Witte. Witte recognized that in order to remain a strong empire, Russia had to develop its industry and build railroads. Under his direction, heavy industry was developed, and the railroad network doubled in mileage, including the completion of the Trans-Siberian line. Thus, industrialization did not come about spontaneously, but as the result of government policies and decrees and foreign investment.

The completion of the Trans-Siberian Railroad enabled Russia to engage in more aggressive and adventurous policies in the Far East. These policies culminated in the outbreak of the Russo-Japanese War (1904–1905). The Tsar initially welcomed the onset of the war to distract the public from problems at home, but the war also extracted a heavy price on the already strained economy. In a surprise attack, the entire Russian Pacific fleet was sunk in the harbor of Port Arthur in 1904. The Tsar then dispatched his Baltic fleet to the Pacific. After making the long journey from the Baltic, through the Atlantic, around the Cape of Good Hope, through the Indian Ocean, to the Sea of Japan, the antiquated fleet was destroyed in a single battle. The peace treaty ending the hostilities ceded Korea and the southern half of Sakhalin Island to Japan.

THE REVOLUTION OF 1905

The humiliating loss to the Japanese compounded problems in Russia and resulted in the first popular revolt against the tsarist government—the Revolution of 1905. Opposition to the Tsar's regime had become more hostile and organized toward the turn of the century. A devastating famine in 1891 and 1892 drove many peasants to the cities in search of employment and food. A formative labor movement began to develop as industrialization took place. By 1900, more than two million industrial workers were concentrated in a few major cities of European Russia.[10] Strikes spread throughout the country, and student protests became more frequent. Sporadic peasant disturbances disrupted rural life and gave added support to the Socialist Revolutionary party, which favored populist and agrarian elements. Some factions of the Party resumed terrorist activities, assassinating several prominent government officials, including Nicholas II's second cousin. In 1902 and 1903, doctors, teachers, and other professional groups began to demand social and political reforms and a voice in the policy-making process.

The labor movement was instrumental in the introduction into Russia of Marxist ideas, advocated by the Social Democratic party. In 1898, Georgii Plekhanov founded the Social Democratic party, the first Marxist party in Russia. A historic split occurred in the Social Democratic party at the

Second International, held in Brussels and London in 1903. Lenin and his faction, who came to be called the *Bolsheviks* (from *bol'shinstvo*, meaning "majority"), argued that the Party should be tightly organized and composed solely of professional revolutionaries. Lenin strongly opposed incorporating "mere trade unionists," liberals, and others who might blunt the Party's revolutionary objectives. The Mensheviks (from *men'shinstvo*, meaning "minority") preferred a broader, looser party structure, incorporating a wide spectrum of liberal and socialist elements. Lenin's faction carried the argument and thereafter adopted the name Bolshevik.

The Bolsheviks and Mensheviks also clashed over issues of Marxist doctrine. While the Mensheviks maintained that Russia must first proceed through the stage of capitalism before advancing to socialism, the Bolsheviks advocated skipping the capitalist stage of development and proceeding directly to socialism by harnessing and guiding the revolutionary potential of the Russian peasantry.

Russia was on the brink of an explosion on January 22, 1905, when a priest, Father Gapon, led thousands of workers on a march to the Winter Palace to petition Tsar Nicholas II for bread and land. Many of the marchers carried icons and portraits of the Tsar; they were his faithful subjects petitioning him for redress and assistance. The palace guards were ordered to fire on the peaceful, unarmed demonstrators, and they killed 130 people and wounded several hundred others.[11] This incident, known as "Bloody Sunday," forever eradicated the view that the Tsar was basically a good and honest man who was simply out of touch with the suffering of the Russian people. His government lost all credibility.

The massacre sparked spontaneous strikes and violence throughout the country. For the first time, millions of ordinary Russian citizens took part in a mass movement in opposition to the regime, thus giving support to the more radical parties. Facing increased pressure, Nicholas II declared his intention to convoke a Duma, or Constituent Assembly. He also repealed some of the more coercive legislation relating to non-Orthodox religious groups and ethnic minorities. However, it was a case of too little, too late. Strikes and peasant uprisings continued throughout 1905. The Duma had no real powers and did not satisfy the masses clamoring for the end of autocracy. In the fall, a general strike was called throughout Russia. In the cities, electricity and water were cut off, and railroad service came to a halt. Leadership of the strike was organized by a council (*sovet*) comprised of the heads of the various socialist parties and representatives of the workers. The leader of the strike movement was Lev Bronstein, later known as Leon Trotsky.

Due to the initiative of Count Witte, a manifesto was issued on October 30, 1905, which amounted to a capitulation by the government to the demands of the populace. The manifesto recognized civil liberties, legalized the formation of political parties, and created a Duma with full powers. The manifesto was a tentative step toward transforming the tsarist regime into a constitutional monarchy. In practice, however, these innovations did not significantly impinge on the powers of the Tsar.

Elections were held for the first time in Russian history, and the results were not encouraging to the regime. Of the 497 representatives elected to the Duma, only 10 percent came from the parties of the Right. Both the Socialist Revolutionaries and the Social Democrats boycotted the election, giving the largest bloc of votes to the Constitutional Democrats (*Kadets*). The First Duma, which convened in May 1906, was dissolved by the Tsar after only seventy-three days of futile bickering and factionalism.

Another round of elections was called; this time, the Socialist Revolutionaries and the Social Democrats participated. Leftist parties increased their representation to approximately 43 percent of the elected representatives. The Second Duma lasted for little more than three months before reaching an impasse with the government over granting immunity to sixteen Social Democratic deputies arrested for treason. On the same day that Nicholas II dissolved the Second Duma, he arbitrarily and unconstitutionally changed the electoral law, justifying his action on the principle that he had the right to abrogate what he had granted. The electoral law was rewritten to reduce drastically peasant and worker representation, while increasing the representation of the gentry.

Having emasculated the Duma, the government initiated its own legislative program. The chief architect of the program was Pyotr Stolypin, Minister of the Interior. Stolypin placed much of the country under martial law. Thousands were imprisoned or executed, and many leading revolutionaries (including Lenin) were forced to flee abroad. Once relative calm had been restored, Stolypin introduced land-reform legislation aimed at counteracting revolutionary influences by granting the peasantry private plots of land. Stolypin hoped that a class of well-to-do peasants would have a stabilizing influence in the countryside. The reform was a partial success, but it did not lead to the calm that Stolypin had anticipated. In 1911, less than one year after the enactment of his agrarian reform, Stolypin was assassinated in the presence of the Tsar by a revolutionary.

THE TWO REVOLUTIONS OF 1917

The domestic difficulties that troubled the tsarist regime at the turn of the century were compounded by the outbreak of World War I in 1914. In the initial days of the war, there was a rapprochement between the government and the public. This soon broke down, however, due to the Tsar's stubborn intransigence in refusing to cooperate with the Duma. Against the advice of his aides and ministers, the Tsar went to the front to command the Russian forces, leaving the capital and the government in the hands of the tsarina, Alexandra, and the infamous monk Gregori Rasputin. Initially, the war effort went well for the Russians; they advanced through Poland and were pressing toward Hungary when the Germans and Austrians mounted a counteroffensive in May 1915. The Russians were then forced to retreat, surrendering control of the newly won regions as well as of much of the western portion of the empire. There were staggering casualties—two million in 1915 alone. More than three million civilian refugees retreated with the Russian army, placing an additional burden on the already overcrowded cities and towns.[12]

Famine and disease were widespread through the winter of 1916–

1917. From March 8 through March 11, 1917, shortages of coal and bread sparked riots and demonstrations in the capital, whose name had been changed from the German "St. Petersburg" to "Petrograd." Troops sent to quell the disturbances joined forces with the protesters, and all authority collapsed. On March 12, in an effort to restore order, the Duma created a Provisional Government headed first by Prince Lvov and later by Aleksandr Kerensky, a Socialist Revolutionary. Three days later, on March 15, the Tsar bowed to the inevitable and abdicated his throne. The tsarist regime fell without a single shot being fired.

In Petrograd and in numerous other cities and regions throughout the country, dual sets of political institutions arose: the Provisional Government and the workers' councils (soviets), which arose more or less spontaneously and were dominated by the Mensheviks and Social Revolutionaries. Order No. 1 of the executive committee of the Petrograd soviet provided that the military orders of the Provisional Government should be obeyed only if they did not conflict with those of the soviets. Throughout much of 1917, nevertheless, the soviets did not openly oppose the Provisional Government, but neither did they allow it to consolidate power.

Word of the Tsar's abdication reached Lenin, who was in exile in Zurich. He had spent most of the war years there, having been declared persona non grata by the Tsar's secret police. Ironically, Lenin had confessed in a lecture just two months earlier: "We of the older generation may not live to see the decisive battles of this coming revolution."[13] Upon hearing the news of the collapse of the Tsar's government, Lenin set out for Russia with the assistance of the Germans, who were more than happy to provide a special train to transport him through the war zone. Lenin arrived at the Finland Station in Petrograd on April 16 and was met by a huge throng. On the train platform, he made a speech demanding that the Bolsheviks and their followers oppose the Provisional Government. In his April Theses, Lenin reiterated his call for opposition to the Provisional Government and declared, "All Power to the Soviets!" That is, he recognized the legitimacy of the soviets and hoped to transform them into revolutionary institutions dominated by the Bolsheviks.

Throughout 1917, the population was demanding "peace, bread, and land," but the Provisional Government was reluctant to withdraw Russia from the war and to redistribute land without first obtaining a mandate from the people. Chaos and the collapse of all civilian authority, however, made holding elections extremely difficult. In July 1917, Kerensky's vacillation and inaction led to an attempt by the Bolsheviks to overthrow the Provisional Government.

During the July Days affair, soldiers and sailors, together with the Bolsheviks, tried to seize power in Petrograd. However, the Petrograd soviet, which was then dominated by Mensheviks, remained loyal to the Provisional Government. Kerensky used the police to root out his opponents, forcing Lenin to flee to Finland, where he continued to direct the Bolsheviks. The Provisional Government moved its base of operations to the former Winter Palace—a decision of immense symbolic importance. The July Days episode convinced Lenin more than ever that a successful revolution in Russia could not occur as a spontaneous popular uprising; it must be the work of a tightly organized, conspiratorial band of professional revolutionaries. His efforts from July through the autumn of 1917 were devoted to creating such an organization.

Meanwhile the Provisional Government continued to promote the war effort and refused to recognize the redistribution of land going on in the countryside. Finally, on the night of October 25 (November 7 on the new calendar), the battleship *Aurora*, moored in the Neva River across from the Winter Palace, fired a signal.* Bolshevik-led troops from the Petrograd garrison and sailors from Kronstadt stormed the palace. A handful of people were killed in the unsuccessful attempts of the Provisional Government to resist what was in essence a palace coup. Two days later, the Bolsheviks formed the Council of People's Commissars, headed by Lenin, who had returned to Petrograd.[14]

The new regime acted quickly to secure peace and redistribute land—the two pressing needs that the Provisional Government had been unwilling or unable to fulfill. On December 5, a preliminary armistice agreement with the Germans was reached at Brest Litovsk. A decree transferred all private and church lands to the state and granted peasants as much land as they could till. This decree merely ratified what was already occurring in the countryside, where peasants were ransacking the large estates of the gentry and confiscating the land and personal property for their own use.

A number of social reforms were quickly instituted, destroying any vestiges of the old regime. The marriage and divorce laws were repealed, and only civil marriages were recognized; the Gregorian calendar was adopted; and the Cyrillic alphabet was simplified. The government proclaimed the separation of church and state, and placed all former parochial schools under secular control. Banks were nationalized, and large factories were placed under the direction of workers' committees. Revolutionary tribunals replaced the tsarist judicial system and were instructed to decide cases based on "revolutionary conscience and the revolutionary concept of justice."[15]

The Constituent Assembly, in which the Social Revolutionaries held an absolute majority, was disbanded. The Bolsheviks solidified their control of the soviets, which sprang up in most cities, towns, villages, and rural districts. The Cheka (Extraordinary Commission to Combat Counterrevolution), a secret police organization under the direction of Felix Dzerzhinsky, was authorized to hunt down Constitutional Democrats, Socialist Revolutionaries, Mensheviks, and other "counterrevolutionaries." Lavrov's prediction of a transitional dictatorship was rapidly becoming a reality.

THE CIVIL WAR: 1918–1921

The Russian Revolution arrived in the countryside not through the popular uprising of the peasants, but by telegraph. After the collapse of the tsarist regime, most areas of the empire were not in the firm hands of the

---

*At the time of the Revolution, Russia still used the Julian calendar. In 1918, the Gregorian calendar was adopted, and today the Great October Revolution is actually celebrated on November 7.

Bolsheviks, but were experiencing the breakdown of all civil authority. Many of the ethnic nationalities seized this opportunity to assert their national independence.

Counterrevolutionaries, frequently referred to as the White forces, resisted Bolshevik attempts to consolidate their hold on the country. The Whites consisted of army officers, members of the bourgeois class of merchants, and a wide array of political groups, including reactionary monarchists on the extreme right and Socialist Revolutionaries on the left. The struggle of these White forces with the Reds culminated in a civil war that ravaged Russia from 1918 to 1921.

The Civil War was complicated by foreign interventions and a war with Poland. In 1918, troops from fourteen countries (primarily Japan, Great Britain, France, and the United States) landed at various ports of Russia. The intervention was supposedly intended to prevent war materiel from falling into the hands of the Germans, with whom the Western powers were still fighting. However, there is little question that the primary aim of the intervention was to lend assistance to the White forces trying to topple the Bolsheviks. The Allied intervention, an episode that every Soviet student learns about at an early age, reinforced the Bolsheviks' fears of capitalist encirclement—that the bourgeoisie capitalist powers would go to any length to reverse socialist successes.

In the first heady days of the Russian Revolution, the Bolsheviks believed that it would be a catalyst, inspiring the workers of Germany, Great Britain, France, and the United States to rise up and overthrow their governments. Trotsky, who assumed the title of Foreign Commissar, glibly pronounced that his job would be exceedingly easy: all he would have to do was issue a few revolutionary proclamations and then close up shop. Once the worldwide socialist revolution came, there would be no need for diplomats or foreign commissariats. Revolutionary activity was strong elsewhere. In Germany, the Social Democratic Party and the Spartakus League commanded a large following, especially among the industrial laborers. In late 1918, a coalition of leftist parties staged an attempted revolution in Berlin. Two of the movement's leaders, Karl Liebknecht and Rosa Luxemburg, were assassinated, however, and the police crushed the abortive revolution. The failure of the German revolution shocked Lenin and the other Bolshevik leaders, who slowly realized that they might remain the only socialist state in a world dominated by capitalist powers.

In 1919, the Third International (Comintern) was convened in Moscow. Marxist parties from all over the world sent representatives to be "officially recognized" by the Comintern leadership. Headed by Lenin's associate Grigorii Zinoviev, the Comintern proclaimed its intentions to foster international revolution.

THE NEW ECONOMIC POLICY (NEP): 1921–1928

The end of the Civil War brought a much-needed period of reconstruction. World War I, the revolutions of 1917, and the Civil War wreaked havoc on Russian society and on the economy. Industrial production was only 14 percent of pre–World War I levels; steel production fell to just 5 percent of prewar levels.[16] The fields lay untended, and what little agricultural production the peasants were able to carry out was done for their own consumption. Few agricultural commodities made their way to the cities.

Lenin recognized that a new direction was required. Resurrecting an earlier doctrine, he advocated "taking one step forward, two steps back." In other words, the Bolsheviks had achieved a major step forward with the Revolution, but now they needed to retreat from socialist revolutionary goals, at least temporarily, in order to gain the support of the peasants. Lenin introduced the New Economic Policy (NEP) to restore order, consolidate Bolshevik political gains, and reconstruct the devastated economy. The NEP represented a partial restoration of capitalism. Peasants were granted the right to farm their own plots, and small- and medium-sized industries were allowed to function much as they had prior to the Revolution. The "commanding heights of the economy," however, remained in the hands of the State.

The agricultural problem was exacerbated by drought and famine in 1921 and 1922. Lenin appealed to the League of Nations for humanitarian relief for his fledgling government, but aid was denied. The United States, under the leadership of President Herbert Hoover, provided some aid for victims of the famine. American businessman Armand Hammer (later chief of Occidental Petroleum) also organized a relief mission to deliver food and medical supplies to Russia. Lenin himself met Hammer at the port of Petrograd when the freighter arrived, and Hammer has maintained close personal contacts with Soviet leaders ever since.

The NEP also entailed a relaxation in social policies. Censorship was lifted, and the arts flourished. After a long period of suppression and turmoil, the creative energies of Russian society were released. There was a heady sense of being part of a new social experiment, of creating a just and equitable social order. Madame Kollontai, the outspoken Bolshevik authority on the "women's question," advocated the abolition of marriage and the communal rearing of children. In her view, children were "the common possession of all the workers."[17] During the NEP period, women achieved their first real prominence in the arts and other professions.

The NEP also spawned the futurist and the constructivist schools of art and literature. The former depicted the glorious future society that would be created by the new socialist order. The latter group applied their artistic talents and abilities in the service of the Revolution by constructing futuristic buildings and designing factories that incorporated revolutionary concepts of architecture.

During the NEP years, the regime was continually troubled by internal political dissension. In March 1921, the sailors at Kronstadt mutinied and had to be put down by garrisons of the Red Guards. Within the Party, opposition to NEP emerged. To many, the NEP represented an unacceptable retreat from the gains the Bolsheviks had achieved in the Revolution. Others, called the Workers' Opposition, who were closely aligned with Trotsky, criticized the increasing centralization of power and favored turning power over to the trade unions. All of these divergent views erupted at the Tenth Party Congress in March 1921. In an attempt to silence his critics,

Lenin hammered through the Decree on Party Unity, which prohibited the formation of political factions to oppose party policies. In short, the decree supported relatively open discussion of policies before they were ratified by the Party, but outlawed any criticism of policies once they were enacted. The decree, however, prohibited the existence of factions with their own organizations and policy goals. Furthermore, the Central Committee was given the power to expel party members who violated this rule. The decree was used to silence Lenin's critics, and it succeeded for a short time.

In 1922, with the New Economic Policy scarcely underway, Lenin suffered a debilitating stroke. Joseph Stalin at that time occupied the post of General Secretary of the Central Committee, a largely bureaucratic position responsible for the management of internal party affairs. Nevertheless, Stalin used his powers to recruit and dismiss party members, thereby strengthening his position among the ruling elite. In fact, Stalin's tactics were so ruthless that Lenin wrote a letter from his deathbed to his comrades on the Central Committee, warning them of Stalin's dangerous ambitions. On January 21, 1924, Lenin died, and the regime confronted its first succession crisis.

FROM AUTOCRACY TO AUTOCRACY

The cycle of rebellion and repression and of revolution and counter-revolution that had characterized Russia throughout the nineteenth century continued into the twentieth. It is ironic that the Bolsheviks, who succeeded in overthrowing the tsarist autocracy, should witness the methodical and relentless reinstitution of autocratic dictatorship under Stalin.

Stalin moved quickly to divide Lenin's successors. First, he split with Trotsky over the issue of supporting international revolution. Whereas Trotsky saw the main hope for socialism in worldwide revolution, Stalin reflected more nationalistic sentiments and favored "socialism in one country." The left and right also disagreed in their stances toward the NEP. Trotsky, Grigorii Zinoviev, and Lev Kamenev denounced the NEP as a retreat from the gains of the Revolution, while Nikolai Bukharin, Mikhail Tomsky, and Aleksei Rykov allied with Stalin in support of the NEP. Stalin launched an attack first on Trotsky, then Zinoviev, then Kamenev on the left. In 1926, Trotsky was forced to resign as War Commissar, and the next year he and Zinoviev were removed from the Party. In 1928, Trotsky fled into exile. (Still troublesome even in exile, he was assassinated in Mexico City in 1940.) Having defeated his adversaries on the left, Stalin then turned on his former allies on the right.

At the Fifteenth Party Congress in December 1927, Stalin declared that the economy had been restored to prewar levels and that the next task was to undertake bold new directions. He advocated the amalgamation of small peasant farms into large-scale agricultural enterprises and the vigorous construction of new industry. Stalin's departure from the NEP alarmed Bukharin and other members of the right, who supported the construction of socialism, but "at a snail's pace."

Throughout 1928, grain deliveries to the cities were inadequate. Stalin used this as a pretext for advocating "emergency measures." He mounted a coercive campaign against the *kulakhs,* the wealthiest of the peasants, while attacking the right for opposing his plans. Gradually, during 1929 and 1930, Stalin succeeded in removing Bukharin, Rykov, and Tomsky from their top leadership posts.

In October 1928, Stalin announced the end of the NEP and the collectivization of agriculture and forced industrialization under the First Five-Year Plan. Collectivization was met with widespread opposition in the countryside. Many of the peasants slaughtered their cattle and burned their crops rather than have them handed over to the collective. Partly as a result of this opposition, famine devastated the country in 1932 and 1933. Stalin later boasted to Winston Churchill that more people were killed in the battle over collectivization in the Ukraine than were killed in the Battle of Stalingrad during World War II. In all, more than five million people perished during Stalin's forced collectivization.[18]

Collectivization was not so much a "revolution from above," as Stalin claimed, as a way to extend control over the peasants. In addition, by lowering the peasants' standard of living, Stalin was able to generate revenue to finance the rapid expansion of industry.

During the 1920s, Stalin demonstrated remarkable flexibility in manipulating policies and forming alliances with various factions in order to isolate and defeat his adversaries. He also used his position as General Secretary of the Party to promote loyal followers into influential positions. Stalin was a preeminent organizational infighter, and it was exactly this cunning and ruthless drive for power that had prompted Lenin to advise his comrades to find a way to remove him.

Having eliminated all major opposition, Stalin emerged in the 1930s as a bold and forceful leader committed to expanding the Soviet Union's industrial might as rapidly as possible. Like Lenin, Stalin believed that the construction and survival of communism in Russia was dependent upon harnessing the power of the peasantry. Thus, in many respects, Stalin represented a logical extension of currents established under Lenin. Even Stalin's authoritarian concentration of power had precursors in Lenin's Decree on Party Unity and the purge of 1921. Collectivized agriculture, nationalized industries, and centralized planning were consistent with the Bolsheviks' aims; they were moderated during and immediately after the Revolution solely to avoid alienating the peasants and the middle class. In this sense, Stalin's "departure" represented the fulfillment of the Revolution.

As hostilities rose in Europe during the 1930s, however, Stalin's push to industrialize the economy and his preoccupation with power became more of an obsession. At the Seventeenth Party Congress in 1934, there was an abortive effort to oust him as General Secretary. Rumors abounded that Sergei Kirov, the Leningrad party chief, was a likely candidate to replace him. In December 1934, Kirov was murdered. Stalin used the murder as a pretext for unleashing a new and more violent wave of purges. By 1938, the top and middle ranks of the Party were decimated. As war neared, Stalin's rule became increasingly conservative, nationalistic, and traditionally autocratic. Ranks were reinstituted in the Red Army and in the civil service in order to reestablish reliable command and control. Among the first to fall victim to Stalin's purges of the 1930s were the Old Bolsheviks, who had joined the Party before the Revolution. In policies reminiscent of those of Nicholas I, Stalin supported Great Russian nationalism and suppressed non-Slavic ethnic groups. During World War II, he forged friendly relations with the Russian Orthodox church and replaced the "Internationale" with a new national hymn of the Soviet Union.

Historians have viewed some of these changes as a retreat from the goals of the October Revolution, but they can also be seen as largely symbolic and expedient departures undertaken to enhance the Soviet state during the war effort. Nevertheless, some of these "temporary" departures became firmly entrenched and were defining characteristics of the Soviet political system during the last decade of Stalin's rule.

Although he rose to power within the Communist Party, Stalin ruled through the State toward the end of his reign, and he preferred the title of Premier or Marshal to that of General Secretary. From early 1939 until his death in 1953, only one Party Congress was convened. Stalin enlarged the Politburo to twenty-five members and changed its name to the Presidium of the Central Committee. Many of the new members held powerful posts in the state apparatus, rather than in the Party. Stalin's "counterrevolution" represented not a victory of the Party, but a victory of the State over the Party.

Although Stalin was fond of comparing himself to Peter the Great and Ivan the Terrible, his autocratic rule was not a simple return to tsarist autocracy. Stalin's dictatorship was a twentieth-century form. Technological advances in communication, the development of more effective social and governmental organizations, and the emergence of a modern industrial economy allowed him to extend dictatorial control over the country more completely than any previous ruler. The Bolshevik Revolution died under the weight of Stalin's authoritarian regime. What emerged forms the foundation of the present political system of the Soviet Union.

Notes

1. Cited in Nicholas V. Riasanovsky, *A History of Russia,* 2d ed. (New York: Oxford University Press, 1969), 357.

2. It is noteworthy that Lenin came into contact with the ideas of the *narodniki* before he was exposed to the works of Marx.

3. Figures of Vasilii Ivanovich Semevsky cited in Riasanovsky, *A History of Russia,* 410.

4. One dessiatin equals 2.7 acres. Statistics of Petr Ivanovich Liashchenko cited in Riasanovsky, *A History of Russia,* 414.

5. See Ivan Turgenev, *Fathers and Sons* (Moscow: Progress Publishers, 1977).

6. Cited in Riasanovsky, *A History of Russia,* 434.

7. Ibid., 437.

8. Pseudonyms were commonly employed by Russian revolutionary leaders to protect them from persecution by the police. The name "Lenin" comes from the Lena River in Siberia.

9. Mikhail Saltykov-Shchedrin cited in Richard Pipes, *Russia under the Old Regime* (London: Weidenfeld and Nicolson, 1974), 284–285.

10. Cited in Riasanovsky, *A History of Russia,* 474.

11. Ibid., 451.

12. Donald W. Treadgold, *Twentieth-Century Russia,* 2d ed. (Chicago: Rand McNally, 1964), 116.

13. Cited in Edmund Wilson, *To the Finland Station* (New York: Farrar, Straus, and Giroux, 1972), 533.

14. The term "people's commissar" was chosen rather than the more traditional "minister" because of the latter's association with the tsarist regime.

15. Decree of D. S. Kurskii cited in Peter H. Juviler, *Revolutionary Law and Order* (New York: Free Press, 1976), 21.

16. Cited in Treadgold, *Twentieth-Century Russia,* 200.

17. Cited in Theodore H. Von Laue, *Why Lenin? Why Stalin?* (Philadelphia: Lippincott, 1971), 159.

18. Cited in Treadgold, *Twentieth-Century Russia,* 272. Robert Conquest, in *The Harvest of Sorrow* (New York: Oxford University Press, 1986), 306, puts the combined death toll of the dekulakhization campaign and the 1932–1933 famine at some 14.5 million.

Selected Bibliography

Berdyaev, Nicolas. *The Origin of Russian Communism.* London: Geoffrey Bles, 1937.

Brinton, Crane. *The Anatomy of Revolution.* New York: Vintage, 1952.

Carr, E. H. *A History of Soviet Russia.* London: Macmillan, 1950–1953.

Conquest, Robert. *The Harvest of Sorrow.* New York: Oxford University Press, 1986.

Fainsod, Merle. *How Russia Is Ruled.* Cambridge: Harvard University Press, 1953.

Herzen, Alexander. *My Past and Thoughts.* New York: Alfred S. Knopf, 1973.

Pipes, Richard. *Russia under the Old Regime.* London: Weidenfeld and Nicolson, 1974.

Rabinowitch, Alexander. *Prelude to Revolution.* Bloomington: Indiana University Press, 1968.

Reed, John. *Ten Days That Shook the World.* New York: International Publishers, 1919.

Riasanovsky, Nicholas V. *A History of Russia.* 2d ed. New York: Oxford University Press, 1969.

Schapiro, Leonard. *The Origin of Communist Autocracy.* Cambridge: Harvard University Press, 1955.

Solzhenitsyn, Alexander. *Lenin in Zurich.* New York: Farrar, Straus, and Giroux, 1976.

Treadgold, Donald W. *Twentieth Century Russia.* 2d ed. Chicago: Rand McNally, 1968.

Ulam, Adam. *The Bolsheviks.* New York: Macmillan, 1965.

Von Laue, Theodore H. *Why Lenin? Why Stalin?* 2d ed. Philadelphia: Lippincott, 1971.

Wilson, Edmund. *To the Finland Station.* New York: Farrar, Straus, and Giroux, 1972.

Wolfe, Bertram D. *Three Who Made a Revolution.* New York: Dell Publishing, 1948.

3

Ideology and Political Socialization

No element of Soviet political life has preoccupied Western observers as much as communist ideology. Children in the West learn to value democracy and to renounce communism even before they understand the meaning of those complex concepts. Western television-news reports of parades from Red Square show banners devoted to Lenin and Marx, and viewers conclude that ideology in the USSR is ubiquitous. Westerners assume that Marxist ideology is used to "brainwash" Russian citizens, keeping them under control and encouraging them to support the regime. In addition, the West tends to view Soviet ideology either as a body of mistaken and dogmatic creeds or as crude rationalizations used to legitimize the self-interested actions of the political leadership. Westerners contrast this picture with their own society, which they generally consider to be free of ideology.

Ideology may be defined as a set of values and beliefs held in common and used to guide political action.[1] In this sense, ideologies exist in all societies and perform a variety of functions. Ideology explains the nature of reality, defining the individual's place in the social universe and providing a framework of values and identity for its adherents. By validating a particular distribution of power, ideology legitimizes the political regime. Finally, it orders the goals of political action and mobilizes adherents in support of the regime.[2]

Soviet society is not unique in manifesting an ideology. On the contrary, all societies espouse values and beliefs that undergird their systems. In the United States, for example, elements of a democratic ideology include individualism, laissez-faire, freedom of travel, freedom of speech, freedom of religion, resolution of conflicts by majority rule, and competitive two-party elections.[3] What distinguishes the ideology of the USSR from that of most other societies? The answer is the degree to which it has been formalized into an "official ideology"—a doctrine that is defined, interpreted, and defended by the state and the Communist party. Hereafter, the term *ideology* will refer to this body of official doctrine, rather than to the popular ideology or political culture of the Soviet people.

The official ideology of the USSR is Marxism-Leninism. Grounded in the ideas of Karl Marx and Friedrich Engels and adapted by Lenin, it has undergone a continuous process of evolution and revision since 1917. In order to assess the impact of Marxism-Leninism on the USSR today, it is essential to understand the origin and development of Marxist thought.

MARXISM

Karl Marx was born in Germany in 1818. Educated at the University of Bonn and the University of Berlin, he was heavily influenced by the German philosophers Georg Hegel and Ludwig Feuerbach, by radical French thinkers and historiographers, and by such English economic philosophers as David Ricardo and Adam Smith. The trauma of the Industrial Revolution—child labor, long workdays in dangerous and unhealthy conditions, urban overcrowding, and virtually nonexistent public education and health care—provided the background for Marx's thought and writing.

During his career, which spanned more than thirty-five years, Marx produced voluminous scholarly works and political tracts.[4] Ironically, it is for one of his least scholarly works, *The Manifesto of the Communist Party*, published in 1848, that Marx is most frequently remembered.

Marx posited that there are identifiable laws governing human historical development and that these laws are determined by the mode of material production.[5] The economic character of a society (i.e., its base or *infrastructure*) determines, or at least strongly affects, everything else about the society (i.e., its *superstructure*). In other words, the economic system of a society shapes its social classes, political institutions, laws, and social norms. As a result, changes in the economic system inevitably lead to changes in social and political institutions.

Marxist philosophy fuses two essential elements: dialectical materialism and historical materialism. Drawing on the work of Hegel and Feuerbach, Marx argued that contradictions in the physical, material world result in constant change. Using historical materialism, Marx attempted to explain the historical development of societies. Combining the two philosophical arguments, Marx described the evolution of all human societies based upon a dialectical process of the clash of economic forces or classes.[6] A change in economic systems, argued Marx, would bring about economic contradictions and economic conflict that, in turn, would give rise to social classes and class conflict. The opening lines of *The Communist Manifesto* proclaim: "The history of all hitherto existing society is the history of class struggles."[7]

Marx noted that the most primitive tribal societies were founded on a communal economy. The sheer difficulty of sustaining life forced primitive people to hunt together and to share equally in the reward. In time, however, hunting-and-gathering tribes developed more efficient methods of farming. Tribes became consolidated into city-states, accompanied by sharp class distinctions between citizens and slaves. In addition to communal ownership, the concept of private property gradually developed.

In contrast to city-states with slave-based economies, feudalism developed in the sparsely populated countryside. Feudal society was divided between the landlords, who owned the land, and the peasants or serfs, who farmed it. As in all societies, Marx argued, one's economic status defined one's class.

Feudalism, like primitive communal society, manifested contradictions. As Marx phrased it, each society "contains the seeds of its own destruction."[8] In time, a middle class of artisans and industrial entrepreneurs emerged to challenge the two existing classes.[9] Capitalism is the resulting economic system. Under capitalism, there are also two dominant social classes, which Marx defined in terms of ownership of the means of production.[10] He called the two classes the *bourgeoisie* and the *proletariat*. The bourgeoisie consists of those people who own the means of production—the land, the housing, and the factories. The proletariat is the working class that staffs the factories and rents the land and the housing. Its members do not own the means of production; rather, they own only their labor, which they must sell on the labor market.

Not only does the bourgeoisie own the means of production, it also controls the political institutions, utilizing them to preserve and promote its own economic interests. In Marx's view, law, courts, police, legislatures, and other governmental institutions serve primarily to protect the economic interests of the dominant class and to suppress other classes.

Like earlier societies, however, capitalism contains the seeds of its own destruction. Marx maintained that the number of people in the bourgeois class would diminish as capital accumulated in fewer and fewer hands. Monopolies would replace competing economic interests, thus concentrating more power in the hands of a minority. The portion of powerless, disenfranchised, and alienated workers would increase until they constituted the vast majority of the population. Their alienation would eventually explode in a socialist revolution in which the workers would take over the means of production and hold them in common, public ownership.

Marx devoted most of his writings to analyzing existing capitalist society. His descriptions of socialism and communism are both sketchy and vague. In his "Critique of the Gotha Programme," he suggested that socialism may be defined by the principle "From each according to his ability, to each according to his work."[11] That is, each citizen will contribute his or her talents and creative energies to the society and will be paid on the basis of how much he or she works. Socialism was, for Marx, merely a transitory stage in the progression toward the final development of a classless, communist society.

In the same tract, Marx defined communism by the principle "From each according to his ability, to each according to his needs."[12] In other words, every citizen under communism will work for the benefit of the society and will be paid in accordance with how much he or she needs. It is recognized that the disabled, the sick, the elderly, and the young, who are able to contribute less to society, also have greater needs for social services than do healthy, able-bodied workers. Communism presupposes an abundant society in which goods and services are more than adequate to satisfy citizens' demands, as well as provide for necessary capital investment. Communism also assumes that citizens will have a new outlook; they will be ready and willing to work diligently for the society and not hoard or take more than they need. Most Western critics view Marx's vague references to communism as utopian. The absence in his writings of a concrete, detailed analysis of how communist society would work has resulted in numerous interpretations, many of which are markedly simplistic. For instance, Nikita Khrushchev once declared that communism will be achieved when workers can go into the bread stores and take as much bread as they need without paying.[13]

Under communism, all the means of production will be held in common ownership. Consequently, Marx predicted, there will be no basis for making class distinctions; everyone will be equal. There will also be no internal class tensions. Communism is, in short, the highest stage of economic, social, and political development. Because there is no longer a ruling class with privileges to protect, all institutions of the state will "wither away." There will be no courts, no law, and no police, because these are merely tools used by one class to subjugate other classes. Communist society will be free of exploitation and coercion; it will be a society of true equality for men and women of all ethnic groups, regions, occupations, and levels of education. In short, communism will allow its citizens the maximum freedom to express their creative abilities.

Marx considered this evolution of societies based on economic character not a theory, not a hypothesis, not even a policy to be followed. He argued that the evolution of societies toward communism is a proven scientific fact; it is inevitable. The evolution of all societies toward communism may suffer temporary setbacks, he maintained, but the internal contradictions in capitalist society ordain that a socialist revolution will occur eventually. From this perspective, the Soviets feel that their social system is more advanced than that of the capitalist West and that time is on their side.

Given the logic of Marx's theories, one would have expected (and Marx did expect) that socialist revolutions would appear first in the most-developed capitalist states, such as Germany or Great Britain.[14] During most of the nineteenth century, Russia was still a feudal society, far from having a well-developed and well-organized class of industrial workers. Despite the country's economic backwardness, however, Russian revolutionaries of the 1880s and 1890s were attracted to Marxism because it espoused the revolutionary transformation of society. The early Russian Marxists differed from the Socialist Revolutionaries in that they favored industrialization and considered the peasants the least likely class to support revolution. They also split from terrorist groups such as the People's Will because they believed the transformation of Russian society would come about only through a broad-based social revolution, not through sporadic terrorist acts.

Georgii Plekhanov, founder of the first Marxist party in Russia, the Social Democratic Workers' party, spoke of a double yoke of oppression: the Russian people were oppressed both by the tsarist autocracy and by capitalism. Thus, he maintained, the revolution must come in two phases. In the first, the bonds of the tsarist regime would be cast off; in the second, the capitalist economy would be replaced by socialism. But he cautioned that a genuine socialist revolution would not come about soon in the backward Russian state.[15]

Some Marxists even argued for cooperating with liberals in speeding the development of capitalism in Russia.[16] But such a position, while consistent with Marxist philosophy, was unacceptable to such impatient revolutionaries as Lenin and Trotsky, who were seeking to overthrow the tsarist government. Plekhanov warned that an attempt to skip the capitalist stage of development and pursue a socialist revolution prematurely might result in a dictatorship by a small revolutionary minority.[17] By 1917, however, the leadership of the Social Democratic Workers' party in Russia had shifted from theoreticians to political activists. Although Lenin and his comrades continued to use Marxist references in their speeches and writings, they introduced an ideology that diverged significantly from Marxism.

LENINISM

Lenin's chief talent was as a political organizer and charismatic leader, not as a philosopher. He had devoted his life to overthrowing the tsarist regime. Succeeding in this, however, he then had to begin the difficult job of building the new socialist order. Marxist ideology offered little guidance in this task. Most of Marx's writings, including his greatest work, *Das Kapital,* contain only vague descriptions of socialist society. Should the new Soviet state create a new police force or abolish the police altogether? How should crime and other antisocial behavior be handled? Should income be set by the State, and if so, should they be made equal and uniform? Should banks be allowed to make loans, and if so, should they charge interest? These were just a few of the many mundane questions confronting Lenin, questions to which Marx provided no clear answers.

Lenin's most notable contributions to Marxist theory consisted of defining the nature of the Party and the State in socialist society. Lenin conceived of the Party as a tightly knit, centralized organization comprised of dedicated, professional revolutionaries. He advocated the formation of party cells in every factory, village, and military unit. The functions of the party cells were twofold: (1) to mobilize the rank-and-file workers, peasants, and soldiers in favor of the Bolshevik cause, and (2) to relay information from the grass-roots level to the Party's top leadership. Rather than a mass party of the working class, Lenin's party was an elitist party, open only to a small portion of the workers, whom it purported to represent. Reflecting the earlier ideas of Peter Tkachev and Peter Lavrov, Lenin argued that a broadly based party could accomplish nothing. Instead, the Party was described as the "vanguard of the working class," made up of a relatively select group of revolutionaries who could see the plight of the workers more clearly than the workers themselves and who would help raise the class consciousness of the workers and peasants.[18] The inherent dangers in this concept of the vanguard party were soon apparent. Lenin proclaimed that because the Party represented the working class, the workers were obliged to accept the Party's leadership.[19]

The potential for authoritarian rule was evident not only in Lenin's concept of the vanguard party, but also in his theory of the State and the "dictatorship of the proletariat."[20] As Lavrov had argued thirty years earlier, the Party must first seize power and then use the power of the State to transform society. Lenin had no qualms about promoting dictatorship because, as a Marxist, he considered all forms of government to be coercive and dictatorial. He justified the "dictatorship of the proletariat" on the grounds that, unlike capitalist dictatorships in which a minority rules over a majority of the people, Russia would need a period in which the majority would rule over the minority. The coercive power of the State would be required to strip the former privileged class of its ill-gained wealth and power. Lenin anticipated that this transitional stage of proletarian dictatorship would continue for quite a long time. In the end, as Georgii Plekhanov had predicted, it was not so much a dictatorship of the proletariat as a dictatorship of the Communist party.

Unlike Marx, who placed hopes for revolution solely on the working class, Lenin proposed forging an alliance of all the social classes that had suffered under the tsarist regime. In short, he advocated an alliance of peasants (who constituted a majority in Russia) and workers, under the leadership of the Communist party.

Although Lenin was instrumental in laying the ideological foundations of the Party and the socialist state and in defining the tactics of revolution, he died before he was able to complete the socialist transformation of Russian society. The nature and the structure of the Soviet regime today bear the imprint of Lenin's successors more than that of Lenin himself.

TROTSKYISM

Of the early revolutionary leaders, Leon Trotsky was clearly the most distinguished for his ideological and philosophical insights. He justified socialist revolution in Russia by noting that the communal heritage of the people, the weakly ingrained notions of private property, and the willingness of a well-organized revolutionary group to seize power might enable the country to skip "bourgeois democracy" and proceed directly to socialism.[21] Although capitalism was only in a rudimentary stage of development in Russia, Trotsky argued that a socialist revolution was both possible and desirable. He noted that the capitalist powers comprised a huge international imperialist system; to destroy the system, it was necessary to attack its weakest link, its least developed member—namely, Russia.[22]

Recognizing Russia's backwardness, Trotsky maintained that the success of the revolution was dependent upon revolutions elsewhere. As long as capitalism existed, it would perceive socialism in Russia as a threat and would seek to overthrow it. He predicted, "Without the direct State support of the European proletariat, the working class of Russia cannot remain in power."[23] The Bolsheviks were confident that a successful socialist revolution in Russia would inflame the workers of Great Britain, France, and the United States and thus usher in a worldwide socialist revolution.[24]

It was over the issue of supporting international revolution that Trotsky first clashed with Joseph Stalin. A dedicated revolutionary, Trotsky despised nationalism. He declared more allegiance to a British worker or a German worker than he did to a member of the Russian gentry. However, when socialist revolutions in Germany and elsewhere proved unsuccessful, the momentum shifted to Stalin, who advocated building "socialism in one country."

Despite—or perhaps because of—Trotsky's ideological brilliance, he was perceived as a threat to Stalin, removed from power, and forced to emigrate. Later, he was brutally murdered in Mexico City, allegedly at Stalin's command. Today, Trotsky is considered a nonperson in the USSR. His published works have been removed from libraries, and his name has been excised from official histories and textbooks. In addition, many of his ideological innovations are now attributed to Lenin. Stalin even had Trotsky "removed" from a group portrait of early Bolshevik leaders that hangs above the main staircase of the Lenin Library in Moscow; where Trotsky once stood, there now appears a potted plant.

STALINISM

Stalin's proclamation of "socialism in one country" was a major turning point in Soviet ideology. As initially set forth in 1924, this doctrine asserted that the Bolsheviks had to push on to socialism whether or not the world revolution came about, or else the regime was doomed to continue the policies of the New Economic Policy. Stalin argued that, drawing on its vast resources and protected by its physical isolation, Russia could achieve socialism and was not dependent upon the success of a worldwide revolution. The right wing of the Politburo supported Stalin's theory, but they were in no hurry to leave NEP. Nikolai Bukharin, a leader of the Right, noted: "We shall creep at a snail's pace, but we are building socialism and we shall complete the building of it."[25]

Stalin's aims, however, were hardly those of Bukharin. Having defeated his principal opponents on the Left and Right and secured control over the secret police, the trade unions, and the army, Stalin launched his famed "Second Revolution" in 1928. Although the introduction of the First Five-Year Plan is widely remembered for its goal of rapidly expanding capital goods, it was foremost a plan for radically transforming the economy and the society along socialist lines. Similarly, the collectivization of agriculture was not designed to improve agricultural performance, but to break down the peasants' attachment to their private farms and to enable the regime to squeeze revenues out of the agricultural sector in order to finance rapid industrialization.

Stalin also manipulated Marxist-Leninist ideology to bolster his legitimacy as Lenin's faithful associate and heir. Stalin initiated the "cult of Lenin," which glorified the founder of the Soviet state.[26] He changed the name of Petrograd to *Leningrad* ("city of Lenin") and renamed the small Siberian town of Lenin's birth *Ulianovsk,* derived from *Ulianov,* Lenin's family name. The Order of Lenin was established as the highest civilian honor, and portraits of Lenin began to appear throughout Soviet cities and in most offices and factories.

Consistent with Stalin's determined efforts to develop Russia and rapidly expand its economic and military might, the size and the complexity of the state apparatus grew at a phenomenal rate. Gone were the days when scholars and theoreticians could refer to "the withering away of the state." In his report to the Sixteenth Party Congress in 1930, Stalin clumsily attempted to justify the mushrooming bureaucracy: "We stand for the strengthening of the dictatorship of the proletariat, which represents the mightiest and most powerful authority of all forms of State that have ever existed. The highest development of the State power for the withering away of the State power—this is the Marxian formula. Is this 'contradictory'?

Yes, it is 'contradictory.' But this contradiction springs from life itself and reflects completely the Marxian dialectic."[27]

Abandoning the notion of the "withering away of the state" was just one of Stalin's "deviations" from Marxism.[28] In the 1930s, there was an evident return to traditional Russian values of nationalism, order, isolation, and xenophobia. Stalin formulated the concept of "capitalist encirclement" and the "two camp" theory of world affairs, both of which stressed Russia's isolation in a world dominated by capitalist powers.

Stalin also deviated from Marx in arguing that "subjective factors" were instrumental in achieving successful policies in Russia. He criticized his opponents for a lack of faith in party policies. It was not enough for the Party to enact effective policies. Rather, the public and the leaders themselves must also believe wholeheartedly in the correctness of those policies. This fanaticism, this demand for unswerving support and total belief in the correctness of Stalin's path, raised the use of terror to unprecedented levels. In Stalin's view, those who failed to believe absolutely in his programs were just as dangerous as those who sabotaged his policies. Stalin's preoccupation with power culminated in the development of an elaborate, "cult of personality." He was depicted as the *Vozhd'* (Leader), the visionary leader of socialism, and the modern counterpart to Peter the Great and Ivan the Terrible. Stalinism represented a synthesis derived from the clash of the revolutionary organizational principles of Leninism with the traditionally Russian autocratic and nationalistic values of the tsarist regime.

IDEOLOGY SINCE STALIN

After Stalin's death in 1953, his political heirs moved quickly to dismantle many elements of his autocratic system. Lavrenti Beria, head of the Ministry of Internal Affairs, was arrested, convicted, and executed for treason, and the secret police were brought under party and state control. At the Twentieth Party Congress in 1956, Nikita Khrushchev stunned the delegates with an unprecedented denunciation of "Stalin's crimes." Khrushchev's "Secret Speech" accused Stalin of abuses of authority and of surrounding himself with a "cult of personality." Khrushchev also noted that Marxism-Leninism was conceived as a flexible guide to policy-making, not the inflexible dogma it had become under Stalin.

The de-Stalinization period under Khrushchev witnessed not only a reduction in the use of terror, but also a reversal on several ideological points. At the Twenty-First Party Congress in 1959, Khrushchev announced "the final and complete victory of socialism in the USSR" and the end of capitalist encirclement. No longer could the threat of external pressures be used to justify the extensive party and state controls over the populace. Progress in diminishing class and ethnic divisions in the USSR and in socializing Soviet youth toward socialist values also meant that state coercion was no longer as necessary as it had been under Stalin.

The Twenty-Second Party Congress in October 1961 represented a landmark in Khrushchev's ideological program. At the congress, Khrushchev renewed his attack on Stalin and used the occasion to announce several doctrinal innovations. He declared that the transitory period of the "dictatorship of the proletariat" had been superseded by "the state of the whole people."[29] Khrushchev maintained that all Soviet citizens, not just party members, were actively engaged in constructing communism. Khrushchev's populist notions called into question the need for elitist decision-making that persisted throughout the party and state apparatuses. The new party program ratified by the congress repudiated Stalin's notion of "revolution from above," stressing popular mass participation instead. The work of various state agencies was turned over to public organizations.

All of these changes amounted to an assault on the bureaucratic prerogatives of state officials. As a result, they engendered considerable opposition, but Khrushchev was undeterred. He was, in fact, using the party congress as a forum for playing on the adversarial relationship between the officials and the masses. His doctrinal innovations appear to have been designed primarily to bolster his legitimacy.

In the 1950s and early 1960s, the growing schism between the USSR and other socialist states (most notably Yugoslavia and China) and the rise of numerous national liberation movements in the Third World mandated other doctrinal revisions. Khrushchev recognized that Moscow was no longer the sole authority on ideological matters and that there were "differing roads to socialism," including parliamentary election. He also reversed the doctrine that war between capitalist and socialist systems is inevitable, setting the stage for pursuing peaceful coexistence with the capitalist West. This doctrinal maneuver also allowed Khrushchev to reorient the Soviet economy away from military industries and toward consumer goods.

Soviet ideology continued to evolve and develop after Khrushchev's ouster in 1964. The doctrinal innovations of his successor, Leonid Brezhnev, had important implications on policies. While playing down the mass participation and "campaignism" that had been prominent under Khrushchev, the Brezhnev regime expanded the role of specialists in decision-making. The Party was no longer seen as a "vanguard" that exclusively possessed the knowledge necessary to transform Soviet society.

In 1971, Brezhnev introduced the concept of "developed socialism," and noted that the scientific-technical revolution that was sweeping Western capitalist societies was also transforming the USSR; science had become a direct productive force in the economy.

The Soviet economy began to falter in the mid-1970s, which forced some modifications in Brezhnev's emphasis and ideological focus. Party ideologists and the *agitprop* (agitation-propaganda) apparatus curtailed their glowing representations of "developed socialism" and the scientific-technical revolution because both tended to inflate the public's expectations, especially for consumer goods. Instead, the ideologists attacked "consumerism," avarice, alcoholism, loafing, parasitism, and hooliganism. Greater stress was placed on the labor collective, not only as an economic unit, but also as a social unit for reaffirming the political and moral standards of Soviet society. The increased East-West contact afforded by détente made the leaders, and to a lesser extent the general population, aware of the widening gap in Soviet and Western living standards. The ideologists responded by asserting "the *qualitative* superiority of the socialist way of life."[30]

Although the official ideology of the USSR is quite diverse and has evolved over the years in response to changing political, social, and economic conditions, certain features of Marxism-Leninism have remained consistent since 1917. For instance, the official doctrine today recognizes the absolute primacy of the Communist Party of the Soviet Union. Article 6 of the 1977 constitution proclaims:

> The leading and guiding force of Soviet society and the nucleus of its political system, of all state and public organizations, is the Communist Party of the Soviet Union. The CPSU exists for the people and serves the people.
>
> The Communist Party, armed with Marxism-Leninism, determines the general perspectives of the development of society and the line of domestic and foreign policy of the USSR, directs the great constructive work of the Soviet people, and imparts a planned, systematic, and theoretically substantiated character to their struggle for the victory of communism.[31]

Also essential to Marxism-Leninism today is the continuation of centralized state control of the economy. Although the centralized planned economy has proven to be inefficient, it gives the political leaders direct and powerful control over the rank-and-file citizens and economic enterprises. It also enables the leadership to make investment decisions that have the greatest potential benefit for the society as a whole. More fundamentally, private economic and social activity are discouraged because they are thought to promote individualism and selfishness and to widen class differences in society; they are seen as retarding rather than promoting the development of the collective consciousness necessary for the achievement of communism.

Under Marxism-Leninism, the individual citizen is an important member of a larger social-political group, rather than an independent possessor of rights. Thus, the concept of rights is inextricably tied to the citizens' duties and obligations to the society. For instance, although the Constitution of the USSR guarantees freedom of speech, its exercise must be in accordance with the general interests of Soviet society.

Under Stalin and his successors, traditional Russian nationalism has been merged with Marxism-Leninism. The success of communism is considered synonymous with the success of the Soviet Union. While Marxism-Leninism is no longer the ideology of a cohesive international movement, Soviet ideology does tend to view the world in terms of "progressive" and "regressive" forces. Soviet ideologists speak of "the correlation of forces" that has shifted in favor of the USSR. By this, they mean that many of the countries of the Third World now favor a socialist rather than a capitalist path of development.

Finally, Marxism-Leninism continues to profess atheism. Religion, which underscores values and allegiances that differ from those of Marxism-Leninism, is viewed as contradictory to the interests of the Soviet regime. Extensive efforts have been undertaken to restrict religious practice in the USSR. The most prestigious cathedrals, synagogues, and mosques have been closed, and children below the age of eighteen are prohibited from participating in religious ceremonies or receiving religious instruction outside of the home.

In some respects, Marxism-Leninism has become a secular religion. It provides to its adherents an explanation of the course of human development. It projects a glorious future society, free of exploitation, injustice, and poverty, and asks its adherents to make sacrifices for the attainment of this future society. Even in symbolic ways, Marxist-Leninist ideology attempts to displace Russian Orthodoxy. Just as some Christians wear crucifixes, those who profess their belief in Marxism-Leninism often wear lapel pins (*znachki*) depicting Lenin or other revolutionary themes. Revolutionary leaders are deified; they have become figures larger than life. In a glass coffin in a mausoleum in Red Square, Lenin's embalmed body lies in state. Even in the dead of winter, people stand in line for hours just to file past his bier. For workers, collective farmers, students, and soldiers rewarded with a trip to the capital, Lenin's tomb is an obligatory stop.

The names and pictures of Lenin and Marx appear everywhere. Almost every book published in the Soviet Union begins with a quote from or reference to Lenin or Marx. (Lenin's collected works total fifty-five volumes, so there is no shortage of material to choose from.) Streets and even towns have been renamed to honor revolutionary heroes of the past. On the November 7 celebration of the October Revolution and again on May 1, huge parades in Red Square march past four-story-tall portraits of Marx, Engels, and Lenin. On one extended visit to the USSR, the author met a French exchange student who was the great-great-granddaughter of Karl Marx. She said that Soviet officials simply did not know how to deal with her. "It is as if I were the great-great-granddaughter of God!" she exclaimed.

FUNCTIONS OF IDEOLOGY IN THE USSR

Ideology in the USSR performs several significant functions. It is used to mobilize the public in support of the goals of the regime. Millions of citizens participate in the numerous parades, demonstrations, party meetings, and public lectures, all designed to instill in them a sense of involvement, civic responsibility, support for the CPSU, and the willingness to endure hardship in the struggle to "build communism."

Marxist-Leninist ideology is also used to legitimize the regime and its policies. Lacking the legitimacy of a popularly elected democratic regime, the Soviet leadership must base its legitimacy on the notion that the policies of the vanguard party will benefit the whole society and therefore merit the support of the populace. Political leaders go to great lengths to find appropriate quotes from Lenin to justify their policies. Lenin has been quoted to support collectivization of farms, as well as private farm plots; national self-determination for non-Russian ethnic minorities, as well as Russification; and policies of antagonism with the capitalist West, as well as peaceful coexistence. When no quote is available, as once happened in 1962, one is conveniently "discovered."[32] While two diametrically opposed policies may both be justified ideologically, it is significant that the Soviet leadership feels obliged to legitimize each policy initiative and each new decision in ideological terms.

Ideology serves as a shared language of political discourse. Policy disputes and the conflicting ambitions of aspiring political leaders are often expressed in ideological terms. As noted earlier, the contest between Stalin and Trotsky to succeed Lenin focused not on their respective personal traits and abilities, but on the issue of "socialism in one country" versus "international revolution."

Marxist-Leninist ideology also fulfills an integrating function. It unifies peoples of diverse ethnic origins, classes, regions, and levels of education in a common cause. Social integration and cohesion is especially important in the USSR, where wide ethnic, cultural, regional, and economic differences exist.

Finally, as noted previously, Marxist-Leninist ideology fulfills a symbolic function. It provides Soviet citizens with something to believe in, instilling in them patriotism, national pride, and support for the regime. For succeeding generations of Soviet citizens, however, the ideological appeal of Marxism-Leninism is waning. Increasingly, the legitimacy of the Soviet regime rests not on its ideological foundations, but on its ability to enact effective policies that improve standards of living and maintain the security of its citizens.

IDEOLOGY AND POLITICAL SOCIALIZATION

Marx recognized that the ultimate achievement of communism was dependent upon restructuring the values and behavior of individuals, and the Soviet regime has gone to considerable lengths to inculcate the values of Marxism-Leninism in the people. Soviet writers devote much attention to the concept of the "new Soviet man." This idealized citizen of socialism is an enthusiastic worker, selfless in devoting time to civic activities. He or she is self-disciplined, dependable, and imbued with a sense of collective spirit, rather than individualism. This citizen possesses a firm grasp of party policies and stands vigilant against enemies of the Party and the nation.

The system for instilling these values is extensive. It begins virtually at birth and envelops the Soviet citizen throughout every stage of life. As in all societies, the family is the most important institution of socialization for children. Because approximately 80 percent of all Soviet women work, much of the responsibility for the socialization of children falls to others. Half of all Soviet schoolchildren attend nursery school or kindergarten; the rest receive their early training at home.[33]

Traditionally, Russian families incorporated the grandparents, with the grandmother (babushka) assuming the household chores as well as child-rearing responsibilities. As the Soviet population has become increasingly mobile and urbanized, however, grandparents have often been left behind in the villages. This has placed a heavy demand on child-care programs in the major cities. It is also common for young working couples to send their children to the country to be raised by the babushka until they are of school age. The babushka plays a role in the socialization not only of children, but even adults. Wearing traditional head scarves, babushki have been known to scold strangers for not wearing hats or dressing warmly enough on cold days. They often launch into verbal attacks against public drunkards or chide young women for wearing too much makeup or skirts that are too short. In a sense, the *babushki* are the self-appointed guardians of public morality in Soviet society.

In addition to the home and family, early socialization frequently occurs in child-care centers (*iasli*) for children from six weeks to four years old. These centers are usually clean, well-staffed, and affordably priced. Some are operated by factories or other large enterprises for the children of their employees. Kindergartens for children ages four to six are also readily available and inexpensive. In the kindergartens, the children not only begin to acquire basic skills, but they also are instructed about the Soviet flag, Lenin, and other political topics. They are taught to be orderly, conforming, obedient, and cooperative. Heavy emphasis is placed on the group (*kollektiv*) as opposed to the individual.

In primary schools, the stress on the *kollektiv* is even more pronounced. One row may compete with another row, a class may compete with another class, or the boys may compete against the girls. Within the group, students are encouraged to assist one another. Their efforts are not for their own recognition, but for the group's, and rewards and punishments are handed out, not to individuals, but to groups. The students learn both cooperation and competition, but always in the context of the *kollektiv*.

Several political institutions in the USSR are directly charged with socializing Soviet children and youth. Most children of ages seven to ten join the Young Octobrists. Members of this organization wear red kerchiefs with their mandatory school uniforms, making it easy to identify any child who does not join. A similar organization for youngsters aged ten through fourteen is the Young Pioneers, in which membership is almost universal. Like the Young Octobrists, the Pioneers wear red scarfs and engage in social, civic, and recreational activities similar to those of the Boy Scouts or Girl Scouts. Most cities have Pioneer Palaces where afterschool programs are organized.[34] In the summer, Pioneers attend camps in the countryside or at the beach. The rules of membership in the Pioneers reflect the values the regime wishes Soviet youth to acquire:

> The Pioneer loves his motherland and the Communist Party of the Soviet Union. He prepares himself for membership in the Komsomol [Young Communist League].
> The Pioneer reveres the memory of those who have given their lives in the struggle for the freedom and the well-being of the Soviet Motherland.
> The Pioneer is friendly with the children of all the countries of the world.
> The Pioneer studies diligently and is disciplined and courteous.
> The Pioneer loves to work and to conserve the national wealth.
> The Pioneer is a good comrade, who is solicitous of younger children and who helps older people.
> The Pioneer grows up to be bold and does not fear difficulties.
> The Pioneer tells the truth and guards the honor of his detachment.
> The Pioneer strengthens himself and does physical exercises every day.
> The Pioneer loves nature; he is a defender of planted areas, of useful birds and animals.
> The Pioneer is an example for all children.[35]

At the age of fourteen or fifteen, most Soviet children enter the Komsomol, a more advanced organization for young men and women up to the age of twenty-eight. Membership in the Komsomol is not as universal as it is in the Pioneers or Young Octobrists, although it is expected that any student who wishes to be admitted to a university be a Komsomol member. Interviews with recent émigrés indicate that most Soviet youth join the Komsomol for political and social reasons, rather than opportunistic ones. Many report a "sense of pride" at having been accepted into the Komsomol. One émigré observed, "I joined the Komsomol for purely ideological reasons when I was fourteen or fifteen years old and when I truly believed in the cause of the Party and the general cause of Soviet power."[36] Others indicate that they joined the Komsomol with their entire class; to refuse membership was to isolate oneself. "The road that leads from cradle to Komsomol is a straight one. I did not think about it. . . . What matters is not to separate oneself from the collective. . . . I wanted to be like everyone else."[37] Another émigré observed, "It was more difficult not to join than to join."[38]

Interest in the Komsomol typically tapers off as the student grows older, however. In 1974, for instance, approximately 63 percent of fifteen- to seventeen-year-olds were members, but only 20 to 25 percent of twenty-six-year-olds and twenty-seven-year-olds were.[39] One émigré who had succeeded in avoiding membership in the Komsomol was confronted by her supervisor and told: "In your work you cannot be a nonmember. When you get to be 28 you can do as you like."[40] A former graduate student at Sverdlovsk University observed, "Those who categorically refuse to enter the Komsomol and the Party place themselves outside the frame of the society and close all doors to themselves."[41]

The Komsomol is more overtly political than the organizations for younger children. It is considered the training ground for aspiring party members. In fact, of all new members of the CPSU, almost three-fourths enter through their Komsomol affiliations.[42] The organization of the Komsomol is virtually identical to that of the CPSU, and Komsomol secretaries gain valuable leadership experience, preparing them for future assignments in the Party. To insure effective control over the Komsomol, its highest offices are exempted from the twenty-eight-year-old age ceiling. As a result, many of the Komsomol leaders are in their thirties and even early forties.

The Komsomol directs the energies of Soviet youth in constructive ways and provides a channel to the leaders for information about the attitudes of the young. The organization also mobilizes young men and women in support of the regime. During the summer, Komsomol brigades are sent to work on construction projects in Siberia or to assist in the harvest. In the mid-1950s, Komsomol laborers were used in Khrushchev's Virgin Lands program, in which previously untilled regions of Kazakhstan were plowed and planted in an attempt to solve the Soviet Union's chronic agricultural problems.

The efforts of the Soviet regime to instill socialist values in its citizens do not stop when they reach the age of twenty-eight. In virtually every village and every city neighborhood, there are agitation-propaganda (*agit-prop*) centers. These Soviet equivalents to community centers in the United States organize public lectures on topics ranging from "The Soviet Peace

Program in the Middle East" to "The Crisis of Capitalism in the United States." Propagandists for the *agitprop* centers are trained at the Academy of Social Sciences in Moscow and are invariably party members.

Most cities and towns also have Houses of Culture that offer an array of public lectures and social events. Public interest in such meetings is notoriously low, however; most of the youth attend only if coerced by their Komsomol leaders or if it is necessary in order to gain admission to a dance or rock concert.

For the adult population, public propaganda and agitation work is also carried out in factories, enterprises, housing units, and offices. Members of the CPSU are expected to devote a minimum of one day per week to "party work." A distinguished professor at the Leningrad University law school confessed that she would probably not have joined the Party if her husband had not been killed in World War II and her children had not grown up and moved far away. She simply would not have had enough time for party work—in her case, speaking to workers in factories on such legal topics as the rights of workers under Soviet law, legal problems in divorce, and legal protections of pregnant workers.

The critical question is: How successful are these efforts to inculcate political values in the Soviet people? Western visitors are struck by the omnipresent banners that adorn the tops of most Soviet buildings and proclaim: "Hail the inviolable unity of the Party and the People!" "Glory to Labor!" and "Glory to the CPSU!" But the average Soviet citizen is just as oblivious to these signs as Westerners are to billboards hawking suntan lotion, cigarettes, or dry-cleaning services. Surveys indicate that despite the government's extensive *agitprop* efforts, a large portion of the populace ignores official propaganda. One survey asked respondents to define a number of words commonly used in the press. About one-fourth of the readers could not define *colonialism;* two-fifths did not understand the word *dictatorship.* Almost half were unable to define *imperialism,* and three-fourths of the respondents had no idea what *reactionary* or *liberal* meant.[43]

There appear to be few "true believers" in the USSR. While many citizens feel obliged to defend Soviet policies and offer frequent references to Marxist-Leninist principles, few realistically anticipate the dawn of communism, the withering away of the State, or the sudden eradication of social classes. A whole genre of jokes has developed around "the building of communism." One such story is set at an international industrial trade fair. The General Secretary visits the IBM exhibit and is told of the fantastic ability of the new state-of-the-art computer to answer any question it is asked. Somewhat dubiously, the General Secretary requests that the technicians ask the computer, "When will the Soviet Union achieve full communism?" The computer whirs, blinks, and gives its answer—"500 kilometers." Embarrassed by the obviously inappropriate reply, the IBM representatives try the question again and get the same answer—"500 kilometers." Finally, the chief programmer is called in and consulted on the problem. The programmer reports, "Mr. General Secretary, we programmed several of your speeches into the computer and in one of those speeches you declared that every Five-Year Plan is one step toward communism!"

THE POPULAR IDEOLOGY OF THE SOVIET PEOPLE

That intelligent Soviet citizens do not fully subscribe to the tenets of the official ideology does not mean that all efforts at political socialization are a failure. Many elements of the Soviet popular ideology, or political culture, reflect (and are reinforced by) Marxist-Leninist principles. For instance, Soviet citizens place a heavy stress on collectivism, rather than individualism. Graffiti and vandalism are not as common in the USSR as in the West, because there is a sense that public property belongs to everyone and should be guarded. One former Leningrad University student remarked, "I don't like to drink in public—it doesn't present the best picture of our society."[44] This is not to imply that public intoxication does not occur in the USSR; in fact, it is nearing epidemic proportions.[45] But among many Soviet citizens, there is a greater tendency than in the West to consider the consequences of one's behavior for the society as a whole.

Soviet citizens are also accustomed to turning to the State to guarantee their quality of life. The State functions *in loco parentis,* providing jobs, housing, health care, education, and pensions for its citizens. Many Soviet citizens who have emigrated to the West are so accustomed to the paternalism of their government that they are bewildered by the responsibilities they must assume for themselves. They must find their own jobs, locate their own housing, purchase health insurance, and save for their children's educations. Some émigrés bitterly criticize Western governments for "luring" them to the West without guaranteeing them jobs and housing. Most émigrés do not appear to be seeking political or religious freedom as much as the opportunity to share in the material abundance that the capitalist West offers. In fact, they are often perplexed and offended by the wide diversity of viewpoints allowed to be expressed in a free, open society. One émigré watching a march by a group of neo-Nazis in Chicago exclaimed, "There should be a law against this!"[46]

While Soviet citizens turn to the State and the Party to guarantee their livelihood, they continue to view the political leaders as detached from the masses. In the popular conception, power does not "bubble up" from the people, but "trickles down" from above. It is a classic we-they dichotomy: *we* the people, *they* the leaders. For the vast majority of Soviet citizens, this dichotomization is quite satisfactory. They are content to leave politics to the politicians and concern themselves with locating a larger apartment, buying a car, or acquiring some stylish, imported shoes. As long as the Soviet economy continues to advance slowly but steadily, the populace appears quite content to remain apolitical. Over time, they have been conditioned that to speak out or to assert their demands only brings misery and repression.

Nationalism runs deep in the Soviet people, who possess a strong sense of attachment to Russia, to the soil. While Soviet youth, especially in the cities, are attracted to Western styles and popular culture, they remain patriotic, ardent supporters of their country.

Western visitors to the USSR are constantly bombarded with questions: "How many rooms in your apartment?" (Single-family houses are virtually unheard of in the USSR.) "How many years' salary does it take to buy a car?" "How much do blue jeans cost in the United States?" In one such session with an official in an institute of the Academy of Sciences, the questioner apparently felt uncomfortable that the USSR was not measuring up favorably. He thought a second and then blurted out, "Well, at least in the Soviet Union we don't lynch blacks!" The steadfast loyalty to Russia transcends politics. As one student remarked, "We have lived under autocratic governments for centuries, but this is still Russia; this is our country. We will endure!"

Finally, despite their revolutionary origins and continued revolutionary rhetoric, the Soviet people today are preoccupied with order and stability (*poriadok*). The generation of leaders who rose to prominence as a result of Stalin's bloody purges in the 1930s are the products of bureaucracy, not of revolution. They place a premium on caution, going through channels, and not challenging the status quo. They bear a closer resemblance to corporate boards of directors in the capitalist West today than they do to the fiery Russian intellectuals and revolutionaries of the late 1800s and early 1900s.

The conservatism of Soviet officials is aptly illustrated by an incident recounted by an American professor. In 1968, the professor was asked to lead a visiting delegation of Soviet politicians on a tour of New York City. At one point, the American offered to take the visitors to see Columbia University, where, he explained, a group of leftist students had taken over the administration building. Banners of Marx were draped from the president's office window, and a student strike had halted classes. The Soviet officials, all distinguished members of the Party, were visibly shaken at the prospect of witnessing such a "disturbance." They remarked, "You should have all those hooligans arrested!"

Notes

1. For a discussion of ideology, see Lyman Tower Sargent, *Contemporary Political Ideologies,* 4th ed. (Homewood, Illinois: Dorsey Press, 1978), 3–6.

2. Peter C. Sederberg, *The Politics of Meaning* (Tucson, Arizona: University of Arizona Press, 1984), 168–169.

3. It is common for ideologies to incorporate idealized concepts and values. That the American economic system bears little resemblance today to a laissez-faire economy is not as important as the fact that laissez-faire is still a widely held value in the American popular culture. See Murray Edelman, *The Symbolic Uses of Politics* (Urbana, Illinois: The University of Illinois Press, 1967).

4. Tom Bottomore, Laurence Harris, V. G. Kieman, and Ralph Milliband, eds. *A Dictionary of Marxist Thought* (Cambridge: Harvard University Press, 1983). According to these authors, Marx's work is fraught with ambiguities and contradictions that contemporary readers often overlook.

5. For example, see Karl Marx, "Wage Labour and Capital," in Robert C. Tucker, ed., *The Marx-Engels Reader,* 2d ed. (New York: W.W. Norton, 1978), 207–208.

6. This view of class conflict leading to social evolution was also expressed by Friedrich Engels. See "Socialism: Utopian and Scientific," in Tucker, *Marx-Engels Reader,* 699.

7. Karl Marx and Friedrich Engels, "Manifesto of the Communist Party," in Tucker, *Marx-Engels Reader,* 473.

8. Ibid., 478, 483.

9. This evolutionary process is gradual, according to Marx. One stage of development is not necessarily clearly distinguished from the next, so that, in advanced feudalism, there are not only peasants and landlords but also a growing capitalist class that in time becomes dominant.

10. Karl Marx and Friedrich Engels, "The German Ideology," in David McLellan, ed., *Karl Marx: Selected Writings* (Oxford: Oxford University Press, 1977), 161.

11. Karl Marx, "Critique of the Gotha Program," in *Karl Marx: Selected Writings*, 569.

12. Ibid.

13. *Pravda*, January 28, 1959.

14. Marx suggested that revolutions may be nonviolent in Britain, the United States, or Holland because of the well-established democratic institutions in these countries.

15. Georgii V. Plekhanov, *Sochineniia*, 3d ed., vol. 2 (Moscow: 1923), 329.

16. This view is usually associated with the Mensheviks; however, few Marxists in Russia were prepared to admit the possibility that any major stage might be skipped altogether. Even some of Lenin's early writings support this view.

17. Plekhanov, *Sochineniia*, 329.

18. V. I. Lenin, "What Is to Be Done?" in *Selected Works* (New York: International Publishers, 1967), 189–202.

19. V. I. Lenin, "One Step Forward, Two Steps Backward," in Lenin, *Selected Works*, 257–449.

20. V. I. Lenin, "Two Tactics of Social-Democracy in the Democratic Revolution," in *V. I. Lenin: Selected Works* (New York: International Publishers, 1971), 105.

21. Leon Trotsky, *The Permanent Revolution* (New York: Pathfinder Press, 1970), 194.

22. Ibid.

23. Ibid. This statement was later used by Stalin to engineer Trotsky's demise.

24. In the early twentieth century, rudimentary communist parties and rapidly growing labor union movements existed in all three societies. See Christopher Lasch, *The American Liberals and the Russian Revolution* (New York: McGraw-Hill, 1962).

25. Cited in Donald W. Treadgold, *Twentieth-Century Russia* (Chicago: Rand McNally, 1964), 223.

26. Lenin was modest and believed in collective leadership. He indicated before he died that he did not wish to become immortalized. Stalin, nevertheless, chose to glorify Lenin in order to strengthen his own political position among Lenin's heirs.

27. Joseph Stalin, Political Report of the Central Committee to the 16th Congress of the Communist Party, June 27, 1930.

28. See Nicholas S. Timasheff, *The Great Retreat* (New York: Dutton, 1946). For instance, under Stalin, ranks were reintroduced into the Red Army, "people's commissariats" reverted to the traditional designation as "ministries," and the Party was eclipsed by the state apparatus.

29. *KPSS v rez.* 8 (1961): 273.

30. For a discussion of ideological developments after Khrushchev, see Alfred Evans, Jr., "The Decline of Developed Socialism?" *Soviet Studies* (January 1986): 1–23.

31. Constitution of the USSR (1977), Article 6.

32. The 1962 controversy surrounded Khrushchev's position that economic matters should take precedence over political matters. Khrushchev was accused of violating the tenets of Leninism on this point. However, a "rediscovered" unpublished chapter of Lenin's 1918 article "Immediate Tasks of Soviet Power" conveniently supported Khrushchev's position. See Carl Linden, *Khrushchev and the Soviet Leadership* (Baltimore: Johns Hopkins University Press, 1966), 149.

33. Nigel Grant, *Soviet Education* (New York: Penguin Books, 1964), 88.

34. Soviet juvenile-affairs officials occasionally note that Pioneer Palaces and Komsomol groups need to expand afterschool activities. Because most parents work, youths are often

unsupervised in the late afternoon. Soviet studies indicate that this is the prime time for delinquent acts to be committed by juveniles.

35. Cited in Allen Kassof, *The Soviet Youth Program* (Cambridge: Harvard University Press, 1965), 79.

36. Cited in Aryeh L. Unger, "Political Participation in the USSR: YCL and CPSU," *Soviet Studies* 33 (January 1981): 107–124.

37. Ibid.

38. Ibid.

39. Ibid.

40. Ibid.

41. Ibid.

42. *Pravda,* 26 September 1983, p. 2.

43. Ellen Mickiewicz, "Policy Issues in the Soviet Media System," in Erik P. Hoffmann, ed., *The Soviet Union in the 1980s* (New York: Academy of Political Science, 1984), 114.

44. From a conversation with the author in 1976.

45. See Nick Eberstadt, "The Health Crisis in the USSR," *New York Review of Books,* 19 February 1981.

46. *New York Times,* 10 July 1978, p. 14.

Selected Bibliography

Berdyaev, Nicolas. *The Origins of Russian Communism.* London: Geoffrey Bles, 1955.

Berlin, Isaiah. *Karl Marx.* New York: Time, 1963.

Brzezinski, Zbigniew. *Ideology and Power in Soviet Politics.* New York: Praeger, 1967.

Deutscher, Isaac. *The Prophet Armed.* New York: Vintage, 1959.

———. *The Prophet Unarmed.* New York: Vintage, 1959.

———. *The Prophet Outcast.* New York: Vintage, 1959.

———. *Stalin: A Political Biography.* New York: Vintage, 1949.

Kassof, Allen. *The Soviet Youth Program.* Cambridge: Harvard University Press, 1965.

Lane, Christel. *The Rites of Rulers: Ritual in Industrial Society—The Soviet Case.* Cambridge: Cambridge University Press, 1981.

Lenin, V. I. *Lenin: Selected Works.* New York: International Publishers, 1967.

———. *Lenin: Selected Works.* New York: International Publishers, 1971.

Meyer, Alfred. *Communism.* New York: Random House, 1960.

———. *Leninism.* Cambridge: Harvard University Press, 1957.

Miliband, Ralph. *Marxism and Politics.* Oxford: Oxford University Press, 1977.

Trotsky, Leon. *The Permanent Revolution.* New York: Pathfinder Press, 1970.

Tucker, Robert C. *The Marx-Engels Reader.* New York: W. W. Norton, 1978.

———. *Stalin as Revolutionary, 1879–1929.* New York: W. W. Norton, 1973.

Tucker, Robert C., ed. *Stalinism.* New York: W. W. Norton, 1977.

Ulam, Adam. *The Bolsheviks.* New York: Collier, 1965.

Venturi, Franco. *Roots of Revolution.* New York: Grosset & Dunlap, 1960.

Wolfe, Bertram D. *Three Who Made a Revolution.* New York: Dell, 1948.

4

The CPSU:
The Guiding Force
in Soviet Society

The Communist Party of the Soviet Union (CPSU) is the nucleus of all political activity in the USSR. It proclaims itself the "leading and guiding force of Soviet society."[1] At all levels of government, it is charged with making policies and supervising the prompt, efficient execution of policy decisions. Since 1917, the Party has developed from a handful of professional revolutionaries into a massive bureaucracy incorporating more than 19 million members. Its growth has been accompanied by a proliferation of responsibilities, as well as an erosion of the revolutionary zeal of its members.

CPSU GROWTH

Since its founding in 1898, the CPSU has grown at a phenomenal rate. In January 1917, just prior to the overthrow of the tsarist regime, the Party numbered only 23,600 members.[2] This was partly due to the personal danger associated with membership in revolutionary parties and the secrecy with which the early Party had to operate. Party membership was also restricted by Lenin's belief that party members should be an elite band of dedicated revolutionaries.

The legalization of the Party after the Tsar's abdication led to an influx of 50,000 new members by April 1917. Another massive enrollment occurred after the October Revolution. T. H. Rigby notes that this growth was still highly spontaneous and subject to little guidance by party leaders.[3] Party membership swelled to approximately 350,000 by the Eighth Party Congress in March 1919, which ordered the reregistration of party members to sift out political opportunists, in most cases those who had joined the Party after the October Revolution. The Civil War temporarily diminished party ranks as members were subject to mobilization for the front, and membership fell to less than 150,000 by August 1919 (see Figure 4-1).

Following the successful conclusion of the Civil War, a renewed effort was made to strengthen the Party, especially among peasants and workers. By the Tenth Congress in 1921, the Party totaled three-quarters of a million

Figure 4-1. CPSU Membership, 1917–1986

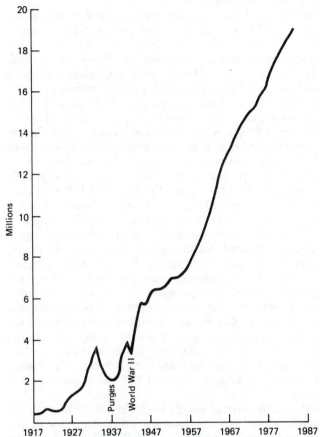

Source: "KPSS v tsifrakh," *Partiinaia zhizn'*, no. 21 (1977): 20–21; and *Pravda*, 26 September 1983, p. 2. Adapted from Ronald J. Hill and Peter Frank, *The Soviet Communist Party* (London: George Allen and Unwin, 1981), 32.

members. Membership was especially attractive to peasants, who could expect rapid upward mobility. However, this also led to an increase in corruption and careerism.

With the normalization of domestic affairs under the New Economic Policy begun in 1921, Lenin instructed the Party to purge from its ranks members guilty of "passivity, careerism, and failure to carry out instructions."[4] Between August 1921 and early 1922, the Party lost almost one-fourth of its membership.

Mass recruitment into the Party has been a feature of every period of crisis in the history of the Soviet regime, and the succession crisis following Lenin's death was no exception. In an effort to pack the CPSU with his supporters, Stalin launched the "Lenin enrollment" in 1924. In three months, the Party expanded by more than 40 percent, and by 1927, the

CPSU totaled 1.3 million members. The major expulsions during this period were Trotskyists and other opponents of Stalin.

The beginning of Stalin's drive for collectivization of agriculture and rapid industrialization in 1928 necessitated better party representation in the countryside and on the factory floor. Between 1928 and 1931, more than 900,000 new party members were recruited—a 70 percent increase.

Having consolidated his position and enforced a strict planning regime in the economy, Stalin launched the purges, which totally reshaped the Party from top to bottom. The purges (*chistki*) lasted from 1933 through 1938 and occurred in three waves, each more far-reaching and violent than the preceding one. In January 1933, a joint resolution of the CPSU Central Committee and the Central Control Commission ordered the verification of party documents of all party members, resulting in the expulsion of 16 percent of the party membership. The "paper purge" took its toll mainly among workers and peasants who had entered the Party in 1929 during the mass recruitment drive that accompanied collectivization and forced industrialization. Older party members were largely untouched by this purge.

In December 1934, Sergei Kirov, the first secretary of the Leningrad party organization, was assassinated. Stalin used the incident as an excuse to launch a new, more violent campaign against his opponents. Grigorii Zinoviev and Lev Kamenev, Stalin's chief opponents in the Politburo, were arrested, and local and regional party organizations were ordered to expel former members of the Trotsky and Zinoviev oppositions. Those eliminated from the party ranks tended to be Old Bolsheviks (those who had joined the Party prior to 1917) and middle-ranking party and state officials. During this second wave of purges, the Party declined by about half a million members. Many of those expelled from the Party were subsequently accused of crimes against the State and disappeared into the Gulag (prison-camp system), never to emerge.

The last and most violent wave of purges began in late 1936, with the show trials of Zinoviev, Kamenev, and fourteen other "enemies of the people." All confessed and were promptly executed. The trials did not end the reign of terror, which came to be called the *Ezhovshchina,* after N. I. Ezhov, Stalin's newly appointed head of the secret police. The *Ezhovshchina* wiped out the elite of virtually all institutions of Soviet society. The military was especially hard hit; an estimated one-fifth to one-half of all officers were purged.[5] In aggregate figures, the CPSU membership dropped from 3.5 million in 1933 to 1.9 million in 1938. More than 100,000 party members were purged in 1937 alone, and the purge appears to have focused on the most prominent members of the Party.

The Central Committee plenum of January 1938 marked the end of the purges. Having eliminated virtually all opposition and eradicated a whole generation of Soviet party and administrative officials, Stalin began to rapidly promote white-collar specialists to fill the posts vacated during the purges. This group, which enjoyed unprecedented upward mobility in the Soviet system, came to be known as the "Class of '38." It counts among its numbers Leonid Brezhnev, Alexsei Kosygin, Andrei Kirilenko, and Mikhail Suslov, all of whom received their first major appointments within the Party in 1938 or 1939.

One of the Party's first responses to the German invasion in 1941 was to instruct local party committees to broaden their recruitment efforts, especially among production workers. The Party's entrance requirements were significantly relaxed. Although the wartime loss of 20 million Soviet citizens included more than 3.5 million party members, an active recruitment campaign more than compensated for the casualties. The Party grew by almost two million members during the period 1941–1945. By 1946, in fact, many local party organizations were experiencing difficulty in assimilating, training, and deploying newly recruited party members, a problem that was exacerbated by the discharge from the armed forces of large numbers of party members. During the immediate postwar years, the Party first achieved a significant representation in the collective farms because the overload of members enabled the leadership to assign extra party personnel to rural areas. Admission standards were toughened again after the war, and expulsions increased to 100,000 per year.

The longest, most sustained increase in the Party's ranks came during the Khrushchev era (1953–1964). Stalin's death in 1953 began a protracted succession struggle, a crisis that was never fully resolved throughout the decade in which Khrushchev served as First Secretary. Although the annual intake of new party members was only a fraction of what it had been during earlier periods of heavy recruitment, the fact that the influx lasted for a full decade resulted in a 70 percent increase in party membership since Stalin's death.

Soon after Khrushchev's ouster in October 1964, the Central Committee's journal *Partiinaia zhizn'* published a decree that signaled renewed restrictive policies on recruitment into the Party. Three changes were introduced into the party rules in order to tighten admission procedures: the vote of the primary party organization to nominate someone for party membership was raised from a majority to two-thirds of the members; sponsors had to have been party members for a minimum of five years instead of three; and the age for admissions through the Young Communist League (Komsomol) was raised from 18–20 to 18–23. The annual rate of party growth steadily diminished from 6.7 percent in 1965 to 1.3 percent in 1973. Since the mid-1970s, the rate of growth has stabilized between 1.5 to 2.5 percent per year.

PARTY COMPOSITION AND SATURATION

As the Party has grown over the years, major changes have occurred in its composition. The social-class profile of the Party in 1917 reflected its proletarian outlook: 60 percent of the membership came from the working class, 32 percent were members of the intelligentsia, and only 8 percent were peasants.[6] During the New Economic Policy, Soviet power was gradually extended to the countryside, and this resulted in the gradual increase of peasant representation to 27 percent by 1927.

Stalin's introduction of rapid industrialization in 1928 signaled a shift to the "proletarianization" of the Party, an effort to enhance worker representation. The percentage of new recruits into the CPSU from the working class jumped from 57 percent in the period from July 1924 to July 1928 to 78 percent in 1929.[7] Despite the tendency for working-class party members to move into supervisory white-collar jobs, 43.8 percent of all party members were actually employed in manual labor by 1932.[8]

In the aftermath of the purges and World War II, the CPSU stabilized its ranks with ever-increasing numbers of white-collar specialists. As Table 4-1 shows, white-collar representation rose to 48.3 percent in 1947, making the intelligentsia the single largest component of the Party. A decade later, Khrushchev allowed the percentage of white-collar experts to slip above the 50-percent mark, a truly startling development in a Party billing itself as the "party of the workers and peasants." Khrushchev justified this trend toward the deproletarianization of the Party by declaring that the concept of the vanguard party was no longer applicable; he introduced instead the concept of "the Party of the whole people."[9]

Of course, the changes in the social composition of the Party reflect ongoing changes in the nature of Soviet society. With the mechanization of agriculture, fewer peasants were needed in the countryside. The cities offered improved housing, running water, central heat, better-quality consumer goods, and access to cultural amenities. Consequently, the 1930s and 1940s witnessed a migration from rural areas to the cities, especially by the young.

During the postwar years, there was also a growing realization that effective decision-making in the CPSU required the participation of the best minds, the most-experienced experts, and the most-able administrators in policy-making. The proliferation of state administrative agencies also created new white-collar positions to be filled by party members.

Since 1957, there has been a small but consistent reduction in both white-collar and peasant representation, while the percentage of workers has risen steadily. However, many of those today classified as workers are engaged in technical fields such as petrochemicals, instrument-making, electronics, and engineering, not in traditional "smokestack" industries. These are the workers most likely to rise out of the ranks of the working class and into white-collar professions.

A better grasp of the social composition of the Party today can be

Table 4-1. CPSU Composition by Social Class, 1917–1983 (in percent)

Year	Workers	Peasants	White Collar
1917	60.2	7.5	32.2
1927	55.1	27.3	32.2
1947	33.7	18.0	48.3
1957	32.0	17.3	50.7
1967	38.1	16.0	45.9
1977	42.0	13.6	44.4
1983	44.1	12.4	43.5

Sources: T. H. Rigby, *Communist Party Membership in the USSR, 1917–1967* (Princeton: Princeton University Press, 1967), 85; "KPSS v tsifrakh," *Partiinaia zhizn'*, no. 21 (1977): 20–43; and *Pravda*, 26 September 1983.

Table 4-2. Employment of CPSU Members by Sector (in percent)

39.2	Industry and Construction
20.0	Agriculture
16.0	Science, Education, Public Health, Culture
8.9	Party and State Administration, Economic Management
8.1	Transportation and Communications
4.7	Trade, Public Catering, Technical Supply
1.9	Housing, Municipal Services
1.2	Other

Source: *Pravda,* 26 September 1983.

gained by considering the sectors in which party members are employed. As Table 4-2 indicates, the largest number of party members are employed in industry and construction, and the nonproduction, service-oriented sectors account for the second-largest share of CPSU members.

The percentage of women in the ranks of the Party has increased gradually from only 7.5 percent in 1920 to 27.6 percent in 1983.[10] Nevertheless, women, who constitute 53.5 percent of the total Soviet population, are still drastically underrepresented. There are several reasons for the small proportion of women in the Party. Party membership entails the commitment of a substantial amount of time to party work, usually one day per week. Approximately 80 percent of all Soviet women work; in addition, they bear the full responsibility for running the household, shopping, cooking, and cleaning. In reality, most Soviet women today are engaged in dual employment and have little time or energy to devote to party affairs.

Those women who are party members tend to be relegated to lower levels in the party apparatus and are placed within traditional women's specializations: cultural affairs, education, the Komsomol, consumer affairs, and light industry. The only woman to reach the Politburo, Ekaterina Furtseeva, served as a Party Secretary and then as Minister of Culture under Khrushchev and Brezhnev. Among the 307 full members elected to the CPSU Central Committee at the Twenty-Seventh Party Congress in 1986, there were thirteen women:[11]

A. P. Biriukova	Secretary, CPSU Central Committee
V. N. Cherkashina	Spinner, Kamyshin Cotton Combine
N. M. Ershova	Adjuster, Perm Machine-Building Production Association
M. A. Golubeva	Milking-machine operator, Katun State Farm
V. N. Golubeva	Weaver, Ivanovo Worsted Combine
M. S. Gromova	Milking-machine operator, Kommunarka State Farm
E. F. Karpova	Deputy Chairman, RSFSR Council of Ministers
Z. M. Kruglova	Chairman, Presidium, Union of Soviet Societies for Friendship and

	Cultural Relations with Foreign Countries
N. V. Pereverzeva	Brigade leader, "Lenin's Way" Collective Farm
V. N. Pletneva	Weaver, Kostroma Flax Combine
V. S. Shevchenko	Chairman, Presidium, Ukrainian Supreme Soviet
V. V. Nikolaeva-Tereshkova	Cosmonaut; Chairman, Soviet Women's Committee; Member, Presidium, USSR Supreme Soviet
R. S. Udalaia	Riveter, Novosibirsk Aviation Plant

In fact, female representation on the Central Committee has declined from 9.7 percent in July 1917 to only 4.2 percent today.[12] In recent years, women have accounted for approximately one-third of all the secretaries of primary party organizations; 20 percent of district party organizations; few, if any, first secretaries of *oblast'* party committees; and only 3.2 percent of all *obkom* bureau members.[13] Women have achieved some limited gains under Mikhail Gorbachev. As noted, the number of women elected to the CPSU Central Committee at the Twenty-Seventh Party Congress increased to thirteen, compared to only eight at the Twenty-Sixth Party Congress in 1981. Gorbachev also promoted Aleksandra Biriukova to the Secretariat, where she is responsible for supervising light industry, the food industry, and consumer services.

In terms of nationality, the Party has always granted a disproportionate share of its membership to Russians, while non-Slavs have been underrepresented. As Table 4-3 shows, Russians are overrepresented by 13.9 percent, while the Central Asian nationalities (especially the Tadzhiks, Uzbeks, and Turkmen) and the Moldavians are seriously underrepresented.

Some progress toward achieving parity has been made over the years. In 1922, Russians were overrepresented in the ranks of the Party by 19 percent.[14] However, recent demographic trends among the Central Asian nationalities will make it difficult for them to achieve full representation in the Party's ranks. The birthrate among the Moslems of Central Asia is four times the national average. By the year 2000, it is estimated, the Islamic peoples will constitute the largest ethnic group in the USSR. These nationality groups have historically been the least likely to assimilate into Soviet society and also the least inclined to join the Party.

In contrast, Georgians and Belorussians have proven very able to assimilate and seek advancement through the Party and are slightly overrepresented. The most highly disproportionate representation in the Party is for Jews, who had more than twice their share of the adult population in the Party.[15] Given the strong correlation between level of education and party membership, much of the apparent variation in party membership by nationality actually reflects the variation in education.[16]

The educational profile of the CPSU indicates that there is still room for improvement. In 1983, a total of 29.5 percent of the Party had a higher (university-level) education, 2.2 percent had an incomplete higher education, 43 percent had a secondary education, 15.7 percent had an incomplete secondary education, and 9.6 percent had only a primary-school education.[17]

Table 4-3. Party Membership by Nationality and Percentage of Overrepresentation or Underrepresentation, January 1, 1983

Nationality	Percent of Population	Percent of CPSU	Overrepresentation or Underrepresentation[a]
Russian	52.4	59.7	+13.9
Ukrainian	16.2	16.0	− 1.2
Uzbek	4.8	2.4	−50.0
Belorussian	3.6	3.8	+ 5.5
Kazakh	2.5	2.0	−20.0
Azerbaidzani	2.1	1.7	−19.0
Armenian	1.6	1.5	− 6.3
Georgian	1.4	1.7	+21.4
Lithuanian	1.1	0.7	−36.4
Moldavian	1.1	0.5	−54.6
Tadzhik	1.1	0.4	−63.6
Turkmen	0.8	0.4	−50.0
Kirghiz	0.7	0.4	−42.9
Latvian	0.6	0.4	−33.3
Estonian	0.4	0.3	−25.0
Other	9.6	8.1	−15.6

[a]The data in this column were calculated by taking the difference and dividing it by the percentage of the population to arrive at the percentage overrepresented or underrepresented in the CPSU.
Sources: Population figures from the 1979 USSR census; CPSU figures from Pravda, 26 September 1983, p. 1.

However, virtually all Party secretaries have higher educations. As Table 4-4 shows, this represents a substantial improvement since World War II.

The stability of cadres promised under Brezhnev resulted in a marked decline in CPSU turnover. Fewer members were expelled or forced to retire, and recruitment dropped to a fraction of the level it had been under Khrushchev. The consequence was the aging of the Party, as indicated in Table 4-5. The percentage of party members over 51 years of age increased 5 percentage points, while the percentage of party members between 31 and 51 decreased 6 percentage points.

The massive influx of the Class of 38, which enjoyed rapid upward mobility at a relatively early age (most of those promoted after the purges were in their early to mid-thirties), filled the party nomenklatura positions for the next thirty to forty years before they retired or died. For the succeeding generation of aspiring party members—those entering the CPSU after World War II—few opportunities for advancement existed until the late 1970s and early 1980s, when the Class of 38 began to pass from the scene.

The Leninist conception of the Party held that membership should be reserved for a relatively small, elite group of professional revolutionaries who would act as the "vanguard of the proletariat." The CPSU is not a mass party; it comprises only 6 percent of the population of the Soviet

Table 4-4. Educational Level of Party Secretaries, 1946–1983 (in percent)

Level	1946	1952	1956	1969	1983
Higher	50.2	77.8	92.6	99.0	99.9
Secondary	39.0	21.5	6.3	1.0	0.1
Primary	10.8	0.7	0.0	0.0	0.0

Sources: Pravda, 26 September 1983, p. 2; and "KPSS v tsifrakh," Partiinaia zhizn', no. 21 (1977): 20–43.

Table 4-5. Age Profile of the CPSU, 1977–1983 (in percent)

Age	1977	1978	1983
25 or younger	5.8	6.0	6.4
26–30	10.8	11.2	11.2
31–40	25.8	24.5	20.8
41–50	26.4	26.1	25.4
51–60	18.1	19.0	21.1
61 or older	13.0	13.2	15.1

Sources: 1977 data from Partiinaia zhizn', no. 21 (November 1977): 31; 1978 data from Kommunist (1978): 203; and 1983 data from Pravda, 26 September 1983, p. 2.

Union. Yet, this figure is misleading. It obscures the extent to which membership in the CPSU affords Soviet citizens a chance to participate in the political process. When one considers factors such as level of education, the Party has a high level of representation among the secondary elite.

The party rules state that the minimum age for joining the Party is 18. Nevertheless, few citizens are permitted to join that early; the average age of admission was 27 years in 1975 (down from 31 years in 1965).[18] At the other end of the age spectrum, the retirement age is 65 for most men and 62 for women. When the young and the retired segments of the population are excluded, the percentage of citizens between the ages of 30 and 65 who are party members is 12.5.[19]

For reasons cited earlier, female representation in the Party is small. Hough found that 21 percent of all Soviet men between the ages of 31 and 60 were in the CPSU, and more than 50 percent of the male college graduates in that age group were party members.[20] This group corresponds to that segment of the population that is upwardly mobile, career-oriented, and most attentive to political issues. Since party membership represents a substantial commitment of time and energy, participation is not casual; it affords a great potential for this segment of Soviet population to affect policies.

Some interesting trends in party membership are revealed by examining the degree of party membership among various occupation groups (see Table 4-6). Rigby classified occupations in the USSR into three types: party-restricted, high-saturation, and low-saturation occupations.[21] Party-restricted occupations are those in which virtually every person is a party member, and membership appears to be a requirement or highly desired for

Table 4-6. Party Saturation by Occupation Group

Occupation	Percent in CPSU
Party officials	100
Komsomol officials	100
Ministers (e.g., Minister of Defense)	100
Judges	90
Public prosecutors	82
Journalists	75
Writers	50
Scientists	50
Composers	33
Engineers	25
Schoolteachers	25
Agronomists, livestock specialists	20–25
Artists	20
Physicians	16.6

Sources: Pravda, 26 September 1983, p. 2. The figures for judges and public prosecutors were reported in Gordon B. Smith, *The Soviet Procuracy and the Supervision of Administration* (Leiden, The Netherlands: Sijthoff & Noordhoff, 1978), 25.

appointment. Examples would include party, Komsomol, ministerial, and high-ranking state administrative officials; judges, public prosecutors, police and military officers, editors and journalists, and directors of major state farms, factories, plants, and enterprises.

High-saturation occupations are those in which 20 to 50 percent of the category are party members. Examples include scientists, scholars and academics, writers, composers, principals and other school administrators, and defense attorneys. Low-saturation occupations encompass the majority of the working class, that is, workers without professional qualifications or those who do not perform managerial or administrative responsibilities.

PARTY RECRUITMENT

The most important political decision a Soviet citizen can make is to join the Party. Joining the Party represents a commitment to the Soviet system and a pledge to support party policy, uphold the values of the society, and abide by party rules. To those who enter its ranks, the CPSU affords many privileges, but also many obligations.

In most cases, aspiring party members do not apply for admission; they are invited to join by their Komsomol organization or the primary party organization (PPO) at work. The Komsomol has increasingly become the major conduit for admission into the Party's ranks. In recent years, three-fourths of all new recruits have come from Komsomol organizations.[22] The admission procedure is long and arduous and designed to ensure that the applicant is, as the Soviets put it, "worthy of the lofty title of communist." The Party prides itself on selecting only the best and the brightest.

Aspiring entrants into the Party must receive letters of nomination from three persons who have been party members for at least five years. For those seeking admission via the Komsomol, references must be provided by the district or city Komsomol committee.

Applicants then fill out formal application forms, which detail their educational backgrounds, awards and honors, job experience, military record, and personal information such as age and date of birth. Also included in the application are a brief autobiography and personal statement.

The application is then presented to the PPO bureau in the factory, office, or institution in which the applicant is employed. The PPO committee or bureau makes an informal recommendation to the full meeting of the PPO; in practice, this recommendation is usually decisive. Soviet authors have stressed that the PPO considerations should be open to nonmembers as well, because it is important to know how the applicant is viewed by his or her peers.[23] The applicant is present at the full meeting of the PPO and may be asked to clarify points of information or to ascertain his or her knowledge of party affairs and sincerity in seeking admission. A vote is held; a two-thirds majority is required for admission. The PPO's decision, if affirmative, must then be confirmed by the district or city party committee superior to the PPO.

After payment of a modest entrance fee and monthly membership dues, the newly elected member begins one year of candidate or probationary membership (*kandidatskii stazh*). At the end of this period, the candidate's application is again brought before the PPO for a final vote. This decision is far from pro forma. One Soviet source reported that between 1966 and 1971, almost 112,000 candidates were denied full membership after their probationary years.[24] Nevertheless, this represents only 3.5 to 4 percent of all candidates.

THE OBLIGATIONS AND PRIVILEGES OF PARTY MEMBERSHIP

CPSU members are obliged to be model workers and take an active part in public life. They are expected to devote much of their leisure time to party meetings, public discussions and lectures, election work, and organizing party affairs. In their personal lives, party members are supposed to be above reproach. Alcoholism or scandal can prompt an investigation by the party committee and can result in a member's reprimand or even expulsion from the Party.

While a CPSU member is expected to be well-versed in Marxist-Leninist ideology and to undertake advanced ideological training at the Higher Party School, being ardent and doctrinaire does not guarantee admission into the Party. The CPSU is intent on admitting only persons who are loyal, capable, and bright, not dogmatic and inflexible.

Although party membership carries many burdens, it also confers some privileges and benefits. Clearly, the greatest benefit is the elite status it conveys. Membership in the CPSU opens the doors to advanced training at the prestigious universities and institutes. It makes possible appointments to influential, well-paid positions in industry and state administration, as well as within the Party. Party membership also affords citizens the opportunity to become politically involved and to influence policy. In particular, it allows them greater freedom in criticizing proposed policies and in speaking out against the ineffective implementation of policies.

Although it is impermissible for party members to abuse their privileges in pursuit of personal aims or gains, such cases are not unheard of. Interviews with recent Soviet émigrés cite numerous examples of party members flaunting their privileged status and abusing their power. For instance, divorces involving childless marriages are usually quite routine in the USSR, but in one such case the wife was unable to obtain an equitable division of property. The husband, a well-placed party member, had used his influence to ensure his private interests.[25]

Party privilege can also interfere in criminal cases. For instance, a Soviet army officer serving in East Germany purchased government bonds and sent them to a bank in his hometown for safekeeping. When he returned home, the officer found that all his bonds had disappeared. The head of the bank turned out to be the thief, but the first secretary of the district party committee permitted the bank manager to return the money and escape criminal prosecution. Why? The bank manager was the first secretary's relative.[26]

ORGANIZATION OF THE CPSU

The CPSU derives much of its power and influence not only from its size and its monopoly hold on the major positions in the society, but also from its highly bureaucratized organizational structure. The CPSU constitutes a pseudo-government parallel to the official organs of the State. Power is invested in its highest offices and is effectively transmitted to every factory and farm in the USSR via a highly centralized and authoritative structure.

The Primary Party Organization. From its inception in Russia, the Party has adopted a cellular structure. That is, in every factory, every collective farm, every student dormitory in which there are three or more party members, a primary party organization (PPO) is formed. The adoption of the cellular structure was initially necessary to facilitate secrecy and minimize the danger to political revolutionaries, whose activities were closely watched by the tsar's secret police. Clandestine workers' meetings were less conspicuous in the workplace than they were after work hours in the homes of fellow revolutionaries.

The cellular structure of the CPSU, as a form of grass-roots organization, has persisted in part due to tradition. Lenin's conception of the Party also retains a powerful ideological appeal. In addition, the Party has been able to use its link to the workplace effectively to mobilize workers in support of party policies. The Party relies on the PPOs in every factory, enterprise, and collective to be its "eyes and ears" at the grass-roots level, reporting on problems, inefficiency, and mismanagement.

Without exception, every member of the CPSU must be a member of a primary party organization. As of January 1, 1983, there were 425,897 PPOs in the USSR.[27] The number of members in the PPOs varies from three in small shops or rural collectives to several hundred in large industrial complexes. The average size of a PPO in industrial enterprises is 103 members; on state farms, 68 members; on collective farms, 60 members; and in construction organizations, 39 members.[28] The percentages of PPOs by sector of the economy are presented in Table 4-7.

In small collectives, shops, offices, and restaurants, the PPOs have a simple structure; party members simply meet periodically to elect a secretary who maintains party records, collects dues, and reports to higher party officials. In such organizations, the PPO secretary's job is not a full-time occupation for which the secretary is paid, but rather a voluntary, civic duty. Approximately 40 percent of all PPOs are of this type, although the trend is clearly away from such simple organizations.[29]

In large industrial plants employing thousands of people, PPOs may consist of several hundred members. Such enterprises are frequently divided into subsections, scattered throughout a city or region. In such instances, the simple model of a PPO described previously is clearly inadequate to fulfill the Party's functions. In large enterprises, PPOs are divided into production-unit party organizations, each headed by a bureau (or executive committee) and a secretary. These production-unit party organizations report to a party committee for the entire industrial plant, which also is chaired by a secretary. In large PPOs such as this, the secretary is a powerful figure who is a full-time party functionary, often serving as deputy director of the enterprise. He or she is assisted by a staff that is responsible for keeping records and organizing political education programs.

Regardless of its size or degree of complexity, the PPO is governed by the general meeting of its members, usually held on a monthly basis. The general meeting formally elects the committee and secretary for a one-year term in small PPOs and two or three years in larger PPOs. The general meeting also admits and expels members. In 1979, only 88 of the 400,000 PPO secretaries were elected by ballot, the rest were nominated by higher party organs and ratified by the general meeting.[30] The general meeting of

Table 4-7. Location of Primary Party Organizations (in percent)

Industrial, transport, communications, and construction enterprises	25.9%
Rural territories and housing management	18.2
Institutions, organizations, and economic agencies	17.2
Educational institutions	16.7
Collective farms	6.2
State farms	5.2
Medical institutions	4.0
Trade and public catering enterprises	3.6
Scientific institutions	1.6
Cultural institutions	1.4

Source: *Partiinaia zhizn'*, no. 8 (April 1983): 20–21.

the PPO also elects delegates to the party conference of the district or town in which the PPO is located.

One of the principal functions of the PPO is investigating shortcomings in the administration of the institution with which it is associated. This is referred to as *pravo kontrolia* ("the right of control"). Soviet sources define *pravo kontrolia* as the "systematic verification of the execution of laws, directives of the Party, and decrees of the government."[31] Until recently, *pravo kontrolia* was granted only to PPOs in economic enterprises, factories, and farms. PPOs within the state bureaucracy did not enjoy the right of control because the State was considered to be under the "control" of the Party's central organs. This changed, however, at the Twenty-Fourth Party Congress in 1971. Under the new party rules, PPOs in state administrative agencies, local Soviets, ministries, and scientific and other institutions were authorized to exercise "control."

In the early years of the Soviet regime, *pravo kontrolia* of the PPOs often brought party secretaries into direct conflict with industrial managers; this came to be called the "red/expert" dilemma. Facing the need to stimulate production in a given factory, the "red" (secretary of the PPO) would halt production for agitation-propaganda sessions to inspire the workers to achieve more. The factory manager, on the other hand, would advocate longer shifts and oppose stopping the assembly lines so that the workers could listen to a political harangue. During the 1920s, the "reds" often controlled the factory manager, but today the two tend to work in tandem.

Recent analysis of career patterns suggests that PPO secretaries are less pivotal in policy-making than are chief administrators and enterprise directors. However, when matters of principle (*prinstipial'nye voprosy*) arise, PPO secretaries participate in discussions. For example, the decision within a machine-tool plant to adopt the brigade form of labor organization and to reward workers not for their individual performance but according to the brigade's performance would involve the PPO secretary. While secretaries cannot veto actions of administrators, they can and do refer matters to higher party organizations. The relatively subordinate role of PPO secretaries is also evidenced by the fact that the office of the secretary is in most cases a part-time (*neosvobozhdennyi*) position.

Complicating this relationship is the fact that most managers and heads of state agencies are themselves party members, and most of them serve on party committees at the district, city, or regional level. As such, they are regarded as "persons trusted by the Party and the State."[32] In most cases, the PPO secretary and the administrative chief occupy *nomenklatura* positions; thus they enjoy the confidence of higher party committees, and each has distinct political resources upon which to draw in case of a conflict.

Many Western specialists have viewed party *kontrol'* primarily as a conflictual relationship between local party officials and state agencies and enterprises. However, Hough indicates that, in practice, the relationship is often a cooperative one, incorporating a degree of division of authority on the basis of expertise.[33] In fact, the principal significance of the PPO in state administrative agencies may not be in controlling administrative activities, but rather in expanding participation in decision-making to a wider circle of persons with practical expertise.

Finally, the PPO is crucial in the recruitment of new party members from the work force. Party cells also identify competent, aggressive party members suitable for promotion into positions of responsibility within the ranks of the CPSU.

LOCAL PARTY ORGANS

Above the PPO level, the CPSU is geographically organized. The lowest level of territorial party organization is the district (*raion*). Every two years, PPOs within a district select delegates to the *raion* party conference. To be named a delegate to the party conference is an honor accorded to exemplary workers and powerful PPO secretaries. The *raion* party conference reaffirms the party line, under the watchful eyes of a representative of higher authority.[34] In addition, delegates to the conference ratify a slate of predetermined candidates to serve as members of the district party committee, including the first secretary, for a term of two years.

At the district level, the real political power rests with the *raikom* (*raion* party committee), which convenes approximately six times per year in plenary sessions to discuss edicts from central party organs, to monitor plan fulfillment in industry and agriculture within the district, and to issue directives to subordinate PPOs. The *raikom* is composed of up to one hundred members, the majority of whom are full, voting members. Candidate or nonvoting members normally constitute 25 to 30 percent of the total and may be consulted on policy matters. These individuals constitute a reserve from which new members may be selected. The membership of the *raikom* typically includes party and state officials of the district; trade union and Komsomol leaders; the directors of major industrial enterprises, collectives, or state farms; a few representatives of the scientific-technical, educational, and cultural establishments; and a few rank-and-file workers and peasants.

Given its large size and its infrequent sessions, the *raikom* delegates much of its day-to-day authority to an executive body, a political bureau (*politburo*) comprising approximately twelve powerful local party and government officials and representatives of major industrial enterprises. The *raikom* bureau meets several times a month to discuss major political and economic issues confronting the district. Frequently, specialists and party functionaries are invited to *raikom* bureau sessions to give reports and to discuss particular problems.

The first secretary presides over the *raikom* and the bureau. The first secretary is the most powerful political figure in the district, the direct link between the district party organization and higher party bodies. The first secretary is ultimately responsible for supervising the efficient implementation of party policies in the district. Success or failure in this major political assignment will determine the first secretary's ultimate career prospects. Should the district prosper, should major industrial concerns fulfill their plan targets, should no major scandals cast a cloud on the administration's performance, the secretary will most likely be promoted, perhaps to a larger, more prominent district or city. Thus, the first secretary functions somewhat as did the boss of a political machine in an American city during the late 1800s and early 1900s.

The first secretary's job also requires the mediation of disputes that invariably arise between various interests within the district. Under the pressure of striving to fulfill their production quotas, various industrial enterprises may come to the first secretary to request extra personnel or resources. Local police and social workers may present the official varying solutions to juvenile delinquency. State farms in the district may complain that they should be granted special allocations to raise the quality of rural housing to the same level as in the cities. Thus, the first secretary is not only a "boss," but also a "broker," allocating resources and setting priorities for the district as a whole.

Attached to the *raikom* is the party *apparat*, the bureaucracy responsible for the day-to-day management of party affairs. The *apparat* is organized into several departments. Among the most important are the propaganda and agitation department (*agitprop*), and the organizational department, which handles local party records and the approval of nominees to PPO secretaryships. District party committees also have departments of agriculture and of industry and transportation, which supervise the economic activities of their respective sectors within the district. While the party secretaries specializing in production matters are not supposed to interfere in or substitute for industrial management, they are concerned with minute details affecting economic performance. The general department handles the internal affairs of the *raikom*, setting the agenda and scheduling meetings of the *raikom* and the bureau, handling correspondence, and duplicating and circulating documents and texts of decisions. The typical structure of a *raion* party committee is presented Figure 4-2.

The outlines of the Party's structure at the district level remain essentially the same at higher levels—in large cities, regions, and republics, as well as at the All-Union level. For instance, the next territorial level above the district is the region (*oblast'*). As of January 1, 1983, there were 151 *oblasti* in the USSR, ranging from 544,000 square miles to 1740 square miles. Thus, an *oblast'* is somewhat larger than a county in the United States, but smaller than most states. It is the modern equivalent of the prerevolutionary province. The regional party committee (*obkom*) is elected by a party conference that convenes every three years. Delegates to the *oblast'* party conference are selected at the district (*raion*) party conferences. Like the *raikom*, the *obkom* meets infrequently, delegating much of its day-to-day decision-making responsibility to the *obkom* bureau, an executive body of approximately ten to fifteen powerful officials that is headed by the regional first party secretary.

The larger territory and more diverse responsibilities of the regional party organization are reflected in a greater number of departments. Attached to the *obkom* is a secretariat—a body comprised of approximately twelve party secretaries, each of whom heads a department. The typical *obkom* secretariat has the following departments: administrative organs, agriculture, construction, culture, general, information, industrial-transportation, light industry and food industry, organizational party work, propaganda and agitation, science and education, trade, and financial and plan-

Figure 4-2. Structure of a District Party Committee

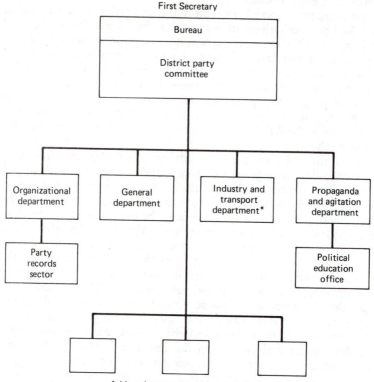

Ad hoc departments and commissions

*May be replaced by an agricultural department in a rural *raikom*.

Source: Adapted from *KPSS—naglyadnoe posobie* (1973): 63, and Ronald J. Hill and Peter Frank, *The Soviet Communisty Party* (London: George Allen and Unwin, 1981), 59.

ning organs. In a region where a particular sector of the economy dominates, there may be a separate department devoted to it (e.g., the coal department in the Donets region of the Ukraine, or the oil department of the Tiumen region in western Siberia).

In the fifteen republics that form the USSR, party organizations are structured much like those at the district and regional levels. Every five years, the republic party congress is held to elect a republic central committee, comprising the leading party, state, educational, industrial, and cultural officials of the republic as well as a few token workers and farmers. The Russian republic (RSFSR) does not have a separate central committee; it is represented instead by the CPSU Central Committee. Like their counterparts at lower levels, the republic central committees delegate authority to a political bureau (*politburo*), while day-to-day administration of party affairs is handled by the republic secretariat.

CENTRAL ORGANS OF THE CPSU

The CPSU is organized according to the principle of *democratic central-ism*. Article 19 of the Party rules defines *democratic centralism* in terms of four criteria: (1) all leading party bodies are elected from below, but elections in the Party are indirect; (2) party organs are expected to make periodic reports of their activities to the general meeting (conference or congress) of its members and to higher-ranking party organs; (3) strict party discipline is observed, and the will of the minority is subordinated to that of the majority; and (4) the decisions of higher party organs are binding on lower-ranking party bodies. The strong centralizing elements in the organization of the Party ensure that supreme power resides in its central organs—the CPSU Congress, the CPSU Central Committee, the Politburo, and the CPSU Secretariat. (See Figures 4-3 and 4-4.)

Party Congress. Every five years, more than five thousand delegates gather in the Palace of Congresses in the Kremlin for the CPSU Congress. According to party rules, the body, which convenes for approximately ten days, wields ultimate political authority over party affairs.[35]

Congress sessions are devoted to formal speeches by the party leadership on domestic and foreign-policy issues confronting the USSR. In recent years, the congresses have featured the presentation of two major reports: one by the General Secretary of the Party dealing with the domestic and foreign-policy concerns of the Central Committee, and one by the Chairman of the Council of Ministers on the new Five-Year Plan.

The congresses also afford local and regional party officials the opportunity to report on the achievements of their regions and to criticize the State Planning Commission or central ministries. Heads of foreign communist parties are also invited to attend and usually address the gathering. The Party Congress serves as a forum for the leadership to articulate new policy directions and reaffirm past decisions. Since the Twentieth Party Congress in 1956, when Krushchev stunned the delegates with his "Secret Speech," an unprecedented denunciation of Stalin and his "crimes," the congresses have tended to be, at least on the surface, rather dull, formal, and above all, predictable. Behind the scenes, however, there is a great deal of informal politicking.

Figure 4-3. Central Organs of the CPSU

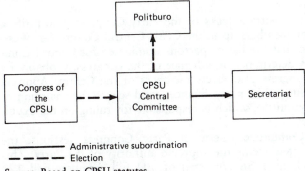

Source: Based on CPSU statutes.

Figure 4-4. The Territorial Structure of the CPSU

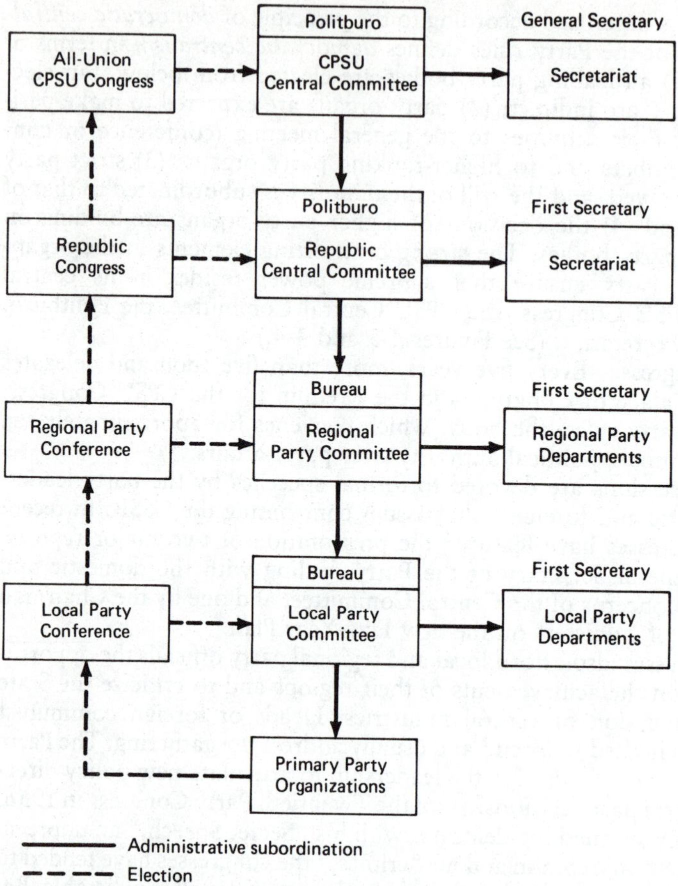

```
                        Politburo            General Secretary
  ┌──────────────┐    ┌──────────────┐    ┌──────────────┐
  │  All-Union   │───▶│    CPSU      │───▶│              │
  │ CPSU Congress│    │   Central    │    │  Secretariat │
  │              │    │  Committee   │    │              │
  └──────────────┘    └──────────────┘    └──────────────┘

                        Politburo            First Secretary
  ┌──────────────┐    ┌──────────────┐    ┌──────────────┐
  │   Republic   │───▶│   Republic   │───▶│              │
  │   Congress   │    │   Central    │    │  Secretariat │
  │              │    │  Committee   │    │              │
  └──────────────┘    └──────────────┘    └──────────────┘

                         Bureau             First Secretary
  ┌──────────────┐    ┌──────────────┐    ┌──────────────┐
  │Regional Party│    │   Regional   │    │Regional Party│
  │  Conference  │    │Party Committee│───▶│ Departments  │
  │              │    │              │    │              │
  └──────────────┘    └──────────────┘    └──────────────┘

                         Bureau             First Secretary
  ┌──────────────┐    ┌──────────────┐    ┌──────────────┐
  │  Local Party │    │  Local Party │    │  Local Party │
  │  Conference  │    │  Committee   │───▶│ Departments  │
  │              │    │              │    │              │
  └──────────────┘    └──────────────┘    └──────────────┘

                      ┌──────────────┐
                      │ Primary Party│
                      │Organizations │
                      └──────────────┘
```

──────── Administrative subordination
─ ─ ─ ─ Election

Source: Based on CPSU statutes. The figure omits the levels of territory (*krai*) and national area (*okrug*). Also, some cities are directly subordinated to republic party committees rather than to regional party committees. Within large cities, there may be district (*raion*) committees between the PPOs and the city party committee.

One of the most important tasks of the Party Congress is to ratify a slate of candidates for membership in the CPSU Central Committee. Western specialists assume that the list of persons nominated for Central Committee membership is determined in advance of the congress, probably by the Politburo. The congress also elects members of the Central Auditing Commission, which supervises party finances, and selects the chairman of the Party Control Committee, which is responsible for ruling on the expulsion of party members.

CPSU Central Committee. Between Party Congress sessions, the CPSU Central Committee wields the supreme authority of the Party. This collective body, which in 1986 consisted of 304 full members and 172 nonvoting candidate members, represents a diverse array of powerful individuals and institutions.[36] The largest group within the Central Committee, accounting for 35 to 40 percent of the membership, is the local, regional, and national party secretaries. The second most prominent bloc is composed of ministers and chairmen of state committees (18 percent); followed by local government officials, such as chairmen of city and regional soviets (11 percent); high-ranking military officials (7 percent); writers, artists, and cultural officials (6.5 percent); and a few scientists, trade-union officials, police, and diplomats. In addition, the Central Committee awards membership as an honor to outstanding workers and peasants, who in recent years have constituted roughly 6 percent of Central Committee membership. The elite status of Central Committee members is reflected in the fact that 76 percent of present members are also deputies to the Supreme Soviet.[37]

Only 4 percent of the Central Committee members are women, and only 5.3 percent of the members are under the age of 50. In 1971, the last year for which data are available, the Central Committee included members of twenty-three nationalities; non-Russians constituted 38 to 39 percent of the total.[38] While this is less than in the Supreme Soviet, it is substantially more than in the Politburo and the Secretariat.

The Central Committee is mandated to convene in plenary sessions at least twice a year, usually for only three to five days per session. Central Committee meetings are devoted to hearing reports on party matters, including the promotion, demotion, and expulsion of members; ratifying Central Committee decrees, which are binding on all party members; and discussing pressing national and international issues. Plenums are normally convened prior to and after major state and party events—Supreme Soviet sessions, Party Congresses, introduction of new Five-Year Plans, and the ratification of a new constitution. Plenums have also been convened to discuss international crises and major new policy initiatives. For instance, plenums were called to consider the Middle East crisis in 1967, the invasion of Czechoslovakia in 1968, the opening of détente with the West in 1971 and 1972, and the invasion of Afghanistan in 1979 and 1980. The purpose of the plenum on these occasions appears not to have been the airing of differing viewpoints, but the demonstration of support for the policies of the ruling Politburo.

Central Committee plenums are a mixture of largely ceremonial functions and meaningful deliberations on policy problems. However, the infrequency and short duration of the committee sessions restrict participation considerably. Thus, on an average, only about one-third of the full members speak at Central Committee plenums.[39] Officials of large or especially important regions are apparently given precedence in speaking to the body. The first secretaries of the largest republics (Ukraine, Kazakhstan, Belorussia, and Uzbekistan) routinely take the rostrum, as do the party leaders of Moscow and Leningrad. Similarly, ministers of prominent ministries and chairmen of influential state committees (e.g., Ministry of Agriculture, Ministry of Defense, and Gosplan) frequently address the Central Committee on economic matters.

Stenographic reports of Central Committee sessions have not been published since the March 1965 plenum, at which agricultural failures were harshly criticized. The secrecy surrounding Central Committee debates suggests that the discussions are still fairly frank and candid. The General Secretary's references to comments made by other speakers during Central Committee discussions imply that regional officials take the rostrum to lobby for increased appropriations for projects in their regions. In his concluding remarks at the June 1976 Central Committee plenary session, for example, Brezhnev noted that not all requests for regional investment could be satisfied and that decisions would have to be made in light of existing resources.[40]

On occasion, the Central Committee may be called upon to resolve matters over which the Politburo is deeply divided. Perhaps the most notable case of this occurred in 1957, when Khrushchev convened an emergency plenum of the Central Committee after a faction within the Politburo attempted to oust him.

Little is known about the process for selecting Central Committee members. One Soviet source indicates that a list of candidates is drawn up before the Party Congress and is discussed by party leaders of the various regional, territorial, and republic delegations before being presented to the congress for a vote.[41]

Candidates to the Central Committee are chosen on the basis of a combination of personal merit and position. Robert Daniels has noted that the Central Committee is merely a collection of individuals selected to represent various functional groups and regional interests.[42] Certain positions and titles appear to confer automatic Central Committee membership; in fact, as much as 90 percent of the body may be determined in this manner.[43] Thus, the Central Committee contains a broad spectrum of policy expertise, experience, skill, and preferences upon which the top leadership may draw. For those Central Committee members whose selection is not explained by position, other factors—personality, ties to the General Secretary, region, nationality, or gender—may weigh heavily in the decision. For example, Valentina Nikolaeva-Tereshkova, the first female cosmonaut and currently the Chairman of the Soviet Women's Committee, is a member, as was the writer Mikhail Sholokhov, who died in 1984. In both cases, membership was most likely determined by their fame. In a study of the party organization in Dnepropetrovsk, the region from which Brezhnev rose to power, Joel Moses found that secretaries from that region enjoyed a much better chance of landing a membership in the Central Committee during the 1960s and 1970s than did secretaries from other regions of the Ukraine.[44]

Since Khrushchev's time, turnover of Central Committee membership has remained very low. Brezhnev rose to power, in part, by promising to bring "stability of cadres." Nowhere is this stability as evident as in the lack of change in the Central Committee. Of the members elected to the body in 1971, 90 percent were reelected in 1976, and 90 percent of the 1976 members were returned to the Central Committee in 1981. The token worker and peasant delegates rotate somewhat more frequently; only five of the twelve worker and peasant Central Committee members elected at the Twenty-Fifth Party Congress were reelected at the next congress. Although individual worker and peasant representatives change over time, the general profile of representation does not vary substantially, as Table 4-8 shows.

The Politburo. The real power over day-to-day decisions in the USSR

Table 4-8. Comparison of Worker and Peasant Members of the CPSU Central Committee Elected at the Twenty-Fifth and Twenty-Sixth CPSU Congresses

Twenty-Fifth Congress	*Twenty-Sixth Congress*
A. V. Chuev, lathe operator, Baltic Shipyard, Leningrad	V. S. Chicherov, brigade leader and fitter, Leningrad Metallurgical Plant for Turbine Construction
L. D. Kazakov, brigade leader, Baikal-Amur Railway Construction Trust, Irkutsk Oblast'	V. A. Zatvornitsky, brigade leader, Construction Administration No. 6, Housing and Civil Construction Trust, Moscow
M. S. Ivannikova, weaver, M. V. Frunze Cotton Factory, Moscow	V. N. Golubeva, weaver, V. I. Lenin Worsted Combine, Ivanovo Oblast'
A. I. Khramtsov, brigade leader and gear cutter, Urals Heavy Machine-Building Plant, Sverdlovsk	A. M. Korolev, brigade leader and lathe operator, Urals Heavy Machine-Building Plant, Sverdlovsk
A. A. Bleskov, Chairman, V. I. Lenin Collective Farm, Stavropol' Krai (RSFSR)	N. S. Popov, Chief Designer, Kirov Steel Plant, Leningrad
G. L. Mikhailov, lathe operator, Kharkov Transport Machine-Building Plant (Ukraine)	V. A. Petrov, brigade leader and lathe operator, Kharkov Transport Machine-Building Plant (Ukraine)
G. Y. Gorban', steelworker, "Azovstal" Metallurgical Plant, Donetsk Oblast' (Ukraine)	G. Y. Gorban', reelected
M. I. Klepikov, brigade leader, "Kuban" Collective Farm, Krasnodar' Krai (RSFSR)	M. I. Klepikov, reelected
E. I. Klimchenko, toolmaker, V. I. Lenin Tractor Plant, Minsk	E. I. Klimchenko, reelected
M. G. Popova, crane operator, Nakhodka Commercial Port, Primor'e Krai (RSFSR)	M. G. Popova, reelected
V. G. Semenov, brigade leader and fitter, Podol'sk Mechanical Plant, Moscow Oblast'	V. G. Semenov, reelected
	S. N. Savin, brigade leader and electrician, Voronezh Radio Components Factory (RSFSR)
	V. P. Tikhomirov, brigade leader and lathe operator, V. I. Lenin Electromechanical Plant, Moscow

(Table continued)

Twenty-Fifth Congress	Twenty-Sixth Congress
	A. Y. Kolesnikov, brigade leader, "Young Guard" Coal Mine, Voroshilov Oblast' (Ukraine)
	I. P. Kudinov, fitter, M. V. Frunze Motor-Building Plant, Kuibyshev (RSFSR)

Source: Compiled from Herwig Kraus, ed., *The Composition of Leading Organs of the CPSU (1952–1982)* (Munich: Radio Liberty Research Bulletin, May 30, 1982).

resides in the Politburo. The body consists of eleven to fifteen full members and roughly six to eight nonvoting candidate members. Like the Central Committee, the Politburo has increased in size over the years. In 1919, it consisted of only five full members and three candidate members. The institution has historically been dominated by Russian males; only one woman has ever served on the Politburo, Ekaterina Furtseeva, Khrushchev's Minister of Culture. Eight of the eleven current members of the Politburo and seven of the eight candidate members are Russians. However, the non-Russian members are fluent in Russian and thoroughly loyal to the center.

The workings of the Politburo remain shrouded in secrecy. Western specialists learned only in 1973 from an interview with Leonid Brezhnev in the *New York Times* that the Politburo meets once a week, on Thursday mornings, with the General Secretary presiding.[45] Iurii Andropov, who was General Secretary from November 1982 to February 1984, lifted the curtain of secrecy somewhat further by permitting the agendas of Politburo meetings to be reported in *Pravda*. Although sketchy, the reports give Soviet citizens an idea of the wide range of issues considered by the political leaders. This report, which appeared in *Pravda* on October 26, 1984, is typical:

> At its regular session, the Politburo of the CPSU Central Committee discussed the performance of Soviet industry for the first nine months of the year. It was noted at the meeting that all ministries and Union republics have fulfilled the plan for sold output. There has been a 4.1% increase in production, compared to an assigned 3.8% for the year, and this has been achieved mainly through increased labor productivity. At the same time, however, the Politburo called to the attention of party committees, ministries, departments and Union republic councils of ministers the fact that a number of enterprises and associations have been operating below capacity in recent months—September included—and it pointed out the need to eliminate quickly the existing lags, in order to complete the 1984 plan and carry out the socialist pledges that were made. A report on industrial performance in the period from January to September 1984 will be carried in the press.
>
> The Politburo examined and approved proposals by the USSR Council of Ministers for ensuring accelerated development in our country of highly automated, large-series production of the modern numerically controlled systems needed to accomplish the tasks involved in automating machine building.
>
> The Politburo approved the results of Comrade A. A. Gromyko's talks with T. Aziz, Deputy Prime Minister and Minister of Foreign Affairs of the

Republic of Iraq. It noted in this connection the positive significance of further developing Soviet-Iraqi relations, including economic relations, and underscored the Soviet Union's unwavering, principled stand on the issues of achieving a comprehensive settlement in the Middle East and putting an end to the war between Iraq and Iran, which would be in keeping with the vital interests of the peoples of these countries.

The Politburo examined a report by Comrade M. S. Gorbachev on his conversation with K. Hager, member of the Politburo and Secretary of the Central Committee of the Socialist Unity Party of Germany, in which they focused on the further expansion of fraternal cooperation between the CPSU and the SUPG.

It approved a report by Comrade V. V. Grishin on the results of the trip to Yugoslavia by a delegation from the Moscow City Party Committee, which took part in events connected with the 40th anniversary of Belgrade's liberation from the fascist invaders.

Comrade G. A. Aliev presented a report on his meeting with the heads of the Japanese delegation of private individuals attending the Soviet-Japanese roundtable conference taking place in Moscow. At its session, the Politburo of the CPSU Central Committee also adopted decisions concerning several other questions of Soviet domestic and foreign policy.[46]

In many respects, the Politburo functions much as a parliamentary cabinet. It is chaired by the General Secretary and includes the Premier (Chairman of the Council of Ministers) and the President (Chairman of the Supreme Soviet). In addition, in recent years the Politburo has included influential ministers: Minister of Defense, Minister of Foreign Affairs, and frequently the Minister of Agriculture and the Chairman of the KGB (security police). Membership is also normally extended to one or two senior-ranking members of the Secretariat, whose functional specializations may include ideological matters or who are closely linked to the General Secretary. Finally, the Politburo includes first secretaries of large and powerful territorial constituencies—Ukraine, Kazakhstan, Moscow, and Leningrad. Thus, in its composition, the Politburo represents a broad mix of regional, economic, and political interests. On occasion, as indicated by the *Pravda* summary, the members invite nonmembers to brief them on problems or issues when additional expertise is needed.

Brezhnev indicated in the *New York Times* interview that Politburo sessions allow for open and detailed discussion in which decisions are reached "99.99 percent of the time" through consensus; votes are rare.[47] Serious policy disagreements do, however, divide the Politburo. For instance, Brezhnev and his supporters were confronted with a faction (including Mikhail Suslov, Andrei Grechko, and Petr Shelest) who opposed détente with the West. Factions within the Politburo are especially evident during succession crises. At the time of Andropov's death in 1984, factions arose around two potential successors: Konstantin Chernenko and Mikhail Gorbachev. Thus, the politics of the Politburo appears to be the politics of coalition-building. This does not lessen the collective nature of decision-making; it merely implies that once the opposing faction sees that it is clearly outnumbered, it is in its interests, as well as the interests of preserving party unity, to acquiesce quietly in the issue, at least in public.

The General Secretary.   There is little doubt that the most prominent, influential figure in the Politburo is the General Secretary. Nevertheless, the party statutes and Soviet textbooks do not mention his power, nor do they define his role. Westerners may find this oversight odd, because the General Secretary dominates the Soviet political scene to an extent unimagined in the West. Huge portraits of the General Secretary adorn many public buildings; factories and even cities are named in his honor. The press glorifies him as "farsighted," "heroic," and "modest."

Despite the honors and accolades heaped on the General Secretary, the emphasis within the Party is on collective decision-making. Lenin established the principle of collective rule by the Politburo, and as is so often the case in the USSR, what Lenin enshrined in 1917 cannot be easily undone today.[48] Even during Stalin's autocratic reign, orders for the execution of high-ranking officials were signed by the entire Politburo.[49]

On many occasions, Nikita Khrushchev violated the principle of collective decision-making. In the process, he lost the support of his most powerful constituency—the local and regional party secretaries. Khrushchev's ill-conceived and often impulsive reforms, including the Virgin Lands program, the bifurcation of the party apparatus, and the decision to place missiles in Cuba, proved to be embarrassing failures that resulted in his ouster in 1964.

Leonid Brezhnev, who was selected to succeed Khrushchev, promised to adhere to the norm of collective decision-making. Brezhnev's leadership style stressed gradualism, going through channels, and consultation with all interested institutions. Greater effort was made under Brezhnev to involve experts in policy-making in order to avoid the problems that had plagued Khrushchev.

One unanticipated consequence of Brezhnev's shift to consultation and collective decision-making, however, was a dramatic dampening of reform and dynamism in decision-making. Problems festered while committees drafted reports, institutions lobbied, and experts were consulted. The immobility of the latter half of the Brezhnev administration can be attributed to the General Secretary's failing health and lack of dynamic leadership. An energetic Brezhnev had been able to enlist the support of Premier Alexei Kosygin and Andrei Gromyko, Minister of Foreign Affairs, in favor of détente to overcome the opposition of conservative military officers and party ideologues. In the late 1970s, however, he was incapable of coping with steadily declining production rates and seriously eroding labor discipline.

Clearly, the General Secretary sets the overall tone and policy agenda of the regime. Iurii Andropov came to power for a brief fifteen-month period in 1982 and 1983, offering dynamic leadership, long-hoped for reforms and innovations, stricter work discipline, and above all, a renewed sense of purpose and vigor. As one Soviet citizen confided, "When Andropov died, everyone cried. He was exactly what we needed. He would have ruled with an iron fist."[50]

The General Secretary's powers in the Politburo depend upon his ability to build a ruling coalition. Politburo decisions usually involve mediating conflicting institutional and regional interests, interests that are often represented by fellow Politburo members. Decision-making in such circumstances entails striking compromises, brokering differences, and bargaining. If the General Secretary is astute in these matters, he is likely to succeed on policy issues of vital importance to him. The limits upon his power appear to be those imposed by the Politburo members' internalized sense of what is proper and improper for him to do, and the collective power of his colleagues in the Politburo to constrain his actions.

The Party Control Committee. The Party Control Committee is the disciplinary arm of the CPSU, overseeing the investigation of violations of party rules and the expulsion of members. The committee also hears appeals of members who have been reprimanded or expelled by lower party organs. The composition of the Control Committee is not made public; only the chairman's name is known. Under Brezhnev, the Control Committee acted more as the passive "supreme court" of the Party, rather than as an aggressive investigatory body.[51] However, Gorbachev's vigorous campaign against corruption has expanded the scope of the Party Control Committee's activities. The Central Committee's journal, *Partiinaia zhizn'*, regularly publishes the decisions of the Control Committee, often in conjunction with an exposé condemning official misconduct or corruption by lower officials.

Secretariat. Of paramount importance among the top party institutions is the Central Committee Secretariat. This organ, headed by the General Secretary, consists of approximately twelve secretaries. Some of the secretaries are also members of the Politburo, but all of them are powerful heads of one or more departments in the Central Committee apparatus. The Central Committee secretaries and officials of their departments act on behalf of the Central Committee. Party secretaries are elected by the Central Committee, while their subordinate officials in the various Central Committee departments (*otdely*) are appointed. The latter are frequently referred to collectively as the *apparat*—the full-time party bureaucrats. The Secretariat meets weekly to discuss the work of the staff.

In 1984, there were twenty-one Central Committee departments, each with responsibility for supervising specific ministries, state committees, and other public organizations (see Table 4-9). Within each department are sectors (*sektory*) that further focus party attention on specialized problems, especially in economic matters. Within the Agriculture Department, for example, there are sectors for land cultivation, mechanization, procurements, reclamation and water conservation, forestry, and agricultural science as well as sectors dealing with each of the major agricultural regions of the USSR.

The Central Committee departments exist as direct counterparts in the Party to the ministries in the state bureaucracy. Western experts even refer to the party secretaries as "shadow ministers." The principal function of this specialized party apparatus is to supervise and direct the work of the state bureaucracy. Thus, there is a close correspondence and frequent contact between the staff members of Central Committee departments and their counterparts in the ministries. Occasionally, a minister who dies or retires will be replaced by the party secretary who supervised his ministry. For example, when Marshal Grechko, the Minister of Defense, died in 1976, he was replaced by Dmitri Ustinov, the party secretary specializing in defense matters.

As stated earlier, one of the chief functions of the CPSU is the supervision of the exact and full execution of party policy by all ministries, state

Table 4-9. Central Committee Departments and the Agencies They Supervise

Central Committee Department	Ministries, State Committees, Etc.
Administrative Organs	Ministry of Civilian Aviation
	Ministry of Defense
	Ministry of Internal Affairs
	Ministry of Justice
	Committee for State Security (KGB)
	Procuracy
	Supreme Court
	Civil defense units
Agriculture	Ministry of Agriculture
	Ministry of Agricultural Procurement
	Ministry of Reclamation and Water Management
	State Committee for Forestry
	All-Union Agricultural Supply Agency
Chemical Industry	Ministry of Cellulose-Paper Industry
	Ministry of the Chemical Industry
	Ministry of the Oil-Refining and Petrochemical Industry
Construction	Ministry of Assembly and Special Construction Work
	Ministry of the Building Materials Industry
	Ministry of Construction
	Ministry of Construction in the Oil and Gas Industry
	Ministry of Construction of Heavy Industry Enterprises
	Ministry of Industrial Construction
	Ministry of Rural Construction
	Ministry of the Timber and Wood-Working Industry
	Ministry of Transportation Construction
	State Committee for Construction
	Union of Architects
	Academy for Construction and Architecture
Culture	Ministry of Culture
	State Committee for Movies
	Writers', artists', and composers' unions
Defense Industry	Ministry of the Aviation Industry
	Ministry of the Defense Industry
	Ministry of the General Machinery Industry
	Ministry of the Machinery Industry
	Ministry of the Means of Communication Industry
	Ministry of the Medium Machinery Industry
	Ministry of the Radio-Technical Industry

Central Committee Department	Ministries, State Committees, Etc.
	Ministry of the Shipbuilding Industry
	State Committee for the Peaceful Uses of Atomic Energy
Foreign Cadres	Ministry of Foreign Affairs
	Ministry of Foreign Trade
	State Committee for Foreign Economic Ties
General	Handles internal secretariat and apparatus housekeeping, routing incoming communications, and security for classified documents.
Heavy Industry	Ministry of the Coal Industry
	Ministry of the Gas Industry
	Ministry of Geology
	Ministry of the Iron and Steel Industry
	Ministry of the Nonferrous Metallurgy Industry
	Ministry of the Oil Industry
Information	The department head serves as press secretary to the General Secretary.
International	Handles ties with communist parties in non-communist countries.
Light Industry and Food Industry	Ministry of Fisheries
	Ministry of the Food Industry
	Ministry of Light Industry
	Ministry of the Meat and Dairy Industry
Machinery Industry	Ministry of the Automobile and Truck Industry
	Ministry of the Chemical and Petroleum Machinery Industry
	Ministry of the Construction, Road, and Communal Machinery Industries
	Ministry of Energy and Electrification
	Ministry of Energy Machinery Industry
	Ministry of the Heavy and Transportation Machinery Industries
	Ministry of the Instrument, Means of Automation, and Control Systems Industries
	Ministry of Machinery for Livestock Raising and the Feed Industry
	Ministry of Machinery for the Light and Food Industries and Consumer Appliances
	Ministry of the Machine-Tool Industry
	Ministry of the Tractor and Agricultural Machinery Industry
Organizational-Party Work	Local party organs
	People's Control Committee
	Party membership records and statistics

(Table continued)

Central Committee Department	Ministries, State Committees, Etc.
	Local soviets
	Komsomol
	Trade unions
Planning and Financial Organs	Ministry of Finance
	State Committee for Labor and Social Questions
	State Committee for Prices
	State Committee for Supplies Procurement
	State Committee for Standards
	State Planning Committee (Gosplan)
	State Bank (Gosbank)
	Central Statistical Administration
	Construction Bank
Political Administration of the Ministry of Defense	Political organs in the armed forces and through them the Ministry of Defense
Propaganda	State Committee for Publishing, Printing, and Book Trade
	State Committee for Television and Radio
	State Committee for Sports and Physical Culture
	Propaganda-agitation work by party, state, and public organizations
	Political education system within the CPSU
	Newspapers and journals
	Cultural work of the trade unions
Science and Education	Ministry of Education
	Ministry of Health
	Ministry of Higher and Specialized Secondary Education
	Ministry of the Medical Industry
	State Committee for Science and Technology
	Academy of Sciences
	Republic ministries of social security
Socialist Countries	Relations with parties of the socialist countries
Trade and Consumers' Services	Ministry of Trade
	Consumers' Coops
	Republic ministries of consumers' services
	Republic ministries of utilities
Transportation-Communications	Ministry of Communications
	Ministry of the Merchant Marine
	Ministry of the Railroads
	RSFSR Ministry of River Transport
	Republic ministries of auto-truck transportation

Source: Jerry Hough and Merle Fainsod, How the Soviet Union Is Governed (Cambridge: Harvard University Press, 1979), 412–417.

committees, and public organizations. The parallel structure of the Central Committee departments and the numerous state agencies enables the CPSU to carry out this supervision effectively.

The Central Committee Secretariat is also charged with drafting decisions and policy memoranda for the Politburo and the Central Committee. Although this may appear to be a mundane, clerical task, in reality it provides the Secretariat with a critical role in policy-making. The Soviet decision-making system is structured so that most power resides in the center. Consequently, the political leaders in the Politburo are constantly flooded with requests, complaints, and appeals from institutions and individuals. Because there is so little delegated decision-making authority at lower levels, the Politburo is the final arbiter. Compounding the overload of decision-making authority in the Politburo was the tendency, originating under Brezhnev and continued by his successors, to allow for widespread consultation on policy decisions by all interested (*zainteresovannye*) institutions. Brezhnev once plaintively observed that so many vested interest groups were included in decision-making that it often delayed the implementation of party policies.[52] The Central Committee departments are frequently called upon to sort out a myriad of conflicting demands and positions and to draft policy statements for Politburo consideration.

The drafting of party proposals is often facilitated by the creation of temporary commissions within Central Committee departments. These bodies, which are under the direction of Central Committee staff but also incorporate experts, scholars, and state officials, have opened the policy-making process to a wider spectrum of the Soviet elite. At the same time, the commissions have enhanced the role of the Central Committee departments vis-à-vis the Politburo.

Finally, the Secretariat and its subordinate secretarial counterparts at the republic, regional, and local levels are responsible for personnel recruitment and selection. Numerous Soviet writers have acknowledged the critical role of the selection of cadres. According to one, "Cadre policy was and remains the key link of party leadership and the powerful lever through which the Party influences all affairs in society."[53] Another has written, "The most important component of the political leadership of the soviets is the active influence of the Party on the selection and placement of cadres in the soviets."[54] A third observer noted, "It is precisely in the realm of cadre policy that the commanding function (*vlastnaia funktsiia*) of the Communist Party as a leading force of socialist society manifests itself."[55]

A leading Soviet study of party-state relations states that regional, city, and district party committees discuss in advance the personnel composition of the executive committees of local Soviets, as well as candidates for heads of administrative departments.[56] The Secretariat must approve all appointments to influential party and state positions, or the *nomenklatura*.

Party committees from the district to the CPSU Central Committee compile two lists, one of political and administrative posts for which the party committee is responsible and one of the names of responsible citizens deemed suitable for filling those posts. A person need not be a party member in order to be considered for a position under the *nomenklatura* system. For example, prior to 1961 those who served as presidents of the USSR

Academy of Sciences had not been party members. Nevertheless, the CPSU considered them sufficiently reliable and competent to be appointed to such an important post.

Although the scope of party control over appointments to various posts is not fully known in the West, nor on what level the *nomenklatura* decisions are made for given positions, it is known that the total *nomenklatura* system is extensive. The *nomenklatura* exercised by the CPSU Central Committee encompasses more than 300,000 positions.[57] The *nomenklatura* systems of the fourteen republic party committees add another 260,000 positions, while *nomenklatura* positions at the regional level are estimated at 76,000 nationwide.[58] Most Soviet cities have several hundred *nomenklatura* positions, and even large factories and enterprises may have as many as four hundred such positions.[59] One observer estimates that the entire *nomenklatura* system in the USSR extends to more than three million positions.[60]

From fragmentary references by Soviet officials, Western specialists have concluded that Central Committee *nomenklatura* extends to most directors and some chief engineers of major plants and factories in the Soviet Union. The chairmen of the executive committees of local, district, and regional soviets (councils); high-ranking police and military officers; judges and public prosecutors; rectors of major educational institutions, editors of newspapers and magazines, and influential officials in social organizations such as the trade unions, the Komsomol, and cultural societies also come under the *nomenklatura* of the Central Committee. Collective-farm managers are appointed through the *nomenklatura* of the regional (*oblast'*) party committees, although it is expected that local and district party committees play an active role in the selection process.

In practice, the *nomenklatura* system has been criticized for promoting persons lacking proper credentials. Connections (*blat*), family ties, regional and ethnic affiliations, and corruption occasionally determine the suitability of candidates more than do experience and ability. Furthermore, the *nomenklatura* system has been criticized for inhibiting the influx of young, dynamic, highly qualified personnel into influential posts. The Soviet leaders are not blind to these problems. Periodic reports published in party newspapers and journals expose abuses of *nomenklatura* by local party organs. In 1967, for example, the Estonian party apparatus was criticized for promoting "poorly trained persons, weak organizers, and people of no initiative."[61] In an effort to curb these abuses, some other socialist countries have decentralized their *nomenklatura* systems on the grounds that local officials are best able to evaluate the suitability of candidates for important party and administrative posts.

CAREER ADVANCEMENT AND THE CPSU

The Party plays an enormous role in making policy and supervising the implementation of policy by officials in the state bureaucracy. The CPSU Secretariat and its subordinate counterparts at all levels are also instrumental in nominating as many as three million individuals to fill critical positions in virtually every institution in the USSR. Given the Party's hold on power, it is important to consider how individuals advance their careers within the Soviet political system.

Western scholars have only recently become aware of the widely varying career specializations associated with various party cadres. If one traces the careers of *obkom* bureau members, both prior and subsequent to *obkom* tenure, five clear patterns or types emerge: agricultural specialists, industrial specialists, ideological specialists, cadre specialists, and generalists.[62]

During their careers, upwardly mobile party members are commonly appointed to positions in both the state and the party apparatuses, while remaining in their fields of specialization. For example, a party member with an advanced degree in agronomy may serve as the deputy director of a regional agricultural administration prior to being named to the agriculture department of the *oblast'* party committee. From this position, he or she may move up to state deputy chairman of a rural district or perhaps director of the state agricultural administration in the region. From this state post, he or she may be promoted to first party secretary in a predominantly agricultural region.

Similar mixed party-state career paths are also typical of party members with specializations in industry, and to a lesser extent in ideological affairs and education. Industrial specialists in the Party may serve interchangeably as *obkom* secretary of industry, first party secretary of an industrial region or city, or chairman of the regional trade union council.[63] Ideological specialists tend to be assigned as *obkom* ideological secretaries in charge of agitation and propaganda activities, editors of regional newspapers, first secretaries of regional Komsomol organizations, or directors of state cultural or educational administrations affiliated with regional governments (soviets).

The mixed career path for the aspiring party leaders provides them with valuable experience not only in the Party, where policy decisions are made, but also in the state administration, where those decisions are implemented. This period of apprenticeship and relatively rapid promotion from position to position gives the party member valuable practical experience in both realms of the Party and State and in virtually every stage of the policy-making process. The appointment of party members to state administrative positions also enhances party control over state administrative bodies, ensuring that they effectively carry out the will of the party leadership.

One unintended consequence of the rapid rotation of party members is that, in a relatively short time, they become acquainted with a large number of upwardly mobile, young party members, all seeking to advance through the system. Informal power networks form, based upon shared experience in a given region or personal affiliations with a powerful figure. Perhaps the best path to success in the Soviet political system is to become the trusted associate, or client, of a powerful and rapidly rising patron. For example, most party members who rose to positions of prominence on Brezhnev's coattails were his long-time associates from his home region in Dnepropetrovsk, from the Eighteenth Army during the war, or from his tenure as first secretary of Moldavia and Kazakhstan.

A prime example of a Brezhnev protégé was General Secretary Konstantin Chernenko. He became associated with Brezhnev in 1950, when the latter was named first secretary for the newly acquired Moldavian republic. Chernenko was Chief of the Propaganda and Agitation Department in Moldavia at the time. When Brezhnev was promoted to candidate member of the Politburo and Party Secretary for heavy industry in 1956, Chernenko followed him to Moscow. Shortly after Khrushchev's ouster and the election of Brezhnev to General Secretary, Chernenko was named Chief of the CPSU General Department and made candidate member of the Central Committee. At the Twenty-Fourth Party Congress in 1971, he was elevated to full member of the Central Committee. Vacancies in the Politburo brought about by the advancing age of the Brezhnev cohort, together with the declining rigor of the General Secretary and his increasing reliance on Chernenko, combined to catapult Chernenko into the Politburo as a full member in 1978.

Of the thirteen full members of the Politburo in February 1981 (excluding Brezhnev), eight can be classified as Brezhnev protégés. Half of those date their association with Brezhnev back to the 1940s, when he was a secretary in the Dnepropetrovsk *obkom* and then first party secretary of the Zaporozh'e *obkom* in the Ukraine.

As the preceding discussion indicates, regional groupings and power bases play a crucial role in the determination of a person's political advancement in the Soviet Union. Lenin warned about the dangers of "family circles"—that is, powerful local and regional bonds between party officials and state administrators. Despite repeated efforts, through the rapid, systematic circulation of cadres, to break up these local and regional constellations of power, they persist today. Gyula Jozsa posits the following eight potential regional groupings in addition to the Dnepropetrovsk group in 1982:[64]

Moscow	V. V. Grishin, I. V. Kapitonov, P. N. Demichev, V. I. Konotop, P. A. Leonov, V. N. Makeev
Leningrad	D. F. Ustinov, G. V. Romanov, V. N. Novikov, K. N. Rudnev, P. V. Finogenov, V. N. Bazovskii, V. M. Falin, A. F. Rumiantsev, V. A. Medvedev, A. K. Antonov
Belorussia	A. A. Gromyko, N. V. Zimianin, V. F. Shauro, N. S. Patolichev, I. E. Poliakov, P. A. Abrasimov, T. Ia. Kiselev
Moldavia	K. U. Chernenko, I. I. Bodiul, P. K. Luchinskii, S. P. Trapeznikov, N. A. Shchelokov, M. S. Tsvigun
Cheliabinsk	N. N. Rodionov, V. G. Afanasev, N. S. Patolichev, N. S. Solomentsev, E. M. Tiazhel'nikov, M. F. Nenashev, M. G. Voropaev
Gorky	I. N. Dmitriev, K. F. Katushev, Ia. N. Khristoradnov
Stavropol	M. A. Suslov, M. S. Gorbachev, V. S. Murakhovskii
Sverdlovsk	A. P. Kirilenko, Ia. P. Riabov, B. N. Eltsyn, N. E. Ryzhkov, G. V. Kolbin

It must be noted that these regional affiliations may on occasion reinforce personalistic patron-client ties, and on other occasions and on other policy issues may cut across those relationships. As might be expected, regional power centers are especially active in lobbying on issues of allocation of resources, capital investment, economic development, housing and consumer affairs, and nationality rights (especially those affecting language).

Clientalism is not unknown in other political systems, of course. Much of Ronald Reagan's cabinet and White House staff had been his associates, friends, and aides when he served as governor of California. Jimmy Carter brought many of his Georgia associates to Washington when he assumed the presidency in 1976. In the Soviet political system, however, the tendency toward clientalism is especially pronounced. Several characteristics of the Soviet political system account for this marked tendency toward the development of patron-client relations. First, promotion within the various bureaucratic hierarchies dominating the Soviet political scene is the only path to power. Second, the decisive criteria for promotion are a mix of objective standards, achievements, and qualifications on the one hand, and loyalty and trust on the other. Third, the rivalries that exist among competing bureaucratic interests are especially evident within the highest political institutions in the USSR—the CPSU Central Committee and the Politburo. Finally, policy-making in such an environment forces officials to conspire and even resort to quasi-legal or illegal means to achieve prescribed goals.[65] In short, the General Secretary is confronted with the task of forging a coalition within his Politburo on virtually every major issue. The Politburo represents in its members a wide variety of institutional, regional, and, in some cases, clientele interests. Consequently, there are enormous pressures to promote those individuals that the General Secretary has long known and trusted and, most importantly, who owe the General Secretary for their career advancement.

THE CPSU AND THE FUTURE

At its pinnacle, the Soviet political system today is experiencing a major generational transfer of power. The Class of 38, which has dominated first *oblast'*-level and then All-Union-level political strata for almost half a century, is rapidly passing from the scene. The generations that are coming to the fore are products of the post–World War II era. Of those currently in the CPSU, 88 percent joined after 1945, and 81.4 percent joined after Stalin's death in 1953.[66] This new breed of party member knew neither the brutality of Stalin nor the sense of national pride and purpose in the drive to industrialize. Instead of the hardships and horrors of World War II, these members experienced the rise of the Soviet Union to a superpower powerful enough to project its military might and political influence globally.

The new generation is a product of the peace and relative affluence that the Soviet Union has enjoyed since Stalin. Its members are better educated and much more knowledgeable about the West. More sophisticated technologically, they are also much more cynical and materialistic than their predecessors, less willing to make sacrifices today for the promise of a glorious communist future.

One sees in Soviet society today the marked erosion of commitment to Marxism-Leninism. One Soviet citizen confided to an American friend, "Soviet society in its middle levels is becoming a society of thieves. . . . The assumption that 'everyone steals' is erasing the nation's sense of right and wrong."[67] A woman in Leningrad repeated the same theme of loss of purpose: "People have become angry because they live badly and in dirt. My mother lived through the Leningrad blockade, which was indescribably worse. But they had something clean in their lives. My generation has no ideals, no beliefs, no hope: they have died. Our children have never had any at all."[68]

Nor is this mood expressed only in private. The Chernenko regime undertook a nationwide campaign to reinstill pride and discipline in Soviet youth. V. V. Shcherbitsky, First Party Secretary of the Ukraine and a Politburo member, has decried Soviet youth's fascination with Western fashion and music, and he has urged Komsomol organizations, teachers, and parents to devote more attention to the correct ideological upbringing of the young.[69]

The succession of fifty-four-year-old Mikhail Gorbachev in 1985 to the post of General Secretary of the CPSU has rapidly accelerated the process of personnel change and infused new life into the Party. Gorbachev's vigorous and dynamic style of leadership may succeed in renewing a sense of commitment and purpose in the Soviet public and the rank-and-file of the Party.

The Communist Party of the Soviet Union today is a far cry from the small band of professional revolutionaries that Lenin envisioned. As it has grown and evolved, so too have its goals and mission changed over the years. But the place of the CPSU at the heart of the Soviet political system has remained immutable. Seven decades after the October Revolution, the Party remains the guiding force in Soviet society.

Notes

1. Preamble to the rules of the Communist Party of the Soviet Union.

2. T. H. Rigby, *Communist Party Membership in the USSR, 1917–1967* (Princeton: Princeton University Press, 1968), 59.

3. Ibid., 65.

4. Ibid., 97.

5. Ibid., 248–250.

6. Cited in Rigby, *Communist Party Membership*, 63.

7. I. N. Iudin, *Sotsialn'naia baza rosta KPSS* (Moscow: Politizdat, 1973), 117, 162. Cited in Jerry Hough and Merle Fainsod, *How the Soviet Union Is Governed* (Cambridge: Harvard University Press, 1979), 327.

8. Rigby, *Communist Party Membership*, 184.

9. For an analysis of the evolution of this concept, see Ronald J. Hill, "The All-People-State and Developed Socialism," in Neil Harding, ed., *The State in Socialist Society* (London: Macmillan, 1984), 104–128.

10. The figure for female membership in the CPSU in 1920 was cited in Hough and Fainsod, *How the Soviet Union Is Governed*, 342. The figure for 1983 comes from *Pravda*, 26 September 1983, p. 2.

11. Herwig Kraus, ed., *The Composition of Leading Organs of the CPSU, 1952–1982* (Munich: Radio Liberty Research Bulletin Supplement, May 30, 1982).

12. Ibid.

13. For a discussion of the status of women in the Party, see Gail Warshofsky Lapidus, "Political Mobilization, Participation and Leadership," *Comparative Politics* (October 1975): 90–118; and Joel C. Moses, "Women in Political Roles," in Dorothy Atkinson, Alexander Dallin, and Gail Warshofsky Lapidus, eds., *Women in Russia* (Stanford: Stanford University Press, 1977), 333–353.

14. Rigby, *Communist Party Membership*, 365–369.

15. Ibid., 386.

16. Hough and Fainsod, *How the Soviet Union Is Governed*, 351.

17. *Partiinaia zhizn'*, no. 15 (August 1984): 14–32.

18. *Voprosy istorii KPSS*, 8 (August 1976): 27, cited in Jerry Hough, *The Soviet Union and Social Science Theory* (Cambridge: Harvard University Press, 1977), 126.

19. Jerry Hough, *Soviet Union and Social Science Theory*, 125.

20. Ibid., 129–131.

21. Rigby, *Communist Party Membership*, 449–453.

22. *Pravda*, 26 September 1983, p. 2.

23. M. I. Khaldeev et al., *Pervichnaia partiinaia organizatsiia: opyt, formy i metody raboty* (Moscow: Politizdat, 1975), 273.

24. A. V. Shumakov and V. V. Zudin, eds., *Knizhka partiinogo aktivista 1974* (Moscow: Politizdat, 1973), 143.

25. Cited in Louise Shelley, "Party Members and the Courts: Exploitation of Privilege," paper presented to a conference on "Ruling Communist Parties and Their Status under Law," Institut fur Recht, Politik und Gesellschaft der sozialistischen Staaten, University of Kiel, Germany, 14–16 June 1984, p. 5.

26. Ibid., 6–7.

27. *Partiinaia zhizn'*, no. 8 (April 1983): 20–21.

28. Ibid.

29. Ronald J. Hill and Peter Frank, *The Soviet Communist Party* (London: George Allen & Unwin, 1981), 49.

30. Ibid., 53.

31. *Iuridicheskii slovar'*, vol. 1 (Moscow: Iuridicheskaia literatura, 1956): 512.

32. Iu. V. Derbinov et al., eds., *Pervichnaia partiinaia organizatsiia—avangard trudovogo kollektiva* (Moscow: Mysl', 1975), 97.

33. Hough and Fainsod, *How the Soviet Union Is Governed*, 505.

34. Hill and Frank, *Soviet Communist Party*, 139.

35. Leonard Schapiro, *The Communist Party of the Soviet Union* (New York: Vintage, 1960), 173. Originally, Party Congresses were held much more frequently and involved a smaller number of members. From 1917 through 1927, congresses were held every year with the exception of 1926, while the number of delegates gradually increased from 267 to 1669.

36. Kraus, *Composition of Leading Organs*, 7.

37. These percentages were compiled from data in Kraus, *Composition of Leading Organs*.

38. Cited in Hough and Fainsod, *How the Soviet Union Is Governed*, 457.

39. Ibid., 462–463.

40. L. I. Brezhnev, *Voprosy upravleniia ekonomikoi razvitogo sotsialisticheskogo obshchestva* (Moscow: Politizdat, 1976), 134, 330.

41. L. A. Apollonov, *Verkhovnyi organ leninskoi partii* (Moscow: Politizdat, 1976), 185–186.

42. Robert V. Daniels, "Office Holding and Elite Status: The Central Committee of the CPSU," in Paul Cocks, Robert V. Daniels, and Nancy Heer, eds., *The Dynamics of Soviet Politics* (Cambridge: Harvard University Press, 1976), 77–95.

43. Ibid.

44. See Joel C. Moses, "Regional Cohorts and Political Mobility in the USSR: The Case of Dnepropetrovsk," *Soviet Union/Union Sovietique* 3, pt. 1 (1976): 63–89.

45. *New York Times*, 15 June 1973, p. 3.

46. *Pravda*, 26 October 1984, p. 1.

47. *New York Times*, 15 June 1973, p. 3.

48. It is frequently noted with approval by Soviet scholars that Lenin often deferred to a majority in the Politburo with whom he disagreed. For example, see L. A. Slepov, "Osnovnye

cherty leninskogo stilia partiinogo i gosudarstvennogo rukovodstva," in I. I. Pronin and S. A. Smirnov, eds., *Zhiznennaia sila leninskikh printsipov partiinogo stoitel'stva* (Moscow: Politizdat, 1970), 222–223.

49. The official name of the Politburo under Stalin had been changed to the Presidium of the CPSU Central Committee.

50. From a conversation with the author, June 1984.

51. Hough and Fainsod, *How the Soviet Union Is Governed*, 418.

52. L. I. Brezhnev, *Ob aktual'nykh problemakh partiinogo stroitel'stva*, 2d ed. (Moscow: Politizdat, 1976), 274.

53. I. Kapitonov, "Rukovodiashchaia napravliaiushchaia sila sovetskogo obshchestva," *Partiinaia zhizn'*, no. 23 (1977): 25–27.

54. N. Vikulin and A. Davydov, "Partiia i sovety," *Partiinaia zhizn'*, no. 4 (1978): 32.

55. P. P. Ukrainets, *Partiinoe rukovodstvo i gosudarstvennoe upravlenie* (Minsk: Belorus', 1976), 65.

56. G. V. Barabashev and K. F. Sheremet, *KPSS: Sovety narodnykh deputatov* (Moscow: Znanie, 1978), 39.

57. Cited in Rolf H. W. Theen, "Party and Bureaucracy," in Gordon B. Smith, ed., *Public Policy and Administration in the Soviet Union* (New York: Praeger, 1980), 42.

58. Bohdan Harasymiw, "Die sowjetische Nomenklatur: I. Organisatien und Mechanismen," *Osteuropa* 27 (1977): 585.

59. Theen, "Party and Bureaucracy," 44.

60. Bohdan Harasymiw, "Nomenklatura: The Soviet Communist Party's Leadership Recruitment System," *Canadian Journal of Political Science* 2 (1969): 511.

61. *KPSS v rez.* 9 (1972): 215–221.

62. See Joel C. Moses, "Functional Career Specialization in Soviet Regional Elite Recruitment," in T. H. Rigby and Bohdan Harasymiw, eds., *Leadership Selection and Patron-Client Relations in the USSR and Yugoslavia* (Boston: George Allen & Unwin, 1983), 17–21.

63. Rigby and Harasymiw, *Leadership Selection and Patron-Client Relations*, 18.

64. Gyula Jozsa, "Political *Seilschaften* in the USSR," in Rigby and Harasymiw, *Leadership Selection and Patron-Client Relations*, 157–158. (Tsvigun, Suslov, and Ustinov are deceased, and several others have subsequently been retired.)

65. These characteristics were first developed by T. H. Rigby in "The Soviet Leadership: Towards a Self-Stabilizing Oligarchy?" *Soviet Studies* 22, no. 2 (1970): 177.

66. *Partiinaia zhizn'*, no. 15 (August 1983): 14–32.

67. Cited in George Feifer, "Russian Disorders," *Harper's* 262, (February 1981): 50.

68. Feifer, "Russian Disorders," 51.

69. V. V. Shcherbitsky, *Rabochaia gazeta*, 22 September 1984, 2–3.

Selected Bibliography

Bialer, Seweryn. *Stalin's Successors: Leadership, Stability and Change in the Soviet Union*. Cambridge: Cambridge University Press, 1980.

Breslauer, George W. *Khrushchev and Brezhnev as Leaders: Building Authority in Soviet Politics*. London: George Allen & Unwin, 1982.

Harasymiw, Bohdan, "Nomenklatura: The Soviet Communist Party's Leadership Recruitment System." *Canadian Journal of Political Science* 2, no. 4 (December 1969): 505–512.

Hill, Ronald J., and Peter Frank. *The Soviet Communist Party*. London: George Allen & Unwin, 1981.

Hough, Jerry F. *Soviet Leadership in Transition*. Washington: The Brookings Institution Press, 1980.

Hough, Jerry F., and Merle Fainsod. *How the Soviet Union Is Governed*. Cambridge: Harvard University Press, 1979.

Linden, Carl A. *Khrushchev and the Soviet Leadership, 1957–1964.* Baltimore: The Johns Hopkins University Press, 1966.

Moses, Joel C. "Regional Cohorts and Political Mobility in the USSR: The Case of Dnepropetrovsk." *Soviet Union/Union Sovietique* 3, pt. 1 (1976): 63–89.

————. *Regional Party Leadership and Policy-Making in the USSR.* New York: Holt, Rinehart & Winston, 1974.

Rigby, T. H. *Communist Party Membership in the USSR, 1917–1967.* Princeton: Princeton University Press, 1968.

Rigby, T. H., and Bohdan Harasymiw, eds. *Leadership Selection and Patron-Client Relations in the USSR and Yugoslavia.* London: George Allen & Unwin, 1983.

Ryavec, Karl W., ed. *Soviet Society and the Communist Party.* Amherst: The University of Massachusetts Press, 1978.

Schapiro, Leonard. *The Communist Party of the Soviet Union.* New York: Random House, 1960.

Tatu, Michel. *Power in the Kremlin: From Khrushchev to Kosygin.* New York: Viking, 1968.

Theen, Rolf H. W. "Party and Bureaucracy." In Gordon B. Smith, ed. *Public Policy and Administration in the Soviet Union.* New York: Praeger, 1980, 18–52.

5

The State Apparatus

If the function of the Communist Party of the Soviet Union is to make policy, control appointments to influential positions, and oversee the implementation of policy, what then is left for the Government to do? In the Soviet Union, more than in any Western political system, there is a blurring of the Party and the State, a tendency for the Party to subsume the role and functions normally associated with governments. The USSR Constitution reveals the contradiction. Article 2 reads:

All power in the USSR belongs to the People.
    The people exercise state power through Soviets of People's Deputies, which constitute the political foundation of the USSR.[1]

Yet, in Article 6, the Constitution states:

The leading and guiding force of Soviet society and the nucleus of its political system, of all state and public organizations, is the Communist Party of the Soviet Union.[2]

Unlike most political systems, the Government, or state apparatus, in the USSR does not make major decisions affecting the domestic or foreign policies of the country. Rather, the principal function of the state apparatus is to implement policies articulated by the party leadership. Nevertheless, the process of executing policies often provides an opportunity for influencing them in meaningful ways.

FEDERAL STRUCTURE OF THE USSR

Occupying such a vast and varied territory, the USSR is divided into a variety of subordinate territorial-political units to facilitate governance and administration (see Figure 5-1). The name of the nation—the Union of Soviet Socialist Republics—implies the existence of a federal state. The territorial-administrative structure of the USSR is organized along two different and sometimes conflicting principles. There are divisions and subdivisions that recognize nationality or ethnic groups, and there are divisions and subdivisions that are purely geographic or territorial. In fact, however, the USSR is not a genuine federal system because each level of government (republic, region, city, and so on) does not have independent powers within its jurisdiction. Rather, many decisions affecting cities and regions are still made in the center (i.e., Moscow).

Figure 5-1. The Union of Soviet Socialist Republics

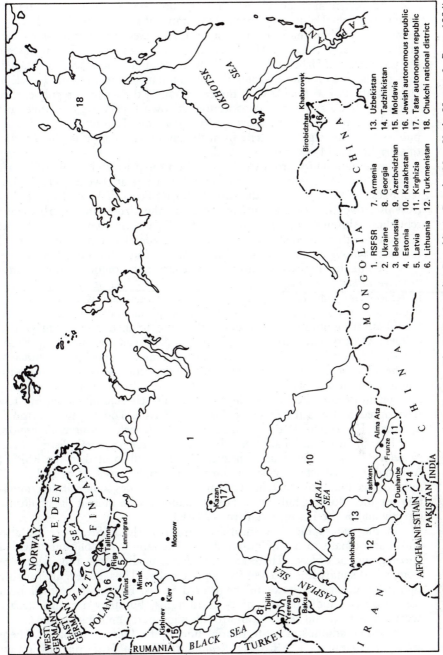

1. RSFSR
2. Ukraine
3. Belorussia
4. Estonia
5. Latvia
6. Lithuania
7. Armenia
8. Georgia
9. Azerbaidzhan
10. Kazakhstan
11. Kirghizia
12. Turkmenistan
13. Uzbekistan
14. Tadzhikistan
15. Moldavia
16. Jewish autonomous republic
17. Tatar autonomous republic
18. Chukchi national district

Source: Hélène Carrère d'Encausse, *Decline of an Empire: The Soviet Socialist Republic in Revolt* (New York: Harper & Row, 1984).

The fifteen most-populous ethnic groups, occupying territory on the perimeter of the USSR, are accorded the status of *union-republics*. They are: Armenia, Azerbaidzhan, Belorussia, Estonia, Georgia, Kazakhstan, Kirghizia, Latvia, Lithuania, Moldavia, Russia, Tadzhikistan, Turkmenistan, the Ukraine, and Uzbekistan. In each union-republic, the official language is that of the major ethnic group (i.e., Ukrainian in the Ukraine, Uzbek in Uzbekistan, and so forth). With the exception of the Russian republic, each union-republic has its own constitution; its own legislative, executive, and judicial institutions; and its own party structure. Theoretically, union-republics have the right to secede from the union, although it is obvious that this "right" could never be exercised.

Large nationality groups not located on the perimeter of the USSR are accorded the status of *autonomous republics*. There are twenty autonomous republics, 16 located within the Russian Soviet Federated Socialist Republic (RSFSR), two in Georgia, and one each in the Uzbek and Azerbaidzhan republics. Although autonomous republics have their own party and state institutions, they do not have the right to secede. The official language of the autonomous republic is that of the majority indigenous nationality.

For smaller nationality groups there are autonomous regions (*avtonomnye oblasti*), of which there are eight today. Most of them are located in remote and underdeveloped areas. Autonomous regions elect their own deputies to the regional soviet, as well as local party officials. Like union-republics, autonomous regions enjoy the right to their own language and culture. One of the more curious twists of Soviet history involves the Jewish autonomous region in the desolate, remote region of Birobidzhan on the Chinese border, more than 4000 miles from Moscow. The Jewish autonomous region was created in 1934 to provide Soviet Jews with their own territory and the limited degree of ethnic self-determination, but few Jews opted to leave the cities of European Russia. Today, Jews constitute less than 10 percent of the population of the Jewish autonomous region.

The smallest nationality-based division is the national district (*natsional'nyi okrug*). There are ten such districts, all located in the RSFSR. Although the districts may be very large, the populations are tiny and primitive. For instance, the Chukchi national district provides some self-determination for the 14,000 Chukchi, or Soviet Eskimos, who inhabit the peninsula directly across the Bering Strait from Alaska.

In the geographic or territorial division of the USSR, there are also units subordinate to the union-republics. The largest republics are divided into regions, or *oblasti*. There are 151 *oblasti* in the USSR, ranging in size from 1,740 square miles to 544,000 square miles.[3] Thus, *oblasti* are roughly equivalent in size to states in the United States. Regions have their own administrative, judicial, and party institutions, but they are also strictly accountable to union-republic and to all-union party and state organs.

Another administrative-territorial unit is the *krai*, or territory. There are eight *kraia* in the USSR today. *Kraia* differ from *oblasti* primarily in that the former are very large but sparsely populated.

At the local level are the cities and rural districts (*raiony*). Each *raion* has its own legislative, administrative, judicial, and party bodies. Large cities are divided into boroughs or urban districts (*gorodskie raiony*), whereas rural districts are comprised of villages and settlements (*sela*).

THE SOVIETS: THE LEGISLATIVE APPARATUS

The Soviet state apparatus is composed of two hierarchies of institutions—the soviets (councils) and the state bureaucracy. The soviets are representative legislative bodies elected on a periodic basis. They date back to the 1905 revolution and came to be dominated by the Bolsheviks in 1917.

The soviets today have little independent power to make policy. Instead, they serve to ratify the Party's policies, enacting them into legislation and providing some legitimacy for the regime. Our examination of the state apparatus in the USSR begins with these legislative bodies.

The Supreme Soviet. The official parliament, or legislature, of the USSR is the Supreme Soviet. The Supreme Soviet of the USSR consists of two chambers: the Soviet of the Union and the Soviet of Nationalities, each having 750 deputies.[4] The Soviet of the Union, or lower chamber, consists of deputies elected every five years in single-member districts throughout the USSR.

In advanced political systems, the upper chamber of the legislature often provides representation for special groups or interests in the society. Fearing a tyranny of the large, populous states over the smaller states, the Founders of the United States gave equal representation in the Senate to all the states. So too in the USSR, the upper chamber—the Soviet of Nationalities—gives special representation to the 109 legally recognized nationality groups that constitute Soviet society. Each of the fifteen constituent republics representing the fifteen most-populous ethnic groups elects thirty-two deputies to the body; each autonomous republic elects eleven deputies; each autonomous region elects five deputies; and each autonomous area elects one deputy.[5]

The Supreme Soviet convenes twice a year for about two or three days per session. Deputies to the Soviet of Nationalities often wear their native costumes, making the body undoubtedly the most colorful, if not the most efficacious, legislative body in the world. Sessions are dominated by the formal presentation of speeches by high-ranking party and state officials. Following the speeches, party decisions are formally presented to be enacted into legislation. For a law to take effect, a legislative proposal must receive an affirmative majority vote in both chambers. Discussions of pending legislation are usually cursory, and all votes are by show of hands. In the entire history of the Supreme Soviet, neither house has recorded a dissenting vote. This fact alone illustrates the chasm that separates the USSR Supreme Soviet from the United States Congress, the British Parliament, or other legislative bodies. Under Soviet law, the Supreme Soviet is the authoritative law-making body of the country. Yet, if a legislature is defined as a forum in which conflicting interests are articulated, mediated, and compromised, resulting in policies, then the legislative functions of the USSR are performed by the CPSU Central Committee and the Politburo, not the Supreme Soviet.

The deputies elected to the Supreme Soviet in 1984 reflect the social composition of the society: 35 percent were workers, 16 percent peasants, and 49 percent white-collar intellectuals.[6] Seventy-one percent were party members.[7] The age profile of the Supreme Soviet indicates a much larger representation of youth than in comparable party bodies: 22 percent of the deputies were thirty years old or younger, and 15 percent were still members of Komsomol organizations.[8] The turnover in the Supreme Soviet membership is much higher than in the CPSU Central Committee, only 35.6 percent of those deputies elected in 1979 were reelected in 1984.[9] Women deputies make up approximately 30 percent of the Supreme Soviet, a substantially higher figure than that for the Central Committee.[10]

To be elected as a deputy to the Supreme Soviet is one of the highest honors the Soviet system can bestow. High-ranking party and state officials (e.g., General Secretary, Minister of Foreign Affairs, President of the Academy of Sciences, and the members of the USSR Supreme Court, among others) are virtually guaranteed seats in the body. Rank-and-file workers are nominated by their factories or state farms in recognition of their hard work and achievements. Invariably, worker deputies to the Supreme Soviet have been active in Komsomol and party affairs. They are model workers and have earned the esteem of their comrades.

Because the turnover rate is relatively high (usually over 50 percent), few of the worker or peasant representatives develop sufficient experience to step into leadership roles within the Supreme Soviet.[11] Instead, these positions tend to be awarded to Central Committee members or other prominent officials within the body.

The December session of the Supreme Soviet normally focuses on the ratification of the plan and budget for the next year, whereas the other session is devoted to ratification of major pieces of pending legislation. For instance, the April 1984 session debated and then adopted a resolution reorganizing university-preparatory and vocational schools in the USSR.[12]

Since 1966, the Supreme Soviet has expanded its standing committees from four in the Soviet of Nationalities and five in the Soviet of the Union, to fifteen in each house. The standing committees deal with the following: agriculture; conservation; construction and building materials industry; consumer goods; credentials; education, science, and culture; foreign affairs; health and social security; industry; planning-budget; trade, consumer services, and utilities; transportation-communication; women's work and living conditions and protection of motherhood and childhood; youth affairs; and legislative proposals. These committees involve almost three-quarters of all the Supreme Soviet deputies.[13] Committee assignments tend to favor persons with the appropriate expertise. Thus, agricultural officials serve on the Agriculture Committee and the President of the Academy of Sciences chairs the Education, Science, and Culture Committee.

Committees of the Supreme Soviet convene twice per year, either to consider their respective portions of the state plan and budget, or to generate advisory recommendations for the consideration of higher state and party officials. In so doing, they frequently solicit the advice of outside experts.

While not as powerful or influential as Congressional committees in the United States, the standing committees of the Supreme Soviet have been able to promote, discourage, and amend policies in many cases. In several instances, policies ranging from education reform to livestock production have been influenced in important ways by the actions of the Supreme Soviet committees. The standing committees also serve as a channel for the expression of parochial interests in such matters as the allocation of resources to local areas or to special projects of local concern. Perhaps the greatest contribution of the standing committees has been the broadening of the range of individuals and viewpoints that are represented in the policymaking process. This expanded participation has now become institutionalized; the various groups that will be affected by prospective decisions now feel they have a right to be heard before such proposals become formalized as policy.

Presidium of the Supreme Soviet. Between sessions of the Supreme Soviet, the highest organ of state authority is the Presidium of the Supreme Soviet. The powers of the Presidium are extensive. It may issue decrees that are legally binding, reorganize ministries and state committees, appoint and demote members of the Council of Ministers, select chairmen for the standing committees of the Supreme Soviet, award state medals and prizes, receive foreign delegations, ratify treaties, and even declare war, all without the approval of the Supreme Soviet. The Presidium meets approximately once every two months.

The Presidium is composed of thirty-nine members, including a chairman, first deputy chairman, fifteen deputy chairmen (one from each republic), a secretary, and twenty-one other members. The other Presidium members elected in 1984 included the first secretaries of the Ukrainian, Belorussian, Kazakh, and Uzbek republic party organizations; the first secretaries of the Tatar and Bashkir autonomous republics; the first secretaries of the Leningrad *oblast'* and the cities of Moscow and Sverdlovsk; the first secretary of the Komsomol; the Chairman of the All-Union Council of Trade Unions; the Chairman of the All-Union Voluntary Society for Cooperation with the Armed Forces; the Chairman of the Chukchi autonomous *oblast'* soviet executive committee; five workers (two of whom are women); and one writer and one scientist.[14]

The Chairman of the Presidium of the Supreme Soviet serves as the titular head of state of the USSR. However, the position is a relatively meaningless, figurehead post, often awarded to an elderly and respected member of the leadership. The current Chairman of the Presidium is Andrei Gromyko, long-time Minister of Foreign Affairs. In 1960, Leonid Brezhnev was demoted from CPSU secretary for heavy industry and defense industry to Chairman of the Presidium, serving in that position until Khrushchev's ouster four years later. Although the move was clearly intended as a setback for Brezhnev's ambitions, he used the post to some advantage by traveling abroad and gaining valuable foreign policy expertise, which is deemed necessary for a candidate for the post of General Secretary. In his travels, Brezhnev also earned prestige by being accorded the full honors befitting a visiting head of state.

The dual roles of head of state and General Secretary of the Party have caused some confusion and awkwardness in the past. When President Richard Nixon visited the USSR in 1972, for example, there was some debate as to whether General Secretary Brezhnev or Nikolai Podgorny, Chairman of the Presidium of the Supreme Soviet, would greet the American President upon arrival. It is assumed that Brezhnev ousted Podgorny and assumed both titles in 1977 in order to claim the full protocol privileges that accompany recognition as a head of state.

The pattern of Soviet state administration at the all-union level is repeated at the republic, regional, and local levels as illustrated in Figure 5-2. Thus, in each of the fifteen republics there is a supreme soviet, which delegates its authority to a presidium. At the regional and local levels, the soviets perform legislative functions analogous to those of the USSR Supreme Soviet and the republic soviets. However, as we will see in Chapter 6, these regional and local soviets and their executive committees do much more than merely rubber-stamp decisions made at the center. At the local level, the soviets offer the potential for meaningful participation in decision-making.

SOVIET ADMINISTRATION: THE EXECUTIVE FUNCTION

Council of Ministers.   The highest executive and administrative institution in the USSR is the Council of Ministers. The 106 members of this body include sixty-two heads of the state ministries, twelve chairmen of state committees, and a number of other high-ranking officials. The large number of ministries in the USSR is explained by the state control and operation of the economy. Thus, in the Soviet Union, there are ministries for each sector of the economy (e.g., the coal industry, the chemical industry, and the automobile industry). More than half of the members of the Council of Ministers occupy positions involving primarily economic responsibilities. This reflects the primary purpose and function of the body—to manage the massive Soviet economy.

The Council of Ministers meets quarterly to hear reports on production and plan fulfillment and to draft the next economic plan. Given its unwieldy size and infrequent meetings, however, the Council of Ministers delegates much of its authority to a presidium, which is not to be confused with the Presidium of the Supreme Soviet. The Presidium of the Council of Ministers is empowered to issue legally binding resolutions and decrees, usually relating to economic activities. Frequently, the most important of these acts are issued jointly with the CPSU Central Committee.

The Chairman of the Presidium of the Council of Ministers is sometimes referred to as the Premier, or head of government (as opposed to the Chairman of the Presidium of the Supreme Soviet, who is President, or head of state). The Premier is responsible for supervising the entire operation of the Soviet economy. The post is currently occupied by Nikolai Ryzhkov.

While Brezhnev and his successors Andropov and Chernenko all assumed the dual titles of General Secretary and President of the USSR, no party leader since Khrushchev has also held the title of Premier. Gorbachev broke with the pattern established by Brezhnev and did not assume the

Figure 5-2. The State Apparatus

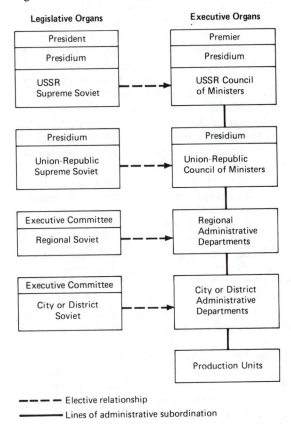

Legislative Organs   Executive Organs

President — Premier
Presidium — Presidium
USSR Supreme Soviet — USSR Council of Ministers

Presidium — Presidium
Union-Republic Supreme Soviet — Union-Republic Council of Ministers

Executive Committee — Regional Administrative Departments
Regional Soviet

Executive Committee — City or District Administrative Departments
City or District Soviet

Production Units

– – – Elective relationship
——— Lines of administrative subordination

additional title of President of the USSR. That title is currently held by Andrei Gromyko.

Executive and administrative functions of the republic governments are carried out by the republic councils of ministers, which also select presidia. Union-republic ministries in every republic report both to the republic-level councils of ministers as well as to the USSR Council of Ministers, through their respective ministries in Moscow.

Ministries and State Committees. The 1977 Constitution of the USSR specifies two types of ministries in the Soviet governmental apparatus: all-union ministries and union-republic ministries. The former have no counterparts at the republic level, operating strictly on a centralized basis out of Moscow; the latter have counterparts in each of the fifteen republics. All-union ministries are generally devoted to industrial matters, while the union-republic ministries are concerned with the traditional jurisdiction of the executive branch of government (e.g., education, health, the interior).

In contrast to party secretaries, ministers tend to spend their careers within a single ministry or sector of the economy. Economic ministers normally have specialized educations and enter the Party's ranks through the factory, rather than through the Komsomol or universities. Unlike regional party secretaries, who may be rotated frequently from one position to another, ministers enjoy a long tenure in office, often fifteen or twenty years.[15] While cabinet members in the United States or other Western political systems may be shifted from agency to agency, Soviet ministers have exceedingly stable careers. For example, Andrei Gromyko served as Minister of Foreign Affairs for twenty-eight years before being named President; Sergei Afanasev has served as Minister of General Machine-Building for more than nineteen years, and Efim Slavskii was Minister of the Medium Machine-Building Industry for twenty-two years.[16] The long tenure and career specialization of ministerial officials help them to acquire an impressive level of expertise. However, career stability in Soviet ministries also impedes the introduction of new blood and may reduce the likelihood of reform and innovation.

Directly under the ministers are *collegia,* small advisory bodies consisting of the minister and his chief deputies. These bodies are somewhat analogous to the ministerial cabinets prevalent in European political systems. The ministerial collegia were established at Lenin's urging, in order to broaden participation in administrative decision-making and as a check on the power of the minister. The collegium advises the minister on important policy matters but it has no independent authority to overrule ministerial decisions. In fact, Soviet state administration functions on the basis of "one-man management" (*edinonachalie*). In other words, state officials are held strictly accountable for their actions and the actions of their direct subordinates. This applies to the manager of a steel mill as well as to the Minister of the Steel Industry. Unlike the Party, which stresses collective decision-making, Soviet state administration emphasizes clearly defined responsibilities resting with individual officials. *Edinonachalie* facilitates directing blame for inefficiency and maladministration, as well as identifying individual administrators who are especially adept and efficient.

Soviet ministries are exceedingly complex bureaucratic organizations, often employing one or two thousand staff personnel in their central and regional offices. To afford the necessary focus and expertise to manage economic matters efficiently, ministries are divided into administrations and departments. The chain of command extends directly from the minister to each factory, farm, and enterprise in the USSR.

Most administrative personnel are recruited directly from specialized technical institutes on the basis of a system of job placement called *raspros-tranenie.* Other administrative officials enter at midcareer or by job transfer; they are hired on the basis of competitive application. There is no civil-service entrance examination in the USSR and no centralized professional training school. Job tenure is not guaranteed, although in practice few state employees are terminated.

The ministries are heavily involved with education and research. Ministries in charge of economic sectors normally have affiliated research institutes that are engaged in research and development, testing, and prototype production. Noneconomic ministries also have research institutes. Thus, the Ministry of Justice has an institute that studies the problems of drafting Soviet legislation and the Procuracy (public prosecutor's office) has an institute that studies the causes and prevention of crime. Most ministries also have subordinate institutes (*vuzy*) offering postgraduate specialized training for midlevel personnel of the ministry. In 1973, the Ministry of Agriculture boasted ninety-nine such institutes.[17] Ministerial personnel undertake specialized training at these institutions as a routine part of their professional development. No tuition is charged, and in most cases the employee is excused from his or her normal responsibilities while at the *vuz*.

State committees in the Soviet Union differ from ministries in that their functions and responsibilities cut across various sectors and agencies. For example, the State Committee for Science and Technology has broad powers to set the agenda for research and development in every sector of the Soviet economy. Similarly, the State Committee for Prices sets prices on items produced in every economic ministry. State committees may be either union-republic or all-union in form; that is, they may have analogous committees at the republic, regional, and local levels, or they may function solely from a centralized office in Moscow. Three of the most important state committees are of the union-republic type: State Planning Committee (Gosplan), the People's Control Committee, and the Committee for State Security (KGB). Although these committees have republic and regional offices, those units have no independent authority and are strictly accountable to the center.

The dynamics of Soviet state administration result in two distinctive features. First, Soviet ministries have accumulated a tremendous amount of expertise that by far eclipses that of the party apparatus. Armed with this expertise, personnel, and material resources, ministries can become powerful advocates of policies affecting their economic sectors. Second, ministerial expertise, social cohesion, and personnel stability can foster the development of clear institutional interests. On appropriations issues, the Ministry of Agriculture and the consumer goods-oriented Ministry of Light Industry frequently oppose a coalition consisting of the ministries of Steel and Defense.[18] Even within a single ministry, departmental interests are often visible. Thus, one department within the Ministry of Agriculture may favor increased capital investment in agricultural mechanization in order to improve production, while another department may favor the increased use of chemical fertilizers and pesticides. At the same time, yet another department may push for increasing the educational standards of agricultural training institutes.

THE SOVIETS AND ELECTIONS IN THE USSR

Elections to the Supreme Soviet and the 50,000 soviets that exist at subordinate republic, regional, and local levels are major political events. Elections to the USSR Supreme Soviet and the supreme soviets of the fifteen constituent republics are held every five years, while elections to regional and local soviets occur every two and a half years.

The Government and Party go to great lengths to ensure virtually universal turnout at the polls. In 1984, a total of 99.99 percent of the eligible voters voted.[19] The figures are even more astonishing when one considers the following: Of almost 8.5 million voters in the Uzbek republic, only thirty failed to vote; in the Turkmen republic, only one voter out of more than 1.5 million registered voters failed to appear at the polls.[20]

Election day is declared a national holiday and is always scheduled on a Sunday in order to minimize conflicts with work schedules and time lost from production. To make it easier for people to vote, polling stations are set up in virtually every housing complex, factory, neighborhood, and village. Polling stations are even set up in hospitals, on ships, on long-distance trains, and in train stations and airports, to enable travelers to vote. Absentee voting is allowed simply by obtaining a certificate, permitting a citizen to vote in another precinct.

Agitprop workers are assigned to each neighborhood and visit every house to make sure that all registered voters come to the polls. They cannot go off duty until they have accounted for each voter. This may require repeated visits to some apartments on election day, with pleas such as "Come and vote. I too have a home and family like you and want to spend the day with them." To entice people to vote, election agitators have even been known to provide babysitting services and transportation. In some cases, the ballot box is brought to voters who are invalids and unable to get to the polling station.[21]

Westerners may well wonder why Soviet officials make such an extensive effort to turn out the vote, when the Party controls the nominating process and all candidates run unopposed. The answer is that the purpose of the electoral process is not to select officeholders, but to mobilize the entire population in support of the regime. As one leading study concluded, "It is the Soviet system and not the individual that is up for election."[22]

Elections in the USSR are symbolic displays of social unity and consensus. The structure of the electoral campaign and the voting process reflect this ritualistic function. Polling places are festively decorated with flags and flowers. Invariably, a large portrait of Lenin hangs above the ballot box. Most voters receive their ballots and deposit them in the ballot box without entering the voting booth. The instructions on the ballot say: "Leave the name of the candidate for whom you are voting, striking out all the others."[23] In other words, voters may vote against the Party's nominee, but no write-ins are allowed. Voters may consider their choices in the voting booth, but eyewitness accounts indicate that only 2 to 5 percent of all voters exercise this option.[24] An even smaller percentage strike out the name of a candidate; negative votes in 1984 amounted to only one in every 1800 ballots.[25] (See Table 5-1.)

In order to be elected, a candidate must receive a majority of the votes cast. Obviously, electoral defeats are extremely rare in the USSR. In 1975, only 68 of almost 2.2 million candidates failed to get half of the votes.[26] That amounts to one electoral defeat in 30,000 races. Most of those failing to receive a majority came from tiny villages, where only a handful of negative votes can defeat a candidate. Negative votes are considered as much an indictment of the Party as of the individual candidate, because the party committee is instrumental in the nomination of candidates.

As undemocratic as Soviet elections appear to Westerners, they do afford citizens some opportunity to express their opinions of the candidates

Table 5-1. Election Results for 1984 Supreme Soviet Elections

Soviet of the Union

Union republic	Total ballots cast for candidates		Votes cast against candidates	Invalid ballots	Deputies elected
	Number	% of vote			
Russian	100,717,650	99.91	93,320	11	405
Ukrainian	36,367,315	99.99	5,184	0	144
Belorussian	6,967,816	99.98	1,185	0	28
Uzbek	8,457,097	99.98	1,495	3	39
Kazakh	9,157,703	99.96	3,999	0	41
Georgian	3,314,931	99.99	147	0	14
Azerbaidzhan	3,439,765	99.99	11	0	15
Lithuanian	2,377,511	99.99	302	0	9
Moldavian	2,673,518	99.97	688	0	11
Latvian	1,863,284	99.97	470	2	7
Kirghiz	2,000,264	99.93	1,333	0	9
Tadzhik	2,078,850	99.99	272	0	9
Armenian	1,854,499	99.99	63	0	8
Turkmenian	1,531,459	99.99	149	0	7
Estonian	1,095,616	99.96	454	1	4
All union-republics	183,897,278	99.94	109,072	17	750

Soviet of Nationalities

Union republic	Total ballots cast for candidates		Votes cast against candidates	Invalid ballots	Deputies elected
	Number	% of vote			
Russian	100,707,315	99.92	80,857	10	32
Ukrainian	36,367,325	99.99	5,174	0	32
Belorussian	6,967,698	99.98	1,304	0	32
Uzbek	8,456,855	99.98	1,734	6	32
Kazakh	8,863,518	99.96	3,584	0	31
Georgian	3,314,915	99.99	160	0	32
Azerbaidzhan	3,439,727	99.99	49	0	32
Lithuanian	2,377,482	99.99	330	0	32
Moldavian	2,673,337	99.97	869	0	32
Latvian	1,863,375	99.98	384	1	32
Kirghiz	2,000,454	99.94	1,143	0	32
Tadzhik	2,078,850	99.99	266	0	32
Armenian	1,854,486	99.99	76	0	32
Turkmenian	1,531,347	99.98	262	0	32
Estonian	1,095,499	99.95	571	1	32
All union-republics	183,592,183	99.95	96,763	18	479

Source: Izvestiia, 7 March 1984, p. 1.

for office. However, citizen input is more extensive and meaningful in the nomination process than in the election itself.

Candidates are nominated by various public organizations: primary party organizations, trade unions, workers' collectives, or military units. Many of the 2.2 million nominations are pro forma; such nominations are reserved for local state and party officials, directors of large industrial plants, and heads of educational and cultural institutions. Well in advance of the formal nomination, party workers solicit opinions about prospective nominees. Rank-and-file workers are asked their opinions of their comrades and their suitability for elective office. The candidates' names are then submitted to a vote of the general meetings of the collectives in their respective factories, collective farms, and enterprises. Soviet sources say that the rejection of candidates by their peers is "frequent," necessitating the identification of other nominees.[27]

The highly controlled nomination process, while decidedly undemocratic, does permit the Party to ensure that certain groups traditionally underrepresented in political institutions are adequately represented. The age, sex, class, and ethnic profile of deputies to the soviets remains remarkably constant throughout the USSR, suggesting that quotas are deliberately set for these groups. Thus, women constitute 49 percent of the deputies to local soviets nationwide. In 1977, female representation ranged from a high of 50.2 percent of all deputies to local soviets in the Russian republic to a low of 46.5 percent in the Azerbaidzhan republic.[28]

Given the controlled nature of the nomination process and the absence of opposing candidates, it is not surprising that Soviet citizens are often apathetic or critical of the election process in the USSR. One Soviet study reported that 18 percent of the workers in a Moscow plant indicated dissatisfaction with the electoral system.[29] Recent émigrés express sentiments ranging from skepticism to contempt of Soviet elections.[30]

Voter apathy is also reflected in the increasingly widespread practice of election avoidance. As many as four million citizens avoid voting by acquiring a certificate to vote elsewhere, which removes their names from the lists of their neighborhood agitators; they then fail to vote.[31] This practice appears to be most common in urban areas, such as Leningrad and Moscow, where citizens would rather spend the day in the country.

INSTITUTIONAL PLURALISM

Clearly, elections are of little significance in the determination of policy in the USSR; rather, they are exercises in mobilizing citizens for symbolic purposes. One may ask then, which institutions of the government do play a significant role in the policy-making process? The Soviet political system has long been viewed as being heavily bureaucratic. In 1961, Alfred Meyer argued that the bureaucratic model should form the basis of our understanding of Soviet society.[32] In another influential work, Carl Friedrich and Zbigniew Brzezinski identified *bureaucratization* as a defining trait of totalitarian autocracy in the USSR.[33] Much of the early focus on bureaucracy in the USSR lent support to the "organizational society" or "administered society" models. These models, which grew out of the totalitarian model, sustained the view that the state bureaucracy is merely the pawn of the leadership and is used to enhance the Party's domination over society. The bureaucracy in this approach was viewed as a uniform, homogeneous organization, devoid of significant powers or interests of its own.

Others viewed the bureaucratic nature of politics in the USSR as presenting the opportunity for multiple power centers to arise. Barrington Moore noted that the technocrats who staff the bureaucracies make decisions on technical and rational criteria; they value predictability and conformity to objective rules.[34] Brzezinski noted that the increasing role of bureaucrats in policy-making threatened to reduce the Soviet political system to "a regime of clerks."[35] Implicit in these notions is the view that the increasing bureaucratization of the Soviet political system places a constraint on the power of the CPSU. There is widespread recognition today that the party leadership is dependent upon the various bureaucracies in the USSR for information and advice in order to enact effective policies. The Party has no independent means of verifying Soviet military projections of American submarine strength, or the capital investment needed to irrigate Central Asia. The various ministries in the USSR, as in other political systems, have a near monopoly on vital information, which gives them some leverage over the political decisionmakers.

Bureaucrats also exert their influence through the implementation of policies. Most policy pronouncements of the Politburo are rather vague, general promises and statements of intent; they strike a new tone, indicate a new direction, or set new priorities. It is up to the staffs of the various ministries and state committees to translate those directives into concrete actions. In defining and shaping party policies, the bureaucrats often wield extensive discretionary powers.

Bureaucrats also have the power to resist new policy initiatives that they do not favor. Bureaucratic inertia, obstructionism, and redefinition of policies can and do deflect the aims of the top leadership. This negative capacity of state bureaucrats can be overcome if the political authorities choose to make an issue of it and are willing to devote the necessary resources to eliminating opposition. More often than not, however, bureaucratic resistance goes unchallenged by the central authorities.

In short, ministries and state committees in the USSR are active participants in Soviet politics. More than mere pawns of the Party, they are self-interested institutions, able and willing to promote their own policies and perspectives. They function as institutional interest groups, representing not a single, uniform bureaucracy, but a diverse array of cooperating and conflicting institutions. On occasion, the interests of one or more of these institutional groups coincides with the interests of certain segments of the CPSU; at other times, they are at odds. This dynamic and multifaceted conception of the Soviet political system has been variously referred to as "institutional pluralism,"[36] "bureaucratic pluralism,"[37] "centralized pluralism,"[38] and "participatory bureaucracy."[39]

These models derive from the interest-group approach to politics, which was first applied to the study of Soviet politics in the 1960s.[40] Unlike the Kremlinologists, who focus solely on factional conflict at the pinnacle of the Soviet system, the interest-group approach looks at conflict among bureaucratic or occupation groups. Thus, potential successors to the General Secretary are assumed to have their own constituencies and organizational bases for support (party apparatus, agriculture, military, secret police, and so forth). Since Stalin's time, power has become deconcentrated among these diverse interests, and policy-making has necessitated the balancing and coalescing of these interests. In the period after Stalin, as Jeremy Azrael observed, there was a "reemergence of politics" in the Soviet system.[41] Conflict and consensus-building replaced the forced unanimity of the Stalin years. Social groups became more assertive and responsive to popular demands. Jerry Hough states that Soviet politics since 1953 has revolved around "conflict among a complex set of crosscutting and shifting alliances of persons with divergent interests."[42] Darrell Hammer notes, "Policy is the outcome of an ongoing political conflict."[43] No longer is political conflict regarded as the "mere personal struggle for power, largely divorced from questions of policy or ideology, or from the interests of social groups."[44] Nor is conflict limited to the highest ranks of the party apparatus.

Where and in what form do conflicts become manifest? While some authors have attempted to examine Soviet pluralism in terms of issue-oriented groups, the majority of the literature examines policy conflicts that find expression in bureaucracies, institutions, or occupations.[45] There are several reasons for the preponderance of this approach. First, strictures on free and open discussion of issues in the Soviet Union tend to reduce the formation of issue-oriented factions and restrict communication and discussion to intra-institutional channels. Second, in Soviet society there is a fusion of institutional and individual interests not found in the West. Third, in the Soviet system, where factionalism is officially outlawed, policy positions must be articulated through legitimate organizational channels. Substantive issues of public policy do divide the Soviet leadership—between "hawks" and "doves"; between those favoring centralization of economic decision-making and those favoring more autonomy for factory managers; between advocates of "law and order" and advocates of rehabilitation of criminals; and between proponents of hard-line literary and artistic policies and proponents of a more liberal stance, for example. But such divisions usually coincide with an occupational or bureaucratic group.

Thus, conflicts in the Soviet political system tend to find expression in the bureaucratic struggle for influence. As Paul Cocks states, there has been a "devolution of authority" to crucial bureaucratic subsystems—the military, factory managers, regional party secretaries, agricultural interests, and jurists.[46] Rather than the monolithic and autocratic system of the Stalin years, there is an oligarchy of conflicting interests, each represented by a powerful bureaucracy. Most policies are the outcome of "compromises and adjustments among these diverse bureaucratic groups and their interests in society."[47] Increasingly, individual party leaders must reach out to these bureaucracies for support and expertise.

Western notions of interest groups and the ways in which they influence the public-policy process have only limited application to the Soviet case. In the West, interest groups are predominantly associational or voluntary; that is, citizens having particular, clearly identifiable demands to articulate form collective organizations to lobby on their behalf. In the Soviet Union, policy conflicts tend to form along institutional lines, rather than among voluntary lobby organizations. In a society that professes the belief that the CPSU and its policies reflect the will and best interests of *all* sectors of Soviet society, associational interest groups that pursue only their own limited interests are not accorded legitimacy in the political process.

The institutional basis for pluralism in the Soviet Union is reinforced by the fusion of individual interests with those of the various institutions within which they exist. The relative welfare of Soviet citizens is closely associated with the power and prestige of the institutions in which they are employed. Not only do people derive their livelihood from their jobs, they also derive a long list of fringe benefits, concessions, perquisites, and connections. For instance, most factories, state farms, institutes, enterprises, and educational institutions provide housing, child-care centers, and polyclinics for their employees. The quality of these services varies with the prestige of the institution. The Soviet military, for example, maintains its own department stores, selling items usually unavailable to the general public. It also has a fund to help military officers build summer cottages or take vacations at the most exclusive resorts. Given the relative equality of Soviet incomes, these preferential policies take on added significance. Workers have been known to transfer from one factory to another in order to take advantage of better housing, better polyclinics, or better day-care centers.

Bureaucratic officials thus become influential, semiautonomous participants in the policy-making and implementing process. They identify with the professional standards of their occupations and the programs they administer, and they strive to represent their clientele in response to broader societal forces. Most bureaucratic groups have special organs through which to voice their institutional interests. For example, the viewpoint of factory managers is expressed in the newspaper *Sotsialisticheskaia industriia* (*Socialist Industry*), the military expresses its demands in the newspaper *Krasnaia zvezda* (*Red Star*), and the literary elite voices its concerns in *Novy Mir* (*New World*) and *Literaturnaia gazeta* (*Literary Gazette*).

As significant as the input of different institutional interests into the policy process are the ways in which bureaucratic officials refine, alter, and reshape policies during the implementation phase, in order to make them coincide more closely with their own perceptions and preferences. In the late 1970s, when industrial ministries were informed that production targets would be lowered and bonuses raised for enterprises manufacturing improved-quality, innovative goods, many factories made minor revisions and improvements in their products; the ministries approved these revisions as "innovations" just so that the factories might receive the special benefits. Nor is bureaucratic opposition manifested only on economic matters. When Khrushchev proposed the extension of secondary education from ten to eleven years, he did so in order that all youth would have to engage in at least one year of "practical" work on a farm or in a factory. When the plan was implemented, however, on-the-job training became voluntary, and the university-bound sons and daughters of the intelligentsia never had to work. In the mid-1980s, Gorbachev's antialcohol campaign ran into extensive opposition from local officials, who adopted pro forma measures instead of vigorously pursuing the new policy direction.

The pluralism that pervades all aspects of Soviet policy-making and implementation raises real questions about the role of the party officials in the policy process. Politics involves making compromises and adjustments among diverse bureaucratic groups and their interests in society. The CPSU is ultimately responsible for mediating these competing interests and striking compromises on policy issues.

PARTY/STATE RELATIONS IN THE USSR

Party guidance of state administration is carried out through a variety of mechanisms and instruments. The exercise of party control through *pravo kontrolia* and *nomenklatura* has already been described. There are also other mechanisms through which the Party exerts its guiding influence over Soviet state administration.

Interlocking Directorates. Party guidance of Soviet state administration at all levels is facilitated by the multiple roles played by party and state officials. This is sometimes referred to as interlocking directorates, a term that originated in reference to the boards of directors of major American corporations. Many corporate board members also serve on the boards of other major corporations, banks, universities, and public institutions, constituting a very influential and interconnected network of powerful individuals. In the USSR, a similar phenomenon exists. One-third of the full members of the Politburo are also members of the Presidium of the Supreme Soviet; another one-third of the Politburo serves simultaneously on the Presidium of the Council of Ministers. In 1980, a total of 79.3 percent of the Central Committee members, 63.9 percent of candidate members, 100 percent of the members of the Central Committee's Secretariat, and 34.6 percent of the Central Auditing Commission were deputies of the USSR Supreme Soviet.[48] In fact, the substantial overlap in party organs and state administrative bodies at all levels leads one observer to view the Party and the State as a single unit.[49] Some Soviet scholars have also referred to the party and state apparatuses in the singular, rather than viewing them as separate entities.[50]

The phenomenon of interlocking directorates ensures the involvement of practical administrative expertise in the formulation of party policies, and facilitates party supervision of the implementation of those policies. Most importantly, the existence of overlapping duties and responsibilities generates informal patterns of horizontal communication that are necessary to transcend the heavily hierarchical and authoritarian vertical channels of communication in the CPSU and in the Soviet ministries and state committees.

Rukovodstvo (Guidance). Pursuant to its role as the "leading and guiding force in Soviet society," the Party must ensure the unity and coherence of policy at all levels. In other words, party secretaries strive to enhance integration in a political system that is both diverse and expansive. The parallel structures of the party and state apparatuses and the functional specialization of party secretaries (e.g., heavy industry, agriculture, consumer services) promote the Party's supervision of state administration. Regional secretaries are responsible for ensuring that party policies are faithfully executed by administrators in their regions and often are directly involved in making decisions. For instance, agriculture departments determine what crops should be planted and set procurement quotas for farms in their regions. Local and regional party committees reportedly play a decisive role in approving or disapproving actions of the KGB and in resolving any political scandal in the area. Local party officials also screen art exhibits and theatrical performances to ensure that they are consistent with the Party's cultural line.[51] Party supervision and verification extends to lower levels as well, where social, economic, local, regional, and administrative policies and plans are formulated and implemented "through the most active participation of Soviet, economic, and public organizations *under the leadership of party committees.*"[52]

In addition, local party committees regularly hold expanded plenums, consisting of party members from state organs, trade unions, the Komsomol, and other nonparty bodies. These sessions meet to discuss specific questions and problems relating to the district, town, or region. Subjects may include organizing local agencies to combat an increase in crime, coordinating resources to ensure the fulfillment of the plan, mobilizing the populace for the harvest, or criticizing the failures of an administrative office.[53] Not only do these expanded plenums widen the circle of officials participating in policy matters, but they also afford party committees an opportunity to supervise administrative bodies, production units, and social organizations.

Informal party-state links are also fostered by party-organized seminars and courses for administrative personnel. State officials often direct unofficial reports to local party committees detailing current problems confronting local soviets, with the aim of "strengthening the cooperation between party committees and state and public organizations."[54] Finally, in most regions and cities, party and state administrative offices are located in the same buildings, which also facilitates party-state communication.

Regional party secretaries play a vital role in ensuring the integration of Soviet regions, towns, and districts. While responsible for the overall performance of their regions, local party organs are dependent upon local administrators and factory managers to fulfill their plans. Effective managers and administrative officials maintain good relations with their ministerial superiors; while dependent upon local party committees for support, they are likely to be deferred to by local party officials. Inefficient administrative offices and production units, on the other hand, are more likely to experience party intervention.

The most significant role of regional party secretaries is in resolving the conflicts that inevitably arise among various local state units. When directives and regulations of local administrators come into conflict, the regional party organs must resolve the institutional conflicting interests. Local party officials must judge the relative priority to be attached to the wide array of projects and activities under their supervision. In an industrial center, such as Leningrad, the city and regional party committees demonstrate far more concern with key industrial plants (e.g., the Svetlana Production Association or the Kirov steelworks) than with the performance of consumer trusts or state farms. Given its significance as a major naval facility and center for defense industries, Leningrad party officials are undoubtedly concerned with providing support for these interests as well. In rural regions, party secretaries are more likely to stress agricultural production, and their education and career backgrounds usually reflect this priority.

The coordination and conflict-resolution functions of local party organs are especially evident on questions of procurement and construction. Annual plans specify supplies and goods to be delivered and quarterly delivery schedules. Nevertheless, conflicts and shortages invariably arise, necessitating the diversion of resources (both material and labor) from lower to higher priority areas. Party secretaries make these authoritative reallocations. Construction projects frequently necessitate party supervision not only in securing the necessary supplies, but also in coordinating the many different organizations involved—construction trusts, suppliers, subcontractors, and trade unions. If the construction project is designated as high priority, a special staff (shtab) is created, headed by a local party official to oversee the project and eliminate bottlenecks.

Podmena. Despite the overriding significance of party guidance of state administrative actions, local and regional party committees cannot issue directives to state administrative agencies within their jurisdictions that contradict ministerial directives. Usurpation of the proper function of state administrative agencies and interference by party officials in the work of administrators is known as podmena and is expressly prohibited by Article 42 of the Party Statutes.[55] Even statements issued jointly by state agencies and party organs are frowned upon when they apply to matters wholly within the competence of administrative bodies.[56] Regional party secretaries, who frequently possess technical expertise superior to that of administrators, may be tempted to interfere in administrative matters when confronted with administrative incompetence. For their part, administrators have been known to defer to party secretaries or to refrain from taking any action lest it anger local party officials. Faced with such administrative paralysis and inertia, the Party is forced to step in. Numerous Soviet commentators have criticized this Party-State relationship, noting that podmena burdens the party apparatus with additional responsibilities that it is ill-equipped to handle. Shakhnazarov notes that podmena breaks down the legal relations governing Party-State relations; although the Party's administrative decisions may be effective, they are, nevertheless, illegal.[57]

Dual Subordination. While party officials supervise the implementation of policy in state administrative agencies, those agencies and departments are also responsible to superior ministries and state committees, as well as to local soviets and party committees. This is referred to as dual subordination (dvoinoe podchinenie). According to the principle of dual subordination, a republic ministry is accountable both to the republic council of ministers and to the counterpart ministry at the all-union level. Not infrequently, the dual accountability of republic and regional administrative agencies confronts them with conflicting choices. The needs and interests of regional governmental and party bodies may mandate certain actions, while the central authorities may demand others. In practice, administrative agencies are literally swamped with directives and instructions from their ministries in Moscow, from the republic ministries, from local and regional soviets, and from party committees at all levels. Many of these directives are mutually conflicting; no agency could possibly satisfy even a small fraction of them. This flood of directives is intended to constrain and limit the authority of administrators, yet paradoxically it may give them a degree of autonomy and discretion in choosing which of the competing directives they wish to fulfill. Anthony Downs refers to this phenomenon in complex bureaucracies as the process of "authority leakage."[58] In complex bureaucracies, the further removed administrators are from the top policymakers, the more latitude they may have in interpreting and implementing policies. The next chapter analyzes how competing institutional interests combine with complex party and state relations to result in policy; it also assesses the degree of latitude regional and local administrators have in making decisions affecting their regions.

Notes

1. Constitution of the USSR (1977), Article 2.
2. Constitution of the USSR (1977), Article 6.
3. Michael Florinsky, ed., *Encyclopedia of Russia and the Soviet Union* (New York: McGraw-Hill, 1961), 391.
4. Constitution of the USSR (1977), Articles 108–119.
5. Constitution of the USSR (1977), Article 110.
6. *Izvestiia,* 7 March 1984, p. 1.
7. Ibid.
8. Ibid.
9. Calculated by the author from Soviet data.
10. *Izvestiia,* 7 March 1984, p. 1.
11. Hough reports that only 19 percent of the workers and peasants elected in 1966 were reelected in 1970, and only 18 percent of those elected in 1970 were reelected in 1974. See Jerry Hough and Merle Fainsod, *How the Soviet Union Is Governed* (Cambridge: Harvard University Press, 1979), 367.
12. *Izvestiia,* 13 April 1984, p. 1.
13. Hough and Fainsod, *How the Soviet Union Is Governed,* 373.
14. *Izvestiia,* 12 April 1984, p. 1.
15. National Foreign Assessment Center, *Directory of Soviet Officials, Volume I: National Organizations* (Washington: November 1979).
16. Ibid.
17. *Ekonomicheskaia gazeta* (August 1973): 15.
18. In November 1985, Gorbachev consolidated five ministries, including the former Ministry of Agriculture, to form the State Committee for the Agro-industrial Complex (*Gosagroprom*).
19. *Pravda,* 7 March 1984, p. 1.
20. Ibid.
21. See Theodore Friedgut, *Political Participation in the USSR* (Princeton: Princeton University Press, 1979), 114.
22. Ibid., 96.
23. USSR Regulations for Election to the Supreme Soviet, Article 79.
24. Peter H. Juviler, *Functions of a Deputy to the Supreme Soviet* (unpublished doctoral dissertation, Columbia University, 1960), 44. Juviler noted that the figure rose to 24 percent in a precinct populated by Moscow University students.

25. *Izvestiia,* 7 March 1984, p. 1.

26. Cited in Friedgut, *Political Participation in the USSR,* 130.

27. Ibid., 86.

28. Based on Soviet statistics cited in Everett M. Jacobs, "Norms of Representation and the Composition of Local Soviets," in Everett M. Jacobs, ed., *Soviet Local Politics and Government* (London: George Allen & Unwin, 1983), 83.

29. Cited in Friedgut, *Political Participation in the USSR,* 75.

30. Zvi Gitelman, "Values, Opinions, and Attitudes of Soviet Jewish Emigres" (unpublished paper presented to the American Association for the Advancement of Slavic Studies, Atlanta, Georgia, October 1975), 25.

31. Friedgut, *Political Participation in the USSR,* 116.

32. Alfred G. Meyer, "USSR, Incorporated," *Slavic Review* 20 (October 1961): 370.

33. Carl J. Friedrich and Zbigniew K. Brzezinski, *Totalitarian Dictatorship and Autocracy,* 2d ed. (New York: Praeger, 1965), 205–218.

34. Barrington Moore, Jr., *Political Power and Social Theory* (Cambridge: Harvard University Press, 1958), 19–20.

35. Zbigniew Brzezinski, "Victory of the Clerks," *The New Republic* (November 14, 1964): 15, 18.

36. Jerry Hough, *The Soviet Prefects* (Cambridge: Harvard University Press, 1969), 27–29.

37. Darrell P. Hammer, *USSR: The Politics of Oligarchy* (Hinsdale, Illinois: Dryden Press, 1974), 223–256.

38. Gordon Skilling, "Interest Groups and Communist Politics," in Gordon Skilling and Franklyn Griffiths, eds., *Interest Groups in Soviet Politics* (Princeton: Princeton University Press, 1971), 17.

39. Robert V. Daniels, "Soviet Politics Since Khrushchev," in John W. Strong, ed., *The Soviet Union under Brezhnev and Kosygin* (New York: Van Nostrand Reinhold, 1971), 22–23.

40. For Example, see Skilling and Griffiths, *Interest Groups in Soviet Politics.*

41. Jeremy Azrael, "Decision-Making in the USSR," in Richard Cornell, ed., *The Soviet Political System* (Englewood Cliffs: Prentice-Hall, 1970), 214.

43. Jerry Hough, "The Soviet System: Petrification or Pluralism?" *Problems of Communism* 21 (1972): 28.

43. Hammer, *USSR: The Politics of Oligarchy,* 286.

44. Skilling, "Interest Groups and Communist Politics," 9.

45. One case-study of issue-oriented interest groups is Joel Schwartz and William Keech, "Group Influence and the Policy Process in the Soviet Union," APSR 62 (1968), 840–851. Examples of bureaucratic conflicts over policies appear in Hammer, *USSR: The Politics of Oligarchy;* Hough, *The Soviet Prefects;* and Daniels, "Soviet Politics Since Khrushchev."

45. Paul Cocks, "The Policy Process and Bureaucratic Politics," in Paul Cocks, et al., eds., *The Dynamics of Soviet Politics* (Cambridge: Harvard University Press, 1976), 158.

47. Sidney Ploss, "Interest Groups," in Allen Kassof, ed., *Prospects for Soviet Society* (New York: Praeger, 1968), 95.

48. Cited in Ronald J. Hill and Peter Frank, *The Soviet Communist Party* (London: George Allen & Unwin, 1981), 115.

49. Mary McAuley, *Politics and the Soviet Union* (New York: Penguin Books, 1977), 186.

50. For example, see *Stanovlenie, razvitie i sovershenstvovanie partiinogo i gosudarstvennogo apparata* (Moscow: 1979).

51. Cited in Hill and Frank, *The Soviet Communist Party.*

52. I. N. Yudin, et al., *Nekotorye voprosy organizatsionno-partiinoi raboty* (Moscow: Politizdat, 1973), 230.

53. For a detailed examination of party control and guidance of the administration of

justice, see Robert Sharlet, "The Communist Party and the Administration of Justice in the USSR," in Donald D. Barry, F. J. M. Feldbrugge, George Ginsburgs, and Peter B. Maggs, eds., *Soviet Law after Stalin,* vol. III (Alphen aan den Rijn, The Netherlands: Sijthoff/Noordhoff, 1979), 321–392.

54. B. A. Kulinchenko, et al., eds., *Voprosy povysheniia urovnia partiinoi raboty na sovremennom etape* (Moscow: Mysl', 1978), 160–161.

55. Article 42 of the Party Statutes was revised at the Twenty-Seventh Party Congress in 1986. Although the reference to *podmena* was deleted, in practice it is still discouraged.

56. N. Kh. Arutiunian, *Partiia i Sovety* (Moscow: Izvestiia, 1970), 30.

57. G. Kh. Shakhnazarov, *Sotsialisticheskaia demokratiia: nekotorye voprosy teorii* (Moscow: Politizdat, 1972), 80–82.

58. Anthony Downs, *Inside Bureaucracy* (Boston: Little, Brown, 1967), 134–135.

Selected Bibliography

Brzezinski, Zbigniew. *Dilemmas of Change in Soviet Politics.* New York: Columbia University Press, 1969.

Brzezinski, Zbigniew, and Samuel P. Huntington. *Political Power: USA/USSR.* New York: Viking Press, 1963.

Cocks, Paul. "Rethinking the Organizational Weapon: The Soviet System in a Systems Age." *World Politics* 32 (January 1980).

———. "The Policy Process and Bureaucratic Politics." In Paul Cocks, et al., eds., *The Dynamics of Soviet Politics.* Cambridge: Harvard University Press, 1976, 156–178.

Downs, Anthony. *Inside Bureaucracy.* Boston: Little, Brown, 1967.

Friedgut, Theodore. *Political Participation in the USSR.* Princeton: Princeton University Press, 1979.

Hammer, Darrell P. *USSR: The Politics of Oligarchy.* Hinsdale, Illinois: Dryden Press, 1974.

Hough, Jerry. *The Soviet Prefects.* Cambridge: Harvard University Press, 1969.

Hough, Jerry and Merle Fainsod. *How the Soviet Union Is Governed.* Cambridge: Harvard University Press, 1979.

Little, D. Richard. "Legislative Authority in the Soviet Political System." *Slavic Review* 30 (March 1971): 57–73.

———. "Soviet Parliamentary Committees after Khrushchev: Obstacles and Opportunities." *Soviet Studies* 24 (July 1972): 41–60.

Mote, Max E. *Soviet Local and Republic Elections.* Stanford: The Hoover Institution, 1965.

Ryavec, Karl W. "The Soviet Ministerial Elite: 1964–1979." Occasional Papers Series, no. 6, Program in Soviet and East European Studies, University of Massachusetts at Amherst, 1981.

Skilling, H. Gordon, and Franklyn Griffiths, eds. *Interest Groups in Soviet Politics.* Princeton: Princeton University Press, 1971.

Smith, Gordon B. *Public Policy and Administration in the Soviet Union.* New York: Praeger, 1980.

Urban, Michael. *The Ideology of Administration: American and Soviet Cases.* Albany, New York: SUNY Press, 1982.

Vanneman, Peter. *The Supreme Soviet.* Durham, North Carolina: Duke University Press, 1977.

Zaslavsky, Victor and Robert J. Brym. "The Functions of Elections in the USSR." *Soviet Studies* 30 (1978): 362–371.

6

Regional and Local Politics in the USSR

Western analysis of Soviet politics invariably focuses on the institutions at the pinnacle of the Soviet system—the CPSU Central Committee and the Politburo. For the average Soviet citizen, however, the machinations of these organs are remote and often irrelevant. It is at the regional and local levels that Soviet citizens most frequently come into direct contact with their political system. Regional and local governments are responsible for a wide range of services that directly affect citizens: the provision of housing, health care, education, the supervision of industrial production, the operation of stores and commercial enterprises, and cultural and recreation facilities.

At the local level, the crosscutting regional and institutional interests come to bear on policies, and it is here that the powers and overlapping jurisdictions of the Party and the State must be worked out. In short, local politics in the USSR represents a microcosm of the larger Soviet political system. Our analysis of local and regional politics in the USSR begins with an examination of the dramatic changes that are shaping Soviet cities.

URBANIZATION IN THE SOVIET UNION

Despite its agrarian roots, Soviet society is rapidly becoming urbanized. In 1926, prior to Stalin's introduction of collectivization, 86.7 percent of the Soviet population lived in towns and villages of fewer than 15,000 people.[1] However, collectivization, the rising demand for industrial workers, and wartime dislocations all tended to accelerate the pace of urban growth. By 1977, only 38.1 percent of the population lived in towns of fewer than 15,000.[2] Since 1926, more than 1,000 new cities have been founded, and the pace of urbanization continues unabated.[3] Thus, within a span of fewer than fifty years, the USSR was transformed from a predominantly rural country to a largely urban one. Somewhat surprisingly, the rate of urbanization today is fastest east of the Urals—in Siberia and the Far East, rather than in European Russia. The rapid development of massive new oil, gas, coal, timber, and other projects linked to the resource wealth of this region has contributed to a growth boom in many Soviet frontier towns.

While the fastest-growing regions of the Soviet Union are to the east, the bulk of the urban population still resides in the European portion of the

114

country. Together, the Russian republic (RSFSR) and the Ukrainian republic account for 68 percent of all Soviet cities and 78 percent of the urban population.[4] These two republics contain fifteen of the nineteen cities currently having populations of more than one million.[5]

The rapid growth of the Soviet urban population is explained by immigration from rural areas—approximately three million new urban residents every year—as well as by a greater than average natural population increase. (Recent immigrants to the cities tend to be young married couples starting families.)[6] Thus, most adults living in Soviet cities today were born in rural areas, which helps to explain the persistence of rural attitudes and behavior among some urban residents. For instance, city people often prefer folk remedies, medicinal herbs, or mustard plasters over modern drugs. One sees Muscovites wearing garlic cloves around their necks to ward off colds, a carry-over from rural customs. A startling reminder of the agrarian roots of Soviet urbanites is that the most common murder weapon in the USSR today is the ax.[7]

Although he or she may live in a huge city, the average Russian is never far from the soil—it is the connection to his or her roots in the countryside. City dwellers may rent a small plot of land (up to one-quarter acre) outside the city for a garden. These plots are an important source of vegetables and fruit, which are otherwise scarce in the summer and nonexistent in the winter in Soviet stores. Soviet citizens often construct tiny toolsheds on their garden plots to double as sleeping quarters on weekend outings.

To cope with the crowded, often bleak urban existence, Soviet citizens seek refuge in the country. On Friday nights, train stations are crowded with urbanites leaving for the weekend. In autumn, they flock to the woods to hunt mushrooms, which is a national pastime. In winter, people of all ages—teenagers, pensioners, middle-aged men and women—don cross-country skis and glide along paths between rows of birch and spruce trees. In summer, urbanites crowd the banks of the Moscow River or the beaches on the Gulf of Finland, or they simply stroll amid the fields and hike through the forests to escape the heat and humanity of the city.

As might be expected, service, trade, and professional occupations in the USSR have been increasing much more rapidly than have blue-collar jobs, and the percentage of the population engaged in agriculture has declined steadily since 1926. Yet, despite the migration of workers from the countryside, Soviet cities still experience serious labor shortages, especially in the service and trade sectors. These shortages further hamper the ability of city governments to meet the needs of their rapidly expanding populations.

In order to moderate the demands on Soviet cities, a system of registration (*propiska*) has been instituted in Moscow, Leningrad, Kiev, and several other large cities. A citizen wishing to move to one of these cities must first obtain a *propiska* (registration document) from an employer. Employers are under pressure to hire from the local population and extend *propiski* to workers from other regions only if they are uniquely qualified for vacant positions. As one might expect, however, such a system is open to widespread abuses through favoritism and nepotism, or what the Soviets call *blat* (connections). Because of the extensive circumvention of the *propiska* restrictions, many cities exceed their planned size. For instance, the plan for

Moscow called for a population of no more than 7.5 million by 1990, which was less than its population in the early 1980s.[8] Soviet authorities acknowledge the ineffectiveness of the *propiska* system as a means of limiting city growth, but they are powerless to stem the tide of urban migration. Many citizens bypass the residence restrictions by living in nearby villages and commuting to the cities to work. Others marry Muscovites or Leningraders simply to obtain the right to reside in one of those cities; still others live in the cities illegally with friends or relatives. Employers, especially in the service sector, may overlook the failure of job applicants to obtain a *propiska* and may even provide them with housing.

The rapid pace of urbanization in the USSR has resulted in the expansion of the activities of local party and state bodies. As the next section indicates, the powers of local governments to set policies affecting the distribution of social services are especially significant and potentially conflictual.

ECONOMIC FUNCTIONS OF LOCAL SOVIETS

Local and regional soviets are charged with a wide array of economic functions, including the allocation of funds, the distribution of goods and services, the control of expenditures by state administrative and social organizations, and the supervision of production in their jurisdictions. Over the past several decades, there has been a steady increase in the budgets of local governments in the USSR. For example, in 1960, local expenditures in Kazakhstan accounted for only 18.7 percent of the republic's total expenditures. By 1974, local budgets had increased to 28.9 percent of the republic's expenditures.[9]

Although relatively few in number, city soviets account for almost one-half of all local spending.[10] Given the heavy demands on social services, housing, and transportation in large cities, it should not be surprising that cities occupy a prominent place in local government expenditure in the USSR. Nationwide, cities account for almost two-thirds of all local expenditures on housing, industry, and other economic services.[11] Such factors as population, economic base, location, and level of administrative subordination, however, account for dramatic disparities among cities. For example, although Sverdlovsk and Minsk are roughly the same size in terms of population, Sverdlovsk is subordinate to regional party and state control, while Minsk, the capital of the Belorussian Republic, is subordinated to republic-level organs. Moscow enjoys a special status, reporting directly to the all-union party and state organs and thus bypassing the Russian Republic level of administration.

Article 147 of the 1977 Constitution states that local soviets have the authority to ensure "the comprehensive economic and social development of their territory."[12] In practice, however, local soviets are an integral and subordinate link in a highly centralized administrative chain that extends from the leading party and state organs and ministries down to the level of factories and enterprises. Most resources for Soviet cities are allocated through a comprehensive and centralized system of economic planning. The budgets for local governments in the USSR are determined at the center, leaving little room for adjustment or alteration by local authorities. Nevertheless, local officials can influence spending in subtle but important ways. Local soviets have three principal sources of revenue: (1) funds allocated through the state budget, (2) state subsidies earmarked for specific projects, and (3) incentives and other funds of branch ministries with enterprises in the area.

The centrally planned budgets for regional and local soviets in the USSR are broken down into specific items, severely restricting the ability of local party and state officials to shift resources from one sector to another. In the short run, the primary method for generating discretionary funds from the state budget is to undertake cost-saving measures. In the long run, local governments can influence future budgets by lobbying the central planning and construction agencies and informing them of local needs that may be raised to a higher-priority status over an extended period of time. The fact of life for most local and regional soviets in the USSR, however, is that they must secure funds for special projects from sources other than the state budget. The ability of local soviets to do this depends greatly on the cooperation and clout of local party officials.

The third source of local revenue, from factories and enterprises, is not inconsequential. In 1979, economic enterprises in the Soviet Union earmarked more than 50 million rubles for subsidizing projects of local soviets.[13] In the Lithuanian city of Kaunas, for example, contributions from factories and local enterprises constituted 12.5 percent of all local outlays for public works projects in the city: lighting, road repair, and landscaping.[14] Soviet sources indicate that enterprises in Bratsk spend five times the city's total budget for capital construction and services.[15]

The distribution functions of local soviets are among the most important and potentially conflict-ridden responsibilities of local governmental and party organs. Cities are responsible for providing a wide array of services: housing, health care, schools, cultural facilities, parks, entertainment enterprises, restaurants, stores, public transportation, utilities, sewage treatment, and garbage-collection services. The city of Moscow, for example, directly provides more than six hundred types of services.[16]

Given the wide scope of social services provided by local governments, they naturally constitute a significant portion of the total income (or benefits) of the average Soviet citizen. As much as 15 to 20 percent of the average industrial worker's aggregate family income is derived from educational, medical, and other services provided free of charge by local governmental agencies, or from housing and consumer services, which are heavily subsidized.[17] Soviet studies have shown that inadequate provision of these social services is the primary reason workers voluntarily terminate employment. For instance, more than 28 percent of all Soviet citizens moving out of the Ukraine in 1979 indicated dissatisfaction with social amenities to be a major factor in their decision to move.[18]

Because most social services are provided either free or for a minimal charge, access to goods and services, rather than cost, becomes the critical factor. While many inner cities in the United States have suffered out-migration and decay, the inner cores of cities in the Soviet Union enjoy advantages over the peripheral areas. In the center of a Soviet city, stores tend to be better stocked than stores in outlying areas, public transportation is better and more accessible, there are more nursery schools and kindergartens, housing tends to be older but roomier, and the quality of construction is superior to the prefabricated apartment blocs that dominate suburban areas. In addition, parks and cultural amenities are more accessible in the heart of the city than in outlying areas.

Local governments in the USSR are responsible for verifying compliance with national policies. The past two decades have witnessed a broadening of these powers of local soviets to encompass enforcement of housing codes, fire regulations, and especially pollution control. The process of urbanization has also fostered increased attention to problems of zoning, urban development, building design, traffic control, industrial siting, and land-use policy.

Despite the extensive responsibilities of local administrative agencies, there is a critical need for regionally based planning in Soviet cities, instead of sectoral planning. Ministries and local governments frequently fail to coordinate their activities, resulting in waste, inefficiency, and bureaucratic squabbling. For instance, the Ministry of Steel may plan to expand production facilities at a given factory and increase the work force substantially. Such a decision may be made independently of local government officials, who are responsible for providing housing, transportation, health care, education, child care, water, electricity, sewage treatment, and other services to the new employees. Similarly, central ministries may reallocate resources originally designated for one region to another region considered to be of a higher priority. The local party secretary in the adversely affected region has little recourse but to appeal to the Central Committee Secretariat or the Politburo; meanwhile, the resulting underfulfillment of the plan in the region may undermine the secretary's political position. In this manner, ministerial officials can exercise a large degree of influence over regional party officials.

GRASS-ROOTS PARTICIPATION IN THE USSR

The Brezhnev era marked the expansion of the role of regional and local soviets in soliciting the input of Soviet citizens. A widely publicized party decree in 1974 encouraged local soviets to broaden citizens' participation in these bodies. In some cases, the expanded participation amounted to more than mere window dressing. For example, deputies to the Tallinn city soviet brought more than five hundred citizens' complaints before the soviet in 1974.[19] In addition, the deputies hold meetings twice per year to hear constituents' complaints and suggestions and to transmit information to the public on the activities of the soviet.

The annual budget meeting of the local soviet serves as an important sounding board for public opinion. Theodore Friedgut observed a local soviet budget session and gave the following account:

> The greater part of the two and a half hour session of the soviet was devoted to the prepared speeches of several deputies, a series of brief questions by other deputies regarding specific items of nonfulfillment of plans, and a detailed reply

by the chairman of the executive committee. The debate began in promising fashion with a vigorously presented critique of conditions in the borough by a deputy who identified herself as speaking "from the point of view of the fifth microraion" (a neighborhood of the borough). The speaker claimed that her constituency should be allotted a larger share in the housing construction budget. She complained of inadequate water supply and decried non-implementation of plans to improve services, dwelling in particular on a promised retail furniture outlet which had been included in the plan for the past three years, but had not been built. The speaker was vehement in her criticisms, using such sharp expressions as "shameful" and "criminal." The effect of her criticism was blunted, however, when at the end of her presentation, she declared that in the name of all her constituents she supported the executive committee's draft budget and proposed that it be unanimously adopted.[20]

In the USSR, where the citizen is dependent on the government for so broad a spectrum of goods and services, which are in short supply, citizens' complaints and petitions to local authorities are very important. One survey of Soviet pensioners found that most sent complaints about problems with their pensions to the local soviet or to social security offices; relatively few addressed their complaints to local party officials. (See Table 6-1.)

Such complaints frequently go unanswered, however. Of all complaints received by the city's office of social security, only 1 to 2 percent were satisfactorily resolved.[21] Complaints sent directly to the RSFSR Ministry of Social Security were even less likely to be resolved satisfactorily.[22] In contrast, complaints made to the Procuracy (prosecutor's office) are investigated; if the prosecutors believe there are sufficient grounds, they will issue protests to the responsible officials. Procuratorial protests are successful in ninety-nine out of a hundred cases.[23]

Citizens may also bring their grievances to the attention of local authorities by writing letters to the press. The Soviet media receive between 60 and 70 million letters each year; *Pravda* alone receives more than 500,000.[24] Obviously, all letters received cannot be published, but Soviet authorities maintain that the letters are read by newspaper personnel and referred to the proper offices for corrective action. Because the editors of most major newspapers also serve on regional party committees, this mechanism is effective in providing feedback to party leaders concerning problems in their regions.

Table 6-1. Where Leningrad Pensioners Send Their Complaints (in percent)

Local Soviets	28
RSFSR Ministry of Social Security	25
Local social security offices	21
Media	20
Party Organs	3
Trade Unions	2
Courts and Procuracy	1

Source: D. M. Chechot, *Administrativnaia iustitsiia* (Leningrad: Leningrad State University, 1973), 105.

Another mechanism linking public demands to the political leadership is the so-called voter mandate (*nakaz izbiratelei*). During the process of nominating candidates, citizens routinely raise issues, make suggestions, and criticize party and state practices. Some of these demands are subsequently ratified by the executive committees of local soviets (*ispolkomy*) and are legally binding on the soviets. In other words, the soviets pledge themselves to satisfy the demands. *Nakazy* relate to specific and often minor demands or complaints: paving roads, changing timetables and routes for public transportation, or constructing additional stores, parks, or cultural facilities in the region. The financing of such projects is not included in the plan but must come from the reserve fund of the local soviet or from donations by major industrial or agricultural enterprises in the region.

During the 1970s, each round of elections generated between 750,000 and 850,000 voter mandates.[25] Despite this large number, between 70 and 80 percent of the mandates were fulfilled within eighteen months.[26] In 1975, for example, local elections in Pavlodar *oblast'* in Kazakhstan generated 5,276 *nakazy*. More than 80 percent of these had been fulfilled by the end of 1976. They included demands for the construction of fourteen new kindergartens, two secondary schools, twenty-nine shops or stores, five cafés or cafeterias, five service shops (shoe repair, tailoring, hairdressing, and so on), and an indoor swimming pool.[27]

The system of voter mandates has become a relatively popular mechanism for citizens to voice their demands and receive prompt attention by elected officials. In the initial draft of the new USSR Constitution, circulated for discussion in 1977, the provision for voter mandates was omitted. A storm of controversy ensued at thousands of workers' meetings called to discuss the new document. The constitutional commission, responding to this overwhelming expression of public protest, reinstated voter mandates in Article 102 of the final document.

REGIONAL DEVELOPMENT

Within the USSR, vast economic, cultural, and demographic differences among regions present Soviet planners with many serious challenges. Regional differences also spark frequent disputes over the allocation of investment funds and the provision of housing and other social services. The Soviet Union is a classic example of uneven economic development. While Moscow is a bustling, modern city with intricate and efficient mass transportation and communications systems and relatively well-stocked stores, not far outside the city, conditions are much more primitive. Just 100 miles to the northeast of Moscow is Vladimir, an *oblast'* capital with a population in excess of 250,000. In downtown Vladimir, women use wooden shoulder yokes to carry buckets of water from a public well. There are few paved streets in the city, and the store shelves are mostly bare. In the winter, women saw holes in the ice of a small river to wash clothes in the freezing water.

The disparities between standards of living in the city and in the countryside are even more evident east of the Urals in Siberia, Central Asia, and the Far East. The republic capitals of Tashkent and Alma-Ata boast sky-scrapers and modern apartment blocs with all the amenities, but just a few miles beyond the city limits people live much as they have for centuries. Urbanization, more than any other factor, accounts for these differences in levels of economic development. The greater the population, the better and more accessible the education, health care, consumer goods, housing, and other services.

Recognizing the vast differences among various portions of the USSR, planners have divided the country into eighteen economic regions in order to promote coordination among economic enterprises within the regions and to facilitate long-range planning. During the period from 1971 to 1985, the Far East, East Siberia, and West Siberia regions were especially targeted for intensive development. Wage and material incentive policies were intro-duced to attract and retain labor in these regions. Workers may receive from 1.2 to 2.0 times their regular salaries for working in the hostile climates and underdeveloped regions of the north.[28] Different industries are able to offer different coefficients, however, so that various occupations in the same city receive different levels of remuneration. The construction industry has been a major proponent of differential wage policies, being one of the chief beneficiaries of the policy. For example, the Baikal-Amur Mainline project, a vast project begun in the late 1970s to build a rail line from the mineral-rich region north of Lake Baikal to the Pacific, is offering wage bonuses of 1.7, even to its office employees.[29]

Young Russian males commonly contract work in one of the northern regions for one or two years in order to amass some money before getting married. However, such a practice results in high rates of labor turnover. Thus, in the far northern city of Norilsk, 19,000 new workers were re-cruited in 1969, but 18,500 workers left during the same year.[30] The consis-tent complaint of those leaving the development zones is inadequate con-sumer goods, medical facilities, housing, child care, and other services.

In Soviet Central Asia, the opposite problem exists: there is an excess of available labor. The 1979 census showed that Central Asians number more than 40 million, and they are increasing at a phenomenal rate—more than four times the national average. It is estimated that, by the year 2000, Central Asians will outnumber Russians in the USSR.[31]

Culturally and economically, the Central Asians are among the most underdeveloped and least urbanized in the USSR. A high proportion of the native population works in traditional occupations such as farming and animal herding. The percentage of Central Asian students admitted to uni-versities and other institutions of higher education is among the lowest of any ethnic group in the USSR. Policies designed to encourage Central Asians to migrate to areas experiencing labor shortages have proven to be ineffec-tive; cultural, familial, linguistic, and religious ties tend to keep the Central Asians in their native regions.

During the early 1970s, the Soviet leadership appeared to favor at-tempts to equalize the standard of living across the entire USSR. Such a policy soon encountered resistance. Party and state officials in the Ukraine, the Baltic republics, Moscow, and Leningrad did not want their budgets cut to assist the development of lagging areas such as Central Asia and Siberia.

The Baltic republics—Estonia, Latvia, and Lithuania—have a well-developed industrial base and thriving small-scale agriculture. This region enjoys the highest standard of living in the Soviet Union. International commerce flourishes, thanks to Baltic shipping, and consequently some goods available in Tallinn, Riga, or Vilnius are unheard of elsewhere in the USSR. In Tallinn, which is only 45 minutes by hydrofoil from Helsinki, Estonians can watch Finnish television programs. Swedish radio stations broadcast to all three republics.

Attracted by its high standard of living, Russians and other Slavic ethnic groups have been immigrating to the region in increasing numbers recently. The influx of non-Balts has raised fears among the indigenous peoples that they will become Russified. For instance, some schools have switched from the Estonian language to the Russian language to serve the needs of the new arrivals. Such conversions have generated storms of protest and anti-Russian sentiment.

Regional economic disparities, demographic trends, and population migration patterns thus raise thorny political problems for regional party officials as well as the top leadership in the USSR. The following case studies illustrate the potency of these regional disputes.

REGIONAL POLITICS: TWO CASE STUDIES

The interplay of regional, ministerial, and party interests is especially evident in decisions affecting large-scale development projects in the USSR. The following two case studies illustrate the intensity of politics at the regional and local levels, as well as the manner in which conflicting interests are articulated and resolved in interactions between central decision-makers and local interests.

The West Siberian Oil and Gas Complex.   During the late 1970s and early 1980s, Soviet leaders were confronted with a critical choice affecting the production and consumption of energy. During the Tenth Five-Year Plan (1976–1980), the coal industry failed to boost its production by the planned 14 percent, raising serious doubts about the strategy of replacing oil and gas with coal as the primary fuel for electrical power plants.[32] This coincided with growing concern over dwindling Soviet petroleum reserves and a leveling off of oil production. In the process of determining energy policy for the Eleventh Five-Year Plan (1981–1985), policymakers faced two major options: investing heavily in the West Siberian oil and gas complex located in Tiumen' *oblast'*, or investing more resources in coal, atomic energy, and hydroelectric power.

In his report to the Twenty-Fifth Party Congress in March 1976, Soviet Premier and leading economic official Alexei Kosygin threw his support to the latter option: "During this five-year plan we will set the foundation for the future growth of our energy potential which will come primarily from hydroelectricity, atomic fuel, and cheap coal. As far as oil and gas are concerned, the growth in their output will be, to a large extent, directed toward technological needs [e.g., the chemical industry]."[33]

The first secretary of the Tiumen' *oblast'* party committee responded in a widely read journal article; he denounced proposals for a crash program to develop and transport Siberian coal to the European portion of the USSR. In his view, this would merely divert scarce capital from the development of gas, which is economically more efficient and environmentally less damaging than coal.[34]

One of the more outspoken proponents of West Siberian oil and gas development was A. A. Trofimuk, director of the Siberian Institute of Geology and Geophysics and deputy director of the Siberian division of the Academy of Sciences. In 1976, Trofimuk called for further increases in the share of oil and gas in the nation's energy mix and discounted charges that the USSR was rapidly depleting its oil and gas reserves.[35] However, geologists and engineers more closely connected with and responsible for actual oil and gas production were more cautious in their assessments. While party secretaries pushed for higher output goals in order to justify greater investment allocations, research geologists stressed the vast potential of hydrocarbons. Engineers and production technicians, meanwhile, argued for more moderate rates of growth. Not only would a slower development rate for oil and gas fields lower their annual production quotas, but it would also enhance ultimate recovery and reduce waste and damage to the oil and gas fields caused by overexploitation.

In his speech to the December 1977 plenum of the CPSU Central Committee, Brezhnev stressed the role of Siberian oil and gas in the Soviet Union's energy future. This was followed in March and April 1978 by his tour of the region. Press accounts gave extensive coverage of his speeches in Tiumen' and Omsk.[36] During his stop in Krasnoiarsk *Krai*, he praised a local hydroelectric project, but failed to mention the territory's huge Kansk-Achinsk coal complex.[37] This was widely interpreted as indicating his support for oil and gas, as opposed to coal. Returning from his tour, Brezhnev addressed the Komsomol Congress; among other things, he urged Soviet youth to volunteer for work on construction projects in Tiumen' *oblast'* and to press for prompt fulfillment of production orders for the West Siberian oil and gas project by industries throughout the USSR.[38]

Several Gosplan officials also threw their support to oil and gas development. Gosplan chairman N. K. Baibakov, who had served as Minister of the Petroleum and Gas Industry during the 1950s, expressed great optimism for oil and gas projects. His chief deputy, Arkady Laviants, noted that oil and gas projects tend to recover their investment costs much faster than coal projects.[39]

In direct opposition to Brezhnev's campaigning for West Siberian oil and gas, Kosygin continued to support policies favoring coal and nuclear power. In his November 1978 speech on the anniversary of the Revolution, he noted:

> The future of our economy depends on a reliable fuel-energy base. . . . The unique deposits of power coal make it possible to ensure the effective reorganization of the fuel balance of the country based on the construction of super-high capacity thermal power stations using the cheap coals of Kansk-Achinsk, Ekibastuz, and other coal deposits. . . . Increasing the share of atomic energy and coal in the fuel-energy balance will also make possible large-scale savings of natural gas and petroleum—irreplaceable sources of chemical feedstocks.[40]

By 1979, the policy debate had begun to sharpen, with clearly identifiable constellations of individuals and interest groups on each side in the debate. Of the twenty members and candidate members of the Politburo, the West Siberian oil and gas complex was supported by nine:

1. L. I. Brezhnev, General Secretary of the CPSU.
2. M. S. Gorbachev, Party secretary with responsibility for agriculture. Gorbachev's support for further oil and gas development was based on the need for petroleum to operate tractors, combines, and other farm machinery. In addition, most herbicides, pesticides, and fertilizers are manufactured from hydrocarbons. Finally, agricultural imports to the USSR are in many cases paid for with hard currency earned by energy exports to Western Europe and Japan.
3. V. V. Grishin, first secretary of the Moscow City Party Committee. The Central Economic Region surrounding Moscow contains more than one-half of the factories of the ministries of petroleum and chemical machine building. Grishin's public statements reflected a strong concern for automobile and truck transport, which are vital to the city. In addition, Moscow and its environs are a major center for automobile and truck production. Grishin also appeared to favor natural gas over coal for power generation in order to reduce pollution.
4. A. A. Gromyko, Minister of Foreign Affairs. Gromyko was a probable supporter of Siberian oil and gas development, although he was never directly quoted on the subject. Yet, the importance of oil and gas in Soviet policies toward Eastern Europe and the capitalist countries makes it likely that he favored their expanded role.
5. N. A. Tikhonov, first deputy of the Presidium of the Council of Ministers. During the 1950s, Tikhonov had been a powerful figure in the ferrous-metals ministry, which depends heavily upon gas. Furthermore, he had risen to power in Brezhnev's home region of Dnepropetrovsk and later worked in Gosplan, giving him close ties to Brezhnev and Baibakov, both of whom supported the Siberian project.
6. D. F. Ustinov, Minister of Defense. Ustinov was an outspoken supporter of petroleum production, which is vital to the operation of the Soviet armed forces. Furthermore, the development of natural-gas pipelines to Eastern Europe lessens their dependence on foreign energy resources and further integrates them into the Soviet sphere.
7. G. A. Aliev, candidate member of the Politburo and first secretary of the Azerbaidzhan Communist Party. The Azerbaidzhan republic is a major center for the production of oil and gas field equipment and pipe.
8. V. I. Dolgikh, candidate member of the Politburo and party secretary in charge of heavy industry. Among Dolgikh's responsibilities was the supervision of the oil, gas, and geology ministries.
9. M. S. Solomentsev, candidate member of the Politburo and Chairman of the RSFSR Council of Ministers. The West Siberian complex fell under his ultimate supervision. In addition, Solomentsev could

be expected to reflect many of the same Moscow-oriented interests of Grishin.

In addition to receiving support from these Politburo members, the project was favored by a relatively cohesive group of at least seventy-seven members of the CPSU Central Committee. They included the abovementioned nine Politburo members and candidate members, two aides to Brezhnev, two Komsomol officials, seven officials of Moscow and Moscow *oblast'*, twenty military officers and defense officials, fifteen officials in various ministries with ties to the oil and gas industries, Baibakov of Gosplan, and twenty-one party officials from oil- and gas-producing regions.

In West Siberia, Tiumen', Omsk, and Tomsk *oblasti* are strongly tied to the oil and gas industries. The first secretaries of the party committees of these three *oblasti* were full members of the Central Committee. Significantly, the project received the unanimous support of other oil- and gas-producing regions. These regions have high concentrations of oil- and gas-related industries (e.g., automobile, aircraft, defense, and chemical) and are the major suppliers of oil- and gas-drilling and production equipment. In addition, the foreign-exchange earnings derived from oil and gas exports from the West Siberian complex could be used to purchase specialized oil and gas equipment needed to enhance recovery from older production regions. The cohesiveness of regional officials on the West Siberian oil and gas complex strengthened its effectiveness as a lobbying force, in contrast to the fragmentation of the pro-coal and pro-nuclear forces.

Within the Politburo, the strongest and most consistent supporters of nuclear power were:

1. A. N. Kosygin, Premier of the USSR (Chairman of the Presidium of the Council of Ministers).
2. A. P. Kirilenko, party secretary with responsibility for economic matters. Kirilenko's public statements reflected concern with nuclear-power generation in Leningrad and Rostov. He also appeared to be a supporter of hydroelectric power and the development of the Kansk-Achinsk and Ekibastuz long-distance power line.
3. G. V. Romanov, first secretary of the Leningrad *Oblast'* Party Committee. Leningrad is the leading center for the manufacture of hydroelectric power turbines and equipment, and also of nuclear power engineering.
4. V. V. Shcherbitsky, first secretary of the Ukrainian Communist Party. Oil and gas reserves in the Ukraine have been declining, while the region (along with Leningrad) is one of the major producers of nuclear technology for power plants. The Ukraine is scheduled to receive almost one-half of all new nuclear-power capacity constructed through 1990.[41]

In addition, there were twenty-four full members of the Central Committee with regional or ministerial positions who had a direct interest in nuclear power.

The pro-coal faction was represented on the Politburo by A. N. Kosygin, Premier of the USSR; A. P. Kirilenko, party secretary; and D. A. Kunaev, first party secretary of the Kazakh Communist Party. In the field of energy, Kunaev was most concerned with the development of the Ekibastuz and Karaganda coal deposits and with the development of oil and gas industries in Central Asia. In addition, the proposal to divert the flow of Siberian rivers to Central Asia for badly needed irrigation projects was opposed by supporters of the West Siberian oil and gas complex because it would disrupt river transport and fish production and would threaten the environment of Tiumen' *oblast'*.

Shcherbitsky, first party secretary of the Ukraine, expressed concern only about the coal industry in the Ukraine. Regional and ministry officials with a direct role in coal production accounted for only seven members of the Central Committee. The first secretaries of two of the most important coal-producing regions, Karaganda and Pavlodar *oblasti,* were not members of the Central Committee. Furthermore, the coal group was divided along regional lines, with Ukrainian coal interests arguing that additional funds for lignite development in Kansk-Achinsk and Ekibastuz could be better used in the Ukraine.

The effect of the West Siberian oil and gas campaign began to be reflected in investment and production figures in 1979. Investment in coal dropped by 0.7 percent in 1979 from the previous year's level.[42] The share of total investment in energy resources that was earmarked for coal declined from 15.2 percent in 1978 to 13.9 percent in 1980.[43]

At the January 1980 meeting of the Council of Ministers, First Deputy Premier N. A. Tikhonov (who succeeded the ailing Kosygin) delivered a report attacking the leadership of the coal ministry for declining production, plummeting labor productivity, and poor management.[44] This served as a prelude to the final exchange between advocates of coal and advocates of oil and gas at the general meeting of the Academy of Sciences in May 1980. A. Aleksandrov, President of the Academy, called attention to serious delays in the construction of the Ekibastuz power line. This key component of the coal strategy involved the construction of massive coal-fired power plants in Siberia and the transmission of electricity to the European portion of the country. Aleksandrov praised the work of the Ministry of Power and Electrification and indicated his concurrence with V. M. Tuchkevich's speech attacking the power and electrification department of Gosplan for hampering the power line's construction through administrative delays and reductions in allocations.[45]

The forces favoring the West Siberian oil and gas complex were too strong, however. The final policy decision in favor of assigning top priority to oil and gas development was made by the Politburo and announced by Brezhnev at the October 1980 plenum of the Central Committee. At the same time, two special commissions were established: the Council of Ministers created the Commission on Questions of the Development of the West Siberian Petroleum and Gas Complex, and Gosplan formed an interdepartmental territorial commission, with headquarters in Tiumen'. The purpose of both commissions was to assist in facilitating coordination among various departments and ministries involved in the project. The commissions also created an organizational base of support. The ministries of the gas industry, petroleum industry, and construction of petroleum and gas industry enterprises all have more than one-half of their production concentrated in West Siberia. The creation of a Tiumen'-based commission under Gosplan (which could bypass these ministerial lines if the ministries were less than cooperative) provided the complex with an organizational means of ensuring adequate capital, equipment, and labor. Similarly, the creation of the commission by the Council of Ministers gave the West Siberian oil and gas complex its own advocate on the highest organ of the Government.

Although the issue of the development of the West Siberian oil and gas complex is resolved today, its aftershocks are still evident from debates in the Soviet press on priorities in allocating capital investment funds. During the Ninth, Tenth, and Eleventh Five-Year Plans, Soviet authorities redirected massive amounts of funds for resource development in West Siberia and the construction of the Baikal-Amur Mainline (BAM). Prior to the promulgation of the Twelfth Five-Year Plan (1986–1990), the ministerial and territorial interests of the European parts of the Soviet Union began to argue strenuously that they had been neglected for too long and that it was now time to shift resources back to the traditional industrial centers of the country. Just as the birth of a Sun Belt coalition in the United States prompted the northeast industrial states to form a Frost Belt coalition, regional disputes over priorities and the allocation of investment funds are an ongoing, never-ending phenomenon in the USSR.

The Ob' River Diversion Project.   In the south-central portion of the USSR lies a massive area called Soviet Central Asia. In this arid region reside more than 40 million Moslems of various nationalities: Uzbeks, Kazakhs, Turkmen, Kirghiz, and Tadzhik. The water supply for Central Asia depends primarily on two rivers, the Amu Darya and the Syr Darya, which flow into the Aral Sea. The two rivers are fed by snowmelt from the Pamir mountains to the southeast and support a thriving cotton economy and a booming population. The water resources of the region are being used to their full capacity, however, and the level of the Aral Sea is falling. Soviet geographers are predicting serious water shortages within the decade, unless new water resources are found.[46] In the face of this situation, Soviet engineers in the mid-1970s proposed an ambitious plan to divert a portion of the Ob' River in western Siberia southward to the Aral Sea basin. The plan calls for the construction of a 1500-mile canal, which in itself raises many difficult technical, engineering, and environmental problems. Preliminary estimates put the cost of the first stage of the project at more than 30 billion rubles.[47] (See Figure 6-1.)

Cost was not the only factor weighing against the plan, however. The thrust of Brezhnev's agricultural program at the time favored the intensive use of lands in European Russia that received regular and dependable rainfall—the so-called non–black-earth (*nechernozem*) zone—and a cutback in irrigation projects in Central Asia. Although the soils in the non–black-earth region are not as fertile as those in Central Asia, the use of chemical fertilizers make that less of a concern than the problem of insufficient precipitation. In addition, during the mid- and late-1970s, investment in agriculture was falling, and it was unlikely that such a massive project could be supported. Finally, the diversion project would inevitably cause environ-

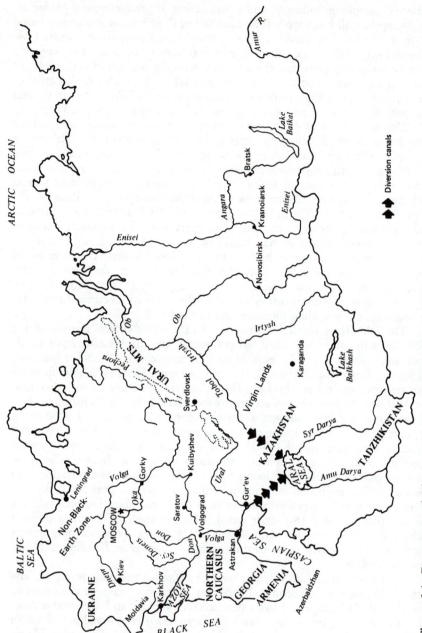

Figure 6-1. European and Siberian Diversion Proposals in the USSR

mental damage in western Siberia, a high-priority development region. Geographers and climatologists warned that withdrawing such large quantities of relatively warm water from the inflow to the Arctic Ocean might change climates the world over.[48] Given these factors, Soviet sources until the early 1980s spoke of the Ob' River diversion scheme as a long-range prospect, a "project for the next century."[49]

Vigorous lobbying by party leaders and local governmental officials in the south, coupled with a growing awareness in Moscow of the grave water resource needs of Central Asia resulted in a reassessment of the project, however. At the Twenty-Fifth Party Congress in 1976, two members of the Politburo, D. A. Kunaev, First Secretary of Kazakhstan, and S. R. Rashidov, First Secretary of Uzbekistan, spoke out strongly in favor of transferring water to the Aral Sea basin. According to Kunaev: "Diversions will provide explosive industrial and agricultural development of new and exceptionally promising areas, in the interests of the entire Soviet nation."[50] Their remarks were echoed by the First Secretary of the Turkmen republic, M. G. Gapurov.[51]

The intervention of southern party leaders may actually have swayed the Politburo. Brezhnev had not mentioned the diversion project in his opening report to the congress. In fact, his remarks implied his rejection of the proposal; he stressed efficiency and intensification of agriculture, discouraged new projects, and urged the rapid completion of old ones. The following day, however, Kosygin called for a detailed study of the Ob' River diversion project, indicating a possible division within the Politburo over the issue.

During spring 1978, the Central Asian project was approved by a review commission of Gosplan, clearing the way for preliminary engineering and economic feasibility studies. This decision was officially ratified in a decree of the CPSU Central Committee and the USSR Council of Ministers in December 1978. The studies were slated for completion in 1980.

Yet the government had not committed itself irrevocably to the project. Opposition interests were strong, although not closely allied. The project would siphon off resources needed for agricultural investment in the Ukraine and the non–black-earth zone, and it would threaten water resources in western Siberia. It may also have been opposed by the powerful oil and gas lobby.[52] Additionally, the military and their seven supporting industrial ministries appear to have been critical of the project's expense, especially in light of estimates that investment capital funds would be exceptionally tight during the 1980s.[53]

Press accounts throughout 1980 appeared to favor more efficient utilization of existing water resources, and they failed to provide much coverage of plans for the diversion project. Beginning in 1981, however, a flurry of articles by regional officials, scientists, and officials of the Ministry of Land Reclamation and Water Resources appeared, indicating a turn in the tide of official opinion in favor of the project.

The chairman of the state commission charged with planning the project, G. V. Voropaev, declared that the project would be enormously important for Central Asia, but he was careful to note that it would also benefit northern Siberian regions—potential opponents of the plan. "By the end of this century, Central Asia could become a major producer of foodstuffs, providing not only for its own needs, but also for those of other regions of the country—first of all, Siberia, which will share its water with Central Asia."[54]

Regional disagreements over the project were evident among the Central Asian republics. A Tadzhik official wrote in 1984 that his republic accounts for nearly 60 percent of Central Asia's hydroelectric power and that its one thousand rivers and more than 1200 cubic kilometers of water stored in glaciers make it a major source of water resources in the region.[55] He argued: "Putting money into irrigation is very profitable. The return per ruble on capital invested is higher in Tadzhikistan than it is anywhere else in Central Asia."[56] He noted, however, that Central Asian regional and republic agencies do not always act in concert; conflicts also arise between the interests of the Ministry of Land Reclamation and Water Resources and the Ministry of Power and Electrification, which is reponsible for hydroelectric projects. He cited several cases in which dams built to generate power were being operated exclusively by the Ministry of Land Reclamation and Water Resources. Water levels were adjusted to meet the needs of irrigation, often resulting in the shutting down of turbines for power generation. When he complained to the chief design institute of the ministry about these matters, "The conversation kept coming around to how the institute is working out a grandiose design for diverting part of the Ob' River to Central Asia and Kazakhstan. But this is a task for the future. For the time being, in the opinion of specialists, we should make maximum use of the water resources of the region itself."[57]

Another article in *Pravda* criticized the Uzbek land reclamation ministry for misusing irrigated land. The report stated that during the Eleventh Five-Year Plan, overzealous officials in the ministry had begun development of more than 170 state farms on irrigated land in the republic. According to the article, it would take thirty to forty years to develop all of these farms to full capacity.[58]

Official, top-level support for the project, which had been noticeably absent under Andropov, resumed under Chernenko. In January 1985, the Soviet press reported that Central Asian engineers and planners were arriving in Tiumen' *oblast'* to begin construction of housing and roads and to plan the construction of the diversion project. With the death of Chernenko in the spring of 1985, many Soviet environmentalists hoped that the new leadership would follow Andropov's course and postpone the project. However, Nikolai F. Vasiliev, minister of land reclamation and water resources, announced on June 5, 1985, that the Soviet Union would go ahead with the plan.[59] Vasiliev's announcement sparked renewed public debate. The daily newspaper *Sovetskaia Rossiia* reported on a newly commissioned study that found the level of the Caspian Sea had actually been rising since 1978.[60] A few days later, the same newspaper published a letter from seven prominent Soviet writers who opposed the plan and another diversion project west of the Urals.[61] They argued that the diversion schemes would flood vast areas of fertile farmland and destroy ancient villages and towns. A decisive blow was struck just prior to the Twenty-Seventh Party Congress in early 1986, when Gorbachev's chief economic analyst, Abel Aganbegian, and a group of other leading academicians publicly opposed the diversion project.[62] The project was again tabled, and funds for the river diversion scheme were not included in the Twelfth Five-Year Plan ratified at the Congress.

MODELS OF SOVIET LOCAL POLITICS

As these cases illustrate, the involvement of local party and state officials, enterprise directors, scientists, academics, and the public in policy debates has important ramifications for our understanding of the nature of the entire Soviet political system. Clearly, the Soviet political system is not completely totalitarian. Party leaders in the Politburo do not simply dictate policies, expecting local officials, enterprises, and workers to obey dutifully. Politics and political conflict exist in the Soviet Union, and policy is the outcome of an ongoing struggle of competing pluralistic interests.

As noted in the previous chapter, the majority of Soviet interests find expression through established bureaucracies, as was evident in both the debate over the Tiumen' oil and gas complex and the controversy surrounding the river diversion project. Geologists, engineers, and economists exerted considerable influence, and their findings were used to reinforce the viewpoints of various regional interests.

Furthermore, these instances illustrate the formation of constellations of regional and industrial interests. The Tiumen' oil and gas complex was favored by several other oil- and gas-producing regions and also by ministries with close ties to hydrocarbons. The river diversion project was supported by a coalition of Central Asian party and state officials, but was opposed by officials from northern Siberia and the industrial heartland west of the Urals, who feared that the mammoth project would absorb a large portion of capital investment funds that could be channeled to their regions. The fusion of personal and regional or institutional interests was apparent: "What is good for the Ministry of Land Reclamation and Water Resources is good for me." "What benefits Tiumen' benefits me."

It is also important to note that such constellations of interests express their demands through legitimate channels. Scientific studies are increasingly influential in policy debates. It is no accident that the original studies forecasting the fall in the level of the Caspian and Aral seas were conducted by researchers with close ties to the Ministry of Land Reclamation and Water Resources. The recent study showing that the water level of the Caspian Sea is actually rising was conducted by the Central Mathematical Economics Institute in Moscow. Many of the views of opponents to the river diversion scheme were published in *Sovetskaia Rossiia* (*Soviet Russia*), the organ of the Russian republic. In recent years, *Sovetskaia Rossiia* has advocated ending expensive Siberian and Far Eastern development projects, favoring instead increased investment in the heavily industrialized regions of the Russian republic west of the Urals.

These case studies also highlight the multiple roles played by regional and local party secretaries. The regional secretary is at the hub of all policy implementation, coordinating regional planning, interpreting central policy guidelines within the context of local conditions, resolving conflicts among enterprises and agencies, bargaining for regional appropriations with state officials, and bearing ultimate responsibility for the success or failure of policies within the region.[63] As the chief political figure in the region, he has been likened to the political bosses that dominated some American cities during the late 1800s and early 1900s.[64] The regional secretary, like the political boss, is the most powerful political figure in the area and thus can break through bureaucratic red tape to support a priority project. In lobbying central authorities for increased allocations for the region and in making appointments to influential posts, the party secretary also resembles a political boss.

Regional party secretaries also perform important coordinating and mediating functions; they act as political brokers. In Soviet society, as elsewhere, politics involves making compromises and adjustments among diverse bureaucratic groups and the interests they represent. Major officials of most of the powerful regional bureaucracies and organizations are represented on local party committees, and these are the arenas in which institutional conflicts are often expressed. In staffing regional party positions, the emphasis appears to be on people who have demonstrated the ability to bargain, to balance competing demands, and to forge effective coalitions in support of policy choices.

The broker model may understate the role and authority of the regional party secretary, whose power derives not only from brokering competing interests and claims on resources, but also from direct contacts to the highest political organs in the USSR. Regional secretaries constitute the single largest group in the CPSU Central Committee. In addition to mediating conflicting interests, they often have their own programs and policy agendas to promote, as the lobbying efforts of the Central Asian party secretaries for the Ob' River diversion project indicate. Regional secretaries are often in a position to use their contacts with top-level policymakers to promote certain programs or terminate others.

On many occasions, regional party secretaries also act as agents for change, applying political pressure to encourage reluctant administrative officials to innovate or to adopt new procedures. The heavily bureaucratized nature of the Soviet system and its centrally planned economy create enormous obstacles to innovation. Local administrators and factory managers see few rewards and many risks in innovation. In the absence of economic incentives that would stimulate innovation, the Party relies on political pressure from central party organs and local party officials to promote change.[65]

Finally, the regional party secretary has been compared to the prefect in France.[66] Structurally, the local and regional party organization shares several features with the prefect system. First, the regional party organization is a superagency over all other administrative units in the region. Second, the regional party organization reports only to its superior party authorities at the republic or all-union levels, not to regional or local soviets. Third, the regional party organization enjoys a comprehensive competence. Virtually no activity occurring within the region falls outside its jurisdiction (the only partial exception to this being the operation of military installations). Fourth, like the prefect, the regional party secretary can cut across the hierarchical lines of authority that exist between central ministries and regional administrators and enterprises, providing a valuable channel of horizontal communication that fosters integration and coordination. The party secretary is responsible for supervising the successful implementation of all policies in the region and reporting problems to the central authorities. He or she will be held accountable for the success or failure of those policies in the region.

Some features of the regional party secretary's role surpass those of the prefect, however. The CPSU, as an institution, is imbued with an ethos that provides regional party secretaries with more prestige and power than prefects. Unlike the prefect system and unlike any other institution in Soviet society, the CPSU maintains cells or primary party organizations in every institution, collective, enterprise, and housing bloc in the Soviet Union. The ability of the Party to extend its influence to the grass roots of the society may be its most significant source of power and authority.

The applicability and usefulness of any one of these models will change from issue to issue and over time. However, the direction of party policy since the 1970s has placed added emphasis on the agent for change and prefect roles of local party officials in relation to administrative agencies and officials. Local party organs and primary party organizations have been under considerable pressure to improve work discipline and quality of economic and administrative performance. These themes were especially pronounced at the November 1982 and June 1983 plenums of the Central Committee, and again at the Twenty-Seventh Party Congress in 1986. As long as systemic, decentralizing reforms that would facilitate innovations and change are not forthcoming, it will fall to local party secretaries to pressure local officials to innovate and change.

Thus, the dynamic interaction and conflict of pluralistic interests affect policy choices at the local and regional levels in the USSR. In many respects, political conflict in the USSR is not so different from policy disputes in other political systems; the differences lie in the style in which those conflicts are expressed and the manner in which they are resolved.

Notes

1. Cited in Robert A. Lewis and Richard H. Rowland, *Population Redistribution in the USSR* (New York: Praeger, 1979), 166.

2. Ibid.

3. Jack Underhill, *Soviet New Towns, Housing and National Growth Policy* (Washington, D.C.: U. S. Government Printing Office, 1976).

4. Cited in Carol W. Lewis and Stephen Sternheimer, *Soviet Urban Management* (New York: Praeger, 1979), 15–16.

5. Ibid.

6. Viktor Perevedentsev, "Novichok v gorode," *Molodoi kommunist* 7 (1971): 91–96.

7. Cited in Leslie Gelb, "What We Really Know about Russia," *New York Times Magazine*, 28 October 1984, p. 78.

8. M. Ia. Vydro, *Naselenie Moskvy* (Moscow: Statistika, 1976), 15.

9. Cited in Carol W. Lewis, "The Economic Functions of Local Soviets," in Everett M. Jacobs, ed., *Soviet Local Politics and Government* (London: George Allen & Unwin, 1983), 50.

10. Ibid.

11. Ibid.

12. Constitution of the USSR (1977), Article 147.

13. A. Miasnikov, "Khoziain dolzhen byt' odin," *Ekonomika i organizatsiia promyshlennogo proizvodstva* 4 (1977): 126.

14. Ibid.

15. Ibid.

16. Cited in Lewis, "Economic Functions of Local Soviets," 61.

17. Ibid., 55.

18. A. Kocherga, "Problemy territorialnogo-planirovania narodnogo blagosostoiania," *Planovoe khoziaistvo* 2 (1979): 92–99.

19. *Kommunist Estonii* 5 (1975): 105–110.

20. Theodore H. Friedgut, "A Local Soviet at Work: The 1970 Budget and Budget Discussions of the Oktiabr Borough Soviet of Moscow," in Jacobs, *Soviet Local Politics and Government*, 159–160. Reprinted by permission.

21. D. M. Chechot, *Administrativnaia iustitsiia* (Leningrad: Leningrad State University, 1973), 104.

22. Ibid., 105.

23. Gordon B. Smith, *The Soviet Procuracy* (Leiden, The Netherlands: Sijthoff Publishers, 1976).

24. Cited in Ellen Michiewicz, "Policy Issues in the Soviet Media System," in Erik P. Hoffmann, *The Soviet Union in the 1980s* (New York: Academy of Political Science, 1984), 114.

25. Cited in L. G. Churchward, "Public Participation in the USSR," in Jacobs, *Soviet Local Politics and Government*, 44.

26. Ibid.

27. Ibid.

28. See John Sallnow, "Soviet Wage Incentives and Regional Development Policies" (Paper presented to the Annual Convention of the American Association for the Advancement of Slavic Studies, Kansas City, October 21–25, 1983).

29. Ibid.

30. Cited in Andrew R. Bond, "Labor Retention, Social Planning, and Population Policy: The Example of the City of Norilsk" (Paper presented to the Annual Convention of the American Association for the Advancement of Slavic Studies, Kansas City, October 21–25, 1983).

31. Murray Feshbach and Stephen Rapaway, "Soviet Population and Manpower Trends and Policies," in *Soviet Economy in a New Perspective* (Washington, D.C.: U. S. Congress, Joint Economic Committee, 1976), 148.

32. Cited in Eric Jones, "The Bureaucratic Politics of Soviet Energy Policy" (Paper presented to the American Association for the Advancement of Slavic Studies, Washington, D. C., October 14–17, 1982).

33. *Materialy XXV-ogo s"ezda KPSS* (Moscow: Politizdat, 1976).

34. G. P. Bogomiakov, *Ekonomika i organizatsiia promyshlennogo proizvodstva* 5 (1976): 5–11.

35. A. A. Trofimuk, *Ekonomika i organizatsiia promyshlennogo proizvodstva* 4 (1976): 170–179.

36. For example, *Pravda*, 31 March 1978, p. 1.

37. *Pravda*, 2 April 1978, p. 1.

38. *Pravda*, 26 April 1978, pp. 1–2.

39. Arkady Lavaiants, "Grand-Scale Projects for Siberia," *Vodny Transport*, 1 January 1979, pp. 1–2.

40. A. Kosygin, *Pravda* and *Izvestiia*, 5 November 1978, p. 1.

41. Jones, "Bureaucratic Politics of Soviet Energy Policy," 45.

42. Cited in Thane Gustafson, "Soviet Energy Policy," in *The Soviet Economy in a Time*

of Change (Washington, D.C.: Joint Economic Committee, 1982), 19; and Office of Technology Assessment, *Technology and Soviet Energy Availability* (Washington, D.C.: OTA, November 1981), 100.

43. Ibid.

44. N. A. Tikhonov, "Povyshat' uroven' khoziaistvovaniia," in N. A. Tikhonov, *Izbrannie rechi i stat'i* (Moscow: Politika, 1980), 419.

45. Cited in Office of Technology Assessment, *Technology and Soviet Energy Availability,* 259.

46. See Thane Gustafson, *Reform in Soviet Politics: Lessons of Recent Policies on Land and Water* (Cambridge: Cambridge University Press, 1981), 76.

47. G. Voropaev, "Chtoby dat' vodu iugu," *Izvestiia,* 13 August 1978, p. 1.

48. See Gustafson, *Reform in Soviet Politics,* 77.

49. Ibid., p. 76.

50. *Materialy XXV-ogo s"ezda KPSS* (Moscow: Politizdat, 1976), 142, 197–199.

51. Ibid., 348.

52. See Gustafson, *Reform in Soviet Politics,* 78.

53. Ibid.

54. *Sovetskaia Rossiia,* 29 August 1984, p. 3.

55. O. Latifi, *Pravda,* 26 November 1984, p. 2.

56. Ibid.

57. Ibid.

58. N. Gladkov, *Pravda,* 24 November 1984, p. 2.

59. *Japan Times,* 7 June 1985, p. 8.

60. *Sovetskaia Rossiia,* 20 December 1985, p. 3.

61. *Sovetskaia Rossiia,* 3 January 1986, p. 3.

62. *Pravda,* 12 February 1986, p. 3.

63. For example, see Philip Stewart, *Political Power in the Soviet Union: A Study of Decision-Making in Stalingrad* (Indianapolis: Bobbs-Merrill, 1968); and Joel Moses, *Regional Party Leadership and Policy-Making in the USSR* (New York: Praeger, 1974).

64. The boss and broker roles of regional party secretaries are described in detail in Lewis and Sternheimer, *Soviet Union Management.*

65. For example, see Gordon B. Smith, "Organizational and Legal Problems in the Implementation of New Technology in the USSR," in Gordon B. Smith, et al. eds, *The Scientific-Technical Revolution and Soviet and East European Law* (Oxford and New York: Pergamon Press, 1981), 240–271.

66. Jerry F. Hough, *The Soviet Prefects: The Local Party Organs in Industrial Decision-Making* (Cambridge: Harvard University Press, 1969).

Selected Bibliography

Cattell, David T. *Leningrad: A Case History of Soviet Urban Government.* New York: Praeger, 1968.

Dienes, Leslie, and Theodore Shabad. *The Soviet Energy System.* New York: John Wiley & Sons, 1979.

Friedgut, Theodore H. *Political Participation in the USSR.* Princeton: Princeton University Press, 1979.

Frolic, Bernard M. "Decision-Making in Soviet Cities." *American Political Science Review* 1 (1972): 38–52.

Gustafson, Thane. *Reform in Soviet Politics: Lessons of Recent Policies on Land and Water.* Cambridge: Cambridge University Press, 1981.

Hill, Ronald J. *Soviet Political Elites: The Case of Tiraspol.* New York: St. Martin's Press, 1977.

Hough, Jerry F. *The Soviet Prefects: The Local Party Organs in Industrial Decision-Making*. Cambridge: Harvard University Press, 1969.

Jacobs, Everett M., ed. *Soviet Local Politics and Government*. London: George Allen & Unwin, 1983.

Lewis, Carol W., and Stephen Sternheimer. *Soviet Urban Management*. New York: Praeger, 1979.

Lewis, Robert A., and Richard H. Rowland. *Population Redistribution in the USSR: Impact on Society, 1897–1977*. New York: Praeger, 1979.

Lewis, Robert A., Richard H. Rowland, and Ralph S. Clem. *Nationality and Population Change in Russia and the USSR: An Evaluation of Census Data, 1897–1970*. New York: Praeger, 1976.

Moses, Joel C. *Regional Party Leadership and Policy-Making in the USSR*. New York: Praeger, 1974.

Powell, David E. "Political and the Urban Environment: The City of Moscow." *Comparative Political Studies* 3 (1977): 433–454.

Remnek, Richard B. *Social Scientists and Policy-Making in the USSR*. New York: Praeger, 1977.

Taubman, William. *Governing Soviet Cities: Bureaucratic Politics and Urban Development in the USSR*. New York: Praeger, 1973.

7

Socialist Legality and the Soviet Legal System

Two legal systems exist in the Soviet Union today, each functioning quite independently and bearing little resemblance to the other. The first, the one about which the average American citizen knows the least, is the legal system that, day in, day out, maintains law and order, enacts and enforces the law, and adjudicates the disputes that inevitably arise among citizens and institutions in modern societies. Existing alongside this legal system is an arbitrary and repressive system used to punish critics of the regime. To call the latter an apparatus for the administration of justice distorts the concept of justice beyond all recognition. In this second legal system, which is discussed in greater detail in Chapter 13, law and legal institutions are used in an arbitrary and brutal manner to suppress political, national, and religious dissent.

The problem confronting observers of Soviet legal policy is differentiating these two systems. All cases do not fall neatly into one system or the other. Rather, there exists a grey area of uncertainty in which an ordinary case may suddenly and unexpectedly take on a political character.

Soviet legal policy must bridge these two systems, providing a framework for the functioning of each. Since Stalin's death in 1953, even the repressive legal system has been limited by law and established procedures. The interests of the first and second legal systems may not always coincide. An advocate charged by law to provide a full and conscientious defense of his client in a political case will undoubtedly feel compromised by political risks to his career. Soviet legal policymakers are fully aware of these conflicts and attempt, where possible, to mediate them when they occur.

Studying Soviet legal policy formulation, then, provides an opportunity to witness the points of contact and divergence between the two legal systems, the varying interests of the bureaucracies charged with legal administration and the maintenance of law and order, and the shifts in power from one system to the other.

Before proceeding to legal policy-making, we must first consider the historical background and the structure of Soviet law and legal administration.

ORIGINS OF SOVIET LAW

Historically, Russian law belongs to the larger family of civil-law systems that are ultimately derived from the rules, principles, and practices elaborated in the ancient Roman Forum. Anglo-American students of Soviet law, who are accustomed to the common-law systems derived from England, are at a disadvantage in understanding Soviet law and legal procedure, while European scholars find the fundamentals of the Soviet legal system quite familiar. Thus, examining any given aspect of Soviet law involves determining whether it is a common characteristic of all civil-law systems or uniquely Soviet. Furthermore, only if no parallel exists in imperial Russian law does this aspect represent a unique trait of socialist law, rather than part of the Russian legal heritage acquired by the Soviets in 1917.

Historians have noted that civil law encouraged autocracy, while common law promoted democracy. The common-law principle was enshrined in the maxim "*Rex no debet esse sub homine sed sub Deo et Lege*" ("The king should not be under any man, but under God and the Law"), while the principle of civil law was "*Quod principi placuit legis habet vigorem*" ("The will of the sovereign has the force of law"). Generally, civil legal systems grant greater authority to state officials than do common-law systems.

Civil law and common law also differ markedly in the origins of laws. In common-law systems, judges make law by establishing precedent decisions. Laws thus change organically, growing as a result of piecemeal judicial decisions. In civil-law systems, all laws are the official enactments of executive or legislative bodies. These laws are gathered into codes and periodically updated and standardized. Greater importance is attached to official documents and reports in civil-law systems, and administrative officials are given broader discretionary powers.

Soviet law also displays many unique characteristics that derive from the existence of a socialist economy in the USSR and reflect the official ideology of Marxism-Leninism. Lenin accepted the Marxist conception of law and the State as instruments of coercion in the hands of the ruling class, the bourgeoisie. He envisaged the eventual transition to a communist society in which coercive instruments of the State and law would no longer be necessary and would, indeed, wither away. The situation Lenin confronted in the lawless and chaotic days following the overthrow of the Provisional Government in November 1917, however, called for a legal system to provide law and order. He wrote:

> There is no doubt that we live in a sea of illegality and that local influences are one of the greatest, if not the greatest obstacle to the establishment of legality and culture. . . . It is clear that in light of these conditions we have the firmest guarantee . . . that the Party create a small, centralized collegium capable of countering local influences, local and any bureaucratism and establishing an actual, uniform conception of legality in the entire republic and the entire federation.[1]

Yet, the writings of Marx and Engels provided only scant guidelines for Lenin to follow in constructing a socialist state. Marx was first and foremost a social critic, not an architect of the new economic and political order. In the area of legal administration, Marx offered even fewer prescriptions. He merely stated that all crime is the result of social and economic contradictions; when those differences are eliminated under socialism, crime will vanish. The only concrete precedents for the administration of justice available to Lenin were the informal, popularly elected revolutionary tribunals established during the Paris Commune (March 28–May 28, 1871) and the 1905 Revolution in Russia.

In 1917, revolutionary tribunals sprang up throughout Russia, spontaneously or under the supervision of the Bolsheviks. To promote participation of the masses in the judicial process, judges and lay assessors (lay judges) were elected by the people for many tribunals. In some instances, accused persons were brought before public gatherings, at which comrades would serve as social accusers or defenders. Guided by a revolutionary sense of justice, the tribunals cracked down on economic crimes. Members of the aristocratic and middle classes were often convicted on flimsy evidence. Crime increased dramatically. One account states that the numbers of robberies and murders in Moscow in 1918 were ten to fifteen times higher than in 1913.[2]

In the face of the deteriorating situation, the Bolsheviks grappled with the problem of coercion and law. Some favored an end to state coercion. For instance, one tribunal official proclaimed, "The socialist criminal code must not know punishment as a means of influence on the criminal."[3] Others were reluctant to abandon punishment altogether. Lenin opted for strict state coercion to stamp out vestiges of bourgeois society. In the political pamphlet *State and Revolution,* he had outlined the fundamental principles of revolutionary justice: smash the old state machine and set up new revolutionary tribunals; make these tribunals simple, informal, and open to mass participation; subordinate law to revolutionary goals and the Party (for all law has a class character; if it does not serve the Bolsheviks' purposes, it will be serving the purposes of counterrevolutionary elements); and use merciless force toward the eventual goal of reaching a society in which there will be no need for coercion. He concluded, "to curb increases in crime, hooliganism, bribery, speculation, and outrages of all kinds . . . we need time and we need an iron hand."[4]

Thus, in the early days of the Soviet regime, there coexisted two countervailing trends in Soviet law: the Marxist, utopian trend, which stressed both the withering away of the state and the creation of popular, informal tribunals to administer revolutionary justice, and the dictatorial trend, which advocated the use of law and legal institutions to suppress all opposition.[5]

The dictatorial trend in Soviet legal policy reached its zenith during the Stalin era. The authoritarian tone of legal policy was voiced by Andrei Vyshinsky, Stalin's Procurator-General and chief prosecutor in the great purge trials of the 1930s. Vyshinsky defined law as a set of rules laid down by the State and guaranteed by the State's monopoly of force.[6] In the wake of Stalin's dictatorial legal policies, utopianism all but vanished. Vyshinsky, speaking before a group of public prosecutors in 1936, stated that "the old twaddle about the mobilization of socially active workers . . . must be set aside; something new is needed at the present time."[7]

Much of the legal administration of the Stalin years was carried on outside of established judicial institutions. Special boards of the Ministry of Internal Affairs were set up to facilitate campaigns against anti-Soviet elements and to silence potential opponents. The boards were given extraordinary powers and were not required to follow established judicial procedure. They had the authority to imprison or exile for a term of up to five years anyone considered to be "socially dangerous." Proceedings of the boards were not public, the accused had no right to counsel, and there was no appeal of verdicts. The boards consigned hundreds of thousands of Soviet citizens to "corrective labor camps." Some Western analysts estimate the prison labor force by 1941 at 3.5 million workers.[8] Thus, the security police apparatus was the single largest employer in the Soviet Union and wielded not only political but tremendous economic power.

The secret police combed the streets at night in their infamous "black marias" (black sedans), stopping at apartments to pick up people whom "informers" had reported. Rumors or a careless comment by a child at school were sufficient to result in imprisonment or death for a parent. Many Soviet citizens recall the years when they had suitcases packed with warm clothing waiting by the door in case they should be awakened by the secret police in the night and taken away.

Change was imminent after Stalin's death in 1953. Stalin's successors moved quickly to destroy the police state and to rebuild party and state organs, including legal institutions. The Party reestablished control over the secret police. Lavrenti Beria, Stalin's head of the Ministry of Internal Affairs, was arrested for crimes against the State and executed.

Having endured constant and pervasive fear for more than two decades, the Soviet people were ready for a respite from dictatorial coercion. Seizing upon the issue of de-Stalinization in order to solidify his position in the struggle for power, Nikita Khrushchev introduced far-reaching legal reforms. Following his lead, Soviet jurists began to attack the coercive use of law to bolster the monopoly on state power and urged changes in Soviet criminal and civil legislation. The special boards of the Ministry of Internal Affairs were abolished. All criminal cases, including political crimes, had to be prosecuted in the people's courts with regular judicial procedure, and the secret police could no longer make arrests without the authorization of a judge or procurator. The Procuracy, which had suffered under Stalin's regime, was strengthened.

A new trend in Soviet law began to take shape during the de-Stalinization of the late 1950s. This new trend, represented by the catchwords "socialist legality," stressed the need for protecting the procedural and substantive rights of citizens in relation to the State and for all laws to be strictly and uniformly enforced. An editorial in the Party's theoretical journal, *Kommunist,* attacked the traditional Soviet interpretation of legality and stressed the need for a concept of legality designed to protect the rights and interests of citizens.[9] A study published by the USSR Academy of Sciences argued that citizens' rights are even binding on state authorities. It concluded: "That the organs of state power be bound by law is an indispensable condition for the existence of legality and the subjective rights of citizens in relations with state authorities. For an organ of power to be bound by law means that it must fully observe the requirements contained in legal standards and unswervingly fulfill all obligations imposed on it by the law in the citizens' interests."[10]

Other Soviet jurists argued that cases involving citizens' personal and property rights should be examined by the courts, rather than by administrative agencies. They further demanded that state officials bear material and criminal responsibility for such violations.[11] Unlike either the utopian or dictatorial concepts of law, socialist legality began to resemble the Western concept of "rule of law."

Socialist legality coexisted with the dictatorial and utopian trends throughout Khrushchev's tenure. It was eclipsed somewhat, however, by a resurgence of legal utopianism in the early 1960s. Khrushchev, a poorly educated, blustery man from a small farming and mining village in the Ukraine, never fully mastered the controls of the complex bureaucracies that dominate the Soviet system. Distrusting bureaucracies and bureaucrats, he turned to the people for support. In order to stem crime, he urged housing units, factories, and shops to resuscitate comrades' courts and other informal tribunals. By the end of 1963, approximately 197,000 comrades' courts were disposing of more than 4 million cases per year.[12] Khrushchev also encouraged the formation of "antiparasite courts," informal tribunals in housing districts and factories that brought pressure to bear on those who refused to work and others deemed to be social "parasites." Voluntary citizens' brigades (*druzhiny*) patrolled the streets to maintain law and order. As if to symbolize the decentralization of legal administration, Khrushchev abolished the All-Union Ministry of Justice, leaving only the fifteen republic ministries.

The legal establishment in general and the Procuracy in particular chafed under Khrushchev's policies. Cases were routinely channeled to comrades' courts for disposition, circumventing the established judicial institutions. Reports of comrades' tribunals meting out prejudicial, arbitrary justice and meddling in nonjudicial matters were common.

With Khrushchev's ouster in 1964, however, the legal profession took steps to bring "popular justice" under control. Jurists attacked the utopian notion of public participation in the administration of justice. A campaign was undertaken to professionalize legal administration and increase the legal competence of judicial personnel. "Socialist legality" again became the principal slogan of the legal apparatus. The return to socialist legality was consonant with the general trend under Brezhnev and his successors of allowing more input from specialists in formulating policy. Legal policies today are carried out primarily through established bureaucratic channels, not through informal, social institutions such as the comrades' courts, although these bodies continue to exist.

Beginning in the early 1960s and extending into the Brezhnev era, there was also a resurgence of the dictatorial trend in law. The powers of the police were expanded, new legislation severely restricted public demonstrations, and capital punishment was reintroduced for a wide variety of offenses, resulting in a rapid increase in the number of executions.

Due to increasing economic pressures and the generally more conservative bureaucratic leadership style of the Brezhnev regime, the emphasis of socialist legality shifted from protecting the interests of individual citizens to protecting the economic interests of the State. The Twenty-Fifth Party Congress in 1976 stressed the need for legal regulation of economic activity to increase production, to strengthen the economic system, and to counter fraud, theft of socialist property, and the padding of accounts and plan-fulfillment reports. R. A. Rudenko, the late procurator-general, noted that the Procuracy had been ordered to strengthen its supervision of legality in all economic organizations.[13] The 1979 Statute on the Procuracy also incorporated several new provisions relating to economic violations. For example, Article 3 states that "the fight against violations concerning the protection of socialist property" is one of the fundamental responsibilities of procurators.[14] Furthermore, the laws protecting socialist property and the punishments for economic crimes were substantially strengthened in the January 1983 revision of the Criminal Code of the RSFSR.

During the fifteen-month rule of Iurii Andropov, legal measures were used to enhance work discipline. Police rounded up idle workers in movie theaters, bathhouses, and stores and demanded to see their work documents. They sometimes called employers to verify that the apprehended workers were not supposed to be on the job. Under Andropov's leadership, new laws were enacted that raised the penalties for absenteeism, tardiness, drunkennesss on the job, managerial incompetence, and theft of state property by workers. The campaign for improving labor discipline culminated in the enactment of the Law on Labor Collectives. The new legislation enlists the support of the labor collectives in the fight for better work discipline by awarding bonuses on the basis of collective, rather than individual, performance. The work discipline and anticorruption campaigns begun by Andropov faltered under his successor, Konstantin Chernenko, but have been renewed with increasing vigor by Mikhail Gorbachev.

While socialist legality is the predominant trend in Soviet legal policy today, the dictatorial and utopian trends are not dead. The recent trials of Soviet dissidents, the house-arrest of Andrei Sakharov in Gorky, and the occasional harassment of Western citizens in the Soviet Union indicate a potential resurgence of dictatorial methods. Another ominous sign of this resurgence is the revision of the law on criminal liability for state crimes, which deals with subversion. In January 1985, the law was amended to add "passing official secrets to foreigners" to the list of antistate crimes. Violation of this provision of the law is punishable by the deprivation of freedom for a term of up to three years.[15] Given the fact that "official secrets" in the USSR include crime statistics; information on fires, plane crashes, and other disasters; health statistics; as well as scientific and technical information, the new law is expected to have a chilling effect on scientific publication and international scientific cooperation.

At the same time, there has been a tendency toward decriminalization of some petty offenses, handing them over to administrative agencies, the comrades' courts, and labor collectives. Alcoholism, drug abuse, and prostitution are now treated more as medical and psychological problems than as criminal violations. Fewer offenses, especially those of minors, are being punished by incarceration. There is a growing awareness today in the USSR among social workers, juvenile affairs officers, the courts, police, and prosecutors that incarceration in a correctional institution may further corrupt, rather than rehabilitate, young offenders.

SOVIET LEGAL INSTITUTIONS

The predominance of socialist legality today in the USSR is in large part the result of an increasing role of jurists in the policy-making process. Legal policy in the Soviet Union is formulated by numerous agencies, bureaucracies, and groups, each representing particular interests. Generally, the interests that come into play in the formulation of legal policy in the Soviet Union coincide with the various occupations and specialties within the legal profession. Thus, the police and other organs of social control are generally proponents of a tough "law and order" stance, while defense lawyers and criminologists tend to favor a less rigid policy. The occupational differences within the Soviet legal profession are accentuated by the existence of large bureaucracies that enjoy a degree of independence from the Party and that have identifiable institutional interests on policy questions. They create a sense of common, professional identity, frequently enhanced by a shared set of values developed in uniform, specialized training. These bureaucratic groups also maintain some form of access to public opinion, through which their interests can be voiced.[16] For example, the views of Soviet prosecutors are expressed in the Procuracy's journal, *Sotsialisticheskaia zakonnost'* (Socialist Legality), while the interests of judges are presented in the journal of the RSFSR Ministry of Justice, *Sovetskaia iustitsiia* (Soviet Justice).

The development of a strong identification of occupational interests is fostered by a high degree of career stability among Soviet jurists. For example, 30 percent of all prosecutors have worked for the Procuracy from three to ten years, and 50 percent have worked for more than ten years.[17] More than half of all advocates have at least ten years of experience in the *advokatura,* while more than 75 percent of all judges have been working in that capacity for five years or more.[18]

Finally, the bureaucracies representing the occupational interests of Soviet jurists provide each group with an "official presence" in the policy-making process. Some, such as the Procuracy and the Ministry of Internal Affairs, have representatives in the Central Committee, the Politburo, or other influential policy-making bodies. The bureaucracies involved in legal policy implementation also include among their numbers many party members, who communicate information relevant to policy-making up through the Party's ranks. Approximately 74 percent of all Soviet jurists are party members.[19]

We now examine the principal bureaucratic groups that are involved in legal policy-making and implementation in the Soviet Union.

The Procuracy. By far the most powerful institution in the Soviet administration of justice today is the Procuracy, the hierarchical organization representing all public prosecutors, from the city or village level up to the Procurator-General of the USSR. The Procuracy's central position in the administration of justice derives from its wide range of functions pertaining to criminal and administrative matters. The procurator is involved at every stage in the criminal process. The arrest of a suspect and the search for evidence require the procurator's written authorization. In Soviet criminal procedure, the prosecution of cases proceeds through two stages: preliminary investigation and trial. The procurator participates in both stages. In most cases, investigators are procuratorial officials. Also falling within the realm of procuratorial action are the review or appeal of criminal and civil cases; the supervision of prisons, prisoner complaints, parole, and the release of prisoners; the supervision of actions of the police and secret police; the supervision of juvenile commissions; and the supervision of the legal operation of all government bodies, enterprises, officials, and social organizations. This latter function, the supervision of administrative and economic officials and bodies, resembles that of the Swedish ombudsman.[20]

The Procuracy employs approximately 15,000 lawyers, or almost 12 percent of the legal profession.[21] Supervised by the Procuracy are another 18,000 investigators, comprising over 14 percent of the legal profession.[22] The power of the Procuracy does not derive solely from its size or extensive functions in the legal system. Procurators also enjoy the greatest prestige of any legal occupation. N. S. Aleksandrov, Dean of the Juridical Faculty of Leningrad State University, reports that most law students want to become procurators.[23] Traditionally, the top law students in each graduating class go to work for the Procuracy, while less-distinguished graduates become jurisconsults, advocates, or judges—in that order.

In addition to having a procuratorial journal, the Procuracy can express its institutional interests through the Procurator-General, the only practicing jurist represented in the CPSU Central Committee.

Advokatura. Gaining in popularity, but without the institutional might of the Procuracy, is the Soviet bar—the *advokatura*. Defense attorneys in the Soviet Union are organized into "colleges" of about 150 lawyers each. These colleges maintain consultation bureaus in virtually every town and city throughout the Soviet Union. Each bureau has a staff of approximately twenty advocates.[24] Here Soviet citizens may seek legal advice on a vast array of questions: divorce, custody, inheritance, property rights, housing disputes, product liability complaints, and so forth. The colleges also provide legal defense for people accused of criminal offenses. The Soviet Constitution, ratified in 1977, provides that a defendant is guaranteed the right to legal counsel and that legal assistance will be provided free of charge if the defendant cannot afford a lawyer.[25] Legal fees in the USSR are determined by the State, based on the salary of the citizen and the amount of time required by the lawyer. Fees are set intentionally very low to make legal services affordable for the average citizen. Soviet émigré jurists note, however, that advocates routinely expect and receive under-the-table payments, "gifts," and other "favors" in exchange for timely and competent legal advice. Such "gifts" can more than double the income of the advocate.[26]

There are approximately eighteen thousand advocates in the Soviet Union.[27] They are not represented by any professional organization, nor do they have a journal or organ through which to express their occupational interests. The absence of an organizational structure prevents Soviet advocates from consolidating their political power and has long been a point of contention among advocates. Most lawyers enter the *advokatura* at an advanced stage of their careers, usually after experience in the Procuracy or the courts. The absence of a standardized training program and this mixed career pattern further retard the development of strong group cohesion.

The Judiciary. According to a 1960s law of the Russian Republic, any Soviet citizen who is at least twenty-five-years-old and possesses electoral rights can be elected to the position of judge for a term of five years. No prior legal experience or education is necessary. In practice, however, more than 95 percent of all judges have a higher legal education.[28]

Given the crucial role of the judge in the Soviet legal system, it is not surprising that the Party carefully screens all candidates for election to the bench. Virtually all Soviet judges above the local level are party members, and all judges fall under the Party's power of appointment, or *nomenklatura*.[29]

As in other civil-law systems, Soviet judges play an active part in judicial proceedings. They are the first to call for evidence, question witnesses, and cross-examine—before either the prosecution or the defense. Their function is not only to determine innocence or guilt, but also to educate the accused and all present in the courtroom. Soviet judges are an important instrument of socialization. When pronouncing sentence, judges often berate the accused for failing to uphold socialist values, for being drunk in public, or for setting a bad example for children.

In the court of first instance, one judge presides with the assistance of two people's assessors. People's assessors are ordinary citizens, elected at general meetings of factories, offices, collective farms, or residential blocs for a term of two years. Their function resembles that of a jury in a common-law system. They do not decide mere guilt or innocence, however, but are full, participating members of the bench with the right to call and question witnesses, examine evidence, and set punishment. All judicial decisions are voted on in closed chambers, so it is not known what impact people's assessors have on the courts' decisions. It is assumed that the judges' prestige and legal education are deciding factors in the resolution of cases. At the appellate level and above, where the questions under review are procedural or involve technical points of law, cases are decided by panels of professional judges. While people's assessors have little input into the policy process, Soviet judges are well-organized and represented by the USSR Ministry of Justice and the fifteen republic ministries.

Other Jurists. Among the remaining legal specialties, two deserve special note—namely, jurisconsults and legal scholars. Jurisconsults are legal advisers who act as counsel to governmental agencies and departments, enterprises, factories, and state farms. Approximately twenty-nine thousand jurisconsults work in the Soviet economy. Although they constitute the single largest portion of the Soviet legal profession, they are not organized into a centralized bureaucracy and do not display any professional cohesion. Rather, jurisconsults tend to identify their own personal and career interests with the interests of the institutions in which they work, so much so that they are periodically criticized and sometimes prosecuted for covering up illegalities in the agencies and enterprises with which they are affiliated.[30]

Legal scholars in the Soviet Union number approximately 3,500. For the most part, they are affiliated with universities or juridical institutes that train jurists. Some juridical scholars are also affiliated with the Ministry of Justice, the Procuracy's Institute for the Study of the Causes and Prevention of Crime, the Institute for the Improvement of Soviet Legislation, or the

Institute of State and Law of the Academy of Sciences.

Although legal scholars do not have a distinct organization to represent their interests, they enjoy a high level of group awareness. This is partly the result of the frequent interaction among members of the scholarly community through symposia, conferences, and numerous legal journals and periodicals. The opinions of Soviet jurists are respected and sought by policymakers, especially in drafting new legislation.

THE PARTY AND LEGAL POLICY-MAKING

Superseding these diverse interest groups in the making and implementation of legal policy is the CPSU. The Party, as Lenin stated, is the self-proclaimed "mind, honor, and conscience of the Soviet people." Political decision-making authority lies in its highest ranks. The Party Program calls for the "further enhancement of the role and importance of the Communist Party as the leading and guiding force of Soviet society." In the realm of judicial policy, the program states: "The strengthening of the legal basis of state and social life, the unswerving observance of socialist legality and law and order and the improvement of the work of the judicial organs, organs of supervision by the prosecutor's office and justice and internal affairs organs have been and remain a matter of constant concern for the Party."[31]

The comments of Mikhail Gorbachev before the recent Twenty-Seventh Party Congress clearly link socialist legality to the economic goals of the regime: "A good deal of work has been done recently to strengthen law and order in all spheres of the life of society. But efforts in this area cannot slacken in the least. We must continue to improve the quality of Soviet laws. Our legislation—civil, labor, financial, administrative, economic, criminal— should more actively help in the introduction of economic methods of management, effective supervision over the measure of labor and consumption, and the implementation of the principles of social justice."[32]

The Party's hegemony in the administration of justice derives from several sources. Party approval is required before a person may be appointed to any influential position in the legal apparatus: judge, procurator, advocate, or police official. This power to fill personnel positions— nomenklatura—is a significant control device that the Party uses to maintain its strict hold on administration. Party organs also directly nominate persons for election, including judges and even people's assessors. The personnel screening process extends to the lowest levels of the party organization. The result is that all those who investigate, prosecute, defend, preside, and even study the administration of justice in the Soviet Union must pass through a system of political filters before they can take office or assume their responsibilities.

The Party also plays a central role in coordinating the work of all judicial bodies. Party officials meet with local law-enforcement bodies on a frequent and regular basis to plan anticrime campaigns. A single campaign against a specific type of crime in a region of the USSR might require the participation of the Procuracy, police, courts, the republic's ministry of trade, factory managers, comrades' courts, trade unions, councils on crime prevention, and primary party organizations. Commissions on juvenile affairs; Komsomol organizations; fire, public safety, and pollution inspection agencies, and the State Standards Committee might also be involved. The Party plays the central role of overseeing the general coordination of these agencies.

Despite the upgrading of the "judicial independence clause" of the 1977 Constitution, Soviet jurists have never fully adopted the notion of an independent judiciary in the Western sense. While overt party interference in nonpolitical cases is generally ruled out, party organs are instructed to play an active role in supervising the judicial process. An editorial in the USSR Ministry of Justice's journal, *Sovetskaia iustitsiia,* stated: "Guidance by the Communist Party surpasses all political and judicial means of assuring that the courts observe socialist legality in their actions. . . . The task of local Party organizations is, while not interfering in the judicial process, actively to influence courts to improve their work, to instill in officers of the court a high sense of discipline, and fulfill Party and government decisions."[33]

In 1956, a study group of the prestigious Institute of State and Law of the Academy of Sciences was impaneled to address the issue of the legal abuses of the Stalin years and to suggest measures to avoid repetitions. While establishing the principle of noninterference in legal cases, the authors concluded that "the court does not stand and cannot stand outside of politics . . . beyond the guidance of the Party."[34]

There is a fine line, however, between party supervision and direction, on the one hand, and party interference, on the other. Impermissible party interference in the administration of justice occurs when a party organ or official directly intervenes in the disposition of an individual case by bringing political pressure to bear on the arresting officer, investigator, prosecutor, judge, or defense attorney. Former Soviet defense lawyers who have emigrated to the West doubt whether judges receive instructions in individual nonpolitical cases. They note, however, a more subtle influence. "Judges get the word from the way the wind is blowing."[35] This is especially the case during organized campaigns against various crimes. During an antibribery campaign, one Soviet advocate privately exclaimed, "If you have a bribery case these days, you might as well give up."[36] Thus, anticrime campaigns tend to blur the line between administration and adjudication. During campaigns, there is the risk that party and police organs will usurp the proper role of judicial institutions.

Party interference is not restricted to anticrime campaigns. Advocates, judges, procurators, police, and investigators are required to make monthly, quarterly, and annual reports to the party apparatus on the cases in which they have been involved. A former advocate from Leningrad observed that too many acquittals are frowned on by party officials.[37] Rapid increases of the crime rate also reflect badly on police officials, procurators, and local party secretaries.

Even more damaging to professional careers than underfulfilling quotas for arrests, convictions, or reduction of the crime rate is the discovery of a major scandal involving official corruption or organized crime. Regional party secretaries are ultimately responsible for coordinating all services of the central ministries in their respective regions.[38] This includes supervision of the orderly fulfillment of economic development programs, provision of social services, and maintenance of law and order. Should top-ranking personnel in a principal industrial enterprise be arrested for embezzlement or theft of property from the factory, should a scandal surface concerning graft and corruption in the allocation of housing or other social services, or should it come to light that the police and the Procuracy in the region have conspired to falsify reports understating the extent of crime, the regional secretary is likely to be held personally accountable. For example, a well-publicized case of high-level corruption in the Azerbaidzhan Republic resulted in five executions and prison sentences for fifty-nine other officials, including several local party secretaries.[39] If the secretary manages to save his or her own position, it will be only because he or she has successfully disassociated from subordinates—the factory manager, the heads of regional social service departments, or the chief of police and the procurator.

SOVIET JURISTS AND THE POLICY PROCESS

Specialist involvement in the making of legal policy varies according to the different levels of Soviet bureaucracy. At the highest levels, specialists are frequently appointed to commissions that draft new legislation. Drafting commissions are usually impaneled by the Supreme Soviet and function under the aegis of its standing Committee on Legislative Proposals. Special temporary commissions are also impaneled by the Presidium of the Supreme Soviet. These special commissions do more than mere technical work, such as drafting or editing; they usually study issues, policies, and tactics and elaborate policy directions.[40] Commissions are likely to be large, frequently numbering over twenty-five members. Their work usually extends over a period of two or more years.

Specialist groups, as well as the general public, often attempt to influence legal policy in the Soviet Union by writing articles and letters to the press. Every year, *Pravda* and *Izvestiia* each receive more than 500,000 letters to the editor. The bulk of these letters suggest policy changes or criticize inept or illegal administrative actions. Letters may bring abuses to the attention of prosecutors, who institute investigations that often end in the prosecution of the officials responsible.

The press is also a legitimate forum for proposing legislative changes at the national level.[41] After the draft of the 1977 Constitution was published, several months of public debate followed. More than 400,000 proposals were received for amending various articles of the draft. Several revisions offered by Soviet citizens in letters to the press were incorporated into the final document, including the formal recognition of voter mandates.[42]

Of course, letters and their contents are subject to careful scrutiny before publication. Real limits are imposed on the range of proposals and criticisms that may be expressed in the USSR. In many cases, the political leadership has used the publication of an article as a means of floating a trial balloon on a policy initiative in order to stimulate responses from various sectors of Soviet society. A well-documented instance of this was Khrushchev's proposed adoption of "production education" in 1959, which precipitated a two-year public debate in the press and behind-the-scenes administrative maneuvering.[43]

The press is not only a forum for affecting policy formation but is also an effective tool in policy implementation. It is largely through the scholarly and popular press that the leadership signals what policies it is pursuing. Sample court cases are carefully selected for publication in order to bring certain types of crime to the attention of prosecutors, judges, and investigators. The press also attempts to mobilize popular involvement in anticrime campaigns. For instance, after the Politburo announced measures to fight alcoholism in the spring of 1985, a flurry of articles appeared in major newspapers and journals depicting the legal, medical, and social consequences of alcohol abuse.[44]

Thus, specialist groups attempt to influence the policy process through their participation on commissions that draft legislation and through their published comments and articles. The most pronounced and continuous influence on policymakers by specialists, however, occurs in regional soviets and party committees. Local soviets frequently include key members of local party committees, chiefs of administrative departments, and managers of crucial factories or enterprises. Similarly, local party committees include deputies of local soviets, factory managers, and chiefs of influential administrative organs. Among the administrative officials represented in these local bodies are the chiefs of the *militsiia* and, frequently, the chief procurators of the respective regions. Thus, members of the legal profession are represented in the state and party organs that coordinate the implementation of national policies at the local level.

Participation of legal specialists in the policy process is also achieved through expanded plenums of local party committees, in which noncommittee members are specifically requested to participate. When a *raion* party committee discusses measures to raise the level of "legal culture" and to combat violations in factories and enterprises, for example, factory managers, procurators, and other key officials are usually invited to attend. Although, as Joel Moses notes, the chance for participation by occupation groups at these expanded plenums is limited, they provide at least some symbolic participation.[45] Since the Yaroslavl Resolution in November 1969, which criticized local party organizations for failing to draw upon expertise from a more varied cross-section of sources, party committees have shown particular interest in broadening the representativeness of plenums.

Local-level integration of legal specialists into the policy process also occurs in periodic conferences and seminars sponsored by local state and party bodies. These conferences and seminars provide information for regional party secretaries and give specialists an opportunity to influence policy by interacting directly with members of local party committees. According to a study by Peter Solomon, legal scholars frequently use presentations at such gatherings for advocating positions on policy issues.[46]

Finally, legal policy in the Soviet Union, as in other countries, is influenced by personal connections and private communications between decision-makers and legal specialists. The various formal meetings, conferences, and seminars that bring together legal specialists and policy-makers allow specialists to maintain and develop important contacts. The private, informal conversations that occur at such gatherings may well prove more significant for the formulation of legal policy than the formal reports and remarks presented at conference sessions.

Overall, the impact of Soviet jurists on legal policy appears to be considerable. Contrary to what some observers suggest, there is often specialist participation before decisions are reached.[47] In fact, the policy process might even be faulted for allowing considerably more specialist involvement on the input side of the process than in policy implementation and evaluation.

LAW AND THE CONSTITUTION OF THE USSR

The present Constitution of the USSR is the fourth such document to be ratified since the October Revolution of 1917. Each of the four constitutions reflected a particular historical phase in the development of Soviet society. Thus, the adoption of new constitutions provides the system with a sense of progress toward the goal of the attainment of communism.

The first constitution of the Russian Soviet Federated Socialist Republic was enacted in 1918 in order to consolidate the victories of the Bolsheviks. The document stressed the revolutionary nature of the society, specified the rights of the "toilers and exploited peoples," placed all power in the soviets, adopted a federal state structure, abolished private ownership of the land, and established the fulfillment of socialism as the immediate goal of the society.

The incorporation of new territories into the republic during and after the Civil War led to the formal adoption of a federation in 1922 and, thus, the need for a new constitution. That document, ratified in 1924, differed from its predecessor primarily in specifying and differentiating the powers of federal bodies and the powers of the constituent republics.

The "Stalin Constitution," ratified in 1936, redefined the USSR as "a socialist state of workers and peasants" and enshrined the CPSU as "vanguard." It reaffirmed socialist ownership of the means of production and created the Supreme Soviet (consisting of two houses) to replace the Congress of Soviets.

During Khrushchev's de-Stalinization drive, Soviet jurists began to urge the ratification of a new constitution that would reflect the achievements of the USSR and also would further extend the notion of citizens' rights. A drafting commission was established in 1962, but the new constitution was not ratified until 1977, in honor of the sixtieth anniversary of the Bolshevik Revolution. The 1977 Constitution does not differ radically from its predecessors; in fact, the preamble stresses the continuity of Soviet law. The document defines the USSR as a "socialist state of all the people" and formally recognizes the CPSU as "the leading and guiding force in Soviet society."[48]

The Constitution of the USSR plays a fundamentally different role in the Soviet legal system than, for instance, the United States Constitution does in the American system. The Soviet Constitution embodies the highest statement of the goals and principles of the Soviet system of government. It defines the powers of various state bodies, including the soviets at all levels, the Council of Ministers, the courts, the Procuracy, and other state bodies. Unlike the United States Constitution, however, the Constitution in the USSR is not a binding legal document in the sense that its articles are cited in court determinations. Constitutional provisions in the Soviet Union have legal force only when they are implemented in one of the codes of law of the various republics. Many constitutional provisions remain unrealized, due to the absence of implementing legislation. For example, Article 58 states: "Actions of officials that contravene the law or exceed their powers, and infringe the rights of citizens, may be appealed in a court in the manner prescribed by law."[49] As yet, however, no code of administrative law has been adopted in any republic to implement the provisions of this "guarantee."

The present Constitution differs from its 1936 predecessor by making explicit the relationship between the rights and the obligations of Soviet citizens. Constitutional rights are bounded or restricted by the extent to which citizens fulfill their obligations to the State. Thus, Article 50 reads: "*In accordance with the interests of the people and in order to strengthen and develop the socialist system,* citizens of the USSR are guaranteed freedom of speech, of the press, and of assembly, meetings, street processions, and demonstrations" (italics added).[50] In other words, freedom of speech is granted only insofar as one does not say anything that might weaken or challenge the social system.

Escorting a group of American political officials on a tour of a Leningrad factory, the author noted a poster that graphically illustrated the connection between rights and duties, as seen by Soviet citizens. The poster depicted a long-haired Russian youth wearing Western jeans. The youth held one briefcase marked *Rights* close to his chest, while he attempted to discard another suitcase marked *Duties*.

The double-edged nature of rights and duties in the USSR is also reflected in the 1979 Statute on the Procuracy. That document states that one of the principal responsibilities of the Procuracy is to protect citizens' freedoms and rights, "which are organically linked with the duty to supervise the fulfillment of their responsibilities."[51]

CRIME IN THE USSR

According to Marx, crime is the manifestation of class antagonisms. With the abolition of classes under socialism, all crime should vanish. While crime has not vanished entirely in the USSR today, certain types of criminal activity are much less prevalent than in Western societies. Comparing crime rates is, however, virtually impossible because crime statistics in the Soviet Union are considered "state secrets." Nevertheless, there appear to be far fewer robberies, murders, and other violent crimes in Soviet cities than in the United States. Strict gun control, the threat of harsh punishment, the omnipresent police, and the low incidence of drug abuse are largely accountable for this. There is also less monetary incentive for violent crime in the USSR than in the West. Most Soviet citizens have ample amounts of money; consequently, there is less motivation to commit robbery. The theft of desirable consumer goods is quite common, however, because they are in great demand and difficult to obtain legally.

Soviet sources indicate that between 80 and 85 percent of all violent crimes are committed under the influence of alcohol and usually involve family members, close friends, or neighbors.[52] Committing a crime under the influence of alcohol is not a mitigating factor, according to Soviet law, but an aggravating factor. Alcohol abuse, which is widespread in the USSR, is listed as the primary cause of almost three-fourths of all divorces.[53] Overcrowded housing conditions combined with alcohol abuse often result in domestic violence.

Anonymous street crime is much less frequent in the Soviet Union than in other societies, although increasingly there are reports in the Soviet press of youth gangs attacking total strangers on the street "simply for something to do."[54] Juveniles account for approximately 12 percent of all murders, 22 percent of all robberies, 59 percent of all burglaries, and 49 percent of all rapes.[55] The portrait of the juvenile offender in the USSR does not differ greatly from that in other societies: the offender is usually male, lives in a city, comes from a broken home, and undertakes delinquent acts while under the influence of alcohol and as a member of a group. School dropouts are twenty-four times more likely to engage in criminal activity than are juveniles who remain in school. Similarly, youths who come from homes in which violence is common are nine to ten times more likely to become juvenile offenders.[56] A Soviet sociological study of juvenile offenders found that three-quarters were introduced to alcohol in the home—almost half before the age of thirteen.[57] As a rite of passage around the age of twelve or thirteen, a boy is expected to split a bottle of vodka with his father to celebrate becoming a man.

As Soviet society becomes increasingly urban, the traditional family structure is breaking down. Grandparents, who were traditionally responsible for child-rearing and supervision, are now often left in the countryside. In urban areas today, fewer than 15 percent of all families have a grandparent living in the house.[58] Approximately 80 percent of all women work, often leaving school-aged children to fend for themselves after school. (Russian men are notorious for failing to assume any household tasks, including child care.) Furthermore, the high incidence of divorce—approaching 50 percent in some cities—results in large numbers of juveniles without fathers in the home, as women almost always get custody in divorce cases. Pioneer and Komsomol organizations try to fill the void by sponsoring afterschool activities, but these programs do not seem to appeal to crime-prone youth.

While violent crime is not as common as in many Western societies, economic crime is widespread. With the average salary of a Russian only $250 per month, many workers consider it their "right" to steal from their employer. The best-quality merchandise is routinely saved under the counter for family and friends in exchange for "gifts" ranging from vodka to money. Automobile assembly-line workers supplement their incomes by stealing spare parts and selling them on the black market. (There are no spare-parts stores in the USSR, and thus headlights, taillights, antifreeze, and windshield wipers are in great demand.) As meat shortages became more prevalent in the early 1980s, some Soviet engineers and technicians reportedly left their posts in research and design bureaus and took menial jobs in cafeterias, restaurants, and other food establishments. The reason? In the research and design bureaus, there is nothing worth stealing, whereas in the food industry, one can always take home a shank of ham in a lunch pail.

The Party has repeatedly launched campaigns against the theft of state property, but they only curtail the activity temporarily and do not stamp it out altogether. Persons who are tried, found guilty, and given criminal penalties tend to be high-ranking party or state officials engaged in grand-scale theft of state property. In most cases, an employee apprehended for petty theft—stealing yarn from a textile factory or meat from a butcher—would receive a warning from a comrades' court, a small fine, or, at most, dismissal. With widespread public acceptance of petty theft, mild penalties, and the small chance of detection, there is little likelihood that the theft of state property will end soon.

PUNISHMENT AND REHABILITATION OF OFFENDERS

Marxist-Leninist ideology is perhaps more evident in sentencing and corrections than anywhere else in the Soviet legal system. Soviet ideology stresses state property over private property, and this is reflected in criminal law. The maximum sentence for the theft of personal property is two years; the maximum sentence for the theft of state property is three years.[59] Negligent destruction of private property may be punished by deprivation of freedom for a term of up to one year, while the term extends to three years for the negligent destruction of state property.[60]

Some activities that are normal in other societies are illegal and strictly punished in the USSR for ideological reasons. According to Marxist-Leninist doctrine, charging interest, speculation, and profiteering are all means of obtaining "unearned income" and are, therefore, exploitative. Speculation is defined as "buying up and reselling goods for the purpose of making a profit" and can result in a prison term of two years, confiscation of property, and a fine of 30 rubles.[61] The penalty for speculation on a grand scale is two to seven years.

Article 154-1 of the Criminal Code of the RSFSR illustrates one of the more Kafkaesque aspects of the Soviet planned economy. In the USSR, the price of bread is artificially kept low in order to make it affordable for the average citizen. The price of feed for chickens and livestock, by contrast, is quite high. Consequently, many Soviet citizens buy bread to feed their animals on their private land plots. Article 154-1 was introduced in 1963 specifically to stop this practice. A fine is levied for the first offense, but for subsequent offenses the penalty may include up to one year of deprivation of freedom.

The maximum sentence for a first-time offender in the USSR is fifteen years, but for most crimes the sentence is no more than seven years. Soviet jurists are highly critical of Western legal systems that routinely mete out life sentences. One prominent jurist exclaimed, "How can you say that you have a system of *corrections* in the United States when you lock up prisoners for life?" By Soviet logic, fifteen years should be adequate time to rehabilitate a criminal.

Soviet law allows for the parole or conditional release of prisoners who have served as little as one-half of their sentences. Parole with compulsory work assignment can also be awarded after serving just one-third of the sentence. In addition, periodic amnesties are granted, usually commemorating a political holiday. In 1970, for instance, the sentences for most inmates were reduced in honor of the hundredth anniversary of Lenin's birth. In 1979, a selective amnesty was announced for many categories of women and juvenile inmates in honor of the International Year of the Child. Presumably, amnesties are intended to underscore socialist values. By releasing a prisoner early in honor of Lenin's birth or some other patriotic event, it is hoped that the former inmate will be more supportive of the Party and the values it seeks to uphold.

The death penalty, by shooting, is applied in the USSR in cases of treason, espionage, terrorist acts, sabotage, and intentional homicide committed under aggravating circumstances (e.g., murder for profit, murder to cover up a previous crime, murder of a pregnant woman, or especially brutal murder). Capital punishment is also occasionally employed to punish state or party officials in extreme cases of theft of state property. Party and state officials are expected to be model Soviet citizens. If they abuse their positions of public trust for their own profit, they are severely punished. For instance, in 1985, the head bookkeeper of a construction firm in the Ukraine was accused of forming a criminal conspiracy with a number of stores in Kiev to steal state property. Over a period of years, the group systematically embezzled more than 327,000 rubles (almost $225,000). The Kiev *oblast'* criminal court sentenced the bookkeeper to death. His accomplices were sentenced to long terms in labor colonies.[62]

The ideological stress in the USSR on the value of labor is reflected in corrections and the punishment of criminals. Few prisons exist in the Soviet Union, and they are only for hardened criminals who are too dangerous to be supervised at the normal labor colonies. The majority of inmates in the USSR serve their sentences in labor camps that are stratified in terms of degree of security, difficulty of work, quality and quantity of food, and privileges. For example, one Soviet source indicates that in a strict-regime camp (maximum security), inmates are expected to work in difficult jobs (frequently involving outdoor work such as construction, lumbering, mining, and so on). At a medium-security facility, the work is usually indoors, and the ration consists of bread, salt, and water with one hot meal every other day.[63] Inmates may be transferred from one regime facility to another as a reward for good behavior. Infringement of the rules of the labor colony can also prolong the sentence of an inmate or even result in a transfer to a stricter-regime facility. Thus, there is every incentive for the inmate to cooperate with the camp authorities. The Soviet correctional system has an astonishingly high success rate. Only 9 to 23 percent of all inmates repeat offenses, compared to more than 60 percent in the United States.[64]

THE EDUCATIONAL ROLE OF SOVIET LAW

As in other societies, law in the USSR both guides and punishes. Whether it is emphasizing the rehabilitation of offenders or communicating a "moral lesson" by executing officials guilty of stealing state property, the Soviet legal system is designed to play an educational role. Law is a teacher; it conveys and enforces societal values and channels behavior into acceptable norms and patterns. Harold Berman notes, a paternalistic strain marks Soviet law and practice:

> The subject of law, legal man, is treated less as an independent possessor of rights and duties, who knows what he wants, than as a dependent member of the collective group, a youth, whom the law must not only protect against the consequences of his own ignorance, but also must guide and train and discipline. . . . It is apparent that the Soviet emphasis on the educational role of law presupposes a new conception of man. The Soviet citizen is considered to be a member of a growing, unfinished, still immature society, which is moving toward a new and higher phase of development. As a subject of law, or a litigant in court, he is like a child or youth to be trained, guided, disciplined, protected. The judge plays the part of a parent or guardian; indeed, the whole legal system is parental.[65]

Paternalism is not a recent development in Soviet law. In 1917, D. I. Kurskii, Lenin's Commissar of Justice, remarked, "It does not matter that many points in our decrees will never be carried out; their task is to teach the masses how to take practical steps."[66] Soviet law, apart from governing the interactions of citizens and the relation of their rights and duties, is concerned with the development of citizens' moral well-being and their "law-consciousness."

The dual purpose of Soviet law—to punish and to educate—surfaces in various concrete legal policies. In 1957, for example, Krushchev initiated "antiparasite" laws aimed at those profiting from the fringe economy: prostitution, begging, vagrancy, private speculation, and other sources of "unearned income." Any able-bodied adult who was found leading an "antisocial, parasitic way of life" could be brought before a general meeting of townspeople and banished. Proceedings were neither trials nor the actions of a court; as such, they were condemned by many jurists as inconsistent with the concepts of "rule of law" and socialist legality. Proponents argued, however, that the parasite laws and their method of enforcement pointed toward realization of the utopian Marxist notion of the withering away of the institutions of the State.

Antiparasite legislation was introduced in nine republics, none of them major republics. With the exception of Latvia, parasite laws were not enacted in any of the European republics of the USSR, where Western traditions of law are more ingrained. While jurists appear to have been unable to alter the draft parasite laws, their objections were heeded in the major republics.

The parasite laws became eclipsed by another significant legal development in the late 1950s—the codification of fundamental principles of criminal law and criminal procedure. A trend toward the "juridization" of law swept Soviet jurisprudence, enhancing the role of established legal institutions and the legal profession. Hereafter, the concern with fringe elements in Soviet society became relegated to the general area of criminal law. On May 4, 1961, the RSFSR enacted a decree on parasitism that subsequently served as a model for similar legislation in most of the other republics. The decree gave jurisdiction over parasite cases to the criminal courts, bypassing the comrades' courts, which could give only light sentences. Also spurned in the legislation were the public meetings of residential units. For cases of parasitism, the new legislation specified punishments of two to five years of exile with compulsory labor.

In the first six months after the enactment of the decree, there were at least 600 convictions.[67] Of those convicted in 1961, more than half received sentences of four or five years.[68] Despite this harsh policy, there apparently was considerable selectivity in enforcement and prosecution, even during a time of increasingly strident public campaigns against parasites. In the first half of 1961, approximately 96 percent of all parasites were given warnings, not prosecuted, because they heeded the warnings and found proper work.[69]

The case of the antiparasite legislation illustrates several aspects of the Soviet legal system. The antiparasite laws were originally initiated to punish antisocial behavior and to socialize Soviet citizens by enlisting their assistance in combating parasitism and hooliganism. In time, however, the professional legal establishment exerted its influence and incorporated the antiparasite laws into regular judicial procedure. Since Khrushchev, such "juridization" has been a hallmark of socialist legality.

The case of the antiparasite laws also illustrates the use of law in the USSR as a means of social engineering—that is, as a means of ordering human relations to further the values of Soviet society. This practice is not unique to the Khrushchev era. Gorbachev's much-publicized antialcohol campaign mobilized the legal establishment in order to discourage alcohol consumption. Prosecutions for public intoxication increased dramatically, and those convicted received harsher penalties.

Nowhere is the educational role of law more evident than in the ordinary courtroom, where the real-life problems of Soviet citizens come into contact with the Soviet legal system. This chapter closes with an account of a typical criminal case—one of many that the author witnessed in the Kalinin *raion* criminal court in Leningrad.

A bell rang, and everyone was asked to stand while the judge and two people's assessors took their places at the bench. They wore no robes; instead, the judge (a woman in her fifties) wore a blue polyester suit with a patriotic lapel pin. The two people's assessors, one a thin-faced, haggard-looking man in his fifties and the other a rotund man in his late forties, wore drab, dark grey suits, but no ties. Behind the bar was a large seal of the Russian republic. In one corner of the courtroom, there was a bust of Lenin with a small pot of flowers in front of it. The accused man, an armed guard at his side, sat at a table with his defense advocate. At another table sat the prosecutor and an investigator, both wearing military-style uniforms. The audience was made up of an odd assortment of approximately twenty-five persons. Several *babushki* wearing brightly flowered kerchiefs and heavy black-flannel coats (even though it was quite warm in the chamber) sat talking quietly among themselves. They appeared to know one another and were most likely regular attendants. In the first row of the spectator gallery sat the defendant's wife, a gaunt woman in her mid-forties. She fidgeted in her seat and coughed occasionally. Beside her, another *babushka* (probably her mother) patted her on the shoulder. A bored-looking man sat by the rear door, reading a newspaper and eating a piece of sausage. He wore a red armband, indicating that he was the doorman and charged with maintaining decorum in the chamber.

The judge called the court into session, announcing that this involved the case of one Boris Mikhailovich Petrov, who had been arrested and charged with assault with a deadly weapon, malicious hooliganism, and public intoxication. Petrov was asked to stand. His shaved head and three- or four-day growth of whiskers gave him a ghostly look. He wore a heavy workingman's coat, made of quilted flannel. Petrov appeared to be in his late fifties, but Russian men generally look older than their age. In fact, he told the judge that he was forty-eight-years-old and was born in Voronezh into the family of a "peasant" (i.e., collective farmer). His parents were killed during the Great Patriotic War, after which he was sent to Leningrad to live with an aunt. He was married and had two children, a girl of seventeen and a boy of thirteen. Petrov stooped over the defense table, his fingers nervously tracing circles on the table as he talked. After Petrov sat down, the judge began to read from the report of the preliminary investigation.

On a Thursday evening two months previously, Petrov had been riding home on the No. 17 tram. According to many witnesses, he was obviously intoxicated. One of the other passengers on the tram, a *babushka* named Olga Nikolaeva Barashkova, began to chide Petrov for his unsightly appearance and disgraceful behavior. Petrov responded crudely, which brought grumblings of censure from several other passengers. According to the report, Petrov then pulled a hunting knife from under his coat, staggered to his feet, and brandished the knife over his head, shouting at Barashkova, "I'll make cutlets out of you!" He was quickly restrained by the female tram operator and several male passengers, and he was arrested at the next stop.

The judge called on Barashkova, who stepped into the witness box. She gave her age, occupation, and address. She recounted the story, pointing out the accused in response to a question from the bench. The judge asked if she thought that Petrov had actually intended to "make cutlets" out of her. She responded: "Yes, I feared for my life." The people's assessors had no additional questions, and the prosecutor declined to ask any further questions. The defense advocate then stood and asked Barashkova whether the tram had been moving at the time of the "assault." She said that it had. This was later corroborated by the testimony of the tram driver. The defense attorney asked Barashkova how far away from her Petrov had been when he threatened her. She estimated it had been three or four meters.

"Did he ever actually point the knife at you?"

"No, he was waving it wildly over his head." She was dismissed.

Petrov took the stand. In response to questions from the judge, he said that he had been arrested twice previously, once as a juvenile for hooliganism, for which he was sentenced to two years in a juvenile facility, and once for assault, the result of a drunken brawl on the street. The latter offense resulted in a three-year prison term. He had been out of prison less than one year. As for the tram incident, Petrov said that he recalled almost nothing. He remembered being chastised by some *babushki,* but that was all.

The prosecutor stood and asked Petrov about the knife. Yes, it was his, a gift from his uncle who had used it on hunting and fishing trips. The prosecutor then began to ask about Petrov's criminal record and his history of alcoholism. Petrov admitted that several times he had been suspended from work and fined for absenteeism and for showing up for work drunk. (This was substantiated by his work records, which were submitted in evidence.)

After Petrov stepped down, the tram driver, several witnesses, and Petrov's supervisor were called to testify. Only one of the witnesses offered an alternative description of the story. A teenage girl who had been on the tram said that she thought Petrov was so inebriated that he could not possibly have posed a threat to Barashkova or anyone else. This elicited several remarks from the audience. One *babushka* exclaimed, "But what about the knife?" Another joined in, "He's a rascal. Just look at him!" The judge warned them to be quiet and rapped the gavel. The doorman looked up from his paper, unperturbed. Asked by the judge whether Petrov had "lunged" at Barashkova with the knife, the witness replied, "The tram lurched, and he was staggering, trying to keep his balance." The audience again offered various opinions on the testimony. This time, the judge banged her gavel fiercely and warned the women to keep their opinions to themselves. If there was another "outburst," she said, she would have them removed from the court.

Finally, after all the witnesses had testified and been cross-examined, the prosecution and defense attorneys made their closing statements. The prosecutor noted Petrov's long history of "violence" and his chronic alcoholism. He indicated that Petrov was a serious recidivist and called for the maximum sentence—seven years in a strict-regime labor colony. The defense advocate contended that the *babushka* Barashkova was certainly correct that Petrov's public drunkenness was disgraceful, and that his rude remarks and carrying of a dangerous weapon were inexcusable. He asked the court, however, to lower the charge to public intoxication and hooliganism—a crime punishable by one to two years' imprisonment. The defense advocate noted that it was not reasonable for Barashkova to have considered herself in imminent danger of her life. Petrov had been very drunk and hardly able to stand. He had not pointed the knife at Barashkova, and he had been a safe distance away from her.

The judge and two people's assessors retired to their chamber behind the bench. The audience talked quietly among themselves. Petrov sat dejectedly at the defense table, the armed guard still at his side. After approximately thirty minutes, the judge and people's assessors reemerged. Everyone stood. Petrov was asked to face the bench, and the judge announced that he was found guilty of assault and malicious hooliganism. In anger, she shook her finger at him and called him a disgrace to Soviet society. "You have two children, and yet you are ignoring your responsibility to them and to your long-suffering wife. Twice before you have run afoul of the law and been 'rehabilitated' in correctional institutions. Yet, your behavior indicates that you have not changed your ways." She sentenced him to the maximum of seven years in a strict-regime labor colony for repeat offenders. Petrov was immediately led away in handcuffs. His wife sobbed quietly and was comforted by the old woman at her side. The *babushki* in attendance chatted contentedly among themselves and waited for the next case, while the doorman put the newspaper down and went into the corridor to smoke a cigarette.

Notes

1. V. I. Lenin, "O dvoinom podchinenii i zakonnsti," reprinted in *Sovetskaia prokuratura: sbornik vazhneishikh dokumentov* (Moscow: Iuridicheskaia literatura, 1972), 100–102.

2. Cited in Peter Juviler, *Revolutionary Law and Order* (New York: Free Press, 1976), 18–19.

3. Ibid.

4. V. I. Lenin, *Polnoe sobranie sochinenii,* 4th ed., vol. 36 (Moscow: Politizdat, 1958–1965), 195.

5. See Darrell P. Hammer, "Bureaucracy and the Rule of Law in Soviet Society," in Clifford M. Foust and Warren Lerner, eds., *The Soviet World in Flux: Six Essays* (Atlanta: Southern Regional Education Board, 1966), 87–110.

6. Cited in Zigurds Zile, *Ideas and Forces in Soviet Legal History* (Madison, Wisconsin: College Printing, 1967), 250–256.

7. Andrei Vyshinsky, "Raise Higher the Banner of Socialist Legality," *Sotsialisticheskaia zakonnost'* 11 (1936).

8. Naum Jasny, "Labor and Output in Soviet Concentration Camps," *Journal of Political Economy* 59 (October 1951): 405.

9. "Ukrepleniie sotsialisticheskoi zakonnosti i iuridicheskaia nauka," *Kommunist* 11 (November 1956): 20.

10. S. Kechekian, *Pravootnosheniia v sotsialisticheskoi obshchestve* (Moscow: Iuridicheskaia literatura, 1958), 68.

11. For example, see *Izvestiia,* 19 December 1961, p. 2.

12. V. Kazin, "Sud tovarishchei," *Pravda,* 13 November 1963, p. 4.

13. R. A. Rudenko, "Leninskie idei sotsialisticheskoi zakonnsti, printsipy organizatsii i deiatel'nosti sovetskoi prokuratury," in *Sovetskaia prokuratura* (Moscow: Iuridicheskaia literatura, 1977), 25–26.

14. Statute on the Procuracy of the USSR (1979), Article 3.

15. *Vedomosti Verkhovnovo Soveta SSSR,* No. 3, item 58 (January 18, 1985): 91–93.

16. For a definition of bureaucratic groups, see Darrell P. Hammer, *USSR: The Politics of Oligarchy* (Hinsdale, Illinois: Dryden Press, 1974), 224–225.

17. M. P. Maliarov, ed., *Organizatsiia roboty raionnoi (gorodskoi) prokuratury* (Moscow: Iuridicheskaia literatura, 1974), 44.

18. These approximate figures are calculated from statistics cited in I. I. Martinovich, *Advokatura v BSSR* (Minsk: 1973); and "Narodnogo doveriia—dostoiny," *Leningradskaia pravda,* 13 April 1976, p. 1.

19. This figure is approximate and calculated from statistics cited in Gordon B. Smith, *The Soviet Procuracy and the Supervision of Administration* (Leiden, the Netherlands: Sijthoff, 1978), 23–25; Donald D. Barry and Harold Berman, "The Jurists," in Gordon Skilling and Franklyn Griffiths, eds., *Interest Groups in Soviet Politics* (Princeton: Princeton University Press, 1971), 311; and A. Ia. Sykharev, ed., *Rol' i zadachi sovetskoi advokatury* (Moscow: Iuridicheskaia literatura, 1972), 37.

20. See Walter Gellhorn, *Ombudsman and Others* (Cambridge: Harvard University Press, 1966).

21. Smith, *The Soviet Procuracy,* 23.

22. Ibid.

23. Consultation with N. S. Aleksandrov, Dean of the Juridical Faculty, Leningrad State University, November 6, 1975.

24. For a discussion of the *advokatura,* see Zigurds Zile, "Soviet *Advokatura:* Its Situation and Prospects," in Donald Barry, George Ginsburgs, and Peter Maggs, eds., *Soviet Law after Stalin,* vol. 3 (Leiden, the Netherlands: Sijthoff, 1979).

25. Ibid.

26. See Konstantin Simis, *USSR, The Corrupt Society* (New York: Simon and Schuster, 1982).

27. Smith, *The Soviet Procuracy,* 23.

28. M. A. Kopylovskaia, *Nauchno-prakticheskii kommentarii k osnovam zakonodatel'stva o sudoustroistve soiuza SSR, souiznikh avtonomnikh respublik* (Moscow: Iuridicheskaia literatura, 1961), 67.

29. T. H. Rigby, *Communist Party Membership in the USSR, 1917–1967* (Princeton: Princeton University Press, 1968), 425.

30. V. G. Rozenfeld, *Prokurorskii nadzor za sobliudeniem zakonnosti dolzhnostnykh lits predpriiatii* (Voronezh: Voronezh University, 1973), 49–51.

31. Program of the CPSU, *Pravda,* 7 March 1986, pp. 3–10.

32. *Pravda,* 26 February 1986, pp. 2–10.

33. Cited in Robert Sharlet, "The Communist Party and the Administration of Justice," in Barry, Ginsburgs, and Maggs, *Soviet Law after Stalin,* 3: 323.

34. M. S. Strogovich, ed., *Pravovye garantii zakonnsti v SSSR* (Moscow: Iuridicheskaia literatura, 1962), 179.

35. George Feifer, *Justice in Moscow* (New York: Simon and Schuster, 1964), 248–249.

36. Ibid.

37. Ibid.

38. See Jerry Hough, *The Soviet Prefects* (Cambridge: Harvard University Press, 1969).

39. *New York Times,* 28 December 1975, p. 7.

40. Peter H. Solomon, *Soviet Criminologists and Criminal Policy* (New York: Columbia University Press, 1978), 119–122.

41. For a discussion of the press in criminal policy-making, see Ibid., 122–125.

42. John N. Hazard, "A Constitution for Developed Socialism," in Barry, Ginsburgs, and Maggs, *Soviet Law after Stalin,* 2: 1–33.

43. For a thorough analysis of the debate on Khrushchev's education reform, see Joel Schwartz and William Keech, "Group Influence and the Policy Process in the Soviet Union," *American Political Science Review* 62 (1968): 840–851.

44. See *Pravda,* 5 April 1985, p. 1, for announcement of the antialcohol campaign.

45. Joel C. Moses, *Regional Party Leadership and Policy-Making in the USSR* (New York: Praeger, 1974), 33–34.

46. Solomon, *Soviet Criminologists and Criminal Policy,* 118.

47. Samuel P. Huntington and Zbigniew Brzezinski, *Political Power USA/USSR* (New York: Viking Press, 1963), 216.

48. The new CPSU Program drops the reference to the "state of all the people." CPSU Program, *Pravda,* 7 March 1986, p. 1.

49. Constitution of the USSR (1977), Article 58.

50. Ibid., Article 50.

51. Statute on the Procuracy of the USSR (1979).

52. Cited in David Shipler, *Russia: Broken Idols, Solemn Dreams* (London: Macdonald, 1983), 237.

53. *Molodoi kommunist,* no. 9 (September 1975): 102.

54. See comments by S. Gusev, First Vice-Chairman of the USSR Supreme Court, *Izvestiia,* 19 April 1984, p. 2.

55. These figures were compiled by Il'ia Zemtsov in "Problems of Soviet Youth," *Radio Liberty Research Paper*, no. 125 (March 1975), p. 10.

56. *Sotsiologicheskie issledovaniia*, no. 3 (1977).

57. Ibid.

58. Cited in Shipler, *Russia: Broken Idols, Solemn Dreams*, 237.

59. Criminal Code of the RSFSR, Articles 89 and 144.

60. Ibid., Articles 99 and 150.

61. Ibid., Article 154.

62. Selskaia zhizn', 24 March 1985, p. 4.

63. M. S. Studenikina, *Zakonodatel'stvo ob administrativnoi otvestvennosti kodifikatsiia* (Candidate dissertation, All-Union Scientific Research Institute on Soviet Legislation, Moscow, 1968), pp. 250–251.

64. Cited in Walter Connor, *Deviance in Soviet Society* (New York: Columbia University Press, 1972).

65. Harold J. Berman, *Justice in the USSR* (Cambridge: Harvard University Press, 1966), 283–284.

66. D. I. Kurskii, cited in Eugene Kamenka, "The Soviet View of Law," in Richard Cornell, ed., *The Soviet Political System* (Englewood Cliffs, New Jersey: Prentice-Hall, 1970), 315.

67. Cited in Leon Lipson, "Hosts and Pests: The Fight Against Parasites," *Problems of Communism*, no. 9 (March–April 1965): 78–79.

68. Ibid., 80.

69. Ibid., 78–79.

Selected Bibliography

Barry, Donald, William Butler, and George Ginsburgs, eds. *Contemporary Soviet Law*. The Hague, the Netherlands: Martinus Nijhoff, 1974.

Barry, Donald, George Ginsburgs, and Peter Maggs, eds. *Soviet Law after Stalin*. Leiden, the Netherlands: Sijthoff, 1977–1979.

Berman, Harold J. *Justice in the USSR*. Cambridge: Harvard University Press, 1966.

Berman, Harold J., and James W. Spindler, eds. *Soviet Criminal Law and Procedure*. 2d ed. Cambridge: Harvard University Press, 1972.

Chalidze, Valery. *Criminal Russia: Crime in the Soviet Union*. New York: Random House, 1977.

Conquest, Robert, ed. *Justice and the Legal System in the USSR*. New York: Praeger, 1968.

Feifer, George. *Justice in Moscow*. New York: Simon and Schuster, 1964.

Feldbrugge, F. J. M., et al., eds. *Encyclopedia of Soviet Law*. 2d rev. ed. Dordrecht, the Netherlands: Martinus Nijhoff, 1985.

Grzybowski, K. *Soviet Legal Institutions*. Ann Arbor: University of Michigan Press, 1962.

Hazard, John N. *Communists and Their Law*. Chicago: University of Chicago Press, 1969.

Hazard, John N. *Managing Change in the USSR: The Politico-Legal Role of the Soviet Jurist*. New York: Columbia University Press, 1983.

Hazard, John N., Isaac Shapiro, and Peter Maggs. *The Soviet Legal System*. Dobbs Ferry, New York: Oceana, 1969.

Ioffe, Olimpiad S. *Soviet Law and Soviet Reality*. Dordrecht, the Netherlands: Martinus Nijhoff, 1985.

Johnson, Edward L. *An Introduction to the Soviet Legal System.* London: Methuen, 1969.

Juviler, Peter. *Revolutionary Law and Order.* New York: Free Press, 1976.

Kucherov, Samuel. *The Organs of Soviet Administration of Justice: Their History and Operation.* Leiden, the Netherlands: E. J. Brill, 1970.

Sharlet, Robert. *The New Soviet Constitution of 1977: Analysis and Text.* Brunswick, Ohio: King's Cross, 1978.

Shelley, Louise I. *Lawyers in Soviet Work Life.* New Brunswick, New Jersey: Rutgers University Press, 1984.

Simis, Konstantin. *USSR, The Corrupt Society.* New York: Simon and Schuster, 1982.

Smith, Gordon B. *The Soviet Procuracy and the Supervision of Administration.* Leiden, the Netherlands: Sijthoff, 1978.

Solomon, Peter H. *Soviet Criminologists and Criminal Policy.* New York: Columbia University Press, 1978.

Zile, Zigurds L., ed. *Ideas and Forces in Soviet Legal History.* 2d rev. ed. Madison, Wisconsin: College Printing, 1970.

8

The Uniformed Services

With the succession of Iurii Andropov, the former chief of the KGB, to the head of the CPSU in 1982, Western observers speculated about the growing role and prominence of the "uniformed services" in the Soviet political system. Three main elements comprise the uniformed services—the security police (KGB), the regular police (militia), and the Soviet armed forces. Although each exists as a distinct entity, the three share several characteristics. Each is hierarchically organized and follows a code of strict discipline. The three services hold a monopoly on weapons and intelligence-gathering technology, and they control information vitally important to the policymakers. They also perform essential social control functions, frequently adopting similarly tough stances on law-and-order issues, dissent, and détente. Order and control have always been highly desired values in Soviet society, which helps to explain the size and power of the uniformed services. This chapter will examine these three institutions, analyzing for each its organizational structure, degree of party control, relative prestige, and influence on policy matters. We begin with the most notorious of the three, the KGB.

THE COMMITTEE ON STATE SECURITY (KGB)

The present-day Committee on State Security (KGB) has its roots in the *Oprichnina* established by Ivan the Terrible in 1565. The *Oprichnina* consisted of a corps of approximately six thousand men who were loyal to the Tsar.[1] The corps existed outside of—or above—the law, and its members were permitted to commit crimes or use violent means with absolute impunity in order to protect the Tsar's interests. To emphasize their function as an instrument of terror, the *Oprichniki* were clad in black and rode black horses. In addition, they carried emblems that depicted a dog's head and a broom, symbolizing their duty to sniff out opposition and sweep it away. The *Oprichnina* was thus created not only to investigate and punish individual political dissidents, but also to instill fear and obedience in the entire populace. In this respect, the *Oprichnina* anticipated Stalin's dreaded political police organization, the NKVD. The parallel is not lost on Soviet citizens, who even today privately refer to the security police as the *Oprichnina*. By 1570, Ivan came to fear the growing power of the *Oprichnina* and ordered the execution or imprisonment of many of its members, just as Stalin would later eliminate many of his own former NKVD commissars.

The *Oprichnina* was abolished in 1572, and no formal organization replaced it until the establishment of the Preobrazhensky Office in 1697 under Peter the Great. An outgrowth of two special military units, the Preobrazhensky Office was initially created to monitor and do away with political adversaries during Peter's eighteen-month tour of Western Europe. Torture and execution were common punishments, as was exile to Siberia. During more than thirty years of operation, the Preobrazhensky Office investigated thousands of cases.[2]

The functions of the secret police were transferred to the Chancellery for Secret Investigations under Peter's niece, Empress Anna (1730–1740). The new Chancellery had an expanded staff; unlike its predecessor, the Preobrazhensky Office, it was not saddled with duties other than ensuring political security. The volume of cases investigated rose to a thousand per year.[3] Under Peter III, the Chancellery was reorganized as the Secret Bureau and placed under the supervision of the Senate. Alexander I, in an apparent move to reduce political oppression, abolished the Secret Bureau in 1802, released many prisoners, and issued a decree forbidding the use of torture. Secret-police activity continued, however, under the Ministry of the Interior, the security forces of the Governor-General of St. Petersburg, and the Special Chancellery of the Ministry of Police. Thus, secret-police activity under Alexander I was far from curtailed; it merely became a matter of confusing, overlapping jurisdictions among competing organizations.

In the wake of the Decembrist uprising in 1825, Nicholas I established a new centralized organization to prevent further attempts to overthrow the regime. Reluctant to grant police powers to a separate bureaucracy, the Tsar authorized the creation of the Third Section within his own Imperial Chancellery. The Third Section supervised the gendarmerie—or "higher police"—which were given precedence over the regular police of the Ministry of the Interior. This division of special police and regular police functions resulted in bureaucratic feuds between the Third Section and the Ministry of the Interior. A similar division resulting in similar bureaucratic tensions has existed periodically between the KGB and the Ministry of Internal Affairs (MVD) in the USSR.

In the middle and late 1800s, the Third Section became an important instrument for investigating and punishing dissident writers and intellectuals who dared to criticize the regime openly. With the rise of anarchist groups, however, criticism grew more violent and the Third Section was unable to stem political threats to the imperial family. One such threat resulted in the assassination of Tsar Alexander II in 1881.

In the aftermath of Alexander's assassination, a statute was issued whereby a state of emergency could be declared. Under the conditions of a state of emergency, the Governors-General and the gendarmerie assumed far-reaching powers, including the right to order summary arrests, to forbid public and private gatherings, and to issue binding decrees for the maintenance of public order. These emergency powers also included the establishment of special units subordinate to police departments for the investigation of political crimes. These units were termed "protective sections" (*okhrannie otdeleniia*) and eventually evolved into the *Okhrana*, the Russian political police during the last thirty-six years of the monarchy.

In one of its first acts after seizing power, the new Bolshevik government abolished the *Okhrana* and arrested most of its officers. Within six weeks after the October Revolution, however, Lenin found it necessary to establish his own security-police organization, the Cheka. (This name is derived from the first two letters of the organization's full name, the Extraordinary Commission for Combating Counterrevolution and Sabotage.) In his famous decree on the "Red Terror" in 1918, Lenin justified the use of police surveillance and summary punishment in order to suppress counterrevolutionary elements: "There is no other way to the liberation of the masses, except by the suppression of exploitation by means of force."[4]

The Cheka's primary powers, like those of the *Okhrana* before it, were investigatory rather than punitive, although it was empowered to impose such penalties as confiscation of property, deprivation of ration cards, and publication of lists of enemies of the people. The first chief of the Cheka was Felix Dzerzhinsky, a Polish revolutionary and longtime associate of Lenin. In 1918, the Cheka's headquarters were moved to Moscow, the new capital, occupying the building of a former insurance company on Lubianka Lane. The present-day KGB headquarters still occupy "the Lubianka," although an enormous new addition was constructed after World War II. The basement of the structure houses the infamous Lubianka prison, a holding facility where suspected political criminals are detained during interrogation and trial, until they are sent to corrective labor camps. As is typical of the Russian ability to find humor in the horrendous, it is said that Lubianka is the tallest building in Moscow—you can see all the way to Siberia from the basement.

In the six months following the Revolution, regional branches of the Cheka were established in more than four hundred cities. The Cheka itself became more formally bureaucratic; specialized divisions were created to deal with such responsibilities as transport, defense of the frontier, and control of the armed forces. The principal task of the Cheka, nonetheless, was to liquidate all opposition. In June 1918, Dzerzhinsky declared: "We stand for organized terror.... Terror is an absolute necessity during times of revolution.... The Cheka is obliged to defend the Revolution and conquer the enemy even if its sword does by chance fall upon the heads of the innocent."[5]

On August 30, 1918, Fania Kaplan, a Socialist Revolutionary, wounded Lenin twice in an assassination plot. The same day, another Socialist Revolutionary succeeded in killing M. S. Uritsky, the head of the Petrograd Cheka. These events prompted the Bolshevik regime to unleash the secret police in what has been called the "Red Terror." On September 3, *Izvestiia* announced that more than five hundred people had been shot in Petrograd in reprisal for the death of Uritsky. Similar massacres followed in Moscow and the provinces. The chief targets of the Red Terror were not Socialist Revolutionaries, however, but members of the middle class, capitalists, factory owners, and former ministers under the Tsar. During its five years of operation, the Cheka was responsible for an estimated 50,000 executions.[6]

With the conclusion of the Civil War in 1921, Lenin began to emphasize a greater degree of legality in the operations of the political police. The

Cheka was abolished in early 1922, and its functions were taken over by a newly created branch of the People's Commissariat of the Interior, the General Political Administration (GPU). The transformation of the Cheka into the GPU left many aspects of political police activities unchanged. Dzerzhinsky retained his title as head of the organization. The GPU was, however, prohibited from executing criminals; the secret police were to confine their activities to making arrests and conducting investigations, turning over all offenders to the regularly constituted courts. One observer argues that, despite this prohibition, the political police continued to operate outside and above the law.[7]

Dzerzhinsky and Stalin forged a close alliance, the former assisting Stalin in bending the Georgian Communists to his will. After Lenin's death in 1924, the use of the political police was stepped up in order to eliminate potential rivals to Stalin. Trotsky was ousted from his post as Commissar of War in 1924; his successor, Mikhail Frunze, died mysteriously while undergoing surgery on a stomach ulcer. The doctors treating Frunze were on the staff of the political police, and they overruled Frunze's personal physicians, who had advised against the operation because Frunze had a heart condition. This lent credence to allegations that Frunze's death was a medical murder.

During the 1920s and 1930s, the OGPU also began to devote considerable attention to the political activities of Russian émigrés and of foreign citizens inside the USSR, two responsibilities of the political police today.* In 1925, in an early example of the use of "disinformation," the OGPU lured Vasilii Shulgin, a noted Russian émigré and right-wing politician, back to the Soviet Union by allegedly establishing meetings between him and a bogus underground resistance network referred to as "the Trust." For several months, Shulgin traveled around the Soviet Union, meeting with representatives of the Trust, who were in fact OGPU agents. The elaborate scheme was intended not to entrap Shulgin on Soviet soil, but to destroy his credibility when he returned to the West. In Berlin, Shulgin published a book on the powerful political underground in Russia. The book and the Trust were quickly exposed by the OGPU. The episode not only discredited Shulgin, but seriously demoralized the politically active Russian émigré groups in Europe.[8]

Dzerzhinsky died in 1926, but for the last two years of his life he had forfeited much of the power over the secret police to Stalin. Dzerzhinsky's successor was also largely a figurehead; Stalin relied instead on the deputy head of the OGPU, Henry Iagoda.

With Stalin's consolidation of power in 1928 and the initiation of rapid industrialization and collectivization of agriculture, the OGPU's responsibilities expanded from political to economic crime. It also adopted harsher methods of repression. Stalin's main weapon against the peasants who resisted collectivization was the secret police. In 1942, he told Winston Churchill that during collectivization the OGPU had had more than 10 million peasants killed, put into labor camps, or forced into exile. The secret police were also responsible for the Gulag (the Main Administration of Camps).

---

*In 1923, the word *Ob"edinennye* ("United") was added to the name of the General Political Administration, which was thereafter known as the OGPU.

The camps themselves changed as their populations swelled to the millions. The inmates tended to be simple peasants rather than well-educated political rivals, and the labor resources of the camps became a major resource in the economy. Most of the showplaces of Moscow—the subway stations, Moscow University, and ironically, even the new Lubianka—were built with convict labor.

Under Stalin's lead, the OGPU resumed the practice of shooting its victims without trial, most frequently for supposedly sabotaging Stalin's economic campaigns. Among those secretly tried and executed and those executed without trial were: bacteriologists charged with causing an epidemic among horses; officials of the food industry charged with sabotaging food supplies; and several agricultural experts, state farm officials, and academics accused of mismanagement and "wrecking."[9] Higher-level officials charged with sabotage were treated to elaborate show-trials at which most confessed after long periods of interrogation and torture by the secret police.

In July 1934, the OGPU was abolished and its functions were incorporated into the People's Commissariat for Internal Affairs (NKVD). The NKVD thus assumed responsibility for both the secret police and the militia (regular police). As in earlier reorganizations, however, the change of name did not signal the cessation of repression. Rather, it was merely a prelude to the most bloody period of Soviet history—the infamous purges of the 1930s. Henry Iagoda was named head of the NKVD, and he presided over the wave of arrests and executions that followed the murder of Leningrad party chief Sergei Kirov in 1935. Stalin, traveling with Iagoda to Leningrad to supervise the investigation into Kirov's death, issued a decree providing for the speedy prosecution of political criminals and the immediate execution of the condemned without the right of appeal. The episode was exploited by Stalin and Iagoda to remove adversaries not only from Leningrad but elsewhere, including many within the ranks of the secret police itself. In April 1935, a new provision was introduced into law that extended criminal penalties, including execution, to children as young as twelve. The purpose of the law was to allow police interrogators to threaten those under investigation with the prosecution of their children.

The terror culminated in three major show-trials of Stalin's political rivals during the period from 1936 to 1938. The first trial began on August 19, 1936. Sixteen persons, including Zinoviev and Kamenev, were charged with being members of a Trotskyite terrorist circle. The trial was held in the October Hall of the House of Trade Unions and heard by the Military Collegium of the Supreme Court. The audience consisted of a group of carefully selected, well-rehearsed employees of the NKVD and approximately thirty foreign journalists and diplomats.[10] With only two exceptions, the accused pleaded guilty to a long list of charges, including organizing the murder of Kirov and plotting the murder of Stalin and several other members of the Presidium. No evidence was offered in the trials other than the confessions wrested from the accused while they were held by the NKVD. All were convicted and executed within 24 hours.

With Zinoviev eliminated, Stalin turned his attention to two remaining adversaries, Bukharin and Rykov. Before plotting their elaborate show-trials, however, he first dismissed Iagoda and replaced him with Nikolai Ezhov as head of the NKVD. Six months after his dismissal, Iagoda was arrested and later tried and executed. He thus carried to his grave extensive knowledge of Stalin's involvement in Kirov's murder and countless other atrocities.

The second major show-trial took place in Moscow in January 1937. Among the seventeen persons arraigned were Gregori Piatakov, Deputy Commissar for Heavy Industry, and the publicist Karl Radek. In a new twist, many of the defendants were accused of economic sabotage (wrecking trains, introducing gas into coal mines, and so on). All were found guilty, and most were shot.

Throughout 1937, Ezhov rounded up and liquidated Iagoda's former senior subordinates in the NKVD. More than three thousand NKVD officers were executed in 1937 alone.[11] Many others committed suicide, some by leaping from the windows of their Lubianka offices in full view of the Moscow populace. The purge, known as the *Ezhovshchina* after the newly appointed secret police chief, reached a climax in May through September 1937. Arrests, exile, imprisonment, and execution affected all sections of the population, but focused especially on the elite.

The purge did not spare foreign residents in the USSR. Polish and German Communists who had sought refuge in the Soviet Union because their parties were illegal in their home countries, were arrested and imprisoned or shot. So too, the *Ezhovshchina* liquidated Soviet citizens who had become contaminated by contact with the West. Diplomatic officials and NKVD spies abroad were ordered or lured back to Moscow for arrest; those who refused to return to the USSR were marked for assassination.

One estimate places the number of arrests in 1937 and 1938 at seven million, and at least five million people had been arrested prior to the *Ezhovshchina*. Some two million persons probably perished in forced labor camps during 1937 and 1938.[12]

Ezhov's demise came in late 1938, but the facts surrounding his disappearance and death are still unclear. The Georgian deputy chief of the NKVD, Lavrenti Beria, assumed the post vacated by Ezhov in December 1938. Following Ezhov's precedent, Beria eliminated most of the high-ranking officials in the NKVD and replaced them with his own trusted clients from the Caucasus.

The German invasion of the Soviet Union in 1941 caught Stalin unaware, despite the numerous reports and warnings of NKVD agents in Germany and Japan. During the war, special NKVD units assigned to back up the Red Army were ordered to shoot any soldiers who deserted or retreated. Another prominent task of the NKVD during the early war years was to destroy all prisons, labor camps, and inmates in the path of the rapidly advancing German army.

As the tide of the war turned after the battle of Stalingrad, the NKVD faced a new responsibility—the execution and imprisonment of Red Army soldiers who had fallen into German hands. Many Soviet soldiers were liberated from German concentration camps only to be charged with collaboration and thrown into similar facilities in the USSR.

Some inmates of the Gulag were offered the opportunity to earn their freedom by fighting in the so-called *shtrafnoi* battalions (i.e., penal battalions), which were often used to spearhead military offensives. Only a fraction of the members of the battalions survived these charges; they were then reconstituted into new battalions, and so on, until the end of the war.

Following the war, the people's commissariats were renamed *ministries;* the secret police were thus subordinated to the Ministry of State Security (MGB) and the Ministry of Internal Affairs (MVD). MGB/MVD activities extended to the newly occupied states of Eastern Europe, where parallel intelligence and police apparatuses were established, reporting to Moscow. The MGB/MVD also had to contend with anti-Soviet émigrés and Western intelligence agents who parachuted or were otherwise smuggled into Eastern Europe and the USSR.

A reorganization of the secret police occurred in 1950, with major responsibilities reassigned from the MVD to the MGB. These included the militia (i.e., regular police), the frontier troops, special purpose troops, and possibly the railroad troops.[13] The effect was to leave the MVD a more exclusively economic agency, responsible for the operation of the huge Gulag system, which was engaged in major construction projects.

In January 1953, *Pravda* announced the arrest of a group of Kremlin physicians who had supposedly confessed to the murder and attempted murder of various leading Soviet figures. Stalin was apparently planning to use the alleged "doctors' plot" as an excuse to launch a new wave of purges in 1953, but his death in March of that year put an end to the plan.

Two days after the death of the *Vozhd'* (Leader), *Pravda* announced sweeping changes in the Party and State. The MVD and MGB were fused into a single ministry—the MVD, with Beria as minister. Stalin's successors moved quickly to reduce the level of purge hysteria. The accused Kremlin doctors were released, and within three months Beria himself was apprehended and executed.

A decree of March 1954 again separated regular police functions from those of the security police, granting the latter to a new body, the KGB (Committee on State Security). In the wake of Nikita Khrushchev's attacks on Stalin at the Twentieth Party Congress in 1956, the KGB was subjected to careful legal and political controls. Ivan Serov, a trusted associate of Khrushchev, was named the new head of the organization. In December 1958, Serov became head of the GRU (i.e., the military intelligence agency), and a new director, Alexander Shelepin, assumed control of the KGB. Shelepin's appointment was notable due to his relatively young age—forty—and his lack of previous experience in police work (he had served in the Komsomol for most of his career). The appointments of both Serov and Shelepin appear to have been motivated by Khrushchev's desire to extend party control over this extremely powerful and potentially violent organization. It was probably at this time that the KGB became not only a tool of the political leadership, but also a major bureaucratic voice on police matters. On the eve of Khrushchev's renewed attack on Stalin at the Twenty-Second Party Congress in October 1961, Shelepin was promoted to the CPSU Secretariat, and another former Komsomol official, Vladimir Semichastny, assumed leadership of the KGB.

During the earlier period of de-Stalinization, a limited degree of literary and artistic freedom had been encouraged. In contrast, however, the early 1960s witnessed crude attacks on Nobel laureate Boris Pasternak and the arrest and trial of poet Joseph Brodsky.

The KGB also began to use its position on occasion to thwart Khrushchev's foreign-policy initiatives. In the autumn of 1959, while Khrushchev was visiting the United States—the first visit ever by a Soviet party chief—the KGB expelled an American embassy official in Moscow. One observer concludes that the incident and the accompanying press campaign on the need for vigilance against capitalist tricks was "so out of keeping with the diplomatic atmosphere of the moment that the timing cannot be regarded as accidental."[14]

On October 13, 1964, Khrushchev's political career came to an abrupt end with his ouster from the Presidium.[15] A collective leadership emerged with Leonid Brezhnev as General Secretary of the Party and Alexei Kosygin as Premier. The coup was most likely accomplished with the knowledge and cooperation of Khrushchev's trusted KGB chief Semichastny and former KGB chief Shelepin. In the aftermath of the overthrow, Semichastny was promoted to the Central Committee, and Shelepin was named to the Presidium without having served the usual term as a candidate member.

Having consolidated their positions, however, Brezhnev and Kosygin apparently sensed a threat in the Shelepin-Semichastny KGB team. Thus, they moved to extend their control over the security apparatus. In June 1967, Shelepin was appointed Chairman of the Central Trade Union Council, a dead end for any aspiring politician, while Semichastny was demoted to First Deputy Premier of the Ukraine. Semichastny's successor as head of the KGB was none other than Iurii Andropov. At the same time, Andropov was promoted to candidate member of the Politburo, thus becoming the first head of the security police since Beria to sit on the highest party body. Once again, a trusted appointee was placed in charge of the security police. Andropov, who had served as Soviet ambassador in Hungary during the 1956 invasion, had no previous experience with the security police.

In 1973, Andropov was elevated to full-member status in the Politburo; in May 1982, he relinquished the KGB chairmanship to assume the unofficial title of "Second Secretary" of the Central Committee Secretariat. In November 1982, he succeeded Brezhnev as General Secretary. Thus, Andropov established two impressive firsts: he served an unprecedented fifteen years as chief of the security-police apparatus, and he used the power and expertise acquired in that position to assume the most powerful post of General Secretary of the CPSU. Succeeding Andropov as KGB chief was Vitalii Fedorchuk, who in December 1982 was named to head the MVD, while another longtime Andropov KGB deputy, Viktor Chebrikov, became the director of the security police.

KGB ORGANIZATION

The present structure and function of the KGB are very much a product of its long, often turbulent evolution. The KGB today is a massive organization, performing functions that, in the United States, fall within the purview of the Central Intelligence Agency, the FBI, the National Security Agency, and a number of other federal and state agencies. Western intelligence services estimate that the KGB employs over 90,000 staff officers and another 400,000 clerical staff, building guards, border guards, and special troops. The number of informants officially working in other organizations but cooperating with the KGB is probably several hundred thousand.[16] There are reported to be more than 250,000 KGB operatives working abroad.[17] In 1983, the FBI was said to be watching the activities of 450 Soviet spies operating in the United States under diplomatic cover.[18] However, the exact personnel strength of the KGB is impossible to determine from available information.

The KGB is headed by the chairman, who is an *ex officio* member of the Council of Ministers. The chairman of the KGB is assisted in his duties by a collegium, consisting of the chiefs of each of the agency's many directorates.

As a result of its size and complexity, the KGB is divided into several directorates, each with its own distinct responsibilities:

The First Chief Directorate is responsible for foreign operations, including clandestine activities abroad, and the theft or purchase of Western scientific, technical, and military-related hardware. The First Chief Directorate is also responsible for counterintelligence—that is, penetrating and neutralizing the activities of foreign security and intelligence services. One element of this task is carried out by the Active Measures Department (formerly known as the Disinformation Department), which plans and implements campaigns to influence the decisions of foreign governments or to demoralize groups hostile to the interests of the USSR. Another division within the First Chief Directorate, the Executive Actions Department (Department V), is responsible for planning and carrying out political murders (sometimes referred to as *mokrye dela,* or "wet work"), kidnappings, and sabotage. In addition to these functional divisions, the First Chief Directorate is also divided into ten departments specializing in various regions of the world.

The Second Chief Directorate is generally responsible for monitoring the activities of Soviet citizens and foreigners within the Soviet Union. Like the First Chief Directorate, this directorate is subdivided into many departments for various geographic regions and functional specializations. For example, the First Department focuses on diplomats from the United States and Latin America in the USSR. The Seventh Department monitors the activities of foreign tourists in the USSR and includes among its staff members KGB agents working for foreign airline offices, hotels, and Intourist, the Soviet tourist agency. The Second Chief Directorate is also responsible for authorizing foreign travel for all Soviet citizens, except senior party members.

The Third Directorate, one of the largest and most important units in the KGB, is usually referred to as the Armed Forces Directorate.[19] It oversees the activities of military units through a network of agents in every echelon of the armed forces, down to the company level. KGB officers are responsible for education and ideological training of the forces, and they also keep the Party informed about the reliability and loyalty of the troops. KGB officers within the military report through their own chain of command, giving them a degree of independence that is sometimes unpopular with the regular military officers.[20]

The KGB has neither a Fourth nor a Sixth Directorate. There is no known reason for these omissions.

The Fifth Chief Directorate specializes in surveillance and operations directed against Soviet citizens in the USSR. This directorate was created in 1969 to uncover and stamp out political dissent in the country. Its activities include monitoring and eliminating uncensored publications and unauthorized gatherings of underground organizations, and limiting the contacts between Soviet citizens and their relatives living abroad, as well as with foreigners within the USSR. Through its network of KGB informants and agents, the Fifth Chief Directorate has infiltrated the Russian Orthodox church and other religious organizations and nationality groups. In the face of growing requests from Jews to emigrate from the USSR, a special Jewish Department was established in 1971. Its functions include discouraging emigration, halting public protests, and general intimidation.

The Seventh Directorate, or Surveillance Directorate, employs more than 3500 men and women whose sole occupation is to follow particular individuals in the USSR. The directorate is divided into departments by geographic region; the First Department thus specializes in following citizens of the United States and Latin America, and so on. The Fifth Department supervises the militia assigned to guard foreign embassies and residences and to prevent unauthorized visits by Russians. The Seventh Department is responsible for the maintenance of cars, hidden microphones, and other surveillance equipment. The Ninth Department patrols streets and buildings near the residences and offices of high-ranking party and state officials. Finally, the Tenth Department covers the Moscow region, focusing on sites that foreigners are likely to visit.

All foreign scholars in the USSR experience the attention of the Seventh Directorate at one time or another. During a stay as a research scholar at the Leningrad University Juridical Faculty, the author was followed periodically. Soon after arriving in Leningrad, he was befriended by an American family working in the U.S. Consulate. On weekends, they often invited him to go cross-country skiing with them outside the city. The arragements were usually confirmed by telephone, which was bugged both in the author's dormitory and in the U.S. Consulate. The Americans usually were accompanied on these ski outings by a dull grey sedan carrying one or two KGB agents. Uncertain as to the Americans' true plans, the KGB "tails" would wear business suits and overcoats, but would also bring along skis. The image of KGB agents huffing and puffing on their skis to keep pace with the Americans was more comical than sinister. After one especially arduous afternoon of skiing, the author and his friends bought some beer at a nearby kiosk and left two bottles in a snowbank for their lagging companions.

Although there is rarely face-to-face contact, a rapport sometimes develops between the KGB tails and their assignments. Western diplomats have reported that KGB agents following them have assisted them in changing flat tires or making emergency auto repairs. In a few cases, KGB surveillance has even prevented Westerners from being mugged or having their automobiles stolen.

The Eighth Directorate, or Communications Directorate, specializes in intelligence-gathering by "national technical means": satellite, "fishing trawlers" monitoring United States naval operations, and sophisticated devices placed on top of Soviet embassies and consulates in most Western capitals. The Ninth Directorate, or Kremlin Guards, comprises a body of elite troops that function as bodyguards for prominent Soviet officials. The Kremlin Guards are the only individuals in the Soviet military allowed to carry loaded weapons in the presence of the political leaders.

In addition to these directorates, the KGB maintains four unnumbered directorates. The Border Guards Chief Directorate patrols Soviet borders to prevent not only the unauthorized entry of foreign agents into the Soviet Union but also, more importantly, the unauthorized exit of Soviet citizens. The Technical Operations Directorate is responsible for researching, designing, and manufacturing the various gadgets used in spying. The Personnel Directorate recruits and trains KGB employees, while the Administration Directorate handles travel arrangements, the management of property, resorts, and apartments, and other routine functions.

THE KGB AND SOVIET SOCIETY

Despite its coerciveness and intrusions into their lives, most Soviet citizens appear to accept, if not like, the KGB. Some Russians still fear being called into the "Big House" to explain their "fraternization" with foreigners, so they prefer to keep such contacts discreet. Others simply maintain, "I have nothing to hide," and instruct their foreign friends to come and go as they please, even if they are being followed.

Increasingly, new recruits to the KGB come from well-educated, white-collar families, often families in which the father is already working in the agency. Midcareer entry into the KGB from other organizations is rare.[21] Thus, the KGB has become a closed bureaucracy of specialists. The one exception remains at the highest ranks of the agency, where the political appointment of party officials is considered necessary to ensure control by the CPSU over the security police.

Employment in the KGB has obvious advantages, including good pay, travel opportunities, and numerous other perquisites. For example, the starting salaries of law-school graduates entering the KGB are two to three times higher than those of their classmates working in other legal agencies.[22] KGB employees also have access to special stores, where there is an abundance of goods unavailable to the general public. The agency also maintains social clubs and resorts that feature the finest food and most luxurious accommodations in the USSR.

Since Stalin's time, there has been a concerted effort to bring the KGB under party control. Political control over the security police is exercised by the Department of Administrative Organs of the Central Committee, primarily through its power over personnel and appointments (*nomenklatura*). All major appointments in the KGB must be cleared by the Department of Administrative Organs. Until the rise of Andropov, KGB officers were restricted to positions within the security apparatus. It was most unusual for a career KGB officer to assume a position of responsibility as a regional party secretary or chairman of an executive committee of a local soviet. Under Andropov, however, several of his former associates in the security apparatus were promoted to regional party posts. The most notable was Geidar Aliev, who served in the KGB until 1969, when he was promoted to First Secretary of the Azerbaidzhan Republic.

Another noteworthy trend began under Brezhnev and continued thereafter: the tendency toward increased representation of KGB officials in party leadership bodies at all levels. This phenomenon indicates that the KGB is no longer viewed simply as an organ for carrying out the Party's policies, but is increasingly being integrated into the policy-making process.[23] This new role, combined with the strong sense of solidarity and esprit de corps within the ranks of the KGB, signals the growing power and influence of the security police in policy matters in the Soviet Union.

THE POLICE (MILITIA)

Compared to the activities of the KGB, the regular police functions of the Ministry of Internal Affairs may seem bland and uninteresting. In recent years, however, the militia has taken on a new and expanded role in carrying out the anticorruption campaigns initiated by Andropov and Gorbachev.

The militia is charged with a wide array of duties: detecting crime, apprehending criminals, supervising the internal passport system, maintaining public order, combating public intoxication, supervising parolees, managing prisons and labor colonies, and controlling traffic. Since 1956, local police departments have been subject to dual subordination; consequently, they must report both to the executive committees of their respective local soviets and to their superior offices within the Ministry of Internal Affairs (MVD).

Local police departments are organized into sections, as described in the following pages.

Section for the Regular Police (Uniformed Police). This section supervises the activities of the regular police forces, who are distinguished by their grey uniforms with red piping. The duties of the uniformed police include patrolling public places to ensure order and arresting persons violating the law, including vagrants and drunks. Resisting arrest or obstructing a police officer from executing his duties is a serious offense in the Soviet Union and can result in a sentence of one to five years.[24]

Especially visible to the foreigner in the USSR are the uniformed police posted outside foreign embassies. They are responsible for checking the documents of all persons entering embassies; on many occasions, they have manhandled Soviet citizens attempting to make "unauthorized" visits. The militia also maintain checkpoints on all roads leading out of Soviet cities. Foreigners in the USSR are restricted to the area within a 25-mile radius from the center of the city. In order to travel beyond the 25-mile limit, a special internal travel permit must be obtained from the police. Approximately 97 percent of the Soviet landmass is "closed" to foreigners, and foreign citizens traveling from one city to another may often do so only during nighttime hours, when it is impossible to see or photograph anything.

Soviet authorities are especially sensitive to foreigners taking photographs. The official list of prohibited subjects includes airports, train stations, bridges, electrical power plants, large factories, military facilities, and persons in uniform. Taking photographs from an airplane over Soviet territory is also strictly prohibited. In addition to these restrictions, past experience has proven that even a seemingly innocuous photograph may be alarming to the Soviet police. An American scholar in Leningrad was apprehended by the police for taking pictures in a meat market. The proprietress suspected that his intent was to illustrate the long lines and shortages of food in the USSR. The author once happened to be on a street in downtown Moscow when a fire broke out on the third floor of a nearby apartment building. The fire trucks arrived, and a crowd gathered. The author pulled out his camera and was about to take a picture when the meaty hand of a stern-looking middle-aged woman covered the lens. "It's not good to take pictures of tragedies!" she commanded.

Local police departments are also responsible for supervising parolees living in their precincts and for registering potentially dangerous items, such as firearms, explosives, and photocopying machines.

Criminal Investigation Section.   This section assists the Procuracy, and on occasion the KGB, in the investigation of criminal cases. The duties of this section may entail gathering evidence, interviewing witnesses, questioning suspects, and writing reports.

Section for the Struggle Against the Theft of Socialist Property.   This section of the militia was established in the 1970s in order to combat such white-collar crime as embezzlement, falsification of plan records, and so on. Economic crimes have been a particular focus of police activity in recent years.

Sections for Passports, Visas, and Registration (OVIR).   OVIR is responsible for registering Soviet citizens and foreigners residing in each precinct of a Soviet city. Foreigners wishing to travel within the USSR and Soviet citizens wishing to emigrate from the USSR must apply to OVIR for the proper authorizations. OVIR is also responsible for issuing internal passports to Soviet citizens. An internal passport, which is issued at the age of sixteen, includes the picture of the citizen, name, date and place of birth, nationality, marital status, children, military service, and place of residence. In an effort to stem the tide of rural out-migration, until 1974 internal passports were not issued to workers on collective farms or state farms; thus, they found it especially difficult to gain permission to travel within the country. Since new legislation governing passports took effect in 1974, people living in rural areas have been treated the same as those living in the cities.

Section for Motor Vehicles.   This section is responsible for the registration of automobiles, safety inspections, and policing of the highways.

Section for Prosecution and Preliminary Investigation.   This section assists in the preparation of materials for court hearings in relatively minor cases, such as traffic offenses, in which the public prosecutor's office does not wish to be involved.

Section for Recruitment and Training.   This section supervises the recruitment of new members of the militia. Candidates are thoroughly screened by local party and Komsomol bodies to ensure their political reliability.

Section for Administration.   This section handles routine administrative functions.

THE POLICE AND POLICY-MAKING

The MVD has never achieved the power nor engendered the degree of fear the KGB has, and its political influence is also much less than that of the security police. The Minister of Internal Affairs normally is a member of the CPSU Central Committee and the USSR Council of Ministers, but, in contrast to the KGB, no police official has ever risen to Politburo status. This would indicate that, at the national level, the police are viewed more as executors of party policy, with little voice in the making of policy. At the local level, however, the police chief generally is included on both the executive committee of the local soviet and the party committee, where he may have a considerable impact on decisions affecting local law enforcement.

The KGB and the MVD appear to have played a major role in the accessions of both Andropov and Gorbachev to the post of General Secretary. Andropov built a solid power base during his fifteen years in the KGB, which has close ties to the MVD and the armed forces. From 1978 until Andropov's assumption of the top party post in November 1982, eleven of fourteen republic KGB chiefs were replaced; in 1982 alone, three new republic KGB chiefs were appointed. There were also substantial changes in the MVD; eleven republic MVD ministers were replaced since 1978. These new appointments strengthened Andropov's power base in both bureaucracies.[25]

After becoming General Secretary, Andropov used his power base in the security police and the militia to launch a campaign against economic crime and official corruption. It was not coincidental that many of the targets of this campaign were officials in Krasnoiarsk and Moldavia, regions in which Andropov's principal rival, Konstantin Chernenko, maintained his power base.

The anticorruption and work-discipline campaigns transcended the power struggle among the ruling elite, however. By mobilizing the coercive power of the KGB and the MVD, Andropov hoped to revive the sagging Soviet economy. For the fifteen months Andropov was in office, the discipline campaign was prominently displayed in the pages of the Soviet press. In 1984, for example, *Pravda Vostoka* announced that a two-year investigation in the Uzbek republic had resulted in the firing of many party and state officials, including the Minister of Finance, Minister of Internal Affairs, Chairman of the State Committee for Publishing, the First Secretary of the Dzhizak City Party Committee, and fifty-nine deputies of local soviets.[26] In addition, the First Secretary of the Tashkent regional party committee reported that 1056 employees of stores, warehouses, pharmacies, and hospitals had been removed from their posts, and charges had been brought against them for accepting bribes, theft of socialist property, and official corruption.[27] Similar investigations in Bukhara resulted in the expulsions of 461 party members, including three prominent regional first secretaries.[28]

The discipline and anticorruption campaigns lost some momentum during the brief interlude of Konstantin Chernenko's leadership (February 1984–March 1985), but they resumed under Mikhail Gorbachev. The prominent role played by the KGB and the MVD in recent successions, coupled with the high visibility of both institutions in the ongoing discipline campaigns, has enhanced their status and influence in the Soviet political system.

THE ARMED FORCES

The Soviet political leadership has always manifested an ambivalent attitude toward the armed forces. The military is seen as a tool for furthering the revolutionary goals of the regime, but it also represents a disciplined, hierarchical, centralized, and powerful institution that could perhaps challenge the Party. This fear of the military's potential counterrevolutionary influence has resulted in a consistent policy of careful subordination and control of the armed forces by the CPSU. We begin our examination of the role of the armed forces in the Soviet political system by analyzing the evolution of Party-military relations.

Party-Military Relations in the USSR.   Immediately following the Bolshevik seizure of power in 1917, Lenin dispatched military commissars to the Petrograd garrison to arrest reactionary officers. The first centrally controlled organization of military commissars began two days later, with the creation of the All-Russian Bureau of Military Commissars. Initially, the Party established the commissar system to assure the loyalty of military officers, many of whom had served in the imperial Russian army. Responsibilities of the political commissars included the ideological training and supervision of military personnel (though in time, many became involved in strictly military matters). During this period, the political commissar and the commander operated on a dual-command principle, which meant that all commands had to be approved by both officers. Needless to say, such an awkward system of control resulted in frequent conflicts between the Party and the professional military. From the beginning, even its proponents felt that the commissar system hindered the ability of the military commanders and that it would eventually give way to a single, unified command structure.

From 1930 to 1936, the armed forces gained greater independence, in part because of Stalin's rising concern with Hitler and his consequent desire for increased professionalism within the Red Army. In addition, during the early 1930s, the political administration evolved into an integral part of the armed forces and did not concern itself with military matters, thus reducing tensions.[29]

The trend toward greater professionalization in the Soviet armed forces came to an abrupt end on May 10, 1937, however, when the principle of a unified command was abolished. During this period, the purges began to take their greatest toll among the military. It is estimated that about one-third of the officer corps were executed between 1935 and 1938, and military intelligence was crippled.[30] The political administration was also severely hit by the purge. The heads of all political sections and most members of military districts were arrested. In addition, all seventeen army commissars, twenty-five of twenty-eight corps commissars, and thirty-four of thirty-six brigade commissars were removed.[31] There have been many explanations offered for Stalin's purge of the Soviet armed foces, but one important factor may have been his fear of this trend toward greater independence and professionalism within the officer corps.

The military's position improved somewhat following the Russo-Finnish conflict of 1939. The Red Army's embarrassing performance against the vastly outnumbered Finnish troops prompted serious reconsideration of political controls over the military. At the urging of Marshal S. K. Timoshenko, Stalin agreed to loosen some party controls and place greater emphasis on military preparedness and less on political indoctrination. Nazi Germany's surprise attack in June 1941 reinforced this trend. By October 1942, the principle of a single, unified command was reestablished, and the military commissars were replaced by political assistants (*zampolity*).

The *zampolit* system and the principle of a unified command have existed to the present, although the degree of party control has fluctuated. The relative influence of military commanders seems to have increased during particularly difficult periods, when the Soviets were on the defensive (e.g., World War II prior to Stalingrad and again during the Korean War); the *zampolity* regained greater influence during peacetime or when the USSR was on the offensive.

Stalin's death marked a significant change in Party-military relations in the USSR. With no designated heir, the military became an important institution in the succession struggle. In particular, the military was needed to crush Beria's bid for power.

The resurgence of the Red Army after Stalin is symbolized by the rise of Marshal G. K. Zhukov to the post of Minister of Defense in 1955. The role of the political administration was further weakened during Zhukov's tenure; in 1955, he reorganized the *zampolity* under his direct supervision. Meanwhile, the armed forces were playing an even more visible political role by removing the potential threat posed by Beria and the security police and by crushing the Hungarian Revolution in 1956. In June 1957, the military, under Zhukov's direction, assisted Khrushchev in foiling an attempted coup by the so-called Anti-Party Group. Air-force planes were mobilized to fly members of the Central Committee to Moscow for an emergency session. At this plenum, the Central Committee, which was dominated by pro-Khrushchev regional-party secretaries, overruled the Presidium and reinstated Khrushchev as First Secretary. For his assistance, Zhukov was rewarded with full membership in the Presidium, the first time this honor was bestowed upon a professional soldier. Not long after, however, Khrushchev became wary of Zhukov's growing power. Zhukov was demoted and accused of Bonapartism, just as Trotsky had been accused of using the Red Army to launch a counterrevolutionary bid for power many years earlier. In the case of Zhukov's forced political exile in 1957, there remains no conclusive evidence that a military coup was being planned under his auspices.

After Zhukov's ouster, party controls over the military were again reinforced, but not to a degree that would irritate those who had assisted in his dismissal.[32] In April 1958, the political administration was renamed the Main Political Administration of the Soviet Army and Navy; it was headed by Marshal Filip Golikov, an associate of Khrushchev from his days in Stalingrad. In October 1958, new instructions to political officers strengthened their position relative to the professional military commanders. Political education became mandatory, and an officer's promotion depended on political as well as military expertise.[33]

In 1961, Khrushchev adopted a military doctrine of minimum deterrence, which reflected his conviction that the effectiveness of conventional forces in deterring war and influencing international relations had diminished in light of the development of intercontinental ballistic missiles. Consequently, he proposed reducing the ground forces of the Soviet army by one-third, from 3.6 to 2.4 million troops; the Strategic Rocket Force was established to fill the void. Thus, Khrushchev's military doctrine emphasized nuclear weapons at the expense of conventional forces, a doctrine that was sure to antagonize powerful factions within the armed forces. The lack of support for Khrushchev's doctrine was evident in both the professional military and the Main Political Administration, as well as among conservative elements of the Party.

The Cuban missile crisis in October 1962 illustrated the weaknesses of Khrushchev's defense policies and further alienated him from the majority of the Soviet armed forces. By 1964, Khrushchev had lost the support of virtually all segments of the Soviet ruling elite, and he was replaced by Brezhnev and Kosygin. On this occasion, the armed forces refused to come to Khrushchev's rescue, as they had in 1957.

In the aftermath of the Cuban missile crisis and Khrushchev's ouster, the Soviet Union pursued a policy designed to achieve military parity with the United States. Military allocations and priority increased substantially. The MPA also increased its prestige and influence during this period. The new head of the MPA, Marshal A. A. Epishev, and a number of his associates gained membership in the Central Committee in 1966.

With the achievement of strategic parity in the late 1960s, Brezhnev moved to improve relations with Western Europe and the United States. Détente was not popular with the armed forces, however, and the MPA, rather than supporting the position of the party leadership, actively opposed Brezhnev's policy.[34] Détente also divided the Politburo into a pro-détente faction led by Brezhnev and an anti-détente faction led by senior ideologist Mikhail Suslov. Military opposition to détente can also be inferred from the numerous hard-line statements made by such high-ranking military officers as Epishev.

The military's opposition to détente resulted in a crackdown on the influence of the armed forces in 1969. The military portion of the traditional May Day parade was canceled. The absence of huge missiles and tanks rolling through Red Square was seen in the West as a conciliatory gesture by the Brezhnev regime. It is likely, however, that Brezhnev intended to send a signal as much to his own military as to Western leaders. Shortly after the May Day parade, an MPA conference on the importance of ideological training in the armed forces was called off. Brezhnev, meanwhile, garnered more accolades. In 1971, he was promoted to the military rank of four-star general, and later the same year, he received the Marshal Star, an honor customarily awarded only to those in active military service. These moves signified his desire to subordinate the armed forces to the Party's control. The signing of the SALT I accord in 1972 further illustrated Brezhnev's willingness to overrule his military advisers.

In 1973, Brezhnev apparently sought to restore the balance in Party-military relations by proposing Foreign Minister Andrei Gromyko, KGB chief Iurii Andropov, and Minister of Defense A. A. Grechko to full membership in the Politburo. Grechko's appointment was clearly intended to assure both the professional army and the defense industries that the military needs of the country would be met regardless of the course of relations with the West.

Two decisions in 1976, however, further symbolized the preeminence of the Party over the armed forces. In May 1976, Brezhnev decorated himself with the highest rank in the Soviet Union, Marshal of the Soviet Union; in July, Dmitri Ustinov, a civilian expert on the defense industry, was made Minister of Defense and Marshal of the Soviet Union, replacing Grechko, who had died a short time earlier. At the time that Brezhnev and Ustinov became Marshals, it had been eight years since the last Soviet commander received such a distinction. This fact signifies the Party's determination to keep the military under control.[35]

The invasion of Afghanistan in 1979 demonstrated the willingness of the party leadership to use military power in support of its perceived national interests. The decision to intervene was political and was apparently opposed by some junior members of the High Command, although the majority of military commentators have been very supportive of the Soviet intervention.[36]

The tensions between the political leadership and the military became even more evident in 1982, when Marshal Nikolai Ogarkov, First Deputy Minister of Defense and Chief of the General Staff, openly championed the merits of fighting a nuclear war.[37] Strategic doctrine is generally considered the purview of the political leaders, and Ogarkov's position challenged the official strategy articulated by Defense Minister Ustinov that nuclear war, even a limited nuclear war, would be suicidal.[38]

Shortly thereafter, on August 31, 1983, Soviet aircraft shot down Korean Airlines Flight 007. While not condemning the action, the Party clearly held the military in general, and Ogarkov in particular, responsible. The shooting down of the airliner came at a particularly awkward moment, as the political leaders were attempting to repair badly damaged relations with the United States. This fact reinforced Western suspicions that the decision to shoot the plane down was made by the military with a minimum of consultation with the political leaders.

The Korean Airlines disaster apparently raised some concern within the Soviet armed forces that the Party would move to reinstitute more stringent political controls. An article published in the military's newspaper, *Krasnaia Zveda* (Red Star), extolled the merits of a unified command structure and warned against a return to the days when "political watchdogs" impeded the efficiency of military command.[39] It is likely that the appearance of this article was meant to persuade Andropov not to use the incident as an excuse to reorganize the military.

While the fortunes of the military as a whole did not suffer a noticeable decline following the Korean Airlines incident, Ogarkov's did. He was demoted in September 1984, accused of "unpartylike tendencies," and reassigned as a commander of Western theater forces, a command that existed largely on paper. After less than a year, however, he was rehabilitated by Gorbachev and assigned as First Deputy Minister of Defense and Commander of the Warsaw Pact Forces. The appointment may indicate that Gorbachev favored Ogarkov's stance, especially that the Soviet armed forces must modernize all aspects of the nation's defense in order to respond to the technological challenge posed by the United States. Equally important, by restoring Ogarkov to an influential post in the Ministry of Defense, Gorbachev could be assured of Ogarkov's support and loyalty. In another surprising move, Gorbachev named Alexei Lizichev to replace the seventy-seven-year-old Epishev as head of the Main Political Administration. Lizichev, head of the political section of Soviet forces in East Germany, had been considered an unlikely candidate for the MPA post. His appointment was consistent with other promotions made by Gorbachev, however, and seemed to signify Gorbachev's desire to promote younger, more competent officials. Rather than replacing retiring executives with deputies who faithfully follow in their predecessors' footsteps, Gorbachev apparently favored promoting from without. Such a policy shakes up the entrenched bureaucracies, promotes innovation, and at the same time reinforces the central position of the Party.

THE SOVIET MILITARY AND POLICY-MAKING

As we have seen, the division of power and responsibilities between the CPSU and the armed forces in the USSR is complex and has fluctuated over time. The Politburo is thought to make most major decisions relating to Soviet foreign policy, including military matters. In reality, however, the role of the Politburo probably is limited to accepting, rejecting, or modifying proposals and recommendations of various military and quasi-military bodies.

Within the CPSU Secretariat, two secretaries have important responsibilities relating to the operation of the Soviet armed forces. The "second secretary" is usually in charge of cadres and thus approves major military appointments. In addition, one of the senior members of the Secretariat is charged with supervising the activities of the agencies relevant to foreign policy—the Ministry of Foreign Affairs, the KGB, and the Ministry of Defense.

The highest-level policy and planning organ for the Soviet military is the Defense Council of the USSR, about which little is known. (See Figure 8-1.) In fact, its existence was not confirmed until 1976, when Brezhnev was identified as Chairman of the Council. In addition to the General Secretary of the CPSU, who serves as its Chairman, the Defense Council is thought to

Figure 8-1. Organization of the Soviet Armed Forces

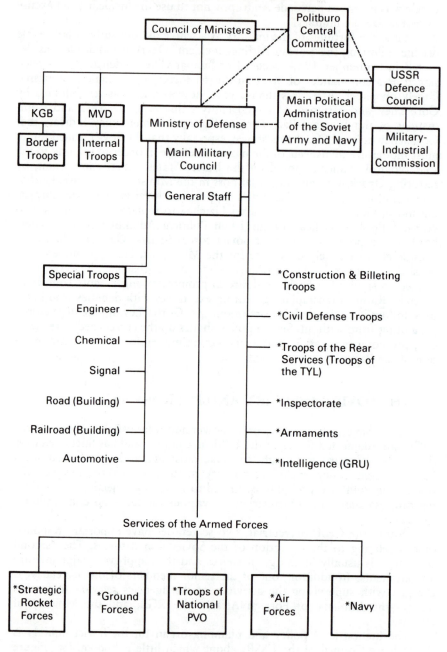

*Each headed by a Deputy Minister of Defense.
Source: Based on material from Harriet Fast Scott and William F. Scott, *The Armed Forces of the USSR.* 2d rev. ed. (Boulder: Westview Press, 1984), 143.

consist of the Minister of Defense, the "second secretary" of the Central Committee Secretariat, the secretary specializing in foreign policy and defense matters, the Premier of the USSR (Chairman of the Presidium of the Council of Ministers), and probably the Chief of the General Staff. Other military and civilian officials may be called upon to attend meetings, depending on the subjects to be discussed. Among these are the Minister of Foreign Affairs, the Chairman of the KGB, the Minister of Internal Affairs, and the Commander of the Warsaw Pact Forces. The fact that the Defense Council includes a number of party officials and other noncareer military officers underscores its role as a policy-making and advisory body, one in which the Party can benefit from the considerable expertise of the professional military without giving them official and extensive representation on the Politburo. The Defense Council seems to focus on overseeing military policies and making recommendations to the Politburo. An especially important aspect of the council's work is designing programs for the development of new weapons systems.

Subordinate to the Defense Council is the Military-Industrial Commission, which includes representatives of the various defense-related industries, the State Planning Commission (Gosplan), the Ministry of Defense, and the Party. The commission supervises the procurement of armaments and material, ensuring that sufficient resources are available to meet production targets and coordinating delivery schedules to meet the needs of the military.

A second influential military body is the Main Military Council within the Ministry of Defense. This body, which is chaired by the Minister of Defense, is responsible for the overall command and control of the armed forces in peacetime. This includes resolving interservice disputes, allocating funds and personnel, and determining how best to implement decisions of the Politburo and the Defense Council. Members of the Main Military Council include the head of the Main Political Administration, the commanders of the five services, other branch chiefs, deputy ministers, chiefs of the General Staff, and the Commander-in-Chief of the Warsaw Pact Forces. In time of war, the Main Military Council would be replaced by the *Stavka*, or Headquarters of the Supreme High Command.

Also within the Ministry of Defense is the General Staff of the Armed Forces. Modeled on its imperial Russian predecessor, this body is responsible for strategic planning and coordinating the activities of the five services.

Subordinate to the General Staff are several directorates, including the influential Main Intelligence Administration (GRU). The GRU gathers intelligence information on enemy forces, technological developments, and combat conditions, and estimates enemy capabilities. Although its functions are much narrower than those of the KGB, there is a degree of overlap in their operations; this has, on occasion, resulted in interagency disputes.

The following are the military services or branches of the Soviet armed forces:

- Strategic Rocket Forces
- Ground Forces
- Air Defense Forces

- Air Forces
- Navy

Soviet publications always list the five services in this order, which roughly approximates their relative prestige and influence, although the navy has been gaining influence in recent years.

The structure of the Main Political Administration has changed little since its reorganization in 1958. Below the highest officers of the MPA, the chief (*nachal'nik*) and his deputies, there exists a hierarchy of full-time political officers that parallels the command structure of the armed forces. At each level, a single political officer is in charge of all political work. The MPA currently employs more than 40,000 political officers.[40] In addition, the MPA supervises the activities of some 62,000 primary party organizations within military units.[41] Party membership is especially common among the officer corps. It is estimated that 40 percent of all party members in the military are officers in staff organizations.[42] In contrast, the Komsomol organizations within the armed forces are primarily for rank-and-file soldiers and noncommissioned officers. Eighty percent of all enlisted personnel are members of the Komsomol.[43]

THE ROLE OF THE ARMED FORCES IN SOVIET SOCIETY

For the Westerner, it is difficult to understand the degree of public, as well as official, praise that is heaped upon the Soviet armed forces. The massive military parades on November 7 and May 1 and the public celebrations on Armed Forces Day can all be rationalized as the result of well-orchestrated efforts of party workers to mobilize support for the military. But much of the adulation of the armed forces appears to be voluntary and spontaneous. Next to the Kremlin wall in Moscow is a memorial to the Soviet war dead. A perpetual flame burns, guarded by young Komsomols. It is the custom for brides to lay their bouquets at the memorial in tribute to the Soviet fighting men. On any given day, several happy brides still wearing their wedding dresses pose for pictures at the memorial. One can hardly imagine a bride in the United States or elsewhere going straight from her wedding to a war memorial.

People in the United States are not accustomed to seeing large numbers of military men in uniform on the streets. Yet, in the USSR, military personnel constitute a large and visible portion of the population, especially in cities such as Leningrad. Members of the armed forces wear their uniforms proudly and are seldom seen in public in civilian attire. Veterans of World War II, which the Soviets still refer to as the Great Patriotic War, are encouraged to wear their medals.

The military establishment in the USSR is estimated to consume from 12 to 15 percent of the gross national product, and this unquestionably results in a lower standard of living for the average citizen. Yet, even among the author's acquaintances in the Soviet Union who are quite liberal on most issues, the "defense of the Motherland" and the level of defense spending are never questioned.

Children are taught respect for the armed forces from an early age. In elementary schools and Pioneer organizations, children march and practice military drills using toy rifles. Mandatory military training for both boys and girls begins in the ninth grade. The program includes instruction in basic drill, weapons operation, field exercises, and civil defense. In addition, boys are required to attend summer camp where they learn to fire weapons using live ammunition.

All males are eligible for the military draft as of age eighteen, and almost all are conscripted. The normal term of service is two years, followed by reserve duty until the age of fifty. Universal service in the Soviet military results in a very large standing army—more than 3.7 million in 1982. Military service is considered important, not only to provide the armed forces with the necessary personnel, but also to instill in the citizen a sense of responsibility for the defense of the USSR.

Service in the Soviet armed forces is also intended as one way in which non-Russian ethnic minorities can become assimilated into Soviet society. The command language throughout the armed forces is Russian; military units are not supposed to be configured on the basis of ethnicity or native language. All non-Russians are to have had a minimum of six years of Russian-language training in school before entering the army. Nevertheless, recent experience in Afghanistan has demonstrated the inability of Central Asian troops to understand their Russian officers. De facto segregation of some ethnic groups (especially Central Asians) has occurred simply in order to facilitate communication and control.

A sizable portion of the military conscripts in the Soviet Union work in construction battalions, building housing, digging ditches, and building highways. In 1980, Soviet soldiers were employed in the construction of the Olympic Village in Moscow, and more recently they were put to work on sections of the Baikal-Amur Railroad in Siberia. In the autumn, army units are often mobilized to assist in the harvest. The majority of Central Asian inductees are assigned to these "pick-and-shovel brigades," where language problems are less troublesome.

Long-term personnel prospects for the Soviet armed forces are not bright. It is estimated that non-Russians will constitute almost three-quarters of the draft-age population by the year 2000.[44] In contrast, the officer corps of the Soviet armed forces is dominated by Russians—at least 80 percent.[45]

Future officers receive their military education in one of the 140 higher military schools, most of which entail four or five years of training and result in a commission as lieutenant. In addition, sixteen higher military academies have been created in the various branches and divisions of the armed forces. In recent years, it appears that the majority of persons entering the officer-training programs are Russian, Ukrainian, or Belorussian; well-educated; and from white-collar families, often military families. Some Western experts have even characterized the higher officer pool as a "new class" that discourages penetration by "outsiders."[46]

Given the high esteem with which the Soviet armed forces are held and the sizable percentage of the budget they consume, it should be no surprise that the members of the military are relatively well compensated. The salaries of top-level officers are among the highest in the Soviet Union, while middle- and lower-level officers live more modestly, but nonetheless comfortably. An especially significant component of income for officers is access to military department stores, clubs, resorts, hospitals, and housing, which provide a much better quality of goods and services than is generally available to civilians. Soviet military officials justify these perquisites as appropriate rewards for enduring the difficulty and danger of military service and as necessary to entice talented youth into seeking military careers.

It is too early to tell whether the Soviet involvement in Afghanistan has tarnished the image of the armed forces in the eyes of Soviet citizens. A handful of Soviet defectors indicate that morale among Soviet forces in Afghanistan is very low. Drug and alcohol abuse appear to be widespread. Furthermore, the normally tightly controlled and ever-optimistic Soviet press has recently reprinted letters in which former soldiers who served in Afghanistan complained that they were treated with indifference upon returning home.[47] For every bitter relative of a soldier killed in Afghanistan, however, there are many more that see their loss as a noble sacrifice made in defense of the Motherland.

With such widespread public and official support, a dynamic and professionally competent leadership, and a commitment to creating a technologically sophisticated defense establishment, the armed forces in the USSR appear to be quite strong. Whether this will translate into expanded influence in policy-making, however, is difficult to judge. The energy, imagination, unpredictability, and power displayed by Gorbachev suggest that the Party will retain its central role as the guiding force in all affairs, including those relating to the military.

Notes

1. Ronald Hingley, *The Russian Secret Police* (London: Hutchinson, 1970), 3.

2. Ibid., 10.

3. Ibid., 15.

4. V. I. Lenin, *Polnoe sobranie sochinenii,* vol. 37 (Moscow: Politicheskaia literatura, 1965), 174.

5. Hingley, *The Russian Secret Police,* 122.

6. Estimate of W. H. Chamberlin, *The Russian Revolution, 1917–1921,* vol. 2 (New York: Macmillan, 1952), 75.

7. E. H. Carr, *The Bolshevik Revolution,* vol. 1 (London: Macmillan, 1953), 181.

8. This episode is recounted in Hingley, *The Russian Secret Police,* 141–142.

9. Robert Conquest, *The Great Terror* (London: Macmillan, 1969), 551–552.

10. Hingley, *The Russian Secret Police,* 161.

11. Ibid., 166–167.

12. Conquest, *The Great Terror,* 532.

13. Robert Conquest, *The Soviet Police System* (New York: Praeger, 1968), 22.

14. Michel Tatu, *Power in the Kremlin* (New York: Viking Press, 1968), 198.

15. In the period from 1952 to 1966, the Politburo was enlarged and its name was changed to the Presidium of the CPSU Central Committee.

16. John Barron, *KGB Today: The Hidden Hand* (New York: Holt, Rinehart & Winston, 1983), 41. *The Economist* claims that the total number of KGB officers, agents, and informants may be as high as 1.5 million. See *The Economist,* 27 November 1982, pp. 105–106.

17. Barron, *KGB Today,* 41.

18. *Washington Post,* 21 June 1983.

19. The Soviets distinguish between Chief Directorate and Directorate. The significance of this distinction is obscure, however. Rather than present the KGB Chief Directorates first, followed by the Directorates, the author has opted to present them in numerical order.

20. Barron, *KGB Today,* 15–16.

21. Amy W. Knight, "The CPSU and Cadres Policy in the State Security Organs," (Paper presented to the annual convention of the American Association for the Advancement of Slavic Studies, New York, November 1–3, 1984), 31.

22. Consultation with students in the Juridical Faculty, Leningrad State University, February 3, 1976.

23. Knight, "The CPSU and Cadres Policy," 32.

24. Criminal Code of the RSFSR, Article 191-1.

25. Amy W. Knight, "Andropov: Myths and Realities," *Survey* 28, no. 1 (Spring 1984): 40.

26. *Pravda Vostoka,* 26 June 1984, pp. 1–3.

27. *Pravda Vostoka,* 15 July 1984, p. 1.

28. *Pravda Vostoka,* 31 July 1984, p. 2.

29. Michael J. Deane, *Political Control of the Soviet Armed Forces* (New York: Crane, Russak, 1977), 38–39.

30. Bill Murphy, "The Political-Military Relations in the USSR," *Radio Liberty Research Bulletin,* October 24, 1984, p. 3.

31. Deane, *Political Control of the Soviet Armed Forces,* 43.

32. Ibid., 66.

33. Ibid., 67.

34. For a discussion of the impact of détente on the military see Deane, *Political Control of the Soviet Armed Forces,* chapters 7 and 8.

35. Murphy, "Political-Military Relations in the USSR," 6.

36. Alfred L. Monks, *The Soviet Intervention in Afghanistan* (Washington: American Enterprise Institute, 1981), 41.

37. Ogarkov's views were expounded in his book *Vsegda v gotovnosti k zashchite otechestva* (Moscow: Voenizdat, 1982).

38. Ustinov's position is articulated in D. F. Ustinov, *Serving the Country and the Communist Cause* (New York: Pergamon Press, 1983).

39. Cited in Murphy, "Political-Military Relations in the USSR," 11.

40. Cited in Timothy J. Colton, *Commissars, Commanders, and Civilian Authority: The Structure of Soviet Military Politics* (Cambridge: Harvard University Press, 1979), 15.

41. Ibid., 17. This figure is for 1945.

42. Ibid., 18.

43. Ibid., 21.

44. D. R. Jones, ed., *Soviet Armed Forces Review Annual,* vol. 2 (Gulf Breeze, Florida: Academic International Press, 1978), 39.

45. S. E. Wimbush and Alex Alexiev, *The Ethnic Factor in the Soviet Armed Forces* (Santa Monica: Rand Corporation, 2787/1, March 1982), 22.

46. Michael Voslensky, *Nomenklatura* (New York: Doubleday, 1984), 107–109.

47. For example, an article entitled "Duty" by a soldier paralyzed in Afghanistan generated 969 letters to the editors. See *Komsomolskaia pravda,* 26 February 1984, p. 4.

Selected Bibliography

Barron, John. *KGB Today: The Hidden Hand.* New York: Holt, Rinehart & Winston, 1983.

Carlson, John E. "The KGB." In James Cracraft, ed. *The Soviet Union Today.* Chicago: Bulletin of the Atomic Scientists, 1983, 81–91.

Colton, Timothy J. *Commissars, Commanders, and Civilian Authority: The Structure of Soviet Military Politics.* Cambridge: Harvard University Press, 1979.

Conquest, Robert. *The Great Terror.* London: Macmillan, 1969.

––––––. *The Soviet Police System.* New York: Praeger, 1968.

Deane, Michael J. *Political Control of the Soviet Armed Forces.* New York: Crane, Russak, 1977.

Golitsyn, Anatoliy. *New Lies for Old.* New York: Dodd, Mead, 1984.

Hingley, Ronald. *The Russian Secret Police.* London: Hutchinson, 1970.

Holloway, David. *The Soviet Union and the Arms Race.* New Haven: Yale University Press, 1983.

Knight, Amy W. "Andropov: Myths and Realities." *Survey* (Spring 1984): 22–44.

––––––. "The CPSU and Cadres Policy in the State Security Organs." Paper presented to the annual convention of the American Association for the Advancement of Slavic Studies, New York, November 1–3, 1984.

––––––. "The KGB's Special Departments in the Soviet Armed Forces." *Orbis* (Summer 1984): 257–280.

––––––. "Powers of the Soviet KGB," *Survey* (Summer 1980): 138–155.

Scott, Harriet Fast, and William F. Scott. *The Armed Forces of the USSR.* 2d rev. ed. Boulder: Westview Press, 1984.

Suvorov, Victor. *Inside Soviet Military Intelligence.* New York: Macmillan, 1984.

9

The Economy and the Workers

The Soviet Union represents the first major experiment in devising a centrally planned socialist economy. The development of a Marxist economy, however, did not occur immediately after the Bolsheviks seized power in 1917. In fact, prior to the Revolution, few if any socialists had seriously considered how to organize and plan an economy; they were too preoccupied with overthrowing the existing capitalist system. Some elements of the new Marxist economic order were predictable, however. State ownership of the means of production would replace private ownership, and the State would dictate allocations of investment capital and labor resources, as well as set prices. Centralized state planning was not a fundamental tenet of Marx and came to be a prominent feature of the Soviet economy only in 1928.

The appallingly difficult problems confronting Lenin and his colleagues in the early days after the Revolution forced the new leadership to improvise. The land, large factories, and housing were declared public property. The agricultural production of the peasants was requisitioned, and resources were allocated by the central authorities. Because of the conditions of civil war and the widespread resistance among the peasants, however, attempts to institute centralized planning or collectivized agriculture were abandoned.

Under the New Economic Policy (NEP), from 1921 to 1928, peasants were allowed to farm as they wished and sell their produce on a relatively free market. Small-scale private enterprise was legalized, while large-scale industry, banking, and foreign trade remained in the hands of the State. State enterprises produced in response to consumer demand, not in response to centrally issued directives.

The relatively relaxed atmosphere of NEP gave way to a more ambitious system of centralized planning under Stalin, with the introduction of the First Five-Year Plan in 1928. Stalin set the USSR on a course of rapid industrial development with greater investment in heavy industries than could be achieved in a market economy. His goal was accomplished, but not without exacting a high price in political coercion, neglect of the consumer goods and agricultural sectors, and a depression in urban and rural living standards. During the period from 1928 to 1931, 25 million peasant farms were forcibly combined into 250,000 collective farms (*kolkhozy*)—one or two per village.[1] Agricultural machinery, formerly the property of individual peasants, was pooled in state-directed machine-tractor stations (MTS); land and cattle were held in common ownership by the collective. Collective farms were required to deliver a large portion of their produce to the State at centrally set low prices. Crops were requisitioned to feed the rapidly growing urban labor force. Compulsory grain deliveries also enabled the regime to expand exports in order to generate foreign currency for purchasing imported equipment and industrial materials. At the same time, by organizing the peasants into state-controlled collectives, Stalin destroyed all vestiges of economic and political resistance to his regime that remained in the rural areas.

In industry, the introduction of the First Five-Year Plan in 1928 facilitated the transfer of materials, equipment, and labor to high-priority factories and construction sites. Consumer production all but ceased as every available resource was pressed into the program of rapid industrial expansion in capital-intensive heavy industries (e.g., steel, coal, and machinery).

Virtually all the resources of Soviet society were mobilized to support Stalin's development program. With such slogans as "There are no fortresses Bolsheviks cannot storm!" workers constructed mammoth hydroelectric dams, forged steel, and dug irrigation canals. Artists and writers were directed to portray "the glories of labor" and forsake the artistic experimentation that had characterized the NEP period. Some Soviet citizens became so imbued with the spirit of industrialization in the 1920s and 1930s that they gave their children such unlikely names as Elektrosila (Electric Power), Dynamo, Traktor, or MEL (in honor of Marx, Engels, and Lenin).

In many respects, Stalin's policies of rapid growth and economic development were successful. From 1928 through the mid-1930s, the average annual increase in the Soviet national income was estimated at 14 to 18 percent. In contrast, during the most intensive period of industrialization in the United States, from 1865 to 1914, the economy grew at a rate of only 5 percent per year. GNP growth rates in Germany and Japan since 1960—8 and 9 percent, respectively—come closest to matching Soviet performance.[2]

The Stalinist economic policies favored extensive growth, that is, growth by increasing inputs: labor, raw materials, factories and plants, and investment capital. With a large pool of unemployed or underemployed workers, seemingly endless supplies of oil, gas, coal, and other raw materials, ample land for cultivation, and capital squeezed from the rural sector through collectivization, Soviet planners during the 1930s and 1940s treated inputs as virtually infinite and inexhaustible.

In the 1950s, however, the Soviet economy began to slow down. In part, this was the result of natural maturation: the larger the total GNP of a country, the more difficult it is to sustain large percentage increases. In addition, it was becoming increasingly apparent by the mid-1950s that Soviet economic resources were not inexhaustible. The leadership began to confront serious shortages in investment capital, labor, and arable land. The rate of growth of the national income fell from 9.9 percent in 1958 to 3.9 percent in 1959, 5.0 percent in 1960, 6.5 percent in 1961, and 2.2 percent in 1962.[3] Not only did the overall economic growth rate decrease, but worker productivity also declined, from 5 percent in 1958 to 3.3 percent in 1962.[4]

There were many indications that the problems confronting the Soviet economy in the 1950s and 1960s were more than simply the "aging" of a rapidly growing economy. The capital-output ratio (an index that measures how many inputs are required to produce a given amount of outputs) increased steadily. Furthermore, the Soviet economy in the 1960s exhibited very low and declining rates of consumption as an ever-larger portion of the productive resources was devoted to producers' goods and defense, rather than to consumer items. In 1962, the Soviet national income was approximately half that of the United States, yet per capita consumption was only one-quarter that of the United States.[5] The problems in the Soviet economy were clearly systemic.

For years, the Stalinist model of economic growth had been predicated on the scarcity of goods. Soviet citizens were poorly clothed and fed, so increases in production of clothing and food, regardless of quality, would be consumed. By the 1960s, however, the Soviet economy had succeeded in satisfying the basic needs of the population. Per capita consumption and housing standards had risen substantially. The number of people moving into new apartments each year more than doubled from 1950 to 1960, while the average consumption of meat and shoes increased by 53 and 64 percent, respectively, over the same period.[6] Economic plans continued to stress quantity over quality, resulting in the production of ever-increasing amounts of low-quality goods, which the public simply refused to buy.

Responding to this situation, Evsei Liberman, an economist from Khar'kov, published an article in *Pravda* in September 1962 in which he called for greater autonomy for factory managers in deciding what style, assortment, quality, and quantity of goods to produce. Liberman also proposed that factories be evaluated not on the basis of gross output, but on the basis of profitability. Records would be kept by stores to indicate which merchandise sold and which did not. Producers of good quality, desirable goods would be rewarded, while those who continued to turn out unattractive, low-quality items would suffer. Profitability was also intended to ensure the efficient use of inputs.

Liberman's proposals in *Pravda* had undoubtedly been cleared by Khrushchev and the Politburo and were presented as a trial balloon to see how the public, industrial managers, economic planners, and party officials would react. A vigorous public debate ensued for three years, with economists, factory managers, consumers, party officials, and central planners voicing their views. In time, two diametrically opposed schools emerged, referred to here as the conservatives, or neo-Stalinists, and the liberals. The conservatives favored central determination of the level of investment, size of the labor force, wages, and production, while the liberals preferred to give decision-making power to local officials and factory managers. On the question of "success indicators," or how performance should be assessed, the conservatives favored gross output and labor productivity as the major criteria, while the liberals proposed a single measure: profitability. Conservatives and liberals also disagreed over investment priorities. The former favored heavy industry and defense, while the latter put more emphasis on consumer goods and agriculture.

The conservatives were led by a group of Soviet computer specialists who maintained that the USSR could retain its heavily centralized planning apparatus but implement a more rational and efficient planning process through the use of computers. Chief among these scientists were A. M. Birman, L. V. Kantorovich, and V. S. Nemchinov—all mathematical modelers and proponents of cybernetics.

In the early 1960s, cybernetics—the science of communication and control theory—became a national fad in the USSR. Books were published on a wide array of subjects, including cybernetics and the economy, cybernetics and law, and cybernetics and the achievements of socialism. Initially, Birman, Kantorovich, and Nemchinov envisioned the day when the entire Soviet Union, every farm and every factory, would be linked by a massive computer network through which would flow commands coordinating all economic units to ensure optimal utilization of resources.

Given the size and complexity of the Soviet economy, however, computer simulation or modeling of economic interactions would be virtually impossible. A group of mathematicians in Kiev calculated that in order to draft an accurate and fully integrated plan of material-technical supply for one year for the Ukrainian Republic alone would require the labor of the entire world population for ten million years.[7] Undoubtedly, this estimate overstates the problem, but the general point is well taken: Soviet planning efforts almost inevitably fall short of the optimum. In time, the Soviets came to hold more modest and practical hopes for the application of computers in the economy.

Debate over the Liberman reforms continued until late 1965, when a compromise position was introduced that included profitability as one of several factors by which factories and enterprises were evaluated. Factory managers were also afforded a slightly greater degree of discretion over production decisions. Nevertheless, the economy remained heavily centralized and bureaucratic.

Pressures were growing in the mid-1960s to shift away from the Stalinist model of extensive growth. The USSR no longer enjoyed excess labor, land, or capital resources waiting to be exploited. New gains in production had to be achieved through intensive growth—that is, through the more efficient use of existing resources—by increases in labor productivity, automation, mechanization, and the application of new technologies. In announcing the directives of the Eighth Five-Year Plan in 1966, Premier Alexei Kosygin, a proponent of intensive growth, stressed the increasing role of technology in rejuvenating the sluggish Soviet economy: "Rapid introduction of scientific and technical achievements into production has now become the main condition for raising the productivity of social labor."[8]

The story of the Liberman proposals provides several useful insights into the ways in which Soviet leaders approach policy innovation in the economy. The political leadership occasionally floats a reform proposal in order to stimulate discussion by a wide spectrum of the public. After a lengthy period of debate, a moderate (or even minimal) compromise solution is implemented. Reforms themselves seem to be assessed in light of three considerations:

1. Will the proposed reform alter the power structure (i.e., the position of the CPSU in the political system)?
2. Is the proposal ideologically acceptable?
3. Will the reform result in substantial economic, social, or military improvements?

It is likely that Liberman's proposals, if adopted, would have significantly improved the quality of production in the USSR, but they would have given a great deal of independent authority to factory managers and may have resulted in problems in coordinating interrelated industries. The proposals also risked creating unemployment or inflation as industries sought to lower production costs and respond to pent-up consumer demands for high-quality products. Finally, the incentives to meet consumer demands may have ultimately raised the portion of Soviet economic resources allocated to consumer goods, thereby reducing allocations for defense and heavy industry. These factors explain why Liberman's proposals were never fully implemented.

In the early 1970s, the Soviet economy experienced further retardation in growth, and the leadership responded with a new round of reforms and organizational reshufflings. Détente with the West and expanded contacts between economic officials in the USSR and Western corporations heightened Soviet awareness of the advantages of large, diversified production units. Thus, in 1973, Soviet economic officials began to consolidate factories and enterprises into production associations, patterned after Western multinational corporations. The aggregation of several steel mills into one association, for instance, was intended to eliminate redundant administrative posts; facilitate procurement, repairs, and coordination among plants; and allow enterprises to pool their resources in order to create research and design bureaus.

Since their introduction in 1973, production associations have grown to encompass almost half of all factories and enterprises in the USSR, representing a drive toward greater concentration of industrial production. By 1979, enterprises employing more than a thousand workers accounted for more than 70 percent of all industrial output, employed almost three-quarters of the industrial labor force, and used more than 80 percent of all capital funds.[9] The average number of employees in a Soviet enterprise is 565, compared to 48 in the United States. In metal-working enterprises, the contrast is even more dramatic—2608 employees in the USSR, compared to 74 in the United States.[10] The creation of the production associations reflects this Soviet preference for large-scale production complexes—what some Western scholars have dubbed "gigantomania."

The massive scale of the Soviet industrial system created under Stalin is responsible both for many impressive achievements and for many of the USSR's present economic difficulties. In the relatively short span of thirty years, Stalin transformed the USSR from a backward, weak, primarily agricultural nation into an industrial and military superpower. Under his system of centralized planning, all resources were harnessed in the drive to modernize the economy. The Soviet economy, however, has now developed to the point where the myriad of economic activities are too complex to be coordinated by a central plan. Nevertheless, planning remains a fundamental feature of the Soviet economy today.

PLANNING IN THE USSR

It is difficult for the Westerner to grasp the extent of Soviet centralized planning. In the USSR, the State, not individual factory managers, entrepreneurs, or corporate officials, decides what and how much should be produced, and in what assortment of sizes, qualities, and colors. The State determines what portion of output should be devoted to consumption and what portion to investment, and the State allocates consumption and investment funds to every district, city, region, and republic of the USSR. The State also fixes the prices on more than nine million types of raw materials, finished goods, and services.

As one might imagine, the apparatus required to carry out these tasks is enormous and often cumbersome. Yet, the centrally planned nature of the Soviet system also gives the leadership powerful and direct means to affect policy. If the planners wish to stimulate employment in the far north or Siberia, for example, they institute pay incentives and increase factory personnel budgets in the region. If they decide to develop the country's natural gas and oil reserves rather than invest in nuclear power and coal, investment capital funds are allocated accordingly. If the leadership wishes to curb alcohol consumption, as Gorbachev advocated, breweries and distilleries find their work forces and purchasing budgets slashed, wholesalers are told to cut back on deliveries to stores, and liquor stores are ordered to reduce their hours and raise prices. In contrast, when Western governments wish to alter economic or social conditions, they usually must rely on such indirect methods as increasing or decreasing the money supply, altering taxes, or manipulating government spending.

Since the initiation of planning by Stalin in 1928, overall growth targets for each sector of the Soviet economy have been specified in five-year plans. The Five-Year Plan (currently the Twelfth Five-Year Plan, 1986–1990) contains detailed production targets for each branch of the economy (chemicals, petroleum, steel, agriculture, and so forth). Plan projections are typically stated in terms of the percentage increase over production levels of the previous five-year period. Thus, the Twelfth Five-Year Plan calls for a 30 to 32 percent increase in chemical production, a 20 to 23 percent increase in public consumption, and a 14 to 16 percent increase in agricultural output over the five-year period.[11] These aggregate projections are then broken down into annual plans, which are in turn disaggregated into quarterly and monthly plan quotas. Five-year and annual plans are also broken down for each republic, territory, region, city, district, and enterprise (factory, state farm, or collective) in the USSR. For instance, the Red Proletariat Machine-Tool Plant in Moscow receives numerous directives from the State Planning Committee (Gosplan) and the Ministry of General Machine-Building specifying quotas not only for production but also for sales, investment, wages and labor, profits, incentives, technical innovation, and productivity. These directives are obligatory for management; failure to fulfill the plan targets may result in demotions or financial penalties. During Stalin's reign, failure to fulfill plan targets was a criminal offense punishable by imprisonment or death.

The Soviet planning system employs "taut planning"—in other words, the target level of production is set intentionally high, given the amount of labor and resources allocated. The rationale behind taut planning is that workers will have to make efficient and maximum use of resources in order to fulfill their production quotas.

Bonuses and rewards for overfulfilling the plan range from salary bonuses to preferential access to vacation facilities, increased investment funds, and political favor. Bonuses constitute an important portion of a worker's income—as much as one-third of total earnings.[12] Currently, 40 percent of all profits above an enterprise's planned level may be used by the enterprise as the manager sees fit (e.g., to purchase new machinery, to provide salary bonuses, or to build new housing for enterprise employees).[13]

The plan is devised through a complicated interaction of officials in numerous bureaucracies, including the Gosplan, the State Committee on Prices, the State Bank, the Ministry of Finance, the State Committee on Material and Technical Supplies (Gossnab), and approximately forty-eight ministries that oversee the various branches of the Soviet economy (e.g., Ministry of the Electronics Industry, Ministry of the Chemical Industry, and Ministry of Ferrous Metallurgy). (See Figure 9-1.) These ministries then disaggregate the plan targets into individual plans for each enterprise and association. On the basis of these general targets, enterprises outline their own production and input requirements in allocation requests called *zaiavki;* these are passed on to the respective ministries, which aggregate them and finally communicate them to Gosplan. Enterprises normally overestimate their personnel and other input needs; when added together, the total resources requested usually exceed the total available resources in the economy. Consequently, the plan typically goes through several rounds of adjustment, lowering production quotas as well as appropriations until a balanced plan is achieved.

The construction of the plan is a highly politicized process. Ministries lobby on behalf of their industries' needs and development programs; republic and regional state and party officials push proposals benefiting their respective areas; domestic and foreign trade organizations request more for their sectors to satisfy customers. All these decisions have important economic and political implications. For instance, the decision to export more gas may require additional investment in drilling and pipe-laying, more foreign currency for buying pipe from the West, and less gas for domestic consumption. In addition, such a decision would likely benefit gas-producing regions while siphoning resources from coal-producing areas.

Gosplan is responsible for balancing these competing demands by reducing requests to practical levels, but it does not make these important distributive decisions independently. Through the Council of Ministers and the Politburo, the political leaders communicate to Gosplan the priorities they wish to pursue. Such priorities may relate either to particular sectors

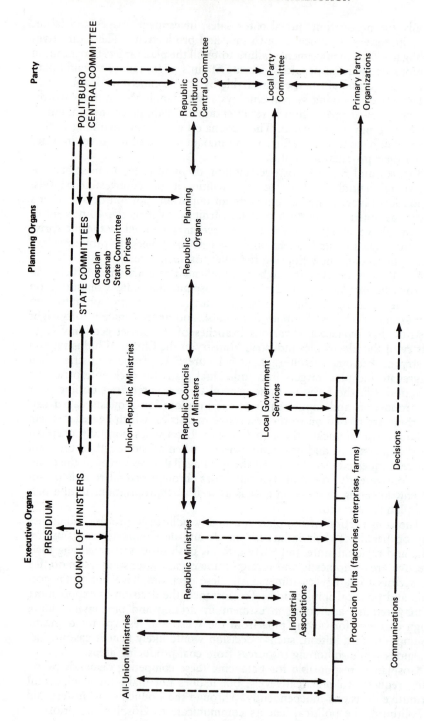

Figure 9-1. Structure of the Soviet Economy

(e.g., gas versus coal and nuclear energy) or particular regions (e.g., Siberia versus European Russia), as we saw in Chapter 6.

It should be emphasized that the targets set forth in the Five-Year Plan are by no means unchangeable. In fact, they are usually altered once, twice, or even several times during the course of the plan period. In contrast, however, annual plans are binding and seldom altered. The process of formulating the annual plan requires almost twelve months, while the Five-Year Plan usually requires two years to complete.[14]

For the annual plan, Gosplan prepares balances for some two thousand of the most important products, while Gossnab constructs more than eighteen thousand balances for items of lesser importance.[15] These centrally set allocations are transmitted to the various industrial ministries, which in turn must decide how many resources and what output levels will be assigned to individual enterprises and collectives. Ideally, it is Gossnab's responsibility to link suppliers to customers, but in practice these relationships have formed over the years through the ad hoc arrangements of Gossnab, Gosplan, the ministries, and the individual enterprises and collectives themselves. Producer-consumer relations in the USSR are notoriously inefficient and inflexible. In an effort to streamline the supply system, Premier Kosygin proposed in the mid-1960s that enterprises purchase inputs through a wholesale system, freeing them from mandated purchase orders issued by Gosplan and Gossnab. By 1973, however, wholesale trade extended to a scant 3 percent of all producers' goods, and it has not increased substantially since then.[16] Most producers and consumers are content to rely on their proven channels and contacts, no matter how inefficient.

While the division of ministerial jurisdictions over various sectors of the Soviet economy appears on the surface to be quite rational, there is a great deal of overlap, which complicates planning considerably. Enterprises producing farm machinery are likely to be subordinated to any number of ministries, including the Ministry of Defense Industries. Refrigerators are manufactured in factories operated by the Ministry of the Radio Industry, and televisions are produced by some defense plants. This diversity of production comes about when a factory has excess production capacity or personnel and uses those resources to manufacture an unrelated product. Redundancy and overlapping production can also result when enterprises are continually frustrated in obtaining necessary components, equipment, or other items. For instance, A. I. Shokin, former Minister of the Electronics Industry, noted that when his ministry could not get adequate measuring and testing equipment from outside suppliers, they began to manufacture the necessary equipment themselves.[17] Factories under the jurisdiction of the Ministry of the Electronics Industry are now producing equipment that would normally fall under the purview of the machine tool, chemical, nonferrous metallurgy, instrument-building, and radio-technical industries.

The performance of enterprises in the USSR is judged across a wide array of indicators. Currently, twelve measures of performance are used:

1. total output
2. assortment
3. proportion of high-quality or export-quality output

4. labor productivity
5. profit, profitability
6. capital construction
7. introduction of new technology
8. investment
9. material incentive fund
10. improvements in technical qualifications of workers
11. sociocultural activities
12. fulfillment of delivery schedules

All of these indicators are not weighted equally by central planners, however. A factory that introduces new techniques, raises the level of worker qualifications and labor productivity, but suffers a decline in total output will be reprimanded; a factory that fails to modernize and improve product quality or worker qualifications but overfulfills its production plan is likely to be rewarded with bonuses, even if its products are of poor quality and not purchased by consumers.

Even when focusing solely on the most important indicator—gross output—Soviet planners have continually encountered difficulties in measuring performance so that desirable results are achieved. Soviet economists sometimes illustrate the "success indicator" problem by referring to the case of a fictitious factory—the May Day Nail Factory. If the output of the May Day Nail Factory is specified in the plan in terms of the number of nails produced, this will encourage factory managers to produce small tacks. On the other hand, if output is specified in terms of the gross weight of nails produced, it is more advantageous for the factory to produce railroad spikes. The Soviet satirical journal *Krokodil* ("Crocodile") poked fun at this sort of behavior in a cartoon depicting a plan manager congratulating the workers in a nail factory for overfulfilling their plan, as a single, huge nail rolls off the assembly line. Such absurdities, unfortunately, do exist in reality. During the 1930s and 1940s, furniture in the USSR was among the heaviest in the world. Some bed frames were constructed from lead. The reason—the performance of furniture factories was judged by total weight of furniture produced. When this indicator was changed under Khrushchev, furniture suddenly appeared in the stores made of lightweight plywood.

The combination of illogical plan incentives and pressure to fulfill plan quotas on time results in other distortions as well. On one visit to Leningrad, the author noticed row after row of concrete slabs on the outskirts of town. When he asked a woman in the neighborhood what the slabs were for, she explained that the central planners measure the performance of housing construction firms by the number of housing starts (i.e., the number of foundations laid). A housing construction firm that had fallen behind in its production had laid the foundations, even though they would never have apartments built upon them. Russians call this phenomenon of pushing to fulfill plan production quotas at all costs "storming." One Soviet source indicates that 35 percent of all housing starts occur in the last quarter of the plan year, and 70 percent of those are in the last week of December—hardly an ideal time for pouring concrete.[18]

Pressures to fulfill plan targets result in a variety of other distortions.

One of the most enduring features of the Soviet economy is hoarding. Supply channels in the USSR are not well established, and factories continually confront shortages of inputs. If an automobile plant has not received a shipment of sheet steel, it has little recourse but to cut back production. If the factory falls short of its production target because of the nondelivery of steel, the workers are penalized nonetheless. Consequently, factories stockpile large quantities of raw materials, spare parts, and other goods to cover this contingency.

Spare parts are generally not available for automobiles, trucks, and tractors in the USSR, because the output of automobile factories is measured in terms of the number of automobiles produced, not the number of parts produced. State farms and factories are forced to "cannibalize" their tractors and other machinery for spare parts. If a state farm manager calls to inquire whether a neighboring state farm has a spare carburetor for a tractor, the manager is likely to respond: "Yes, but I can't give it to you. What if one of *our* tractors breaks down and needs a carburetor?"

The lack of spare parts has given rise to a thriving black market, often supplied with goods stolen by production workers. There is such a demand for windshield wipers that citizens do not dare to leave them attached to their cars for fear they will be stolen. Most drivers keep their wipers in the glove compartment. When it begins to rain, all traffic stops for a few seconds while drivers jump out and hurriedly reattach their wipers.

The hoarding of resources also applies to labor. As noted earlier, the most important indicator of economic performance is total output. The profitability and labor productivity indices, which would be affected adversely by employing excess numbers of workers, are only secondary in importance. Consequently, most factories, stores, and state farms hire more workers than necessary, in case extra workers are required at the end of the plan period for "storming" to fulfill the plan. In addition, it has been reported that on any given day as much as 20 percent of the labor force shows up to work drunk or fails to show up at all; thus, excess labor is needed just to ensure a full complement of workers.[19] The underutilization of workers, however, seriously erodes the efficiency of the economy, especially in the service sector. For example, a pancake (*bliny*) shop on Nevsky Prospekt, the main street of Leningrad, employs seven people (two cooks, three waitresses, and two dishwashers), even though it has a seating capacity for only six customers.

Plan pressures combined with shortages of components have also caused some factory managers to produce incomplete products or falsify their plan fulfillment reports. During the final days of the plan period, production will continue in an automobile assembly plant even if it means that the "finished" automobiles have no headlights, taillights, or windshield wipers because the plant has run out of the necessary parts (often due to pilfering by the workers). When the cars arrive to be sold, the officials will report that the parts were stolen while the cars were being shipped. Having waited two or three years to buy a car, it is unlikely that customers will refuse to accept the automobiles; they will simply try to acquire the missing parts on the black market.

Soviet economists admit that their planning efforts are often insufficient. Ultimately, however, the level of acceptable economic performance is a political issue. Although a shoe factory that overfulfills its production quota may be rewarded even when the products are of low quality, it runs the risk of being singled out for chastisement by political officials. It is the uncertainty of political reprisals as much as plan directives that keeps industrial managers in line. In some areas, such as stimulating enterprises to adopt new technologies, political pressures can be more effective than the economic incentives built into the plan.[20]

Planning violations can be very serious and even entail criminal prosecution. Several years ago, for instance, violations by a manufacturer of surgical sterilization machines resulted in criminal action. The factory ran out of critical electrical coils that were necessary for proper functioning of the machine, but the pressures to fulfill the production quota were so great that the factory produced and delivered a shipment of incomplete sterilization machines anyway. After several hospital patients died of massive postoperative infections, an investigation uncovered the cause. The factory manager, the chief engineer, and the quality control chief were all convicted of gross negligence and executed.[21]

Planning in the USSR extends into virtually every facet of life. Lawyers have a plan for the number of clients they serve; hospitals are evaluated on the number of patients they treat, and artists by the number of paintings they produce. At the end of every Five-Year Plan, the faculty of the Leningrad University law school meets to "review faculty performance in light of the plan." One by one, each faculty member rises and reads a memo detailing his or her accomplishments during the past five years—the number of books and articles published, public lectures presented, and so on. After each recitation, the faculty votes on whether or not the individual has fulfilled the plan. On most occasions, faculty members receive unanimously favorable evaluations.

The incorporation of the plan mentality into the Soviet mind-set is evident even on some solemn occasions. At the conclusion of burial services, it is often proclaimed, "Rest in peace, comrade. Your plan has been fulfilled!"

SECTORAL PRIORITIES

For planning purposes, the Soviet economy is divided into two large sectors: heavy industry and defense (sometimes referred to as Group A industries) and consumer goods, light industry, and agriculture (Group B industries). The following section analyzes the performance and problems of the principal sectors of the Soviet economy.

Heavy Industry. Economically, politically, and ideologically, the backbone of the Soviet system is heavy industry. Stalin's model of extensive growth was predicated upon the development of primary industries—steel, coal, electricity, and machinery production. Throughout the 1930s and 1940s, steel output was seen as a barometer of the general growth in the economy. Because the Soviet economy at that time was confronting shortages virtually everywhere, the problem of satisfying demand for particular types and grades of steel was of secondary concern; whatever was produced would find a ready buyer. By the 1950s and 1960s, however, scarcity in the Soviet economy, while still prevalent in some areas, was less evident in others. Nevertheless, gross output of steel and other basic industrial producers' goods continued to occupy—and still occupies today—a central place in the economy.

While the Soviet national income is roughly half that of the United States, total Soviet industrial output is over 80 percent of that in the United States.[22] The Soviet Union outproduces the United States in steel, oil, cement, and textiles. Despite repeated efforts to shift resources into agriculture, consumer goods, and service industries, heavy industrial production is still clearly the highest-priority sector of the Soviet economy. More than 70 percent of Soviet industrial output consists of producers' goods.[23] In other words, most Soviet industrial enterprises produce goods for other industrial enterprises, not for public consumption.

The Gorbachev regime recognized the need to revitalize the consumer economy. Rather than simply launch a series of political campaigns on product quality, as Brezhnev had done, Gorbachev proposed a different course. The centerpiece of his strategy was to raise productivity by renovating factories and introducing advanced technology. The share of total investment funds used for reequipping existing enterprises was projected to increase from 35 percent to 50 percent or more.[24] Gorbachev's policy entailed an important shift in resources away from construction industries to machine-building and equipment-supplying industries, especially in high-technology fields.

Defense Industries in the USSR.   Closely tied to heavy industrial production are the defense industries. Since the mid-1930s, defense has been a major drain on the productive resources of the Soviet economy. It is difficult to assess the exact amount allocated to defense, because only a small portion of defense production is included in the budget of the Ministry of Defense. There are nine ministries whose primary responsibility is producing for the defense establishment:

- Ministry of Defense Industries
- Ministry of General Machine Building
- Ministry of Medium Machine Building
- Ministry of Heavy Machine Building
- Ministry of Aviation
- Ministry of Shipbuilding
- Ministry of the Electronics Industry
- Ministry of the Radio-Technical Industry
- Ministry of Means of Communication

Virtually all ministries play some role in defense production, however. Conversely, the ministries that are primarily geared toward military production also manufacture some nondefense items.

The Central Intelligence Agency currently estimates that defense spending in the USSR constitutes 12 to 13 percent of the national income, compared to 6 to 8 percent in the United States.[25] Such a level of defense spending inevitably interferes in a spectacular way with advances in consumption, research and development, and investment. During the Tenth Five-Year Plan (1976–1980), Soviet planners apparently cut back on capital investment to allow continuing growth in military expenditures, despite a deceleration in the economic growth rate.

The cuts in capital investment may also have been intended, in part, to stimulate greater consumption. The CIA has revised its estimates of the growth rate for Soviet defense spending from the previous level of 4 percent to approximately 2 percent, while allocations for military hardware have remained virtually stable since the late 1970s.[26] If it is true that the Soviet leadership is holding down defense spending in order to allocate investment capital to the consumer-goods sector, this would indicate the seriousness with which economic planners perceive the need to stimulate the economy by increasing domestic consumption.

Western analysts have tended to view the military sector as a separate, sacrosanct segment of the Soviet economy. Defense industries command the best-quality materials, the best-trained labor force, and more than one-half of all resources devoted to research and development. Unlike its civilian counterparts, the Ministry of Defense has the right to refuse shipment of substandard goods. Military inspectors and quality-control engineers work side by side with plant inspectors in assessing the quality of production. The defense sector is subject to planning arrangements similar to those in the civilian economy; however, some significant adjustments have been made to stimulate the introduction of new products and processes. In addition to their general plan targets, industries producing for the Ministry of Defense have specific production orders that carry considerable political weight. Finally, enterprises producing under contract with the Ministry of Defense are afforded more administrative and organizational flexibility than are their counterparts in the civilian economy.

Despite its special features, however, the defense sector cannot be separated from the rest of the Soviet economy. Some of the same problems that plague other sectors of the economy are evident in the realm of military production. The military is dependent upon the civilian economy for a host of technologies and products—materials, electronic components, instruments, steel, and chemicals. Weaknesses in these sectors can create bottlenecks in military production programs. Furthermore, a lagging civilian economy generates fewer resources for investment in research and development, while the military budget threatens to expand to the detriment of the economy as a whole.

Recently, Soviet military authorities have acknowledged that the health of the Soviet defense establishment is linked to the health of the general economy. In a widely read article, the Deputy Minister of Defense for Procurements, General V. M. Shabanov, noted that the strengthening of the USSR's defenses is possible only on the base of a highly developed economy.[27] Rather than lobbying for increased military appropriations, Shabanov lauded the Party's decisions at the Twenty-Sixth Party Congress to give first priority to strengthening basic branches of energy, metallurgy, machine buildings, and agriculture.

Soviet Agriculture—The Persistent Troublespot.   Dramatic shifts in economic resources are not easy to sustain and do not always bring about immediate improvements. Nowhere is this more clear than in the agricultural sector.

Soviet agriculture today is still organized very much along the lines established by Stalin during collectivization. In addition to collective farms (*kolkhozy*), however, state farms (*sovkhozy*) now exist. *Sovkhozy* are state-owned institutions, rather than cooperatives, and employees are paid a salary, just as industrial workers receive a salary. While the incomes of collective farmers may fluctuate from year to year due to varying growing conditions or crop prices, state farm employees receive a steady, set income. Since 1966, however, collective farmers have been guaranteed a minimum income from the state to protect them from disastrous harvests, flood, drought, or other calamities.

Although collective farms are closer to the Marxist vision of a self-managing socialist institution, they have not been favored by Soviet planners. The average collective farm today covers approximately 15,000 acres and employs 500 persons.[28] State farms are much larger, averaging 92,500 acres and employing many more people.[29] Collectives are subjected to higher compulsory delivery quotas at lower prices and must buy fertilizer, seed, fuel, and other supplies from the State at higher prices than state farms pay. Collectives also find it more difficult to receive investment funds for purchasing new buildings and machinery. The number of collective farms has fallen steadily over the last thirty years, until today there are roughly equal numbers of state farms and collective farms (approximately 25,000 of each).

Sovkhozy appear to be favored by central planners precisely because they are not self-governing; they respond to directives issued by Gosplan and the State Committee for the Agro-Industrial Complex. Because they are eligible for state investment funds, they are also better able to mechanize and modernize production, whereas collectives must finance machinery purchases from their modest revenues. Finally, due in part to the influx of investment funds and their larger size, state farms are more efficient than collectives.

In recent years, funds have been poured into the agricultural sector in an effort to repair the damage caused by its long neglect under Stalin and Khrushchev. The portion of total investment allocated to agriculture grew from 19 percent in 1961–1965 to more than 27 percent in 1976–1980.[30] If the investment in agriculturally related industries is included, the allocations constituted 34 percent of total investment during the Tenth Five-Year Plan (1976–1980). Yet, for all the investment in agriculture, the returns have been disappointing to say the least.

Since 1970, agricultural production has barely kept pace with population growth; over the same period, the USSR changed from being a net exporter of grain to the world's largest importer. Milk production has fallen steadily and is now below 1974 levels.[31] The Soviet Union's poor agricultural performance is often attributed to poor climatic conditions. On an average, Soviet planners can expect substantially reduced harvests due to drought, flood, or inclement weather in one out of every four years.

Agricultural production is also hampered by poor land management, inadequate agricultural infrastructure and equipment, and a low level of training of agricultural workers. The poor quality and inadequate maintenance of farm machinery results in an average service life of one-third to one-half that of comparable equipment in the United States.[32] Soviet agricultural experts estimate that one-fifth of the gross harvest in grain, vegetables, and other produce is lost or damaged in transport, storage, and processing.[33] The heavy investment in agriculture during the 1960s and 1970s tended to stress the production of fertilizers, herbicides, and pesticides, rather than the development of an efficient farm-to-market rail and highway system, refrigerated railroad cars, storage bins, and grain elevators.

Soviet agriculture today remains very labor-intensive compared to that in the United States. As of 1975, a total of 25.4 percent of the Soviet labor force was engaged in farming, compared to only 4.6 percent in the U.S.[34] The enormous number of farm workers in the USSR is, nevertheless, insufficient. In 1979, some 15.6 million nonagricultural workers had to be mobilized to assist with the harvest.[35]

In the late 1970s, Brezhnev introduced measures to improve agricultural production, reduce waste, and alleviate the gap between the standards of living of urban and rural workers, in an effort to stem the out-migration of youth from the countryside. The hallmark of Brezhnev's proposals was the "agro-industrial complex." Drawing on his earlier experience in Moldavia, Brezhnev advocated relocating light industry, especially food-processing industries, in agricultural regions. Thus, canning plants were built near vegetable farms, processing plants for sugar beets were located close to the fields, and so forth. The complexes also merged collective and state farms into still-larger units in an effort to enhance efficiency and productivity. So far, the agro-industrial complexes have been limited to meat, dairy, fruit, vegetable, and wine production.

In November 1985, in a move to restructure Soviet agriculture, Gorbachev consolidated the Ministry of Agriculture, four other agriculturally related ministries, and one state committee into a gigantic new State Committee for the Agro-Industrial Complex (Gosagroprom). The reorganization was undertaken to facilitate the formation of agro-industrial complexes throughout the agricultural sector and to eliminate overlapping ministerial jurisdictions. No matter how extensively they are adopted, however, the agro-industrial complexes cannot solve all of the problems that confront Soviet agriculture. What is required is continued heavy investment in the agricultural infrastructure (silos, grain elevators and milling facilities, and a more efficient rail system). But such investments are likely to encounter strong opposition from advocates of the powerful heavy-industry and defense sectors.

TRADE UNIONS IN THE USSR

One of the principal mechanisms by which the Soviet regime controls the workers is the trade unions. Trade unions existed in Russia prior to the Revolution, but their function changed dramatically from radical antigovernment agitation prior to 1917 to tools of the Bolshevik regime after the Revolution. Lenin viewed the unions not as independent organizations representing the workers, but as "schools of Communism"; Stalin referred to them as "transmission belts" for transferring the demands of the party leadership to the masses. Soviet trade unions are often criticized in the West for being mere "puppets" of the regime. They do not engage in the open clashes with government and management that characterize unions in the United States, Britain, France, Italy, or other democratic societies. Further-more, central trade union officials are thoroughly incorporated into party and state organs and play an active role in developing economic plans. At the highest levels, Soviet trade unions frequently form alliances with their respective ministries in lobbying for their sectoral interests.

Although they do not play an adversarial role on behalf of workers in their relationship to management, Soviet trade unions do represent the workers' interests in expanding social services and consumer production. They are also charged with administering sick-leave and maternity benefits, compensation for job-related injuries, family allowances, as well as pensions and disability payments. In addition, trade unions supervise the observance of health and safety regulations in industry. Finally, trade unions organize numerous social activities and maintain resorts and recreational facilities for workers and their families.

Membership in Soviet trade unions is voluntary. In practice, however, membership is expected of all workers, and more than 98 percent of all Soviet workers are members of a union.[36] There are thirty-one trade unions in the USSR, covering not only industrial sectors, but also white-collar and service professions. Unions are organized by industry; unlike their American counterparts, all employees of a given industry are members of the same union. Thus, an electrician working in a steel mill will be a member of the steelworkers' union. An exception is medical personnel, who are members of the Health Workers' Union regardless of whether they work in a hospital or in a clinic of a large factory.

The structure of the Soviet trade unions parallels that of the CPSU. Trade unions operate on the basis of democratic centralism—that is, they are hierarchically structured from the All-Union Congress of Trade Unions down to the primary union organizations in the workplace. In relatively small factories, trade union committees are elected directly by the workers, but in large industrial complexes they are elected indirectly by deputies chosen by union members. Factory committees nominate delegates to re-gional conferences of trade unions, and these bodies, in turn, nominate delegates to trade union congresses at the republic and all-union levels. (See Figure 9-2.)

As in the Party, overall trade union policy is made and directed not by these elective bodies, but by the Central Committee of the Trade Union Congress. The Central Committee has an administrative staff not only at the All-Union level, but also at lower echelons.

It is at the enterprise level where differences between workers and management increase the importance of unions as representatives of workers' interests. Enterprise management does not set wages in the Soviet Union; thus, one of the major points of worker-management conflict has been removed. Nevertheless, conflicts often occur between unions and fac-tory administrators over the designation of grades or levels for various jobs,

Figure 9-2. Structure of Soviet Trade Unions

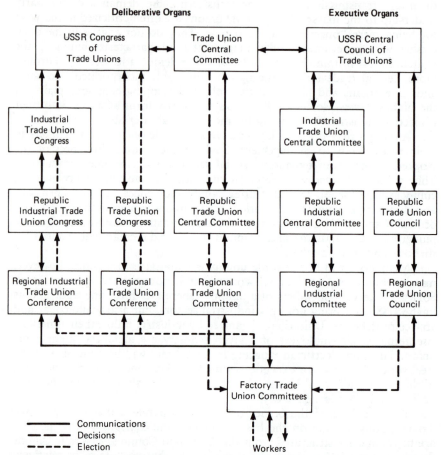

Source: Based on material in Blair A. Ruble, *Soviet Trade Unions* (Cambridge: Cambridge University Press, 1981); and E. C. Brown, *Soviet Trade Unions and Labor Relations* (Cambridge: Harvard University Press, 1966).

as well as over safety and health conditions, overtime work and "storming," and the allocation of bonus funds. Individual grievances may be brought before labor dispute boards. Grievances usually relate to infringement of holidays, wages, dismissals, deductions from pay, bonuses, work transfers, and disciplinary actions. Analysis of cases heard by the boards indicates that nearly twice as many decisions are resolved in favor of aggrieved workers as against them.[37] Workers may appeal unfavorable decisions to a higher-level appeal panel, and from there to a people's court.

Soviet labor law goes to great lengths to ensure the rights of Soviet workers. Factory managers may not fire workers without the approval of the local trade union committee. Pregnant women cannot be dismissed under any circumstances. Enterprise managers often complain that the provisions of Soviet labor law protecting workers are so strong that they find it impossible to fire incompetent and unreliable workers.[38]

Strikes are not expressly prohibited in the USSR, although in the few known instances of industrial strikes, workers were arrested and charged with a variety of offenses ranging from hooliganism and disorderly conduct to anti-Soviet agitation. Most strikes in the USSR have been sparked by economic conditions, rather than by labor disputes. For instance, in Sverdlovsk a riot broke out in 1956 to protest poor living conditions. In 1962, strikes in Novocherkassk followed price rises and increases in work norms. More recently, strikes and work stoppages have occurred at the Tol'iatti automobile plant over shortages of meat and dairy products. Similarly, a strike occurred at the Kama River truck factory in 1980 over food shortages. In the latter two cases, the authorities responded to the strikes with prompt remedial action; store shelves suddenly overflowed with produce and goods not normally available.

Rather than strike, Soviet workers typically demonstrate their dissatisfactions in other ways: absenteeism and tardiness, poor work discipline, frequent job changes, and alcoholism. A study conducted by the USSR Ministry of Internal Affairs estimated that 37 percent of all male workers abuse alcohol and that in the Russian republic 11 percent of the population over the age of 15 can be classified as alcoholics.[39] A poll conducted by the monthly journal *Zhurnalist* revealed that 25 percent of those surveyed drank before arriving at work and 20 percent admitted to drinking on the job.[40] Not only is alcohol abuse responsible for the vast majority of all absenteeism, but it also accounts for more than two-thirds of all on-the-job accidents.[41] Soviet authorities estimate that alcohol abuse costs the State $100 billion per year in economic losses and sagging production.[42]

Soviet authorities report that 25 million workers—almost 20 percent of the nation's labor force—change their places of work each year.[43] Trade union committees have sought to reduce the turnover rate by applying informal pressure on workers who wish to leave and by delaying their departure by initiating "investigations" into their work records.[44] In 1983, the amount of advance notice required from anyone leaving a job was extended from one month to two months, but these measures have only marginally affected the high rate of labor turnover.

In an effort to instill more responsibility in workers, the Andropov regime introduced a campaign on work discipline and enacted the USSR Law on Labor Collectives. The law, which went into effect in August 1983, increased the power of the labor collective or brigade in applying sanctions to workers who do not do their fair share of the work. Bonuses for overfulfilling the plan are now allocated not to individual workers, but to the labor brigade, which divides bonuses equally. Such a system uses peer pressure to enforce greater efficiency and discipline among workers. Although the brigade system is not popular with some workers, it appears to have achieved some increases in worker productivity since its introduction. In the shipbuilding industry, the introduction of the brigade system is credited with a 20 to 30 percent increase in labor productivity and a 10 to 12 percent increase in wages.[45] Nevertheless, good workers are sometimes reluctant to join a brigade for fear that their personal achievements will be diminished by the lackadaisical attitudes of their comrades, while some managers have not been enthusiastic about the brigade system. In their view, increased productivity merely results in higher plan quotas in the future.

WORK LIFE IN THE USSR

The Bolshevik Revolution of 1917 was ostensibly carried out on behalf of the workers and peasants in order to create the first workers' state. Lenin and his colleagues perceived of themselves as the champions of the working man and woman. The Revolution was intended to free the workers' creative energies to work for their own benefit, rather than for the benefit of a ruling class. Even today the image of "the worker" is at the center of political propaganda. Banners on buildings, tram cars, and construction cranes proclaim "Glory to Labor!" or "Our Labor Is for the Motherland!" Yet, for all the lofty rhetoric, the reality of work life in the Soviet Union is that most workers are employed in menial, dreary, and low-paying jobs.

The normal workweek in the Soviet Union averages 42 hours; Soviet employees work a five-day week except for the last week of the month, when they must also work on Saturday—colloquially referred to as "black Saturday." Overtime work is common, and many workers are coerced into working overtime toward the end of a plan period, although it is officially not mandatory. In April each year, workers are expected to devote an additional Saturday of uncompensated work in honor of Lenin's birthday (April 22). The practice of "Lenin Saturday" extends even to university students, who are mobilized by their Komsomol organizations into brigades and assigned to rake lawns in parks, pick up litter, and spruce up public places.

Salaries and wage rates of Soviet workers are set by central authorities according to the difficulty, degree of danger, and technical qualifications of the job. In addition, elaborate gradation systems exist for various jobs, depending on seniority, past performance on the job, and range of responsibilities. Thus, taxi drivers are ranked first class, second class, third class, and so on, and pay levels vary accordingly.

The average salary nationwide is approximately 215 rubles per month, or about $280. Although this may seem to be very low, one must also consider the benefits that Soviet citizens receive free of charge or at minimal cost. Health and dental care are provided free of charge, and rent and utilities are heavily subsidized in the USSR. Whereas rent accounts for more than one-quarter of the average wage earner's monthly salary in Washington, D.C., rent constitutes only about one-sixteenth of a worker's monthly salary in Moscow.[46] (See Table 9-1.) Public transportation, cultural activities, and basic foodstuffs are subsidized in order to make them affordable for average citizens. In 1987, the subway cost 5 kopeks (6 cents), a ticket to hear the Moscow Philharmonic could be purchased for only $2.50, and a loaf of bread cost 35 cents.

Salaries in the Soviet Union reflect, in part, the Marxian notion of rewarding manual labor more than white-collar labor. For instance, a coal miner is paid more than a teacher or doctor because of the dangerous and difficult nature of the work. Income differentials exist in the USSR, but they are not nearly as dramatic as in the West. The ratio of Soviet workers in the bottom 10 percent of wage earners to the highest 10 percent has declined to approximately 3:1, compared to roughly 4.5:1 in the United States.[47] The relative equality of incomes in the USSR is evident in Table 9-2, which presents some average salaries for various types of workers and officials.

Bonuses and salary increments are offered to encourage workers to seek employment in priority sectors or in far-off regions. The chief driller on an oil rig north of the Arctic Circle, for example, receives 1200 rubles per month—five times the national average.[48] He works a four-day shift, is off one day, and then works four more days. Young men are often attracted to these high-paying jobs in order to amass some savings prior to getting married.

Salary figures, however, mask the substantial inequalities that exist in access to special perquisites and benefits. For example, high-ranking party officials are provided with spacious apartments, summer houses in the country, limousines with chauffeurs, maids, cooks, gardeners, and extensive entertainment allowances.

Public officials, top military officers, well-known scientists and artists, and foreign diplomats in the USSR are granted access to special stores that carry export-quality merchandise not normally found in stores. The author was in one of the "diplomatic stores" on a bitterly cold February day shopping for a few "luxury" goods—tomatoes and cucumbers—when a limousine pulled up to the front door and an important-looking woman got out. The woman approached the salesclerk and asked for fresh strawberries. The clerk hurriedly motioned her into the back room. In a short time, she emerged carrying a small package. When the author boldly approached the same salesclerk and asked for fresh strawberries, he was told: "Young man, you must be crazy. We don't have strawberries at this time of year!"

How well one lives in the USSR depends a great deal on who one is and who one's friends are. Russians call this *blat*—connections. Nevertheless, compared to top corporate executives or political officials in the West, prominent figures in the Soviet Union enjoy a rather modest standard of living. At the other end of the income scale, the policy of relative equality of incomes and provision of extensive social welfare benefits has virtually eliminated poverty in the USSR.

WOMEN AND WORK

Women play a major role in the Soviet labor force, constituting more than 51 percent of all workers.[49] Approximately 85 percent of women under the age of 55 work outside the home.[50] Women are heavily represented in clerical, sales, and catering professions, as well as in teaching and health care. Women account for 68 percent of all doctors (*vracha*), 71 percent of all teachers, and 33 percent of all engineers.[51]

In addition, women are heavily represented in the construction trades, light industry (e.g., textiles), and in menial jobs. Most bricklayers, carpenters, painters, crane operators, and plasterers in the USSR are women. In

Table 9-1. Retail Prices in Moscow: Weekly Basket (for Four Persons) of Consumer Goods at Soviet Level of Consumption in March, 1982, Expressed as Work-Time Units

Item	Kilograms	Washington	Moscow	Munich	Paris	London
			(Minutes of Work-Time)			
Flour	1.0	5	28	9	6	6
Bread	7.0	112	119	189	126	112
Noodles	2.0	28	68	32	22	28
Beef	1.0	69	123	150	119	115
Pork	1.5	63	176	150	108	117
Minced Beef	1.0	37	123	70	80	63
Sausages	1.0	33	160	75	75	51
Cod	1.0	61	47	45	118	72
Sugar	3.3	30	191	33	30	36
Butter	0.5	28	111	26	24	25
Margerine	2.0	46	222	34	36	64
Milk (liters)	12.0	72	264	84	96	108
Cheese	2.0	200	370	130	118	130
Eggs, cheapest (units)	18.0	14	99	22	23	29
Potatoes	9.0	63	63	36	36	27

Cabbage	3.0	27	36	21	27	30
Carrots	1.0	11	19	10	7	13
Tomatoes	1.0	23	62	28	25	32
Apples	1.0	10	92	15	15	23
Tea	0.1	10	53	10	17	5
Beer (liters)	3.0	33	48	24	21	54
Gin/Vodka (liters)	1.0	87	646	106	153	187
Cigarettes (units)	120	54	90	96	48	150
			(Hours of Work-Time)			
Weekly basket, as above		18.6	53.5	23.3	22.2	24.7
Weekly basket for "statistically average" family of 3.5 persons		16.3	46.8	20.4	19.4	21.6
Rent, monthly		51	12	24	39	28
Color TV		65	701	143	106	132
			(Months of Work-Time)			
Small car		5	53	6	8	11
Medium car		8	88	9	12	18

Source: Keith Bush, "Retail Prices in Moscow and Four Western Cities in March 1982," Radio Liberty Research Supplement, June 4, 1982, p. 7.

Table 9-2. Average Monthly Income of Soviet Workers (in rubles)

Marshal of the USSR	2000
General Secretary of the CPSU	900
First Secretary, Union of Composers	800
Director, scientific-research institute	700
First Secretary of a Union-Republic	600
Major General	600
Colonel	500
Well-known ballet dancer	500
Director, large industrial enterprise	450–500
Professor	325–525
Attorney	250
Editor, Union-Republic newspaper	240
Coal miner	210
Doctor	183
Chairman, collective farm	180
Steel worker	145
Taxi driver	140
Secondary school teacher	140
Collective farmer	122
Fork-lift operator	110
Clerical worker	90
Janitorial worker	70

Sources: Mervyn Matthews, *Privilege in the Soviet Union* (London: George Allen & Unwin, 1978), 23, 26 and 27; and Murray Yanowitch, *Social and Economic Inequality in the Soviet Union* (New York: M. E. Sharpe, 1977), 30, 32, 34–35, and 39.

the winter, it is common to see a brigade of women shoveling snow into a dumptruck while the male driver sits in the heated cab reading a book. In the spring, armies of women use crowbars to chip away at the thick layers of ice and packed snow that have accumulated on the sidewalks and streets during the winter.

One senses that it is the strength of its women that has enabled the Soviet Union to survive. During World War II, women operated lathes and forged steel while the men were on the front. Women in Russia have traditionally been responsible for planting and harvesting the crops, even when this requires long hours of swinging a scythe or baling hay and shocking wheat by hand. While the women worked the fields, the men were responsible for the livestock and machinery. In agricultural areas, this division of labor is still evident today.

Although they occupy a major role in the work force, relatively few women rise to supervisory positions. Fewer than 2 percent of collective farm managers, 9 percent of enterprise directors, 12 percent of construction supervisors, and 28 percent of school principals are women.[52] Women invariably receive lower salaries than their male counterparts; the average Soviet woman earns about 65 percent as much as the average male worker.[53] Women pensioners often find that they have to take low-paying jobs such as museum guards, coatroom attendants, or janitors in order to supplement their pensions.

Although women's rights are loudly proclaimed by the government, most Soviet women in fact find themselves in inferior jobs and saddled with second jobs at home. The average Soviet apartment lacks modern conveniences such as a dishwasher, washing machine, and clothes dryer that have greatly simplified the tedious work of housewives elsewhere. Shopping for a single meal can easily consume two hours of standing in lines at the bakery, the dairy, the meat market, and the vegetable store. Russian husbands are notorious for refusing to assist in household or child-rearing chores, preferring instead to drink with their buddies. The Soviet press has in recent years encouraged more men to assume their fair share of household duties, but change comes slowly.

This combination of circumstances has left many Soviet women bitter and cynical. March 8, International Women's Day, was originated by radical leftist women during the Paris Commune, but in the USSR today it bears a closer resemblance to Mother's Day in the United States. Moscow Radio plays an endless barrage of syrupy songs with such lyrics as, "Oh, our women, how sweet they are!" The songs are interrupted by occasional political statements that Soviet women have more rights than women anywhere else on earth and by reminders to husbands to buy their wives flowers and chocolates (two commodities that never seem to be in short supply). Attending a reception in honor of International Women's Day at Leningrad University law school, the author extended salutations to one of the female faculty members. She scoffed in reply, "International Women's Day, indeed! That is when all the men invite their drinking buddies over for dinner and the woman has to cook and clean up afterwards!"

THE CONSUMER ECONOMY

The predominant characteristic of the Soviet economy is the ever-present shortage of decent-quality consumer goods. With little incentive to produce desirable goods, manufacturers simply produce in order to fulfill plan targets. Similarly, stores and shops have no incentive to assist shoppers; long lines and surly clerks make shopping even for simple, everyday items an ordeal.

Lines have become a national institution in the USSR. Most stores are organized so that customers must stand in three lines just to buy one item. They must stand in one line to place their orders, in another line to pay the cashier, and in a third line to pick up their merchandise. The enterprising Soviet shoppers have developed an elaborate etiquette for standing in line. When someone joins the line behind you, you turn to them and say, "I'm in front of you," and your place in line is thus reserved. You are then free to establish a place in another line by following the same procedure. The object of the exercise is to time your spots in line so that you place your order before you pay for it and that you pay before you pick up your order. In a large Kiev department store with numerous departments and cashier booths, the author once managed to hold places in nine lines simultaneously.

Lines perform both an economic and a social function. Because prices are centrally determined, there is no need to shop around. A bottle of milk costs the same in a store in the dairy region of Lithuania as it does in Tashkent, in the south, or in Murmansk, above the Arctic Circle. Most items have the price stamped on them indelibly to prevent stores from overcharging. Prices are artificially set and bear little relation to demand or cost of production. Thus, the cost of meat does not determine who buys steak and who buys hamburger; rather, allocations are determined primarily by availability. Buying steak in the meat market is a combination of luck, timing, and patience.

Because prices are fixed, there is no inflation in the USSR. Yet, hidden inflation exists and can be measured in longer lines and poorer quality. Western journalists have noted over the past several years that the quality of bread is deteriorating while the size of the loaves is getting smaller. Russian bread that once was golden brown and very tasty today is tasteless and often has a slightly grey color—the result of adding sawdust to make the flour go further.

While standing in line, Soviet citizens gossip, chat, and share their woes or offer helpful hints as to where to find garlic or toilet paper. Soviet stores are filled with the constant hum of conversation among the shoppers in line. The author never had occasion to consider the social function of standing in line until he returned to the United States after a long stay in the USSR. He was accompanying a newly arrived Soviet émigré family to a large super-market to show them how to shop *po-Amerikanskii* (American-style). In the produce section, the family was wide-eyed at the sight of mountains of apples, oranges, bananas, and pears. They had never seen a pineapple, and the author had to explain how to cook artichokes. In the canned-goods section, they were impressed by the variety and colorful packaging. They looked a bit bewildered, however, by the rows of frozen dinners, pizzas, and juice containers; with the exception of small bricks of ice cream, frozen foods do not exist in Soviet stores. In the meat section, the author noticed that the wife was frowning. Glancing over an assortment of neatly wrapped cuts of beef and pork, she asked, "Why is everything packaged?" The author cited the convenience and sanitary advantages, to which she replied, "But we have been in this store 20 minutes and haven't said a word to anyone. Maybe you Americans wrap your meat so you won't have to talk with the butcher." There is some truth in her observation; it illustrates the extent to which shopping in the Soviet Union represents an important way in which Soviets interact. Shopping provides immediate, interpersonal contact with fellow citizens; it gives a feeling of belonging.

The Soviet economy functions strictly on a cash basis. Checking accounts and credit cards do not exist. As a consequence, Soviet shoppers carry wads of rubles, in case they should happen to be in the produce store when strawberries go on sale or in the department store when a shipment of Italian shoes arrives. Many of the most desirable items never reach the store shelves; they are sold from the backs of delivery trucks. The author was once on a street in downtown Leningrad when a truck pulled up outside a department store. A line immediately began to form at the back of the truck, even before anyone knew what was inside. Word was passed back through the line, "We're in luck! It's toilet paper! Ten rolls maximum." The author bought the maximum and passed them out as presents to his friends back in the dormitory. Over the course of the year, his friends repaid the favor when they were lucky enough to find imported oranges in January or when they received a package of home-canned tomatoes from an aunt on a collective farm.

"Deficit items" also are sold *na levo,* or "on the left"—that is, illegally through an extensive "second economy." Sales clerks save the Italian shoes in the back room or under the counter for friends and relatives. The butcher in the local meat market told the author that he knew how much Americans love steak, so he would save the best cuts for the author. With a wink, the butcher told the author not to stand in line, but to come directly to him. As is customary, the author repaid the butcher occasionally with a bottle of scotch.

The scarcity of some food items has sparked a thriving unofficial distribution network, as Uzbeks, Georgians, and others from the warmer regions of the south bring produce to Moscow or other cities to be sold at an attractive profit in the farmers' markets (*rynki*). With their profits, these enterprising people purchase rugs, pots and pans, clothing, and other goods that are not available in their home regions. Because Soviet airline tickets are quite cheap (and regulations governing carry-on baggage are quite lax), many of these people fly to the big cities carrying huge net bags filled with tomatoes, cucumbers, oranges, and even live chickens.

The farmers' markets are the only places in the Soviet economy where market forces appear to work relatively unimpeded. Each collective farmer is entitled to a private land plot of up to 1.5 acres. The produce from these plots may be sold at the farmers' markets for whatever price the seller wishes to charge. Consequently, one can find fresh vegetables at the market virtually any time of the year, although the prices may be four or more times higher than the same item at a state store. The difference is that the state stores are virtually barren much of the year.

The private plots play no small role in Soviet agriculture, contributing approximately 25 percent of total production.[54] They account for 30 percent of all milk, 31 percent of all eggs, 32 percent of all vegetables, 41 percent of all fruit, and 63 percent of all potatoes produced in the USSR.[55] While some see this as proof of the superiority of the free market, it is also true that collective farmers routinely shirk their duties on the collective farmland and devote their time to tending their private plots. Fertilizer, seed, and pesticides are often stolen from the collective's storehouses and used on private plots. The collective's harvest may suffer as a result, but the lower earnings of the *kolkhozniki* are more than compensated for by increased earnings from the produce from their private plots.

The extensive "second economy" in the USSR consists of a wide variety of illegal or quasi-legal economic activities operating beyond the realm of state regulations and directives. By far the most prevalent form of illegal economic activity is theft of state property. Given the low salary levels of

Table 9-3. Colored Markets in the USSR

Nature of Market	Commodity	Source	Method of Sale	Example
White (legal)	Legal	Legal	Legal	Sale of food in a state store or farmers' market
Grey (semi-legal)	Legal	Legal	Semi-legal	Selling Italian shoes "under the counter"
	Legal	Semi-legal	Legal	Providing dental treatment on the side, using state-owned equipment and supplies
	Legal	Semi-legal	Semi-legal	Purchase of blue jeans from foreign tourist
Black (illegal)	Legal	Legal	Illegal	Speculation—selling vodka for more than the mandated price
	Legal	Semi-legal	Semi-legal	Selling blue jeans purchased from foreign tourist
	Legal	Illegal	Illegal	Sale of stolen auto parts
	Illegal	Illegal	Illegal	Prostitution; narcotics

Source: This table is a revised version of a typology of colored markets developed by A. Katsenelinboigen in "Coloured Markets in the Soviet Union," *Soviet Studies* 29, no. 1 (1977): 63.

most workers and the chronic shortages of numerous items, workers often feel they are justified in stealing from their employers. Collective farmers steal seed and tools; automobile assembly-line workers steal spare parts; waiters and cooks in restaurants steal food; physicians steal medicine; taxi drivers steal gasoline and use state-owned cars as unofficial "gypsy" taxis. Theft of state property is becoming so prevalent that some engineers and technicians are reportedly leaving their posts in research and design bureaus to work in restaurants, where they will have the opportunity to steal food.[56]

While theft of state property entails a high cost to the State, it fuels an enormous black market in agricultural products, spare parts, food, medicine, gasoline, and other commodities. This illegal network unquestionably is more efficient than the state bureaucracy would be at distributing such items.

Grey market activities—that is, economic transactions that are technically legal but outside the structure of the official Soviet economy—are especially common in the service sector. Doctors, lawyers, dentists, mechanics, repair people, dressmakers, and hairdressers provide services on the side, often on state time and using state-owned tools, equipment, and materials. Similarly, the service trades are notorious in the Soviet Union for requiring bribes or "gifts" in order to provide good service.

Officials can use the power of their positions to acquire special favors. Whether it is the director of a construction trust who has his workers build him a summer cottage or the director of a collective farm who gets first pick of the collective's garden plot, officials and influential people are the recipients of many benefits of the grey market. A former Soviet economist who emigrated to the West developed a typology of colored markets in the "second economy," as shown in Table 9-3.

ECONOMIC REFORM

The ascendancy of Mikhail Gorbachev to the General Secretaryship of the CPSU sparked widespread speculation in both the East and the West that reforms would be implemented to improve Soviet economic performance. Over the past thirty years, there have been repeated attempts and proposals to reform the Soviet economy, but these reforms either were never implemented or were so compromised by bureaucratic opposition and inertia that they proved ineffective.

Reforms of the Soviet economy can take one of two forms. On the one hand, there are reforms in the structure of planning and economic management. On the other hand, economic reforms can focus on revamping the plan incentives designed to induce enterprises and workers to perform better. The first type of reforms—structural reforms—usually center around the degree of centralization or decentralization in decision-making. The Soviets are quite fond of organizational reforms and often consolidate ministries, divide ministries, or bring together various enterprises into production associations, all in an attempt to increase efficiency and expand control.

Perhaps the most well-known example of an organizational reform in the Soviet economy was the creation of regional economic councils (sov-

narkhozy) under Khrushchev. In 1957, Khrushchev abolished the economic ministries and transferred their functions to 105 regional economic councils, which were in turn subordinated to the union republics. The *sovnarkhozy* were intended to supervise plans made by Gosplan and enhance coordination among all enterprises in the region. Prior to the reform, Khrushchev had severely criticized economic ministries for lack of coordination, duplications of effort, and "empire-building." He cited cases in which ministries sent parts and components all over the USSR to "their" enterprises, rather than use items produced by local enterprises reporting to another ministry. The *sovnarkhoz* reform, however, simply replaced ministerial empirebuilding with regional empire-building. *Mestnichestvo,* or localism, hindered coordination between and among enterprises in different regions. The *sovnarkhozy* were finally abolished by Khrushchev's successors in 1965.

The abolition of the *sovnarkhozy* and the return of the economic ministries prompted a vigorous debate over the degree of managerial autonomy that should prevail in enterprise decision-making. Throughout the Brezhnev period, most of the organizational restructuring reforms in the Soviet economy tended to enhance, rather than reduce, the powers of central authorities. When things begin to go awry in the USSR, the immediate reaction often is to call for more vigilant, centralized control. Most observers in the West agree, however, that one of the basic problems of the Soviet economy is an excessive degree of centralization of economic decision-making.

This centralization and mounting economic difficulties have again sparked debate over decentralizing reforms. Advocates of economic decentralization frequently propose that market forces play a greater role in economic decision-making and that the influence of central planners be diminished. Such proposals envision enterprises coordinating their activities in response to market forces, rather than through a vertical administrative chain of command. Most Soviet officials, economists, and media commentators, however, renounce such radical "market-oriented" reforms and even avoid the use of the term "reform." Instead, they refer to "improvements in the economic mechanism"—that is, minor adjustments in the structure of the planning apparatus, plan fulfillment indicators, and bonuses.

Over the years, various attempts have been made to revise performance indicators and other incentives for managers and workers, with varying degrees of success. The chapter has already described Liberman's proposals in the early 1960s to measure enterprise performance using a profitability indicator. The Liberman reform proposal was merely one of many similar suggestions for altering the incentives for workers and managers by revamping plan indicators.

Another widely publicized reform—the Shchekino experiment—was instituted at a chemical combine in Tula in 1967. As noted earlier, the Soviet economy suffers from the inefficient utilization of inputs—both labor and material. At the Shchekino plant, managers were allowed to decide how many people to hire and what to produce. Savings achieved by employing fewer people were used to increase salaries and social benefits. In the first months of the experiment, managers laid off almost one-third of the labor force and raised wages by 45 percent.[57] Over the ten-year period of the experiment, chemical output at the plant rose by 170 percent, and labor productivity increased by 240 percent.[58] Housing, vacation facilities, and other social benefits were improved, and labor turnover dropped to low levels. Other enterprises have adopted the Shchekino method on an experimental basis. During the Ninth Five-Year Plan, nearly a thousand enterprises adopted the Shchekino plan, freeing more than 50,000 workers, and during the Tenth Five-Year Plan, almost one million people were released from 11,710 enterprises.[59] At the same time, labor productivity at plants employing the Shchekino method increased at an average rate of 3.4 percent per year, compared to only 1.5 percent at other enterprises.[60]

If the Shchekino experiment was so effective in raising wages, increasing social benefits of workers, and increasing output, then why has it not been adopted across the entire Soviet economy? One reason is that the sudden and universal adoption of the Shchekino method would free more workers than the economy could absorb, creating massive unemployment. Many managers also resisted the introduction of Shchekino methods because the prestige of their enterprises and the size of their budgets is determined, in part, by the number of people employed in their factories. Given the unreliability of the Soviet labor force, managers also wanted to keep extra workers in reserve for "storming" in case their enterprises fell behind in production. Finally, managers opposed the adoption of the Shchekino method because increased output and productivity would merely result in higher plan targets in the future.

Yet another reform experiment was inaugurated in July 1983 by Iurii Andropov. This experiment, which was limited to two all-union machine-building ministries and three republic-level consumer-goods ministries, was aimed at expanding the rights of production associations and enterprises in planning and increasing their responsibility for the results of their work. In practice, the reform entailed relatively minor modifications in planning, supply, performance indicators, pricing, wage and bonus funds, distribution of profits, and investment. For instance, enterprises were given greater leeway in determining how to distribute wages and bonuses among their employees. Bonuses for exemplary performance by workers could range up to 24 percent of base wages, while bonuses to engineers and other white-collar employees could go as high as 50 percent.[61]

After the first year, the experiment was hailed as a great success and was extended to twenty more ministries, but its aggregate effects on sagging economic performance are questionable. Such economic experiments normally occur in an ideal setting, with privileged access to the best-quality labor and supplies. As with the 1965 reforms, the success of economic experiments may derive less from better structures or incentives, and more from the political priority attached to the highly publicized experiments.

Another widely publicized experiment in the Baltic republic of Estonia has legalized small-scale "private enterprise" in the service trades. Soviet authorities report that when workers in one television repair shop were allowed to run their own business, productivity increased by 15 percent in one year.[62] In part, such "privatization" reforms are an attempt by the State to legalize the flourishing business—estimated at 6 to 7 billion dollars per year—in services being provided "on the left."[63] Yet, legal private enterprise in the USSR extends only to small-scale farming, handicraft, and service trades, and it is unlikely that it will be expanded to medium- or large-scale industrial firms.

Most recently, a Siberian economist, Tatiana Zaslavskaia, voiced outspoken criticism of the Soviet economic system and called for fundamental reform, in what is referred to as the Novosibirsk Report. Leaked to a Western journalist in August 1983, the report appears to have been a highly confidential paper presented to a closed seminar organized by the economic departments of the CPSU Central Committee, the USSR Academy of Sciences, and Gosplan. In her report, Zaslavskaia argued that the problems that have plagued the Soviet economy since the late 1960s reflect general weaknesses in the structure of the Soviet economic system.[64] She noted that the present Soviet economy is largely the product of Stalin. Since Stalin's time, minor changes and adjustments have been made in the economy, but "not once has it undergone a qualitative restructuring which would reflect fundamental changes in the state of productive forces."[65]

The report implied that the outmoded economic structure itself is to blame for encouraging shoddy work, idleness, and dishonesty in the workplace. Although the labor force is better educated and able to make decisions more effectively than ever before, it has not been allowed to use its own discretion. According to Zaslavskaia, "It is in the interests of socialist society, while regulating the key aspects of the socioeconomic activity of workers, to leave them a sufficiently wide margin of freedom of individual behavior."[66] This can only be achieved "with the help of incentives which would take into account the economic and social demands or workers."[67]

In particular, she cited the overly centralized character of economic decision-making, heavy reliance on gross-output plan indicators, and the weak development of market mechanisms as key to Soviet economic woes. Since Stalin's time, she argued, the size and complexity of the Soviet economy have increased to the point where a command economy is no longer workable. "The structure of the national economy long ago crossed the threshold of complexity when it was still possible to regulate it effectively from one single center."[68] She advocated more extensive reliance on "automatic" or market regulators.

Decentralizing reforms and the introduction of market mechanisms have not occurred, Zaslavskaia noted, largely due to the opposition of powerful vested interests that wish to perpetuate the existing situation. In particular, she pointed blame at the middle levels of Soviet economic administration—that is, at officials in economic ministries and branch administrative offices. These officials, she maintained, "occupy cozy niches with ill-defined responsibilities, but thoroughly agreeable salaries."[69] Zaslavskaia called for strengthening the role of Gosplan, at the top of the economic hierarchy, and of enterprises at the bottom, while reducing the number and powers of mid-level economic administrators.

The Novosibirsk Report was significant for two reasons. It demonstrated a surprising degree of frankness in the discussion of economic problems and policies in the USSR today. Second, it served as the core for several of the policy initiatives undertaken by Gorbachev after he came to power in early 1985.

The economic policy direction of the Gorbachev regime began to emerge in the months leading up to the Twenty-Seventh Party Congress in February 1986. In a series of key addresses on economic matters, Gorbachev indicated that the powers of Gosplan would be strengthened and enterprises would be granted more autonomy and discretion in decision-making, while the powers of middle-level economic administrators to ministerial and branch offices would be severely cut back.[70] Apparently, Gorbachev agreed with Zaslavskaia's criticisms of this powerful and conservative stratum in the economic bureaucracy.

Gorbachev also advocated an end to the extensive increases in agricultural investment that characterized previous five-year plans. He appeared to favor a moderate reduction in agricultural investment, a stable rate of investment in energy and raw materials, and dramatic increases in investments in high-technology engineering industries. The latter were slated to rise by 80 to 100 percent during the Twelfth Five-Year Plan (1986–1990).[71] While investment in engineering was to increase substantially over this five-year period, so too was planned industrial output. In other words, Gorbachev was providing more resources to enterprises in the computer, electronics, chemicals, and other "new technologies" sectors, but he was also expecting those resources to result in even larger increases in production. A major thrust of the increased investment was targeted toward reequipping existing factories and enterprises and introducing automated production techniques to increase quality and efficiency.

As dramatic as these changes are, however, Gorbachev still faces many economic challenges. He has not yet broached fundamental reforms in plan performance indicators, the introduction of market mechanisms, redevised incentives for workers and managers, and adjusted prices—all of which are necessary in order to reorient and improve Soviet economic performance. Whether Gorbachev will tackle these remaining stumbling blocks depends, in large measure, on whether he is able to solidify his power sufficiently to overcome the opposition of those conservative mid-level economic bureaucrats occupying their "cozy niches."

While many commentators in the West welcomed Gorbachev's rise to power and spoke of his "liberal" policy orientations, the possibility remained that Gorbachev would rely on coercive measures to rectify the Soviet Union's economic problems. One of Gorbachev's first acts upon assuming the top party position was to renew the campaign on work discipline begun by Andropov. The number of economic officials and factory managers who were denounced, removed, and punished for poor performance increased dramatically. In the first six months of his administration, Gorbachev fired or otherwise replaced eight ministers of key economic sectors as well as the two principal officials responsible for economic policy—the Premier (Chairman of the Presidium of the Council of Ministers) and the Chairman of Gosplan. The replacement of a large number of regional and local party secretaries at the Twenty-Seventh Party Congress appeared to have been designed to enhance the Party's ability to hold enterprise managers and local economic officials accountable, even if the incentives built into the plan do not. With his own personnel in place, Gorbachev was uniquely positioned to impose wide-ranging economic reforms from above, using a combination of positive incentives and political pressure.

Notes

1. A. A. Baikov, *The Development of the Soviet Economy* (Moscow: Statistika, 1946), 327.

2. Alexander Gerschenkron, "The Rate of Industrial Growth in Russia since 1885," *The Journal of Economic History* 7, supplement (1947): 167. In the USSR, economic planners refer to national income rather than GNP.

3. For Soviet national income data, see *Narodnoe khoziaistvo v SSSR, 1974* (Moscow: Statistika, 1975), 5.

4. Ibid.

5. Ibid.

6. *Strana Sovetov za 50 let: Sbornik statisticheskikh materialov* (Moscow: Statistika, 1969), 251, 253–254.

7. O. K. Antonov, *Dlia vsekh i dlia sebia: o sovershenstvovanii pokazatelei planirovaniia sotsialisticheskogo promyshlennogo proizvodstva* (Moscow: Ekonomika, 1965), 23.

8. *23rd Congress of the CPSU* (Moscow: Novosti, 1966), 171.

9. Andrew Freris, *The Soviet Industrial Enterprise: Theory and Practice* (London: Croom Helm, 1984), 8.

10. Cited in Alec Nove, *The Soviet Economic System* (London: George Allen & Unwin, 1977), 84.

11. *Izvestiia,* 9 November 1985, pp. 1–6.

12. See Paul R. Gregory and Robert C. Stuart, *Soviet Economic Structure and Performance* (New York: Harper & Row, 1974), 199.

13. See Freris, *Soviet Industrial Enterprise,* 23.

14. Ibid., 13.

15. Cited in Nove, *Soviet Economic System,* 39.

16. Ibid., 42.

17. *Pravda,* 27 May 1984.

18. V. Kim and L. Ivanov, "Nadzor za ispoleneniem zakonov ob otvetstvennosti za nedobrokachestvennoe stroitel'stvo," *Sotsialisticheskaia zakonnost'* (May 1975): 35–38.

19. Cited in Fydor Turovsky, "Society without a Present," in Leonard Schapiro and Joseph Godson, eds., *The Soviet Worker from Lenin to Andropov,* 2d ed. (London: Macmillan, 1984), 197.

20. See Gordon B. Smith, "Organizational and Legal Problems in the Implementation of Technology in the USSR," in Gordon B. Smith, Peter B. Maggs, and George Ginsburgs, eds., *Soviet and East European Law and the Scientific-Technical Revolution* (New York: Pergamon Press, 1981), 240–271.

21. Cited in M.S. Studenikina, "Zakonodatel'stvo ob administrativnoi otvetstvennosti kodifikatsii" (Moscow: Candidate dissertation, VNIISZ, 1968).

22. *Narodnoe khoziaistvo, 1922–1982* (Moscow: Statistika, 1982), 91–92.

23. Cited in Nove, *Soviet Economic System,* 33.

24. See *Ekonomicheskaia gazeta,* no. 17 (1985).

25. U.S. Congress, Joint Economic Committee, *Allocation of Resources in the Soviet Union and China, 1981* (Washington, D.C.: U.S. Government Printing Office, 1982), 252–258.

26. U.S. Congress, Joint Economic Committee, *Allocation of Resources in the Soviet Union and China, 1983* (Washington, D.C.: U.S. Government Printing Office, 1984), 230.

27. See *Ekonomicheskaia gazeta,* no. 8 (1985): 5.

28. Cited in Nove, *Soviet Economic System,* 27.

29. *Narodnoe khoziaistvo SSSR v 1979 g.* (Moscow: Statistika, 1980), 237.

30. David W. Carey, "Soviet Agriculture: Recent Performance and Future Plans," in U.S. Congress, Joint Economic Committee, *Soviet Economy in a New Perspective* (Washington, D.C.: U.S. Government Printing Office, 1976), 586–587.

31. Cited in D. Gale Johnson, "Agriculture," in James Cracraft, ed., *The Soviet Union Today* (Chicago: Bulletin of the Atomic Scientists, 1983), 197.

32. Ibid., 203.

33. V. Tikhonov cited in Johnson, "Agriculture," 203.

34. Cited in James R. Millar, "Prospects for Soviet Agriculture," *Problems of Communism* (May–June, 1977): 8.

35. Johnson, "Agriculture," 197.

36. S. Shalaev, *Pravda,* 12 October 1983.

37. Mary McAuley, *Labour Disputes in Soviet Russia, 1957–1965* (Oxford: Clarendon Press, 1969), 156.

38. See *Bulletin' Verkhovnogo Suda SSSR,* no. 6 (1968).

39. Cited in David E. Powell, "A Troubled Society," in Cracraft, *The Soviet Union Today,* 326.

40. Reported in *Time,* 23 September 1985, p. 45.

41. Cited in Basile Kerblay, *Modern Soviet Society* (New York: Pantheon Books, 1983), 291.

42. *Time,* 23 September 1985, p. 45. Vladimir Treml puts the figure at 8 to 9 percent of the national income for 1980. See Vladimir G. Treml, "Alcohol Abuse and Quality of Life in the USSR," in Helmut Sonnenfeldt, ed., *Soviet Politics in the 1980s* (Boulder: Westview Press, 1985), 61.

43. Cited in William Moskoff, *Labor and Leisure in the Soviet Union* (London: Macmillan, 1984), ix.

44. Reported in McAuley, *Labour Disputes in Soviet Russia,* 126–127.

45. *Ekonomicheskaia gazeta,* no. 45 (1980): 6.

46. Keith Bush, "Retail Prices in Moscow and Four Western Cities in March 1982," Radio Liberty Research Supplement, June 4, 1982.

47. J. G. Chapman, "Recent Trends in the Soviet Industrial Wage Structure," in A. Kahan and Blair Ruble, *Industrial Labor in the USSR* (New York: Pergamon Press, 1979), 175.

48. Cited in Murray Seeger, "Eyewitness to Failure," in Schapiro and Godson, *The Soviet Worker,* 94.

49. Cited in Gail Warshofsky Lapidus, *Women in Soviet Society* (Berkeley: University of California Press, 1978), 55.

50. Iu. B. Riurikov, "Family Matters? No Matters of State!" *Ekonomika i organizatsiia promyshlennovo proizvodstva,* no. 10 (October 1982): 149–170.

51. *Zhenshchiny v SSSR* (Moscow: Politizdat, 1983), 12–13; and *Zhenshchiny v SSSR* (Moscow: Politizdat, 1975), 78, 86.

52. Alastair McAuley, *Women's Work and Wages in the Soviet Union* (London: George Allen & Unwin, 1981), 87–89.

53. Ibid., 21.

54. *Istoriia SSSR,* no. 5 (September–October 1984): 120–126.

55. Ibid.

56. Cited in George Feifer, "Russian Disorders: The Sick Man of Europe," *Harper's* (February 1981): 48.

57. *Pravda,* 28 March 1977.

58. Ibid.

59. R. Batkev and S. Semin, "Shchekinski metod v usloviiakh sovershenstvovaniia khoziaistvennogo mekhanizma," *Sotsialisticheskii trud,* no. 1 (1983): 44.

60. Ibid.

61. Cited in Fyodor I. Kushnirsky, "The Limits of Soviet Economic Reform," *Problems of Communism* (July–August, 1984): 41.

62. *Izvestiia* article cited in *The Japan Times,* 7 September 1985.

63. Ibid.

64. English text of the Novosibirsk Report, *Survey* (Spring 1984): 88–108.
65. Ibid., 88.
66. Ibid., 95.
67. Ibid., 96.
68. Ibid., 91.
69. Ibid., 99.
70. Speech by Mikhail Gorbachev on Moscow Television, June 11, 1985.
71. Ibid.

Selected Bibliography

Bergson, Abram, and Herbert S. Levine, eds. *The Soviet Economy: Toward the Year 2000*. London: George Allen & Unwin, 1983.

Bornstein, Morris, ed. *The Soviet Economy: Continuity and Change*. Boulder: Westview Press, 1981.

Campbell, Robert W. *Soviet-Type Economies: Performance and Evolution*. New York: Houghton, Mifflin, 1974.

Colton, Timothy. *Dilemma of Reform in the USSR*. New York: Council on Foreign Relations, 1985.

Freris, Andrew. *The Soviet Industrial Enterprise: Theory and Practice*. London: Croom Helm, 1984.

Kahan, A., and Blair A. Ruble, eds. *Industrial Labor in the USSR*. New York: Pergamon Press, 1979.

Lane, David. *Soviet Economy and Society*. Oxford: Basil Blackwell, 1985.

Lane, David, and Felicity O'Dell. *The Soviet Industrial Worker*. Oxford: Martin Robertson, 1978.

Lapidus, Gail Warshofsky. *Women in Soviet Society*. Berkeley: University of California Press, 1978.

McAuley, Alastair. *Women's Work and Wages in the Soviet Union*. London: George Allen & Unwin, 1981.

Matthews, Mervyn. *Privilege in the Soviet Union*. London: George Allen & Unwin, 1978.

Moskoff, William. *Labor and Leisure in the Soviet Union*. London: Macmillan, 1984.

Nove, Alec. *The Soviet Economic System*. 2d ed. London: George Allen & Unwin, 1984.

Ruble, Blair A. *Soviet Trade Unions*. Cambridge: Cambridge University Press, 1981.

Schapiro, Leonard, and Joseph Godson, eds. *The Soviet Worker from Lenin to Andropov*. London: Macmillan, 1984.

U.S. Congress, Joint Economic Committee. *Soviet Economy in the 1980s: Problems and Prospects*. Washington, D.C.: U.S. Government Printing Office, 1982.

Yanowitch, Murray. *Social and Economic Inequality in the Soviet Union*. New York: M. E. Sharpe, 1977.

10

Science, Technology, and Education

From its founding, the Soviet regime has manifested an ambivalent attitude toward science and scientists. On the one hand, science has been accorded a prominent role in Soviet ideology. Marx noted that the progression to socialist society depended on the general condition of science and technology and their application to production.[1] Lenin echoed this stress on science and technology by urging Bolsheviks "to take all science, technology, knowledge" because communism could not be built without them.[2] Lenin frequently referred to a "technical revolution," which would change the nature of the society. Throughout the Bolshevik period, science and technology were seen as the great transformers of society. The Bolsheviks expected the development of a "new," revolutionary science, free of ties to bourgeois society, to unleash the creative powers of science on behalf of all social classes. A clear illustration of Lenin's views on the revolutionizing effect of technology was the GOELRO (electrification) plan. For Lenin, electrification was not simply a technical problem, but a socioeconomic one with profound political and social implications.

On the other hand, however, scientists have often been at odds with official policies in the USSR, and a few have become outspoken critics of the Soviet system. Lenin and his successors have found that creative, scientific minds cannot be channeled exclusively toward technical and scientific problems; scientists who are capable of envisioning revolutionary scientific discoveries are also capable of analyzing and criticizing social and political issues as well.

At the same time, the expertise of the Soviet scientific and technical community has proven invaluable to policymakers. Resolving the complex issues that confront the leadership demands minds and talents of the highest quality. Yet, the policymakers are sometimes not pleased with the advice they receive from the experts. Thus, while Soviet scientists are indispensable to the Soviet regime, they also pose many challenges for the leadership. The study of the role of science and scientists in Soviet society illustrates the policy-formulation process in a dynamic and vitally important field.

THE DEVELOPMENT OF SOVIET SCIENCE

As in so many other fields, the Bolsheviks inherited a scientific establishment that had been created under the imperial government. Prior to the Revolution, Russian science was closely tied to the State; all universities and research institutes, as well as the Imperial Russian Academy of Sciences, fell under the direct supervision of the government. Scientists were members of a privileged elite. Although they occupied a broad range of the political spectrum, from ultraconservatives to radicals, the largest group supported the Constitutional Democrats (Kadets). During the Civil War, professors and academics were considered enemies of the Bolshevik regime, and many were arrested and died during the Red Terror. Nikolai Koltsov, the famous biologist, was condemned to death, but he was spared due to Bolshevik writer Maxim Gorky's personal appeal to Lenin.

The repression of scientists during the early years of the Soviet regime resulted in the emigration of a large number of distinguished scientists, including Igor Sikorsky, the prominent aircraft designer; V. Korenchevsky, a biologist and noted specialist on gerontology; G. B. Kistiakovsky, a chemist who would later serve as science adviser to President Eisenhower; Pitirim Sorokin, a sociologist; and Wasily Leontiev, who would later receive the Nobel Prize in economics. Recognizing the damage caused by this "brain drain," Lenin introduced a resolution at the Eighth Party Congress in 1919 that signaled a more moderate stance toward science: "The problem of industrial and economic development demands the immediate and widespread use of experts in science and technology whom we have inherited from capitalism, in spite of the fact that they inevitably are impregnated with bourgeois ideas and customs."[3]

Meanwhile, the foundations were being laid for training a new generation of "revolutionary" scientists and technical experts, who would eventually replace the scientists held over from the tsarist period. Despite the precarious status of Soviet science during the Civil War period, many new research institutes were established, often housed in large estates confiscated from wealthy industrialists and former members of the aristocracy.

The end of the Civil War, the introduction of the New Economic Policy (NEP) in 1921, and the liberalized political climate combined to create favorable conditions for the development of science. International scholarly cooperation and exchanges of scientific literature were resumed. Financial support for new research institutes and laboratories was increased, and ideological strictures were eased in the natural and physical sciences. The humanities and social sciences, however, continued under strict ideological controls enforced by Bolshevik political activists, few of whom had any scientific training.

Science policy during NEP was directed by *Glavnauka*, a special department of the People's Commissariat of Education. *Glavnauka* was responsible for allocating government research contracts as well as authorizing foreign travel for scientists. Under the leadership of A. V. Lunacharsky, chief of *Glavnauka*, Soviet science flourished. The number of scientific papers, conferences, and journals increased rapidly. Major advances were made in the fields of genetics, biochemistry, physiology, biology, physics, chemistry, mathematics, geology, and geophysics.

Like virtually every other sphere of Soviet life, however, science changed dramatically in 1928 with Stalin's introduction of forced industrialization, centralized state planning, and collectivization of agriculture. In March 1928, a major purge of scientists, engineers, and technical personnel began with the arrest, trial, and execution of eleven persons accused of sabotaging coal mines. Émigré Soviet scientist Zhores Medvedev argues that the campaign directed against scientific experts was part of Stalin's plan to replace the older generation of scientists with a new generation of "red" experts.[4] Supposed anti-Soviet organizations were "exposed" and with them many prominent scientists, including the historian M. S. Grushevsky; S. A. Efremov, vice-president of the Ukrainian Academy of Sciences; the economist N. D. Kondratiev; agricultural specialists A. V. Chaianov and A. G. Diarenko; L. K. Ramzin, director of the Heat Engineering Research Institute; and numerous professors in universities and technical colleges. The arbitrary and groundless arrests of scientists often encouraged their opponents and enemies to declare whole branches of science or theoretical approaches "bourgeois" or "reactionary." For instance, in 1929 when the noted biologist and founder of the Russian school of genetics, S. S. Chetverikov, was arrested and exiled to a remote region of the Urals, the whole field of genetics also came under attack. Koltsov, A. Serebrovsky, and many other geneticists were subsequently arrested and replaced by a younger generation of poorly trained, but ideologically "pure" specialists. Largely because of the elimination of a whole generation of geneticists, T. D. Lysenko was able to rise to prominence, advocating a dubious theory (later proved erroneous) of the inheritance of acquired characteristics. Lysenko and other members of the new breed of scientists offered false hopes to Stalin that by subordinating pure science to practice (*praktikat*), science would dramatically and immediately enhance industrial and agricultural performance.

In 1929, the Leningrad Party Committee organized a special commission to investigate the USSR Academy of Sciences, whose headquarters were still located in the city. The commission found the Academy to be a "center for counterrevolutionary work against Soviet power."[5] Hundreds of academicians and staff members were either arrested or dismissed. Prior to 1928, the Academy had managed to remain apolitical, but with new elections scheduled, great pressure was brought on the Academy to elect party members as academicians. Political controls over the Academy further increased in 1934, when the Academy was moved to Moscow and merged with the Communist Academy, a Party-controlled body that had attempted unsuccessfully to duplicate the functions of the Academy.

The need for scientific and technical expertise grew under Stalin's industrialization program, and the repression of scientists eased somewhat after 1932. A few scientists were released from prison, while others, such as L. K. Ramzin, were allowed to continue their research in prison. While confined, Ramzin developed a revolutionary model boiler for heat engines for which he was later given an award.

The easing of pressure on scientists was, however, only temporary.

Stalin's Great Terror of 1936–1938 wiped out many thousands of scientists and other academics, decimating every branch of science and learning. While the economy continued to function, all new research and development came to an abrupt end. International scientific and technical ties were severed. Technological development, even in such important fields as aircraft design, were halted with the arrest, imprisonment, and execution of leading experts. What little research and development was performed during the war years occurred within the confines of Stalin's Gulag prison system. Medvedev describes the absurdities of prison research centers. The chief engineers of these centers, although prisoners, headed large teams of experts, some of whom were not prisoners themselves. After the long working day, the free employees would return home to their families while their superiors were taken to their prison cells.[6]

The prison research network is credited with designing new series of tanks, aircraft, artillery, and locomotives as well as laying the groundwork for the early Soviet missiles. Scientists and academicians in fields with no potential military applications were sent to work in mines or to harvest timber in Siberia. S. P. Korolev, who would later design the first sputniks and the Soviet Union's first intercontinental missiles, spent the war years working in the notorious mines of Kolyma, north of the Arctic Circle. By the time the war ended and he was released, he was close to death from fatigue and malnutrition.

The war demonstrated to Stalin the inferiority of Soviet technology, and from 1946 all branches of military-oriented technology received highest state priority. Allocations for science increased dramatically, and the powers of the Academy were extended. The salaries of scientists were doubled or even tripled. New institutes and research centers sprang up, and the scientific community suddenly became a privileged elite.

Especially prominent in the post–World War II emphasis on scientific advancement was the program to develop an atomic bomb. The program, headed by Igor Kurchatov, drew on the finest available talent, including several captured German physicists. One of the Germans was later awarded the title "Hero of Socialist Labor" and appointed head of a nuclear research team in East Germany, but soon escaped to West Germany.[7] Lavrenti Beria, Stalin's infamous chief of secret police, was responsible for mobilizing prison labor to increase uranium production. Beria also utilized the resources of the prison-camp system in the years following the war to construct massive science and space complexes.[8]

The development of Soviet atomic capability also benefited other branches of science. The sudden availability of isotopes spurred new advances in chemistry, biochemistry, physiology, and medicine. These fields, however, did not receive the high priority accorded to the Soviet atomic project.

In lower-priority branches of Soviet science, political intrusions were frequent. Stalin considered himself an authority in many scientific fields, including biology, evolution, linguistics, philosophy, and the social sciences, and he did not hesitate to impose his theories. Furthermore, he extended his own authoritarian style of leadership to each branch of science. "Scientific leaders" in each research field were charged not only with administering their respective research projects, but also with developing the "correct" theoretical line to be followed by all researchers. In the natural sciences, all research had to be based on the principles of "dialectical materialism" as expounded in Stalin's political tract on the subject. From the late 1940s until Khrushchev's ouster in 1964, Lysenko, the scientific leader in the fields of biology and agricultural sciences, exerted dictatorial powers over research, and a number of his pseudo-scientific theories became official dogma. Under Lysenko, genetics research stopped for almost twenty years, doing irreparable damage to the field in the Soviet Union.

A new wave of purges of Soviet scientists was planned in conjunction with the "Doctors' Plot" but was cut short by Stalin's death in March 1953. The more relaxed political climate introduced by Khrushchev spurred scientific and technological development. At the Twentieth Party Congress in 1956, the First Secretary shocked the delegates with a stinging denunciation of Stalin's crimes, including the arrest and imprisonment of thousands of the Soviet Union's leading scientists. Many scientists were "rehabilitated" during Khrushchev's de-Stalinization campaign. For others, however, the rehabilitation came too late—they had already been executed or had died in the camps.

Reflecting the new, more open attitude toward science, international scientific communication and cooperation resumed after 20 years of isolation imposed by Stalin. Expanded contacts with the American and European scientific communities, however, further illustrated the scientific and technological gap that existed between the USSR and the West. Khrushchev initiated a program of actively assimilating foreign technology in an effort to narrow the gap. Technical and agricultural attachés were assigned to Soviet embassies abroad, scientific exchanges were initiated, Western scientific journals were made available to Soviet scientists, and specialists were allowed to attend international conferences and symposia abroad.

Khrushchev's emphasis on duplicating Western scientific and technological achievements, while well-intentioned, further widened the technological gap in some cases. Medvedev notes that while Soviet scientists were busy trying to copy imported instruments and equipment, Western scientists were introducing many innovations, resulting in equipment that was several generations ahead of the Soviet efforts.[9]

The Soviet thrust in scientific and technical fields under Khrushchev was impressive nevertheless. In 1957, the Soviets shocked the world with the first successful launching of an unmanned satellite, Sputnik I. During the Khrushchev years, the number of research workers almost tripled, while the number of research institutes doubled.[10] The proliferation of institutes under the jurisdiction of the USSR Academy of Sciences burdened its budget and managerial resources to the point that in 1961, about half of the institutes were shifted from the Academy to various industrial ministries, where they were to conduct applied research to enhance the performance of their respective industrial sectors. Thus, the Institute of Fisheries was transferred to the Ministry of Fisheries and the Institute of Oil was placed under the aegis of the Ministry of the Petroleum Industry. Institutes remaining under the jurisdiction of the Academy tended to focus on pure or basic research rather than applied research.

Khrushchev also promoted the decentralization of the Soviet scientific establishment. Under Stalin, the concentration of scientific research centers in Moscow had reached high levels. For instance, 70 to 80 percent of all biologists lived in that city.[11] Khrushchev considered this concentration unhealthy and even dangerous, so he ordered the construction of several gigantic science centers far from Moscow. The best-known example is Akademgorodok (Academy Town), near Novosibirsk in Central Siberia. The new planned community was the site of the prestigious Siberian Division of the Academy of Sciences, and several noted scientists were encouraged to establish research institutes there. In order to attract scientists and technical personnel to the region, Khrushchev authorized salary bonuses of 50 to 100 percent.[12]

The Khrushchev era was also marked by extensive discussions of the dynamic role of science and technology in altering Soviet society and ushering in communism. In the mid-1950s, books and articles began to appear discussing the "scientific-technical revolution" (STR) that was sweeping the modern world and would radically transform social and economic relations. The Program of the Twenty-Second Party Congress in 1961 stated, "Humanity is entering a period of scientific and technical revolution connected with the mastering of nuclear power, the conquest of space, the development of chemistry, the automation of production, and other achievements of science and technology."[13] This official recognition by the Party stimulated even more research on the STR.

Specialists during this period were sensitive to the political and cultural ramifications of the scientific-technical revolution. A leading Czechoslovakian scholar referred to the STR as "a cultural revolution of unprecedented proportions."[14] Inherent in this revolution were changes affecting not only industrial production, but also the full range of people-machine relations, interpersonal relations, and the relationship of people to their environment. During the late 1960s, a team of Soviet and Czech specialists working on the STR noted that it involved a "fundamental transformation of science and technology . . . leading to the application of science as a direct productive force" in the economy.[15]

Some authors saw the STR as the rational, planned outcome of centralized state policies in the area of science, technology, and production. Consequently, they maintained that the STR was subject to manipulation in order to fulfill specific economic, social, and political goals. Others referred to the scientific-technical revolution as a societal, diffuse, and autonomous process that was affecting all advanced industrial societies. This view held that the STR was a permanent and irreversible revolution that was not subject to manipulation. Nevertheless, these authors maintained that only under socialism could the fruits of the STR be fully and equitably realized.

During the 1960s and early 1970s, there was a veritable flood of monographs, texts, research symposia, and newspaper articles devoted to the scientific-technical revolution. Discussions of the STR were not limited to economists, engineers, scientists, and others most directly affected by it; rather, they left virtually no discipline untouched. Legal scholars, urban planners, sociologists, health-care specialists, artists, and writers all speculated on the impact of the STR on their respective fields.

As research on the scientific-technical revolution gained momentum, however, it became apparent that expectations of its accomplishments were outpacing actual societal change. A conservative backlash occurred under Brezhnev, and the early optimism that had permeated discussions of the STR became clouded with cautionary statements. In 1968, a major philosophical journal warned against "illusions" about the omnipotence of science and technology in effecting change.[16] Other authors chose to downgrade the ambitious scope of the STR and instead began referring to "scientific and technical *progress.*"[17]

The history of Soviet science is replete with examples of scientific fads and trends (like the STR or cybernetics) that begin with the imaginative work of Soviet scientists but soon expand to dominate all scientific discussions. As a fad takes hold, it becomes the subject of an intensive campaign and is thus transformed into an element of the official ideology. Inevitably, scientific fads fail to live up to expectations, and they eventually generate conservative reactions and are superseded by other trends or fads.

In the late 1960s and early 1970s, the emerging policy of détente under Brezhnev greatly facilitated international scientific contacts and cooperation. Because of these increased contacts, Soviet science gradually shifted from the duplication of Western achievements to cooperation and integration into worldwide developments in scientific and technical progress.

The Brezhnev leadership recognized that the numerous and embarrassing failures of Khrushchev's policies had occurred in large part because of a failure to consult with scientific experts or to heed their advice. Consequently, the Brezhnev regime began to incorporate technical specialists in policy-making to a degree never before seen in the USSR.

Throughout the 1960s, the Soviet scientific community also became increasingly vocal on political matters, using their privileged status and scholarly credibility to support various political causes. In 1966, a group of twenty-five prominent scientists, literary experts, and artists sent a strongly worded letter to the CPSU Central Committee protesting Stalin's rehabilitation. Scientists also protested the trial of the prominent Soviet writers Andrei Siniavsky and Iurii Daniel and the harassment of Alexander Solzhenitsyn. But the event that crystallized opposition within the scientific community more than any other was the 1968 Soviet invasion of Czechoslovakia. Hundreds of Soviet scientists signed letters or attended meetings protesting the suppression of the liberal reforms that had occurred during the "Prague Spring."

The Brezhnev regime responded to this rising criticism with a crackdown on dissident scientists. Scientists who signed petitions or spoke out publicly were often called in by party authorities and asked to retract their statements. Those who refused were expelled from the Party, stripped of security clearances (making them ineligible to work in most institutes that conducted classified research), and blacklisted by government censors. Some dissident scientists were even dismissed, arrested, and convicted of anti-Soviet agitation. Academician Andrei Sakharov, father of the hydrogen bomb in the USSR, lost his security clearance and was not allowed to enter his institute in Moscow.

The Brezhnev regime's crackdown on intellectual dissent also resulted in a policy of abolishing the separate, privileged status of the Soviet scientific community. The isolated, scholarly towns were "proletarianized" by relocating industries and by transferring thousands of working-class families there to alter their social composition. Akademgorodok was incorporated into Novosibirsk, losing its autonomy and even its name.

At the same time, the Brezhnev leadership began to criticize the over-concentration of Jews in the scientific and academic professions. Measures were taken to restrict the admission of Jews to colleges and universities and in hiring. The number of Jews entering universities declined from 112,000 in 1968 to 105,800 in 1970, 88,500 in 1972, and an estimated 50,000 in 1980.[18] Jewish scientists and researchers were dismissed from their institutes, and quotas on hiring were instituted in some cities.[19] These harsh and restrictive measures prompted a sudden outpouring of demands by Jewish intellectuals to emigrate from the USSR, creating another thorny political issue to complicate Brezhnev's foreign-policy objectives and catalyzing even greater dissent within the scientific and scholarly community.

The stagnation of the Soviet economy during the latter Brezhnev years also took its toll on Soviet science. The rate of annual increase in the number of scientists dropped from the phenomenal figure of 7.8 percent in the period from 1963–1968, to 6.1 percent from 1968 to 1973, and to 3.2 percent from 1973 to 1978.[20] The average annual increase in budget allocations for scientific and technological research fell from 15 percent in the 1950s and early 1960s to 8 percent in the mid-1960s, to a low of 1.7 percent in 1976.[21] Despite the reduced growth rates, however, more than 1.3 million scientists are employed in research institutes in the USSR, almost 60 percent more than in the United States.[22]

SCIENTISTS AND POLICY-MAKING

As we have seen, the role of scientists and other specialists in the policy-making process has waxed and waned in the years from 1917 to the present. Despite these fluctuations, however, there has been a general increase over the long run in scientists' influence over policymakers. This trend was especially evident during the Brezhnev period.

Academicians first became involved in advising the Soviet government in the early 1930s, when Stalin began to emphasize tying research to the industrial needs of the country. The range of issues on which scientists could express opinions was limited to technical matters, however, and policy-making retained its highly centralized character. Khrushchev's failure to allow specialists to become involved in policy-making and his disregard for their advice when it was offered accounts for many of his disastrous policies.

Brezhnev heeded the advice of specialists much more extensively than had previous Soviet leaders. Whether it was agronomists advising the leadership on the potential of the non–black-earth zone, criminologists on policies to counteract juvenile delinquency, or environmental scientists on the potential detrimental impact of the diversion of Siberian rivers, specialist involvement in the policy-making process became institutionalized under Brezhnev. With their growing influence, various Soviet research institutes have developed reputations for supporting certain positions on issues, and inter-institute rivalries are common, especially in attempting to influence the political leadership. While one's title or position within a given research institute is important, the biggest determinant of an individual scientist's degree of influence on policy questions appears to be his or her reputation and personal connections to the ruling elite.

In addition to being more involved in policy-making in recent years, scientists have also been given a freer hand in setting their own research agendas and managing research institutes. There is a fine line between party coordination of scientific research activities and *podmena*—party interference in questions of pure research. The political intrusions into the realm of science that characterized the Stalin and Khrushchev eras have been largely absent under Brezhnev and his successors. Speaking to a congress marking the two hundred and fiftieth anniversary of the Academy of Science, Brezhnev said: "We have no intention of dictating to you the details of your research subjects, nor how to go about it—that is a matter for the scientists themselves."[23]

In contrast to earlier periods, there is relatively little pressure on young scientists to join the Party. Yet, the presidents of the Academy since 1961 have all been party members. In addition, scientific personnel are expected to attend periodic meetings and political lectures organized by the party committee in each research institute.

Under Brezhnev, the role and functions of academic councils (*uchenye sovety*) in scientific institutes were expanded. These councils, which consist of the institute director, academicians and corresponding members of the Academy, and other leading specialists, advise institute directors on administrative as well as scientific matters. Since 1972, the academic councils have met jointly with local party bureaus to discuss budgetary allocations, planning, and fulfillment of research programs.

The Party's primary mechanism for influencing research and development (R&D) policies is the party committee (*partkom*) within each scientific research institute. Chairmen of *partkomy* act as liaisons between institute directors and local party officials. They report to their superiors on plan fulfillment, labor discipline, and worker morale within their research institutes. In addition, they can use party connections and influence to acquire additional personnel, larger budgets, and better equipment. Party committees also participate in many administrative and managerial decisions, including selecting and assigning projects, awarding promotions and raises, and distributing bonuses and social funds.

Innovations in the USSR are greatly facilitated when research institutes find powerful patrons in the higher party apparatus or obtain contracts from powerful ministries. When a minister or a member of the Central Committee throws his or her support behind an R&D project, bureaucratic obstacles are more easily overcome and rival institutes are less able to attack the project. Similarly, much of the innovative research in the Soviet Union is performed under contract. There is intense competition among research institutes over contracts, especially for defense projects, because of the defense sector's political clout, abundance of funds, and general openness to innovative ideas.

THE MANAGEMENT OF SCIENCE IN THE USSR

Scientific and technological research in the USSR is carried out through three main administrative structures: the Academy of Sciences of the USSR, the industrial ministries and their affiliated research institutes, and universities and technical colleges. The latter are relatively minor and are engaged primarily in graduate-level training rather than in conducting major research projects.

Traditionally, the power and prestige of the Academy of Sciences has far surpassed that of the other research organizations. The Academy comprises approximately 260 "academicians," or full members, and approximately 480 "corresponding members."[24] It convenes twice a year in a General Assembly to discuss major trends and problems of science policy in the USSR. In addition, the General Assembly elects new members by secret ballot and resolves organizational matters. The policy-making and administrative functions of the Academy are delegated to a presidium, chaired by the President of the Academy.

The Academy is divided into four branches: (1) physics, engineering, and mathematics; (2) chemistry and biology; (3) geosciences; and (4) social sciences. The Academy directly supervises more than three hundred of the most prestigious research institutes.

Each of the republics of the USSR (with the exception of the Russian republic) has its own academy of science, which reports to the USSR Academy of Science in Moscow. Research institutes that are subordinate to the republic academies tend to focus on scientific or technical problems relevant to their regions. Thus, the Azerbaidzhan Academy of Sciences is noted for its work in petrochemicals, while the Armenian Academy operates an observatory high in the mountains and is noted for its research in astrophysics.

In addition, the USSR Academy of Sciences maintains branches throughout the Soviet Union. The three largest of these are the Siberian Division in Novosibirsk (formerly Akademgorodok), the Far Eastern Center in Khabarovsk, and the Urals Center in Sverdlovsk. In aggregate, the Academy system, including institutes subordinated to the republic academies and regional branches, contains approximately 1500 research institutes and employs more than 49,000 scientists and 150,000 staff.[25]

In recent years, research institutes affiliated with industrial ministries have grown in numbers and importance. Many of these institutes were originally under the authority of the Academy; they were transferred to the jurisdiction of industrial ministries in 1961 in an effort to separate institutes engaged in applied research from those conducting fundamental research. This division of institutes, which is responsible for some of the present problems of Soviet science, created the need for a new organization, parallel to the Academy, to coordinate the activities of institutes engaged in applied research. Such an institution, the State Committee for Science and Technology, was created in 1965. The State Committee, which reports directly to the Council of Ministers, is responsible for formulating and directing science policy, assisting Gosplan and the Academy in allocating funds for research, identifying high-priority research projects, coordinating R&D efforts, and supervising the acquisition of technology from the West. Although the State

Committee can influence scientific and technological work in important ways, it does not directly supervise the operations of the industrial institutes. Those institutes frequently concentrate on the narrow interests of their ministries or industrial sectors, placing more emphasis on short-term production goals rather than on the long-term innovation favored by the State Committee.

Brezhnev and his successors emphasized the need for improving economic performance through technological innovation. Soviet political leaders have become more and more insistent that research projects have practical payoffs. As a result, the State Committee has grown in power and prestige and can now occasionally challenge the dominance of the Academy of Sciences. The trend toward applied research has also strengthened the position of some of the industrial institutes. Their status and their level of financial support now equal that of many of the Academy institutes.

During the early 1980s, the Academy came under considerable pressure to devote greater attention to the potential industrial applications of its research. In his speeches A. P. Aleksandrov, President of the Academy from 1960 to 1986, stressed the need for rapid advances in the fields of energy, computer technology, genetic engineering, and agriculture—all of which have direct industrial or agricultural applications.[26] In what has been interpreted as a jab at the role of the State Committee in encouraging technology imports from the West, Aleksandrov also warned about the dangers of relying too heavily on imported technology. He reported that 70 percent of the technical apparatuses, measuring devices, and instruments used in Soviet laboratories are of foreign origin.[27]

In June 1985, the Central Committee sponsored a special conference to discuss how the assimilation of science and technology into the economy might be improved. One of the central points made by many speakers at the conference was the need to shift the emphasis toward indigenous development of science and technology, rather than reliance on foreign sources.[28]

At the level of the enterprise or production association, R&D has been enhanced since the early 1970s by the creation of science-production associations (*nauchno-proizvodstvennie ob"edineniia-NPO*). NPOs were formed by amalgamating different research institutes, design bureaus, and production units under the leadership of a single research institute. By creating larger R&D units, it was hoped that redundancy would be reduced, bureaucratic staff would be cut back, coordination and cooperation would be facilitated, and the research-production cycle would be shortened. The reform has been credited with substantial improvements. For example, at Pozitron, a leading microelectronics firm in Leningrad, the introduction of an NPO shortened the average lead-time for a R&D project from 4 years to 1.7 years.[29] NPOs play a prominent role in electronics, chemical engineering, and instrument-building, and in the radio and communications industries to a lesser extent.

The adoption of the NPO system in other sectors and branches has been hampered, however, by bureaucratic interests that wish to preserve the status quo. Some industrial ministries opposed the divestiture of their research institutes because these institutes provided a source of revenue through their contract research activities. Many enterprises and small design bureaus also opposed amalgamation into NPOs, fearing the loss of their independent status.

PROBLEMS AND PROSPECTS FOR SOVIET SCIENCE

With all the resources that are devoted to science and technology in the USSR, one might wonder why Soviet scientists do not perform better than they do. By most measures—numbers of Nobel prizes, major scientific or technical breakthroughs, citations by fellow scientists, or sheer volume of scientific publication—American scientists in most fields far surpass their Soviet counterparts.[30] The reason for this relatively lower level of Soviet scientific achievement stems not from political intrusions into science, but from the organization and management of science in the Soviet Union.

This chapter has already alluded to some of the problems in Soviet science. For instance, there is a relatively sharp distinction among Soviet research institutes between fundamental research and applied research. Scientists working in research institutes of the Academy of Sciences frequently disregard potential industrial applications of their research. Similarly, research institutes attached to industrial branches frequently focus on narrow, applied problems, such as how to eliminate production bottlenecks in existing technologies or processes, rather than pursuing more revolutionary and innovative research. Not only are fundamental and applied research separated organizationally, but there are few financial incentives for fundamental scientists to be concerned with applications, and for applied scientists to keep abreast of developments in basic theoretical research.

Organizational fragmentation also hampers scientific achievement by reducing coordination among research institutes. A research institute within the Ministry of the Electronics Industry, for example, will find it virtually impossible to acquire the assistance of specialists from institutes affiliated with other ministries. The development of an electrical component may be delayed by years or even scrapped altogether because the Ministry of the Chemical Industry does not produce the necessary polymers or other elements, or the Ministry of Instrument-Making and Control Systems does not manufacture a specialized measuring device.

Furthermore, scientific discoveries and breakthroughs in one field are often not reported to the other branches of science for which they may have important consequences. In part, this is because the majority of R&D projects are conducted under security classifications, but it is also because of an inadequate system for publicizing research findings within the scientific community. One study found that it took Soviet enterprises one to two years longer to introduce new processes that were first developed in other branches or ministries than those that were developed in house.[31] It simply takes enterprises longer to learn about innovations that occur outside their respective ministerial chains of command.

In order to facilitate the dissemination of technical information within the research community, the All-Union Institute of Interbranch Information (VIMI) was created. The Institute acts as a clearinghouse for information received from industrial ministries concerning their innovations. VIMI sends copies of this information to other ministries and research institutes that may find it useful. The system, however, has proved overly cumbersome and bureaucratic.

Scientific progress is also retarded in the USSR by inadequate equipment, instruments, and supplies. A survey of 300 Soviet institutes found that 85 percent had no photocopiers; thus, designs and technical drawings had to be reproduced by hand.[32] Partly as a result of chronic shortages of equipment, Soviet scientists excel in the theoretical, or "blackboard," sciences, including theoretical condensed-matter physics, theoretical astrophysics, theoretical seismology, mathematical psychology, elementary particle theory, and plasma physics. These fields do not require extensive laboratory equipment or elaborate computer technology. However, in the experimental sciences (e.g., astronomy, interferometry, experimental physics, computer science, the social sciences, and all fields of engineering) where equipment needs are vital, the Soviets lag considerably behind their American and European counterparts. Even when Soviet scientists make a crucial breakthrough, they are often unable to maintain their lead due to the inadequate infrastructure. For example, although Soviet scientists are credited with founding the field of low-temperature physics, their leadership in the field has declined, in part, because of a lack of high-vacuum components and other ancillary technologies.[33]

Despite the impressive achievements of Soviet science in some fields, the technological level of the Soviet economy is far from uniform. Traditional values, a poorly trained labor force, and primitive operating conditions frequently render advanced technology useless or seriously impair its efficiency. Several years ago, for example, the Soviets imported a multimillion-dollar American computer system and installed it in a research institute. The system was plagued by breakdowns, however, because the room in which the computer was installed was not "climate controlled." In addition, the Soviets decided to use their own paper in the printer. The paper was of poor quality, and when the humidity in the room increased, the paper swelled and jammed the printer.[34] The transmission of computerized information by telephone is commonplace in the United States, but in the Soviet Union the telephone lines are so inefficient (partly because of the KGB's tapping of the lines) that computers often malfunction or send erroneous information.

Some advanced technology in the USSR exists primarily as "decorative technology," or window dressing. On a visit to the Soviet Union, the author stayed at the Cosmos Hotel in Moscow, which was built for the 1980 Olympics. He was impressed to see that the attendant on each floor had a computer terminal on her desk. When the author asked one attendant what she used the terminal for, she replied that it was empty and she kept her purse in it.

Finally, Soviet performance in engineering and other technical fields has been hampered by the practice of following the lead of Americans, Japanese, and Europeans. In computer technology, genetic engineering, as well as military technologies, the Soviets appear to be engaged primarily in copying Western developments rather than pursuing their own innovations.[35] By choosing to follow the technological lead of the West, the USSR assures the West a critical lead-time advantage.

The economic stringencies confronting the Gorbachev regime will prob-ably further retard the rate of growth of Soviet science and technology in the years ahead. Yet, the Soviet system is still capable of mobilizing massive resources in a few specially targeted areas. Major efforts are currently under way in the fields of computer engineering and microelectronics, lasers and charged particle beam technology, and genetic engineering. The Soviet re-gime is discussing the possibility of creating a new ministry devoted solely to genetic engineering. The obvious driving factor in each of these cases is the fear of falling behind American efforts in such critical, militarily-related technological fields.

The future will likely see the continuation of the struggle for dominance between the Academy of Sciences and the State Committee for Science and Technology. Because of the latter's responsibility for technology imports, its influence seems to increase during periods of détente and expanded trade with the West and diminish with heightened East-West tensions.

Gorbachev has made it clear that he intends to harness the potentials of science and technology in order to improve economic performance through technical innovation. The emphasis on applied research will undoubtedly continue for the foreseeable future. While the focus on applied research may help invigorate the faltering Soviet economy in the short run, the long-term consequences for fundamental, basic research are troubling to many in the Academy of Sciences and to Western observers of Soviet science. The Soviet Union is not alone in shifting its emphasis from fundamental to applied research, especially in light of the ever-increasing share of research funds supporting the development of new weapons systems. A similar trend has occurred in the United States in the past decade. It is too early to determine the long-term effects of this trend on scientific and technological develop-ment in either the East or the West.

EDUCATION IN THE USSR

One of the early goals of the Soviet regime was the provision of univer-sal education to all citizens. At the time of the Revolution, approximately 70 percent of the population was illiterate.[36] Education was provided through a modest but growing educational system. Primary schools oper-ated by the central government, local authorities, and the Church enrolled approximately one-half of the children between the ages of eight and eleven.[37] Secondary schooling was provided through a variety of public and private gymnasia, military schools, technicums, and teachers' colleges to a significantly smaller percentage of Russian youth—primarily the sons of the aristocracy and the emerging middle class.

After the 1917 Revolution, Marxist-Leninist doctrine not only radically altered the content of the school curriculum, but also dictated the form and style of instruction. Individual achievement was denounced as a bourgeois concept. Instead, communist education stressed collective activities and val-ues. The school and class were seen as a cohesive whole. In addition, Lenin-ist principles of education emphasized the unity of theory and practice. Consequently, efforts were made to include "polytechnic" practice in the educational experience. Students were organized into brigades and set to work on "productivity activities bearing a class, proletarian character."[38] In other words, students were made to work in factories or on farms.

A decree of September 1931, however, refocused education on the abstract sciences, language, history, and geography. Manual labor gradually disappeared from the curriculum. Under Stalin, the Soviet educational system was centralized. Pupils no longer had a hand in managing school affairs; instead, the role of school director was enforced. Standardized curricula, textbooks, attendance policies, and examinations were dictated by central authorities.

Soviet education today still bears Stalin's imprint; the structure of the school system has changed little since the 1930s. Soviet schoolchildren enter the general secondary school system at the age of seven. Approximately 50 to 55 percent of the students entering first grade have attended nursery schools or kindergartens, but neither is mandatory.[39] Students in general secondary education are expected to complete a ten-year course of study and receive the equivalent of a high-school diploma at the age of seventeen or eighteen. There are, however, various tracks by which students may complete the last two years of their general secondary education. After eight years in the general secondary school, students may:

- enroll in two additional years of general secondary education, preparing them for the intensely competitive examination to enter universities and other institutions of higher education (about 60 percent of the pupils take this option).
- enroll in three to four years at a specialized secondary school (technicum), which provides general education along with technical training for a middle-level job.
- enroll in two to four years at a vocational-technical school offering practical training preliminary to entering the labor force.
- enter the labor force and complete their education in evening or correspondence courses.

As many as one-half of the students who go to work after the eighth grade fail to complete their secondary education, however.[40] The dropout rate is highest in rural and non-Russian areas, and special efforts are being made to improve education coverage in those regions.

The 1984 Education Reform extended general secondary education to eleven years. The reforms were to be gradually phased in between 1984 and 1990. Under these reforms, students begin school at the age of six, rather than seven. In the final two years of secondary school, vocational education is required, even for students bound for universities. Those students who do not pursue higher education are required to take an additional year of vocational training.[41]

Educational achievement in Soviet secondary schools is quite impressive. A nationwide standardized curriculum places a heavy emphasis on mathematics, the natural sciences, and language. By the time Soviet students have completed ten years of pre-university schooling, they have taken six years of a foreign language, two years of algebra, two years of geometry, one year of trigonometry, one year of calculus, one year of physics, one year of chemistry, and one year of biology. The humanities and social science courses tend to be ideological in orientation. Thus, upper-level Russian history courses are dominated by the history of the CPSU. Approximately 10 percent of class time is devoted to such political subjects.[42]

Pupils in secondary schools also take required courses in physical education, art (mandatory through the sixth grade), music (mandatory through the seventh grade), and on-the-job training. All ninth- and tenth-graders are required to have two hours of military training per week. For boys, this consists of basic drill and target practice, while for girls it stresses civil defense and first aid.

The school year is long—approximately 235 days, compared to an average of 178 days in the United States. Students attend school six days per week, from September 1 to early June. Extracurricular activities are scheduled after school hours. Discipline in Soviet schools is strict. Students wear uniforms, and the class is designed to form a cohesive unit. All students in a given first-grade class will remain together throughout their secondary-school years, although the teachers rotate from year to year and from subject to subject. (In the first three grades, however, one teacher teaches the class all subjects each year.)

Optional courses and programs from the seventh grade onward allow students to develop their skills in computer science, natural science, physics, mathematics, foreign languages, the humanities, and the arts. Beginning in the second grade, students can also apply to attend special schools (*spetsshkoly*) for foreign languages. In the *spetsshkoly*, courses in history and social studies are conducted in a foreign language (English, German, French, Spanish, Portuguese, or several other languages), while Russian literature, mathematics, and science courses are taught in Russian. As early as the first grade, pupils with exceptional aptitude in sports or the arts are recruited for special schools. A few special schools have recently been created for students who are especially gifted in science, mathematics, and computer programming. The system of scientific competitions, called Olympiads, has also promoted the achievements of students in mathematics, physics, and other scientific disciplines.

As a result of the tracking options available after the eighth grade and the special schools and programs for gifted and talented pupils, Soviet education has lost much of its early egalitarian character. A highly stratified system exists today that tends to favor children from urban, ethnically Russian, white-collar families.

The Soviet Constitution guarantees citizens the right to receive instruction in their native languages. With more than one hundred ethnic groups in the USSR, however, multilingual education poses a real challenge. In practice, schools currently offer instruction in approximately sixty languages.[43] Schools using languages other than Russian are, for the most part, located in the union-republics, territories, autonomous republics, and regions dominated by non-Russian ethnic groups, while Russian-language schools exist throughout the USSR. In native-language schools, Russian is taught as a mandatory second language.

Russian is the language of instruction in the universities and other institutions of higher education, except in the Ukraine, Georgia, and Latvia, where some universities still use the native language of the republic. The predominance of the Russian language in institutions of higher learning puts non-Russians at a distinct disadvantage. Consequently, many non-Russian parents wishing to enhance their child's chances of being accepted at a university opt to send the child to Russian schools rather than native-language schools.

The language of instruction in general secondary schools has been a contentious political issue in recent years, especially in the Baltic republics. The large influx of Russians and other Slavic peoples and the declining birthrate among the indigenous Latvians, Lithuanians, and Estonians have resulted in a shift in the composition of the population in the three republics. In order to meet the resulting increased demand for Russian-language schools, some school officials have attempted to change the language of instruction from the indigenous language to Russian. Such attempts, have provoked storms of protest from the ethnic minorities.

Technical Secondary Education. The technical education system in the USSR is very large, encompassing more than 4000 schools and 9 million students—almost half of all secondary-school pupils.[44] These schools fall under the jurisdiction of the State Committee for Vocational and Technical Education, rather than the Ministry of Education, which supervises the general secondary schools.

In the late 1970s, there was a resurgence of "polytechnization," much as existed under Khrushchev in the mid-1950s. In 1977, the Minister of Education suggested that all secondary schools must prepare pupils for work directly in the factory or on the state farms.[45] The head of the Academy of the National Economy, M. Rutkevich, projected: "In the near future the implementation of universal secondary education is to be combined with the implementation of universal vocational education."[46] The educational reforms enacted in 1984 required vocational education in the ninth and tenth grades for all students.

Technical education in the Soviet Union is free, and more than three-quarters of the students in technicums receive stipends and dormitory accommodations at a nominal charge.[47] Upon graduation, technicum students must accept the positions assigned to them by the placement officers in their schools. After the mandatory minimum of two years, however, they are free to move to other jobs.

Technical education in the USSR extends to a much broader range of disciplines and fields than in the United States or many other Western nations. Thus, engineering, nursing, medical technology, journalism, agricultural sciences, business, accounting, law enforcement, library science, dietetics, home economics, and military science all fall within the scope of technical secondary education, as opposed to general secondary or higher education.

Higher Education in the USSR. Institutions of higher education (*vysshie uchebnye zavedeniia-VUZy*) in the USSR consist of two types—universities and institutes. Universities, which are generally more prestigious than institutes, number about sixty-five, while there are more than eight hundred institutes awarding degrees equivalent to the American bachelor's degree.[48]

Universities are organized into colleges and departments and offer programs in the social sciences and humanities, natural sciences, mathematics, and law. Most university degree programs are five years in duration, and the curriculum is much more narrowly focused than in undergraduate programs in the West. Soviet university students normally are required to take six courses in ideological subjects (history of the CPSU, Marxism-Leninism, political economy, scientific communism, scientific atheism, and Soviet law), one foreign language, and physical education. All other courses are concentrated in the student's major field. As a result, Soviet university graduates normally have much more intensive training in their fields of specialization than their American counterparts, but their overall education lacks the breadth of the Western liberal-arts education.

Advanced degree programs in the Soviet Union are organized differently than those in the United States. The initial postgraduate degree is the *Kandidat Nauk* (Candidate of Sciences), which is conferred upon completion of three years of graduate-level coursework, three comprehensive examinations, and a dissertation. Many observers equate the *Kandidat* degree with the Ph.D. in the United States. The highest degree in the USSR, the *Doktor Nauk* (Doctor of Sciences), resembles the doctorate in European academic systems and is awarded to established scholars well advanced in their careers.

Admission to universities is by competitive written and oral examinations that are given twice a year. Both examinations concentrate on the applicant's intended field of specialization. Applications must be filed to specific programs in specific universities, and a student cannot apply to more than one program at a time. The level of competition varies considerably from program to program and from university to university. Perhaps the most difficult programs to enter are those in English or other Western languages at the two most prestigious universities, Moscow State University and Leningrad State University. The number of entrants into each program is set by central authorities in the Ministry of Higher and Specialized Secondary Education in light of Gosplan's projections of the economy's future needs for persons with various specialties. Thus, the entering class in English literature at Leningrad State University is usually limited to fewer than thirty-five, while many more students are accepted in physics or mathematics. In some of the most popular fields, there may be as many as two hundred applicants for each seat in the entering class. Consequently, many students are forced to apply to less prestigious universities or less competitive programs. It is not unusual to hear Soviet university students say that they wanted to major in literature or philosophy but the competition was so intense that they applied instead to the program in physics or Chinese language. Once a student has been admitted, he or she cannot switch programs.

Although merit is the primary criterion for admission to the universities, the Ministry of Higher Education also sets quotas for each nationality group and for the social composition of the student population at institutions of higher education. This amounts to a kind of Soviet affirmative action policy, designed to grant better access to education for non-Russian minorities and children from working-class and peasant families. Quotas for various nationality groups, however, as well as the introduction of the oral examination, have resulted in discrimination against Jewish students, who have traditionally been very successful in attaining admission to the universities.[49]

Periodically, the Soviet press prints letters charging favoritism in university admissions for the sons and daughters of influential families. Children of the political elite and the intelligentsia frequently receive better-quality secondary educations, often through the *spetsshkoly,* which attract the best teachers, materials, and equipment. As a group, students from urban, white-collar families with well-educated parents demonstrate a higher level of achievement and more frequently aspire to complete their university educations, while students from rural, working-class backgrounds whose parents are not well-educated may decide not to pursue advanced training.[50]

Political pull undoubtedly plays a part in gaining admission to some particularly prestigious universities and institutions. For instance, admission to the Moscow Institute for International Relations, which trains future diplomats, requires the recommendation of a *raion* party secretary plus considerable influence even at the Central Committee level. It is not uncommon to find "diplomatic families" in which several generations have all followed the same educational and career course. The military academies display similar tendencies in admissions and family ties.

University education is free, and students receive stipends to help them meet their living expenses. The amount of the stipend varies depending on the student's year, program, and level of performance.

In contrast to higher education in the United States, which is centered around the university, advanced training in many professional and technical fields in the USSR is provided only through specialized institutes. Medicine, education, engineering, agriculture, architecture, international relations, nursing, pharmacy, journalism, library science, management science, and military science are taught exclusively in special professional institutes and academies. Advanced training in the arts (music, theater, ballet, and the visual arts) is provided through conservatories and art academies. Professional and technical institutes are supervised both by the Ministry of Higher and Specialized Secondary Education and the relevant ministry for that field. Thus, the conservatories report to the Ministry of Culture, while the Azerbaidzhan Oil and Chemistry Institute reports to the Ministry of Petroleum Refining and the Petrochemical Industry.

The curriculum of the professional schools and technical institutes varies in length from five to six years, depending on the program. As in the universities, all students are required to take a basic core of ideological courses, at least one foreign language, and physical education. In contrast to university programs, which tend to stress theoretical approaches, professional and technical institutes emphasize practical, applied training. Some professional and technical institutes, although not all, offer advanced degrees—the *Kandidat Nauk* and the *Doktor Nauk.*

Graduates of the universities as well as the technical and professional institutes are placed into jobs by an appointment commission attached to each VUZ. Gosplan and the various ministries develop a list of job vacancies and communicate the list downward through the Ministry of Higher

Table 10-1. Placement of University Students (in percent)

Assignment	History Graduates		Biology Graduates	
	Desired	Received	Desired	Received
Teacher (secondary)	18.0	65.6	0.0	25.0
Production	2.6	10.3	5.0	37.0
Research	18.0	5.8	67.7	5.7
University teaching	40.0	2.3	33.0	4.3
Other	21.4	16.0	0.0	28.0
Total	100.0	100.0	105.7*	100.0

*Discrepancy not explained.
Source: Mervyn Matthews, "Soviet Students—Some Sociological Perspectives," Soviet Studies 27 (January 1975): 107.

and Specialized Secondary Education to the appointment commission in each institute. The commission then interviews each graduate and typically proposes one or more positions on the list. The most desirable positions tend to be offered to the students with the highest records of academic achievement. The commission may consider any request a student makes, and family, health, or other factors may be taken into account. Fulfillment of the placement plan is, however, of utmost importance; students are obliged to accept their assigned positions whether or not they find them satisfactory.[51]

The separation of husband and wife is not always sufficient reason to be released from a job assignment. A Soviet graduate student lamented to the author that he was obliged to return to his teaching job in a secondary school in Kemerovo in Central Siberia upon completion of his *kandidat* degree, despite the fact that his wife was being assigned to a teaching post in Murmansk, near the Finnish border, some 2000 miles away.[52]

Inevitably, many graduates find themselves assigned to jobs they do not want or in locations they do not like. A survey of university graduates in Gorky demonstrates the discrepancies that exist between desired placements and actual appointments. (See Table 10-1.)

Mandatory appointments are for a term of two years, after which time graduates are free to seek other employment. Many students, however, are able to circumvent the system of job placement. Students can approach prospective employers and ask them to make personal requests for their services. Children of the elite are more likely to know persons in influential positions and are also better able to bring pressure to bear on employers to make such requests.

Despite its imperfections, the Soviet system of job placement ensures all graduates a job. At the same time, it provides a steady flow of trained workers to remote regions that might otherwise not attract doctors, lawyers, dentists, engineers, teachers, and others whose skills are needed by the local population.

Turnover among young graduates sent to remote regions is high, however. The disparities in living standards in the USSR are so vast that many people are willing to accept positions beneath their levels of training as long as the jobs are located in Moscow or Leningrad.

An often-aired criticism of the Soviet education system at all levels is that it is overly structured and stresses rote learning rather than creative, inquisitive thinking. A group of American educators visiting a "model" Soviet kindergarten were struck by the uniformity of the children's paintings that were on display. All the trees were green and round, all the houses were brown with red roofs, and there was a fox by the tree in most of the paintings. The children had obviously been told not only what to paint, but how to paint it. When an American teacher asked whether Soviet kindergartners use finger paints, the answer was, "No, it is too unstructured for them."[53] In secondary schools, children stand beside their desks, face the teacher at the front of the classroom, and recite from their texts. Rote learning exists even at the university level. In classes the author attended at Leningrad University law school, teachers read directly from the textbooks, rather than lecture, while students took verbatim notes. The only available copies of the textbooks were on reserve in the law-school library. Besides being deadly boring, such teaching methods discourage analytical inquiry. Furthermore, Soviet textbooks often fail to note that some questions in various disciplines are open to controversy and dispute within the Soviet scholarly community. Students tend to acquire a simplistic, one-dimensional view of their fields. Leaders in the scientific community have expressed concern that the regimentation of education in the USSR is stamping out creativity and, thus, jeopardizing future scientific and technological progress.

The shortage of textbooks also illustrates the woeful inadequacy of educational materials in the USSR. With photocopying virtually nonexistent, there is a heavy demand for carbon paper, but this is a "deficit" item only rarely found in stationery stores. Typewriters are similarly hard to find. While planners in Moscow talk glowingly about the computerized classroom of the future, local school officials complain about shortages of such basic supplies as chalk.[54] University professors and research scientists charge that inadequate laboratory equipment and limited access to computers are seriously eroding the quality of the training that the next generation of scientists and engineers is receiving.

The problems confronting the Gorbachev leadership in the areas of science, technology, and education have crucial implications for the regime. The proliferation of computer technology in the United States, Japan, and Europe in recent years is speeding communications, improving economic efficiency, and radically altering the workplace. Many technological fields today (e.g., microelectronics and fiber optics) revolve around improving access to information. In the West, these technologies have developed as a reflection of the diverse and decentralized character of those societies. Yet, in the USSR, strict centralized control over the flow of information is a key to the power of the Party. The same technologies that enable a Soviet factory to coordinate the delivery of necessary materials from its suppliers in Siberia could also permit a Soviet dissident in Moscow to plug into a nationwide electronic network of dissidents, each with his or her own personal computer. Soviet authorities are fully aware of this potential and have urged caution. Academician A. P. Ershov, head of a program to introduce computer training in Soviet schools, cautioned that the spread of computer literacy "should be a matter of careful observation and not be allowed to get out of control."[55]

Meanwhile, in the field of genetics, Soviet scientists have reopened the nurture vs. nature debate—whether social environment or inherited traits explain human behavior. Marxist ideology holds that the social environment determines a person's "consciousness." By creating a new social and economic order, the Bolshevik revolutionaries hoped to develop "a new Soviet man." Yet, social ills such as alcoholism, crime, corruption, prostitution, and laziness persist today in what Soviet ideologists call a "mature socialist society." Some scientists have recently switched from the official "nurture" position to favor "nature" as an important determinant of behavior. One scientist even suggested that persons of superior intellect could be developed through genetic engineering.[56] Criminologists are studying the link between criminal behavior and genetic factors. The thrust of these inquiries calls into question a fundamental tenet of Marxism-Leninism and, thus, an important part of the foundation of the entire political system. A counterattack was launched in the late 1970s by Elena Chernenko, daughter of the future General Secretary. She defended the nurturist doctrine as "the uniquely correct Marxist solution to the problem of human behavior."[57] Her father echoed this position in 1983 in a speech criticizing the explanation of human behavior on the basis of genes.

These issues illustrate some of the significant dilemmas that science, technology, and education pose for the Soviet leadership. How can the Soviet system develop advanced communications technologies without creating the potential for informal, decentralized information networks? How can the regime draw on the expertise and knowledge of Soviet scientists, but continue to silence their demands on human rights? How can the system educate a new generation of creative thinkers, but restrict their creativity and analytical abilities to only those questions deemed "open to debate"? How can the regime utilize advanced technology without undercutting the ideological premises upon which the regime is based? As the Soviet Union is swept along by the force of the scientific-technological revolution, these issues will not become any easier to resolve.

Notes

1. Karl Marx, *Capital,* vol. 1 (New York: Modern Library, 1906), 475–476.

2. V. I. Lenin, *Collected Works,* vol. 23 (Moscow: Foreign Language Publishing House, 1960), 70.

3. See *Communist Party of the USSR in Statements and Decrees of Congresses, Conferences, and Plenums of the Central Committee,* vol. 2 (Moscow: Politizdat, 1970), 52.

4. Zhores A. Medvedev, *Soviet Science* (New York: W. W. Norton, 1978), 23–24.

5. Cited in Loren R. Graham, *The Soviet Academy of Sciences and the Communist Party, 1927–1932* (Princeton: Princeton University Press, 1967).

6. Medvedev, *Soviet Science,* 35–36.

7. Ibid., 46–47.

8. Ibid., 57.

9. Ibid., 67.

10. *Narodnoe khoziaistvo SSSR v 1974* (Moscow: Statistika, 1975).

11. Medvedev, *Soviet Science,* 73–74.

12. Ibid., 76.

13. *Programma kommunisticheskoi partii sovetskogo soiuza* (Moscow: Pravda, 1961), 27.

14. Radovan Richta et al., *Civilization at the Crossroads: Social and Human Implications of the Scientific and Technical Revolution* (White Plains, NY: International Arts and Sciences Press, 1969).

15. *Chelovek—nauka—tekhnika* (Moscow: Politizdat, 1973), 352.

16. See Robert F. Miller, "The Scientific-Technical Revolution and the Soviet Administrative Debate," in Paul Cocks et al., *The Dynamics of Soviet Politics* (Cambridge: Harvard University Press, 1976), 150.

17. Ibid.

18. William Korey, "Jewish Emigration and Soviet Policy Models," *Survey* (Winter 1976): 128–129; and U.S. Congress, House of Representatives, Committee on Foreign Affairs, Subcommittee on Human Rights and International Organizations, testimony of Theodore R. Mann, Chairman, National Conference on Soviet Jewry (Washington, D.C.: U.S. Government Printing Office, June 23 and 28, 1983), 40.

19. According to numerous accounts of Soviet émigrés, the Leningrad Party Secretary ordered the percentage of Jews in scientific research institutes reduced to less than 1 percent, roughly the percentage that Jews constitute in the general population. For example, see Henry Firdman, *Development of Microelectronics in the USSR* (Washington, D.C.: Delphic Associates Monograph Series, 1985).

20. Louvan E. Nolting, *Sources of Financing the Stages of Research, Development and Innovation Cycle in the USSR,* Foreign Economics Report, no. 3 (Washington, D.C.: U.S. Department of Commerce, 1973).

21. Ibid.

22. Louvan E. Nolting and Murray Feshbach, "R&D Employment in the USSR," *Science* (February 1, 1980): 493–503.

23. *Pravda,* 8 October 1975, p. 2.

24. In addition, there are approximately seventy honorary foreign members. Cited in *The Cambridge Encyclopedia of Russia and the Soviet Union* (Cambridge: Cambridge University Press, 1982), 259.

25. *Narodnoe khoziaistvo SSSR, 1922–1982* (Moscow: Statistika, 1982), 125.

26. For example, see A. P. Aleksandrov, "Vstupitel'noe slovo," *Vestnik akademii nauk,* no. 4 (1983): 8.

27. Cited in U.S. Congress, Senate, Committee on Foreign Relations, *The Premises of East-West Commercial Relations* (Washington, D.C.: U.S. Government Printing Office, 1982), 104.

28. See *Pravda,* 12 June 1985, p. 1.

29. V. I. Kushlin, *Uskorenie vedreniia nauchnykh dostizhenii v proizvodstvo* (Moscow: Ekonomika, 1976), 123.

30. Thane Gustafson, "Why Doesn't Soviet Science Do Better Than It Does," in Linda L. Lubrano and Susan Gross Solomon, eds., *The Social Context of Soviet Science* (Boulder: Westview Press, 1980), 33.

31. John A. Martens and John P. Young, "Soviet Implementation of Domestic Inventions: First Results," in U.S. Congress, Joint Economic Committee, *Soviet Economy in a Time of Change* (Washington, D.C.: U.S. Government Printing Office, 1979), 499.

32. *Pravda,* 3 January 1975.

33. Gustafson, "Why Doesn't Soviet Science Do Better," 33.

34. This account was related to the author by a representative of Control Data Corporation in 1981.

35. This argument is made by David Holloway in "Innovation in the Defense Sector," in Ronald Amann and Julian Cooper, eds., *Industrial Innovation in the Soviet Union* (New Haven: Yale University Press, 1982), 350.

36. Cited in Basile Kerblay, *Modern Soviet Society* (New York: Pantheon Books, 1983), 147.

37. Cited in Mervyn Matthews, *Education in the Soviet Union* (London: George Allen & Unwin, 1982), 2.

38. Ibid., 5.

39. Cited in Kerblay, *Modern Soviet Society*, 152.

40. Cited in Matthews, *Education in the Soviet Union*.

41. "Basic Guidelines for Reform in the General Education and Vocational Schools," *Pravda*, 10 April 1984, pp. 3–4.

42. Matthews, *Education in the Soviet Union*, 47–48.

43. Cited in Vadim Medish, *The Soviet Union* (Englewood Cliffs, NJ: Prentice-Hall, 1981), 205.

44. *Narodnoe khoziaistvo SSSR, 1922–1982*, pp. 499–500.

45. M. A. Prokof'ev, "Novyi uchebnyi god," *Narodnoe obrazovanie*, no. 9 (1977): 10–11.

46. *Sovetskaia Rossiia*, 21 September 1983, pp. 1–2.

47. Cited in Medish, *The Soviet Union*, 209.

48. Cited in Harley D. Balzer, "Education, Science, and Technology," in James Cracraft, ed., *The Soviet Union Today* (Chicago: Bulletin of the Atomic Scientists, 1983), 238.

49. For a discussion of inequalities in university admissions, see Murray Yanowitch, *Social and Economic Inequality in the Soviet Union* (New York: M. E. Sharpe, 1977), 58–99. Concerning discrimination against Jews in education, see Robert O. Freedman, ed., *Soviet Jewry in the Decisive Decade, 1971–1980* (Durham, North Carolina: Duke University Press, 1984).

50. Yanowitch, *Social and Economic Inequality*.

51. Matthews, *Education in the Soviet Union*, 170.

52. The student told the author about this case while he was at Leningrad State University in 1975–1976.

53. Comment made by a teacher to a group of visiting Americans, November 1978. For official criticism of rote learning, see *Literaturnaia gazeta*, 22 February 1984, p. 11.

54. Balzer, "Education, Science, and Technology," 237.

55. *Pravda*, 8 February 1985.

56. Cited in Loren Graham, "The Return of Genetics: A New Revolution in Soviet Science," *The Washington Post* (National Weekly Edition), 7 October 1985, pp. 23–24.

57. Ibid.

Selected Bibliography

Afanas'ev, V. G. *The Scientific and Technological Revolution—Its Impact on Management and Education*. Moscow: Progress, 1975.

Amann, Ronald, and Julian Cooper, eds. *Industrial Innovation in the Soviet Union*. New Haven: Yale University Press, 1982.

Berliner, Joseph S. *The Innovation Decision in Soviet Industry*. Cambridge: MIT Press, 1976.

Churchward, L. G. *The Soviet Intelligentsia*. London: Routledge & Kegan Paul, 1973.

Fleron, Frederic J., ed. *Technology and Communist Culture*. New York: Praeger, 1977.

Graham, Loren R. *Science and Philosophy in the Soviet Union*. New York: Knopf, 1972.

Grant, Nigel. *Soviet Education*. 4th ed. London: Penguin Books, 1979.

Gvishiani, D. M., ed. *The Scientific Intelligentsia in the USSR*. Moscow: Progress, 1976.

Hoffmann, Erik P., and Robbin F. Laird. *The Politics of Economic Modernization in the Soviet Union*. Ithaca: Cornell University Press, 1982.

Hoffmann, Erik P., and Robbin F. Laird. *Technocratic Socialism: The Soviet Union in the Advanced Industrial Era*. Durham: Duke University Press, 1985.

Hutchings, Raymond. *Soviet Science, Technology, Design*. London: Oxford University Press, 1976.

Jacoby, Susan. *Inside Soviet Schools*. New York: Hill & Wang, 1974.

Kassel, Simon, and Cathleen Campbell. *The Soviet Academy of Sciences and Technological Development*. Santa Monica, CA: Rand Corporation, 1980.

Kneen, Peter. *Soviet Scientists and the State*. London: Macmillan Press, 1984.

Kuzin, N. P. *Education in the USSR*. Moscow: Progress, 1972.

Lampert, Nicholas. *The Technical Intelligentsia and the Soviet State*. New York: Holmes & Meier, 1979.

Lubrano, Linda, and Susan Gross Solomon, eds. *The Social Context of Soviet Science*. Boulder: Westview Press, 1980.

Matthews, Mervyn. *Education in the Soviet Union*. London: George Allen & Unwin, 1982.

Medvedev, Zhores. *Soviet Science*. New York: W. W. Norton, 1978.

Parrott, Bruce. *Politics and Technology in the Soviet Union*. Cambridge: MIT Press, 1983.

Remnek, Richard B., ed. *Social Scientists and Policy-Making in the USSR*. New York: Praeger, 1977.

Thomas, John R., and Ursula Kruse-Vaucienne, eds. *Soviet Science and Technology*. Washington, D.C.: National Science Foundation, 1977.

Zajda, J. I. *Education in the USSR*. New York: Pergamon, 1980.

11

The Social Welfare State

In the twentieth century, advanced industrialized nations increasingly have sought to guarantee to all citizens certain minimum living standards. The Soviet Union is no exception; in fact, in several respects it epitomizes the social welfare state. The 1936 Constitution guaranteed Soviet citizens the right to a job, health care, education, maintenance in old age, and leisure. The 1977 Constitution added to these fundamental human rights the right to housing and access to cultural achievements. To what extent has the Soviet system translated the formal pronouncement of these social and economic rights into reality? This chapter seeks to answer that question by analyzing Soviet policies and performance in three areas of social policy: housing, health care, and social security.

HOUSING IN THE SOVIET UNION

Bolshevik housing practices initially reflected the experimental family policies of Madame Kollontai, who advocated the radical transformation of the family, with familial ties subordinated to those of the collective or commune. Kollontai envisaged house-communes, rather than the traditional single-family houses or apartments.

Communal housing was indeed prevalent during the 1920s, but it was more the result of economic realities than a reflection of revolutionary ideology. The day after the Bolshevik seizure of power, Lenin issued a decree confiscating all large urban houses and townhomes from the aristocracy and the middle class. These were used to house workers and peasants who had been dispossessed by the ravages of World War I and the Revolution. The Civil War destroyed even more housing. From 1918 to 1921, the housing stock in Petrograd (currently Leningrad) declined by 17 percent, while in Moscow it declined by 30 percent.[1] Famine in the countryside prompted a massive exodus from rural areas to the cities, worsening the already overcrowded situation. Urban homes and apartments initially intended for one family had to accommodate several families per room—all sharing a single bath and kitchen. Workers in the newly established industrial areas were forced to live in hurriedly constructed barracks.

The fledgling Soviet regime proved incapable of managing the existing housing supply, much less making repairs or building new residential units. During the New Economic Policy (NEP), housing was, in effect, denationalized in an effort to stimulate residents to take responsibility for the repair and upkeep of their own units. In 1922, individuals were given the right to construct houses, and land was provided free of charge. By 1926, two-thirds of all new housing was privately built.[2]

The moderate policies of NEP ended abruptly in 1928, when Stalin redirected the emphasis to industrialization. Private leases were terminated, and building supplies were absorbed by Stalin's ambitious development projects. During the First Five-Year Plan (1928–1932), private construction of housing fell from 40 percent of total housing construction to less than 1 percent.[3] Collectivization further drove peasants from the countryside to the city, adding to the strain on the existing housing supply.

Under Stalin, the social welfare goals of the USSR were inevitably subordinated to the realities of rapid industrialization, collectivization, and social modernization. In order to finance his program of rapid industrial development, Stalin asked Soviet citizens to make "serious sacrifices" and imposed a "regime of the strictest economy."[4] Investments in housing, health care, and other social programs fell sharply, while massive amounts of capital were funneled into industrial production. As a proportion of total investment in the economy, housing fell from 17 percent in the 1920s to 9 percent during the First Five-Year Plan, to 8 percent by 1939.[5] Plans for housing construction routinely went unfulfilled—by as much as 50 percent.[6] The economic stringency of Stalin's policies forced hard choices among various competing social policies. Stalin favored education and health care because they had a more immediate impact on worker productivity. Consequently, greater efforts were made in those spheres, while housing languished.

Under Stalin, the gap widened between the quality of housing provided to the political elite, high-ranking military officers, and the intelligentsia and that provided to the average workers and peasants. Thus, members of the elite strata were insulated from the generally poor living conditions that prevailed in the country.

While private housing construction tapered off under Stalin, industrial enterprises were encouraged to construct housing for their employees, especially in the new towns springing up around the country. By the beginning of World War II, factory housing represented 20 percent of all residential units.[7]

The war devastated the housing supply in the USSR. More than 1710 cities and towns were destroyed, including more than 6 million dwellings—one-quarter of the total housing in the USSR.[8] More than 25 million people were displaced and without housing after the war.[9] Millions more lived in severely damaged or substandard accommodations. The bulk of capital and resources, however, was earmarked for reconstructing the Soviet Union's demolished industrial base, rather than its housing. Private construction was again encouraged in order to alleviate the situation, but the impoverished citizens could not afford to build their own houses, and supplies were scarce or nonexistent.

At the time of Stalin's death in 1953, the living conditions of the average Soviet family were actually worse than they had been in 1926.[10]

Western experts estimate that Soviet housing in the mid-1950s was roughly comparable to that of tenement dwellers in the United States in the 1890s.[11] John Gunther describes the deplorable condition of Soviet housing:

> Every citizen is supposed to have nine square meters of floor space, but most do not have even half of this . . . people are crowded three, four, five or even more to a room, with disastrous social consequences. Young people cannot marry, because they can find no place to live. Scarcely any Soviet family is without a covey of in-laws living on the premises, and it is rare for any family to have its own private bath and kitchen . . . sometimes a single doorway leads to a nest of stalls where a dozen people live. . . . One reason why the streets are so thronged at night, even in the winter . . . is that homes are so unbelievably crowded, squalid, and uncomfortable.[12]

Under the populist leader Nikita Khrushchev, housing and other social policies were finally given high priority. A resolution of the CPSU Central Committee and the USSR Council of Ministers in 1957 acknowledged that housing conditions in the Soviet Union were intolerable for the vast majority of the population and promised to rectify the situation. The decree reorganized the housing construction industry, shifting production to favor prefabricated units. Thanks to the new thrust, housing construction during the late 1950s for the first time exceeded planned levels; approximately 2 million units were being built per year, more than in any other country. Investment in housing during the Sixth Five-Year Plan (1956–1960) reached a high of 23.2 percent of total capital investment.[13]

Between 1956 and 1970, 34.2 million housing units were built in the USSR.[14] These units were occupied by 126.5 million citizens, more than one-half of the entire population of the Soviet Union. This represents a stunning achievement and a major commitment by the Khrushchev and Brezhnev regimes to improve living conditions for average citizens.

During the building boom under Khrushchev and Brezhnev, large numbers of single-family apartments (*otdel'nye kvartiry*) were constructed, with the goal of entirely eliminating communal apartments. Quality of construction, square footage, attractiveness, and access to social services and public transportation were sacrificed to meet this primary objective. "Khrushchev houses," as they came to be called, were uniform, prefabricated, grey concrete apartment buildings, usually five to seven stories tall (with no elevators). These apartment buildings were situated on the fringes of the major cities, where land was readily available. The units normally consisted of two-room apartments—living room and one bedroom, with a small entrance hall, bath, and kitchen. The average size of the apartments was approximately 45 square meters, less than the minimum sanitary norm established by housing authorities.[15] Most apartments housed at least four people, often as many as six or seven. Shoddy workmanship gave rise to numerous complaints, but with pent-up demand for housing still unsatisfied, the authorities continued to focus on new construction rather than repairing existing housing.

Planners organized "Khrushchev houses" into microdistricts (*mikroraiony*) in which several apartment buildings formed a cluster. In the middle of the cluster, buildings to accommodate stores, libraries, polyclinics, schools, kindergartens, and community centers were planned. In the rush to satisfy the demand for housing, however, these amenities were accorded low priority. Most of the new neighborhoods also lacked playgrounds, parks, and access to public transportation. Nevertheless, they were an improvement over the overcrowded communal flats in the center-city areas, and there were long waiting lists of people requesting the new units.

Khrushchev attempted to centralize the management of housing through the local soviets, thus stripping industrial enterprises of housing they had built at Stalin's urging. In the 1950s, the state managed almost half of all housing; in rural areas, the majority of housing remained privately owned, and most new construction was undertaken by individuals or collective farms.

Under Brezhnev, housing construction advanced considerably. The typical apartment buildings constructed during the 1970s were nine to fourteen stories tall (with elevators), containing slightly larger two-room apartments. Each apartment building might house as many as seven hundred families. Given this phenomenal population density, concerted efforts were made to improve the quality of social services and public transportation in the newly established microdistricts.

Overcrowding in housing units has serious social consequences in the USSR today. Soviet youth complain of a lack of privacy. It is virtually impossible for a single young adult to locate a private apartment or even a room in a communal flat. Most young people do not leave their parents' home until they are married. Once a young couple is married and their names are placed on the waiting list for housing, it may still be another two or three years before they actually receive a separate apartment.

Because bars and other drinking establishments are few in the USSR, most alcohol is consumed at home. Cramped living conditions combined with alcohol abuse frequently erupt into domestic violence. Most murders and other violent crimes are committed under the influence of alcohol, in the home, and among people who are related or close friends. Alcohol abuse is reported to be the most common cause of divorce. Not surprisingly, the divorce rates in urban areas are rising rapidly, exceeding one out of every three marriages.[16]

The crowded housing conditions often preclude more than two generations living in the same apartment. Young couples who are attracted to the cities tend to leave their parents behind in the countryside. Without the assistance of the grandmother (*babushka*), who was traditionally responsible for child care, cooking, and cleaning, these tasks fall to the mothers, who are also employed full-time in other jobs in most cases. In addition, the lack of supervision of children in after-school hours has resulted in increased incidence of juvenile delinquency.

The housing boom under Brezhnev barely kept pace with the urban population growth caused by out-migration from rural areas. In order to restrict the growth of urban centers, a *propiska* system has been enforced in Moscow, Leningrad, Kiev, and several other cities. Persons wishing to move to one of the "closed" cities must first acquire a *propiska,* usually from an employer. The registration system has had only marginal success, however, in stemming the flow of people to urban areas. Individuals find various ways to circumvent the system and obtain the necessary documentation for a *propiska*. Some even arrange fictitious marriages with Muscovites or Leningraders in order to obtain authorization to live in those cities.

The influx of people has kept demand for housing high despite the government's efforts to build more housing. Many urban residents still live in substandard accommodations. One-quarter of all urban families, most of them newly married couples, live in communal apartments and must share a kitchen and bath with others.[17] Shoddy workmanship continues to characterize housing construction; the Soviet press frequently prints letters to the editor complaining about newly constructed buildings in which the plumbing is faulty or even nonexistent. In 1971, a total of 23 percent of all urban housing lacked running water, 18 percent lacked central heat, 35 percent had no bath or shower, and 27 percent had no toilet facilities.[18]

Housing space has risen gradually from 4.7 square meters per capita in 1950 to 8.6 square meters per capita today, but this is still below the minimum sanitary standard of nine square meters per person established by the government in 1928.[19] The sanitary norm is currently met in only five of the fifteen republics.

Investment in housing has declined steadily since the mid-1950s, as Table 11-1 shows. Declining rates of growth of national income coupled with ever-increasing demands for investment capital in the military and industrial sectors have resulted in drastically reduced investments in housing and other social services.

The average age of the housing stock is rapidly growing, making upkeep a serious problem in Soviet housing today. The "Khrushchev apartments" built in the 1950s were in a serious state of decay soon after they were built; today more than thirty years old, they may soon be uninhabitable if major renovations are not undertaken.

Repairs and upkeep are complicated by the low rents on housing in the USSR. Rent is calculated on the basis of square footage; in Moscow, rents average only 7 rubles ($8.50) per month. Utilities are likewise subsidized

Table 11-1. Investments in Housing as a Percentage of Total Capital Investment

Sixth Five-Year Plan (1956–1960)	23.2
Seventh Five-Year Plan (1961–1965)	18.3
Eighth Five-Year Plan (1966–1970)	17.0
Ninth Five-Year Plan (1971–1975)	14.7
Tenth Five-Year Plan (1976–1980)	13.6
Eleventh Five-Year Plan (1981–1985)	13.3
Twelfth Five-Year Plan (1986–1990)	12*

*Estimate.
Sources: Henry W. Morton, "What Have Soviet Leaders Done about the Housing Crisis?" in Henry W. Morton and Rudolf L. Tokes, eds., *Soviet Politics and Society in the 1970s* (New York: The Free Press, 1974), 168; *Narodnoe khoziaistvo v SSSR v 1983* (Moscow: Finansy i statistika, 1984); and "Stroiteli v startovom godu piatiletki," *Ekonomika stroitel'stva*, no. 1 (1986): 3–11.

and average 10 to 15 rubles per month.[20] With rents so low, money for repairs and upkeep must come from state housing budgets, but officials are reluctant to divert money for repairs when there is still pent-up demand for new housing.

Much of the funds for housing are distributed to high-priority industrial sectors or regions to stimulate labor productivity and to attract workers. In 1980, for example, Soviet planners announced a three-year plan for accelerating housing construction in the oil and gas region of Tiumen *oblast'*. More than 1.5 million square meters of new housing were planned, tripling the level of housing construction in the region.[21] The apartments built there were also larger than the national norm, averaging 10 square meters per capita.[22]

The quality of housing of a factory or institution is directly related to its prestige. Thus, the apartments owned by the Academy of Sciences for its researchers are among the nicest in Moscow. Similarly, award-winning factories and production associations boast attractive and relatively spacious apartments for many of their workers, while low-priority enterprises and state farms receive fewer housing funds and provide apartments of much poorer quality to their employees.

Factories and enterprises also maintain furnished dormitory-style hostels for young single workers. Approximately 3.5 million young people reside in these institutions.[23] The hostels are managed by "commandants" and have a curfew; nevertheless, they are often dirty and noisy. Life in the worker hostels was depicted in a popular Soviet movie, *Moscow Does Not Believe in Tears*. In the movie, several young women, attracted by the glamour of city life, leave their villages and move to Moscow. There they discover that life in a worker hostel and dreary jobs in a factory are all they can expect. Some return home disillusioned; others manage by luck, wheeling and dealing, or marriage to escape the hostel.

Local soviets and enterprises manage 78 percent of all urban housing, while 22 percent remains privately owned. In rural areas, however, 85 percent of the housing is privately owned.[24]

Local soviets administer their housing stock through housing commissions in each *raion* of a city. The commissions screen applicants and place those eligible on a waiting list. Single young people and persons already occupying housing that meets minimum standards are not eligible to apply for accommodations. Once placed on the waiting list, citizens can expect to wait from one-and-a-half to three years to secure new lodging. Certain categories of citizens are entitled to extra space, priority on the waiting list, or other special consideration. These include people suffering from certain diseases, the handicapped, and families with many children. The largest group of persons exempted from the normal housing regulations and waiting period, however, are party and state officials, high-ranking military officers, scientists, writers, and artists. In some of the newer apartment blocs, the top floors have higher than average ceilings, large windows, and ample floor space and are reserved for artists' studios.

Citizens who do not wish to wait three years to obtain cramped and poorly constructed apartments can pool their resources to form a building society and hire a construction firm to put up an apartment building for them. Residents in such "condominiums" own their units and may sell them at a price established by the local housing commission, thus preventing speculation. This option is expensive and available only to relatively wealthy citizens in urban areas. Cooperative housing currently accounts for only 6 percent of all new construction.[25]

Given the intense demand for urban housing and the cumbersome system for assigning apartments, it is perhaps inevitable that many housing transactions occur "on the left" in the "second economy." In Leningrad, the author became acquainted with a young couple who lived in a communal apartment off Herzen Street. One night over dinner, the conversation turned to a familiar subject—housing. The couple had been on the waiting list for an apartment for more than two years. The author asked them what would happen if they did not like the apartment offered to them when their name came up on the housing list. What if it were located on the opposite side of the city from where they worked, or on the top floor of a seven-story walk-up? They both looked at him in astonishment. After waiting so long, it was inconceivable to them that anyone would turn down an offer for any apartment. The husband responded, "If our new apartment does not suit us, we will simply exchange it on the black market."

In an old section of Leningrad not far from the Kirov Ballet Theatre, the street fills every Sunday with people wishing to exchange apartments. Carrying placards advertising their apartments, they mill around chatting, occasionally gathering to overhear a transaction being conducted. A typical placard reads: "Will exchange two-room apartment in Kalinin *raion* for two-room apartment in Lenin *raion.*"

Some of the placards tell of personal or family joys or troubles. A pregnant woman has a sign pinned to her wool coat: "Will exchange two-room Stalin apartment for three-room apartment." "Stalin apartments," built during the 1930s and 1940s, are in great demand. In contrast to the prefabricated "Khrushchev apartments," they have large rooms, high ceilings, good-quality construction, and are located close to the city center. A woman carrying a sign reading "Will exchange two-room apartment for two single apartments" is most likely getting a divorce. The demand for housing is so great that frequently couples who get divorced have to live together for a long time before they can locate separate housing.

Housing exchanges can become dehumanizing affairs. For instance, the Soviet press reported the case of an elderly woman who was dying of cancer. Her son switched apartments with her, moving her from her spacious two-room "Stalin apartment" in the center of the city to his cramped and noisy "Khrushchev apartment" on the outskirts of town. The "exchange" had to be finalized with the local housing authorities prior to the woman's death, or her apartment would have reverted to the housing commission for reassignment to someone on the waiting list.[26]

Some enterprising "speculators" acquire one-room apartments and build partitions in them, creating small two-room apartments. They then attempt to trade these apartments on the black market for legitimate two-room apartments, and so forth. Mikhail Bulgakov, the satirist, describes just such an "entrepreneur" in his novel *The Master and Margarita.*

One man in this town was given a three-room flat on the Zemlianoi Rampart and he had turned it into four rooms by dividing one of the rooms in half with a partition. Then he exchanged it for two separate flats in different parts of Moscow, one with three rooms and the other with two. . . . He then exchanged the three-room one for two separate two-roomers, and thus became the owner of six rooms altogether, though admittedly scattered all over Moscow. He was about to pull off his last and most brilliant coup by offering six rooms in various districts of Moscow in exchange for one five-room flat on the Zemlianoi Rampart when his activities were suddenly and inexplicably curtailed. He may have a room somewhere now, but not, I can assure you, in Moscow.[27]

Bulgakov's hapless real estate tycoon notwithstanding, the authorities in the USSR today generally allow the black market to operate without intervention. Black marketeers run afoul of housing officials only when they speculate in housing to earn a profit.

HEALTH CARE IN THE SOVIET UNION

The goals of the Soviet health system from its inception in 1918 have been the provision of comprehensive medical care by a unified state health service free of charge to all citizens. Initially, Soviet medicine was founded on the ideological notion that disease was a product of capitalism and that clinical intervention would eventually wither away under socialism, to be replaced by preventive medicine and public health education. The Commissariat of Health was established in 1918 to oversee health policies, but the Bolsheviks decided that health services should be run by local soviets in order to increase "the broad participation of the masses" in implementing health services.

The health of the Soviet population after the Revolution was a serious problem. The prerevolutionary health-care system collapsed during the turmoil of World War I and the revolutions of 1917. The Civil War brought about further famine and disease. Epidemics ravaged the country. Between 1916 and 1924, an estimated 10 million people died in epidemics—primarily typhus, typhoid, smallpox, and relapsing fever.[28] Addressing the second Congress of Medical Workers in 1920, Lenin declared, "Either the lice will defeat Socialism, or Socialism will defeat the lice!"[29]

It was neither socialism nor the efforts of the newly established public health system that defeated the lice, however, but the improved living standards resulting from NEP. Medical schools resumed instruction in the return to normalcy of the NEP period, and the number of doctors tripled between 1917 and 1928. The combination of these factors helped to eradicate most epidemics in urban areas by the end of the 1920s. Health services in rural areas, however, remained in a primitive state. Medical care was provided by "feldshers"—traveling medical paraprofessionals. Low living standards and the poor quality of transportation, housing, and educational facilities discouraged most doctors from working in the countryside.

Predictably, the emphasis within the health-care system changed dramatically under Stalin. Stalin rejected several elements of Bolshevik health policy: the ideological assumption that illness resulted from capitalism, the preference for mass participation in health-care policy-making, the decentralized system for delivering health services, and the stress on preventive medicine. Instead, Stalin ordered that the quality of health services within industrial enterprises be upgraded. The number of medical personnel within factories quadrupled during the first six months of 1932.[30] As more and more women were added to the industrial work force, special efforts were made to improve health services to them and to their children. In addition, greater emphasis was placed on sanitation in rapidly growing urban areas.

Soviet authorities made it clear, however, that the principal goal of industrial medicine was to ensure a healthy labor force, which was necessary to achieve Stalin's ambitious economic aims. One of the primary functions of industrial medical personnel, therefore, was to detect fraudulent requests for sick leave.

The proletarianization of the Soviet health-care profession during the 1930s lowered the status of doctors relative to other occupations (especially engineers), and the pay and the quality of training of doctors declined precipitously. Medical education was removed from the universities and relegated to special institutes in 1929. As the status of doctors dropped relative to engineers, so too did the availability of drugs and instruments. Because most males were employed in the industrial labor force, women were actively recruited into the health professions during the 1930s. By 1934 three-quarters of all doctors were women.[31]

Administratively, the health services became more centralized during Stalin's reign. The Ministry of Health was charged with making and administering health policy, while the operations of polyclinics and the public health service were subordinated to local hospitals.

The health-service sector received a large share of the funds earmarked for social services throughout the Stalin and Khrushchev periods, and the results are reflected in various health statistics. Prior to the Revolution, the life expectancy of women was only 33 years; by the time of Khrushchev's ouster in 1964, it was 75.6 years.[32] In 1913, more than one out of every four babies died before the age of one. By 1971, infant mortality in the USSR had fallen to 2 percent.[33] In 1964, the mortality rate for the Soviet population was less than that in the United States and many other developed nations of the West, leading Khrushchev to boast that the USSR "long ago left the capitalist countries behind" in the provision of health services.[34]

The achievements of Soviet health care are impressive. Indeed, during the 1950s and 1960s, Soviet health care was one field in which Western experts acknowledged Soviet successes and even suggested that Western societies could learn from the Soviet example in providing inexpensive, high-quality health services to the entire population.

The Soviet health-care delivery system has remained essentially unchanged since Stalin's time. Primary health care is provided through polyclinics located in microdistricts and industrial enterprises. Polyclinics provide initial treatment for common, minor ailments—colds, flu, sprains, and so on. They are staffed with general practitioners (vracha) and nurses and have basic equipment for routine treatments and laboratory tests. Citizens may choose to receive medical treatment either at the polyclinic in their microdistrict or the polyclinic attached to their place of employment. All medical care in the USSR, including treatment at a polyclinic, is provided free of charge. There is, however, a minimal charge for drugs.

Polyclinics refer patients with more-serious illnesses and those requiring more-specialized treatment to the general hospital located in each town and city. (In Moscow and other large cities, there are general hospitals in various parts of the city.) Hospitals provide a wide range of services—both inpatient and outpatient. Hospitalization rates in the Soviet Union are high. In contrast to trends in other developed countries, the average length of hospital stays has increased in recent years and is double that of the United States.[35] Two factors account for this phenomenon: Housing conditions are so overcrowded that people prefer to recuperate in the hospital, and in rural areas, where polyclinics are poorly staffed and equipped, it is more difficult for patients to receive qualified care outside of the hospitals.

In addition to the general hospitals, specialized hospitals exist for a variety of diseases and conditions. The most common specialized health facilities are maternity hospitals. Other specialized facilities exist for the treatment of cancer, tuberculosis, mental illness, kidney disease, and geriatrics. Admission to one of these facilities is on a referral basis.

Several years ago, the author was accompanying a group of American officials on a tour of a specialized cancer-treatment hospital being built on the outskirts of Moscow. It was truly an impressive complex. One building for pediatric patients had already been completed, and a high-rise tower for adult patients was under construction. In a corridor of the tower building, they came across two women busily plastering the walls. One of the American physicians asked whether there was asbestos in the plaster. One of the women, splattered with the grey plaster, replied, *"Konezhno"* ("of course"). The American then asked whether she was aware that asbestos was a proven cause of lung cancer. She was not. She simply shrugged and went back to her job.

The number of hospitals and physicians has continued to grow since the 1960s, although at a slower rate. The number of hospital beds per 10,000 of population has increased from 80 in 1960 to more than 128 today. At the same time, the number of physicians per 10,000 of population has increased from 20 in 1960 to more than 40 today, roughly twice as many doctors per capita as in the United States.[36] There are fewer auxiliary medical personnel in the USSR than in the United States, however, and many Soviet doctors perform duties that in the United States are the responsibility of nurses, laboratory technicians, physical therapists, and other medical professionals.

The vast majority of physicians in the USSR are general practitioners (*vracha*), who are responsible for providing primary health care through the polyclinics and general hospitals. All students in medical school are expected to specialize in one of three fields: general clinical medicine, obstetrics-gynecology-pediatrics, or public health medicine. The level of training within these specializations is, however, generally considered inferior to that of specialists in the United States. Approximately 70 percent of all general practitioners are women.[37] By Western standards, Soviet general practitioners are very poorly paid; their average salary is only 183 rubles per month ($229), far less than that of the average industrial worker.[38]

Medical-school training consists of a seven-year program that includes one year of internship. Doctors who wish to pursue more intensive specializations usually do so after several years of general practice. Specialist doctors constitute a relatively small percentage of all physicians in the USSR, and the vast majority of them are men. Women account for only 20 percent of medical-school professors, 40 percent of all tertiary-care physicians, and 50 percent of all hospital administrators.[39] Some medical schools have recently instituted separate entrance examinations for men and women, and others have imposed quotas to ensure that 50 percent of all admissions are men.[40]

Medical-school training is free, and most students also receive a living allowance to cover food and housing expenses. After graduating, however, they are obliged to fulfill a three-year assignment, usually in a rural area.[41] Regional disparities have plagued the delivery of health services in the Soviet Union since 1917. The quality of health care provided in rural areas still lags far behind that in the cities.

In the countryside, the number of doctors per capita is approximately one-half that of urban areas, despite the fact that doctors in rural areas receive 15 percent incentive bonuses. It was recently reported that twenty-five rural hospitals in Soviet Georgia, did not have even one trained physician.[42] In Krasnoiarsk *krai*, Gorbachev's home region, polyclinics that were designed to handle 260 patients per day are seeing more than 1300.[43]

In 1977, in an effort to encourage more physicians to stay in rural areas, new policies were introduced allowing rural physicians three times the salary of their urban counterparts after ten years of service, a free apartment, priority in purchasing an automobile, and the right to buy food directly from state farms in the vicinity. Nevertheless, few doctors appear to be taking advantage of this opportunity.

Even in the cities, the quality of health-care services varies dramatically from polyclinic to polyclinic. Polyclinics associated with large, industrial complexes and prestigious institutions tend to be well-staffed and well-equipped, while polyclinics in small, marginal factories suffer from persistent staffing and supply problems.

Hospitals also vary in terms of quality. In Leningrad, for instance, foreigners are usually treated at Hospital No. 1, which caters to influential politicians and members of the intellectual elite. The surgical ward of Hospital No. 1 is equipped with the latest American, Swiss, and German equipment, surgical instruments, and pharmaceuticals. In contrast, other hospitals can be dirty, overcrowded, ill-equipped, and understaffed.

Under Brezhnev, Soviet health care deteriorated markedly. In the 1970s, the defense and industrial sectors of the economy absorbed a steadily increasing portion of the state budget, placing a strain on health services. The percentage of the state budget earmarked for health care fell from 6.5 percent in 1965 to 5.2 percent in 1975, and to 5.0 percent in 1980.[44]

The impact of reduced funding for health care was apparent in rising infant mortality and decreasing life expectancy. Infant mortality, which had decreased steadily since 1917, almost doubled between 1971 and 1980. (See Table 11-2.)

Table 11-2. Infant Mortality in the Soviet
Union (deaths per 1000 live births)

1950	60.0
1971	22.9
1974	28.0
1976	31.1
1980	39–40 (estimated)

Source: Christopher Davis and Murray Feshbach, *Rising Infant Mortality in the USSR in the 1970s*, U.S. Bureau of the Census, Series P-95, no. 74 (Washington, D.C.: U.S. Government Printing Office, September 1980).

At the same time, adult life expectancy for men decreased from 67.0 years in 1964 to 61.9 years in 1980; for women it fell from 75.6 years in 1964 to 73.5 years in 1980.[45] Soviet authorities were sufficiently embarrassed by these trends so that, since 1976, they have refused to release statistics on infant mortality and life expectancy.

The causes of the alarming deterioration of the health of Soviet citizens are several. In addition to declining allocations for health care, other important contributing factors include alcohol abuse, environmental pollution, and the high incidence of abortion.

Alcohol consumption in the USSR is among the highest in the world. Unlike France, which records high levels of wine consumption, or Germany, which favors beer, the preferred alcoholic beverage in the Soviet Union is vodka, drunk straight from the bottle. The USSR ranks first in the world in the consumption of distilled spirits. Furthermore, alcohol consumption is growing at an alarming rate. From 1940 through 1980, the Soviet population increased by 36 percent, while alcohol consumption rose by more than 800 percent.[46] A report by the USSR Ministry of Internal Affairs estimates that 37 percent of all male workers abuse alcohol.[47] Alcohol consumption is highly differentiated by region, with the worst problem centered in the Slavic and Baltic regions; wine consumption is high in Moldavia, Armenia, and Georgia.

Especially troublesome is the recent increase in alcoholism among women and teenagers. Alcohol abuse is currently growing more rapidly among women than men and is being blamed for increasing incidence of birth defects (including brain damage), miscarriages, and premature births.[48]

Public health officials as well as the press and local party organs have launched repeated campaigns to educate Soviet citizens about the dangers of alcohol abuse—without noticeable effect. Sales of alcohol have been curtailed, and prices increased to discourage consumption. Demand for alcohol, however, appears to be inelastic. In other words, when the price of vodka is increased, it simply means that alcohol consumes a larger share of the average family's budget, threatening to reduce money spent on food, clothing, and entertainment for other family members.

Persons who are apprehended for public intoxication or drunk driving are taken to sobering-up stations (*vytreziteli*). They are fined, and their names are reported to their employers. In 1979, 16 to 18 million drunks, or 12 to 15 percent of the adult population, was processed through the stations.[49]

Most drinking is done at home or outdoors, given the limited number of bars and pubs. It is not unusual on a winter evening to see clusters of middle-aged men in heavily padded wool coats standing on the street sharing a bottle of vodka "three ways." Workers refer to this as a form of "primitive communism." By splitting a bottle among three people, it is relatively affordable, and the amount of alcohol, while sufficient to get a person quite drunk, is not normally enough to kill one.

Government efforts to curb alcohol abuse often unwittingly encourage even more dangerous practices, such as the consumption of home-brewed alcohol (samogon) or alcohol surrogates. An estimated 1.7 billion liters of 80-proof samogon are produced every year in the USSR.[50] Vladimir Treml notes that in 1978 there were 51,000 deaths in the Soviet Union due to alcohol poisoning—or 19.5 deaths per 100,000 of population (compared to 400 instances in the United States, or 0.18 per 100,000).[51]

As the price of alcohol has increased to discourage consumption, Russians have begun to consume large quantities of alcohol surrogates, such as lotions, medical alcohol, shellac, varnish, and brake and deicing fluids. Treml estimates that 1,200 people died in 1976 from drinking ethylene glycol (antifreeze), cleaning fluids, and solvents.[52] Another 5000 died from ingesting vinegar concentrate, considered to be a good (although sometimes permanent) remedy for hangover.[53]

With the exception of alcoholism, the biggest health risks in the USSR are related to diet and lack of exercise. The leading cause of death in the USSR is heart disease, followed by cancer and alcohol-related illnesses. The typical Russian diet is heavily laden with starch and dairy products, while fresh fruits and vegetables are difficult to come by most of the year. Furthermore, few Soviet citizens exercise on a regular basis after leaving secondary school. A Soviet medical official recently estimated that more than 40 percent of all Soviet men are overweight.[54] Compounding the risks of heart disease are alcohol abuse and the relatively widespread use of cigarettes by Soviet males. As with alcohol consumption, smoking is increasingly common among young women.

Also affecting the health of the female population is the widespread practice of abortion. Lenin and his chief adviser on family and women's issues, Madame Kollontai, considered abortion to be the legal right of every Soviet woman. Abortion was officially decriminalized in 1920, and since that time, abortion has been the most widely practiced form of birth control in the Soviet Union.[55] Other forms of birth control suffer from the same problems that beset other consumer goods—poor quality, lack of consideration of consumers' preferences, and sporadic availability. Soviet birth-control pills, although effective, have a variety of unpleasant side-effects such as hair loss, cramps, and nausea. Yet, Soviet pharmaceutical companies appear reluctant to produce a better pill. In addition, shortages are chronic, so one can never count on being able to obtain birth-control pills on a regular basis. The same problems plague other forms of birth control. In contrast, abortions are readily available, cheap or free (depending on one's income level), and they do not carry the social stigma that they often do in other societies. On the average, every Soviet woman has six abortions during her child-bearing years.[56] In urban areas, the abortion rate may be even higher. Abortions entail obvious health risks to women and reduce the chances of subsequently delivering a healthy baby; thus, they may be a primary factor in the increase of infant mortality.

Environmental pollution also affects infant mortality rates in the USSR. In the push to industrialize and match its adversaries in the arms race, the USSR has accorded scant attention to environmental concerns. Soviet researchers report increasing numbers of "birth abnormalities" and respiratory conditions linked to air and water pollution and increasing exposure to radiation.[57]

Dental care is another problem area in the Soviet health-care system. While recent émigrés have generally given Soviet health care high marks, the same is not true for Soviet dentistry. Examinations conducted by Soviet dental researchers found that 70 to 90 percent of all Soviet citizens are in need of dental work.[58] The USSR has roughly one-half the number of dentists per capita as has the United States.[59] Because dental care is not essential to the productivity of the labor force, it was not accorded a high priority under Stalin and his successors. While routine fillings (using silver or gold) are performed, more complicated procedures, such as root canals or orthodontia, are not widely available. Dentists treat an abscessed tooth by extracting the tooth and replacing it with a gold or stainless-steel model.

The Soviet health-care system is not immune to the workings of the "second economy." Most doctors and dentists perform private practice "on the left" and may be paid in antiques, rare books, vodka, meat, or even live chickens. It is widely known that when a woman goes in for an abortion, she must "tip" the doctor in order to receive a double dose of anesthetic so that she will not experience any pain. With the normally prescribed dosage, the procedure is painful, but not excruciating.

Perhaps the two most underdeveloped areas of the Soviet health-care system are the production of medical supplies and pharmaceuticals and medical transport. There are chronic shortages of sophisticated medical equipment and instruments, such as kidney dialysis machines and intensive-care monitoring devices. Modern, effective drugs are often unavailable or extremely difficult to obtain. Even such relatively basic supplies and drugs as X-ray film, thermometers, insulin, and novocaine are often unavailable. In Moscow, it may take as long as nine months to receive a pair of glasses, and much longer in more remote areas.[60]

In recent years, some effort has been devoted to reverse-engineering of Western drugs. On one trip to the USSR, the author noticed customs officials at the Leningrad airport collecting samples of all prescription drugs brought in by foreigners. When the author asked a customs officer why he was taking the samples, he responded that they were aware of "serious drug problems in the West" and wanted to be certain that no illegal drugs were being smuggled into the USSR. It is more likely, however, that the drugs were being collected in an effort to copy Western pharmaceuticals.

Soviet authorities have also instituted educational campaigns to impress upon citizens the need for regular check-ups. Regular physical examinations were not common until recently and are still not universal. Consequently, many illnesses often reach an advanced stage before citizens seek treatment.

Despite the impressive achievements of the Soviet health-care system and the extensive efforts of the government to improve the quality of citizens' health, many problems persist and may actually be increasing. Some of these problems can be resolved by increasing appropriations, training more health-care professionals, and enforcing stiffer environmental and occupational safety regulations. However, many of the problems, such as alcoholism, smoking, and abortion, are more difficult to tackle because they reflect ingrained habits, values, and behavior. Educational efforts such as Gorbachev's antialcohol campaign, mounted soon after he came to office in March 1985, may help; they are unlikely to eradicate the problems entirely, however. The social costs associated with the deteriorating state of health in the USSR are more and more evident and will undoubtedly continue to command the attention of the leadership in the future.

SOCIAL SECURITY IN THE SOVIET UNION

Social insurance benefits and relief for the poor under the tsarist regime were the responsibility of local authorities through the *zemstva* (county councils). The resources of the *zemstva* were, however, clearly inadequate for the task. The dislocations created by World War I, compounded by famine in the countryside, drove millions of peasants to the cities, where most were unemployed and lived in squalor.

In his address to the sixth conference of the Russian Social Democratic Party in Prague in 1912, Lenin outlined a plan for a socialist system of social security. Such a system should, he declared, provide the following:

1. assistance in all cases of incapacity—including old age, accidents, illness, and death of the breadwinner—as well as maternity and birth benefits
2. comprehensive coverage to *all* wage earners and their families
3. compensation equal to *full* earnings, with *total* costs to be borne by employers and the state.[61]

Furthermore, Lenin stipulated that social security should be uniform throughout the country and administered by local soviets with the widespread participation of workers in the management of the system. Excluded from coverage under Lenin's social security plan were peasants—the vast majority of Russian society—and self-employed artisans.

Less than a month after the Bolshevik seizure of power in 1917, two laws on social insurance guaranteed comprehensive unemployment, sickness, and maternity benefits as well as death grants to all Soviet wage earners. Initially, the social insurance programs were administered by local trade unions.

In an effort to gain the support of the peasantry during the Civil War, Lenin expanded social security coverage to the entire population and broadened coverage to include all major risks—unemployment, sickness, maternity, disability, old age, and loss of the breadwinner. The scheme was to be financed mainly from employers' contributions supplemented with earnings derived from confiscated private property. In practice, however, Soviet industry was unable to pay for such extensive social security programs. The economic chaos wrought by the Civil War forced the government to assume the burden of supporting social security programs through general revenues. Despite the government's intervention, most eligible recipients failed to receive their benefits; top priority was given to providing relief for families of those who died fighting with the Reds during the Civil War. As the government assumed financial responsibility for social security programs, it also assumed administrative control. Administration of social security programs was gradually transferred from local trade unions to offices of the local soviets.

With the conclusion of the Civil War in 1921, the social security system was scaled down to make it more financially feasible. Peasants and self-employed persons were no longer eligible to receive benefits and, instead, were encouraged to join self-financed mutual aid societies. As the economic conditions of the country improved under NEP and more and more workers returned to their jobs, the coverage of social security programs broadened. By 1928, it encompassed some 11 million workers.[62]

Stalin's drive to industrialize the economy resulted in important modifications in Lenin's original conception of social security. Gone was the stress on egalitarianism. Instead, social benefits were structured to favor shock workers (Stakhanovites) and laborers with long and exemplary work records. In other words, social security benefits were considered a reward bestowed on the best workers and denied to shirkers.

In 1930, unemployment benefits were abolished, and sick leave required a medical certificate. In 1938, maternity leave was reduced from 16 weeks to 9 weeks. Furthermore, length of uninterrupted employment became an important factor in determining eligibility for most social benefits. Stalin introduced these changes in order to reinforce work discipline and cut down on unemployment and high labor turnover.

When some social service departments of local soviets failed to institute all of Stalin's directives, he ordered the administration of social security programs transferred to the trade unions, which were placed under the strict hierarchical control of central party and trade union officials. Despite this restructuring of the social security system, the growth of the industrial labor force under Stalin resulted in more and more people being covered. The number of persons eligible to receive social security benefits increased from 10 million in 1928 to over 30 million in 1940.[63]

Changes in social security in the USSR followed Stalin's death in 1953. Revamping social programs became one of Khrushchev's high-priority items. In a series of legislative changes, social security coverage was extended to most workers and their dependents (collective farm workers were, however, still excluded). The level of pensions doubled, while disability and survivor allowances increased substantially. Furthermore, efforts were made to eliminate inequalities in benefits. These expansions of social security coverage under Khrushchev were financed by government funds supplemented with employers' contributions. Between 1964 and 1970, most social security provisions were extended to collective farmers in order to eliminate inequities, stimulate agricultural production, and stem the migration of rural workers to the cities.

No major reforms of social security have been introduced since 1970, although some policies have been altered. Length of employment has been removed as a condition for sick leave and maternity benefits, and a family allowance program has been introduced to reduce the effects of poverty. The following section describes the major social welfare programs in the USSR today.

All civilian state employees (that is, everyone except persons in the armed forces or cooperatives) are entitled to an old-age pension on reaching 60 years of age (55 years for women), provided they have worked at least 25 years (20 years for women). Lower retirement ages are granted to coal miners and certain other types of workers engaged in dangerous and difficult jobs. Since 1967, collective farmers have been entitled to pensions at the same ages and same rates as corresponding state employees.

The pension rate is determined by a person's income during the last 12 months of employment. Those workers earning the minimum wage of 70 rubles per month receive pensions of 45 rubles per month. For persons with higher incomes, the pension rate is 50 percent of salary, to a maximum of 120 rubles per month.[64] In contrast to recipients of social security in the United States, pensioners in the Soviet Union do not lose their benefits if they earn additional income. Thus, as many as one-third of all pensioners continue to work to supplement their pensions.[65] There is no mandatory retirement age in the USSR; in fact, with a declining birthrate and a slowing rate of growth in the labor force, pensioners are encouraged to continue in their jobs. They play a major role in the service sector. Many elderly citizens work as museum guards, hotel and coatroom attendants, or even as public service workers, raking leaves in parks.

Social welfare benefits are also awarded to dependent children, grandchildren, parents, and surviving spouses upon the death of state employees. The amount of the "survivors' pension" varies with the number of dependents and the income of the deceased.

Disability pensions are paid to persons who, due to industrial accidents, occupational diseases, or other incapacity, are unable to continue to work. Benefits vary depending on the degree of incapacity, and they are higher if the disability was work-related. In 1970, the disability benefits of collective farmers were brought into line with those of state employees.

Sickness benefits in the USSR cover the entire period of illness. Benefit levels are tied to salary, type of employment, and cause of illness, and may range as high as 90 percent of a worker's normal earnings.[66] In addition, mothers can receive up to seven days of paid leave to care for sick children at home. These provisions were also extended to collective farmers in 1970.

In the last two decades, the birthrate in the USSR has fallen, raising concerns among officials about the impact on future labor resource needs. Child allowances have been instituted to encourage larger families. Mothers with two children are paid 20 rubles on the birth of their third child. Upon the birth of a fourth child, the grant is 65 rubles plus an allowance of 4 rubles per month until the child is five years old.[67] Benefits increase up to the tenth child. The Soviet government has also introduced the "Hero Mother Medal," which is awarded to a woman upon the birth of her tenth child.

Surveys of Moscow working women reveal that the majority would like to have two children; only 3 percent favored having just one child.[68] Crowded living conditions and the fact that 80 percent of all women work outside of the home create strong disincentives to having large families. Approximately 60 percent of all families in the USSR are composed of two or three persons.[69]

A notable exception to small family size, however, is the Central Asian ethnic minorities, who have a birthrate four times the national average. A survey of young Uzbek women conducted by a team of Soviet sociologists found that more than half hoped to have six or more children, and almost one-third wanted more than ten children.[70] It is estimated that Russians will constitute less than half of the population by the year 2000, while the Muslims of Central Asia will represent one out of every three Soviet citizens.

Finally, family allowances have been instituted to assist low-income families. Families below the poverty line of 50 rubles per person per month receive 12 rubles per month for each child under eight years of age. Approximately 37 percent of all children now qualify for relief.[71]

Taken together, total social welfare benefits in the USSR account for approximately 18 percent of personal income. Including medical, educational, housing, and other social services, Soviet social welfare programs constitute as much as 30 percent of the total annual income of the average family.[72]

The welfare system is financed from payroll taxes and budgetary revenues, which are, in turn, derived from indirect taxes and profit taxes. It is difficult to assess precisely how progressive or regressive Soviet social welfare programs and the taxation system are. Some evidence suggests that because many of the benefits are tied to a person's income, high wage earners tend to receive more benefits than low wage earners. In addition, the taxation scheme that supports the Soviet social welfare system appears to place a relatively heavier burden on those with lower incomes. Regardless of whether the combined effects of social welfare programs and taxation are neutral or regressive, it is clear that the Soviet social welfare system does not radically pursue Lenin's original goals of income redistribution and egalitarianism.[73]

The biggest changes in Soviet social security in recent years are the increased demand for existing social security benefits and the emerging needs for new kinds of programs, which have occurred as a result of demographic changes. As in many other industrialized societies, the Soviet population is aging. On the eve of World War II, approximately 9 percent of the population were of retirement age; today, some 15.5 percent are of retirement age and the percentage continues to grow.[74] The "greying" of the population has resulted in a serious reduction in the rate of growth of the Soviet labor force and has increased the amount of social security funds being paid out in pensions.

Total expenditures on social welfare programs in the USSR have increased in recent years at a rate of 6 to 7 percent per year. (See Table 11-3.)

Table 11-3. Social Welfare Expenditures in the USSR, 1940–1983 (in billions of rubles)

Year	Pensions	Assistance	Other	Total
1940	0.3	0.5	0.1	0.9
1960	7.1	2.6	0.2	9.9
1970	16.2	6.1	0.5	22.8
1975	24.4	9.2	1.0	34.6
1980	33.3	11.0	1.3	45.6
1981	35.4	11.3	1.6	48.3
1982	37.8	11.9	1.6	51.3
1983	40.0	13.2	1.9	55.1

Source: Narodnoe khoziaistvo v SSSR v 1983 (Moscow: Finansy i statistika, 1984), 408.

Pensions account for the largest share by far of these expenditures. As a result of the increased number of pensioners in the Soviet Union, social security expenditures have increased from approximately 8 percent of the national income in 1970 to more than 10 percent today.[75]

In comparison, other social programs have not been keeping pace with pensions. In particular, the increased incidence of divorce and the absence of provisions for either alimony or child support have created a drastic need for increased public support for divorced women with children.

As noted earlier, the official poverty level in the USSR is 50 rubles per person per month. Western estimates based on Soviet statistics indicate that in the mid-1960s as much as one-third of the working class was below the poverty line.[76] While poverty remains a real problem in the USSR, it must also be recognized that a poverty level of 50 rubles per month is relatively high when compared to the average industrial wage, and when compared to poverty levels in other industrialized countries.

A large portion of the Soviet population below the poverty level falls into one of two groups: single-parent families and pensioners. The government has sought to reduce the burden on these two groups by increasing family allowances and day-care services for working single mothers and by encouraging pensioners to continue working. Those who are either unwilling or unable to work, however, will continue to fall below the minimum level of income deemed necessary for subsistence by Soviet authorities and will have to rely on private support from relatives.

On the whole, the Soviet social welfare system today meets the provisions established by Lenin in 1912. It provides comprehensive assistance to all workers in most cases of incapacity, illness, accident, or death of the breadwinner. The system falls short of Lenin's ideal, however, over the principles that workers should be compensated for 100 percent of their salaries, that citizens should be actively engaged in making and implementing policies, and that the system should reduce inequalities in the standard of living among various social classes and groups. In these respects, the Soviet welfare system in the USSR does not differ markedly from those of many West European states; as in social welfare programs in the West, the two groups most likely to fall through the safety net are single women with children and the elderly.

This chapter began by asking whether the Soviet social welfare system has translated social and economic rights into reality. Having assessed Soviet performance in housing, health care, and social security, the answer must be a qualified yes. Given the abysmal level of public services prior to the Revolution, Soviet achievements in the past seventy years have been truly remarkable.

Despite these achievements, however, problems persist. In several cases, these problems are growing faster than the regime's ability to solve them. Many of the problems, including increased divorce, alcoholism, abortion, rural migration, declining birthrates, and the aging of the Soviet population, are social or demographic phenomena that cannot be resolved simply by increasing budgetary allocations. Other social problems, such as housing shortages, inadequate medical facilities, and persistent poverty, are more amenable to resolution through expanded welfare programs and increased expenditures. The Soviet economy, however, has entered a stage of dramatically reduced growth rates, necessitating stringent controls on government spending.

At the same time, increased industrialization and improved living standards have led to the growth of special interests. Soviet society is no longer divided simply into workers, peasants, and the intelligentsia, but into numerous regional, occupational, ethnic, and bureaucratic subgroups. Under conditions of economic stringency, competition between the demands of the industrial, defense, agricultural, and social service sectors has grown more intense.

Further complicating the dilemma confronting the leadership is the fact that the progress achieved in raising the living standards of Soviet citizens may not be enough to keep up with public expectations. To a considerable degree, the legitimacy of the Soviet system rests on its ability to deliver a better life to its citizens. In his public statements, Gorbachev acknowledges this and responds, in effect, "If you want to live better, you will have to work harder."

Many of the social problems in the USSR today require complex, comprehensive solutions that entail public education and rehabilitation—in short, "social engineering." The founders of the Soviet system often spoke of the Revolution as ushering in a grand experiment in social engineering that would relegate alcoholism, crime, prostitution, and poverty to the capitalist past. The persistence of these social ills today, seven decades later, can be seen (depending on one's outlook) as either proof of the failure of Lenin's experiment or as testimony to the intractability of social problems in a modern, diverse, and complex society like the Soviet Union.

Notes

1. Alexander Block, "Soviet Housing—I," *Soviet Studies* 3, no. 1, (July, 1951): 12.

2. Alexander Block, "Soviet Housing—II," *Soviet Studies* 3, no. 3, (January, 1952): 248–249.

3. T. Sosnovy, "Housing in the Workers' State," *Problems of Communism* 5, no. 6, (1956): 52–55.

4. J. V. Stalin, *Works,* vol. 13 (Moscow: Foreign Languages Publishing House, 1955), 178.

5. Sosnovy, "Housing in the Workers' State," 57.

6. Ibid., 66.

7. A. Block, "Soviet Housing—I," 7.

8. M. F. Parkins, *City Planning in Soviet Russia* (Chicago: University of Chicago Press, 1953), 56.

9. Ibid.

10. Henry W. Morton, "What Have Soviet Leaders Done about the Housing Crisis?" in Henry W. Morton and Rudolf L. Tokes, eds., *Soviet Politics and Society in the 1970s* (New York: The Free Press, 1974), 170.

11. Cited in Gertrude E. Schroeder, "Consumption in the USSR: A Survey," *Studies on the Soviet Union* 10 (1970): 16.

12. John Gunther, *Inside Russia Today* (New York: Harpers, 1958).

13. Morton, "What Have Soviet Leaders Done," 168.

14. Ibid., 164.

15. Hedrick Smith, *The Russians* (New York: Ballantine, 1976), 98.

16. David K. Shipler, *Russia: Broken Idols, Solemn Dreams* (New York: Times Books, 1983), 91.

17. Smith, *The Russians*, 98.

18. Ibid.

19. Gertrude E. Schroeder, "Consumption," in Abram Bergson and Herbert S. Levine, eds., *The Soviet Economy: Toward the Year 2000* (London: George Allen & Unwin, 1983), 313.

20. Calculated from figures in *The Cambridge Encyclopedia of Russia and the Soviet Union* (Cambridge: Cambridge University Press, 1982), 348.

21. *Sotsialisticheskaia industriia*, April 17, 1980, cited in Leslie Dienes, "Regional Economic Development," in Bergson and Levine, *The Soviet Economy*, 250.

22. Ibid.

23. Cited in Basile Kerblay, *Modern Soviet Society* (New York: Pantheon Books, 1983), 63.

24. *The Cambridge Encyclopedia*, 348.

25. Cited in Carol Nechemias, "Welfare in the Soviet Union: Health Care, Housing, and Personal Consumption," in Gordon B. Smith, ed., *Public Policy and Administration in the Soviet Union* (New York: Praeger, 1980), 189.

26. A similar case forms the basis for Iurii Trifonov's short story "The Exchange."

27. Mikhail Bulgakov, *The Master and Margarita* (London: Fontana, 1983), 265–266.

28. Mark G. Field, *Soviet Socialized Medicine* (New York: The Free Press, 1967), 52.

29. V. I. Lenin, *Sochineniia*, vol. 30 (Moscow: Politicheskaia literatura, 1950), 375–376.

30. G. Hyde, *The Soviet Health Service* (London: Lawrence & Wishart, 1974), 99.

31. V. Navarro, *Social Security and Medicine in the USSR* (Lexington, MA: Lexington Books, 1977), 48.

32. Cited in Murray Feshbach and Stephen Rapawy, "Soviet Manpower Trends and Policies," Joint Economic Committee, U.S. Congress, *The Soviet Economy in a New Perspective* (Washington, D.C.: U.S. Government Printing Office, 1976).

33. Christopher Davis and Murray Feshbach, *Rising Infant Mortality in the USSR in the 1970s*, U.S. Bureau of the Census, Series P-95, no. 74 (Washington, D.C.: U.S. Government Printing Office, September 1980).

34. N. S. Khrushchev, "Report to the Central Committee of the CPSU at the 22nd Congress," in *Materialy XXII S"ezda KPSS* (Moscow: Gospolitizdat, 1961), 73.

35. Murray Feshbach, "Issues in Soviet Health Problems," in U.S. Congress, Joint Economic Committee, *Soviet Economy in the 1980s: Problems and Prospects* (Washington, D.C.: U.S. Government Printing Office, 1982), 216.

36. *Narodnoe khoziaistvo SSSR v 1983* (Moscow: Finansy i statistika, 1984), 446.

37. *Cambridge Encyclopedia*, 394.

38. Cited in Christopher Davis, "The Economics of the Soviet Health System," U.S. Congress, Joint Economic Committee, *Soviet Economy in the 1980s*, 244.

39. Navarro, *Social Security and Medicine*, 76.

40. Cited in *Zaria Vostoka*, 15 July 1984.

41. During their three-year obligation, Soviet doctors earn a regular salary.

42. Cited in Feshbach, "Issues in Soviet Health Problems," 209.

43. *Sovetskaia Rossiia*, 30 September 1981, p. 1.

44. Cited in Davis, "Economics of the Soviet Health System," 250.

45. Feshbach, "Issues in Soviet Health Problems," 205.

46. Cited in David E. Powell, "A Troubled Society," in James Cracraft, ed., *The Soviet Union Today* (Chicago: Bulletin of the Atomic Scientists, 1983), 326.

47. Ibid.

48. B. Levin and M. Levin, *Literaturnaia gazeta*, 20 December 1978, p. 12.

49. Cited in Vladimir G. Treml, "Alcohol Abuse and Quality of Life in the USSR," in Helmut Sonnenfeldt, ed., *Soviet Politics in the 1980s* (Boulder: Westview Press, 1985), 59.

50. Vladimir G. Treml, "Death from Alcohol Poisoning in the USSR," *Wall Street Journal*, 10 November 1981.

51. Treml, "Alcohol Abuse," 57.

52. Treml, "Death from Alcohol Poisoning."

53. Ibid.

54. Reported by John Kenneth Galbraith in "Reflections: A Visit to Russia," *The New Yorker*, 3 September 1984, p. 59.

55. Abortion was outlawed from 1936 to 1955.

56. Davis and Feshbach, *Rising Infant Mortality*.

57. For example, see M. S. Bednyy, *Mediko-demograficheskoe izuchenie narodonaseleniia* (Moscow: Statistika, 1979), 128.

58. *Pravda*, 14 February 1974, p. 3.

59. Ibid.

60. Feshbach, "Issues in Soviet Health Problems," 209.

61. V. I. Lenin, *Polnoe sobranie sochineniia*, vol. 17 (Moscow: Foreign Languages Publishing House, 1963), 476.

62. Cited in Vic George and Nick Manning, *Socialism, Social Welfare and the Soviet Union* (London: Routledge and Kegan Paul, 1980), 38.

63. Ibid., 41.

64. *Cambridge Encyclopedia*, 397.

65. Ibid.

66. Ibid.

67. Ibid.

68. *Problemy ekonomiki* 24 (November 1981): 180–181.

69. *Vestnik statistiki*, no. 11 (1981): 60.

70. V. A. Belova et al., *Skol'ko detei budet v sovetskoi sem'e: Sbornik statei* (Moscow: Statistika, 1977).

71. *The Cambridge Encyclopedia*, 380.

72. Ibid., 398.

73. This assessment is reached by George and Manning in *Socialism, Social Welfare and the Soviet Union*, 60.

74. Stephen Sternheimer, "The Graying of the Soviet Union: Labor and Welfare Issues for the Post-Brezhnev Era," *Problems of Communism* (September–October, 1982), 81–82.

75. Calculated from Soviet statistics in *Narodnoe khoziaistvo v SSSR v 1983* (Moscow: Finansy i statistika, 1984), 407, 410.

76. Mervyn Matthews, *Class and Society in Soviet Politics* (London: Allen Lane, 1972), 88.

Selected Bibliography

Andrusz, Gregory D. *Housing and Urban Development in the USSR*. London: Macmillan, 1984.

Brine, Jenny, Maureen Perrie, and Andrew Sutton. *Home, School and Leisure in the Soviet Union*. Boston: Allen & Unwin, 1980.

Davis, Christopher, and Murray Feshbach. *Rising Infant Mortality in the USSR in the 1970s*. Washington, D.C.: U.S. Bureau of the Census, 1980.

Dimaio, A. J. *Soviet Urban Housing*. New York: Praeger, 1974.

Field, Mark G. *Soviet Socialized Medicine*. New York: The Free Press, 1967.

Field, Mark G., ed. *Social Consequences of Modernization in Communist Societies*. Baltimore: The Johns Hopkins University Press, 1976.

George, Vic, and Nick Manning. *Socialism, Social Welfare and the Soviet Union*. London: Routledge & Kegan Paul, 1980.

Hyde, G. *The Soviet Health Service*. London: Lawrence & Wishart, 1974.

Kaser, Michael. *Health Care in the Soviet Union and Eastern Europe*. London: Croom Helm, 1976.

Kerblay, Basile. *Modern Soviet Society*. New York: Pantheon Books, 1983.

Komarova, D. P. *Social Security in the USSR*. Moscow: Progress, 1971.

Lane, David. *Soviet Economy and Society*. London: Basil Blackwell, 1985.

Lisitsin, Y. *Health Protection in the USSR*. Moscow: Progress, 1972.

Littlejohn, Gary. *A Sociology of the Soviet Union*. London: Macmillan, 1984.

Madison, Bernice Q. *Social Welfare in the Soviet Union*. Stanford: Stanford University Press, 1968.

Matthews, Mervyn. *Class and Society in Soviet Russia*. London: Allen Lane, 1972.

Mc Auley, Alastair. *Economic Welfare in the Soviet Union*. London: George Allen & Unwin, 1979.

Navarro, Vicente. *Social Security and Medicine in the USSR*. Lexington, MA: Lexington Books, 1977.

Osborn, Robert J. *Soviet Social Policies: Welfare, Equality, and Community*. Homewood, IL: Dorsey Press, 1970.

Rimlinger, G. V. *Welfare Policy and Industrialization in Europe, America, and Russia*. Boston: Wiley & Sons, 1971.

Ryan, T. M. *The Organization of Soviet Medical Care*. London: Basil Blackwell, 1978.

Smith, Gordon B., ed. *Public Policy and Administration in the Soviet Union*. New York: Praeger, 1980.

Zhukov, K., and V. Fyodorov. *Housing Construction in the Soviet Union*. Moscow: Progress, 1974.

12

The Politics of Culture

The arts in the Soviet Union serve a political as well as an aesthetic purpose. Music, literature, the visual arts, film, theater, as well as the mass media reflect the official policies and goals of the regime. Yet, at the same time, the arts are a mirror of the society and its people; the arts reflect social trends, human emotions, and the complexities of Soviet society. From the founding of the Soviet regime, these two functions of culture and the arts have coexisted in an uneasy contradiction. A dualism exists between the regime's need for art in service to the State and the intellectual community's need for artistic self-expression. An earlier chapter noted the existence of a similar duality in the Soviet legal system between the competing currents of rule of law and the suppression of dissent. Another chapter analyzed the intricate interrelations of the "first" and "second" economies. In the arts and cultural fields, the dual forces have resulted in a division between "official" and "unofficial" art. The arts have also been an important field upon which battles over larger political issues have been waged. These battles illustrate the political leadership's need for the arts and the media in order to mobilize the population as well as the intelligentsia's ability to affect policies. This chapter will examine the Soviet arts and the media, noting in particular the contradictions between the "official" and "unofficial" realms of art and policy.

FROM REVOLUTION TO REVOLT

From the inception of the Bolshevik regime in 1917, culture and the arts have been drafted into the the service of the State. In some respects, in fact, the cultural revolution in Russia predated the political revolution. In the relatively free climate that followed the 1905 Revolution, Russian artists, writers, dramatists, and musicians experimented with revolutionary new forms. Symbolist writers and artists, such as Alexander Blok and Vasilii Kandinsky, believing in a higher realm of existence, saw literature and art as a means of raising the political and aesthetic consciousness of the society.

The futurists, a brashly iconoclastic movement, tended toward nihilism both politically and aesthetically, as evidenced by the stark, cubistic canvases of Mikhail Larionov, Natalia Goncharova, and Kasimir Malevich. Just as Malevich sought to liberate art from depicting objects, the futurist poet V. V. Khlebnikov experimented with "non-sense" and "trans-sense" poetry in a revolutionary attempt to liberate words from their meanings.

Sergei Esenin, whose lyrical poetry reflected his peasant origins, became the voice of "wooden" (peasant) Russia prior to the Revolution.

The Revolution of 1917 was welcomed by virtually all segments of the intelligentsia as introducing a bold social experiment in which the arts would be allowed to flourish and play a central role in the construction of the new social order. The poet Vladimir Maiakovsky, one of the founders of Russian futurism, joined the Bolshevik Party at the age of fifteen, was arrested three times, and spent eleven months in prison for underground propaganda activity. Maxim Gorky, another pro-Bolshevik poet and playwright, became a personal friend and associate of Lenin. Blok, like many of the symbolists, supported the Revolution as a prelude to the spiritual fulfillment of Russia's messianic destiny. His work, and that of other writers of the period, reflects a curious mix of Christianity and revolutionary zeal. His poem *The Twelve,* for example, depicts twelve Red Guards, led by Christ, patrolling the streets of Petrograd, brutally sweeping away remnants of the former corrupt society. Esenin likewise supported the Revolution as a force for spiritual renewal and the rejection of Western values.

Artists also enthusiastically supported the new regime. On the first anniversary of the October Revolution, the square in front of the Winter Palace in Petrograd was bedecked in cubist and futurist banners and posters. Museums devoted to avant-garde art were opened, and several noted suprematist and futurist painters assumed influential positions in newly established art academies and collectives. Some volunteered their talents to create poster art promoting literacy, encouraging enlistments in the Red Army, celebrating May Day, and exhorting the peasants to deliver grain to the cities. Most notable were the constructivists with their pronounced strain of *proletkult* (proletarian culture), which sought to imbue art with a utilitarian purpose. The supreme example of constructivism was Vladimir Tatlin's design for a spiraling tower to commemorate the Third International. Other constructivists turned their talents to designing factories and futuristic public buildings.

At the same time, *proletkult* writers sought to create a literature for the working class that stressed the collective, rather than individual characters. The best known of the *proletkult* authors was Mikhail Sholokov, whose epic *And Quiet Flows the Don* is one of the most popular twentieth-century Russian novels.[1]

The honeymoon between artists and the Bolshevik regime lasted only four years, however. Censorship, which had been reimposed by Lenin within weeks of the Revolution, became more stringent after the Civil War. In the early 1920s, avant-garde literature and art were denounced for confusing the citizens. Lenin decreed: "Art belongs to the people. It must penetrate with its deepest roots into the very midst of the toiling masses. It must be intelligible to these masses and moved by them. It must unite the feeling, thought, and will of these masses and elevate them. It must awaken in them artists and develop them."[2]

Although experimental art and literature continued to exist throughout the 1920s, it was no longer encouraged by the regime. The experimentation in the arts during the Civil War and NEP spawned a countermovement for more realistic art and literature, designed to be more intelligible to the workers and peasants. This movement, which was spearheaded by the conservative Russian Association of Proletarian Writers (RAPP), helped to promote socialist realism long before it became the sole official literary style under Stalin. As RAPP grew more conservative and gained strength, new controls were imposed.

For many of the Soviet intelligentsia, the enthusiasm of the early NEP years turned to despair and ended in tragedy. By the early 1920s, both Blok and Esenin had grown deeply disillusioned with the course of the Revolution. Blok had fallen from favor by the time of his death in 1921; Esenin's tempestuous marriage to the dancer Isadora Duncan and his growing disillusionment with industrialization and urbanization in Russia contributed to his dramatic suicide in 1925—he wrote a farewell poem in his own blood. Khlebnikov died in 1922 from dropsy, complicated by malnutrition and starvation. Maiakovsky was harassed by RAPP and grew increasingly disillusioned with the regime. He committed suicide in 1930. The satirical writers Mikhail Zoshchenko and Evgenii Zamiatin depicted with cynical humor the cold, hunger, and misery of war communism and the bleakness of life in Soviet Russia. Zamiatin's independent viewpoint brought him into conflict with the Party. *We,* his futuristic novel not unlike Orwell's *1984,* had to be published abroad, and he emigrated to France in 1931.

The novelist Boris Pilniak originally welcomed the Revolution as ushering in a renewal of social justice and morality. By 1926, however, he was publicly denounced; the publication in Berlin of his major work, *Mahogany* (1929), led to his expulsion from RAPP. Pilniak later publicly recanted his "errors," but under Stalin he was arrested and died in a labor camp in 1937.

Isaak Babel, an orthodox Jew, won acclaim for his collection of chilling short stories, *Red Cavalry,* based on his experiences in the Soviet-Polish War of 1920–1921. When his work came under attack in the mid-1920s, Babel opted for the "genre of silence." Silence was not enough to protect him, however; he too disappeared into Stalin's Gulag and died in 1941.

During the early NEP years, the People's Commissar of Enlightenment, Anatolii Lunacharsky, argued strenuously for artistic diversity and eclecticism, fearing the imposition of a single artistic dogma. By the mid-1920s, however, his influence was waning; he resigned in 1929.

Repression was not limited to literature, but was also aimed at other genres. The conservative Association of Artists of the Russian Revolution (AKhRR) gained increasing influence during the late 1920s. In 1929, all artists, sculptors, and architects were united in a single cooperative to enforce greater uniformity. Also in 1929, Malevich was granted his last one-man show. The long-awaited exhibit of Pavel Filonov, however, scheduled for 1930, was canceled due to pressure from AKhRR. Filonov was not allowed to display any works in public after 1934. Many artists, including Marc Chagall, Larionov, Goncharova, Kandinsky, and Ivan Puni, emigrated to Western Europe. Others who stayed in the Soviet Union were impoverished and often the target of mounting repression. Olga Rozanova died of diphtheria in November 1918; Liubov Popova died of scarlet fever in 1924; Filonov died of pneumonia during the siege of Leningrad; Gustav Klucis died in a labor camp in 1944; Malevich died in poverty in Leningrad in

1935. His paintings, like those of other futurist and suprematist artists, are still not displayed in the Soviet Union.

In music, the period immediately preceding the Revolution was rich and diverse. Major compositions by Sergei Rachmaninoff, Alexander Scriabin, Sergei Prokofiev, and Igor Stravinsky brought worldwide acclaim. After the Revolution, however, emigration and mounting repression soon dissipated the musical talent of the country. Rachmaninoff emigrated in 1917 to the United States, where he died unrecognized and impoverished. Prokofiev left Russia in 1918, but returned in 1932. Throughout the 1930s, he was reprimanded for "formalism," and some of his works were suppressed. Dmitri Shostakovich escaped the crackdown by composing works on revolutionary themes. In 1927, for instance, he was commissioned to write a symphony to commemorate the tenth anniversary of the Revolution. Nevertheless, he fell into disgrace in 1936 when a *Pravda* review entitled "Confusion Instead of Music" denounced his work. He was later rehabilitated during World War II and restored to full prominence after 1956.

From the turn of the century to the mid-1920s, Russian theater led the world in originality and innovation. Directors such as Konstantin Stanislavsky, Evgenii Vakhtangov, Alexander Tairov, and Vsevolod Meierhold pioneered in the use of sparse settings, stripping theater of its decorativeness in order to focus attention on the actors. Stanislavsky helped to create the Moscow Arts Theatre (MKhAT), which was instrumental in building the reputations of Anton Chekhov and Maxim Gorky. Gorky's early symbolist plays, such as *The Lower Depths,* gave way to more tendentious and crudely heroic works, such as the novel *Mother,* which is hailed today in the USSR as a forerunner of socialist realism. During the Civil War, Gorky used his personal ties to Lenin to intercede on behalf of many starving members of the intelligentsia; however, in 1921, Gorky left Russia. Lured back in 1928, he died in 1936 under mysterious circumstances while receiving medical treatment.

The introduction of centralized economic planning and the drive for rapid industrialization and collectivization of agriculture destroyed the relative diversity and eclecticism in the arts in the Soviet Union. Signs of a monolithic official cultural doctrine were already evident by 1932, when a party decree "On the Reconstruction of Literary and Artistic Organizations" established exclusive unions for artists, writers, musicians, and architects. All privately or cooperatively owned printing presses were brought under the centralized control of the Association of State Publishing Houses, thus facilitating the work of the censors. Two years later, at a congress of the Union of Soviet Writers, Stalin imposed the concept of socialist realism. A resolution adopted at the congress affirmed: "We must depict reality in its revolutionary development and create works with a high level of craftmanship, with high ideological and artistic content."[3] The content of socialist realism, whether in the graphic arts or literature, centered around the glorification of the workers and the peasants, on the one hand, and the glorification of Lenin and Stalin, on the other. An anonymous observer defined socialist realism more caustically as "a method of portraying our leaders in a way they will understand."[4] However defined, socialist realism was the sole official cultural policy for at least the next twenty years.

Socialist realist novels such as Nikolai Ostrovsky's *How the Steel Was Tempered* and F. V. Gladkov's *Cement* played on the themes of heroism and selfless striving for the goals of the society. Artists produced murals, posters, and other public art that depicted men with bulging muscles working in steel mills and women (also with bulging muscles) working in the fields or milking cows. Perhaps the closest equivalent in the United States to socialist realist art is the WPA murals painted in many public buildings during the Depression.

Stalin's cultural policies concerning poetry were particularly oppressive. Boris Pasternak was censured for producing overly introverted and aesthetic work. Refusing to conform to socialist realism, he published nothing but translations of classics, especially Shakespeare, until World War II. Osip Mandelshtam, another prominent poet, was arrested in 1934 for producing a vicious anti-Stalin poem. He died four years later in a prison camp. Anna Akhmatova, whose husband was shot as a White conspirator in 1921, was denounced beginning in the mid-1920s for her personalistic poems. Under Stalin, her son was arrested and spent fourteen months in a labor colony. In the 1930s, Akhmatova became the voice of Russian women whose husbands and sons had been imprisoned or shot during the purges. The twin themes of her poems—sensual pleasures and atonement for sin—prompted A. A. Zhdanov, Stalin's watchdog over the arts, to characterize her as "half nun and half whore."[5] Marina Tsvetaeva's husband, like Akhmatova's, was linked to an anti-Bolshevik group, forcing Tsvetaeva to emigrate to Paris in 1926. She returned to the Soviet Union in 1939 but committed suicide after learning that her husband had been shot as a double agent.

World War II introduced a new theme for socialist realism—Russian nationalism. Artists depicted past Russian victories over foreign invaders, while composers such as Shostakovich composed heroic symphonies in honor of the people of Leningrad and other patriotic subjects.

After the relatively relaxed period of World War II, Stalin again clamped down on the arts. A resolution of the CPSU Central Committee in August 1946 initiated a campaign against Zoshchenko, Akhmatova, and other writers. New norms of socialist realism required literary and other artistic works to reflect official optimism, nationalism and patriotism, and glorification of Stalin.

Stalin's cultural dictates did not totally destroy independent artistic expression, however, they simply drove it underground. Within a matter of weeks after Stalin's death, there appeared rebellious stirrings of an artistic and cultural renaissance.

The death of the *Vozhd'* in 1953 and Nikita Khrushchev's "secret" speech at the Twentieth Party Congress in 1956 opened the floodgates of long-suppressed artistic grievances and sparked a flurry of creativity in the arts. The metaphor most often used to describe the post-Stalin revival in the arts is *ottepel'* (the thaw), taken from a novel of that title by Ilia Ehrenburg. The thaw was, however, selective. Not all of the Stalinist strictures were lifted, just those that suited Khrushchev's purposes. The central theme of the period echoed the new party line denouncing Stalin's cult of the personality and abuses of socialist legality. Representative was Aleksandr Solzhenitsyn's *One Day in the Life of Ivan Denisovich,* a semiautobiographical account of a political prisoner's day in one of Stalin's labor camps. This was, however, the only one of Solzhenitsyn's novels to be officially published in the USSR; *The First Circle, Cancer Ward,* and *The Gulag Archipelago* appeared only in the West. Boris Pasternak's epic novel *Doctor Zhivago* came close to being approved for publication in the liberal literary journal *Novy Mir,* but a new crackdown was under way before final authorization could be obtained. The novel was relegated to the growing category of unofficial *samizdat* (self-published) literature, which circulated relatively freely in typewritten copies.

With the thaw, Soviet art also began to show real diversity. Although official art under Khrushchev and Brezhnev remained realistic and even heroic, membership in the Union of Soviet Artists or Union of Soviet Writers did not preclude experimentation with unofficial styles. The 1960s saw a proliferation of artistic trends, most of which depicted reality through a prism of surrealism, expressionism, the grotesque, or fantastic realism. A small group adopted abstractionism, not attempting to portray reality but instead embracing pure form.

Under Khrushchev, Soviet society became more open and accessible to Western ideas, values, and artistic trends. Peaceful coexistence resulted in exchanges of American and European scholars, literary critics, writers, art exhibitions, and performing groups, all of which were eagerly welcomed by the Soviet intelligentsia.

The explosion in the arts raised concerns among the conservative watchdogs of official ideology, especially within the USSR Academy of Arts. Some members of the Academy convinced Khrushchev that a crackdown was needed. Viewing a major exhibition of modern art at the Manege in 1963, they pointed out for Khrushchev these "dangerous" developments in modern Soviet art and assailed them as ideological deviations and corruptions introduced from the capitalist West. Khrushchev lashed out, denouncing all abstract art as "doodling" and modern artists as "pederasts." In reality, Khrushchev had been manipulated by those who wished to preserve many of the tenets of socialist realism and who needed a strong political ally to counter the dynamic and innovative artistic movement that had sprung up in the USSR.

Those who refused to capitulate to the new, more stringent artistic norms were ejected from the Union of Soviet Artists and the Union of Soviet Writers and became members of the growing unofficial artistic community. Among them were Ernst Neizvestny, Vadim Sidur, and Boris Birger. Ironically, it was Neizvestny (whose name means "unknown") who was commissioned to sculpt Khrushchev's tombstone. It is a stunning, cubistic monolith composed of two halves—one of pure white marble, one of pure black marble, representing the two sides of the First Secretary's character.[6]

The Brezhnev regime reinforced the prevailing conservative line on the arts, with more subtle, but no less coercive, means. The works of some authors who had fallen from favor during earlier periods of repression were published in limited numbers after their deaths. For example, Mikhail Bulgakov's biting satirical novel *The Master and Margarita* appeared in a censored version; a very small number were published. Volumes by the novelist Pilniak and poets Tsvetaeva and Mandelshtam also appeared, but they were never accorded the praise they were due. The only notable appearances in print by living writers were limited editions of volumes of poetry by Boris Pasternak and Anna Akhmatova. By publishing very small numbers of these works, the Brezhnev regime was attempting to placate a restive intelligentsia, but still shield the general public from nonconformist ideas.

Brezhnev's cultural policy took an ominous turn in 1965 with the arrest of two noted writers, Andrei Siniavsky and Iurii Daniel, for having their works smuggled out of the USSR and published in the West. The Siniavsky-Daniel trial set a precedent for criminal prosecution of writers for publishing work abroad (although there was no such provision in the criminal codes). Moreover, it signaled a more vigorous policing of cultural standards under Brezhnev.[7] In the face of this cultural offensive, artists and writers were confronted with three options: complete artistic conformity, silence, or writing "for the drawer." The latter option means writing with no intention of seeking official publication, instead circulating works privately (*samizdat*) and hoping that they might be accepted for publication during a period of more relaxed censorship in the future.

Détente brought a massive influx of Western culture that, according to the Party's chief ideologists, threatened to further erode traditional Marxist-Leninist values. The authorities tightened their grip on the intellectual community in the early 1970s, preferring cultural isolation to overexposure to the capitalist West. Increasing numbers of Soviet artists, writers, and other members of the intelligentsia were driven into the world of unofficial art, a move that many found to be liberating and exhilarating. Freed from the constraints of official dogma and stimulated by greater access to ideas and artistic trends in the West, Soviet unofficial art exploded in the 1970s and 1980s with pop art, photo-realism, conceptualism, and even artistic installations and "happenings."

On September 15, 1974, a group of unofficial artists staged an impromptu exhibition of their work on a vacant lot in Moscow. Within minutes, the exhibition was disrupted by bulldozers and fire trucks, which used their hoses to disperse the crowd. Several paintings were burned on the spot by plainclothes KGB officers. The authorities are powerless, however, to curtail private exhibitions in the apartments of artists and their friends. Since the early 1970s, some of the most exciting art shows and poetry readings have taken place in cramped and smoke-filled apartments in Moscow and Leningrad.

Recognizing the growing phenomenon of unofficial art, the Brezhnev regime moderated its policies slightly. Beginning in 1976, annual public exhibits of artwork by unofficial artists were allowed in Moscow and Leningrad.

The 1976 Leningrad exhibit was held at a Komsomol "palace" in a working-class district far from the center of town.[8] Despite the fact that there had been no public announcements of the exhibition, there was a line two blocks long waiting to be admitted. An army of KGB agents guarded the doors, closely observing the crowd and limiting the number of persons allowed into the small room on the second floor that housed the exhibit. The exhibition consisted of approximately eighty paintings by some twenty unofficial Leningrad artists. All of the paintings had been screened in advance, and a few "offensive" works had been removed by the authorities. The styles of the works on display varied widely, including surrealism, montages, abstract expressionism, and cubism. There were even some lyrical pieces with Hebrew and Yiddish titles by a Jewish artist.

In comparison to the visual arts, Soviet literature is accorded a wider range of latitude despite the omnipresent censors. Soviet citizens are avid readers. One sees people reading in subways and while waiting in lines at the meat market. With little competition from television for entertainment, there is a great demand for pulp fiction. Although low in terms of artistic creativity and style, pulp fiction purveys social values and has a large and steadfast audience. The themes of pulp fiction usually revolve around tales of World War II heroism, Western espionage, nationalism, village life, labor, and romance. In contrast to the writers of the Stalinist period, pulp fiction writers today deal frankly with such social problems as divorce, alcoholism, housing shortages, philandering, and petty politics in the work place. I. Gerkova's novellas *The Ladies' Hairdresser* and *The Mistress of a Hotel,* for example, feature themes such as the difficulties of reconciling career demands and the duties of a single mother.

Since the 1960s, there has been a proliferation of journals that serve the interests of specialized audiences. This allows the authorities to publish works on a restricted scale that they wish neither to ban outright, nor disseminate widely. Of the national literary journals, *Literaturnaia gazeta* is best known. Ostensibly devoted to literature, this weekly is, in reality, the liveliest political and social publication in the Soviet Union. Its editor, Alexander Chakovsky, is a prolific writer and one of few remaining Jews in an influential position in the USSR. During the 1960s, *Novy Mir,* under the editorship of Alexander Tvardovsky, published many liberal writers. In 1970, however, the editorial board was disbanded, and the journal now is politically moderate.

The generation of writers of the 1950s, 1960s, and early 1970s who were concerned with social justice (e.g., Solzhenitsyn, Siniavsky, Vasili Aksyonov, Anatoli Gladilin, Joseph Brodsky, and Viktor Nekrasov) are all in exile abroad. The talented writers remaining in the Soviet Union today tend to restrict themselves to less overtly political themes, focusing instead on personal emotions. Many of these writers, like Iurii Trifonov (*House on the Embankment* and *The Old Man*), paint a gloomy portrait of contemporary society with the underlying message that human unhappiness is the result of lack of will and the corrupting influence of "consumerism" and affluence. The latter theme appears to be encouraged by the political leadership as an attempt to lower the public's expectations in light of the growing stagnation of the Soviet economy. The message is clear: Money doesn't buy happiness—to which an unofficial writer in Leningrad rejoins: "Poverty doesn't either!"[9]

Poverty is a fact of life for any Soviet writer who refuses to join (or is denied membership in) the Union of Soviet Writers. Without membership, a person is simply not recognized as a professional writer and therefore is not paid. Similarly, artists who are not members of the Union of Soviet Artists are not provided studios, cannot show their work in galleries, and are not allowed to sell their work. Thus, unofficial artists, writers, and otehr members of the creative intelligentsia must support themselves by working as assembly-line workers, doormen, or taxi drivers. A few artists are able to survive by selling their works discreetly to established musicians, writers, scientists, and other members of the intelligentsia. Some writers who find official restrictions too confining but wish to remain in the writers' union have gravitated to science fiction and children's literature, two genres in which surrealism and the fantastic are still permissible.

Finally, the long tradition of underground journals and newspapers in Russian has been revived with the publication of *The Chronicle of Current Events*. The journal documents violations of human rights, focusing especially on ethnic discrimination and the persecution of religious believers in the Soviet Union. The political orientation of the *Chronicle* is liberal democratic and has been linked to Andrei Sakharov, the unofficial leader of the so-called Democratic Movement. Other underground journals of various political persuasions exist in the USSR today, most notably *The Political Diary* on the left and *Veche* on the right.

The performing arts have not enjoyed the same explosion of creative activity during the 1970s and 1980s that has occurred in either literature or art. Ballet, opera, music, and theater cannot be performed in a cramped apartment; nor can works be written "for the drawer" or passed from person to person in *samizdat* form.

Iurii Liubimov, the embattled director of Moscow's Taganka Theatre, built a reputation during the 1970s and early 1980s for staging bold experimental productions that played to packed houses. The popularity of the Taganka was reflected in its box-office receipts and gave it a degree of financial independence from the Ministry of Culture, which subsidizes most performing arts groups. Nevertheless, Liubimov came under attack for slighting contemporary Soviet playwrights and was relieved of his position on March 7, 1984, while he was in London. The next day, he announced his intention to stay in the West. The firing of Liubimov coincided with a campaign under Chernenko to urge writers and playwrights to create more "positive heroes," characters worthy of emulation.[10]

Much of Soviet ballet today is also rather stagnant in repertoire, choreography, and direction. Having rejected the early experimentation by such visionaries as Vaslav Nijinsky and Sergei Diaghilev, Soviet ballet has restored nineteenth-century classical forms, complete with elaborate sets and standard choreography, combined with Soviet gymnastic virtuoso. Many of the Soviet Union's most talented dancers, including Rudolf Nureyev, Natalia Makarova, Mikhail Baryshnikov, and Valery and Galina Panov, have emigrated to the West in search of fame, fortune, and artistic freedom.

Cinema, which Lenin considered the most important of all the arts, today is dominated by overly sentimental romances (e.g., Ilia Maslin's *Love and Lies*) and countless films of World War II heroism. Some films of note have been produced, but they are often not shown to Soviet audiences. Andrei Tarkovsky's epic *Andrei Rublev*, based on the life of the medieval icon painter, was completed in 1966; a heavily edited version was not shown in the USSR until some five to ten years after it was released in the West. While the film was criticized for glamorizing religion, its undercurrent of Russian nationalism struck a positive chord with the Brezhnev leadership.

Dersu-Uzala, a 1970 film, was a joint Japanese-Soviet venture and a by-product of détente. It relates the experiences of a nineteenth-century Russian explorer who befriends Dersu-Uzala, a Siberian native. The film was directed by the distinguished Japanese director Akira Kurosawa and filmed in Siberia. Highly acclaimed abroad, it was shown in the USSR, in part, because of its graphic portrayal of Chinese brutality against the native populations of Siberia. In contrast, Sergei Pradzhanov's *Shadows of Forgotten Ancestors,* although shown abroad, never appeared in the USSR because of its prominent theme of Ukranian nationalism, which the government finds offensive.

The staple of the Soviet film industry today remains films based on classics of Russian literature. As the Western literary scholar Maurice Friedberg observes, however, undue preoccupation with literature of the past may signal a refuge from the present.[11]

THE MANAGEMENT OF CULTURE

When it was created in 1953, the USSR Ministry of Culture was responsible for formulating and implementing cultural policies in all artistic fields. Today, however, it deals primarily with literature, music, dance, and theater. Separate state committees now supervise radio and television (*Gostelradio*), cinema (*Goskino*), and publishing (*Goskomizdat*).

In addition to supervising the arts and cultural fields, the Ministry of Culture is responsible for maintaining museums, libraries, parks, clubs, and "palaces of culture," and for the training of personnel for these establishments. In Soviet jargon, the latter function is known as "cultural-enlightenment" work and consumes a major portion of the ministry's time and attention. Of some seventy educational institutions in the arts (art academies, conservatories, and so forth) in the USSR, fifty fall under the administrative aegis of the Ministry of Culture.[12]

Subordinate to the USSR Ministry of Culture are ministries in each of the fifteen republics, which have particular responsibility for managing culture in their respective regions. The interaction of the central ministry and the fifteen subordinate republic ministries is complex and fraught with conflict and confusion.

Policies and decisions made at the republic and local levels are subject to approval by the central ministry in Moscow. Normally, local cultural departments are responsible for supervising museums, theaters, and other artistic and cultural institutions in their cities or regions. There are exceptions, however, especially for very prominent institutions. For example, the Kirov Ballet in Leningrad reports directly to the USSR Ministry of Culture, rather than to the culture department of the Leningrad city soviet.

All creative arts and literary organizations at the republic level are encouraged to reflect the nationality composition of their respective republics. Thus, newspapers, books, magazines, and journals are published in each of the fifteen major languages of the Soviet Union. The effort to make the arts accessible even to smaller ethnic groups is impressive. Scholarly journals in the USSR appear in forty-five languages, while books are published in sixty-eight languages, theatrical performances are presented in forty-seven languages, and radio broadcasts in seventy languages.[13] Theaters, ballet companies, and orchestras have been established in virtually every major city and town in the USSR. The quality and level of professional traning varies widely, but many of the regional companies have won acclaim at home and abroad.[14] Dance, dramatic, and musical troupes also tour remote areas that cannot support residential performing-arts companies.

Although they are technically public organizations and not a formal part of the state machinery, the unions for members of the various artistic professions play an integral role in the management of Soviet culture. There are separate unions for artists, dancers, musicians and composers, architects, and actors (including both cinema and drama). The unions receive ample support from the State in the form of offices, health resorts, and vacation facilities, as well as direct financial support.

The Ministry of Culture has considerable influence over the professional unions. For example, the ministry has the right to "assist" unions in planning and to present proposals for consideration by their members.[15] All top-level officials within the various unions occupy *nomenklatura* positions, which furthers their sensitivity to "proposals" coming from the ministry and from the Party's Culture Department.

In addition to organizing artistic performances and sponsoring symposia and other professional activities, the unions provide a variety of services for their members. The unions manage pension programs and administer social insurance and welfare programs for the creative intelligentsia. Unions also operate exclusive resorts, health spas, clubs, restaurants, retirement homes, and summer cottages for their members, as well as special stores through which members can purchase everything from rare books to automobiles.

The Soviet regime places great emphasis on making the arts accessible to all citizens, rather than keeping them the exclusive preserve of the intelligentsia. Concerts and theater and ballet performances are usually scheduled to begin in the early evening in order to attract workers coming home from their jobs. It is not unusual to see office workers, military officers, and even manual laborers attending performances still wearing their work clothes or uniforms.

Accessibility of the arts is also assured by holding down the cost of admission. Tickets to concerts by the Leningrad or Moscow Philharmonic Orchestra usually range from approximately $1.00 to $3.50. Ballet and opera tickets cost slightly more, especially at the prestigious Bolshoi or Kirov theatres, but even the most expensive ballet ticket costs less than $5.00. Many cultural events are open to the public free of charge.

One consequence of low ticket prices in the USSR is that most performing-arts companies operate at a loss and are dependent upon the Ministry of Culture for subsidies (*dotatsiia*). Subsidies are one of the most influential means by which the Ministry of Culture shapes the artistic policies of performing-arts companies. Indirect subsidies are also received in the form of rent-free buildings, equipment, and even routine maintenance costs borne by the central ministry. By threatening to withhold subsidies, the ministry can wield decisive power over most artistic groups.[16] Ironically, however, the most avant-garde and controversial companies, such as the Taganka Theatre, play to packed houses and are the least dependent upon the ministry's subsidies.

No matter how profitable, however, all artistic insitutions are subject to censorship. Censorship extends to every form of printed or reproduced material in the USSR and is the responsibility of Glavlit, the Main Literary Department of the Main Directorate for the Protection of State Secrets in the Press.[17] All books, magazine articles, scholarly and scientific publications, news stories, textbooks, and even photocopied material must be cleared by Glavlit and display the number and seal of the censor. Publication or reproduction of printed matter without prior authorization by Glavlit is a serious criminal offense punishable by up to seven years in prison.

Because information on Glavlit itself falls into the category of unpublishable material, little is known about its organization, staffing, or operations. Although the guidelines established by Glavlit are quite vague, most authors and editors know what will and will not pass the censors. Consequently, writers commonly engage in self-censorship. The editorial boards of publishing houses and journals mediate between the writers and the literary standards set by the Ministry of Culture and enforced by Glavlit. Thus, editors make many of the most vital decisions as to what shall be published and what shall not.[18] Editorial boards are appointed by and answerable to the writers' union. Editors and high-ranking officials of the writers' union meet frequently with personnel of the Central Committee's Culture Department to discuss the Party's latest authoritative directives. The editors are responsible for communicating those directives to writers and policing the standards in their respective publications, thus reducing the amount of work for the censors.

In the performing arts, the censorship function—usually referred to as "repertoire policy"—is the responsibility of the Ministry of Culture, which must approve all theatrical, musical, dance, and cinematic productions. Performing-arts companies, following general guidelines set by the Ministry of Culture, submit annual "repertoire plans" to the ministry for approval. New plays, musical scores, and screenplays are carefully reviewed by the central authorities. The primary task of repertoire policy, however, is not to censor scripts, but to ensure the proper balance among contemporary Soviet works, foreign works, and classics.[19]

Before a play or other artistic performance can be given a public premiere, it is presented at a closed performance attended by local cultural officials, the artistic council of the theater (or orchestra, ballet company, and so on), and invited members of the public (normally including local party and governmental officials). In the visual arts, the Ministry of Culture, through its Directorate of Art, follows a similar procedure of approving annual plans for art exhibitions and screening all works of art prior to the opening of exhibits.

This extensive supervision of culture in the Soviet Union is justified by officials on two grounds: It ensures that only works of high artistic quality are performed or displayed, and it protects the Soviet public from "incorrect" and "potentially harmful" ideas and influences.

Despite the tremendous influence and authority of the USSR Ministry of Culture in literature and the arts, the broad outlines of Soviet cultural policy are made within the highest levels of the CPSU. In 1955, the Culture Department was established within the CPSU Central Committee Secretariat in order to centralize party supervision over the arts. Today, the Culture

Department has broad responsibility for overseeing all aspects of cultural policy, including those falling outside the purview of the Ministry of Culture (e.g., film, radio, television, and the press). The Culture Department largely implements policies enacted by the Politburo and the Central Committee, but it is also in a position to shape those policies by formulating proposals to be submitted to and discussed by those bodies.

At the republic and local levels, party cultural officers are primarily responsible for supervising artistic performances and institutions in their respective areas and have little actual impact on policies. They do, however, influence cultural affairs in their jurisdictions by screening films and dramatic, musical, dance, and artistic productions before they may be opened to public view. Local cultural officers also communicate party policies to the artistic community so that those themes can be incoporated into their work.

The party leadership relies on the arts to support its policies and political campaigns. For example, soon after the inception of Gorbachev's antialcohol campaign, there was a noticeable increase in the number of artworks, films, plays, and books devoted to the problem of alcoholism.

The Party can directly promote such works through its use of state orders. Every year, for example, the Party issues state orders to the State Committee on Cinematography for the production of films that are "of great topical and ideological significance."[20] A state order gives the production of a film, book, or play highest priority; actors, directors, and others working on the production receive handsome bonuses.

Art also mirrors political life in the USSR. In 1984, at a time when the Soviet Union was languishing under a series of elderly and feeble leaders, an article in *Pravda* by a noted drama critic decried the lack of focus on ordinary workers, teachers, and citizens in contemporary plays. The critic candidly observed: "Needless to say, this tendency is connected with a problem that our society and press have been discussing heatedly of late—the problem of leadership, of the fitness of leaders for their positions, and of potential leaders."[21]

The arts are inextricably bound to the ideological underpinnings of the Soviet system; thus, they frequently command the attention of the political leadership. As noted in Chapter 3, much of the early allure of Marxism-Leninism has waned. Although the intellectual community as well as the general public is still expected to pay ritual obeisance to the ideology as a symbol of the regime, the meaning of Marxism-Leninism today has changed. The leadership is confronting a morass of social and moral problems—dishonesty in the workplace, alcoholism, divorce, abortion, consumerism, and loss of faith in "the communist future." As a consequence, the leaders may allow somewhat greater voice to the creative intelligentsia that has traditionally acted as the collective conscience of the society.

THE MASS MEDIA

Like culture and the arts, the mass media play a central role in conveying the policies of the political leaders and mobilizing the population in support of those policies. Lenin recognized the power of the media and edited several underground newspapers prior to the Revolution. He observed, "A newspaper is not only a collective propagandist and collective agitator; it is also a collective organizer."[22]

On November 9, 1917, Lenin's newly established regime issued a "Decree on the Press," which outlawed all opposition newspapers. By May 1919, the regime had seized all printing presses and duplicating machines. Since 1919, all the mass media have come under the monopolistic control of the State.

The extent of development of the mass media in the USSR is closely linked to its primary function—the dissemination of propaganda. Today in the Soviet Union, more than 8,000 newspapers are published, with a combined circulation of 170 million.[23] The largest newspaper, *Pravda* (Truth), is the official organ of the CPSU Central Committee and boasts more than 12 million readers.[24] *Izvestiia* (News) is the official organ of the State. Its circulation is between 8 and 9 million.[25] *Trud* (Labor), the newspaper representing the trade union organizations, also attracts between 8 and 9 million readers.[26] *Komsomolskaia pravda* (Komsomol Truth), with a circulation of more than 10 million, is the organ of the communist youth organization.[27] It focuses especially on the concerns of Soviet youth. *Krasnaia zvezda* (Red Star) represents the views of the Soviet armed forces and is noted for its hawkish stances on foreign policy issues. *Sel'skaia zhizn'* (Rural Life) is directed to the peasants. The popular newspaper *Sovetskii Sport* (Soviet Sport) reports on sporting events both inside the USSR and abroad, and includes as well the obligatory party-political-editorial coverage.

In addition to these central newspapers, there are more than 7,000 regional and local papers, most of which are organs of party, state, or trade union organizations in their respective areas. Thus, *Pravda Vostoka* (Truth of the East), published in Tashkent, is the party newspaper for Uzbekistan. Evening papers, such as *Vecherniaia Moskva* (Evening Moscow), published by the Moscow city soviet, carry a wider range of entertainment and political commentary than many of the morning newspapers. Regional newspapers and translations of the major central newspapers are published in some fifty-five languages.[28]

Despite the apparent diversity of the Soviet press, the reportage, editorial content, and format are remarkably standardized. *Pravda* serves as the prime model for all other publications. The front page is devoted to reports of production achievements, an "agitational" editorial, and occasional announcements of government or party decrees and resolutions. Once a week (usually on Tuesdays), there is a brief article entitled "In the Politburo of the CPSU," which mentions some of the major agenda items brought up in the Politburo session held the previous Thursday. The remaining five pages of *Pravda* cover party affairs, editorial commentaries, correspondence, foreign news, sports reports, and the weather. Even specialized newspapers adhere to this general content and format. For example, the front page of *Sovetskii Sport* may carry an article on Soviet athletes working to organize sports activities in light of the decisions of the Twenty-Seventh Party Congress.

There are two news agencies in the Soviet Union, TASS and Novosti. In reality, Novosti is a propaganda agency with close ties to the KGB; it is primarily responsible for supervising the activities of foreign correspondents in the USSR. TASS, with its gigantic network of reporters and foreign correspondents, is the major news source for Soviet newspapers.

As in other aspects of Soviet society, the better connections one has, the more information one receives. The regular TASS service, known as "Blue" or "Green" TASS, is highly censored and sanitized for public consumption. "White" or "Service" TASS is a special, classified news-and-information service provided to selected ministers, military officers, party secretaries, and other high-ranking officials. "White" TASS contains accurate information on Soviet domestic affairs, including statistics on crime, economic problems, accidents, and epidemics that never appear in open sources.[29] "White" TASS also carries detailed international coverage from TASS correspondents as well as reprints of editorial commentary from foreign media. At the pinnacle of this news hierarchy is the highly classified "Red" TASS, which is distributed only to chief editors of the major newspapers and the highest state and party leaders.

Although foreign coverage is obviously biased, the Soviet media usually do not fabricate stories; they rely instead on selective reporting to demonstrate their points. Thus, the Soviet reader is bombarded by daily reports of unemployment, racial strife, and social malaise in the United States.

Soviet newspapers are very strictly controlled in what types of news events they may report. Official censorship regulations are summarized for foreign correspondents in five long typewritten pages. Taboo subjects include economic problems, shortages, lines, price increases; salaries; inequities and special benefits (especially those received by party and state officials); crime statistics and other adverse social indicators; foreign policy involvements of the USSR (e.g., the invasion of Afghanistan, arms sales, international aid); details of the private lives of Soviet leaders and their families and advance word about their traveling schedules; dissidents, religious believers, and their activities; statistics or reports on illnesses such as cholera; the activities of the KGB and the Soviet military; and censorship (acknowledging the existence of censorship is itself taboo).[30]

Under Gorbachev, press censorship has been substantially reduced. Previously forbidden subjects such as earthquakes, shipwrecks, and civil disturbances have been covered accurately and promptly in the Soviet press, lending credibility to Gorbachev's policy of glasnost'—or candor.[31] A major purpose of the glasnost' campaign, however, goes byond the simple desire for more accurate reportage; the frank reporting on mismanagement, incompetence, and corruption is designed to put pressure on officials to perform better.

Soviet newspapers attract a large and diverse audience. A study conducted in Leningrad found that 75 percent of those polled read at least one newspaper every day, and that official communications by party and state bodies attract the largest audience.[32] The Soviet media have developed an elaborate array of "catchwords," metaphors, and Aesopian language to convey the true views and policy disputes within the leadership. Soviet readers pride themselves on their ability to read between the lines of news reports in order to ascertain what direction policies might take in the future.

Soviet newspapers are not generally sold by subscription, but are purchased at sidewalk kiosks. Pravda costs a mere 3 kopeks—4 cents. The latest editions of the major newspapers are also pasted up on bulletin boards near bus stops and in public buildings.

One important function of Soviet newspapers is to receive and publish letters from Soviet citizens. Letters to the editors relate to a wide variety of subjects: suggestions, petty grievances, complaints about housing conditions, consumer complaints, and criticisms of mismanagement by low-level officials. Soviet authorities report that between 60 and 70 million letters are received every year; *Pravda* alone receives more than half a million.[33] Although only a small portion of the letters can actually be printed, all letters are supposed to be answered. Many are referred to local party, state, industrial, legal, and other officials for action. There are many instances reported every year in which corrupt officials are dismissed following probes into citizens' complaints.

The great importance attached to the propaganda and mobilizing functions of the press in the USSR also extends to other media. More than five thousand journals and magazines are published in forty-five different languages of the USSR and twenty-three foreign languages, covering a wide array of specialized and regional audiences.[34] The most prominent political journal, *Kommunist* (Communist), carries ideological as well as political articles. Its editorials are closely scrutinized by party members to reveal policy shifts. *Krokodil* (Crocodile) is a popular satirical journal that features cartoons, articles, and poems lampooning consumerism, alcoholism, bureaucratic red tape, and black-market activities.

There are more than three hundred radio stations in the USSR broadcasting in seventy languages.[35] All radio stations rely heavily on the eight main national networks for their programs. These networks provide news and political commentary, educational programs, and cultural performances, as well as programs for special audiences (children, youth, women, peasants, and so forth).

The television audience in the USSR has grown rapidly since 1960, when only 8 percent of all families owned a television set.[36] Today, there are some 85 million television sets in the USSR (more than the number of households), and television broadcasts reach approximately 98 percent of the population.[37] There are four main channels covering a wide variety of news, economic and political reporting, educational programs, cultural performances, sporting events, and documentary films. The major evening news program *Vremia* (Time) attracts a large audience, despite its bland format and ubiquitous reports on the grain harvest in Kazakhstan or steel production in Vitebsk. Soviet literary officials have recently criticized the television networks for showing too many sporting events and films, especially reruns. In 1983, Soviet television broadcast only eight ballets, while 116 soccer matches and 100 hockey games were aired.[38] Another recent development in Soviet television programming is the talk show. Programs such as *Critical View, Candid Talk,* and *Facts and Commentary* invite officials to appear and be questioned by callers in an attempt to increase official accountability to the public for their actions and decisions.[39]

Soviet citizens have only limited access to foreign newspapers, magazines, and radio. Customs officials at the airports normally confiscate Western newspapers and magazines; nevertheless, copies find their way into the country and are avidly read by Soviet citizens. Rather than being read and discarded, issues of foreign magazines circulate from person to person even after they are long out of date. Often the news content of Western magazines is less interesting to Soviet readers than the glossy and glamorous advertisements.

Western uncensored news reports are available from foreign broadcasts such as those of Voice of America, the BBC, and Radio Liberty. Soviet authorities intermittently jam such transmissions, but many broadcasts—especially musical and cultural programs—are received without interference. Western rock music programs are especially popular with Soviet young people, who frequently tape them on their portable tape recorders. People in the Baltic republics and other northern regions can receive radio and television broadcasts from Finland and Sweden, while citizens in the Far East can pick up Japanese radio and television shows.

THE CREATIVE INTELLIGENTSIA AND POLICY-MAKING

Throughout Russian history, members of the creative intelligentsia have been deeply involved in political affairs. The eighteenth-century poet Gavrila Derzhavin served as Minister of Justice under Alexander I. The most famous Russian poet, Alexander Pushkin, despite being occasionally exiled, came under the personal patronage of Nicholas I and was named a "Gentleman of the Chamber." The nineteenth-century playwright Alexander Griboedov was dispatched to Tehran as the Russian ambassador, where he was later beheaded by an angry mob. Moreover, the many writers who criticized the tsarist regime and were banished or imprisoned, such as Alexander Radishchev, Mikhail Lermontov, and Fyodor Dostoyevsky, helped bring about gradual social and political reforms. So too in the USSR today, the creative intelligentsia plays a role in shaping policies both as supporters and critics of the regime.

The ability of an individual or group to influence policies in the Soviet Union depends on four factors: the status or prestige of the indiviudal (or group); whether the individual (or group) seeking to influence policies is acting autonomously or as a representative of a recognized organization; the level of administration that the individual (or group) is seeking to influence; and the degree of political conflict and division within the political leadership.[40]

The higher the status of the individual or group, the greater the ability to influence policy. Thus, writers generally enjoy greater influence than ballet dancers or librarians, and nuclear physicists more than foreign-language teachers.

Many members of the creative intelligentsia have been named to prominent positions that bring them into close and frequent contact with high-ranking party and state officials. The CPSU Central Committee, elected at the Twenty-Seventh Party Congress in 1986, includes more than twelve members of the intelligentsia, including the editors of *Pravda, Kommunist,* and *Literaturnaia gazeta;* the secretary of the writers' union; several members of the Academy of Sciences as well as two scientists; and the rector of Moscow State University. Beneath the level of national politics, directors of major orchestras, museums, theaters, and libraries are powerful figures in local decision-making because they speak on behalf of highly respected institutions or groups.

The intelligentsia appears to have the greatest impact at the local level. Here, contacts with party and state officials are more likely to be informal, personal, and direct; attempts to influence the Politburo or the Minister of Culture, on the other hand, are usually indirect and formal.[41]

Finally, the more divided the political leadership, the greater the opportunity for interest groups to influence policies.[42] Even during a period of unified leadership, however, the Party must rely on the intelligentsia for its expertise in formulating cultural policies. Under Brezhnev, policy-making became more bureaucratized; the stature of the Ministry of Culture and the professional unions thus increased in the realm of cultural policy.

Today, there are numerous channels through which Soviet artists, writers, musicians, and other members of the creative intelligentsia can attempt to influence cultural policy. Most members of the intelligentsia join the Party because it affords them an opportunity to discuss important issues and affect policies. Komsomol membership is expected of virtually all students enrolling in universities, conservatories, art academies, and other institutions that train future members of the intelligentsia. For these students, the road from Komsomol member to party member is natural and easy.

The intelligentsia also has direct links to top decision-making bodies through numerous artistic and literary bureaucratic organizations, including the Ministry of Culture, the professional unions (e.g., the writers' union), the Academy of Art, the Academy of Sciences, the State Committee on Radio and Television, and the State Committee on Cinematography. Furthermore, prominent artists, writers, and other intellectuals are named to serve on standing commissions of the Supreme Soviet. During the 1960s, for example, of the thirty-one members of the Standing Committee on Foreign Affairs there were four writers—Alexander Korneichuk, Mikhail Sholokhov, Nikolai Tikhonov, and Ilia Ehrenburg. In the past twenty years, these standing commissions have become more active and less dominated by political officials.[43] Similarly, ministries have "scientific councils" that assist and advise the minister on policy matters. The "scientific council" of the Ministry of Culture includes several writers, artists, composers, playwrights, and directors. Occasionally, the council undertakes research projects and writes reports that influence the course of the ministry's policies.

Integration of the artistic, intellectual community and the political system is also enhanced by the existence of mixed career patterns in the USSR. It is not uncommon for the Party to raid the ranks of the creative intelligentsia for new blood and talent. These recruits are frequently placed in the Party's Culture Department or are assigned as cultural officers in regional and city party organizations.

Soviet political leaders have, in the past, cultivated close personal ties to many members of the creative intelligentsia. In the late 1960s, the KGB arrested Andrei Voznesensky after a reading of his protest poems at a Moscow concert hall. Within hours, however, Voznesensky was released after the personal intervention of Politburo member A. N. Shelepin.[44]

The immense popularity of some Soviet writers, poets, ballet dancers, and actors both gives them a powerful political voice and shields them from blatant repression by the authorities. The poets and balladeers Bulat Okudzhava, Evgenii Evtushchenko, and Vladimir Vysotsky attracted huge and enthusiastic followings, bordering on becoming cults. Vysotsky was hailed as the "true bard of the people." Unfortunately, like many of his fellow citizens, Vysotsky died of alcoholism at any early age. On the day of his funeral, some 30,000 people crowded into Taganka Square in front of the theater where he had so often performed.[45] Vysotsky's verse spoke of the trials of daily life in the Soviet Union. His friend, the Russian poet Bella Akhmadulina, wrote: "Their love of him is a sign of a profound weariness in our people of all the offficial gloss, a profound hunger to be told about things as they are."[46]

Finally, the creative intelligentsia can influence the course of Soviet policies through criticism and dissent. Acting as the conscience of society, the Soviet intelligentsia has become a potent political force, calling for official adherence to Soviet laws, recognition of human rights, and the relaxation of censorship. Members of the intelligentsia have also used their prestige on occasion to speak out against environmental pollution and to denounce the invasion of Afghanistan. The fact that Soviet authorities go to such lengths to silence dissident members of the intelligentsia itself suggests that their demands have weight. The next chapter examines dissent in greater detail, focusing not only on political dissent, but also on ethnic and religious dissent.

Notes

1. Sholokhov was later accused of plagiarizing the work from an author killed during the Civil War.

2. V. I. Lenin, cited in Edward J. Brown, *Proletarian Episode in Russian Literature, 1928–1932* (New York: Columbia University Press, 1953), 178–179.

3. Cited in *The Cambridge Encyclopedia of Russia and the Soviet Union* (Cambridge: Cambridge University Press, 1982), 1976.

4. Ibid.

5. Cited in Maurice Friedberg, "Cultural and Intellectual Life," in Robert F. Byrnes, ed., *After Brezhnev* (Bloomington: Indiana University Press, 1983), 283.

6. The monument stands in a cemetery near the Novodevichy Monastery. Because the cemetery became the site of numerous protest vigils by intellectuals during the 1960s and 1970s, it has been closed to the public.

7. For an analysis of the Sinyavsky-Daniel case, see John E. Turner, "Artists in Adversity: The Sinyavsky-Daniel Case," in Theodore Becker, ed., *Political Trials* (Indianapolis: Bobbs-Merrill, 1971), 107–133.

8. The author attended the exhibition, and this account is based on his observations.

9. From a conversation in Leningrad with the author, January 1976.

10. For example, see *Literaturnaia gazeta*, 18 April 1984, p. 3; *Literaturnaia gazeta*, 25 April 1984, p. 3; *Literaturnaia gazeta*, 19 September 1984, p. 6; and Z. Antonov, *Teatr*, no. 4 (1984): 20–36.

11. Friedberg, "Cultural and Intellectual Life," 276–277.

12. Darrell P. Hammer, "Inside the Ministry of Culture: Cultural Policy in the Soviet Union," in Gordon B. Smith, ed., *Public Policy and Administration in the Soviet Union* (New York: Praeger, 1980), 63.

13. Cited in John L. Scherer, ed., *USSR Facts and Figures Annual*, vol. 9, (Gulf Breeze, FL: Academic International Press, 1985), 311.

14. Western critics have noted the high degree of sophistication of theaters in the Baltic republics and Georgia. Tbilisi's Rustaveli Theater has performed Brecht in Berlin and Shakespeare in London to critical acclaim. See Irwin Weil, "A Survey of the Cultural Scene," in James Cracraft, ed., *The Soviet Union Today* (Chicago: Bulletin of the Atomic Scientists, 1983), 255.

15. Hammer, "Inside the Ministry of Culture," 62.

16. Ibid., 69.

17. The Main Directorate for the Protection of State Secrets in the Press is directly subordinate to the USSR Council of Ministers.

18. For example, Solzhenitsyn's autobiography contains vivid descriptions of his negotiations with Alexander Tvardovsky, editor of *Novy Mir*. See Aleksandr Solzhenitsyn, *The Oak and the Calf: Sketches of a Literary Life in the Soviet Union* (New York: Harper & Row, 1980).

19. Hammer, "Inside the Ministry of Culture," 70.

20. See Resolution of the CPSU Central Committee and the USSR Council of Ministers, "On Measures to Further Raise the Ideological and Artistic Level of Motion Pictures and to Strengthen the Material and Technical Base of Cinematography," *Pravda*, 6 May 1984, pp. 1–2.

21. B. Liubimov, *Pravda*, 11 July 1984, p. 3.

22. Cited in *Cambridge Encyclopedia*, 406.

23. Ibid., 407.

24. Based on figures in *Cambridge Encyclopedia*.

25. Ibid.

26. Ibid.

27. Ibid.

28. Scherer, *USSR Facts and Figures Annual*, 311.

29. Hedrick Smith, *The Russians* (New York: Ballantine Books, 1976), 474–475.

30. Ibid.

31. See *Izvestiia*, September 2, 1986, p. 3; *Pravda*, September 2, 1986, p. 1; and *Pravda*, December 19, 1986, p. 6.

32. Cited in *Cambridge Encyclopedia*, 47.

33. Ibid.

34. Scherer, *USSR Facts and Figures Annual*, 311.

35. Ibid.

36. *Cambridge Encyclopedia*, 408.

37. Ibid.

38. L. Polskaia and E. Iakovich, *Literaturnaia gazeta*, 21 March 1984, p. 8.

39. See *Pravda*, 2 November 1984, p. 3.

40. These factors are examined in greater detail in L. G. Churchward, *The Soviet Intelligentsia* (London: Routledge and Kegan Paul, 1973), 111.

41. Ibid.

42. Ibid.; and Thane Gustafson, *Reform in Soviet Politics* (Cambridge: Cambridge University Press, 1981).

43. Churchward, *The Soviet Intelligentsia*, 114–115.

44. Ibid., 122–123.

45. David K. Shipler, *Russia: Broken Idols, Solemn Dreams* (New York: Times Books, 1983), 388.

46. Cited in Ibid.

Selected Bibliography

Brown, Deming. *Soviet Russian Literature since Stalin*. Cambridge: Cambridge University Press, 1978.

Brown, Edward J. *Russian Literature since the Revolution*. rev. ed. Cambridge: Harvard University Press, 1982.

Churchward, L. G. *The Soviet Intelligentsia*. London: Routledge and Kegan Paul, 1973.

Cohen, Lewis H. *The Cultural-Political Tradition and Development of the Soviet Cinema, 1917–1972*. New York: Arno Press, 1974.

Dewhirst, Martin, and Robert Farrell. *The Soviet Censorship*. Metuchen, NJ: Scarecrow Press, 1973.

Gleason, Abbott, Peter Kenez, and Richard Stites, eds. *Bolshevik Culture: Experiment and Order in the Russian Revolution*. Bloomington: Indiana University Press, 1985.

Hammer, Darrell P. "Inside the Ministry of Culture: Cultural Policy in the Soviet Union." In Gordon B. Smith, ed. *Public Policy and Administration in the Soviet Union*. New York: Praeger, 1980, 53–78.

Johnson, Priscilla. *Khrushchev and the Arts, 1962–1964*. Cambridge: MIT Press, 1965.

Mickiewicz, Ellen P. *Media and the Russian Public*. New York: Praeger, 1981.

Schwartz, Boris. *Music and Musical Life in Soviet Russia, 1917–1970*. New York: W. W. Norton, 1973.

Sjeklocha, Paul, and Igor Mead. *Unofficial Art in the Soviet Union*. Berkeley: University of California Press, 1967.

Slonim, Marc. *Soviet Russian Literature*. 2d ed. Oxford: Oxford University Press, 1977.

Solzhenitsyn, Aleksandr. *The Oak and the Calf: Sketches of a Literary Life in the Soviet Union*. New York: Harper & Row, 1980.

13

Dissent: Political, Ethnic, and Religious

Dissent has a long and honorable tradition among the Russian intelligentsia. From the time of Alexander Radishchev in the eighteenth century to the present day, intellectuals have spoken out against the policies and practices of the regime. The tactics of dissident groups and the responses of the government, whether the tsarist regime or the Soviet, have also been remarkably consistent over the years. Radishchev, whose *Journey from St. Petersburg to Moscow* depicted the poverty of the serfs, was condemned to death, but Catherine the Great commuted the sentence to exile in Siberia. Like Radishchev, thousands of persons who have written or voiced their criticism of the Soviet regime have been imprisoned or exiled since the 1960s. Even the ghoulish practice of interning opponents in psychiatric hospitals has historical antecedents. The nineteenth-century philosopher, biologist, and leader of the Westernizers, Peter Chaadaev, was arrested, condemned as insane, and placed in an asylum. He emerged several years later to write his scathing *Apology of a Madman*. Neither are *samizdat* (self-published) tracts criticizing the regime a new development in the Soviet Union. In the mid-nineteenth century, Alexander Herzen, another Westernizer who had been forced to emigrate to the West, began publishing an underground newspaper, *The Bell*. Copies of *The Bell* were smuggled back into Russia and helped to arouse greater opposition to the tsarist regime. In 1896, Lenin was imprisoned and spent three years in exile in Siberia. Following his release, he fled to Zurich and founded the Social Democratic newspaper *Iskra* (The Spark). Trotsky also engaged in criticism from abroad. He was expelled from the Soviet Union in January 1929 and began publishing the Russian-language newspaper *Bulletin of the Opposition* from exile. The *Bulletin*, which was similar to today's *Chronicle of Current Events,* focused on abuses of power by the party leadership.

Dissidence in the USSR has emerged in the past several decades as a complex, heterogenous, and potent political force. It is not a unified movement, but a diverse assemblage of groups and individuals, embracing political opponents from a wide ideological spectrum, ethnic groups seeking greater autonomy, and religious sects demanding the right to practice their faiths free of harassment. The sole factor uniting them is that they publicly voice their opposition to policies of the Soviet government. This chapter will analyze dissent in the USSR, looking in particular at the three major forms in which it is manifested—political, ethnic, and religious dissent.

POLITICAL DISSENT

By the time of World War II, Stalin had silenced virtually all opposition within the USSR. His death in 1953 and Khrushchev's policy of de-Stalinization announced at the Twentieth Party Congress in 1956 allowed modest expressions of political dissent to reemerge. Khrushchev chose to rule by persuasion rather than by terror; consequently, he had to follow a moderate line. He began by releasing almost 10 million political prisoners and drastically limiting the number of new arrests.[1] The most notable exceptions to Khrushchev's relatively tolerant approach to political dissent occurred when he was politically most vulnerable—in the wake of the Hungarian uprising in 1956 and again just prior to his ouster in 1964. In contrast to his policy of relaxing political repression, however, Khrushchev adopted an aggressive stance against religion and religious dissent.

The Brezhnev regime also began on a conciliatory note. For almost a year after Brezhnev came to power, no leaders of dissident nationality or religious groups were arrested. Some two hundred Baptists who were in prison at the time of Khrushchev's ouster were released early. The Brezhnev regime also indicated a willingness to listen to (if not act upon) the grievances of the Crimean Tatars and other disgruntled ethnic groups.

This period of relative tolerance toward divergent political views was short-lived, however. In June 1965, the leadership permitted the KGB to resume arresting dissidents. The process began in Leningrad and continued in the Ukraine with more than thirty arrests. The crackdown culminated in September 1965 with the arrest of authors Andrei Siniavsky and Iurii Daniel in Moscow. The authors, whose books had been smuggled out of the USSR and published in the West, were charged with "anti-Soviet agitation and propaganda." The arrest and trial of Siniavsky and Daniel were a watershed in the development of dissent in the USSR. Rather than quietly mourning the loss of the two, friends and supporters undertook a petition campaign on their behalf and organized a protest demonstration in Moscow's Pushkin Square on December 5—Soviet Constitution Day.

Despite the flurry of activity, Siniavsky and Daniel were convicted and sentenced to long terms in a labor colony. Alexander Ginzburg, who compiled a transcript of the trial and had it smuggled to the West, was arrested on January 22, 1967. Vladimir Bukovsky was arrested one week later for demonstrating against Ginzburg's arrest, while Pavel Litvinov, grandson of Maxim Litvinov, Stalin's foreign minister, was threatened by the KGB for circulating a *samizdat* transcript of Bukovksy's trial. By this time, more than a thousand Soviet citizens had signed petitions against the mounting repression.[2]

The Soviet invasion of Czechoslovakia in August 1968 sparked a new wave of demonstrations and arrests. The "Prague Spring" with its slogan "Communism with a human face" had been closely watched by political dissidents in the USSR, who hoped that liberalization in Eastern Europe would lead to greater tolerance at home. When the Czech experiment was brutally crushed by Soviet tanks, Russian intellectuals reacted in anger and disillusionment. Litvinov and six others were arrested for demonstrating in Red Square against the invasion.

In the late 1960s, the embryonic dissent movement began to employ Soviet law as an instrument for promoting democratization and securing civil rights. This practice, which was advocated initially by the distinguished Soviet mathematician Alexander Esenin-Volpin, in effect put pressure on the regime to abide by its own laws. The dissident journal *The Chronicle of Current Events* was founded in 1968, in large measure, to document violations of socialist legality. Nonetheless, the authorities were undeterred. While administering a psychiatric examination to dissident Bukovsky, one psychiatrist declared: "You keep talking about the Constitution and the laws, but what normal person takes Soviet law seriously? You are living in an unreal world of your own invention; you react inadequately to the world around you."[3]

In the politically charged atmosphere of the late 1960s, two figures rose to prominence in the dissent movement—Alexander Solzhenitsyn and Andrei Sakharov. They had come to be dissidents for different reasons, and they held fundamentally opposed views of what type of government they favored. Nevertheless, they found themselves united in their opposition to the Soviet regime.

Alexander Solzhenitsyn was born in 1918 in Kislovodsk, the son of an artillery officer. He graduated from the Physics and Mathematics Faculty of Rostov University in 1941 and was drafted into the army shortly thereafter. In 1945, Solzhenitsyn was arrested in East Prussia when authorities intercepted some of his letters to friends in the USSR that contained unfavorable references to Stalin. He was tried *in absentia* and sentenced to eight years in a labor colony. After being released in 1953, he accepted a teaching post in Kazakhstan. Three years later, he moved to a village near Vladimir and then to Riazan', where he completed his novel *The First Circle*. Although Solzhenitsyn's stories and poems had appeared in official journals, it was not until 1963 that one of his novels was approved for publication. Alexander Tvardovsky, editor of the literary journal *Novy Mir*, published Solzhenitsyn's *One Day in the Life of Ivan Denisovich*, a searing account of life in a labor camp. The more open political and literary climate soon vanished, however. In 1965, the authorities ransacked the house of one of Solzhenitsyn's friends and confiscated several manuscripts and archives. In 1966, the writers' union reviewed the first part of his novel *Cancer Ward* and recommended publication; the decision was overruled at higher levels, however, and the work appeared only in *samizdat* form. By 1967, Solzhenitsyn realized that he would not be allowed to publish any more of his writing in the USSR and chose to undertake a risky strategy of public confrontation with the regime. In May 1967, in an open letter addressed to the writers' union, he denounced literary censorship and sharply criticized the union for its acquiescence to literary controls. The letter was endorsed by more than a hundred writers and members of the union. The press campaign of slander and denunciation of Solzhenitsyn intensified, but no reprisals were taken against the author directly.

Solzhenitsyn's bold and militant stand encouraged others to speak out, resulting in the birth of the modern human rights movement in the USSR. The Brezhnev leadership clearly had not anticipated these events. The KGB chief, Vladimir Semichastny, was fired in May "for causing small matters to be blown up out of proportion."[4] His successor, Iurii Andropov, followed a moderate policy initially, but as the events of the Prague Spring unfolded and reaction to the Bukovsky trial mounted, the authorities gradually tightened their grip. Solzhenitsyn was expelled from the writers' union, and the editorial board of Novy Mir was purged.

The other pillar of the dissent movement in the 1970s was Andrei Sakharov, the noted physicist and father of the Soviet hydrogen bomb. Sakharov was born in Moscow in 1921. His father was a physics teacher, and the young Sakharov followed his father's interest, graduating in physics from Moscow State University in 1942. He received his doctorate in physics in 1953. After a brief period working in a military factory, Sakharov went on to distinguish himself as a physicist; in 1948, he was selected to be a member of a research team working on the production of thermonuclear weapons. In 1953, Sakharov was elected to the USSR Academy of Sciences, and he was awarded the Order of Lenin for his work in developing the hydrogen bomb.

In 1961, during a conference attended by top atomic scientists, Sakharov passed a note to Khrushchev in which he insisted that atmospheric tests of nuclear devices were not necessary and could have harmful environmental consequences, as well as accelerate the arms race. Khrushchev publicly rebuked him for his views. During the next several years, Sakharov continued his efforts in vain to halt nuclear testing. Official disregard or public rebukes prompted Sakharov to broaden his criticisms. In 1966, along with some twenty-five other intellectuals, he signed a letter to Brezhnev warning against the rehabilitation of Stalin. The next year, Sakharov appealed to the CPSU Central Committee to dismiss the case against fellow dissidents Ginzburg and Daniel. In 1968, he circulated an essay, "Progress, Peaceful Coexistence, and Intellectual Freedom," which advocated an end to the arms race and supported détente. The addition of such a highly respected voice as Sakharov's to the growing chorus of dissidents apparently alarmed the authorities sufficiently to step up reprisals. The KGB focused particularly on those in the human rights movement who were trying to forge links between various dissident elements, including ethnic and religious groups with grievances against the regime. As a result of the publication in the West of his essay, Sakharov lost his security clearance, which was tantamount to dismissal from his research institute. With little to lose, he became an active supporter of other dissidents who had been arrested, imprisoned, and confined in psychiatric hospitals.

A third group of dissidents, represented by the twin brothers Roy and Zhores Medvedev, challenged the Soviet regime from a Marxist position. The Medvedevs, whose father was a Marxist philosopher and professor, were born in 1925. When they were just twelve years old, their father was arrested during the purges and died in the notorious Kolyma mines. Zhores Medvedev became a biologist and headed a laboratory on molecular radiobiology in Kaluga oblast'; Roy Medvedev studied philosophy at Leningrad State University. During Khrushchev's de-Stalinization campaign, their father, along with many others who had died in Stalin's prison camps, was posthumously declared innocent. Both brothers joined the Party, and Roy began to work on his monumental study of Stalinism, Let History Judge.

Before he could finish the project, however, the political climate had changed. When *Kommunist* published an article in 1969 defending Stalin, Roy wrote a letter to the editor in protest. He was then expelled from the Party. The following year, Zhores was confined to a mental institution. Roy masterminded an international campaign that eventually succeeded in persuading the authorities to release his brother. After his release, Zhores received permission to go to England to conduct research. While he was abroad, he was stripped of his citizenship. Roy eventually lost all hope of publishing *Let History Judge* in the USSR, but it appeared in the West in 1971. Despite repeated harassment by the KGB, he continues to live and work in Moscow.

While the dissent movement in the USSR had been shaped by such prominent figures as Solzhenitsyn, Sakharov, and the Medvedevs, it has also been influenced by the repression of Jewish intellectuals. Beginning in the late 1960s, harsh restrictions were imposed on Jews wishing to gain admission to the most prestigious universities and institutes. In some cities, quotas were established for the percentage of employees who could be Jews. These repressive measures sparked demands for the right to emigrate. The grievances of the Jewish population in the USSR were dramatized in 1970 by the attempted hijacking of a Soviet airliner by several Jews from Leningrad. Two of the hijackers were condemned to death, but the sentences touched off such a storm of protest in the West that their appeal was hurriedly arranged only six days later. At the Politburo's direction, their death sentences were commuted.[5]

The rising tide of militancy among Soviet Jews not only set a damaging precedent for the other disaffected groups in the eyes of party leaders, but also threatened to derail Brezhnev's newly inaugurated policy of détente. The General Secretary was fully aware of the sensitivity in the West to human rights issues, especially the question of Jewish emigration. On the eve of the Twenty-Fourth Party Congress, which was to ratify the détente policy, in early 1971, it was decided to allow Jews to emigrate to the West. Over the next decade more than one-quarter of a million Jews would emigrate.[6] Germans and Armenians fell under the provisions of the new policy and also emigrated in large numbers.

Numerous obstacles, however, made the road to the West a difficult one for Soviet citizens seeking to emigrate. Those who filed applications to emigrate with the passport office (OVIR) were usually dismissed from their jobs. Often, the loss of one's job also resulted in the loss of housing, polyclinic, and other benefits. Consequently, those applying to emigrate had to find temporary jobs as taxi drivers, janitors, doormen, or menial laborers. The period between applying for an exit visa and actually leaving the country averaged between two and three years. Many applicants, however, were denied exit visas, sometimes on the grounds that they had been stationed at secret installations during military service. Sometimes no reason whatsoever was given for an official rejection. By 1986, a total of 400,000 Soviet Jews had applied to emigrate, and an estimated 20,000 had been denied exit permits repeatedly.[7] Many of the *refuzniki*, such as Anatolii Shcharansky, vented their anger by becoming increasingly active in Jewish and dissident organizations.

For those who succeed in emigrating to the West, the problems do not cease. Distinguished Soviet scientists, engineers, lawyers, and doctors often are forced to accept low-level, low-status positions in the West.[8] They must worry about matters that they seldom concerned themselves with in the USSR—crime, finding a job, locating decent and affordable housing, and paying medical bills. Neither do the émigrés fully understand the freedom and pluralism afforded in the West. Many bring along deep-seated prejudices, dogmatism, and intolerance, making them critics not only of their former country, but of their new one as well.

Following the 1972 Nixon-Brezhnev summit, which culminated in the signing of the SALT I treaty and a trade agreement, Soviet authorities again clamped down on dissent. An education tax was imposed on all Soviet citizens seeking to emigrate. Because university education is provided free of charge in the USSR, it was reasoned that Jewish doctors, lawyers, scientists, and engineers leaving the country should have to reimburse the government for the cost of their training. For some, the "tax" was as high as 20,000 rubles, equivalent to five to ten years salary.[9] The education tax provoked much negative publicity in the West and provided the impetus in the United States for the Jackson-Vanik Amendment of 1974, which sought to link trade with the USSR to emigration.

The mid-1970s witnessed Soviet official efforts to shore up détente in the face of rising criticism in the West. Soviet authorities, under intense pressure from Secretary of State Henry Kissinger and the United States Congress, withdrew the education tax and promised to remove obstacles to emigration for Soviet Jews. Brezhnev was particularly interested in putting the best-possible face on human rights issues in advance of the Conference on Security and Cooperation in Europe, set to meet in Helsinki in the summer of 1975. In the Helsinki Final Act, the USSR pledged, among other things, to facilitate the reunification of families, to permit greater freedom of communication, to recognize political and civil rights, and to act in conformity with international commitments on human rights.

The following year, Iurii Orlov, a specialist in high-energy physics and designer of particle accelerators, formed the Helsinki Watch Group to monitor Soviet compliance with the accords on human rights. Other groups were established in Leningrad, the Ukraine, Georgia, Armenia, and the Baltic Republics. Soon after the first review of the accords were held in Belgrade, Yugoslavia, in 1977, however, Orlov, Ginzburg, Shcharansky, and several other members of the Helsinki Watch Group were arrested. In less than a year, Ginzburg was released, while Orlov was sentenced to seven years in a labor camp plus exile. Shcharansky was sentenced to thirteen years in a labor colony. In February 1986, he was exchanged for several East European spies being held in the West and emigrated to Israel.

During the 1970s, the KGB mounted several counteroffensives against the dissidents. In 1970, the Fifth Main Directorate was created. It was devoted solely to combatting dissent, an indication that the leaders viewed the phenomenon as a serious threat and one that was unlikely to dissipate soon. The following year, the KGB was instructed to close down the *Chronicle of Current Events* and through arrests and harassment managed to suspend its publication for eighteen months. In the absence of the *Chronicle*,

Solzhenitsyn and Sakharov came to personify the human rights movement and were the subjects of daily virulent denunciations in the press. Both men were so well known in the West, however, that they enjoyed a degree of immunity from the harsher treatments doled out to lesser dissidents.

In the face of mounting criticism from abroad, the regime limited somewhat the abuse of psychiatric hospitals, at least for political dissidents who were well known in the West. Leonid Pliushch, a mathematician from the Ukraine, was confined in a psychiatric hospital where he was repeatedly injected with sulfur to induce high fevers. Mathematics societies throughout the world as well as professional psychiatric associations bombarded Soviet authorities with demands for his release. The French Communist Party felt compelled to add its support. Finally, in January 1976, Pliushch was released and allowed to emigrate to Paris. Similar campaigns won the release of Valentin Moroz, Pyotr Starchik, and Vladimir Borisov, all of whom had suffered similar treatments in psychiatric institutes. No one in the West knows the exact extent of Soviet abuse of psychiatry. Bloch and Reddaway document 210 cases of dissidents being subjected to psychiatric "treatment" between 1962 and 1976.[10] Another estimate places the figure between 1,000 and 2,000.[11]

In the mid-1970s, the authorities began using another weapon against prominent dissidents—deportation. In February 1974, Solzhenitsyn and his family were forcibly expelled from the USSR, an action reminiscent of Stalin's deportation of Trotsky in 1929. The authorities had apparently been considering stripping Solzhenitsyn of his citizenship for two years but repeatedly delayed carrying out the expulsion for fear of escalating tensions with the West.[12] Solzhenitsyn had steadfastly proclaimed his desire to stay in Russia no matter what; he had even refused an offer from the authorities allowing him to go to Norway to accept the Nobel Prize for Literature in 1970 for fear he would not be allowed back into the country. The deportation of Sakharov had also been considered, but it was apparently concluded that his supporters in the West were too powerful, especially in the scientific and economic spheres, in which Brezhnev hoped to reap some advantages from détente.

A series of changes in Soviet laws in the 1970s also signaled the tougher stance on dissent. These measures increased penalties for illegal use of telephones and printing presses;[13] strengthened residency restrictions for released prisoners, making it more difficult for them to live in major cities;[14] and altered the law on citizenship to make it easier to deprive "those who defame the lofty title of citizen of the USSR" of citizenship.[15]

For his part in promoting the human rights movement in the USSR, Andrei Sakharov was awarded the Nobel Peace Prize in October 1975. Like Solzhenitsyn, he was unable to accept the award in person for fear he would not be permitted back into the USSR. His wife, Elena Bonner, accepted the award and made a presentation on his behalf.

From 1976 through 1979, the authorities indicated a willingness to trade dissidents for trade concessions or to improve the political climate in order to increase the chances of Senate ratification of the SALT II agreement. For example, dissident Bukovsky was freed and allowed to emigrate in exchange for the release of Chilean communist leader Louis Corvalan.[16]

The failure of SALT II to gain ratification in the Senate and the trade sanctions imposed by the United States and its allies in response to the Soviet invasion of Afghanistan further damaged East-West relations and worsened the situation for Soviet dissidents. With little to lose by angering the West over its treatment of dissidents, Soviet authorities mounted a new offensive. Sakharov was placed under house arrest and moved to the city of Gorky, some 300 miles southeast of Moscow. Because Gorky is strictly off limits to all foreigners, Sakharov was effectively isolated from his contacts with Western correspondents and the world. As part of a general relaxation of repression under Gorbachev, however, Sakharov was allowed to return to Moscow in December 1986.

The 1980 Moscow Olympics provided another pretext for sweeping up dissidents. In the spring of 1980, the KGB was averaging five to ten arrests per week.[17] Among those arrested on the eve of the Olympics was Anatolii Koriagin, a psychiatrist who had documented the torture of dissidents in psychiatric hospitals. He was sentenced to twelve years of imprisonment and exile. Koriagin was released in February 1987, having served seven years of his sentence.

The succession of Iurii Andropov to the post of General Secretary of the CPSU was viewed with dismay by many who had suffered under attacks from the KGB while he was its chief. Soviet dissidents recalled that he would on occasion summon critics to his office and carry on lengthy, informal, and even pleasant conversations with them. Within a matter of days, however, the same individuals would generally find themselves behind bars.

An ominous note was introduced in 1984 with the enactment of new legislation that restricted contacts between Soviet citizens and foreigners, especially foreign correspondents.[18] Andropov's strategy, which was continued by his successors, Chernenko and Gorbachev, was designed to break down the dissidents through a combination of steady pressure and isolation. This strategy seems to have succeeded, at least to a degree, in demoralizing the dissent movement.

Several generalizations can be made on the basis of this brief historical survey of dissent in the Soviet Union. First, political dissidents in the USSR hold widely divergent ideological views.[19] On occasion, as with the exchanges between Solzhenitsyn and Bukovsky, both in exile in the United States, the clash of opinions on political grounds has been heated.

On the political right, the best-known figure is Solzhenitsyn, who frankly declares that Western-style democracy is inappropriate for Russia. Instead, Solzhenitsyn appears to favor a nationalistic and authoritarian regime based on the principles of Orthodox Christianity.

The largest component of the political dissent movement is composed of those who favor liberal democratic values, especially the recognition of the civil and political rights of all citizens. Andrei Sakharov is the chief proponent of this view and is joined by many other scientists and academics, including Pliushch, Esenin-Volpin, Orlov, Shcharansky, and Litvinov.

A significant portion of dissidents in the USSR remain staunch socialists but criticize the ruling bureaucratic oligarchy for disregarding genuine Marxist forms of political participation. They also contend that free political discourse would promote, rather than hinder, the development of communism in the USSR. The authorities find these criticisms particularly disquieting and have brutally suppressed many Marxist dissidents. Chief among the opponents on the left are Roy and Zhores Medvedev, Andrei Amalrik, Ginzburg, and Bukovsky.

Whereas Poland experienced the growth of a broadly based working-class movement in the 1980s, dissent in the USSR is overwhelmingly dominated by members of the intelligentsia. This was also the case in prerevolutionary Russia. The reasons rank-and-file workers do not support dissident causes are complex. The right to strike is not recognized in Soviet labor law, and any strikes that workers have attempted have been brutally broken up. For example, when the workers in Novocherkassk mounted a protest against price increases and wage cuts in 1962, army units were called in. The strikers refused to disperse, and the troops opened fire, killing more than seventy people.[20] In 1978, Vladimir Klebanov and several other workers formed the Free Trade Union Association. Within a week, however, Klebanov was arrested and confined to a psychiatric hospital, thus avoiding an embarrassing trial. Similarly, Alexander Nikitin, a coal miner from the Ukraine, was arrested and "placed under psychiatric observation" for airing grievances to a *Washington Post* correspondent about safety violations and working conditions in the mines.

Andrei Amalrik, a Marxist critic of the Brezhnev regime, compiled a profile of some seven hundred dissidents who signed letters of protest during the trials of Alexander Ginzburg and Iurii Daniel. Amalrik's data showed that the vast majority of dissidents were well-educated members of the intelligentsia; only 6 percent were workers. (See Table 13-1.) The low level of worker involvement in the dissent movement in the USSR is explained in part by workers' low salaries; they simply cannot afford to be dismissed from their jobs. Instead of striking, workers tend to express their frustrations with the regime and with life in general through drunkenness, poor work, and frequent absences.

The evolution of dissent in the USSR demonstrates that the regime modifies its approach to the problem in response to both internal and external pressures. When a new leader emerges and is attempting to consolidate his power, there is often a respite in repression. On the other hand, when a leader is struggling to maintain his power and is being pressured

Table 13-1. Composition of Dissident Movement in the USSR (in percentages)

Occupation	Percentage
Academics, scientists, professors	45
Writers, artists, musicians	22
Engineers and technical specialists	13
Editors, teachers, doctors, lawyers	9
Workers	6
Students	5

Source: Andrei Amalrik, *Will the Soviet Union Survive Until 1984?* (New York: Harper & Row, 1970), 14.

from conservative, doctrinaire elements (as Khrushchev was in 1956 and 1963–1964), a crackdown on dissent is often undertaken. Similarly, the degree of repression of dissidents is a good barometer of East-West relations. During the period of détente, Brezhnev was reluctant to be too repressive for fear of arousing opposition in the West. When East-West tensions rose after the Soviet invasion of Afghanistan and the declaration of martial law in Poland, Soviet leaders felt no such constraints on their treatment of dissidents. These shifts and turns in official strategies for coping with dissent indicate that the leaders are sensitive to the problem and that the dissidents have managed to articulate their interests effectively.

The personal histories of Solzhenitsyn, Sakharov, the Medvedev brothers, and many other dissidents are as diverse as their political ideologies, but there is a common thread to all of them. Many dissidents had originally been fully integrated into Soviet society and only gradually came to be disillusioned, often because of official indifference to their moderate and cautious requests for redress of some injustice. For Shcharansky, it was the refusal to allow him to emigrate; for Solzhenitsyn, it was the failure of the censors to approve Cancer Ward for publication; for Sakharov, it was Khrushchev's rebuke of his concern about the environmental effects of atmospheric testing; and for Roy Medvedev, it was the refusal to publish Let History Judge. Once expelled from their unions, fired from their jobs, or publicly denounced, dissidents feel they have little more to lose by becoming outspoken critics of the regime.

In recent years, the leadership has learned from earlier cases, such as those of Solzhenitsyn and Sakharov. Now, as the first line of defense against dissent, local officials, party secretaries, and trade unions are being urged to deal promptly and judiciously with citizens' grievances.[21] The authorities obviously want to avoid creating future dissidents and prevent the formation of a large group or network demanding redress through illegitimate channels.

The second line of defense against dissent is the KGB. The secret police have demonstrated carefully graded steps to be followed in dealing with dissidents. These measures begin with cajoling and warning dissidents and escalate to threats, demotions, dismissals, searches, physical attacks, attacks on relatives and friends, formal warnings, arrest, imprisonment, exile, internment in psychiatric hospitals, and deportation. The KGB thus goes to considerable lengths to avoid arresting political dissidents since arrests create martyrs, generate undesirable publicity, and inspire even more people to speak out.

It must be acknowledged that the number of known dissidents in the USSR is small, probably not exceeding 3,000 people.[22] Furthermore, the number of dissidents may have decreased in the past decade due to emigration, deportations, and arrest. Medvedev points out that only twenty people signed petitions on behalf of Sakharov when he was exiled to Gorky, while thousands of people protested the political trials of the 1960s.[23] The number of "latent dissidents"—that is, people who sympathize with the dissidents but are not active critics of the regime—is impossible to estimate. The overwhelming majority of the Soviet population views dissidents as "spoiled" or "social misfits" who would be unhappy in any society. The dissident Alexander

Zinoviev recently observed, "The majority of the Soviet population has no use whatsoever for [Western democracy and liberalism]."[24] Jews who have applied to leave the USSR are generally ostracized and accused of trading their devotion to country for the materialistc "baubles" of capitalist society. The party leadership's intolerance toward divergent views and values in the USSR is shared (perhaps even exceeded) by the intolerance displayed by the citizens themselves.

The Gorbachev regime initiated a markedly different approach toward dissent in late 1986 and early 1987. In a series of surprise actions, more than 150 prominent dissidents were released from labor colonies and psychiatric institutions and several were allowed to emigrate to the West.[25] This more tolerant approach was designed to bolster the USSR's image internationally as well as to engender greater public support at home. These actions may also affect the growing maturity and confidence of a Soviet regime which recognizes that dissidents are a tiny proportion of the Soviet population and that by repressing them, the regime simply draws more attention to their views.

NATIONALITY POLICY AND DISSENT

The Bolsheviks inherited from the tsars a diverse multiethnic empire comprising more than a hundred distinct nationalities. Since 1903, the Bolshevik party program proclaimed the right of self-determination and national autonomy for the nationality groups that lived within the Russian Empire, but this was largely a political ploy to win greater support among disgruntled ethnic groups. The Bolsheviks considered any concessions granted to nationality groups as minor since they believed the nationality problem was a short-term one. In the long run, with the triumph of socialism, national boundaries and differences would wither away; under communism, nationalities would merge into a homogeneous culture.

The downfall of the tsarist regime, and the ensuing political chaos during the Revolution and the Civil War, permitted several nationality groups to establish independent governments. At the time of the Revolution in 1917 and the conclusion of a separate peace treaty with Germany, the Baltic nations—Latvia, Lithuania, and Estonia—were under German occupation. The peoples in these areas expressed strong anti-Russian sentiments; consequently, they were not incorporated into the Bolshevik state. Finland, which had been a largely autonomous province of the Russian Empire until the Revolution, fought and won its national independence in 1920.

Despite its earlier pledges to honor national self-determination and autonomy, the Bolshevik regime forcibly incorporated into the Soviet Republic various nationality groups that tried to assert their national independence. In 1917, for example, the Ukrainian nationalist assembly (*Rada*) established a Ukrainian People's Rebpulic and supported the Whites during the Civil War. Less than one month later, however, the Red Army seized control of the entire Ukraine, and the region was incorporated into the Soviet Republic. Numerous national governments also arose in the Caucasus, in some cases with the support of Britain, Germany, and Turkey. Soviet forces intervened in Azerbaidzhan and Armenia, however, and these regions became Soviet republics in 1920. The Georgian Menshevik government was toppled the following year.

The 1924 Constitution established the federal structure for the USSR, and each republic was granted (in theory, if not in fact) the right to conduct diplomatic relations and the right to secede. The present version of the Constitution retains these rights, but few people take them seriously.

Cultural and linguistic autonomy of nationality groups, however, does exist to a considerable extent in the USSR today. Unlike the United States, which prides itself on being a melting pot in which diverse nationalities merge to become "American," the Soviet Union has an official policy of fostering and preserving diverse nationality cultures and languages. This policy, however, inevitably produces dilemmas: How can ethnic minorities be encouraged to maintain their unique languages and cultures but still be assimilated into Soviet society in order to enjoy upward mobility? How can national self-determination be promoted without allowing parochial, ethnic identities to supersede loyalty to the USSR? How can investments be allocated to benefit the least-developed areas but at the same time maximize the benefits to the general economy? In short, how can the centrifugal forces of nationalism be reconciled with the centripetal forces of Russification and the Soviet state?

The Soviet definition of a "nation" or nationality group is the same as that promulgated by Stalin in 1913: "A nation is a historically constituted, stable community of people formed on the basis of a common language, territory, economic life, and psychological make-up, manifested in a common culture."[26]

Today, there are some 126 officially recognized nationalities in the USSR. They are usually categorized in terms of language groups.

The Slavs.   The dominant nationality groups in the USSR, accounting for some 70 percent of the total population, are Slavic nationalities (Russians, Ukrainians, and Belorussians). For the most part, they live in the European part of the USSR (west of the Urals) and are by tradition Orthodox. According to the latest census, taken in 1979, Russians constitute slightly more than half of the total population. Their proportion of the population has steadily declined since World War II, and it is expected that by the next census they will fall below the 50 percent mark. The territory that is assigned to the Russians, the Russian Soviet Federated Socialist Republic (RSFSR) stretches from the Baltic to the Pacific and encompasses 76 percent of the total area of the country. Although Russians constitute 83 percent of the population of the RSFSR, more than a hundred other nationality groups reside within the republic as well.[27]

Because of modernization and population migration over the decades, Russians now reside in significant numbers in every republic of the USSR. Only in Lithuania and the Caucasus do they constitute less than 10 percent of the population.[28] Russians outside of the RSFSR tend to live in large urban centers. Thus, more than two-thirds of all Russians living in Central Asia reside in urban areas.[29] In Alma-Ata, the capital of Kazakhstan, over 70 percent of the population is Russian and only 12 percent Kazakh.[30]

Ukrainians constitute the second-largest nationality group in the USSR.

The Ukraine, a rich agricultural region in the southwestern portion of the Soviet Union, gave rise to an ancient culture that subsequently formed the basis for Russian society. In the tenth century, Kiev dominated Moscow and other Russian principalities; through this influence, Orthodoxy was introduced into Russia. Later occupations and annexations of the Ukraine by Poland and Austria-Hungary introduced Catholicism. Partly due to its history of domination by neighboring powers, a fierce sense of national pride exists in the Ukraine. For a few, this translates into the desire for autonomy and national independence.

Belorussians, the third major Slavic nationality in the USSR, occupy the western region of the country bordering on Poland. Belorussians today are thoroughly integrated into Soviet society; marriages between Belorussians and other Slavic groups are quite common.

Western Nationality Groups. On the Western fringes of the USSR reside four non-Slavic, Western nationalities, who were incorporated into the country as a result of World War II. Three of these nationalities are often referred to collectively as the Baltic republics, although the religious, cultural, and linguistic heritages of the Latvians, Lithuanians, and Estonians are quite distinct. The Estonians are closely related to the Finns and are predominantly Lutheran. The Estonian language is part of the Finno-Ugric family of languages that also includes Finnish, Magyar (Hungarian), and Mongolian. In medieval times, the capital of the Estonian Republic, Tallinn, was a member of the Hanseatic League. Thus, the Estonians have always been more oriented toward Scandinavian and Germanic culture than to that of the Slavic regions to the east.

In modern history, the Estonians have displayed the lowest rate of population growth of the major nationalities in the Soviet Union. At the same time, the region's high standard of living (the highest in the USSR) has attracted large numbers of Slavic immigrants. As a result, the percentage of Estonians in the republic is declining rapidly, and this has led to some expressions of concern by the native population.

The Latvian and Lithuanian languages belong to the Baltic group of Indo-European languages. Latvia is predominantly Lutheran, while Lithuania is overwhelmingly Catholic. Immigration has also adversely affected Latvia, but is less of a problem in Lithuania, the least urbanized of the three republics, because Slavic immigrants prefer to resettle in urban areas.

The fourth Western nationality group, the Moldavians, occupy a small mountainous region that was annexed into the USSR during the Soviet military occupation of Romania in 1940. Of the various nationalities in the Soviet Union, it is the most artificial; the Moldavians are linguistically, culturally, and historically indistinguishable from Romanians, and the Moldavian republic was created solely to justify Soviet annexation of the region.

The Caucasian Peoples. The Caucasus region comprises the Georgian, Armenian, and Azerbaidzhan republics. Their cultures have origins in prehistory. Armenia, which borders on Turkey, once had an empire that stretched from the Mediterranean to the Caucasus. The national symbol of Armenia, Mount Ararat (thought to be the site of the landing of Noah's Ark), is now located in Turkey, although it is visible from the Armenian capital, Yerevan. The Armenian Apostolic church embodies Armenian nationalism and attracts a large and powerful following among Armenians both inside and outside the USSR. The Georgian Orthodox church, while less of a nationalistic rallying symbol, has its own patriarch and is independent of the Russian Orthodox church in Moscow.

The Armenians have demonstrated a high propensity for assimilation and upward mobility in Soviet society; together with the neighboring Georgians, they enjoy the highest levels of education in the USSR. Unlike the Georgians, however, one-third of the Armenians have migrated to other areas of the country; they also have the highest rate of intermarriage of any of the fifteen major nationalities.[31]

The third Caucasian group, the Azerbaidzhanis, are Islamic, and their language is Turkic. The capital of the Azerbaidzhan SSR is Baku, a city whose industry centers around the oil fields of the Caspian Basin.

Central Asian Nationalities. Soviet Central Asia is comprised of five republics—the Turkmen, Kirghiz, Uzbek, Kazakh, and Tadzhik republics. With the exception of the Tadzhik, these nationality groups speak Turkic languages. (Tadzhik was derived from Persian.) All of the Central Asian nationalities are Muslim, and some of the most cherished mosques in the Islamic world are located in the ancient cities of Samarkand and Bukhara. The Central Asian peoples exhibit very high birthrates and retain family and cultural traditions. Consequently, they are the least assimilated into Soviet society. Many Central Asians in urban areas speak Russian, work in technical and professional jobs, and have adopted a modern, Russian standard of living; in their homes, however, native dietary and religious practices, as well as traditional family relations, persist.

Other Territorial Nationality Groups. The remaining territorially based nationality groups in the USSR are extremely diverse. They include the Buriats and Kalmyks, whose languages and cultures are Mongolian and whose religious practices are either Buddhist or Shamanist; the Iakuts, a seminomadic people living in the far north of Siberia; the Chukchi, who are similar to the American Eskimos; the Turkic-speaking Tatars, who are clustered in the Tatar Autonomous Republic 500 miles east of Moscow; the Komi, who live off their reindeer herds like the Lapps of Scandinavia; and the Karelians, Finns who occupy a region taken over by the Soviets during the "Winter War" of 1939–1940. The ethnic groups below the level of the fifteen major nationalities are accorded varying levels of regional representation and autonomy, generally in accordance to their size and level of development. These ethnic groups range in size from several million to just one or two hundred.

Nonterritorial Nationality Groups. A persistent problem in the USSR is how to cope with nationality groups that are not concentrated in a single region. Groups such as the Germans, Poles, and Jews reside throughout the European portion of the USSR. Granting these groups the right of autonomy and self-determination is thus impossible. In rural areas in which Poles and Germans are sufficiently populous, Soviet authorities allow a few schools to operate using those languages; newspapers and books appear in both German and Polish in these regions. The majority of the 1.8 million Jews in the USSR live in large urban centers in the European portion of the country. Linguistically, the Jews have been fully assimilated into Russian society for more than 150 years. The demand for Hebrew or Yiddish schools and publications today is extremely limited. In order to grant some degree of autonomy and self-determination to the Jews, Stalin created the Jewish Autonomous Region in a desolate area on the Chinese border, some 4,000 miles from Moscow. In Birobidzhan, the capital of the region, there are some Yiddish schools and a thriving Yiddish theater, but few European Jews have been enticed to settle in the area. Rather than seeking the right to a separate cultural identity, Soviet Jews have clashed with the regime over educational quotas and job restrictions that have barred Jews from becoming further integrated into the society. For some Jews, however, the systematic discrimination has renewed a sense of Jewish consciousness.

Soviet nationality policy is frequently torn between the dual goals of promoting economic growth for the country as a whole and fostering greater economic equality among the diverse nationality groups in the USSR. At times, the regime has allocated resources to favor the least-developed regions; at other times, it has invested resources strictly on the basis of economic efficiency. In the realm of social policy, however, the regime remains committed to eliminating class and ethnic divisions and continues to support national self-determination.

National self-determination and autonomy today apply primarily to language rights. Article 36 of the Constitution states: "Citizens of the USSR of different races and nationalities have equal rights. Exercise of these rights is ensured by a policy of all-round development and drawing together of all the nations and nationalities of the USSR, by educating citizens in the spirit of Soviet patriotism and socialist internationalism, and by the possibility of using their native language and the languages of other peoples of the USSR."[32] In the various republics, nationality regions, and territories, newspapers, books, and cultural performances use indigenous languages. Primary and secondary schools provide instruction in native languages as well as in Russian. Courses at the universities, however, with the exception of those in the Ukraine, Georgia, and Latvia, are taught in Russian, and fluency in Russian is necessary for upward mobility in most career fields. While governmental bodies at all levels function bilingually (in Russian and in the indigenous language), the official language of the CPSU, the security organs, and the military is exclusively Russian.

Evidence of the persistence of linguistic diversity in the Soviet Union is impressive. Almost 94 percent of all Soviet citizens use their native language as their primary language.[33] At the same time, more than three-fourths of the non-Russian population speak Russian fluently.[34] Experts disagree as to the long-term prospects for bilingualism in the USSR. The French scholar Hélène Carrère d'Encausse considers the adoption of Russian a temporary phase in a larger movement toward the elimination of ethnic identities.[35] The British linguist E. G. Lewis sees bilingualism as a stable and enduring feature of Soviet society.[36]

The official policy of the regime does not envisage the elimination of national languages, but it does emphasize bilingualism and word-borrowing among all of the languages in the Soviet Union. Recently, however, there has been a renewed emphasis on promoting the use of Russian in non-Russian areas. Conferences in Baku in 1981 and Riga in 1982 called for greater use of Russian language in schools and more publications in Russian. Since 1976, authorities in some areas have been restricting the circulation of non-Russian newspapers and magazines.[37]

Soviet authorities distinguish between the "drawing together" (*sblizhenie*) of nationalities and the "merger" (*sliianie*) of nationalities. The former implies the retention of national identities but the narrowing of social and economic differences among ethnic groups and the prevention of outbursts of national sentiment.[38] Merger refers to the elimination of all national differences and the assimilation of all nationalities into a uniform culture. Khrushchev resurrected the notion of the merging of nationalities in the 1961 Party Program; subsequent leaders, however, have adopted the much more cautious "drawing together" approach. Brezhnev once candidly observed, "Nationality relations, even in a society of mature socialism, are a reality that is constantly developing and raising new problems and tasks."[39]

Soviet nationality policies have also tended to heighten regional competition for resources. Since the 1930s, tremendous amounts of resources have been poured into Central Asia and other less-developed regions of the USSR. In part, these investments have been dictated by national economic priorities; they also have been motivated by the desire to create a uniform standard of living throughout the country and in response to a vigorous lobbying effort by Central Asian leaders. In recent years, however, investment capital has become increasingly scarce and the competition for resources more acute. In the Baltic republics, Leningrad, Moscow, Kiev, and other well-developed areas of the USSR, local officials argue (with ample justification) that they have not been receiving their fair share of the state budget, but instead have been forced to pay (with reduced allocations) for development projects in Central Asia and Siberia.

Preferential treatment has also stirred some controversy within the ranks of the CPSU. Numerous articles by party officials have appeared stressing the importance of a nondiscriminatory cadre policy.[40] A party secretary in Tashkent may well be transferred to Moldavia or Moscow and, thus, must be able to function effectively outside his or her native republic. Being Uzbek, in and of itself, should not be a ticket for easy admission into the Party, they argue. The authors of such articles are invariably Slavic, and one suspects from their plaintive tone that there is an undercurrent of resentment against the Party's efforts to recruit non-Slavic elites into party posts.

The potential emergence of Russian nationalism in the 1970s was indicated by the leadership's frequent references to the concept of a *Soviet* people (*Sovetskii narod*). With developed socialism, it is believed, narrow ethnic and national identities will diminish and be replaced by a single, uniform, *Soviet* culture based on:

1. a common territory (USSR)
2. a single ideology (Marxism-Leninism)
3. a single, unified political party (CPSU)
4. a common goal (building communism)
5. a single, planned economic system
6. harmonious relations among all classes
7. proletarian internationalism

Efforts to foster such an all-encompassing Soviet nationality, however, have often amounted simply to Russification. In 1978, the drafts of the new constitutions for the union republics were circulated for public discussion and criticism. Minority nationalities quickly pointed out that the new versions of the constitutions dropped the guarantees that the official language of each republic would be the language of the indigenous people. After several months of heated discussion, these provisions were reinserted in the constitutions. An official announcement proclaimed that it was not the intent of the party leadership to undermine the languages of the national republics; rather, it had simply been assumed that the official language of each republic would be that of the native population.[41]

Concerns of incipient Russian nationalism were again raised in June 1985 when Gorbachev, speaking to a group of citizens in the Ukrainian capital of Kiev, twice slipped and referred to the Soviet Union as "Russia." After apparently realizing his mistake, Gorbachev offered the clumsy explanation that "Russia" and "the Soviet Union" are now synonymous. Perhaps this was merely a slip of the tongue, but it is surprising that Moscow television broadcast the General Secretary's remarks unedited on the major evening news program *Vremia*.[42]

Concerns have also been raised in Central Asia over the appointment of a Russian as first secretary of the Tashkent city party organization. In virtually all non-Russian republics, it has been a longstanding practice to elect a native as the head of the party committee in the capital city. Not since 1955 has a non-Uzbek served in this post.

In December 1986, the removal of D. A. Kunaev as first secretary of Kazakhstan and his replacement with a Russian sparked widespread riots in the republic capital, Alma-Ata. According to Soviet accounts, several hundred students burned cars and set fire to a foodstore.[43] The episode illustrated not only the Gorbachev regime's commitment to openness or *glastnost'*, but more importantly the volatile state of ethnic relations, especially in Central Asia.

Russification is a major source of nationality dissent, especially in those areas where the influx of Russian immigrants and the low birthrate of the indigenous population combine to raise fears of the loss of national identity. These conditions exist particularly in the Baltic states. In Lithuania, a movement has been formed fusing Lithuanian nationalism and Catholicism, much as has occurred in Poland. The much more decentralized structure of the Lutheran church in Estonia and Latvia prohibits the formation of comparable movements in those republics. Protests against Russification in Estonia and Latvia center primarily around the designation of languages for schools. As more Russians move into these republics, there is a greater demand for Russian-language schools. When local officials have attempted to change a school's language from Estonian or Latvian to Russian, however, a storm of protest has often ensued.[44]

In the Ukraine, strong dissident and nationalistic sentiments have existed for centuries. Under the tsars as well as today, many Ukrainians have longed for national independence and sovereignty. Soviet authorities have dealt harshly with Ukrainian nationalism, reducing the extent of Ukrainian language usage in schools and universities in the republic and allowing many monuments of Ukrainian culture to be neglected or destroyed. In 1965 and again in 1972, there were widespread arrests of Ukrainian writers and historians who were attempting to preserve the Ukrainian cultural heritage. The arrests in 1972 succeeded in terminating publication of the *Ukrainian Herald,* the Ukrainian counterpart of the *Chronicle of Current Events.*

The cause of Ukrainian nationalism has been promoted in recent years by the death under mysterious circumstances of a young Ukrainian poet, Volodymyr Ivasyuk. The twenty-five-year-old poet and composer was immensely popular for his arrangements of Ukrainian folk songs. In 1979, he was asked to compose an oratorio marking the fortieth anniversary of the "reunification" of the Ukraine under Soviet rule after the defeat of Hitler. Ivasyuk refused. A few days later, he was found hanging from a tree; the authorities claimed it was a suicide. More than 10,000 people attended Ivasyuk's funeral. Two of the prominent organizers of the funeral and members of the Ukrainian Helsinki Watch Group—Petro Sichko and his son Vasyl—were arrested after the funeral, convicted of "anti-Soviet slander," and sentenced to three years in a labor camp.[45]

In Central Asia and other regions of the USSR, economic development has worked against the emergence of nationalistic resentments and dissent. What dissent does exist in Central Asia usually centers around religious persecution.

The repressive acts of Soviet authorities, whether in restricting the activities of the Catholic church in Lithuania or in silencing nationalistic sentiments in the Ukraine, often generate even more dissent. Two of the most ardent dissident nationality groups in the USSR are the Crimean Tatars and the Volga Germans. These groups were accused of collaboration with the Germans during World War II and were forcibly deported en masse to a desolate region in Central Asia. More than 200,000 Crimean Tatars (mostly women and children) were transported some 2,000 miles in closed trucks and cattle cars with little food or water. Almost half of the people died during the journey.[46] Despite the fact that they were officially exonerated in 1967, they have not been allowed to relocate to their native region in Crimea.

While the plight of Soviet Jews and the Crimean Tatars is well known in the West, they are relatively isolated cases. The major points of friction today between the Soviet government and non-Russian ethnic groups are not, for the most part, over the right to emigrate, but over demands for more regional autonomy, curbs on Slavic migrations, use of native language, and claims on investment funds.[47] Just as economic problems in the USSR seem to represent gnawing structural deficiencies rather than point to catastrophic collapse, nationalistic sentiments may continue to be expressed without necessarily signaling the disintegration of the Soviet system.

RELIGION AND RELIGIOUS DISSENT

From its inception in 1917, the Bolshevik regime has been hostile toward religion. The Russian Orthodox church was closely allied to the tsarist government, and the clergy actively opposed the Bolsheviks after the Revolution. Marx and Lenin both denounced religion as "the opium of the people," numbing them to social injustices and undermining the cause of revolution.[48] Religion represents a belief system that is at odds with official Marxist-Leninist ideology.

In practice, Soviet policies toward religion have vacillated between extreme hostility and reluctant tolerance. This vacillation reflects a lack of consensus within the leadership on what to do about religion and religious believers. Policies have also fluctuated in relation to the stability and degree of authority of the regime. In 1917, the Bolsheviks nationalized all church property. The following year, the separation of church and state became law; religious schools were taken over by the State. During the Civil War, the Church supported the Whites, and many clergy were arrested as counterrevolutionaries.

During NEP, the persecution of the Church lessened. The regime recognized the right of citizens to espouse religious beliefs, but it also guaranteed the right of citizens to conduct antireligious propaganda. The League of the Militant Godless was formed in 1920 to organize atheistic propaganda. A compromise was reached during NEP, under which the Russian Orthodox church would declare its loyalty to the Soviet government and refrain from intruding into political matters in exchange for greater religious tolerance and recognition by the State.

Shortly after Stalin's consolidation of power, however, stringent new controls were introduced. A Council of Religious Affairs was established, and all religious groups were required to be registered. Unregistered groups were considered illegal and subject to arrest. Thousands of churches, synagogues, and mosques were closed and the buildings put to "public use" as offices, warehouses, and even grain-storage facilities.

The Russian Orthodox clergy were decimated during the purges; by 1941, tens of thousands of priests and several million believers had been arrested.[49] With the outbreak of World War II, however, Stalin relaxed his stance toward the Church. The Russian Orthodox church, as a bastion of Russian nationalism, was allowed more freedom in order to mobilize the citizens in support of the war effort. Priests were asked to bless the troops as they left for the front and offer prayers for the defense of "Holy Russia." By the end of the war, more than 18,000 Orthodox parishes had been reconstituted and seminaries and monasteries reopened.[50] The wartime relaxation of policies toward religion also benefited other denominations, including Evangelical Christians, Baptists, the Georgian Orthodox, and the Armenian church, but it did not extend to the Jews and the Ukrainian Uniates.

From 1959 to 1964, the Khrushchev regime mounted a virulent antireligious campaign, with the officially stated goal of abolishing all religion in the USSR by 1980. More than half of the remaining churches and seminaries were closed, and restrictions on church activities even harsher than those of Stalin were introduced.[51] Executive committees were established to manage church affairs, relegating the clergy to strictly liturgical matters. Invariably, the executive committees were staffed by atheists and party members in order to undermine religious institutions from within.

The Brezhnev regime restored the uneasy coexistence with religious groups, while continuing to conduct antireligious propaganda. In 1975, the

Law on Religious Associations was liberalized slightly. By the early 1980s, however, new restrictions were being drafted and implemented by Andropov. Symbolic of the crackdown, a new abbot was named to the Caves Monastery near Pskov, and he subsequently cooperated in efforts by the KGB to curtail pilgrimages to the monastery.[52] Similar pressures have been applied to the monastery in Zagorsk.

Despite the past policies and practices of the regime, there are today in the USSR substantial numbers of religious believers—by some estimates, they constitute as much as one-half of the Soviet population.[53] The Russian Orthodox church claims more than 50 million members, organized into eighty dioceses. Currently, however, there are fewer than 7,000 "working" churches and 6,500 clergy, compared to more than 54,000 churches and 51,000 clergy in 1917.[54] The number of seminaries has declined from fifty-seven to three, while only six monasteries and ten convents are permitted to operate, compared to more than one thousand before the Revolution.[55] The Church does not have its own printing presses but must have its printing done by state-run publishing houses; all publications are subject to strict censorship.

The Partriarchate, located in Moscow, is supervised by the Council for Religious Affairs, a ministerial-level organization charged with keeping religious groups under control. In exchange for relaxed restrictions on the Church, the Patriarchate has on several occasions been called on to support Soviet foreign policy goals. Thus, the Church publicly denounced the Vietnam War and is on record as supporting national liberation movements in the Third World as well as the Soviet involvement in Afghanistan.

The Georgian Orthodox church commands the following of an estimated 3 million people, while the Armenian church claims another 2.1 million adherents inside the USSR.[56] The Armenian church enjoys the greatest degree of freedom of any religious institution in the Soviet Union, in part, because of the large and influential community of Armenians outside the USSR. Unlike any other church in the Soviet Union, the Armenian church operates its own printing presses.

There are some 4 million Roman Catholics in the USSR, located primarily in Lithuania and on the borders of Poland. Although the Catholic church attracts three-quarters of all Lithuanians, the authorities have restricted the number of priests, and only one seminary is still in operation there.[57]

Some 600,000 Lutherans reside in Latvia, Estonia, and Karelia, on the Finnish border.[58] Scattered throughout the USSR are Baptists, Evangelical Christians, and Pentecostals, who total more than one million.[59] There are also small congregations of Seventh-Day Adventists, Methodists, and the Reformed churches.

After the Russian Orthodox church, the largest group of believers are Muslim, totaling an estimated 45 million. The majority of Soviet Muslims are of the Sunni rite, although some Shiite Muslims reside in the Azerbaidzhan Republic on the northwestern border of Iran. Only 400 mosques are in operation today, compared to more than 26,000 in 1917.[60] The number of mullahs has declined from 45,000 to fewer than 2,000.[61] In recent years, the Soviet authorities have informally agreed to limit overt persecution of Muslims; in return, the Muslim leaders are to refrain from intruding into political affairs. Nevertheless, Muslim women have been encouraged to receive advanced educations and discouraged from wearing the chador (veil), while customs such as the bride price and self-flagellation are considered violations of Soviet law and are absolutely prohibited. In addition to the officially recognized Muslim groups, there exist "unofficial" Islamic sects, such as the highly disciplined and clandestine Sufi brotherhoods, whose antisecular views are considered fantical and anti-Soviet by the authorities.

Some 1.8 million Jews still reside in the USSR, but in the official view they are considered (with some justification) a nationality group more than a religious group. Only 1 to 3 percent are practicing Jews.[62] Some fifty synagogues still operate in the USSR and are served by a handful of trained rabbis, while Jewish literature is scarce to nonexistent.[63]

Soviet Jews have suffered periodically from state-supported anti-Semitism. The emigration movement of the 1970s, however, fostered greater identification of Jewishness among the population. The curtailment of emigration in the 1980s has also forged closer links among members of the Jewish community and focused their frustrations. So far, however, the new-found solidarity within the Jewish community has not translated itself into greater involvement in religious activities.

On the border of Mongolia and China, there are more than 400,000 Buddhists, primarily Buriats by nationality. Buddhists in the USSR tend to inhabit remote regions and sensitive areas that are strictly off-limits to foreigners, so little is known about the status of religious practice among them today.

In addition to these religious groups and denominations, several unregistered "illegal" religious groups struggle to survive in the Soviet Union. The largest unregistered group is represented by the Council of Churches of Evangelical Christians and Baptists (a rival organization to the officially sanctioned All-Union Council of Evangelical Christians and Baptists). "Illegal" Baptist churches are thought to claim 100,000 members and operate several underground printing presses that produce Bibles in numerous languages, as well as other devotional literature. The Jehovah's Witnesses have been declared illegal, presumably because of their ardent anticommunist stance, prodigious evangelistic activity, and refusal to recognize aspects of the secular state. The Ukrainian Uniates, who are Catholic but follow the Eastern rite, are declared illegal because of their support of Ukrainian nationalism. Finally, the True Believers, an Orthodox sect living in Siberia, have come into conflict with the regime because they do not recognize the legitimacy of secular government. Consequently, they refuse to swear allegiance to the USSR, to register their churches, and to be conscripted into military service.

Soviet officials today acknowledge that religious belief and practice continue to exist, although they usually portray religious communities as being enfeebled and dominated by old, superstitious grandmothers (babushki). Many of the current restrictions on religious practice appear to focus on preventing the propagation of religious faith among the young. Baptism is discouraged, and religious instruction outside the home is illegal. Similarly, the use of children under eighteen years of age in religious ceremonies is prohibited. Nevertheless, many religious practices persist, and not only among the elderly. Approximately one-half of all marriages are performed in religious ceremonies (a civil service is also required to make such marriages legal).[64] According to one report in the Gorky region, 60 percent of all babies are baptized; in Armenia, the figure exceeds 70 percent.[65]

Open religious activity, while legal, is not advisable for those seeking admission to a university or career advancement. Not surprisingly, then, the majority of people who regularly attend church services are elderly. For every generation of elderly believers that dies, however, there appears to be a new generation that replaces them.

The regime has tried to curtail the appeal of religious institutions by not allowing them to grow and change in relation to the needs of society. No periodicals exist in which theological issues can be raised and debated. Consequently, the Russian Orthodox church's liturgy has not changed appreciably since the Revolution. During the 1970s, some Russian youth criticized the Church for being out of touch and experimented with their own services in private apartments. In the 1980s, there has been an upsurge of interest in religion, especially among the educated classes and the youth, who are searching for the roots of Russian national culture and a non-Marxist system of ethics.

The 1977 Constitution recognizes the right of Soviet citizens to practice their religious beliefs, but it also grants citizens the right to conduct atheistic propaganda. Antireligious campaigns, conducted regularly, mobilize the Komsomol, educators, and the trade unions for support. Courses in "scientific atheism" are required at all levels of schooling, from elementary through the university. Some of the country's most famous churches, including the imposing Kazan Cathedral in downtown Leningrad, have been turned into museums of atheism and the history of religion.

On Easter Sunday, the few "working" churches in the USSR are thronged with worshippers wishing to participate in or observe services. This presents the KGB with a difficult task. In 1976, the author attended Easter services at St. Nikola Church in Leningrad and witnessed firsthand the KGB's attempts to discourage religious practice. The authorities, assisted by red arm-banded *druzhiniki* (voluntary militia), encircled the church and refused to admit anyone without an official invitation. Apparently, the church leaders had agreed to this scheme, which involved turning over to the KGB a list of all regular members of the congregation. When the author produced an American passport and asked to be allowed through the phalanx of secret police at the front gate, a plainclothes officer, obviously embarrassed, rationalized the police measures as necessary in order to guarantee space for regular church members. Nevertheless, the officer gladly allowed the author through so that he could see "how we live up to our laws on religious freedom." In other churches, the KGB adopts the opposite tactic, packing churches with officers and party *aktiv*, leaving no room for worshippers. The presence of police and KBG at St. Nikola did not, however, seem to deter several teenagers on motorcycles, who rode a circuit around the cathedral, revving their engines to deafening levels in order to disrupt the services.

The size of a religious denomination in the USSR does not appear to account for its involvement in dissident activities. Although they constitute less than 1 percent of all believers, Baptists make up almost half of all religious dissidents.[66] Similarly, Catholics represent only 3 percent of all believers, but they have been active and outspoken critics of the regime. Since 1972, one-half of all the Catholic priests and more than 200,000 parishioners have signed petitions against restrictions imposed on the Church in Lithuania.[67] Jews also represent a tiny segment of the Soviet population but have enjoyed a disproportionate degree of influence through dissent and emigration. For the most part, however, Jewish dissidents raise grievances over violations of their civil rights, rather than over religious repression.

The proportion of Russian Orthodox dissidents is quite small, and dissent is actively discouraged by the Church hierarchy. The Moscow Patriarchate has been reluctant to become involved in individual cases involving religious dissidents; its subservience to the Party has been bitterly criticized by numerous members of the human rights movement.

Political, ethnic, and religious dissent in the USSR are not mutually exclusive; rather, they are often mutually reinforcing. In Lithuania, Armenia, Georgia, and Central Asia, it is virtually impossible to separate ethnic elements from religious elements. The rise of the human rights movement in the 1970s encompassed all three groups. The denial of civil rights to certain ethnic and religious groups, such as the Jews, has heightened their sense of national and religious solidarity. The specter of a unified dissent movement including disaffected intellectuals, nationality groups, and religious believers is a threat the leadership takes seriously. In order to combat this threat, the regime has adopted a multifaceted, integrated approach that includes both preemptive and punitive measures.

Soviet authorities attempt to minimize dissent of all kinds by anticipating problems and eliminating them before they become major points of dissension. Economic development in Central Asia and antireligious education are two examples of the regime's attempt to anticipate and nullify potentially explosive sentiments.

The regime allows a limited degree of political, ethnic, and religious self-expression as a "pressure valve." This policy also permits the Soviet government to proclaim its recognition of civil, ethnic, and religious rights in propaganda disseminated both inside and outside the country.

The regime also attempts to co-opt political, ethnic, and religious leaders and institutions in order to undercut potential opposition. The recruitment of minority nationalities into the Party, the offer to the Ukrainian poet Ivasyuk to compose a major work commemorating the defeat of Nazi Germany, the awarding of the Red Banner of Labor to Russian Orthodox Patriarch Pimen, the tacit agreement to restrict persecution of the Russian Orthodox church in exchange for the nomination of compliant bishops and abbots to critical posts, all have a common element—they attempt to foster greater control via co-optation.

When all of these preemptive strategies fail, the regime applies more punitive sanctions—arrests, imprisonment, exile, and psychiatric treatment. Even these measures have an important deterrent character. They isolate dissidents from their supporters in order to preclude the formation of dissident networks that could pose a significant challenge to the authorities.

Punishment of dissidents also sets an example for others and may have some deterrent value in the eyes of Soviet officials.

Chapter 2 of this book noted the recurring cycle of repression and dissent in eighteenth- and nineteenth-century Russia, which culminated in the Revolution of 1917. On a much more limited scale, a similar pattern is discernible in the Soviet response to dissent in the past several decades. The persecution of prominent dissidents in the USSR—whether political critics, nationalists, or religious leaders—has more often than not fostered increased dissent, rather than silenced the opponents of the regime. Dissent, in all its forms and manifestations, has been a remarkably constant feature in Russian and Soviet politics; like religion and nationalism, it is not likely to wither away soon. On the contrary, religious faith and nationalistic sentiments may well prove more enduring and attract more ardent supporters in the decades ahead than Marxist-Leninist ideology.

Notes

1. Cited in Peter Reddaway, "Policy towards Dissent since Khrushchev," in T. H. Rigby et al., eds. *Authority, Power, and Policy in the USSR* (London: Macmillan, 1980), 161.

2. Cited in Joshua Rubenstein, "Dissent," in James Cracraft, ed., *The Soviet Union Today* (Chicago: Bulletin of the Atomic Scientists, 1983), 66.

3. Ibid.

4. *Politicheskii dnevnik* I: 243.

5. Reddaway argues that the decision to commute the sentences was made by the Politburo, "Policy towards Dissent since Khrushchev," 170.

6. Robert O. Freedman, *Soviet Jewry in the Decisive Decade, 1971–1980* (Durham, NC: Duke University Press, 1984).

7. Reported in *The Japan Times*, 4 January 1986, p. 4.

8. See Theodore Friedgut, "The Welcome Home: Absorption of Soviet Jews in Israel"; and Zvi Gitelman, "Soviet-Jewish Immigrants to the United States: Profile, Problems, Prospects," in Freedman, *Soviet Jewry in the Decisive Decade, 1971–1980*, 68–78, 89–98.

9. Cited in Reddaway, "Policy towards Dissent since Khrushchev," 174.

10. Sidney Bloch and Peter Reddaway, *Psychiatric Terror: How Soviet Psychiatry Is Used to Suppress Dissent* (New York: Basic Books, 1977), 258.

11. Harvey Fireside, "Psychiatry and the Soviet State," *Problems of Communism* (July–August 1981): 58.

12. Andrei D. Sakharov, *Sakharov Speaks* (New York: Alfred Knopf, 1974), 165–230.

13. *Chronicle of Current Events* 27: October 15, 1972, 337–338; and *Vedomosti Verkhovnogo Soveta i Pravitel'stva Estonskoi SSR* (1977), no. 37, resolution 436.

14. See the *Chronicle of Current Events* 34 (1974): 92–93, for a discussion of the revised Article 190–1 of the Criminal Procedure Code.

15. See George Ginsburgs, "The New Soviet Citizenship Law and the Universal Declaration of Human Rights," in *A Chronicle of Human Rights in the USSR* (1979), no. 33, pp. 47–54.

16. Freedman, *Soviet Jewry*, 50.

17. Cited in Rubenstein, "Dissent," 70.

18. See Radio Liberty Research Bulletin, no. 31 (August 1, 1984). Specifically, the law makes it a criminal offense to pass unauthorized information to foreigners.

19. For two classifications of Soviet dissidents by political ideologies, see Rudolf L. Tokes, *Dissent in the USSR* (Baltimore: The Johns Hopkins University Press, 1975), 13; and Andrei Amalrik, *Will the Soviet Union Survive until 1984?* (New York: Harper & Row, 1970), 37.

20. Rubenstein, "Dissent," 69.

21. Reddaway, "Policy towards Dissent since Khrushchev," 160–161.

22. The *Biographical Dictionary of Dissidents in the Soviet Union, 1956–1975,* compiled by S. P. de Boer, E. J. Driessen, and H. L. Verhaar (Dordrecht, the Netherlands: Martinus Nijhoff, 1982). Contains some 3,400 dissidents.

23. Roy Medvedev, *On Soviet Dissent* (New York: Columbia University Press, 1980), 147.

24. Ibid., 123.

25. Bill Keller, "Moscow Resolves a Dissident Case; Delay in Another," *New York Times,* February 18, 1987, p. 1.

26. J. V. Stalin, "Marxism and the National Question," in *Collected Words,* vol. 2 (Moscow: Politizdat, 1952–1955), 307.

27. Based on 1979 census data cited in Peter Zwick, "Soviet Nationality Policy: Social, Economic, and Political Aspects," in Gordon B. Smith, ed. *Public Policy and Administration in the Soviet Union* (New York: Praeger, 1980), 153.

28. Ibid.

29. Cited in Robert A. Lewis et al., *Nationality and Population Change in Russia and the USSR* (New York: Praeger, 1976), 147.

30. Cited in Zev Katz et al., eds., *Handbook of Major Soviet Nationalities* (New York: The Free Press, 1975), 11.

31. 1979 census data from Zwick, "Soviet Nationality Policy," p. 153.

32. Constitution of the USSR (1977), Article 36.

33. Cited in Peter Rutland, "The Nationality Problem and the Soviet State," in Neil Harding, ed., *The State in Socialist Society* (London: Macmillan, 1984), 164.

34. Ibid.

35. Hélène Carrère d'Encausse, *The Decline of an Empire* (New York: Newsweek Books, 1979), 192–193.

36. E. G. Lewis, *Multilingualism in the Soviet Union* (Elmsford, NY: Mouton Publishers, 1972).

37. See Ann Sheehy, "Call for More Education and Publication in Russian in Non-Russian Republics," Radio Liberty Research Bulletin, no. 121 (April 17, 1985): 2. For a recent campaign for Russian-language use in Estonia, see *Sovetskaia Estonia,* 26 February 1985.

38. This definition comes from Peter Zwick, "Soviet Nationality Policy: Social, Economic, and Political Aspects," in Gordon B. Smith, ed., *Public Policy and Administration in the Soviet Union* (New York: Praeger, 1980), 144.

39. L. I. Brezhnev, *Pravda,* 22 December 1972, p. 3.

40. For example, see A. F. Dashdamirov, *Pravda,* 7 August 1981, p. 2.

41. The most widely publicized protests of the new republic consitutions occurred in Georgia, where on April 14, 1978, several thousand people took to the streets of Tbilisi to voice their opposition. The next day, the authorities backed down and reestablished Georgian as the official language of the republic.

42. Radio Liberty Research Bulletin, no. 221 (July 3, 1985).

43. *Pravda,* December 16, 1986, p. 2.

44. Local education officials in Tallinn reported this to the author in November 1978.

45. This case was reported in Rubenstein, "Dissent," 73–74.

46. Tokes, *Dissent in the USSR,* 82.

47. Mary McAuley, "Nationalism and the Soviet Multiethnic State," in Harding, *The State in Socialist Society,* 180.

48. Cited in Robert Conquest, *Religion in the USSR* (New York: Praeger, 1968), 7.

49. Cited in Paul A. Lucey, "Religion," in Cracraft, *The Soviet Union Today,* 294.

50. Ibid.

51. John Lawrence, "Religion in the USSR," in Curtis Keeble, *The Soviet State* (London: Gower, 1985), 61.

52. Lawrence claims that the appointment of Abbot Gavriil was arranged by the KGB. Ibid., 65.

53. Ibid., 59. Calculations based on the numbers of members of various churches cited in this chapter results in a figure closer to 40 percent.

54. Lucey, "Religion," 295.

55. Ibid.

56. Ibid., 298.

57. Ibid., 299.

58. Ibid., 297.

59. Walter Sawatsky, *Soviet Evangelicals since World War II* (Scottsdale, PA: Herald Press, 1981).

60. Lucey, "Religion," 301.

61. Ibid.

62. Ibid., 300.

63. Ibid.

64. Conquest, *Religion in the USSR.*

65. Lucey, "Religion," 299.

66. Barbara Wolfe Jancar, "Religious Dissent in the Soviet Union," in Tokes, *Dissent in the USSR,* 196.

67. Lucey, "Religion," 299–300.

Selected Bibliography

Alexeyeva, Ludmilla. *Soviet Dissent.* Middletown, CT: Wesleyan University Press, 1985.

Allworth, Edward. *Ethnic Russia in the USSR.* New York: Pergamon, 1980.

Amalrik, Andrei. *Will the Soviet Union Survive until 1984?* New York: Harper and Row, 1970.

Azrael, Jeremy. *Soviet Nationality Policies and Practices.* New York: Praeger, 1978.

Bennigsen, Alexandre, and Marie Broxup. *The Islamic Threat to the Soviet State.* London: Croom Helm, 1983.

Bloch, Sidney, and Peter Reddaway. *Psychiatric Terror: How Soviet Psychiatry Is Used to Suppress Dissent.* New York: Basic Books, 1977.

Bociurkiw, B. R., and J. W. Strong, eds. *Religion and Atheism in the USSR and Eastern Europe.* London: Macmillan, 1975.

Bourdeaux, Michael. *Patriarchs and Prophets.* New York: Praeger, 1970.

Carrère d'Encausse, Hélène. *The Decline of an Empire.* New York: Newsweek Books, 1979.

Chalidze, Valery. *To Defend These Rights.* New York: Random House, 1974.

Conquest, Robert. *Religion in the USSR.* New York: Praeger, 1968.

Dunn, Dennis J. *Religion and Modernization in the Soviet Union.* Boulder: Westview Press, 1977.

Freedman, Robert O., ed. *Soviet Jewry in the Decisive Decade, 1971–1980.* Durham, NC: Duke University Press, 1984.

Katz, Zev, et al., eds. *Handbook of Major Soviet Nationalities.* New York: The Free Press, 1975.

Lane, Christel. *Christian Religion in the Soviet Union.* London: George Allen & Unwin, 1978.

Lewis, Robert A., et al., *Nationality and Population Change in Russia and the USSR.* New York: Praeger, 1976.

Medvedev, Roy. *On Socialist Democracy.* New York: Alfred A. Knopf, 1975.

————.*On Soviet Dissent.* New York: Columbia University Press, 1980.

Reddaway, Peter. *Uncensored Russia.* London: Cape, 1972.

Roi, Yaacov. *The USSR and the Muslim World.* London: George Allen & Unwin, 1984.

Sakharov, Andrei. *My Country and the World.* London: Collins, 1975.

————.*Sakharov Speaks.* New York: Alfred A. Knopf, 1974.

Sharlet, Robert. "Dissent and the 'Contra-System' in the Soviet Union," in Erik P. Hoffmann, ed. *The Soviet Union in the 1980s.* New York: The Academy of Political Science, 1984, 135–146.

————."Varieties of Dissent and Regularities of Repression in the European Communist States." In Jane Curry, ed. *Dissent in Eastern Europe.* New York: Praeger, 1983.

Silver, Brian. "Social Mobilization and the Russification of Soviet Nationalities." *American Political Science Review* 68 (March 1974): 45–66.

Tokes, Rudolf, L., ed. *Dissent in the USSR.* Baltimore: The John Hopkins University Press, 1975.

Zwick, Peter. *National Communism.* Boulder: Westview, 1982.

————."Soviet Nationality Policy: Social, Economic, and Political Aspects." In Gordon B. Smith, ed. *Public Policy and Administration in the Soviet Union.* New York: Praeger, 1980, 142–171.

14

Whither Gorbachev? Whither the Soviet Union?

The horses fly like a whirlwind . . . and the troika dashes away. . . . Russia, art not thou also flying onwards like a spirited troika that nothing can overtake? What is the meaning of this terrifying onrush? Russia, whither flyest thou?

NIKOLAI GOGOL, *Dead Souls*

An oak is a tree. A rose is a flower. A deer is an animal. A sparrow is a bird. Russia is our motherland. Death is inevitable.

VLADIMIR NABOKOV, "The Gift"

Death came to Leonid Ilich Brezhnev on November 10, 1982. Just three days earlier, looking frailer than usual, the man whom the press had come to refer to in the most grandiose terms as General Secretary of the CPSU, President of the USSR, Chairman of the USSR Defense Council, Marshal of the Armed Forces, and farsighted leader of socialism, had stood atop Lenin's mausoleum in an icy drizzle. From there, he had reviewed the seemingly endless procession of troops, gymnasts, and workers marching through Red Square in honor of the sixty-fifth anniversary of the Bolshevik Revolution. Rumors had been circulating for ten years about the failing health of the General Secretary. At the Twenty-Fifth Party Congress in 1976, Brezhnev's speech had been slurred and at times unintelligible. References to "socialist legality" (*sotsialisticheskaia zakonnost'*) sounded instead like "sausage legality" (*sosiskaia zakonnost'*). Reports circulated that Brezhnev suffered from cancer of the jaw. Some observers speculated that he might use the occasion of the Party Congress to step down voluntarily, retiring with all the pomp and circumstance befitting a leader who had guided the USSR for more than a decade, raising the country from a position of military inferiority to the status of superpower. But the General Secretary held onto the reins of power and the next year ratified a new Constitution—widely referred to as "the Brezhnev Constitution"—and also assumed the title of President of the USSR.

By the time of the Twenty-Sixth Party Congress in 1981, Brezhnev's subordinates were jockeying for position to succeed him. Konstantin Chernenko, Brezhnev's trusted right-hand man, rose to the third-ranking position within the Politburo behind Brezhnev and the senior party "second secretary" and chief ideologist Mikhail Suslov. Suslov's death on January

25, 1982, precipitated a rapid series of shifts within the ruling elite. Iurii Andropov, the former KGB chief, gradually assumed Suslov's former responsibilities within the CPSU Secretariat and presented himself as a clear alternative to Chernenko.[1]

Muscovites first suspected that Brezhnev had succumbed to failing health when Radio Moscow and the central television channels interrupted their scheduled programming and switched to solemn music. Within hours, the public announcement was made. Portraits of the fallen leader, which had become increasingly prominent and numerous on public buildings during the latter half of the Brezhnev regime, were draped in black crepe. Lines formed at the Hall of the Trade Unions, where the body lay in state. Andropov was named to head the funeral commission, signaling his selection as the next General Secretary. The succession was confirmed by an extraordinary plenum of the CPSU Central Committee on November 12. Thus, by the time Brezhnev was buried beside Lenin's mausoleum on November 15, the succession had been largely resolved.

Brezhnev's death resulted in the transfer of power at the pinnacle of the CPSU, but it also symbolized a generational transfer of power, which had begun in the mid-1970s and would continue into the mid-1980s. In 1981, at the time of the Twenty-Sixth Party Congress, the average age of Politburo members was seventy years. The remarkable continuity and stability of the Brezhnev generation, "the Class of '38," which had been propelled into positions of power by Stalin's purges, had resulted in long tenures in office, as well as the aging, not only of the top officials, but of officials throughout the party and state apparatuses. By the mid-1970s, however, the Brezhnev generation of leaders began to die or retire. For the most part, they were replaced by other senior officials from the same generation.[2]

Reflecting the growing incapacity of the General Secretary, the Soviet political system appeared to lose its momentum and sense of direction in the late 1970s and early 1980s. As in past leadership transitions in the USSR, most party and state bodies adopted a cautious and conservative approach. With the future of Brezhnev's leadership in doubt, state and party administrators, not wishing to undertake any long-term plans or policy commitments, muddled through with short-term, interim decisions until the new leader had clearly established his policy orientation. Meanwhile, unresolved problems continued to mount.

The extent to which elite politics pervades into even low levels of administration is not often appreciated outside the USSR. For example, in 1978 a researcher in the Institute of State and Law of the USSR Academy of Sciences complained privately that in the absence of decisive and dynamic leadership "from the top," the Institute could not plan its long-range research agenda. "Everyone is just waiting for Brezhnev to die," he said.[3]

With Brezhnev's death, the time was ripe for widespread personnel and policy changes. In fact, the general consensus among all levels of society that change and resolute leadership were long overdue considerably weakened support for Konstantin Chernenko, who had been Brezhnev's closest protégé and had pledged himself to continue "on the Brezhnev course." In contrast, Iurii Andropov represented a break from the Brezhnev past in two important respects: he promised to crack down on the corruption and black-market activities that had proliferated during the Brezhnev era and to undertake meaningful economic reforms. An air of expectancy and enthusiasm pervaded the USSR in early 1983. At long last, it was hoped that the stagnation of the Brezhnev years would give way to the dynamic and forceful leadership of Iurii Andropov. Andropov's short-lived rule, however, precluded the realization of his ambitious plans. After only eight months in office, the General Secretary dropped from public view, reportedly suffering from "a cold." He died in February 1984.

At the time of Andropov's death, there were two principal rivals for the office of General Secretary: Konstantin Chernenko and Mikhail Gorbachev. Chernenko, whose power and influence in the Politburo had waned during the early months of Andropov's rule, was able to stage a political comeback during the General Secretary's long absence. Chernenko stood in for the ailing Andropov at the parade marking the anniversary of the October Revolution and reportedly chaired the weekly meetings of the Politburo. At the same time, the Gorbachev faction was also solidifying its position. In late 1983, several pro-Gorbachev officials were named to the Central Committee Secretariat and Politburo, as well as to the influential regional party posts.

The choice of Chernenko to succeed Andropov appears to have been supported by a coalition of former Brezhnev associates and conservative party secretaries within the ruling Politburo. It is not known how strongly Gorbachev contested Chernenko's selection. It is likely that in return for acquiescing in the succession of Chernenko, he was rewarded with expanded responsibilities and powers and, most importantly, was recognized as the heir apparent.

During Chernenko's brief thirteen months in office, Gorbachev played an increasingly visible role. In addition to his responsibilities within the Secretariat in supervising cadre policy and economic policy, he added foreign policy, ideological affairs, and cultural policy to his portfolio. When Chernenko's health began to fail, Gorbachev assumed the leading role in the Politburo and became much more active and visible in foreign affairs. The fact that Gorbachev's election to General Secretary occurred on the same day that Chernenko's death was made public also suggests that the succession had been agreed to in advance.[4]

The future course of the Soviet Union now lies in the hands of Mikhail Gorbachev. The direction of Gorbachev's policies to date has been shaped to a considerable degree by the enduring contradictions and historical continuities noted throughout this book. Before assessing the policies of the new generation of Soviet leaders, this chapter will consider the context in which those policies are being made, a context that includes Gorbachev's struggle to consolidate his leadership and expand his authority. Underlying this struggle is a fundamental contradiction in the Soviet political system between the need for reform and resistance to change.

LEADERSHIP CONSOLIDATION AND THE DILEMMA OF CHANGE

Political patronage has long been recognized as a crucial element in the succession process in the USSR. A newly named General Secretary must garner sufficient support within various powerful party and state bodies to consolidate his or her political position and begin to enunciate a policy agenda. A General Secretary can gain the support of these diverse interests by two principal courses: (1) by proposing policies that are favored by those interests and thus building an alliance based on shared values, or (2) by offering the leaders of those institutions promotions, perquisites, and other career rewards in return for their support. Stalin, Khrushchev, Brezhnev, Andropov, Chernenko, and Gorbachev all employed both of these techniques, but to varying degrees. A fundamental problem with the former strategy is that it is usually a zero-sum situation. A General Secretary who strives to garner support among consumer interests by promising greater investments in that sector will automatically erode support among influential military and heavy-industrial interests. Similarly, a General Secretary who advocates ambitious development projects in Siberia and Central Asia risks alienating officials from regions in the European portion of the Soviet Union. Neither is political patronage a guaranteed means of consolidating one's power position. Bureaucratic inertia and vested interests can dissipate the General Secretary's authority, even if the Secretary appoints loyal supporters to top-level posts in those bureaucracies. Although policy strategies and political patronage are important factors in leadership consolidation and authority building in the USSR, there are limits that constrain both strategies.

Authority building—that is, the process by which leaders seek to legitimize their policy programs and demonstrate their competence—rests on a combination of factors, including the leader's proven ability to solve problems and the leader's ability to project an image of confidence and dynamism. The latter has often been overlooked by Western scholars, who believe that public perception of Soviet leaders and their ability to manipulate symbols has little impact on their legitimacy or power. However, mounting evidence to the contrary warrants a reassessment of the role of symbols and public images in Soviet politics. In discussing the Soviet succession process since Stalin, one factor of particular importance is the manner in which contenders to office have portrayed themselves on the issue of reform versus stability. The important distinction is not whether post-Stalin regimes have been liberal or conservative—those labels have virtually no meaning in the Soviet context. Instead, a more useful distinction among post-Stalin leaders is whether they have adopted status quo or pro-change positions.[5]

During most of the post-Stalin leadership transitions, a broad regime consensus existed on the question of change or stability.[6] Within these points of general consensus, however, personal, regional, bureaucratic, and policy differences existed. Stalin's successors, for example, seemed to agree that a diminution of the powers of the secret police was necessary and that a devolution of responsibility in decision-making was long overdue. Nevertheless, the leading contenders—Nikita Khrushchev, Georgi Malenkov, Nikolai Bulganin, and Lazar Kaganovich—strongly split over agricultural policy, investment priorities, industrial management, and the role of the Party.[7]

Undoubtedly, the determinants of Soviet leaders' orientation on the question of reform versus stability are complex. Much depends on the psychological makeup of the leader and the leader's relative ability to be comfortable with uncertainty and change. This line of inquiry is difficult to pursue in the Soviet case, however.

Historical circumstance can also shape predispositions toward either reformist or status quo orientations. A recurring pattern of vacillation between the reformist and status quo positions is evident in the USSR.

This contradiction between reformist and status quo tendencies gives rise to a dialectical process of policy change. The Soviet political system is characterized by an ongoing political struggle between proponents of reform and proponents of the status quo, which results in a series of syntheses or compromises. Each synthesis on this reform/status quo continuum is only partial and transient and forms the background against which the struggle between the two forces will be carried out in the future.[8] These vacillations between reformist and status quo positions have been reflected in both the personnel and policy choices of Soviet leaders since the Stalin era.

After almost three decades of Stalin's rule, the Soviet public and many officials in powerful bureaucratic organizations as well as the CPSU hoped for a general relaxation of the political climate. Khrushchev offered such a reform, making de-Stalinization the centerpiece of his populist attempt to secure a firm hold on the reins of power. In contrast to the terrorism and authoritarianism of the Stalin regime, the Khrushchev regime abolished the security police, elevated regular judicial procedure, broadened mass participation in politics, ushered in a "thaw" in the arts, and radically restructured the Party and economic ministries. Although many of Khrushchev's policies, including the suppression of religious practices, were distinctly conservative, his overall administration was reformist; he proposed radical changes and attempted to use his reform agenda to enhance his legitimacy and stature as a leader.

Khrushchev also undertook sweeping personnel changes within the party and state apparatuses, beginning with the dismantling of the NKVD (secret police). Prior to the Twentieth Party Congress in 1956, Khrushchev replaced half of the republic party secretaries and almost two-thirds of the regional party secretaries.[9]

The dangers inherent in Khrushchev's reformist strategy soon become apparent, however. De-Stalinization unleashed strong anti-Soviet sentiments in Eastern Europe, and Soviet troops were eventually forced to put down uprisings in Hungary. Khrushchev's overly ambitious Virgin Lands program, the Cuban missile crisis, the demoralizing effect of the division of the Party into agricultural and industrial wings, and the regular rotation of party personnel contributed to his ouster in 1964.

Khrushchev's outster prompted a period of collective leadership, with Brezhnev and Kosygin assuming the top leadership posts in the Party and the State, respectively. It took Brezhnev several years to consolidate his political power. One of the key elements in Brezhnev's attempt to enhance his legitimacy and expand his authority was the promise to restore stability in Soviet politics. Brezhnev criticized Khrushchev for, among other things, "the unjustified transferring and replacing of personnel" and pledged to restore "respect for cadres."[10] Consequently, relatively few personnel changes were immediately forthcoming. In his first ten months in office, Brezhnev replaced only 9 percent of the regional party secretaries and only two of the fourteen republic first secretaries.[11] More-extensive organizational and personnel changes were undertaken in the state apparatus, however. Brezhnev abolished the regional economic councils that Khrushchev had created and reestablished the industrial ministries along pre-1957 lines, necessitating the promotion of numerous people to ministerial posts. Yet, approximately two-thirds of the ministers appointed in 1965 had been ministers or deputy ministers in 1957.[12] Continuity and stability, rather than the infusion of new blood, appear to have been the principal motivating factors in the appointments and personnel changes of the early Brezhnev period.

The emphasis on restoring stability in the Soviet political system was also evident in Brezhnev's policies. Brezhnev denounced Khrushchev's "hare-brained" schemes, which were often undertaken without proper consultation with experts. Under Brezhnev, the stress shifted from mass participation in politics, which Khrushchev had championed, to expanded involvement of specialists in decision-making. Scientific councils and collegia were established within ministries and research institutes to broaden the range of expertise and opinions on which policymakers relied. In contrast to Khrushchev, Brezhnev promised stability, professionalism, and conservatism.

By the late 1970s, however, the "stability of cadres" promised by Brezhnev had become tantamount to stagnation. Many of the party secretaries and ministers named to their posts in 1965 were still in office when Brezhnev died seventeen years later.[13] In the early 1980s, the economic growth rate slowed to the lowest level since World War II, and this was accompanied by chronic shortages of meat, dairy products, vegetables, and other staples. Lagging economic performance gave rise to a burgeoning "second economy" and widespread theft and other economic crimes. Labor productivity declined as a result of chronic absenteeism, alcoholism, and the lack of incentives. Workers routinely left their jobs early to shop for groceries, a task that could require two to three hours every day. While average Soviet citizens confronted these difficulties, however, the elite enjoyed more and more privileges. Special stores were opened, carrying difficult-to-find items ranging from meat and caviar to imported shoes and cameras. Usually, Soviet citizens are either cynical about such privileges or accept them grudgingly as a fact of life, but the ostentatiousness, the flaunting of wealth and position by the elite under Brezhnev, sparked increasing resentment among the populace.[14]

In foreign affairs, policy problems also accumulated with the demise of détente, the increasing defense deployments in the United States and Western Europe, the failure of arms negotiations to reach any concrete reductions, the continued tense relations with China, and the protracted involvement of Soviet forces in Afghanistan. The need for change—both in policy and personnel—was the chief agenda item confronting Brezhnev's successors.

The Andropov leadership moved quickly to rejuvenate the party and state apparatuses and to set a new tone of leadership style. During his fifteen months in office, Andropov replaced one-fifth of all regional party secretaries, one-fifth of all ministers, and one-third of the department heads of the Central Committee Secretariat.[15] The chief targets of Andropov's firings were corrupt party and state officials. The consumer and transportation industries were particularly hard hit by the firings. Andropov's prolonged illness and short term in office, however, precluded further, more-sweeping personnel changes.

In his policies and style of leadership, Andropov represented a sharp contrast to his predecessor. The tough-minded former KGB chief shed many of the luxurious trappings that Brezhnev had enjoyed. Andropov's limousine drove at normal speeds down Moscow's streets, rather than racing along the specially designated center lane that had been reserved for Brezhnev's motorcades. Andropov visited factories and government offices to appear to be more in touch with average citizens. He also clamped down on the special privileges of the elite.

In order to reverse the negative economic trends plaguing the USSR, Andropov adopted a two-part strategy stressing discipline and reform. He mobilized the KGB, police, and trade unions for a massive crackdown on absenteeism, alcoholism, shoddy work, and black-market activities. At the same time, he advocated economic reforms. In particular, Andropov called for greater independence for factories, enterprises, and state and collective farms; he pointed to the successes of economic experiments in East Germany and Hungary as meriting closer scrutiny. Ultimately, however, Andropov's policy agenda remained unfulfilled because of his declining health and long absence from power.

Konstantin Chernenko, succeeding Andropov, built his power base on a return to the stability of the Brezhnev era, particularly the policy of "stability of cadres." The sudden personnel and policy changes that had occurred under Andropov, the widely publicized shake-up of several regional party organizations, and the disclosure of official corruption had aroused considerable trepidation within the ranks of the CPSU. In contrast to the extensive personnel changes under Andropov, only four new ministers were appointed during Chernenko's thirteen-month tenure and no changes were forthcoming in the composition of the Politburo and the Central Committee Secretariat.[16] At regional and local levels of the Party, only a few new appointments were made.

Chernenko's status quo orientation was also evident in his lack of a coherent policy program. The new General Secretary inherited from his predecessor the discipline campaign and economic experiments in several ministries, but he pursued both with less vigor. One of the few policy initiatives linked to the Chernenko regime was a campaign to improve education and "upbringing."[17] Curiously, this campaign undermined the drive to improve labor discipline by implying that the declining performance of Soviet workers was the fault of improper socialization and indoctrination rather than the fault of the workers themselves.

This cycle of change and status quo would suggest that Gorbachev, coming to office after a conservative and antireformist leader, enjoyed a mandate to undertake meaningful reforms in the USSR. There is much evidence to support such a contention.

GORBACHEV THE REFORMER

Gorbachev's statements both prior to and after becoming General Secretary indicated his willingness to consider moderate economic and political reforms. In a speech on February 20, 1985, he blamed the Soviet economic slowdown in part on the failure of economic officials to undertake necessary changes.[18] On many occasions, he advocated granting greater decision-making authority to factory, state-farm, and collective-farm managers, which would free central planners and ministerial officials to concentrate on larger problems, such as investment priorities, regional development, living standards, and foreign economic policy.

Gorbachev advocated consolidating the more than sixty industrial ministries and state committees into five to seven "superministries," thus reducing the fragmentation of the economy that impedes the development of advanced technology and undermines coordination among sectors. In his first year in office, he succeeded in creating three such "superministries"—in agriculture, machine-building, and energy.[19]

Gorbachev's reformist orientation was also confirmed by his support for the reform-oriented Institute of Economics and Organization of Industrial Production of the Siberian division of the USSR Academy of Sciences. Abel Aganbegian, the former director of the Institute and a widely recognized advocate of fundamental economic reforms, was brought from Novosibirsk to Moscow to be Gorbachev's chief economic adviser. Many proposals for reforming the economy were openly discussed after Gorbachev took office. These proposals included greater self-financing of R&D and capital expansion projects; reduction in the number of output indicators, placing greater emphasis on labor productivity, profitability, and contract fulfillment; and greater stability in plan inputs and targets. In agriculture, Aganbegian noted that a land rent was being considered to stimulate agricultural units to use land more efficiently.[20]

In order to actually undertake fundamental economic reforms, however, Gorbachev would have to overcome the opposition of the status-quo-oriented interests. The ministries and mid-level economic administrators in industrial associations represent the single most-consistent obstacle to the introduction of economic reforms in the USSR. They are the most conservative segments in the economy and are also the groups criticized by Aganbegian and Gorbachev.[21] Past reforms, such as those introduced in 1973 and 1979 and the "economic experiments" launched in five ministries in 1984, encountered foot-dragging and outright opposition; ministers refused to delegate power to enterprise managers and fought to preserve their powers to shift inputs and adjust enterprise production plans in order to ensure overall plan fulfillment by the ministry. Gorbachev's ability to overcome this opposition depended on his success in expanding his authority and extending his power through patronage.

Under Gorbachev, changes occurred rapidly in the makeup of the ruling elite. In fact, Gorbachev's record in making personnel changes early in his tenure eclipsed that of any previous leader of the USSR. In his first year in office, Gorbachev removed 47 of 121 regional party secretaries and replaced more than one-half of the CPSU Central Committee.[22] Sweeping changes occurred at the city and local levels, with younger, better-educated party *apparatchiki,* many with experience in agriculture and industry, assuming influential party posts. Gorbachev's purge was not restricted to the ranks of the Party. The number of newly appointed ministers rose to forty-two—more than one-half of the Council of Ministers, compared to only twelve under Andropov and four under Chernenko.[23] The average age of Gorbachev's new ministerial appointees was fifty-six years, while the ministers who were dismissed averaged sixty-nine years of age and had held their posts for an average of twelve years.[24]

Gorbachev's ministerial changes did not hit each sector of the economy equally; rather, they were concentrated in the agricultural, construction, energy, and basic-industries sectors. It is notable that the defense industries were not subject to Gorbachev's ministerial personnel changes. The defense sector may have been spared because it operates on a fundamentally different basis than civilian industries and is more efficient and technologically progressive.

In his appointments, Gorbachev has promoted capable specialists from within various ministries. In a few crucial ministries (e.g., Foreign Affairs, Internal Affairs, and Agriculture), he relied on the appointment of trusted party secretaries.

The career backgrounds of Gorbachev's ministerial appointees also provided a signal as to his goals and motivations. Several of the newly appointed officials had distinguished themselves in the most productive and technologically advanced industrial enterprises in the USSR—such "showcase factories" as the gigantic Uralmash machine-building complex in Sverdlovsk, whose former director, Nikolai Ryzhkov, became Premier of the USSR. Such appointments indicated that Gorbachev acknowledged the successes of these prestigious factories and enterprises and wanted to see them more widely emulated. In effect, he may well have been saying, "These industries and enterprises have succeeded in operating within the existing economic structure, and they are efficient and technologically advanced. Why can't others do the same?"

Gorbachev's personnel changes in the party apparatus reflected similar trends and priorities in reshaping the state apparatus. After coming to power, Gorbachev replaced more than half of the heads of Central Committee departments charged with overseeing various economic sectors. The party secretaries of many of the principal industrial regions and cities were also changed during the first year of the Gorbachev regime, including the secretaries of Ivanovo, Kemerovo, Leningrad, Moscow, Orel, Sverdlovsk, Minsk, and Gorky. Many of the new secretaries had had some previous training and experience in industry or agriculture as well as extensive experience in party work. Approximately one-half had served as inspector (*inspektor*) in the CPSU Central Committee, a position that entails conducting investigations of local and regional party organizations to ferret out graft, corruption, and inefficient management.[25] These positions are few in number and held by rapidly rising party *apparatchiki* for a period of two to three years. The Gorbachev regime, manifesting both the ability and the will to introduce economic reforms, was clearly placing new personnel in key industrial ministries and regional party apparatuses in order to impose "reforms from above" on reluctant ministries, managers, and economic administrators.

Yet, there were also grounds for questioning how extensive Gorbachev's reforms would be. The stresses and strains between the need to enact reforms and stubborn resistance to change were visible within the Gorbachev regime, even in the speeches of the General Secretary. In his public statements, Gorbachev assiduously avoided using the word *reform*, preferring instead the phrase "improving the economic mechanism." Aganbegian's positions also seemed to have become more moderate and compromising after he came to Moscow. He too avoided using *reform* and instead talked of a "major structural rebuilding" of the economy.[26] Gorbachev's appointments of industrial ministers also reflected his recognition that efficient, high-technology production was possible within the existing organization and incentive structures of the Soviet economy. Had his appointees come from enterprises that were models of experimentation or reform (e.g., the Shchekino Chemical Combine), there would have been more grounds for concluding that Gorbachev favored basic reform of the economic system. The fact that the majority of the newly appointed ministers were promoted from within cast some doubt upon the likelihood of fundamental or radical changes in the economy.

The Gorbachev regime confronted the problem of revitalizing the economy and instilling a greater sense of urgency and purpose in political organs without shedding the fundamentals of the Soviet political and economic system, without abandoning central planning, without introducing market mechanisms, and without threatening the leading role of the Party. In sum, Gorbachev had to define a course that would rejuvenate the economy and the political system, but one that would not deviate from the essential nature of the political and economic system established by Stalin in the 1920s and 1930s. After one year in power, the lines of Gorbachev's policies had begun to emerge.

TWENTY-SEVENTH PARTY CONGRESS

The Twenty-Seventh Party Congress convened in late February and early March 1986, just one year after Gorbachev had risen to power. Having consolidated his leadership, Gorbachev used the congress to demonstrate his command of the political system, to set a constructive tone, and to announce new policy directions. Prior to the congress, several major personnel questions had already been resolved. In July, Gorbachev had succeeded in removing his principal rival in the Politburo, Georgii Romanov, the former chief of the Leningrad party organization; just a few weeks before the congress, a second adversary, Viktor Grishin, head of the Moscow party apparatus, was dropped from the Politburo. Similarly, major personnel changes in regional and local party organs as well as in state ministries had occurred prior to the congress and were ratified after the fact by the 5000 delegates in attendance.

While Gorbachev acted quickly and decisively in making personnel changes in the party and state apparatuses, many observers anticipated more extensive changes in the Politburo than actually occurred. In this sense, the congress was an exercise in caution and confidence. Only one new member was named to the Politburo at the Twenty-Seventh Party Congress—Lev Zaikov, the new party leader from Leningrad. That appointment brought the membership to twelve. (During most of the Brezhnev era, the Politburo had consisted of fifteen to sixteen members.) Further-more, Gorbachev retained the Ukrainian party secretary, V. V. Shcherbit-skii, and the Kazakh first secretary, D. A. Kunaev, despite their advanced ages (seventy-five and sixty-eight, respectively) and despite the fact that they had been strong supporters of Brezhnev and were thus out of step with Gorbachev's policies. Whether the leadership continuity in the Politburo reflected Gorbachev's attempt to follow a low-key course to avoid alienat-ing key figures or whether it was a sign of his lack of strength in the Politburo is much debated.

More-substantial changes occurred in the Central Committee Secretar-iat, indicating that it has become more important in policy-making. Nine of eleven members of the CPSU Secretariat (excluding Gorbachev) were newly elected or reassigned to new positions within the body. Experienced offi-cials, such as long-time ambassador to the United States Anatolii Dobrynin, were brought in to supervise foreign affairs; dynamic party *apparatchiki,* such as G. P. Razumovsky, were assigned to spearhead efforts to seek out careerists and corrupt party officials. Alexandra Biriukova, the first woman to hold a top leadership post since the Khrushchev regime, was also named to the Secretariat to supervise light industry, consumer services, and the food industry. In a departure from past practice and reflecting Gorbachev's faith in the ability of high technology to revitalize the Soviet economy, V. A. Medvedev, the head of the Central Committee Department of Science and Education, was elevated to secretary status.

As previously noted, an important aspect of authority building is ma-nipulating diffuse appeals in order to project the image of a confident and dynamic leader. The Twenty-Seventh Party Congress was most significant in this respect. After coming to office, Gorbachev had strived to project the image of a vigorous, candid, confident, pragmatic, and demanding leader. A general consensus seems to have existed since the late 1970s that these characteristics were lacking in Soviet politics. As Brezhnev grew more feeble and less involved in policy matters, the cult of Brezhnev increased apprecia-bly. The General Secretary accumulated more and more titles and awards, his books were reviewed in glowing terms in all newspapers, art exhibits depicting his life were organized, and the media heaped praise on his accom-plishments at home and abroad. In contrast, Gorbachev deliberately tried to project a self-assured, modest, and less regal image. In fact, he initiated a "cult of modesty." At the Twenty-Seventh Party Congress, he chided one speaker for making too many references to his name during an address.[27]

In another departure from past practice, Gorbachev called for more openness (*glasnost'*) and candor in discussing the problems confronting the USSR. In a country in which information about airplane crashes, earth-quakes, and crime is strictly censored, such frankness is startling. A *Pravda* editorial on the new policy stated: "Timely and frank release of information is evidence of trust in the people, respect for their intelligence, and feeling for their ability to assess events."[28]

The first big test of Gorbachev's *glasnost'* policy was the accident at the Chernobyl nuclear reactor in the Ukraine in April 1986. Initially, the leader-ship maintained tight secrecy on news coverage of the near-disaster and even denied that there was a problem. In the weeks following the accident, however, press reports, television coverage, and news conferences gradually reconstructed the events surrounding the accident. While the Soviet handling of the Chernobyl episode represented a departure from previous practice, it clearly fell short of what some Western observers had expected.

The stress on *glasnost'* was also used to apply public pressure to ministers, factory managers, and economic officials. For example, ministers and factory officials were asked to appear on television and radio programs to answer consumer complaints. Unlike Brezhnev and Chernenko, who promised the bureaucrats stability, Gorbachev expected results. For that reason, it is unlikely that all of those he promoted to high-level posts will still be in office after ten or fifteen years. As Gorbachev boldly stated in a 1985 address in Leningrad: "Those who do not intend to adjust and who are an obstacle to the solution of these new tasks simply must get out of the way, get out of the way and not be a hindrance."[29]

In terms of setting a new policy agenda, the Twenty-Seventh Party Congress offered few departures from the past. The overriding concern of the Gorbachev regime was revitalizing the stagnating economy in the face of serious shortages of labor, investment capital, and hard (foreign) currency. Gorbachev's solution was fourfold. First, Gorbachev and Premier Ryzhkov called for a "radical restructuring of the economy," consolidating numerous cumbersome ministries into a handful of "superministries" and giving greater autonomy to factory and farm managers. Second, the Twelfth Five-Year Plan, which was ratified by the congress, redirected economic resources to favor the development and application of high technology and the renovation of existing factories. No new grandiose projects were envisaged in the plan, and the bulk of investment funds were slated for the European portion of the country, rather than for Siberia. Third, Gorbachev renewed the campaign begun under Andropov to improve work discipline and cut down on alcoholism, one of the chief causes of absenteeism and low labor productivity. Finally, the new leadership noted that the revitalization of the economy required the revitalization of the society in general, and the CPSU in particular. Party officials were urged to be more vigilant over economic performance, holding factory managers and workers strictly accountable for fulfilling their production plans. At the same time, Gorbachev cautioned party members to limit their involvement to supervision and not to intrude in administrative matters. The distinction between party supervision and party interference, however, remained fuzzy. The fact that many of the newly appointed regional party secretaries had distinguished records in agricultural and industrial management indicated both the rising level of expertise within the Party and a greater degree of sensitivity by party secretaries to the problems confronting the productive sector.

On the political front, the Twenty-Seventh Party Congress was particularly noteworthy in two respects. First, the delegates ratified a new Party Program, substantially revising the previous program, which had been enacted under Khrushchev in 1961. Work on the new Party Program was begun under Brezhnev and continued under the direction of his successors. Both Brezhnev and Andropov noted that some provisions of the 1961 document "had not stood the test of time," particularly the promises that, by

1970, the Soviet economy would overtake that of the United States in per capita production and that, by 1980, communism, complete with an abundance of housing, consumer goods, and social services, would be largely realized.[30]

During the drafting phase of the new program, a heated debate occurred over the wording of a clause referring to "socialist self-administration." There were disagreements as to whether workers should be allowed to have a direct say in the appointment of managers and in managerial decisions. The Party Program as enacted by the congress called for increased participation of workers in administration and also reflected Gorbachev's stress on *glasnost'* in calling for greater openness in the press and increased attention to public opinion.

In contrast to Khrushchev's utopian predictions, the new document acknowledges that the advance of humanity toward communism is "uneven, complex, and controversial."[31] The program does, however, propose that national income and industrial output be doubled by the year 2000. These goals are to be achieved by granting greater independence to enterprises, abandoning wage equalization among workers, introducing the brigade method of labor organization more widely, using material incentives to encourage the population to work harder, and applying advanced technology in production.

A second dominant political feature of the Twenty-Seventh Party Congress was the tendency to blame the Brezhnev leadership for the economic, social, and political problems confronting the country. While not mentioning the former General Secretary by name, Gorbachev criticized the "inertness" of the Brezhnev years and noted that the Kremlin leaders had tried "to improve things without changing anything."[32]

Blaming one's predecessors has become routine in the USSR since Khrushchev's famed denunciations of Stalin at the Twentieth and Twenty-Second Party Congresses. But the criticisms of Brezhnev marked the first time that he was singled out for public reproof at a party gathering. On the third anniversary of Brezhnev's death, *Pravda* published an article entitled "Flattery and Obsequiousness" that attacked the idolatry that had characterized the Brezhnev era.[33] Delegates to the Twenty-Seventh Party Congress were urged to develop a new "cult of modesty" and to shy away from the "self-congratulatory ways of the past."[34]

Gorbachev's policy agenda began to emerge more clearly in his second year in office. In 1986, he began to speak more forcefully in favor of decentralizing economic planning, granting greater power to factory managers to make decisions.[35] Serious efforts were undertaken to revamp wages and prices in order to create greater incentives for workers to work diligently, while pensions were modified to prevent price increases from impoverishing the Soviet Union's large retired population.

In a major address to the January 1987 plenum of the CPSU Central Committee, Gorbachev described the problems confronting the USSR with brutal honesty, even using the word *crisis* to describe the USSR's social and economic predicament.[36] He noted that the political leaders had grown "deaf to social issues." Housing, health care, education, and consumer needs had been neglected. Furthermore, he observed that this "social corrosion" profoundly affected public morale, resulting in cynicism, consumerism, alcoholism, corruption, and infringements of labor discipline.

Gorbachev placed the blame for these conditions at the top: "Comrades, it is the leading bodies of the Party and the State that bear responsibility for all this."[37] Gorbachev's proposed remedies were nothing short of revolutionary: He proposed "democratizing" the political system by instituting multiple-candidate elections for local soviets and party posts, involving more nonparty members in the government and the economy, allowing workers to select their factory directors, and expanding the sphere of private economic activity.

In the arts, Gorbachev encouraged a thaw unparalleled in the past thirty years. Long-suppressed works such as Boris Pasternak's *Doctor Zhivago* and Anatolii Rybakov's *Children of the Arbat* were approved for publication. The latter was just one of several works published that reexamined the trauma of the Stalin years. A shake-up of Goskino, the Soviet film agency, resulted in the release of several previously banned movies. Among them was the widely acclaimed movie *Repentance,* a chilling examination of Stalin's purges.

Famous émigrés, such as ballet Mikhail Baryshnikov and Natalia Makarova and Iurii Liubimov, former director of the Taganka Theater, were invited to return to the USSR. At the same time, repression of dissidents was reduced appreciably, and barriers to emigration were relaxed.

The *glasnost'* campaign continued to gather momentum during 1986 and 1987 with unprecedented coverage of misconduct by KGB officials in arresting a Soviet reporter who uncovered corruption in a coal-mining region of the Ukraine and anti-Russian rioting in the Central Asian city of Alma-Ata.[38] Television coverage of the West was also less polemical. Favorable reports were broadcast on a variety of subjects including Western fashion, rock music, and fast-food restaurants.

All of these developments did not come without stiff opposition, however. Gorbachev's speeches were replete with references to inertia, bureaucratic opposition, and foot-dragging.[39] In a 1986 address to a conference of social scientists, Gorbachev indicated that "an acute, uncompromising struggle of ideas" was under way between "the old ways" and "profound and revolutionary changes in Soviet society."[40] Sergei Zalygin, editor of the literary journal *Novy Mir,* recently characterized Soviet society as split between "progressives and conservatives."[41] The press also reported numerous cases of efforts to "sabotage" Gorbachev's ambitious economic and political reform.[42]

Gorbachev responded to these challenges by vigorously implementing a policy of "exchange of cadres" in order to break up local patronage networks. He made sweeping personnel changes throughout the party and state apparatus, in most cases appointing officials from Moscow to local posts. At the January 1987 Central Committee plenum, he succeeded in securing the promotion of three allies (one to candidate of the Politburo and two to the Party Secretariat) and the removal of Kazakh Party First Secretary D. A. Kunaev from the Politburo. However, none of Gorbachev's protegés were elevated to full, voting status on the Politburo, indicating that the Central

Committee members still had reservations about the scope and pace of Gorbachev's proposed reforms.

During his first two years in office, Gorbachev dramatically altered the makeup of the Council of Ministers, Gosplan, and most of the important industrial ministries, as well as the party apparatus charged with overseeing economic performance. With his own personnel in place, Gorbachev was well-positioned to use his extensive powers to impose reforms from above and to use political pressure to hold local party and state officials strictly accountable for implementing his policies. Whether he succeeds in overcoming his opponents remains to be seen. No one doubts his abilities, vigor, and resolve. During his speech nominating Gorbachev to office, former Foreign Minister Andrei Gromyko observed, "This man has a nice smile, but he has iron teeth."[43] A former classmate of Gorbachev characterized Gorbachev as "a reformer who considers politics as a means to an end, with its objective being to meet the needs of people."[44] These two sides of Gorbachev's character—the reform-oriented, flexible, pragmatic politician and the tough-minded disciplinarian—emerged in his speeches and in his policies. Gorbachev recognized that discipline alone would not solve the country's nagging economic, social, and political problems; he also recognized that reform without firm discipline and controls could be politically dangerous. Both approaches are necessary if a leader is to be successful in resolving the challenges that confront the Soviet Union today.

The Soviet Union is a society divided by many contradictory forces and ideals, and the manner in which those contradictions are manifested has shown remarkable continuity throughout history. The future course of the Soviet political system will evolve out of these contradictions and shape the policy options of the new generation of Soviet leaders. The contradictions between the need for reform and resistance to change, the divisions between center and periphery, the competing appeals of nationalism and internationalism, the ideal of a mass society and the persistence of a class society, the coexistence of official systems and informal arrangements, the paradox of superpower status and fears of insecurity, and the contradiction of revolutionary rhetoric and bureaucratic reality have characterized past regimes and will continue to influence the Soviet political system in the future. The Soviet Union remains a land of contradictions.

Notes

1. See Archie Brown, "Andropov: Discipline and Reform," *Problems of Communism* (January–February, 1983): 18–31.

2. For example, when Minister of Defense Andrei Grechko died at age seventy-three, he was replaced by sixty-eight-year-old Dmitri Ustinov. Similarly, Brezhnev named seventy-five-year-old Nikolai Tikhonov Chairman of the USSR Council of Ministers after the death of Alexei Kosygin, age seventy-six.

3. From a conversation with the author in Moscow in 1978.

4. Archie Brown, "Gorbachev: New Man in the Kremlin," *Problems of Communism* (May–June, 1985): 1–23.

5. For a discussion of political distinctions among elites in the USSR, see Stephen F. Cohen, "The Friends and Foes of Change: Reformism and Conservatism in the Soviet Union," *Slavic Review* (June 1979): 187–202.

6. George Breslauer makes a similar argument in *Khrushchev and Brezhnev as Leaders: Building Authority in Soviet Politics* (London: George Allen and Unwin, 1982), 4.

7. Ibid., 39–60. Also see works of leading Kremlinologists: Robert Conquest, *Power and Policy in the USSR* (New York: St. Martin's Press, 1969); Carl A. Linden, *Khrushchev and the Soviet Leadership, 1957–1964* (Baltimore: The Johns Hopkins University Press, 1966); and Michel Tatu, *Power in the Kremlin: From Khrushchev to Kosygin* (New York: Viking Press, 1967).

8. George Breslauer, "Reformism and Conservatism," *Slavic Review* (June 1978): 216.

9. Cited in Jerry Hough and Merle Fainsod, *How the Soviet Union Is Governed* (Cambridge: Harvard University Press, 1979), 213.

10. *Pravda,* 17 November 1964, p. 1. Also, *Pravda,* 7 November 1964; 27 March 1965; and 28 September 1965.

11. Cited in Hough and Fainsod, *How The Soviet Union Is Governed,* 253.

12. Ibid., 254.

13. Based on biographical data from Borys Lewytzkyj, ed., *Who's Who in the Soviet Union* (Munich: K. G. Saur, 1984).

14. The low point in public respect for Brezhnev may well have been at his funeral. Leading Brezhnev's funeral procession through Red Square, Brezhnev's daughter scandalized the public by wearing knee-high Italian leather boots and a full-length fox fur coat, in sharp contrast to the customary dark wool coat.

15. Lewytzkyj, *Who's Who in the Soviet Union.*

16. Ibid.

17. For example, see *Pravda,* 11 April 1984, pp. 1–2; *Pravda,* 29 May 1984, pp. 1–2; and *Pravda,* 6 November 1984, p. 1.

18. *Pravda,* 21 February 1985, p. 2.

19. In the case of agriculture, all of the former agriculturally related ministries were abolished and placed under the direction of the State Committee for the Agro-Industrial Complex. In the other two sectors, however, the ministries were retained, but were subordinated to an "umbrella" coordinating body within the Presidium of the USSR Council of Ministers.

20. Cited in Elizabeth Teague, "Aganbegian Outlines Gorbachev's Economic Policy," *Radio Liberty Research Bulletin,* no. 338 (1985): 356, 362.

21. For example, see "The Novosibirsk Report," *Survey* (Spring 1984): 88–108; and Abel Aganbegian, "Na novom etape ekonomicheskogo stroitel'stva," *EKO,* no. 8 (1985): 3–24.

22. Based on a survey of TASS announcements published in the Soviet press in 1985 and 1986. Figures for party secretaries are based on data compiled by Professor Nobuo Shimotomai of Seikei University and presented to a conference on Soviet Studies held at the Slavic Research Center, Hokkaido University, Sapporo, Japan, January 31–February 1, 1986.

23. Ibid.

24. Ibid.

25. Ibid.

26. Aganbegian, "Na novom etape ekonomicheskogo stroitel'stva"; and Abel Aganbegian, "Strategiia uskoreniia sotsial'no-ekonomicheskogo razvitiia," *Problemy mira i sotsializma,* no. 9 (1985): 13–18.

27. *Pravda,* 7 March 1986, p. 1.

28. *Pravda,* 27 March 1985, p. 1.

29. *Leningradskaia pravda,* 18 May 1985, pp. 1–2.

30. For example, see Iurii Andropov, "Ucheniie Karla Marksa i nekotorye voprosy sotsialisticheskogo stroitel'stva v SSSR," *Kommunist,* no. 3 (1983): 9–23.

31. "Programma Kommunisticheskoi Partii Sovetskogo Soiuza," *Pravda,* 7 March 1986, pp. 3–10.

32. *Pravda,* 26 February 1986, p. 1.

33. *Pravda,* 10 November 1985, p. 1.

34. *Pravda,* 26 February 1986, p. 1.

35. For example, see *Pravda,* 29 August 1986, p. 1.

36. TASS, 27 January 1987, reported in Elizabeth Teague, "Gorbachev Discusses Personnel Policy," *Radio Liberty Research Bulletin,* 28 January 1987, p. 1.

37. *New York Times,* 28 January 1987, p. 4.

38. See *Pravda,* 4 January 1987, p. 3; and *Literaturnaia gazeta,* 1 January 1987, p. 10.

39. For example, see *Pravda,* 2 August 1986, pp. 1–2.

40. Moscow Television, 1 October 1986, reported in Elizabeth Teague, "Charges of Resistance to Restructuring Intensify," *Radio Liberty Research Bulletin,* 26 January 1987, p. 1.

41. Ibid.

42. *Izvestiia,* 17 January 1987, p. 1.

45. Cited in Michael Dobbs, "Gorbachev: All Smiles, Steel Teeth," *Washington Post,* 10 October 1985.

44. Zdenek Mlynar, "My Fellow Student Mikhail Gorbachev," *L'Unita* (Rome), 9 April 1985, p. 9.

Selected Bibliography

Barghoorn, Frederick. "Problems of Policy and Political Behavior." *Slavic Review* (June 1978): 211–215.

Bialar, Seweryn. *Stalin's Successors: Leadership, Stability, and Change in the Soviet Union.* Cambridge: Cambridge University Press, 1980.

Bialer, Seweryn, and Thane Gustafson, eds. *Russia at the Crossroads: The 26th Congress of the CPSU.* London: George Allen and Unwin, 1982.

Breslauer, George. *Khrushchev and Brezhnev as Leaders: Building Authority in Soviet Politics.* London: George Allen and Unwin, 1982.

Breslauer, George. "Reformism and Conservatism." *Slavic Review* (June 1978): 216–219.

Brown, Archie. "Andropov: Discipline and Reform." *Problems of Communism* (January–February, 1983): 18–31.

Brown, Archie. "Gorbachev: New Man in the Kremlin." *Problems of Communism* (May–June, 1985): 1–23.

Cohen, Stephen F. "The Friends and Foes of Change: Reformism and Conservatism in the Soviet Union." *Slavic Review* (June 1979: 187–202.

Colton, Timothy J. *The Dilemma of Reform in the Soviet Union.* New York: Council on Foreign Relations, 1984.

Hough, Jerry. *Soviet Leadership in Transition.* Washington: Brookings Institution Press, 1980.

Hough, Jerry, and Merle Fainsod. *How the Soviet Union Is Governed.* Cambridge: Harvard University Press, 1979.

Meissner, Boris. "Transition in the Kremlin." *Problems of Communism* (January–February, 1983): 8–17.

Nogee, Joseph L. *Soviet Politics: Russia after Brezhnev.* New York: Praeger, 1985.

Rigby, T. H. "Forward From Who Gets What, When, How." *Slavic Review* (June 1978): 203–207.

Rigby, T. H., Archie Brown, and Peter Reddaway, eds. *Authority, Power, and Policy in the USSR.* London: Macmillan, 1980.

Rush, Myron. "Succeeding Brezhnev." *Problems of Communism* (January–February, 1983): 2–7.

Starr, S. Frederick. "Unity, Duality, or Fragmentation?" *Slavic Review* (June 1978): 208–210.

Zlotnik, Marc D. "Chernenko Succeeds." *Problems of Communism* (March–April, 1984): 17–31.

Appendix A

The Constitution (Fundamental Law) of the USSR, 1977

The Great October Socialist Revolution, made by the workers and peasants of Russia under the leadership of the Communist Party headed by Lenin, overthrew capitalist and landowner rule, broke the fetters of oppression, established the dictatorship of the proletariat, and created the Soviet state, a new type of state, the basic instrument for defending the gains of the revolution and for building socialism and communism. Humanity thereby began the epoch-making turn from capitalism to socialism.

After achieving victory in the Civil War and repulsing imperialist intervention, the Soviet government carried through far-reaching social and economic transformations, and put an end once and for all to exploitation of man by man, antagonisms between classes, and strife between nationalities. The unification of the Soviet Republics in the Union of Soviet Socialist Republics multiplied the forces and opportunities of the peoples of the country in the building of socialism. Social ownership of the means of production and genuine democracy for the working masses were established. For the first time in the history of mankind a socialist society was created.

The strength of socialism was vividly demonstrated by the immortal feat of the Soviet people and their Armed Forces in achieving their historic victory in the Great Patriotic War. This victory consolidated the influence and international standing of the Soviet Union and created new opportunities for growth of the forces of socialism, national liberation, democracy and peace throughout the world.

Continuing their creative endeavors, the working people of the Soviet Union have ensured rapid, all-round development of the country and steady improvement of the socialist system. They have consolidated the alliance of the working class, collective-farm peasantry, and people's intelligentsia, and friendship of the nations and nationalities of the USSR. Socio-political and ideological unity of Soviet society, in which the working class is the leading force, has been achieved. The aims of the dictatorship of the proletariat having been fulfilled, the Soviet state has become a state of the whole people. The leading role of the Communist Party, the vanguard of all the people, has grown.

In the USSR a developed socialist society has been built. At this stage, when socialism is developing on its own foundations, the creative forces of the new system and the advantages of the socialist way of life are becoming increasingly evident, and the working people are more and more widely enjoying the fruits of their great revolutionary gains.

It is a society in which powerful productive forces and progressive science and culture have been created, in which the well-being of the people is constantly rising, and more and more favorable conditions are being provided for the all-round development of the individual.

It is a society of mature socialist social relations, in which, on the basis of the drawing together of all classes and social strata and of the juridical and factual equality of all its nations and nationalities and their fraternal cooperation, a new historical community of people has been formed—the Soviet people.

It is a society of high organizational capacity, ideological commitment, and consciousness of the working people, who are patriots and internationalists.

It is a society in which the law of life is concern of all for the good of each and concern of each for the good of all.

It is a society of true democracy, the political system of which ensures effective management of all public affairs, ever more active participation of the working people in running the state, and the combining of citizens' real rights and freedoms with their obligations and responsibility to society.

Developed socialist society is a natural, logical stage on the road to communism.

The supreme goal of the Soviet state is the building of a classless communist society in which there will be public, communist self-government. The main aims of the people's socialist state are: to lay the material and technical foundation of communism, to perfect socialist social relations and transform them into communist relations, to mold the citizen of communist society, to raise the people's living and cultural standards, to safeguard the country's security, and to further consolidation of peace and development of international cooperation.

The Soviet people, guided by the ideas of scientific communism and true to their revolutionary traditions, relying on the great social, economic, and political gains of socialism, striving for the further development of socialist democracy, taking into account the international position of the USSR as part of the world system of socialism, and conscious of their internationalist responsibility, preserving continuity of the ideas and principles of the first Soviet Constitution of 1918, the 1924 Constitution of the USSR and the 1936 Constitution of the USSR, hereby affirm the principles of the social structure and policy of the USSR, and define the rights, freedoms and obligations of citizens, and the principles of the organization of the socialist state of the whole people, and its aims, and proclaim these in this Constitution.

I. PRINCIPLES OF THE SOCIAL STRUCTURE AND POLICY OF THE USSR

Chapter 1   The Political System

Article I. The Union of Soviet Socialist Republics is a socialist state of the whole people, expressing the will and interests of the workers, peasants, and intelligentsia, the working people of all the nations and nationalities of the country.

Article 2. All power in the USSR belongs to the people.

The people exercise state power through Soviets of People's Deputies, which constitute the political foundation of the USSR.

All other state bodies are under the control of, and accountable to, the Soviets of People's Deputies.

Article 3. The Soviet state is organized and functions on the principle of democratic centralism, namely the electiveness of all bodies of state authority from the lowest to the highest, their accountability to the people, and the obligation of lower bodies to observe the decisions of higher ones. Democratic centralism combines central leadership with local initiative and creative activity and with the responsibility of each state body and official for work entrusted to them.

Article 4. The Soviet state and all its bodies function on the basis of socialist law, ensure the maintenance of law and order, and safeguard the interests of society and the rights and freedoms of citizens.

State organizations, public organizations and officials shall observe the Constitution of the USSR and Soviet laws.

Article 5. Major matters of state shall be submitted to nationwide discussion and put to a popular vote (referendum).

Article 6. The leading and guiding force of Soviet society and the nucleus of its political system, of all state organizations and public organizations, is the Communist Party of the Soviet Union. The CPSU exists for the people and serves the people.

The Communist Party, armed with Marxism-Leninism, determines the general perspectives of the development of society and the course of the home and foreign policy of the USSR, directs the great constructive work of the Soviet people, and imparts a planned, systematic and theoretically substantiated character to their struggle for the victory of communism.

All Party organizations shall function within the framework of the Constitution of the USSR.

Article 7. Trade unions, the All-Union Leninist Young Communist League, cooperatives, and other public organizations, participate, in accordance with the aims laid down in their rules, in managing state and public affairs, and in deciding political, economic, and social and cultural matters.

Article 8. Work collectives take part in discussing the deciding state and public affairs, in planning production and social development, in training and placing personnel, and in discussing and deciding matters pertaining to the management of enterprises and institutions, the improvement of working and living conditions, and the use of funds allocated both for developing production and for social and cultural purposes and financial incentives.

Work collectives promote socialist emulation, the spread of progressive methods of work, and the strengthening of production discipline, educate their members in the spirit of communist morality, and strive to enhance their political consciousness and raise their cultural level and skills and qualifications.

Article 9. The principal direction in the development of the political system of Soviet society is the extension of socialist democracy, namely ever broader participation of citizens in managing the affairs of society and the state, continuous improvement of the machinery of state, heightening of the activity of public organizations, strenthening of the system of people's control, consolidation of the legal foundations of the functioning of the state and of public life, greater openness and publicity, and constant responsiveness to public opinion.

Chapter 2 The Economic System

Article 10. The foundation of the economic system of the USSR is socialist ownership of the means of production in the form of state property (belonging to all the people), and collective farm and cooperative property.

Socialist ownership also embraces the property of trade unions and other public organizations which they require to carry out their purposes under their rules.

The state protects socialist property and provides conditions for its growth.

No one has the right to use socialist property for personal gain or other selfish ends.

Article 11. State property, i.e., the common property of the Soviet people, is the principal form of socialist property.

The land, its minerals, waters, and forests are the exclusive property of the state. The state owns the basic means of production in industry, construction, and agriculture; means of transport and communication; the bank; the property of state-run trade organizations and public utilities, and other state-run undertakings; most urban housing; and other property necessary for state purposes.

Article 12. The property of collective farms and other cooperative organizations, and of their joint undertakings, comprises the means of production and other assets which they require for the purposes laid down in their rules.

The land held by collective farms is secured to them for their free use in perpetuity.

The state promotes development of collective farm and cooperative property and its approximation to state property.

Collective farms, like other land users, are obliged to make effective and thrifty use of the land and to increase its fertility.

Article 13. Earned income forms the basis of the personal property of Soviet citizens. The personal property of citizens of the USSR may include articles of everyday use, personal consumption and convenience, the implements and other objects of a small-holding, a house, and earned savings. The personal property of citizens and the right to inherit it are protected by the state.

Citizens may be granted the use of plots of land, in the manner prescribed by law, for a subsidiary small-holding (including the keeping of livestock and poultry), for fruit and vegetable growing or for building an individual dwelling. Citizens are required to make rational use of the land allotted to them. The state and collective farms provide assistance to citizens in working their small-holdings.

Property owned or used by citizens shall not serve as a means of deriving unearned income or be employed to the detriment of the interests of society.

Article 14. The source of the growth of social wealth and of the well-being of the people, and of each individual, is the labor, free from exploitation, of Soviet people.

The state exercises control over the measure of labor and of consumption in accordance with the principle of socialism: "From each according to his ability, to each according to his work." It fixes the rate of taxation on taxable income.

Socially useful work and its results determine a person's status in society. By combining material and moral incentives and encouraging innovation and a creative attitude to work, the state helps transform labor into the prime vital need of every Soviet citizen.

Article 15. The supreme goal of social production under socialism is the fullest possible satisfaction of the people's growing material, and cultural and intellectual requirements.

Relying on the creative initiative of the working people, socialist emulation, and scientific and technological progress, and by improving the forms and methods of economic management, the state ensures growth of the productivity of labor, raising of the efficiency of production and of the quality of work, and dynamic, planned, proportionate development of the economy.

Article 16. The economy of the USSR is an integral economic complex comprising all the elements of social production, distribution, and exchange on its territory.

The economy is managed on the basis of state plans for economic and social development, with due account of the sectoral and territorial principles, and by combining centralized direction with the managerial independence and initiative of individual and amalgamated enterprises and other organizations, for which active use is made of management accounting, profit, cost, and other economic levers and incentives.

Article 17. In the USSR, the law permits individual labor in handicrafts, farming, the provision of services for the public, and other forms of activity based exclusively on the personal work of individual citizens and members of their families. The state makes regulations for such work to ensure that it serves the interests of society.

Article 18. In the interests of the present and future generations, the necessary steps are taken in the USSR to protect and make scientific, rational use of the land and its mineral and water resources, and the plant and animal kingdoms, to preserve the purity of air and water, ensure reproduction of natural wealth, and improve the human environment.

Chapter 3   Social Development and Culture

Article 19. The social basis of the USSR is the unbreakable alliance of the workers, peasants, and intelligentsia.

The state helps enhance the social homogeneity of society, namely the elimination of class differences and of the essential distinctions between town and country and between mental and physical labor, and the all-round development and drawing together of all the nations and nationalities of the USSR.

Article 20. In accordance with the communist ideal—"The free development of each is the condition of the free development of all"—the state pursues the aim of giving citizens more and more real opportunities to apply their creative energies, abilities, and talents, and to develop their personalities in every way.

Article 21. The state concerns itself with improving working conditions, safety and labor protection and the scientific organization of work, and with reducing and ultimately eliminating all arduous physical labor through comprehensive mechanization and automation of production processes in all branches of the economy.

Article 22. A program is being consistently implemented in the USSR to convert agricultural work into a variety of industrial work, to extend the network of educational, cultural and medical institutions, and of trade, public catering, service and public utility facilities in rural localities, and transform hamlets and villages into well-planned and well-appointed settlements.

Article 23. The state pursues a steady policy of raising people's pay levels and real incomes through increase in productivity.

In order to satisfy the needs of Soviet people more fully social consumption funds are created. The state, with the broad participation of public organizations and work collectives, ensures the growth and just distribution of these funds.

Article 24. In the USSR, state systems of health protection, social security, trade and public catering, communal services and amenities, and public utilities, operate and are being extended.

The state encourages cooperatives and other public organizations to provide all types of services for the population. It encourages the development of mass physical culture and sport.

Article 25. In the USSR there is a uniform system of public education, which is being constantly improved, that provides general education and vocational training for citizens, serves the communist education and intellectual and physical development of the youth, and trains them for work and social activity.

Article 26. In accordance with society's needs the state provides for planned development of science and the training of scientific personnel and organizes introduction of the results of research in the economy and other spheres of life.

Article 27. The state concerns itself with protecting, augmenting and making extensive use of society's cultural wealth for the moral and aesthetic education of the Soviet people, for raising their cultural level.

In the USSR development of the professional, amateur and folk arts is encouraged in every way.

Chapter 4   Foreign Policy

Article 28. The USSR steadfastly pursues a Leninist policy of peace and stands for strengthening of the security of nations and broad international cooperation.

The foreign policy of the USSR is aimed at ensuring international conditions favorable for building communism in the USSR, safeguarding the state interests of the Soviet Union, consolidating the positions of world socialism, supporting the struggle of peoples for national liberation and social progress, preventing wars of aggression, achieving universal and complete disarmament, and consistently implementing the principle of the peaceful coexistence of states with different social systems.

In the USSR war propaganda is banned.

Article 29. The USSR's relations with other states are based on observance of the following principles: sovereign equality; mutual renunciation of the use or threat of force; inviolability of frontiers; territorial integrity of states; peaceful settlement of disputes; non-intervention in internal affairs; respect for human rights and fundamental freedoms; the equal rights of peoples and their right to decide their own destiny; cooperation among states; and fulfillment in good faith of obligations arising from the generally recognized principles and rules of international law, and from the international treaties signed by the USSR.

Article 30. The USSR, as part of the world system of socialism and of the socialist community, promotes and strengthens friendship, cooperation, and comradely mutual assistance with other socialist countries on the basis of the principle of socialist internationalism, and takes an active part in socialist economic integration and the socialist international division of labor.

Chapter 5   Defense of the Socialist Motherland

Article 31. Defense of the Socialist Motherland is one of the most important functions of the state, and is the concern of the whole people.

In order to defend the gains of socialism, the peaceful labor of the Soviet people, and the sovereignty and territorial integrity of the state, the USSR maintains Armed Forces and has instituted universal military service.

The duty of the Armed Forces of the USSR to the people is to provide reliable defense of the Socialist Motherland and to be in constant combat readiness, guaranteeing that any aggressor is instantly repulsed.

Article 32. The state ensures the security and defense capability of the country, and supplies the Armed Forces of the USSR with everything necessary for that purpose.

The duties of state bodies, public organizations, officials, and citizens in regard to safeguarding the country's security and strengthening its defense capacity are defined by the legislation of the USSR.

II. THE STATE AND THE INDIVIDUAL

Chapter 6   Citizenship of the USSR. Equality of Citizens' Rights

Article 33. Uniform federal citizenship is established for the USSR. Every citizen of a Union Republic is a citizen of the USSR.

The grounds and procedure for acquiring or forfeiting Soviet citizenship are defined by the Law on Citizenship of the USSR.

When abroad, citizens of the USSR enjoy the protection and assistance of the Soviet state.

Article 34. Citizens of the USSR are equal before the law, without distinction of origin, social or property status, race or nationality, sex, education, language, attitude to religion, type and nature of occupation, domicile, or other status.

The equal rights of citizens of the USSR are guaranteed in all fields of economic, political, social, and cultural life.

Article 35. Women and men have equal rights in the USSR.

Exercise of these rights is ensured by according women equal access with men to education and vocational and professional training, equal opportunities in employment, remuneration, and promotion, and in social and political, and cultural activity, and by special labor and health protection measures for women; by providing conditions enabling mothers to work; by legal protection, and material and moral support for mothers and children, including paid leaves and other benefits for expectant mothers, and gradual reduction of working time for mothers with small children.

Article 36. Citizens of the USSR of different races and nationalities have equal rights.

Exercise of these rights is ensured by a policy of all-round development and drawing together of all the nations and nationalities of the USSR, by educating citizens in the spirit of Soviet patriotism and socialist internationalism, and by the possibility to use their native language and the languages of other peoples of the USSR.

Any direct or indirect limitation of the rights of citizens or establishment of direct or indirect privileges on grounds of race or nationality, and any advocacy of racial or national exclusiveness, hostility or contempt, are punishable by law.

Article 37. Citizens of other countries and stateless persons in the USSR are guaranteed the rights and freedoms provided by law, including the right to apply to a court and other state bodies for the protection of their personal, property, family and other rights.

Citizens of other countries and stateless persons, when in the USSR, are obliged to respect the Constitution of the USSR and observe Soviet laws.

Article 38. The USSR grants the right of asylum to foreigners persecuted for defending the interests of the working people and the cause of peace, or for participation in the revolutionary and national-liberation movement, or for progressive social and political, scientific or other creative activity.

Chapter 7   The Basic Rights, Freedoms, and Duties of Citizens of the USSR

Article 39. Citizens of the USSR enjoy in full the social, economic, political and personal rights and freedoms proclaimed and guaranteed by the Constitution of the USSR and by Soviet laws. The socialist system ensures enlargement of the rights and freedoms of citizens and continuous improvement of their living standards as social, economic, and cultural development programs are fulfilled.

Enjoyment by citizens of their rights and freedoms must not be to the detriment of the interests of society or the state, or infringe the rights of other citizens.

Article 40. Citizens of the USSR have the right to work (that is, to guaranteed employment and pay in accordance with the quantity and quality of their work, and not below the state-established minimum), including the right to choose their trade or profession, type of job and work in accordance with their inclinations, abilities, training and education, with due account of the needs of society.

This right is ensured by the socialist economic system, steady growth of the productive forces, free vocational and professional training, improvement of skills, training in new trades or professions, and development of the systems of vocational guidance and job placement.

Article 41. Citizens of the USSR have the right to rest and leisure.

This right is ensured by the establishment of a working week not exceeding 41 hours, for workers and other employees, a shorter working day in a number of trades and industries, and shorter hours for night work; by the provision of paid annual holidays, weekly days of rest, extension of the network of cultural, educational and health-building institutions, and the development on a mass scale of sport, physical cultural, and camping and tourism; by the provision of neighborhood recreational facilities, and of other opportunity for rational use of free time.

The length of collective farmers' working and leisure time is established by their collective farms.

Article 42. Citizens of the USSR have the right to health protection.

This right is ensured by free, qualified medical care provided by state health insitutions; by extension of the network of therapeutic and health-building institutions; by the development and improvement of safety and hygiene in industry; by carrying out broad prophylactic measures; by measures to improve the environment; by special care for the health of the rising generation, including prohibition of child labor, excluding the work done by children as part of the school curriculum; and by developing research to prevent and reduce the incidence of disease and ensure citizens a long and active life.

Article 43. Citizens of the USSR have the right to maintenance in old age, in sickness, and in the event of complete or partial disability of loss of the breadwinner.

This right is guaranteed by social insurance of workers and other employees and collective farmers; by allowances for temporary disability; by the provision by the state or by collective farms of retirement pensions, disability pensions, and pensions for loss of the breadwinner; by providing employment for the partially disabled; by care for the elderly and the disabled; and by other forms of social security.

Article 44. Citizens of the USSR have the right to housing.

This right is ensured by the development and upkeep of state and socially owned housing; by assistance for cooperative and individual house building; by fair distribution, under public control, of the housing that becomes available through fulfillment of the program of building well-appointed dwellings, and by low rents and low charges for utility services. Citizens of the USSR shall take good care of the housing allocated to them.

Article 45. Citizens of the USSR have the right to education.

This right is ensured by free provision of all forms of education, by the institution of universal, compulsory secondary education, and broad development of vocational, specialized secondary, and higher education, in which instruction is oriented toward practical activity and production; by the development of extramural, correspondence and evening courses; by the provision of state scholarships and grants and privileges for students; by the free issue of school textbooks; by the opportunity to attend a school where teaching is in the native language; and by the provision of facilities for self-education.

Article 46. Citizens of the USSR have the right to enjoy cultural benefits.

This right is ensured by broad access to the cultural treasures of their own land and of the world that are preserved in state and other public collections; by the development and fair distribution of cultural and educational institutions throughout the country; by developing television and radio broadcasting and the publishing of books, newspapers and periodicals, and by extending the free library service; and by expanding cultural exchanges with other countries.

Article 47. Citizens of the USSR, in accordance with the aims of building communism, are guaranteed freedom of scientific, technical, and artistic work. This freedom is ensured by broadening scientific research, encouraging invention and innovation, and developing literature and the arts. The state provides the necessary material conditions for this and support for voluntary societies and unions of workers in the arts, organizes introduction of inventions and innovations in production and other spheres of activity.

The rights of authors, inventors and innovators are protected by the state.

Article 48. Citizens of the USSR have the right to take part in the management and administration of state and public affairs and in the discussion and adoption of laws and measures of All-Union and local significance.

This right is ensured by the opportunity to vote and to be elected to Soviets of People's Deputies and other elective state bodies, to take part in nationwide discussions and referendums, in people's control, in the work of state bodies, public organizations, and local community groups, and in meetings at places of work or residence.

Article 49. Every citizen of the USSR has the right to submit proposals to state bodies and public organizations for improving their activity, and to criticize shortcomings in their work.

Officials are obliged, within established time-limits, to examine citizens' proposals and requests, to reply to them, and to take appropriate action.

Persecution for criticism is prohibited. Persons guilty of such persecution shall be called to account.

Article 50. In accordance with the interests of the people and in order to strengthen and develop the socialist system, citizens of the USSR are guaranteed freedom of speech, of the press, and of assembly, meetings, street processions and demonstrations.

Exercise of these political freedoms is ensured by putting public buildings, streets and squares at the disposal of the working people and their organizations, by broad dissemination of information, and by the opportunity to use the press, television, and radio.

Article 51. In accordance with the aims of building communism, citizens of the USSR have the right to associate in public organizations that promote their political activity and initiative and satisfaction for their various interests.

Public organizations are guaranteed conditions for successfully performing the functions defined in their rules.

Article 52. Citizens of the USSR are guaranteed freedom of conscience, that is, the right to profess or not to profess any religion, and to conduct religious worship of atheistic propaganda. Incitement of hostility or hatred on religious grounds is prohibited.

In the USSR, the church is separated from the state, and the school from the church.

Article 53. The family enjoys the protection of the state.

Marriage is based on the free consent of the woman and the man; the spouses are completely equal in their family relations.

The state helps the family by providing and developing a broad system of childcare institutions, by organizing and improving communal services and public catering, by paying grants on the birth of a child, by providing children's allowances and benefits for large families, and other forms of family allowances and assistance.

Article 54. Citizens of the USSR are guaranteed inviolability of the person. No one may be arrested except by a court decision or on the warrant of a procurator.

Article 55. Citizens of the USSR are guaranteed inviolability of the home. No one may, without lawful grounds, enter a home against the will of those residing in it.

Article 56. The privacy of citizens, and of their correspondence, telephone conversations, and telegraphic communications is protected by law.

Article 57. Respect for the individual and protection of the rights and freedoms of citizens are the duty of all state bodies, public organizations, and officials.

Citizens of the USSR have the right to protection by the courts against encroachments on their honor and reputation, life and health, and personal freedom and property.

Article 58. Citizens of the USSR have the right to lodge a complaint against the actions of officials, state bodies and public bodies. Complaints shall be examined according to the procedure and within the time-limit established by law. Actions by officials that contravene the law or exceed their powers, and infringe the rights of citizens, may be appealed against in a court in the manner prescribed by law.

Citizens of the USSR have the right to compensation for damage resulting from unlawful actions by state organizations and public organizations, or by officials in the performance of their duties.

Article 59. Citizens' exercise of their rights and freedoms is inseparable from the performance of their duties and obligations.

Citizens of the USSR are obliged to observe the Constitution of the USSR and Soviet laws, comply with the standards of socialist conduct, and uphold the honor and dignity of Soviet citizenship.

Article 60. It is the duty of, and a matter of honor for, every able-bodied citizen of the USSR to work conscientiously in his chosen, socially useful occupation, and strictly to observe labor discipline. Evasion of socially useful work is incompatible with the principles of socialist society.

Article 61. Citizens of the USSR are obliged to preserve and protect socialist property. It is the duty of a citizen of the USSR to combat misappropriation and squandering of state and socially owned property and to make thrifty use of the people's wealth.

Persons encroaching in any way on socialist property shall be punished according to the law.

Article 62. Citizens of the USSR are obliged to safeguard the interests of the Soviet state, and to enhance its power and prestige.

Defense of the Socialist Motherland is the sacred duty of every citizen of the USSR.

Betrayal of the Motherland is the gravest of crimes against the people.

Article 63. Military service in the ranks of the Armed Forces of the USSR is an honorable duty of Soviet citizens.

Article 64. It is the duty of every citizen of the USSR to respect the national dignity of other citizens, and to strengthen friendship of the nations and nationalities of the multinational Soviet state.

Article 65. A citizen of the USSR is obliged to respect the rights and lawful interests of other persons, to be uncompromising toward anti-social behavior, and to help maintain public order.

Article 66. Citizens of the USSR are obliged to concern themselves with the upbringing of children, to train them for socially useful work, and to raise them as worthy members of socialist society. Children are obliged to care for their parents and help them.

Article 67. Citizens of the USSR are obliged to protect nature and conserve its riches.

Article 68. Concern for the preservation of historical monuments and other cultural values is a duty and obligation of citizens of the USSR.

Article 69. It is the internationalist duty of citizens of the USSR to promote friendship and cooperation with peoples of other lands and help maintain and strengthen world peace.

III. THE NATIONAL–STATE STRUCTURE OF THE USSR

Chapter 8   The USSR—A Federal State

Article 70. The Union of Soviet Socialist Republics is an integral, federal, multi-national state formed on the principle of socialist federalism as a result of the free self-determination of nations and the voluntary association of equal Soviet Socialist Republics.

The USSR embodies the state unity of the Soviet people and draws all its nations and nationalities together for the purpose of jointly building communism.

Article 71. The Union of Soviet Socialist Republics unites:
the Russian Soviet Federated Socialist Republic,
the Ukrainian Soviet Socialist Republic,
the Belorussian Soviet Socialist Republic,
the Uzbek Soviet Socialist Republic,
the Kazakh Soviet Socialist Republic,
the Georgian Soviet Socialist Republic,
the Azerbaidzhan Soviet Socialist Republic,
the Lithuanian Soviet Socialist Republic,
the Moldavian Soviet Socialist Republic,
the Latvian Soviet Socialist Republic,
the Kirghiz Soviet Socialist Republic,
the Tadzhik Soviet Socialist Republic,
the Armenian Soviet Socialist Republic,
the Turkmen Soviet Socialist Republic,
the Estonian Soviet Socialist Republic.

Article 72. Each Union Republic shall retain the right freely to secede from the USSR.

Article 73. The jurisdiction of the Union of Soviet Socialist Republics, as represented by its highest bodies of state authority and administration, shall cover:

1) the admission of new republics to the USSR; endorsement of the formation of new autonomous republics and autonomous regions within Union Republics;

2) determination of the state boundaries of the USSR and approval of changes in the boundaries between Union Republics;

3) establishment of the general principles for the organization and functioning of republican and local bodies of state authority and administration;

4) the ensurance of uniformity of legislative norms throughout the USSR and establishment of the fundamentals of the legislation of the Union of Soviet Socialist Republics and Union Republics;

5) pursuance of a uniform social and economic policy; direction of the country's economy; determination of the main lines of scientific and technological progress and the general measures for rational exploitation and conservation of natural resources; the drafting and approval of state plans for the economic and social development of the USSR, and endorsement of reports on their fulfillment;

6) the drafting and approval of the consolidated Budget of the USSR, and endorsement of the report on its execution; management of a single monetary and credit system; determination of the taxes and revenues forming the Budget of the USSR; and the formulation of prices and wages policy;

7) direction of the sectors of the economy, and of enterprises and amalgamations under Union jurisdiction, and general direction of industries under Union-Republican jurisdiction;

8) issues of war and peace, defense of the sovereignty of the USSR and safeguarding of its frontiers and territory, and organization of defense; direction of the Armed Forces of the USSR;

9) state security;

10) representation of the USSR in international relations; the USSR's relations with other states and with international organizations; establishment of the general procedure for, and coordination of, the relations of Union Republics with other states and with international organizations; foreign trade and other forms of external economic activity on the basis of state monopoly;

11) control over observance of the Constitution of the USSR, and ensurance of conformity of the Constitutions of Union Republics to the Constitution of the USSR;

12) and settlement of other matters of All-Union importance.

Article 74. The laws of the USSR shall have the same force in all Union Republics. In the event of a discrepancy between a Union Republic law and an All-Union law, the law of the USSR shall prevail.

Article 75. The territory of the Union of Soviet Socialist Republics is a single entity and comprises the territories of the Union Republics.

The sovereignty of the USSR extends throughout its territory.

Chapter 9   The Union Soviet Socialist Republics

Article 76. A Union Republic is a sovereign Soviet socialist state that has united with other Soviet Republics in the Union of Soviet Socialist Republics.

Outside the spheres listed in Article 73 of the Constitution of the USSR, a Union Republic exercises independent authority on its territory.

A Union Republic shall have its own Constitution conforming to the Constitution of the USSR with the specific features of the Republic being taken into account.

Article 77. Union Republics take part in decision-making in the Supreme Soviet of the USSR, the Presidium of the Supreme Soviet of the USSR, the Government of the USSR, and other bodies of the Union of Soviet Socialist Republics in matters that come within the jurisdiction of the Union of Soviet Socialist Republics.

A Union Republic shall ensure comprehensive economic and social development on its territory, facilitate exercise of the powers of the USSR on its territory, and implement the decisions of the highest bodies of state authority and administration of the USSR.

In matters that come within its jurisdiction, a Union Republic shall coordinate and control the activity of enterprises, institutions, and organizations subordinate to the Union.

Article 78. The territory of a Union Republic may not be altered without its consent. The boundaries between Union Republics may be altered by mutual agreement of the Republics concerned, subject to ratification by the Union of Soviet Socialist Republics.

Article 79. A Union Republic shall determine its division into territories, regions, areas, and districts, and decide other matters relating to its administrative and territorial structure.

Article 80. A Union Republic has the right to enter into relations with other states, conclude treaties with them, exchange diplomatic and consular representatives, and take part in the work of international organizations.

Article 81. The sovereign rights of Union Republics shall be safeguarded by the USSR.

Chapter 10   The Autonomous Soviet Socialist Republic

Article 82. An Autonomous Republic is a constituent part of a Union Republic.

In spheres not within the jurisdiction of the Union of Soviet Socialist Republics and the Union Republic, an Autonomous Republic shall deal independently with matters within its jurisdiction.

An Autonomous Republic shall have its own Constitution conforming to the Constitutions of the USSR and the Union Republic with the specific features of the Autonomous Republic being taken into account.

Article 83. An Autonomous Republic takes part in decision-making through the highest bodies of state authority and administration of the USSR and of the Union Republic respectively, in matters that come within the jurisdiction of the USSR and the Union Republic.

An Autonomous Republic shall ensure comprehensive economic and social development on its territory, facilitate exercise of the powers of the USSR and the Union Republic on its territory, and implement decisions of the highest bodies of state authority and administration of the USSR and the Union Republic.

In matters within its jurisdiction, an Autonomous Republic shall coordinate and control the activity of enterprises, institutions, and organizations subordinate to the Union or the Union Republic.

Article 84. The territory of an Autonomous Republic may not be altered without its consent.

Article 85. The Russian Soviet Federated Socialist Republic includes the Bashkir, Buryiat, Daghestan, Kabardin-Balkar, Kalmyk, Karelian, Komi, Mari, Mordovian, North Ossetian, Tatar, Tuva, Udmurt, Chechen-Ingush, Chuvash, and Yakut Autonomous Soviet Socialist Republics.

The Uzbek Soviet Socialist Republic includes the Kara-Kalpak Autonomous Soviet Socialist Republic.

The Georgian Soviet Socialist Republic includes the Abkhasian and Adzhar Autonomous Soviet Socialist Republics.

The Azerbaijan Soviet Socialist Republic includes the Nakhichevan Autonomous Soviet Socialist Republic.

Chapter 11   The Autonomous Region and Autonomous Area

Article 86. An Autonomous Region is a constituent part of a Union Republic or Territory. The Law on an Autonomous Region, upon submission by the Soviet of People's Deputies of the Autonomous Region concerned, shall be adopted by the Supreme Soviet of the Union Republic.

Article 87. The Russian Soviet Federated Socialist Republic includes the Adygei, Gorno-Altai, Jewish, Karachai-Circassian, and Khakass Autonomous Regions.

The Georgian Soviet Socialist Republic includes the South Ossetian Autonomous Region.

The Azerbaijan Soviet Socialist Republic includes the Nagorno-Karabakh Autonomous Region.

The Tadzhik Soviet Socialist Republic includes the Gorno-Badakhshan Autonomous Region.

Article 88. An Autonomous Area is a constituent part of a Territory or Region. The Law on an Autonomous Area shall be adopted by the Supreme Soviet of the Union Republic concerned.

IV. SOVIETS OF PEOPLE'S DEPUTIES AND ELECTORAL PROCEDURE

Chapter 12   The System of Soviets of People's Deputies and the Principles of their Work

Article 89. The Soviets of People's Deputies, i.e., the Supreme Soviet of the USSR, the Supreme Soviets of Union Republics, the Supreme Soviets of Autonomous

Republics, the Soviets of People's Deputies of Territories and Regions, the Soviets of People's Deputies of Autonomous Regions and Autonomous Area, and the Soviets of People's Deputies of districts, cities, city districts, settlements and villages shall constitute a single system of bodies of state authority.

Article 90. The term of the Supreme Soviet of the USSR, the Supreme Soviets of Union Republics, and the Supreme Soviets of Autonomous Republics shall be five years.

The term of local Soviets of People's Deputies shall be two and a half years.

Elections to Soviets of People's Deputies shall be called not later than two months before expiry of the term of the Soviet concerned.

Article 91. The most important matters within the jurisdiction of the respective Soviets of People's Deputies shall be considered and settled at their sessions.

Soviets of People's Deputies shall elect standing commissions and form executive-administrative, and other bodies accountable to them.

Article 92. Soviets of People's Deputies shall form people's control bodies combining state control with control by the working people at enterprises, collective farms, institutions, and organizations.

People's control bodies shall check on the fulfillment of state plans and assignments, combat breaches of state discipline, localistic tendencies, narrow departmental attitudes, mismanagement, extravagance and waste, red tape and bureaucracy, and help improve the working of the state machinery.

Article 93. Soviets of People's Deputies shall direct all sectors of state, economic and social and cultural development, either directly or through bodies instituted by them, take decisions and ensure their execution, and verify their implementation.

Article 94. Soviets of People's Deputies shall function publicly on the basis of collective, free, constructive discussion and decision-making, of systematic reporting back to them and the people by their executive-administrative and other bodies, and of involving citizens on a broad scale in their work.

Soviets of People's Deputies and the bodies set up by them shall systematically inform the public about their work and the decisions taken by them.

Chapter 13   The Electoral System

Article 95. Deputies to all Soviets shall be elected on the basis of universal, equal, and direct suffrage by secret ballot.

Article 96. Elections shall be universal: all citizens of the USSR who have reached the age of 18 shall have the right to vote and to be elected, with the exception of persons who have been legally certified insane.

To be eligible for election to the Supreme Soviet of the USSR a citizen of the USSR must have reached the age of 21.

Article 97. Elections shall be equal: each citizen shall have one vote; all voters shall exercise the franchise on an equal footing.

Article 98. Elections shall be direct: Deputies to all Soviets of People's Deputies shall be elected by citizens by direct vote.

Article 99. Voting at elections shall be secret: control over voters' exercise of the franchise is inadmissible.

Article 100. The following shall have the right to nominate candidates: branches and organizations of the Communist Party of the Soviet Union, trade unions, and the All-Union Leninist Young Communist League; cooperatives and other public organizations; work collectives, and meetings of servicemen in their military units.

Citizens of the USSR and public organizations are guaranteed the right to free and all-round discussion of the political and personal qualities and competence of candidates, and the right to campaign for them at meetings, in the press, and on television and radio.

The expenses involved in holding elections to Soviets of People's Deputies shall be met by the state.

Article 101. Deputies to Soviets of People's Deputies shall be elected by constituencies.

A citizen of the USSR may not, as a rule, be elected to more than two Soviets of People's Deputies.

Elections to the Soviets shall be conducted by electoral commissions consisting of representatives of public organizations and work collectives, and of meetings of servicemen in military units.

The procedure for holding elections to Soviets by People's Deputies shall be defined by the laws of the USSR, and of Union and Autonomous Republics.

Article 102. Electors give mandates to their Deputies.

The appropriate Soviets of People's Deputies shall examine electors' mandates, take them into account in drafting economic and social development plans and in drawing up the budget, organize implementation of the mandates, and inform citizens about it.

Chapter 14   People's Deputies

Article 103. Deputies are the plenipotentiary representatives of the people in the Soviets of People's Deputies.

In the Soviets, Deputies deal with matters relating to state, economic and social and cultural development, organize implementation of the decisions of the Soviets, and exercise control over the work of state bodies, enterprises, institutions and organizations.

Deputies shall be guided in their activities by the interests of the state, and shall take the needs of their constituents into account and work to implement their electors' mandates.

Article 104. Deputies shall exercise their powers without discontinuing their regular employment or duties.

During sessions of the Soviet, and so as to exercise their Deputy's powers in other cases stipulated by law, Deputies shall be released from their regular employment or duties, with retention of their average earnings at their permanent place of work.

Article 105. A Deputy has the right to address inquiries to the appropriate state bodies and officials, who are obliged to reply to them at a session of the Soviet.

Deputies have the right to approach any state or public body, enterprise, institution, or organization on matters arising from their work as Deputies and to take part in considering the questions raised by them. The heads of the state or public bodies, enterprises, institutions or organizations concerned are obliged to receive Deputies without delay and to consider their proposals within the time-limit established by law.

Article 106. Deputies shall be ensured conditions for the unhampered and effective exercise of their rights and duties.

The immunity of Deputies, and other guarantees of their activity as Deputies, are defined in the Law on the Status of Deputies and other legislative acts of the USSR and of Union and Autonomous Republics.

Article 107. Deputies shall report on their work and on that of the Soviet to their constituents, and to the work collectives and public organizations that nominated them.

Deputies who have not justified the confidence of their constituents may be recalled at any time by decision of a majority of the electors in accordance with the procedure established by law.

V. HIGHER BODIES OF STATE AUTHORITY AND ADMINISTRATION OF THE USSR

Chapter 15   The Supreme Soviet of the USSR

Article 108. The highest body of state authority of the USSR shall be the Supreme Soviet of the USSR.

The Supreme Soviet of the USSR is empowered to deal with all matters within the jurisdiction of the Union of Soviet Socialist Republics, as defined by this Constitution.

The adoption and amendment of the Constitution of the USSR; admission of new Republics to the USSR; endorsement of the formation of new Autonomous Republics and Autonomous Regions; approval of the state plans for economic and social development, of the Budget of the USSR, and of reports on their execution; and the institution of bodies of the USSR accountable to it, are the exclusive prerogative of the Supreme Soviet of the USSR.

Laws of the USSR shall be enacted by the Supreme Soviet of the USSR or by a nationwide vote (referendum) held by decision of the Supreme Soviet of the USSR.

Article 109. The Supreme Soviet of the USSR shall consist of two chambers: the Soviet of the Union and the Soviet of Nationalities.

The two chambers of the Supreme Soviet of the USSR shall have equal rights.

Article 110. The Soviet of the Union and the Soviet of Nationalities shall have equal numbers of deputies.

The Soviet of the Union shall be elected by constituencies with equal populations.

The Soviet of Nationalities shall be elected on the basis of the following representation: 32 Deputies from each Union Republic, 11 Deputies from each Autonomous Republic, five Deputies from each Autonomous Region, and one Deputy from each Autonomous Area.

The Soviet of the Union and the Soviet of Nationalities, upon submission by the credentials commissions elected by them, shall decide on the validity of Deputies' credentials, and, in cases in which the election law has been violated, shall declare the election of the Deputies concerned null and void.

Article 111. Each chamber of the Supreme Soviet of the USSR shall elect a Chairman and four Vice-Chairmen.

The Chairmen of the Soviet of the Union and of the Soviet of Nationalities shall preside over the sittings of the respective chambers and conduct their affairs.

Joint sittings of the chambers of the Supreme Soviet of the USSR shall be presided over alternately by the Chairman of the Soviet of the Union and the Chairman of the Soviet of Nationalities.

Article 112. Sessions of the Supreme Soviet of the USSR shall be convened twice a year.

Special sessions shall be convened by the Presidium of the Supreme Soviet of the USSR at its discretion or on the proposal of a Union Republic, or of not less than one-third of the Deputies of one of the chambers.

A session of the Supreme Soviet of the USSR shall consist of separate and joint sittings of the chambers, and of meetings of the standing commissions of the chambers or commissions of the Supreme Soviet of the USSR held between the sittings of the chambers. A session may be opened and closed at either separate or joint sitting of the chambers.

Article 113. The right to initiate legislation in the Supreme Soviet of the USSR is vested in the Soviet of the Union and the Soviet of Nationalities, the Presidium of the Supreme Soviet of the USSR, the Council of Ministers of the USSR, Union Republics through their higher bodies of state authority, commissions of the Supreme Soviet of the USSR and standing commissions of its chambers, Deputies of the Supreme Soviet of the USSR, the Supreme Court of the USSR, and the Procurator-General of the USSR.

The right to initiate legislation is also vested in public organizations through their All-Union bodies.

Article 114. Bills and other matters submitted to the Supreme Soviet of the USSR shall be debated by its chambers at separate or joint sittings. Where necessary, a bill or other matter may be referred to one or more commissions for preliminary or additional consideration.

A law of the USSR shall be deemed adopted when it has been passed in each chamber of the Supreme Soviet of the USSR by a majority of the total number of its Deputies. Decisions and other acts of the Supreme Soviet of the USSR are adopted by a majority of the total number of Deputies of the Supreme Soviet of the USSR.

Bills and other very important matters of state may be submitted for nationwide discussion by a decision of the Supreme Soviet of the USSR or its Presidium taken on their own initiative or on the proposal of a Union Republic.

Article 115. In the event of disagreement between the Soviet of the Union and the Soviet of Nationalities, the matter at issue shall be referred for settlement to a conciliation commission formed by the chambers on a parity basis, after which it shall be considered for a second time by the Soviet of the Union and the Soviet of Nationalities at a joint sitting. If agreement is again not reached, the matter shall be postponed for debate at the next session of the Supreme Soviet of the USSR or submitted by the Supreme Soviet to a nationwide vote (referendum).

Article 116. Laws of the USSR and decisions and other acts of the Supreme Soviet of the USSR shall be published in the languages of the Union Republics over the signatures of the Chairman and Secretary of the Presidium of the Supreme Soviet of the USSR.

Article 117. A Deputy of the Supreme Soviet of the USSR has the right to address inquiries to the Council of Ministers of the USSR, and to Ministers and the heads of other bodies formed by the Supreme Soviet of the USSR. The Council of Ministers of the USSR, or the official to whom the inquiry is addressed, is obliged to give a verbal or written reply within three days at the given session of the Supreme Soviet of the USSR.

Article 118. A Deputy of the Supreme Soviet of the USSR may not be prosecuted, or arrested, or incur a court-imposed penalty, without the sanction of the Supreme Soviet of the USSR or, between its sessions, of the Presidium of the Supreme Soviet of the USSR.

Article 119. The Supreme Soviet of the USSR, at a joint sitting of its chambers, shall elect a Presidium of the Supreme Soviet of the USSR, which shall be a standing body of the Supreme Soviet of the USSR, accountable to it for all its work and exercising the functions of the highest body of state authority of the USSR between sessions of the Supreme Soviet, within the limits prescribed by the Constitution.

Article 120. The Presidium of the Supreme Soviet of the USSR shall be elected from among the Deputies and shall consist of a Chairman, First Vice-Chairman, 15 Vice-Chairmen (one from each Union Republic), a Secretary, and 21 members.

Article 121. The Presidium of the Supreme Soviet of the USSR shall:
1) name the date of elections to the Supreme Soviet of the USSR;
2) convene sessions of the Supreme Soviet of the USSR;
3) coordinate the work of the standing commissions of the chambers of the Supreme Soviet of the USSR;

4) ensure observance of the Constitution of the USSR and conformity of the Constitutions and laws of Union Republics to the Constitution and laws of the USSR;

5) interpret the laws of the USSR;

6) ratify and denounce international treaties of the USSR;

7) revoke decisions and ordinances of the Council of Ministers of the USSR and of the Councils of Ministers of Union Republics should they fail to conform to the law;

8) institute military and diplomatic ranks and other special titles; and confer the highest military and diplomatic ranks and other special titles;

9) institute orders and medals of the USSR, and honorific titles of the USSR; award orders and medals of the USSR; and confer honorific titles of the USSR;

10) grant citizenship of the USSR, and rule on matters of the renunciation or deprivation of citizenship of the USSR and of granting asylum;

11) issue All-Union acts of annesty and exercise the right of pardon;

12) appoint and recall diplomatic representatives of the USSR to other countries and to international organizations;

13) receive the letters of credence and recall of the diplomatic representatives of foreign states accredited to it;

14) form the Council of Defense of the USSR and confirm its composition; appoint and dismiss the high command of the Armed Forces of the USSR;

15) proclaim martial law in particular localities or throughout the country in the interests of defense of the USSR;

16) order general or partial mobilization;

17) between sessions of the Supreme Soviet of the USSR, proclaim a state of war in the event of an armed attack on the USSR, or when it is necessary to meet international treaty obligations relating to mutual defense against aggression;

18) and exercise other powers vested in it by the Constitution and laws of the USSR.

Article 122. The Presidium of the Supreme Soviet of the USSR, between sessions of the Supreme Soviet of the USSR and subject to submission for its confirmation at the next sessions, shall:

1) amend existing legislative acts of the USSR when necessary;

2) approve changes in the boundaries between Union Republics;

3) form and abolish Ministries and State Committees of the USSR on the recommendation of the Council of Ministers of the USSR;

4) relieve individual members of the Council of Ministers of the USSR of their responsibilities and appoint persons to the Council of Ministers on the recommendation of the Chairman of the Council of Ministers of the USSR.

Article 123. The Presidium of the Supreme Soviet of the USSR promulgates decrees and adopts decisions.

Article 124. On expiry of the term of the Supreme Soviet of the USSR, the Presidium of the Supreme Soviet of the USSR shall retain its powers until the newly elected Supreme Soviet of the USSR has elected a new Presidium.

The newly elected Supreme Soviet of the USSR shall be convened by the outgoing Presidium of the Supreme Soviet of the USSR within two months of the elections.

Article 125. The Soviet of the Union and the Soviet of Nationalities shall elect standing commissions from among the Deputies to make a preliminary review of matters coming within the jurisdiction of the Supreme Soviet of the USSR, to promote execution of the laws of the USSR and other acts of the Supreme Soviet of the USSR and its Presidium, and to check on the work of state bodies and organizations. The chambers of the Supreme Soviet of the USSR may also set up joint commissions on a parity basis.

When it deems it necessary, the Supreme Soviet of the USSR sets up commissions of inquiry and audit, and commissions on any matter.

All state and public bodies, organizations and officials are obliged to meet the requests of the commissions of the Supreme Soviet of the USSR and of its chambers, and submit the requisite materials and documents to them.

The commissions' recommendations shall be subject to consideration by state and public bodies, institutions and organizations. The commissions shall be informed, within the prescribed time-limit, or the results of such consideration or of the action taken.

Article 126. The Supreme Soviet of the USSR shall supervise the work of all state bodies accountable to it.

The Supreme Soviet of the USSR shall form a Committee of People's Control of the USSR to head the system of people's control.

The organization and procedure of people's control bodies are defined by the Law on People's Control in the USSR.

Article 127. The procedure of the Supreme Soviet of the USSR and of its bodies shall be defined in the Rules and Regulations of the Supreme Soviet of the USSR and others laws of the USSR enacted on the basis of the Constitution of the USSR.

Chapter 16   The Council of Ministers of the USSR

Article 128. The Council of Ministers of the USSR, i.e., the Government of the USSR, is the highest executive and administrative body of state authority of the USSR.

Article 129. The Council of Ministers of the USSR shall be formed by the Supreme Soviet of the USSR at a joint sitting of the Soviet of the Union and the Soviet of Nationalities, and shall consist of the Chairman of the Council of Ministers of the USSR, First Vice-Chairmen and Vice-Chairmen, Ministers of the USSR, and Chairmen of State Committees of the USSR.

The Chairmen of the Councils of Ministers of Union Republics shall be ex officio members of the Council of Ministers of the USSR.

The Supreme Soviet of the USSR, on the recommendation of the Chairman of the Council of Ministers of the USSR, may include in the Government of the USSR the heads of other bodies and organizations of the USSR.

The Council of Ministers of the USSR shall tender its resignation to a newly elected Supreme Soviet of the USSR at its first session.

Article 130. The Council of Ministers of the USSR shall be responsible and accountable to the Supreme Soviet of the USSR and, between sessions of the Supreme Soviet of the USSR, to the Presidium of the Supreme Soviet of the USSR.

The Council of Ministers of the USSR shall report regularly on its work to the Supreme Soviet of the USSR.

Article 131. The Council of Ministers of the USSR is empowered to deal with all matters of state administration within the jurisdiction of the Union of Soviet Socialist Republics insofar as, under the Constitution, they do not come within the competence of the Supreme Soviet of the USSR or the Presidium of the Supreme Soviet of the USSR.

Within its powers the Council of Ministers of the USSR shall:

1) ensure direction of economic, social and cultural development; draft and implement measures to promote the well-being and cultural development of the people, to develop science and engineering, to ensure rational exploitation and conservation of natural resources, to consolidate the monetary and credit system, to pursue a uniform prices, wages, and social security policy, and to organize state insurance and a uniform system of accounting and statistics; and

to organize the management of industrial, constructional, and agricultural enterprises and amalgamations, transport and communications undertakings, banks, and other organizations and institutions of Union subordination;

2) draft current and long-term state plans for the economic and social development of the USSR and the Budget of the USSR, and submit them to the Supreme Soviet of the USSR; take measures to execute the state plans and Budget; and report to the Supreme Soviet of the USSR on the implementation of the plans and Budget;

3) implement measures to defend the interests of the state, protect socialist property and maintain public order, and guarantee and protect citizens' rights and freedoms;

4) take measures to ensure state security;

5) exercise general direction of the development of the Armed Forces of the USSR, and determine the annual contingent of citizens to be called up for active military service;

6) provide general direction in regard to relations with other states, foreign trade and economic, scientific, technical, and cultural cooperation of the USSR with other countries; take measures to ensure fulfillment of the USSR's international treaties; and ratify and denounce intergovernmental international agreements;

7) and when necessary, form committees, central boards and other departments under the Council of Ministers of the USSR to deal with matters of economic, social and cultural development, and defense.

Article 132. A Presidium of the Council of Ministers of the USSR, consisting of the Chairman, the First Vice-Chairmen, and Vice-Chairmen of the Council of Ministers of the USSR, shall function as a standing body of the Council of Ministers of the USSR to deal with questions relating to guidance of the economy, and with other matters of state administration.

Article 133. The Council of Ministers of the USSR, on the basis of, and in pursuance of, the laws of the USSR and other decisions of the Supreme Soviet of the USSR and its Presidium, shall issue decisions and ordinances and verify their execution. The decisions and ordinances of the Council of Ministers of the USSR shall be binding throughout the USSR.

Article 134. The Council of Ministers of the USSR has the right, in matters within the jurisdiction of the Union of Soviet Socialist Republics, to suspend execution of decisions and ordinances of the Councils of Ministers of Union Republics, and to recind acts of ministries and state committees of the USSR, and of other bodies subordinate to it.

Article 135. The Council of Ministers of the USSR shall coordinate and direct the work of All-Union and Union-Republican ministries, state committees of the USSR, and other bodies subordinate to it.

All-Union ministries and state committees of the USSR shall direct the work of the branches of administration entrusted to them, or exercise inter-branch administration, throughout the territory of the USSR directly or through bodies set up by them.

Union-Republican ministries and state committees of the USSR direct the work of the branches of administration entrusted to them, or exercise inter-branch administration, as a rule, through the corresponding ministries and state committees, and other bodies of Union Republics, and directly administer individual enterprises and amalgamations of Union subordination. The procedure for transferring enterprises and amalgamations from Republic or local subordination to Union subordination shall be defined by the Presidium of the Supreme Soviet of the USSR.

Ministries and state committees of the USSR shall be responsible for the condition and development of the spheres of administration entrusted to them; within their competence, they issue orders and other acts on the basis of, and in execution of, the laws of the USSR and other decisions of the Supreme Soviet of the USSR and its Presidium, and of decisions and ordinances of the Council of Ministers of the USSR, and organize and verify their implementation.

Article 136. The competence of the Council of Ministers of the USSR and its Presidium, the procedure for their work, relationships between the Council of Ministers and other state bodies, and the list of All-Union and Union-Republican ministries and state committees of the USSR are defined, on the basis of the Constitution, in the Law on the Council of Ministers of the USSR.

VI. BASIC PRINCIPLES OF THE STRUCTURE OF THE BODIES OF STATE AUTHORITY AND ADMINISTRATION IN UNION REPUBLICS

Chapter 17   Higher Bodies of State Authority and Administration of a Union Republic

Article 137. The highest body of state authority of a Union Republic shall be the Supreme Soviet of that Republic.

The Supreme Soviet of a Union Republic is empowered to deal with all matters within the jurisdiction of the Republic under the Constitutions of the USSR and the Republic.

Adoption and amendment of the Constitution of a Union Republic; endorsement of state plans for economic and social development, of the Republic's Budget, and of reports on their fulfillment; and the formation of bodies accountable to the Supreme Soviet of the Union Republic are the exclusive prerogative of that Supreme Soviet.

Laws of a Union Republic shall be enacted by the Supreme Soviet of the Union Republic or by a popular vote (referendum) held by decision of the Republic's Supreme Soviet.

Article 138. The Supreme Soviet of a Union Republic shall elect a Presidium, which is a standing body of that Supreme Soviet and accountable to it for all its work. The composition and powers of the Presidium of the Supreme Soviet of a Union Republic shall be defined in the Constitution of the Union Republic.

Article 139. The Supreme Soviet of a Union Republic shall form a Council of Ministers of the Union Republic, i.e., the Government of that Republic, which shall be the highest executive and administrative body of state authority in the Republic.

The Council of Ministers of a Union Republic shall be responsible and accountable to the Supreme Soviet of that Republic or, between sessions of the Supreme Soviet, to its Presidium.

Article 140. The Council of Ministers of a Union Republic issues decisions and ordinances on the basis of, and in pursuance of, the legislative acts of the USSR and of the Union Republic, and of decisions and ordinances of the Council of Ministers of the USSR, and shall organize and verify their execution.

Article 141. The Council of Ministers of a Union Republic has the right to suspend the execution of decisions and ordinances of the Councils of Ministers of Autonomous Republics, to rescind the decisions and orders of the Executive Committees of Soviets of People's Deputies of Territories, Regions, and cities (i.e., cities under Republic jurisdiction) and of Autonomous Regions, and in Union Republics not divided into regions, of the Executive Committees of district and corresponding city Soviets of People's Deputies.

Article 142. The Council of Ministers of a Union Republic shall coordinate and direct the work of the Union-Republican and Republican ministries and of state committees of the Union Republic, and other bodies under its jurisdiction.

The Union-Republican ministries and state committees of a Union Republic shall direct the branches of administration entrusted to them, or exercise inter-branch control, and shall be subordinate to both the Council of Ministers of the Union Republic and the corresponding Union-Republican ministry or state committee of the USSR.

Republican ministries and state committees shall direct the branches of administration entrusted to them, or exercise inter-branch control, and shall be subordinate to the Council of Ministers of the Union Republic.

Chapter 18   Higher Bodies of State Authority and Administration of an Autonomous Republic

Article 143. The highest body of state authority of an Autonomous Republic shall be the Supreme Soviet of that Republic.

Adoption and amendment of the Constitution of an Autonomous Republic; endorsement of state plans for economic and social development, and of the Republic's Budget; and the formation of bodies accountable to the Supreme Soviet of the Autonomous Republic are the exclusive prerogative of that Supreme Soviet.

Laws of an Autonomous Republic shall be enacted by the Supreme Soviet of the Autonomous Republic.

Article 144. The Supreme Soviet of an Autonomous Republic shall elect a Presidium of the Supreme Soviet of the Autonomous Republic and shall form a Council of Ministers of the Autonomous Republic, i.e., the Government of that Republic.

Chapter 19   Local Bodies of State Authority and Administration

Article 145. The bodies of state authority in Territories, Regions, Autonomous Regions, Autonomous Areas, districts, cities, city districts, settlements, and rural communities shall be the corresponding Soviets of People's Deputies.

Article 146. Local Soviets of People's Deputies shall deal with all matters of local significance in accordance with the interests of the whole state and of the citizens residing in the area under their jurisdiction, implement decisions of higher bodies of state authority, guide the work of lower Soviets of People's Deputies, take part in the discussion of matters of Republican and All-Union significance, and submit their proposals concerning them.

Local Soviets of People's Deputies shall direct state, economic, social and cultural development within their territory; endorse plans of economic and social development and the local budget; exercise general guidance over state bodies, enterprises, institutions and organizations subordinate to them; ensure observance of the laws, maintenance of law and order, and protection of citizens' rights, and help strengthen the country's defense capacity.

Article 147. Within their powers, local Soviets of People's Deputies shall ensure the comprehensive, all-round economic and social development of their area; exercise control over the observance of legislation by enterprises, institutions and organizations subordinate to higher authorities and located in this area; and coordinate and supervise their activity as regards land use, nature conservation, building, employment of manpower, production of consumer goods, and social, cultural, communal and other services and amenities for the public.

Article 148. Local Soviets of People's Deputies shall decide matters within the powers accorded them by the legislation of the USSR and of the appropriate Union Republic and Autonomous Republic. Their decisions shall be binding on all enterprises, institutions, and organizations located in their area and on officials and citizens.

Article 149. The executive-administrative bodies of local Soviets shall be the Executive Committees elected by them from among their Deputies.

Executive Committees shall report on their work at least once a year to the Soviets that elected them and to meetings of citizens at their places of work or residence.

Article 150. Executive Committees of local Soviets of People's Deputies shall be directly accountable both to the Soviet that elected them and to the higher executive-administrative body.

VII. JUSTICE, ARBITRATION, AND PROCURATOR'S SUPERVISION

Chapter 20   Courts and Arbitration

Article 151. In the USSR justice is administered only by the courts.

In the USSR there are the following courts: the Supreme Court of the USSR, the Supreme Courts of Union Republics, the Supreme Courts of Autonomous Republics, Territorial, Regional, and city courts, courts of Autonomous Regions, courts of Autonomous Areas, district (city) people's courts, and military tribunals in the Armed Forces.

Article 152. All courts in the USSR shall be formed on the principle of the electiveness of judges and people's assessors.

People's judges of district (city) people's courts shall be elected for a term of five years by the citizens of the district (city) on the basis of universal, equal and direct suffrage by secret ballot. People's assessors of district (city) people's courts shall be elected for a term of two and a half years at meetings of citizens at their places of work or residence by a show of hands.

Higher courts shall be elected for a term of five years by the corresponding Soviet of People's Deputies.

The judges of military tribunals shall be elected for a term of five years by the Presidium of the Supreme Soviet of the USSR and people's assessors for a term of two and a half years by meetings of servicemen.

Judges and people's assessors are responsible and accountable to their electors or the bodies that elected them, shall report to them, and may be recalled by them in the manner prescribed by law.

Article 153. The Supreme Court of the USSR is the highest judicial body in the USSR and supervises the administration of justice by the courts of the USSR and Union Republics within the limits established by law.

The Supreme Court of the USSR shall be elected by the Supreme Soviet of the USSR and shall consist of a Chairman, Vice-Chairmen, members, and people's assessors. The Chairmen of the Supreme Courts of Union Republics are ex officio members of the Supreme Court of the USSR.

The organization and procedure of the Supreme Court of the USSR are defined in the Law on the Supreme Court of the USSR.

Article 154. The hearing of civil and criminal cases in all courts is collegial; in courts of first instance cases are heard with the participation of people's assessors. In the administration of justice people's assessors have all the rights of a judge.

Article 155. Judges and people's assessors are independent and subject only to the law.

Article 156. Justice is administered in the USSR on the principle of the equality of citizens before the law and the court.

Article 157. Proceedings in all courts shall be open to the public. Hearings in camera are only allowed in cases provided for by law, with observance of all the rules of judicial procedure.

Article 158. A defendant in a criminal action is guaranteed the right to legal assistance.

Article 159. Judicial proceedings shall be conducted in the language of the Union Republic, Autonomous Republic, Autonomous Region, or Autonomous Area, or in the language spoken by the majority of the people in the locality. Persons participating in court proceedings, who do not know the language in which they are being conducted, shall be ensured the right to become fully acquainted with the materials in the case; the services of an interpreter during the proceedings; and the right to address the court in their own language.

Article 160. No one may be adjudged guilty of a crime and subjected to punishment as a criminal except by the sentence of a court and in conformity with the law.

Article 161. Colleges of advocates are available to give legal assistance to citizens and organizations. In cases provided for by legislation citizens shall be given legal assistance free of charge.

The organization and procedure of the bar are determined by legislation of the USSR and Union Republics.

Article 162. Representatives of public organizations and of work collectives may take part in civil and criminal proceedings.

Article 163. Economic disputes between enterprises, institutions, and organizations are settled by state arbitration bodies within the limits of their jurisdiction.

The organization and manner of functioning of state arbitration bodies are defined in the Law on State Arbitration in the USSR.

Chapter 21   The Procurator's Office

Article 164. Supreme power of supervision over the strict and uniform observance of laws by all ministers, state committees and departments, enterprises, institutions and organizations, executive-administrative bodies of local Soviets of People's Deputies, collective farms, cooperatives and other public organizations, officials and citizens is vested in the Procurator-General of the USSR and procurators subordinate to him.

Article 165. The Procurator-General of the USSR is appointed by the Supreme Soviet of the USSR and is responsible and accountable to it and, between sessions of the Supreme Soviet, to the Presidium of the Supreme Soviet of the USSR.

Article 166. The procurators of Union Republics, Autonomous Republics, Territories, Regions and Autonomous Regions are appointed by the Procurator-General of the USSR. The procurators of Autonomous Areas and district and city procurators are appointed by the procurators of Union Republics, subject to confirmation by the Procurator-General of the USSR.

Article 167. The term of office of the Procurator-General of the USSR and all lower-ranking procurators shall be five years.

Article 168. The agencies of the Procurator's Office exercise their powers independently of any local bodies whatsoever, and are subordinate solely to the Procurator-General of the USSR.

The organization and procedure of the agencies of the Procurator's Office are defined in the Law on the Procurator's Office of the USSR.

VIII. THE EMBLEM, FLAG, ANTHEM, AND CAPITAL OF THE USSR

Article 169. The State Emblem of the Union of Soviet Socialist Republics is a hammer and sickle on a globe depicted in the rays of the sun and framed by ears of wheat, with the inscription "Workers of All Countries, Unite!" in the languages of the Union Republics. At the top of the Emblem is a five-pointed star.

Article 170. The State Flag of the Union of Soviet Socialist Republics is a rectangle of red cloth with a hammer and sickle depicted in gold in the upper corner next to the staff and with a five-pointed red star edged in gold above them. The ratio of the width of the flag to its length is 1:2.

Article 171. The State Anthem of the Union of Soviet Socialist Republics is confirmed by the Presidium of the Supreme Soviet of the USSR.

Article 172. The Capital of the Union of Soviet Socialist Republics is the city of Moscow.

IX. THE LEGAL FORCE OF THE CONSTITUTION OF THE USSR AND PROCEDURE FOR AMENDING THE CONSTITUTION

Article 173. The Constitution of the USSR shall have supreme legal force. All laws and other acts of state bodies shall be promulgated on the basis of and in conformity with it.

Article 174. The Constitution of the USSR may be amended by a decision of the Supreme Soviet of the USSR adopted by a majority of not less than two-thirds of the total number of Deputies of each of its chambers.

Appendix B

Rules of the CPSU (Communist Party of the Soviet Union) Approved by the Twenty-Seventh CPSU Congress

The Communist Party of the Soviet Union is the militant and tested vanguard of the Soviet people, uniting on principles of voluntary participation the advanced and most conscious segment of the working class, collective farm peasantry and intelligentsia of the USSR. Founded by V. I. Lenin as the advanced detachment of the working class, the Communist Party has covered a glorious road of struggle and led the working class and the toiling peasants to the victory of the Great October Socialist Revolution and the establishment of the dictatorship of the proletariat in our country. Under the leadership of the Communist Party, in the Soviet Union the exploiting classes were liquidated and the socio-political and ideological unity of the Soviet multinational society was established and is constantly strengthening. Socialism has won full and final victory. The proletarian state has developed into a state of the whole people. The country has entered the stage of developed socialism.

The CPSU, while remaining in its class essence and ideology the party of the working class, has become the party of the whole people.

The party exists for the people and serves the people. It is the highest form of socio-political organization, the nucleus of the political system and the leading and directing force of Soviet society. The party defines the general prospects of the country's development, ensures scientific leadership of the people's creative activity and gives an organized, planned and purposeful nature to their struggle to reach the final goal—the victory of communism.

In all its activity the CPSU is guided by Marxist-Leninist teaching and its Program in which are defined the tasks of the systematic and all-round improvement of socialism and of Soviet society's further advance towards communism on the basis of the acceleration of the country's socio-economic development.

The CPSU builds its work on the basis of strict observance of Leninist norms of party life and the principles of democratic centralism, collectiveness of leadership, the all-round development of intra-party democracy, the creative activeness of communists, criticism and self-criticism and broad publicity.

The immutable law of the life of the CPSU is the ideological and organizational unity and monolithic cohesion of its ranks and the high and conscious discipline of all communists. Any manifestation of factionalism and group activity is incompatible with Marxist-Leninist party principles and party membership. The party rids itself of persons who violate the Program and the CPSU Rules and who by their behavior compromise the high title of communist.

Creatively developing Marxism-Leninism, the CPSU resolutely combats any manifestations of revisionism and dogmatism, which are deeply alien to revolutionary theory.

The Communist Party of the Soviet Union is an integral part of the international communist movement. It is firmly based on tested Marxist-Leninist principles of proletarian and socialist internationalism and actively assists in strengthening the cooperation and cohesion of the fraternal socialist countries, the world system of socialism, and the international communist and workers' movement and displays solidarity with peoples struggling for national and social liberation, against imperialism and for the preservation of peace.

I. MEMBERS OF THE PARTY, THEIR DUTIES AND RIGHTS

1. Any citizen of the Soviet Union who accepts the Party Program and Rules, who actively participates in the building of communism, who works in a party organization, who implements party resolutions and pays membership dues may be a member of the CPSU.

2. The party member has the duty:

a) to implement firmly and unswervingly the party's general line and directives, explain the CPSU's domestic and foreign policy to the masses, organize the working people to implement it and promote the strengthening and expansion of the ties between the party and the people;

b) to set an example in labor, protect and augment socialist property, seek persistently to improve production efficiency, steadily increase labor productivity, improve output quality and introduce into the national economy the achievements of modern science, technology and advanced experience, improve his qualifications, be a vigorous champion of everything new and progressive, and make the greatest possible contribution to accelerating the country's socio-economic development;

c) to take an active part in the political life of the country and in the management of state and public affairs, set an example in doing one's civic duty and actively promote the increasingly full implementation of socialist people's self-management;

d) to master Marxist-Leninist theory, expand his political and cultural horizons and promote in every possible way the raising of the consciousness and the ideological and moral growth of the Soviet people. To wage a resolute struggle against any manifestations of bourgeois ideology, private ownership mentality, religious prejudices and other views and customs which are alien to the socialist way of life;

e) to strictly observe the norms of communist morality, affirm the principle of social justice inherent in socialism, put public interests above personal interests, display modesty and decency, sensitivity and attention towards people, respond promptly to the working people's demands and needs and be truthful and honest to the party and people;

f) to consistently convey to the masses of working people the ideas of proletarian and socialist internationalism and Soviet patriotism, combat manifestations of nationalism and chauvinism and actively help to strengthen the friendship among the USSR's peoples and fraternal ties with the socialist countries and with the proletarians and working people of the whole world;

g) to promote in every possible way the strengthening of the USSR's defense power and to wage a tireless struggle for peace and friendship among the peoples;

h) to strengthen the ideological and organizational unity of the party, protect the party against the penetration into its ranks of people unworthy of the high title of communist, display vigilance and keep party and state secrets;

i) to develop criticism and self-criticism, boldly expose shortcomings and work to eliminate them, fight against ostentation, conceit, complacency and window-dressing, decisively rebuff all attempts to suppress criticism and oppose bureaucratism, parochialism, departmentalism and any activities prejudicial to the party and state and report them to the party organs, right up to the CPSU Central Committee;

j) to pursue strictly the party line on the selection of cadres on the basis of their political, professional and moral qualities. To be implacable in all cases where the Leninist principles of the selection and education of cadres are violated;

k) to observe party and state discipline, equally obligatory for all members of the party. The party has only one discipline and one law for all communists, irrespective of services or office.

3. The party member has the right:

a) to elect and be elected to party organs;

b) to discuss freely at party meetings, conferences, congresses and party committee sessions and in the party press matters regarding the party's policy and practical activity, submit proposals and openly express and defend his opinion before the organization adopts a resolution;

c) to criticize at party meetings, conferences, congresses and committee plenums any party organ or any communist, irrespective of the post he occupies. Persons guilty of suppressing criticism or persecuting others for criticism must be called to strict party account, up to and including expulsion from the ranks of the CPSU;

d) to take part personally in party meeting and buro and committee sessions when the matter of his activity and behavior is being discussed;

e) to address questions, statements and proposals to any party instance up to and including the CPSU Central Committee, and demand a reply on the substance of the application.

4. Admission to party membership is carried out exclusively on an individual basis. Workers, peasants and members of the intelligentsia who are conscientious, active and devoted to the cause of communism are admitted to party membership. New members are admitted from the ranks of candidate members with the required length of candidate party service.

Persons who have reached the age of 18 years are admitted into the party. Young people up to the age of 25 inclusive enter the party only through the all-union Komsomol.

Procedure for the admission of candidates to party membership:

a) persons to be admitted to party membership must produce recommendations from three CPSU members with no less than five years' standing in the party who have been acquainted with the candidate in joint production and public work for not less than a year.

Note 1. Members of the Komsomol entering the party submit the recommendation of the raion or town of Komsomol committee, which is considered equivalent to the recommendation of one party member.

Note 2. Members and candidates for membership in the CPSU Central Committee will refrain from acting as sponsors;

b) the question of admission into the party is discussed and decided by the general meeting of the primary party organization; its resolution is deemed adopted if no fewer than two-thirds of the party members attending the meeting vote for it, and it enters into force after ratification by the raion party committee or, in towns which have no raion division, by the town party committee.

The presence of the sponsors is not obligatory during the discussion of admission into the party. Admission into the party takes place as a rule at open meetings;

c) citizens of the USSR who were formerly members of communist and workers' parties in other countries are admitted into the CPSU on the basis of regulations established by the CPSU Central Committee.

5. Sponsors are responsible to the party organizations for describing objectively the political, professional and moral qualities of the candidates and give them assistance in ideological and political growth.

6. The length of party service of persons admitted into the party dates from adoption of the resolution by the general meeting of the primary party organization admitting the candidate to party membership.

7. The procedure for registering members and candidates for party membership and their transfer from one organization to another is established by the corresponding instructions of the CPSU Central Committee.

8. The matter of party members and candidates for membership who without valid reason have failed to pay membership dues for three months is subject to discussion in the primary party organization. If it is found that a given member or candidate for party membership has in fact lost contact with the party organization, he is then considered to have left the party and the primary party organization adopts a resolution to that effect and submits it to the raion or town party committee for ratification.

9. The party member or candidate for membership is called to account for failure to carry out the duties laid down by the Rules and other offenses and the following penalties may be imposed on him: public warning, reprimand (severe reprimand) or reprimand (severe reprimand) with notation in his report card. The severest form of party punishment is expulsion from the party.

For minor offenses, party educational measures and other means to influence must be applied in the form of comradely criticism, party censure, warning and instruction.

A communist who has committed a misdemeanor answers for it in the first instance to the primary party organization. If a communist is called to party account by a higher organ, the primary party organization is informed of this.

In examining the matter of being called to party account, maximum care and a painstaking examination of the validity of the accusations against the communist must be ensured.

Not later than a year after the imposition of a penalty on a party member the party organization must hear his report on how he is rectifying the shortcomings he committed.

10. The matter of expelling a communist from the party is decided by a general meeting of the primary party organization. The resolution of the primary party organization on expulsion from the party is deemed adopted if no fewer than two-thirds of the party members attending the meeting vote for it, and it enters into force after ratification by the raion or town party committee.

Until the raion or town party committee ratifies the resolution on expulsion from the CPSU, the party card or candidate's card will be retained by the communist and he has the right to attend closed party meetings.

Anyone expelled from the party has the right to appeal within a two-month period to higher party organs, up to and including the CPSU Central Committee.

11. The matter of calling to party account the members and candidate members of a union republican communist party central committee or krai, oblast, okrug, town or raion party committee, and also of the members of the auditing commissions, is discussed in primary party organizations, and resolutions imposing penalties on them are adopted by regular procedure.

The proposals of the party organizations for expulsion from the CPSU are conveyed to the appropriate party committee of which the communist in question is a member. Resolutions on expulsion from the party of members and candidates for membership of a union republican Communist Party Central Committee or krai, oblast, okrug, town or raion party committee and members of the auditing commissions are adopted at a plenum of the appropriate committee by a majority of two-thirds of the votes of its members.

The matter of expulsion from the party of a member or candidate for membership of the CPSU Central Committee or a member of the CPSU Central Auditing Commission is decided by Party Congress and, during the period between congresses, by a plenum of the Central Committee by a majority of two-thirds of the members of the CPSU Central Committee.

12. A party member bears dual liability for violation of Soviet laws—to the state and to the party. Persons committing misdemeanors punishable by criminal proceedings are expelled from the ranks of the CPSU.

13. Appeals of members expelled from the party or penalized by the party and the resolutions of the party organizations on expulsion from the party are reviewed by the appropriate party organs not later than two months from the date of their receipt.

II. CANDIDATES FOR PARTY MEMBERSHIP

14. Persons joining the party undergo a period of candidate service necessary to familiarize them in greater depth with the CPSU Program and rules and prepare them to join the party. The party organization must help candidates prepare for CPSU membership and check their personal qualities as reflected in practical actions and in the implementation of party and public instructions.

The length of candidate service is one year.

15. Procedure for candidate admission (individual admission, submission of recommendations, and resolution of primary organization on candidate admission and its ratification) is the same as for admission to party membership.

16. On the expiration of the period of candidate service, the primary party organization considers and decides on the admission of the candidate to CPSU membership. Should a candidate fail to prove himself during candidate service, and should his personal qualities make him unworthy of CPSU membership, the party organization adopts a resolution refusing him admission to the party and, on ratification of this resolution by a raion or town party committee, he is considered to have left candidate membership of the CPSU.

17. Candidates for membership of the party participate in all activities of the party organization and have a consultative vote at party meetings. Candidates for membership of the party cannot be elected to leading party organs or be delegates to party conferences and congresses.

18. Candidates for membership of the CPSU pay the same party dues as party members.

III. ORGANIZATIONAL STRUCTURE OF THE PARTY.
INTRA-PARTY DEMOCRACY

19. The guiding principle of the organizational structure and of the life and activity of the party is democratic centralism, which means:

a) election of all leading party organs, from the lowest to the highest organ;

b) periodic accountability of party organs to their party organizations and higher organs;

c) strict party discipline and the subordination of the minority to the majority;

d) the decisions of the higher organs are absolutely binding on lower organs;

e) collectiveness in the work of all party organizations and leading organs and personal responsibility on the part of each communist for carrying out his duties and party assignments.

20. The party is structured on the territorial-production basis: primary organizations are formed at the communist's place of work and are united in raion, town and other organizations in a given territory. The organization uniting the communists of a given territory is superior to all party organizations constituting that organization.

21. All party organizations are autonomous in deciding local matters, provided the decisions are not contrary to party policy.

22. The highest leadership organ of the party organization is: the general meeting or conference (for primary organizations); the conference (for raion, town, okrug, oblast and krai organizations); and the congress (for union republican communist parties and the CPSU). The meeting, conference and congress has a quorum if more than half the members of the party organization or elected delegates are present.

23. The general meeting, conference or congress elects the buro or committee, which are the executive organs and guides the entire current work of the party organization.

In the CPSU Central Committee, union republican Communist Party central committees, and krai, oblast, okrug, town and raion party committees an apparatus is created for current work to organize and verify the implementation of party resolutions and assist lower organizations in their activity.

The structure and establishment of the party apparatus are determined by the CPSU Central Committee.

24. The election of party organs is by closed (secret) ballot. At meetings in primary and shop organizations with fewer than 15 party members and in party groups, the election of secretaries and deputy secretaries of party organizations and party group organizers may with the consent of the communists take place by open ballot. In these primary organizations, delegates to raion and town party conferences are elected by the same procedure.

All members of the party have the unrestricted right during elections to reject candidates and criticize them. Each candidacy must be voted on separately. Candidates will be deemed elected if over half of the participants in the meeting, conference or congress vote for them.

In the election of all party organs from primary organizations to the CPSU Central Committee, the principle of the systematic renewal of their composition and of continuity of leadership shall be observed.

25. Members and candidates for membership of the CPSU Central Committee union republican Communist Party central committees and krai, oblast, okrug, town and raion party committees must, in all their activities, justify the great trust shown in them. If the party committee member or candidate member loses his honor and dignity, he cannot remain a member of the committee.

The matter of the removal of a party committee member or candidate member from the party committee is decided at a plenum of the committee. The resolution is deemed adopted if in a closed (secret) ballot no fewer than two-thirds of the party committee members vote for it.

The matter of the removal from these commissions of members of the CPSU Central Auditing Commission and the auditing commissions of local party organizations is decided at their sessions under the procedure laid down for members and candidates for membership of party committees.

26. Free and businesslike discussion of the matters of party policy in the party and in all its organizations is an important principle of intra-party democracy. Only on the basis of intra-party democracy is it possible to ensure high creative activeness on the part of communists, open criticism and self-criticism and firm party discipline, which must be conscious and not mechanical.

Debates on disputed or insufficiently clear issues are possible within the framework of individual organizations or the party as a whole.

Party-wide debate is held:

a) on the initiative of the CPSU Central Committee, if it finds it necessary to consult the whole party on particular matters of policy;

b) at the proposal of several party organizations of republican, krai or oblast level.

Broad debates, especially debates on an all-union level about matters of party policy, must be carried out so as to ensure the free expression of the views of party members and exclude the possibility of attempts to form factional groupings and split the party.

27. The highest principle of party leadership is collectiveness of leadership—an essential condition for normal activity of party organizations, the correct education of cadres and the development of the activeness and spontaneous activity of communists, and a reliable guarantee against the adoption of willful and subjectivist resolutions, the manifestation of the cult of personality and violations of the Leninist norms of party life.

The collectiveness of leadership presupposes personal responsibility for assigned work and constant monitoring of the activity of every party organization and every worker.

28. The CPSU Central Committee, union republican Communist Party central committees and krai, oblast, okrug, town and raion party committees systematically inform party organizations about their work and about the implementation of communists' criticisms and proposals in the period between congresses and conferences.

An immutable rule for party committees and primary party organizations is also the objective and timely briefing of higher party organs and about their own activity and the situation at local level.

29. For discussion of the most important party resolutions and the elaboration of measures to implement them, as well as the examination of matters of local life, meetings are convened of activists of raion, town, okrug, oblast and krai party organizations and union republican communist parties.

30. Standing or temporary commissions and working groups on various matters of party work may be created in party committees, and other forms of involvement of communists in the activity of party organs on a voluntary basis may also be used.

IV. THE HIGHEST PARTY ORGANS

31. The supreme organ of the Communist Party of the Soviet Union is the party congress. Regular congresses are convened by the Central Committee at least once every five years. The convocation of the party congress and the agenda are an-

nounced not less than one and a half months before the congress. Special (emergency) congresses are convened by the Party Central Committee on its own initiative or at the request of no fewer than one-third of the total number of party members represented at the last party congress. Special (emergency) congresses are convened at two months' notice. The congress is considered valid if at least half the total number of party members are represented at it.

The norms of representation at the party congress are laid down by the Central Committee.

32. If the Party Central Committee does not convene a special (emergency) congress within the term specified in Article 31, organizations requesting the convocation of special (emergency) congress have the right to form an organizing committee possessing the rights of the Party Central Committee to convene a special (emergency) congress.

33. The congress:

a) hears and approves the reports of the Central Committee, the Central Auditing Commission and other central organizations;

b) reviews, amends and approves the Party Program and Rules;

c) determines the party line on matters of domestic and foreign policy and examines and decides on the most important issues of party and state life and communist construction;

d) elects the Central Committee and the Central Auditing Commission.

34. The Central Committee and the Central Auditing Commission are elected in the composition established by the congress. In the event of members leaving the Central Committee, its membership is replenished from among candidate members of the CPSU Central Committee elected by the congress.

35. The CPSU Central Committee in the period between congresses leads all the activity of the party and of local party organs; selects and places leading cadres; directs the work of central state and public organizations of the working people; creates various organs, institutions and enterprises of the party and leads their activities; appoints the editorial staff of central papers and journals functioning under its control; and allocates funds from the party budget and monitors its execution.

The Central Committee represents the CPSU in its relations with other parties.

36. The CPSU Central Auditing Commission inspects compliance with the established procedure for the conduct of affairs and work to examine working people's letters, statements and complaints in central party organs, the correct execution of the party budget, including the payment, receipt and accounting of members' party dues, and also the financial and economic activity of enterprises and institutions of the CPSU Central Committee.

37. The CPSU Central Committee holds not less than one plenum every six months. Candidate members of the Central Committee attend the sessions of Central Committee plenums with the right of consultative vote.

38. The CPSU Central Committee elects: the Politburo, to lead the work of the party between Central Committee plenums; and the Secretariat, to lead current work, mainly in the selection of cadres and organization of the verification of implementation. The Central Committee elects the General Secretary of the CPSU Central Committee.

39. The CPSU Central Committee organizes the Party Control Committee under the Central Committee.

The Party Control Committee under the CPSU Central Committee:

a) verifies compliance with party discipline by members and candidates for membership of the CPSU, calls to account communists guilty of violating the Party Program and Rules and party and state discipline, as well as violators of party ethics;

b) examines appeals against the resolutions of union republican Communist Party central committees and krai and oblast party committees on expulsion from the party and on party penalties.

40. In the period between party congresses the CPSU Central Committee may, when necessary, convene an all-union party conference to discuss pressing matters of party policy. The procedure for holding an all-union party conference is determined by the CPSU Central Committee.

V. REPUBLICAN, KRAI, OBLAST, OKRUG, TOWN AND RAION PARTY ORGANIZATIONS

41. Republican, krai, oblast, okrug, town and raion party organizations and their committees are guided in their activity by the CPSU Program and Rules, carry out within the republic, krai, oblast, okrug, town and raion all the work of implementing party policy and organize fulfillment of the CPSU Central Committee's directives.

42. The fundamental duties of republican, krai, oblast, okrug, town and raion party organizations and their leading organs are:

a) political and organizational work among the masses, the mobilization of communists and all working people to implement the tasks of communist construction, accelerate socio-economic development on the basis of scientific and technical progress, increase social production efficiency and labor productivity, improve output quality and fulfill state plans and socialist pledges, and the ensuring of steady growth in the working people's material well-being and cultural level.

b) organization of ideological work; propaganda of Marxism-Leninism; the enhancement of working people's communist consciousness; leadership of the local press, radio and television; and monitoring of the activity of scientific, cultural and educational institutions;

c) leadership of soviets of people's deputies, trade unions, the Komsomol, cooperatives and other public organizations through the communists working in them; increasingly broad involvement of working people in the work of these organizations; and development of the spontaneous activity and activeness of the masses as a necessary condition for the further deepening of socialist democracy;

d) strict observance of Leninist principles and methods of leadership, the establishment of a Leninist style in party work and in all spheres of state and economic management, the ensuring of the unity of ideological, organizational and economic activity, and the strengthening of socialist legality, state and labor discipline, order and organization in all sectors;

e) implementation of cadre policy, the education of cadres in the spirit of cummunist ideological commitment, moral purity and high responsibility to the party and the people for the tasks entrusted to them;

f) organization of various institutions and enterprises of the party in the republic, krai, oblast, okrug, town and raion, and leadership of their activity, allocation of party funds within their organization; systematic reports to the higher party organ and accountability to it for their work.

The Leading Organs of the Republic, Krai and Oblast Party Organizations

43. The highest organ of the republic, krai and oblast party organization is the union republican Communist Party congress and the krai and oblast party conference and, in the period between them, the union republican Communist Party Central Committee and krai and oblast party committee.

44. The regular congress of the union republican Communist Party is convened by the Communist Party central committee at least once every five years. A regular krai and oblast conference is convened by the krai or oblast party committee once every two or three years. Special (emergency) congresses and conferences are convened by decision of the union republican Communist Party central committee, krai or oblast party committee, or on the demand of one-third of the total number of members of the organizations belonging to the republic, krai or oblast party organization.

The norms for representation at the union republican Communist Party congress and krai and oblast conference are established by the appropriate party committee.

The union republican Communist Party congress and krai and oblast conference hear reports from the union republican Communist Party central committee, krai or oblast party committee and the auditing commission, discuss at their discretion other matters of party, economic and cultural construction and elect the union republican Communist Party central committee, krai or oblast party committee and the auditing commission, and delegates to the CPSU congress.

In the period between union republican Communist Party congresses, in order to discuss the most important issues of party organizations' activity, Communist Party central committees may, when necessary, convene republican party conferences. The procedure for holding republican party conferences is determined by the union republican Communist Party central committees.

45. The union republican Communist Party central committees and krai and oblast party committees elect a buro including secretaries of the committee. The secretaries must have had at least five years of party service. At the plenums of the committee heads of committee departments, party control commission chairmen and editors of party papers and journals are confirmed.

Secretariats are established to handle current matters and verify implementation in union republican Communist Party central committees and krai and oblast party committees.

46. A plenum of a union republican Communist Party central committee, or krai or oblast party committee must be convened not less than once every four months.

47. The union republican Communist Party central committee, krai and oblast party committee lead okrug, town and raion party organizations, verify their activities and systematically receive reports from the relevant party committees.

The party organizations of autonomous republics and of autonomous and other oblasts included in union republics and krais work under the leadership of the union republican Communist Party Central Committees and krai party committees.

Leading Organs of Okrug, Town and Raion (Rural and Urban) Party Organizations

48. The highest organ of the okrug, town, and raion party organization is the okrug, town and raion party conference or general meeting of communists convened by the okrug, town or raion party committee once every two to three years, or special ones convened by decision of the committee or by demand of one-third of the total number of party members belonging to the corresponding party organization.

The okrug, town and raion conference (meeting) hears reports of the committee and the auditing commission, at its discretion examines other matters regarding party, economic and cultural construction and elects the okrug, town and raion party committee, the auditing commission and delegates to the oblast or krai conferences and to the congress of the union republic's Communist Party.

The norms for representation at okrug, town and raion conferences are established by the party committee concerned.

49. The okrug, town and raion party committees elect a buro, including secretaries of the committee, and also confirm the heads of committee departments, the chairman of the party commission and newspaper editors. Okrug, town and raion party committee secretaries must have at least five years' party membership. Secretaries of the committees are confirmed by the oblast or krai party committee or union republican Communist Party central committee.

50. The okrug, town and raion party committee create primary party organizations, lead their activities, systematically hear reports on the work of the party organizations and conduct the registration of communists.

51. Plenums of okrug, town and raion party committees are convened not less than once every three months.

VI. PRIMARY PARTY ORGANIZATIONS

52. The primary organizations are the foundation of the party.

The primary party organizations are created at the working place of the party member—in works, factories, state farms and other enterprises, collective farms, units of the armed forces, institutions, educational establishments and so forth—where there are at least three party members. Where necessary, territorial primary party organizations may also be formed at the places of residence of communists.

In individual cases, with the permission of the oblast or krai party committee, or union republican Communist Party central committee, party organizations may be created within the framework of several enterprises belonging to a production association and located, as a rule, on the territory of one raion or several raions in one town.

53. At enterprises, collective farms and institutions with over 50 CPSU members and candidates for membership, party organizations may be created within the overall primary party organization at workshops, sectors, livestock units, teams, departments and so forth with the permission of the raion, town or okrug party committee.

In the workshop, sector and other organizations, as well as within primary party organizations with fewer than 50 members and candidates for membership, party groups may be created within the teams and other production links.

54. The highest organ of the primary party organization is the party meeting, which is held at least once a month. In party organizations which have shop organizations, meetings, both general and shop, are held at least once every two months.

In large party organizations numbering more than 300 communists, general party meetings are called as necessary within periods established by the party committees or at the request of several shop party organizations.

55. To conduct current work, the primary and shop party organization elects for a period of two to three years a buro whose numerical size is established at a party meeting. The primary and the shop party organizations with fewer than 15 party members do not elect a buro but a party organization secretary and a deputy. Elections in these organizations are held annually.

The secretaries of the primary and shop party organizations must have had at least one year of party service.

In primary party organizations with fewer than 150 party members, party work, as a rule, is due by persons not excused from their jobs.

56. Party committees can be established at large enterprises and in establishments comprising over 300 members and candidates for membership of the party,

and in necessary cases, considering production peculiarities and territorial dispersion, also in organizations numbering over 100 communists—with the permission of the oblast or krai party committee or the union republican Communist Party central committee, with the allocation to shop party organizations of these enterprises or institutions of the rights of primary party organizations.

In the party organizations of collective farms, state farms and other enterprises in agriculture, party committees may be created where there are 50 communists.

In party organizations numbering over 500 communists, in individual cases, with the permission of the oblast or krai party committee or union republican Communist Party central committee, party committees may be created in large shops and the party organizations of production sectors are granted the rights of primary party organizations.

Party committees are elected for a term of two to three years and their size is determined by a general party meeting or conference.

Party committees, party buros and secretaries of primary and shop party organizations systematically inform communists about their work at party meetings.

57. Party committees of primary organizations numbering more than 1,000 communists, with the permission of union republican Communist Party central committees, may be granted the rights of a raion party committee on matters concerning admission into the CPSU, the registration of party members and candidates for membership and the examination of communists' personal files.

Within these organizations enlarged party committees may be elected within which a buro is formed for the leadership of current work.

58. The primary party organization is guided in its activities by the Program and Rules of the CPSU. It is the political nucleus of the labor collective, works directly among the working people, rallies them around the party, organizes them to fulfill the tasks of communist construction and participates actively in the implementation of the party's cadre policy.

The primary party organization:

a) admits new members in the CPSU;

b) educates communists in a spirit of devotion to the cause of the party, ideological conviction and communist morality;

c) organizes communists' study of Marxist-Leninist theory in close connection with the practice of communist construction and combats any manifestation of bourgeois ideology, revisionism and dogmatism and backward views and sentiments;

d) shows concern for enhancing the vanguard role of the communists in labor and socio-political life and for their exemplary behavior in everyday life, and hears reports from members and candidates for membership of the CPSU on their implementation of statutory duties and party assignments;

e) organizes working people to resolve the tasks of economic and social development; heads socialist competition to fulfill state plans and pledges, promote the intensification of production, improve labor productivity and output quality and widely introduce into production the achievements of science and technology and leading experience; mobilizes the working people to find internal reserves; seeks the rational and economical use of material, labor, and financial resources; and displays concern for the preservation and augmentation of public wealth and the improvement of people's working and living conditions;

f) carries out mass agitation and propaganda work, educates the working people in a spirit of devotion to the ideas of communism, Soviet patriotism and the friendship of peoples, helps them to develop a high political culture, and enhances their social activeness and responsibility;

g) promotes the development in communists and all working people of habits of participation in socialist self-management, ensures an increase in the labor collective's role in the management of the enterprise or institution and directs the work of trade union, Komsomol and other public organizations;

h) on the basis of the wide development of criticism and self-criticism, wages a struggle against manifestations of bureaucratism, parochialism and departmentalism and breaches of state, labor and production discipline, roots out attempts to cheat the state, takes measures against slackness, mismanagement and waste, and seeks to establish a sober way of life.

59. Primary party organizations of enterprises in industry, transport, communications, construction, material and technical supply, trade, public catering and municipal and consumer services, collective and state farms and other agricultural enterprises, planning organizations, design bureaus, scientific research institutes, educational establishments and cultural enlightenment and medical institutions have the right to monitor the activity of the administration.

Party organizations of ministries, state committees and other central and local government and economic institutions and departments exercise monitoring of the work of the apparatus in implementing party and government directives and observing Soviet laws. They must actively influence the improvement of the work of the apparatus and the selection, placement and education of its employees, enhance their responsibility for their assigned tasks, for the development of the branch and for services to the population, take measures to strengthen state discipline, wage a resolute struggle against bureaucratism and red tape, and promptly inform the appropriate party organs of any shortcomings in the work of the institution or individual workers, regardless of their position.

Note: In primary party organizations, commissions may be formed to exercise the right of monitoring the administration's activity and the work of the apparatus in particular areas of production activity.

VII. THE PARTY AND STATE AND PUBLIC ORGANIZATIONS

60. The CPSU, acting within the framework of the USSR constitution, exercises political leadership of state and public organizations and directs and coordinates their activity.

Party organizations and the communists working in state and public organizations strive to ensure that these organizations fully exercise their constitutional powers and statutory rights and duties and widely involve working people in management and in the resolution of political, economic and social issues.

Party organizations do not supplant local government trade union, cooperative and other public organizations and do not tolerate confusion of the functions of party and other organs.

61. At congresses, conferences and meetings convened by state and public organizations and also in the elected organs of these organizations where there are at least three party members, party groups are organized. The task of these groups is to pursue the party's policy in the relevant non-party organizations, to strengthen communists' influence on the state of affairs in these organizations, to develop democratic norms in their activity, strengthen party and state discipline, struggle against bureaucratism and verify the implementation of party and local government directives.

62. The work of party groups in non-party organizations is led by the corresponding party organs: The CPSU Central Committee, the union republican Communist Party central committee, or the krai, oblast, okrug, town or raion party committee.

VIII. THE PARTY AND THE KOMSOMOL

63. The All-Union Lenin Komsomol is an independently functioning socio-political youth organization which is an active assistant and reserve of the party. The Komsomol helps the party to educate young people in the spirit of communism, involve them in the practical building of a new society and the management of state and public affairs and mold a generation of comprehensively developed people ready for labor and the defense of the Soviet homeland.

64. The Komsomol organizations are called upon to be active promoters of the party's goals in all spheres of production and public life. They have the right of broad initiative in the discussion and submission to the appropriate party organizations of matters regarding the work of enterprises, collective farms, institutions and educational establishments and participate directly in their solution, especially where they concern the labor, life, training and education of young people.

65. The Komsomol works under the leadership of the CPSU. The work of the local organizations of the Komsomol is directed and controlled by the respective republican krai, oblast, okrug, town and raion party organizations.

The local party organs and primary party organizations rely on the Komsomol organizations in work for the communist education of young people and for their mobilization to resolve specific tasks of production and social life, support their useful initiatives and give all-round assistance in their activity.

66. Members of the Komsomol who are admitted into the CPSU leave the Komsomol the moment they join the party unless they are members of elected Komsomol organs and are in Komsomol work.

IX. PARTY ORGANIZATIONS IN THE ARMED FORCES

67. The party organizations of the armed forces are guided by the Program and Rules of the CPSU in their activities and work on the basis of instructions confirmed by the Central Committee. They ensure the implementation of party policy in the armed forces, rally their personnel around the Communist Party, educate servicemen in the spirit of the ideas of Marxism-Leninism and selfless devotion to the socialist homeland, actively assist in consolidating the unity of the army and the people, take care to increase the combat readiness of troops and strengthen military discipline and mobilize personnel to fulfill tasks of combat and political training, master new technology and weapons, and carry out irreproachably their military duties and the orders and instructions of the command.

68. The leadership of party work in the armed forces is carried out by the CPSU Central Committee though political organs. The Main Political Directorate of the Soviet Army and Navy has the rights of a department of the CPSU Central Committee.

The heads of the political directorates of districts and fleets and the heads of the political departments of armies, flotillas and formations must have had five years' party membership.

69. The party organizations and political organs of the armed forces maintain close ties with local party committees and inform them systematically about political work in military units. The secretaries of the military party organizations and leaders of the political organs participate in the work of local party committees.

X. THE PARTY'S FINANCIAL RESOURCES

70. The financial resources of the party and its organizations consist of membership dues, income from party enterprises and other revenue.

The procedure for the use of the party's financial resources is determined by the CPSU Central Committee.

71. Monthly membership dues for party members and candidates for memberships of the CPSU are as follows:

Monthly Income (in roubles)	*Dues*
up to 70	10 kopecks
71 to 100	20 kopecks
101 to 150	1.0% of monthly income
151 to 200	1.5% of monthly income
201 to 250	2.0% of monthly income
251 to 300	2.5% of monthly income
over 300	3.0% of monthly income

72. Joining fees of 2% of monthly income are paid on becoming a candidate member of the party.

Index